Prais  **de**

"In the often resource-constra... ...velopment, solid software engineering practices are essential to success. Ivo's book, with its emphasis on code performance, is refreshing and timely—and it delivers!"

—Bill Draper, Director of Software Development, MICROS Systems, Inc.

"To write mobile, you need to think mobile. This book is a big first step in getting your head into the right gear."

—Jon Skeet, Independent Software Engineer

"*Writing Mobile Code* is an indispensable resource for any programmer, whether or not you are writing mobile code. That's because Salmre not only teaches you how to program mobile devices, he also teaches you how to be a good programmer. Salmre's writing is easy to follow and has real-world application. He teaches the novice how to develop robust applications with the user in mind, and he reminds us veterans that keeping things simple is very important. I am recommending this book to my peers and anyone who needs to write a program."

—Michael Maitland, Sr. Systems Architect, Target Systems

"This book will be your new bible for the rapidly developing world of mobile computing. From design to performance, the information you need to be successful is here."

—Doug Ellis, Area Technical Manager, Cognos Corporation

"A great reference and learning tool that covers all the main issues for software engineering on mobile devices, this is an essential book for anyone who is developing software on mobile platforms. Designing software on a mobile device has a lot of unique challenges; this book walks the developer through all of them."

—Mark Gilbert, Software Designer, Microsoft Corporation

"In this book, Ivo Salmre leverages his experience as a designer of the .Net Compact Framework and teaches us how to develop effective mobile applications. It covers the entire process of designing and developing mobile applications with a focus on performance optimization. Although the examples in this book are given in the C# language, it would prove useful to mobile developers of all platforms. I highly recommend it."

—Michael Yuan, PhD., Mobile Software Consultant

"Just when you thought you knew how to write mobile code, this book makes you reconsider the things you took for granted. Salmre provides a balanced mix of software recipes and forays into the philosophy of mobile development that will help any mobile developer to write better apps."

—Alex Feinman, Software Engineer, OpenNETCF.org

Writing Mobile Code

Writing Mobile Code

Essential Software Engineering for Building Mobile Applications

Ivo Salmre

✦✦ Addison-Wesley

Upper Saddle River, NJ • Boston • Indianapolis • San Francisco
New York • Toronto • Montreal • London • Munich • Paris • Madrid
Capetown • Sydney • Tokyo • Singapore • Mexico City

Many of the designations used by manufacturers and sellers to distinguish their products are claimed as trademarks. Where those designations appear in this book, and the publisher was aware of a trademark claim, the designations have been printed with initial capital letters or in all capitals.

The author and publisher have taken care in the preparation of this book, but make no expressed or implied warranty of any kind and assume no responsibility for errors or omissions. No liability is assumed for incidental or consequential damages in connection with or arising out of the use of the information or programs contained herein.

The publisher offers excellent discounts on this book when ordered in quantity for bulk purchases or special sales, which may include electronic versions and/or custom covers and content particular to your business, training goals, marketing focus, and branding interests. For more information, please contact:

U.S. Corporate and Government Sales
(800) 382-3419
corpsales@pearsontechgroup.com

For sales outside the U.S., please contact:

International Sales
international@pearsoned.com

Visit us on the Web: www.awprofessional.com

Library of Congress Catalog Number:

2004115250

Copyright © 2005 Pearson Education, Inc.

All rights reserved. Printed in the United States of America. This publication is protected by copyright, and permission must be obtained from the publisher prior to any prohibited reproduction, storage in a retrieval system, or transmission in any form or by any means, electronic, mechanical, photocopying, recording, or likewise. For information regarding permissions, write to:

Pearson Education, Inc.
Rights and Contracts Department
One Lake Street
Upper Saddle River, NJ 07458

ISBN 0-321-26931-4
Text composed using FrameMaker 7.1 and printed in the United States on recycled paper at Phoenix Book Tech in Hagerstown, MD.
First printing, February 2005

This work is dedicated to all my teachers, both formal and informal, and most especially to my parents, Aire and William Salmre. If I have been able to see a few new things in useful and different ways, it is only because of the kindness and patience of those who have taken the time to lead me up the hill and point my head in the right direction. Thank you all.

Contents

About the Author

Ivo Salmre has been working for Microsoft for more than eleven years, focusing on the design and production of software development tools—first for desktops and servers and then specifically focusing on mobile device software development. Ivo was the Lead Program Manager in the design of the .NET Compact Framework. He holds a Bachelor of Science in Electrical Engineering from the University of Connecticut and is a frequent speaker at industry conferences. After living for ten years in Seattle and a bit more than one year in London, Ivo now works at the Microsoft European Innovation Center (EMIC) in Aachen, Germany, doing research on advanced mobile device programming models. Ivo was born in Norwalk, Connecticut.

Preface

There is a mobile device revolution underway.

It is only very recently that mobile computing devices have crossed the boundary between fixed-purpose communications devices to compelling and extensible mass-market computing platforms. The upcoming decade will see an explosion of capable mobile computing and communications devices providing ever-richer focused information and services to aid people in their daily work and personal lives. It is difficult to overestimate the impact truly mobile and ubiquitous computing will have on the way we work, the way we live, the way we communicate, and the way we interact with the world around us. Intelligent mobile device software is central to the sea change that is underway.

This book is about how to build great mobile device applications. To achieve this goal, it provides a mix of important conceptual knowledge and concrete practical examples. The examples are developed in C# and Visual Basic .NET and target the Microsoft .NET Compact Framework, but the concepts in the book are relevant to all kinds of mobile computing programming technologies and platforms. Visual Basic and C# developers will get the greatest benefit from this book along with specific technical knowledge, but the book is intended for anyone interested in how to build great mobile device software regardless of the programming technology they choose to use.

If I am allowed to hope for a desired book review, it would read: *Extremely practical yet thought provoking,* Writing Mobile Code *will make you a better software developer and get you excited about building new and innovative software for mobile devices.* The end readers will have to judge how close I have come to meeting this lofty goal.

The goal of *Writing Mobile Code* is to create a "different kind of technical book." In discussing the idea for this project with the publishers and other interested parties, the question was posed, "What do you think is missing from most technical books today and what unique value will this book offer?"

What is missing from most technical books today?

Today technical reference materials about software development abound. There is no shortage of facts and reference information on the Web as well as in the racks of bookstores. We live in a world overflowing with information, but in spite of, or perhaps because of this, real wisdom is hard to come by. The interested person must dig though the heaps of coal to search for the diamonds of insight that are surely hidden in there somewhere. Like coal, raw facts themselves are extremely useful but they are not the precious gems we seek. What is missing, and particularly missing from existing mobile software development literature, is an accessible hands-on engineering book that lays out the principles and methods of good mobile software design using concrete examples to demonstrate theory. This book hopes to give readers the gems of wisdom that will enrich them and spur them on to discover the great possibilities that mobile software development holds. The book offers insights with practical examples, encouraging readers to experiment and make their own observations while learning the key elements of mobile software engineering.

What unique value does this book add?

Writing Mobile Code is about mobile software development and is meant to go beyond the bounds of any specific technology. Although the numerous examples offered in the book are written using the .NET Compact Framework, the general principles discussed are valid for all mobile device technologies. Technologies advance rapidly, but good engineering practices and design wisdom grow slowly through the painstaking learning of trial and error. This book is about learning the design and engineering principles that will prove durable even as technology advances.

The goal of this book is not to flood the reader with a multitude of details devoid of greater context but rather to impart in the reader an appreciation for the proper philosophy and design methods for mobile software development. Detailed examples present the facts and figures, but the main goal is to grow in the reader a deep understanding of how to write great mobile software. There will always be more facts to learn, and specific technologies will always evolve and eventually be replaced; this book concentrates on explaining what is unique and interesting about mobile software development and how to build successful mobile applications.

What Various audiences can expect to gain from reading this book:

- *People presently doing software development for mobile devices—* Mobile software development is rapidly moving from being a specialized black art of the initiated to a mass developer-audience community. This book endeavors to offer a rich and, I believe, new perspective on mobile software development that will be valuable both for developers new to mobile devices as well as to seasoned hands in the mobile software domain.

- *Desktop and server Java, C#, or VB.NET developers considering a move to or moving on to device development*—Desktop and server developers already using any of these languages will be immediately able to follow the examples in this book. What this book offers additionally to these developers is a deep understanding of how mobile software development differs from classical desktop and server development. I believe this book will be an enjoyable test drive for these developers and convince them that mobile device development is an arrow they will want to add to their software development quiver. This book will impart in these developers the knowledge and skills necessary to build great mobile applications.
- *C++ developers looking at moving to a managed runtime language such as C#*—The chances are very good that people doing C/C++ development today will be moving some of their programming work to managed-code languages such as C# in the near future. The productivity and reliability benefits are simply overwhelming. This book offers many examples using C#, and C/C++ developers should easily be able to follow the syntax.
- *Visual Basic developers looking at VB.NET or C#*—The examples in the book are written both in C# and Visual Basic .NET and will serve as a good aid to picking up the fundamentals of these programming languages and the runtime libraries of the .NET Framework. Because the .NET Compact Framework is a rich subset of the desktop and server .NET Framework, working through devices can be a fun way to learn these new programming models.
- *People interested in sharpening their software engineering skills*—This book is fundamentally about imparting good engineering practices in the mind of the reader. Those interested in sharpening their software engineering skills for servers, desktop, and device development will be able to do so in a fun and novel way by looking at software engineering from a mobile device development perspective.
- *Software architects looking to extend existing solutions with mobile device support*—Mobile computing offers an interesting new medium with which to extend desktop and server solutions. For this it is important to understand the things that mobile devices are well suited for and those things they are not. By reading this book, software architects should gain a good understanding of the role that mobile devices can play in their solutions.

Acknowledgments

This book is not just about mobility but is itself the product of mobile computing. Much time was spent in different environments, and ad hoc experiments were done with a backpack and pockets full of various mobile devices for companionship. The book was written over the course of a year spent traveling between two different continents in at least six different countries and with the aid of an eye-popping amount of late-night coffee. On average, I have to acknowledge that the coffee in Europe is generally superior to the variety found in North America; this "coffee gap" is something that merits further study.

I would like to thank the following people without whom this book would never have reached its potential and may not have happened at all:

- The folks at Addison-Wesley and Pearson who encouraged me and kept me on track. Most specifically I want to thank Karen Gettman, with whom I discussed the original proposal to write a "different kind of technical book"; Elizabeth Zdunich, who patiently worked with me through the writing process; and Lori Lyons and Keith Cline for their terrific work editing the book.
- The great people who reviewed earlier drafts of the book. If it is the role of the reviewer to save the end reader from the mistakes, inconsistencies, and folly of the writer, they have done a superior job. I was fortunate enough to have excellent people offer both encouraging and "tough love" feedback on the book. If the effort has been successful, the reviewers deserve a significant part of the credit for it. Specifically, I want to thank Craig Neable, Bill Draper, Jon Skeet, Michael Maitland, Doug Holland, and Alex Feinman for offering detailed feedback on the manuscript along with a myriad of useful suggestions and corrections.
- My managers at Microsoft for being supportive of this work. It is truly a wonderful thing to have been given the freedom to pursue this independent effort, and I am grateful to them.

CHAPTER 1

Introduction

> *"Would you tell me, please, which way I ought to go from here?"*
> *"That depends a good deal on where you want to get to," said the Cat.*
>
> —Lewis Carroll, Alice's Adventures in Wonderland
> (Encarta 2004, Quotations)

Welcome to Mobile Device Software Engineering

Day by day software plays a greater role in peoples' lives, enabling us to access information, make decisions in "real time," and generally live more productive and enjoyable lives. In the early days of computers, there were a few computers to be shared by many users. Now the famous march of Moore's law has brought us to a much more democratized and distributed form of computing, the desktop and portable "personal computer." Today we are in the midst of an even more profound evolution. Personal computers and centralized servers are not going away; instead, they are being surrounded by clouds of mobile devices allowing for further decentralization of computing power. This is bringing the applicability of application software into ever-newer domains. The same people who use desktop computers for browsing the Web, doing e-mail, playing games, shopping, and otherwise interacting with the world of networked information are increasingly bringing targeted pieces of this experience with them when they "go mobile." My long-time employer Microsoft had some years back stated its mission as "A computer on every desk and in every home." It is telling that this mission statement has since been amended with "software, running anytime, anywhere, on any device." This brings us to the subject of devices. What exactly is a mobile device and how is software engineering different for mobile devices?

What is a mobile device? Computationally a mobile device represents a compromise. We have chosen to trade the incredible processing power, storage capacity, and graphical capabilities of a modern desktop computer for a mobile device where size, instantaneousness of response, and battery life matter most. This is not a bad trade. With the continued exponential growth in processing power and decline in prices, we are now at a point where my run-of-the-mill Pocket PC (400MHz XScale processor, 64MB of RAM) is in many ways more powerful than the desktop computers that ran Windows 95 only a handful of years ago. Nevertheless, mobile devices *are* different. Simply running a desktop operating system and applications on a mobile device will not produce a satisfactory experience for the end user. As anyone using a modern mobile phone or PDA is familiar with, the device they are holding is indeed a rich computer, but it is in significant ways different from their desktop or laptop personal computer. The design priorities and user expectations for mobile devices differ from traditional personal computers.

Today, mobile devices offer developers and end users a unique opportunity to take information, entertainment, and knowledge with them in ways that were not possible even a few years ago. Any user who has spent a significant time with today's latest smart phones or Wi-Fi enabled devices can see that fantastic things are coming. Nothing represents the concept of "information at your fingertips" as literally as the ability to pull a device out of one's pocket and interact with that information.

The established principals of software engineering are still valid for mobile devices. There is no need to throw out the existing books on successful coding techniques or security. In fact, it is even more critical that good software engineering principals be followed for mobile device software development. Desktop computers offer such a rich and tolerant environment for application development that developers can just power though many of the problems at hand without thought to good engineering practices. Sloppy design and engineering practices are at least partially forgiven by the overwhelming resources available to the developer. When this happens, the overall user experience suffers due to unnecessarily sluggish performance or poorly thought-out user interface design; *however*, because the desktop computer is so rich in processing power, screen real estate, and data-input capabilities, the user can work around these limitations. This is not so with devices. A sloppy user interface rapidly becomes frustrating to a user who expects rapid and intuitive access to information and has no way to navigate around bad design. Similarly wasteful or thoughtless memory usage will rapidly cause a mobile application's performance to degrade to the point of being useless. Mobile device software design is more demanding.

This book is a software engineering guide focusing on mobile application development because good software engineering is so important for making great mobile applications. It is a topic that has not been addressed yet, and the lack of clear guidelines and techniques is responsible for a great deal of frustration both for developers attempting to move to mobile development as well as for end users who bear the brunt of software developers' design mistakes. Although the examples in this book are written using the .NET Compact Framework, the concepts are general and will be of use to developers building applications regardless of the mobile device framework they choose. Whether developers work using C/C++ native code, the .NET Compact Framework, Java/J2ME, or any other mobile device technology, a good understanding of mobile software engineering practices is essential. The reader will learn how to think about mobile development problems in a clear and insightful way and will be able to navigate the mobile software development process to a successful conclusion. It is my hope that the hard-won knowledge gained by my associates and myself knocking our heads against enough low ceilings and tripping over more than a few unseen pitfalls can be shared to save others the pain. This book's intention is to serve as a guide giving practical advice on how to navigate mobile software development successfully to the very rewarding ends that mobile computing promises.

Success Is Driven by a Few Key Factors

Successful engineering is about making good design decisions. Central to this is the ability to discern what is most important, to separate the wheat from the chaff, and to identify the key areas to spend your valuable time thinking about. In any activity you can easily separate the experts who "make it look too easy" from the struggling novices. The difference is simple: The experts make it look easy because for them it is! They implicitly know what to concentrate on and what can be safely ignored. The novice, on the other hand, does not have this knowledge and so exhausts himself or herself trying to concentrate on everything simultaneously, with predictable results. Anyone who has ever gone from being a beginner skier or windsurfer (two sports with steep learning curves) to a level of expertise will immediately appreciate this. Sometimes the experts are not even aware of what makes them experts; they just implicitly know how to do the right things (something that drives novices looking for tips crazy). Learning what is important to concentrate on is the key to becoming an expert. Looking at this mathematically, the concept is known as "first-order effects" versus "second-," "third-," and "higher-order effects," the idea being that in any given equation with many separate terms there are those factors that matter and those that "really matter." The lowest-order effects drive the overall behavior of the system. So it is with mobile software development; everything matters, but some things matter a great deal more than others.

Success in mobile software development is driven by the following factors. All are important, but the first ones are the most important. In order of decreasing importance, they are as follows:

1. *Scope of application*—It is most important to have a firm idea of what the mobile application is intended to accomplish both in terms of overall vision as well as in concrete user scenarios. This statement may seem self-evident, but "feature creep" and ambiguous goals have persistently plagued modern software development projects; they have brought to ruin many promising projects both big and small. Mobile software development is no different. Successful mobile applications need to have more focused purpose and more specific goals than their desktop and server counterparts. Having a firm vision for what the application is going to enable the user to do is essential. Equally, if not more important, is a firm statement for the things the mobile application is *not* intended to do. Focus of purpose is critically important.

2. *Performance*—Having established the vision and scope for your mobile application, next in line is performance. More than any other application characteristic, performance will govern the success of your mobile application. More than desktop or server applications, mobile applications need to be highly responsive. If you do not achieve *great* performance, none of the other design decisions you make will matter. Think of how frustrated you would be if your phone did not let you dial numbers as rapidly as you can type them on the keypad; mobile device users demand responsiveness. Importantly, performance is *not* a matter of hand optimizing every line of code (often this is self-defeating), but rather understanding what is most critical from an end user's perspective and then concentrating your creativity and design skills in these areas to make the experience great.

3. *Proper UI design*—Mobile device user interfaces need to provide a focused and intuitive experience. The user interface of a mobile device is very different from what desktop applications typically present. Physical differences in mobile device displays and input mechanisms exist along with different user usage patterns. Additionally, end users may have differing degrees of experience and familiarity with using desktop software or the mobile devices you are targeting; this may introduce additional design requirements for your user interface design. It will require practice and iteration to get the user interface right. You will design, redesign, and redesign again before you arrive at a great

user experience for your mobile application. Your code needs to be flexible enough to allow you this freedom to iterate on your design. There is both an art and a science to this.

4. *Data model / memory model*—How your application internally represents its data, how much it holds in its memory at any given time, and when it disposes of data are of fundamental importance to how your application will perform.

5. *Communications model*—Having a good model for how and when data will flow between the device and other computers is a requirement for successfully building great mobile applications. Mobile devices can communicate with desktops, servers, and other devices; each of these interactions needs to be understood and engineered properly. Even more than for desktop applications, you must account for intermittent connectivity, situations where bandwidth is limited or expensive, and unreliable communications channels.

Software engineering techniques for addressing each of the needs above are discussed in the following chapters.

How to Read This Book

The knowledge in this book is hard won though years of personal experience and through lengthy discussions with friends and peers about their own experiences in mobile development. Mobile development is disciplined work but can be great fun. It is very rewarding to see a great application you built pop up and run on a mobile device that fits in your pocket. With technologies such as Microsoft's .NET Compact Framework and Visual Studio .NET, as well as competitive tools and runtime offerings from other venders, mobile device development can be very approachable. The best way to learn and experience these techniques is to put them to use and try them out along with your own ideas.

I suggest committing to memory the success factors listed above and then reading this book in any order you want. If there is a software engineering topic you are particularly interested in, jump right into it. The book is full of useful samples; feel free to jump in anywhere and try things out.

Most importantly, experiment!

Ways to Develop for Devices

Quite a few technologies can be used to build applications for mobile devices. Much like desktop computers, the two primary models for application development are the server-based Web application approach and the smart-client approach. This book specifically concerns itself with smart-client applications for mobile devices, but for comparison it is worth having a brief overview of both application models for mobile devices.

Server-Based Applications for Mobile Devices

Server-based applications are commonly referred to as "browser applications." They offer a great deal of flexibility. Attractively, they require no "on-device footprint" other than the presence of a generic mobile browser application on the device. The downside of this approach is that like other Web-based applications, mobile Web applications require a continual server connection and do not offer the richness and responsiveness of an on-device solution. The connectivity requirement is important to consider because unlike desktop computers mobile devices frequently go in and out of connectivity while their users are roaming around in the physical unwired world. However, if your application only needs to run when the user is connected and you want to target the largest range of devices, it is certainly worth considering a mobile Web-based solution.

NOTE: Many technology choices exist for supporting Web-application development targeting mobile devices. In addition to Microsoft ASP.NET's mobile controls, other Web-application technologies also support application development targeting mobile devices. These offer their own strategies for making Web applications geared toward mobile devices. If there is a popular Web-development technology you are using, chances are that there is a mobile device targeting extension available for it.

Microsoft's technology for Web applications is called ASP.NET (Active Server Pages .NET). ASP.NET offers ASP.NET "mobile controls" for targeting mobile devices. Visual Studio .NET 2003 enables developers to build ASP.NET mobile device applications. Figure 1.1 shows the new project dialog in Visual Studio with the Mobile Web Application option selected.

Creating and designing a mobile Web application works much in the same way as creating and designing Web applications targeted at desktop Web browsers, with the following major differences:

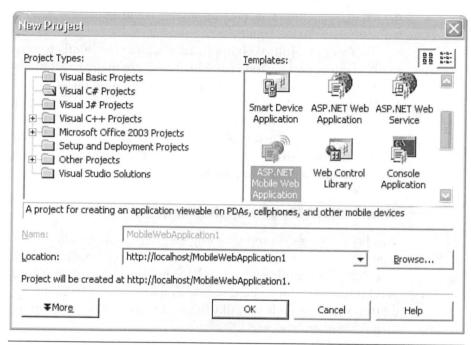

Figure 1.1 Beginning a new ASP.NET mobile Web application.

- *Design surface*—You are provided with a design surface that is specifically mobile device oriented with a simplified and streamlined control layout paradigm suitable for mobile applications.
- *Device-targeted controls*—Instead of the normal HTML set of controls, you are provided with a set of Mobile Web Forms controls to work with. These controls are specifically designed to render properly for a wide range of devices. Also offered are some controls specific to mobile devices, such as PhoneCall control.
- *Rendered markup language*—At runtime, the Mobile Web Forms controls run on the server can generate Wireless Markup Language (WML), Compact HTML (cHTML), or HTML depending on the capabilities supported by the requesting device's browser.

The server-side runtime takes on the burden of determining what the best display experience is for the mobile device interacting with it based on information the mobile Web browser submits with its request. Out of the box, the ASP.NET Mobile Web application technology supports a wide range of devices. Support for new device types can be added by Microsoft, device manufacturers, or end developers wanting to target a device type not yet supported by the framework.

To access mobile Web applications, a device needs to have a capable mobile browser application present. There are many kinds of mobile browsers, the most common being the previously mentioned WML, cHTML, and HTML browsers. Most modern smart phones come with some kind of Web browser technology installed.

You can find a great deal more information on ASP.NET mobile applications in the online documentation. (The "Mobile" section of http://www.asp.net is a great place to start.)

Smart-Client Mobile Applications

This book focuses on software engineering for smart-client mobile applications. When you decide that your mobile-device application will work best as a rich client application, you have another basic decision to make. You need to decide which client-side technology to use. Will the application be written in native code or will you use a managed code solution? Both have benefits and drawbacks.

Native Code

Native code development is usually done in C or C++. Native code is useful when you need the absolute maximum performance from a system or need low-level access to the hardware. However, native code has some significant drawbacks as well, including the following:

- *Native code development is less productive than working with managed code.* Because you are working at a lower level of abstraction, you will spend more time coding.
- *Native code is processor dependent.* When you compile to native code, you are generating instructions specific to the microprocessor you are targeting. This means that if you want to target more than one processor family, you must compile and deploy several versions of your application: This can also be true for different processors in the same processor family. For example, there are several different variants of the very popular ARM chip design that require different native compilers.
- *Native code needs to be stress tested more than managed code.* Working in native code means managing your own memory and other resources. Experience has shown that it is very difficult if not impossible to build a "perfect application." Almost invariably, some

memory or other system resource is occasionally left unreleased in complex systems. Over time even small memory or other resource leaks that occur in repetitive code can strain the finite resources on a device. Many cell phones are never turned off. Many PDAs have instant-on features that keep applications running or in memory even when the device is switched off. With respect to memory leaks, mobile devices behave more like servers than desktop applications because mobile devices are often left on continuously. If you are leaking memory, you will eventually cause the system to become unresponsive or unstable. Native code development on devices requires an extra amount of diligence and 24/7 stress testing.

C++ Tools Available for Mobile Device Development

As of this writing, Microsoft offers a free C/C++ development tool for device developers called eVC++. eVC++ stands for Embedded Visual C++. It is available for free download from Microsoft and enables developers to build native code C/C++ applications for Windows CE, Pocket PC, and the Microsoft Windows Mobile 2003 software for Smartphone (mercifully referred to hereafter simply as the Microsoft Smartphone) devices. This development environment is based on the Visual Studio 6.0 C++ development environment, which predates the Visual Studio .NET development environment. Microsoft's plan is for future versions of Visual Studio .NET (starting with the 2005 "Whidbey" release) to contain support for C++ native code development for devices, thus merging the two into one single environment.

People developing for Windows XP Embedded can use the same Visual Studio .NET development environment that exists for desktop and server development.

Many other companies also make native code development environments for devices, including MetroWorks and WindRiver. A great many command-line tools also exist, some free and some for sale. Typically these development environments are packaged per-development target; for example, a development environment for Windows CE; a different development environment for the Symbian Operating System; and a different development environment for LINUX, FreeBSD, Palm OS, and so on.

Various levels of support for the ANSI C/C++ standards exist in mobile device development tools. If code or library portability is a goal for you:

- *Pay special attention to the level of standards support in the compiler you choose, particularly for sophisticated features such as structured exception handling.* Different compilers will have different levels of support for things such as exception handling as well as potentially for things such as floating-point math support or the standard bit widths for integers.

- *Have well-defined coding guidelines that identify the compiler features and code libraries you will use in your application.* Make sure these features and libraries are supported by all the compilers you plan to use to target different processors or operating systems.

- *Consider using least common denominator features such as only using C (as opposed to C++) or only using a specific simple subset of C++ features.* This will help ensure that the language features you use are present and supported equally on the widest variety of compilers.

- *Test early and test often on each of the compilers/platforms you want to target.* Not all C/C++ compilers are created equal and some may contain bugs that you will only find when running code or debugging. In general C/C++ compilers for devices are not used as widely as desktop and server x86 compilers. The consequence of this is that they do not have as many developers exercising their code-generation capabilities. Practical experience has proven that in general less usage means more subtle bugs and limitations. If you do not test your code early and often on the set of compilers and platforms you want to run on, you are in for nasty surprises!

- *Understand the licensing policy restrictions of the compilers, libraries, and tools you are using.* If you are building code for commercial use, be aware of the licensing policies of the compiler, source and runtime libraries, and build tools you use. As boring as licensing agreements are to read, it is better to find out early than have to redesign or move to another compiler late in a product cycle. Switching compilers sounds easy but is remarkably difficult and time-consuming. This is true for all software development but particularly true for mobile device development because the large variety of different specialist tools that exist with different licensing policies including EULAs (end-user license agreements), royalty restrictions, intellectual property ownership restrictions such as GPL (general public license), LGPL (lesser general public license), FreeBSD, and so forth. *Caveat emptor: Let the coder beware! No one is looking to pull one over on you; just make sure you choose knowingly.*

Native code development for mobile devices is a viable choice and may be appropriate for your needs, but this decision needs to be made deliberately and for the right reasons. If you choose to write your mobile device application in native code, make sure you are doing so for the correct reasons and spend time up front understanding the C/C++ compiler choices you will be making along with the engineering and testing burden this will require. Native code mobile device development is significantly more complex than native code desktop or server development. To be successful, you need to approach it armed with clear goals and an understanding of the tools you will be using.

Managed Code

Managed code is a term describing code running in a managed environment whether on a server, personal computer, mobile device, or in an embedded system. A runtime engine oversees resource allocation, threading, and synchronization needs, and enforces the type safety of executing code, preventing illegal memory access. It is a level of abstraction above native code that greatly increases developer productivity and the reliability of the code produced. The lifetime of objects and other types allocated by running code is tracked by the runtime engine, freeing the developer of the burden of this task. When managed code is compiled, it generates binary instructions that also include rich meta-data descriptions of the classes, types, variables, and any other information necessary to manage the code's execution. This meta data describing the code is what allows a managed-code runtime to perform its administration and supervision services. Rich meta data is a key difference between native code and managed code. Some additional common features of many managed code environments include the following:

- *Processor independence*—Managed code is not compiled into processor-specific instructions but is instead compiled into an intermediate language. Intermediate language is often shortened to IL and also referred to as "byte codes" in some runtime environments; all these terms mean the same thing. This IL is then converted on the device to the appropriate executable format. Compiling into an IL format can allow the same compiled code to run on not just different processors but also different address sizes; for example, the same IL component can run on 32- or 64-bit processors because the instructions are not processor-address-size specific.
- *Operating system independence*—Managed-code runtimes and their programming libraries enable developers to program targeting an abstraction on top of the core operating system. Although "write once, run anywhere" is not a practical goal given the significant differences in user interface and user interaction models on different classes of devices having a degree of abstraction above, the operating system is still very useful for porting applications to target different device classes. In addition, the ability to build headless (headless = no user interface) components that can be run on different devices without recompilation is very useful for building reusable modules. Common code can be placed into headless components leaving only

the need to implement device-specific user interfaces that use those common modules.

- *JIT (just-in-time compilation) and/or interpretation of code*—There are two methods for executing managed code: (1) JITing, where the IL is translated into native processor instructions and then executed; or (2) interpretation, where each IL instruction is looked at and predefined libraries are called to execute the intent of the IL. JITing produces the fastest-executing code, but interpreters are easier to build because they do not need to know how to generate processor-specific instructions. Often an interpreter is first built to quickly port a managed runtime to a new processor and then JIT compilers are built to optimize for specific popular processors. The same IL can either be interpreted or JITed; the choice is up to the implementer of the runtime.

- *Garbage collection*—Garbage collection is the way managed-code environments remove the burden of low-level memory management from application developers. There are many different strategies for garbage collection, each optimized for different scenarios. It is an ongoing research subject to discover ever-more-optimal strategies for important scenarios. A common strategy employed on device runtimes is "mark and sweep," where periodically the runtime will start with the list of all variables currently in scope and trace all of the objects referenced by these objects. Each object that is found this way is "marked" to indicate it is still being used. In this way a live-object tree is built representing the full set of all objects that can be reached by the application's code. When all live objects are marked, a sweep is performed to release all objects not reachable by the application. Garbage collectors can be highly complex systems, and many optimizations are possible to maximize performance on servers, desktops, and devices. Organizations building managed-code runtimes spend a great deal of time tuning their garbage collection strategy for maximum performance and reliability.

- *Versioning*—One of the things meta data can be used for is to supply rich information about the version of a component and the versions of other components that it is dependent on. Managed runtimes with this capability can manage multiple versions of the same components on the same machine, allowing each component to bind to the specific component it was built and tested against. This is important for the long-term stability of machines running multiple applications. Built-in versioning support avoids versioning conflicts and both the subtle and overt kinds of problems improper versioning can bring about.

■ *Security support*—Managed code can also enforce security policy on the device. Managed-code runtimes that have rich security support can set policy for which services any specific piece of code will be granted. This is often referred to as "evidence-based security." Typical examples of security policy include "Code signed by a trusted third party can run with full capabilities," "Code present on the local file system will have access to files in a specific set of folders," "Code downloaded from the Internet that is not signed by a trusted party will run with minimal permissions and generic file i/o is not allowed." Different runtimes have different levels of support for security; for example, J2ME and .NET Compact Framework v1.1 have different support for security. The .NET Compact Framework supports a subset of the desktop and server .NET Framework security policy.

Two of the most common managed-code environments for mobile devices are J2ME (Java Mobile Edition) and the .NET Compact Framework. This book shows the principals of software engineering for mobile devices using the .NET Compact Framework, although most of the principals discussed are valid for all kinds of mobile device development, including native code.

The benefits of managed code cannot be overstated. As a general rule, if it is possible to use managed code for a software development project, use it. Your code will get developed faster, will run with fewer bugs, will be easier to port to new devices, will run safer and with higher stability, and will be more maintainable than the native code implementation would be. Native code development should be used only when absolutely required for performance reasons or for low-level access. Even in these cases it is best to write the small necessary bit of critical code in native code and build the rest of the application in higher-level managed code. As you will see later in this book, with good mobile device software engineering practices as well as managed runtimes supporting JIT compilation, very few tasks should require native code. Even many action-oriented highly animated games are possible in managed code. The benefits the higher-level abstractions of managed code bring are overwhelmingly compelling. Ten to twenty years ago people moved from developing applications in assembly code to writing them in C, reserving assembly code for only the most focused and critical tasks. This increased level of abstraction allowed far more complex applications to be developed more quickly and with greater reliability. The same kind of transition is now underway from native C/C++ to managed-code environments.

The .NET Compact Framework—A Managed-Code Runtime for Devices

This book uses the .NET Compact Framework to demonstrate good mobile software engineering practices, so it is worth giving a high-level overview of the .NET Compact Framework in this introductory chapter. A later chapter is devoted to describing in more detail how the .NET Compact Framework works and how it manages memory, compiles code, and collects garbage. Developers choosing other mobile device programming models will find many of the concepts similar.

The .NET Compact Framework is composed of two major pieces:

(1) a core native code engine, and

(2) a larger set of managed class libraries.

The Core Execution Engine

The .NET Compact Framework core engine is written in native code. Its job is to load managed code, compile it, run it, and perform all the tasks involved in managed-code execution. The .NET Compact Framework has been ported to several different processor families including x86, StrongARM, SH3, MIPS, and others.

Floating Point: What's in a Number?

The .NET Compact Framework's execution engine and runtime libraries have built-in support for floating-point mathematics. This is specifically worth pointing out because not all mobile device runtimes do. If you are coming from the perspective of desktop or server development, this is important to understand.

For example, the Java J2ME CLDC (Common Limited Device Configuration) version 1.0 does not require floating-point support, but the J2ME CLDC v1.1 does. Java's MIDP 2.0 only (Mobile Information Device Profile) requires only CLDC 1.0 support. If you are targeting a mobile device with a J2ME runtime, make sure you know which version it supports.

Most rich mobile applications require some form of decimal arithmetic. Although it is possible to simulate some floating-point operations with fixed-point integer mathematics, this can be cumbersome and is limited in its flexibility to handle advanced needs.

When you are defining your mobile application's runtime requirements, pay careful attention to the math support present in the runtime, not only for floating point but also currency and date/time. Advanced math libraries for subjects such as trigonometry and exponent support are also useful things to verify. The .NET Compact Framework has built-in support for all of these.

The benefit of a runtime not supporting floating-point math is the ability to fit into smaller spaces and run in simpler environments. The big drawback is limited functionality for application developers. Take a careful look at your needs and choose a runtime and target device that offers you the right degree of functionality and flexibility.

The Class Libraries

These are the programming APIs that developers use to build their applications. They can logically be broken into four pieces:

1. *Base class libraries*—These are the nuts and bolts of programming. Support for strings, arrays, collections, file i/o, threading, networking, and pretty much all of the things you expect to be available when writing code are in the base class libraries.
2. *Drawing/forms*—The drawing and forms libraries contain support for 2D drawing, as well as support for rich forms and controls with which to build user interfaces.
3. *Data access*—The data access libraries offer an in-memory relational-tables model called ADO.NET for working with data created in memory, loaded from XML, or queried from a database.
4. *XML and Web services*—These libraries contain support for working with XML as well as making Web service calls to pass information between devices and servers via XML and SOAP.

Portability

The .NET Compact Framework execution engine and class libraries were designed in such a way as to enable the relatively straightforward porting of them to multiple device types and different operating systems. The first devices that have been targeted are Windows CE 4.1, the Pocket PC 2000/

2002/2003/and beyond, and the Microsoft Smartphone operating system. Other non-Microsoft platforms may be supported in the future.

It is also worth pointing out that because the .NET Compact Framework was built on top of the CLI (Common Language Infrastructure) ECMA and ISO standards, it is quite possible for another organization to build its own device-targeted CLI implementation for C# and VB.NET development. Such an implementation would be likely to have the same base class libraries but potentially different higher-level libraries. There are already at least two independent third-party CLI implementations for desktops and servers.

Summary

Today's rich mobile devices offer great opportunities to build compelling mobile software. This software has the potential to entertain, to bring valuable information and decision making to people, and to increase people's productivity by unchaining them from their desks. With all this new technology and potential, this is an exciting time to be a software developer.

Successful mobile applications bring a highly focused experience to their users, enabling them to zero in on and quickly accomplish desired tasks. Performance is a critical aspect of this experience.

When building a mobile application, a primary question that must be answered is "Should it be a local application or a browser-based application?" Local applications enable you to deliver the richest possible experience to the user and also allow the application to run when the device is not directly connected to a communications network but require an on-device footprint.

If a rich local-device application is chosen, the next question to be answered is "Should the application be written in native code or using a managed-code runtime?" The default answer should be to use a managed-code runtime because of the great productivity and reliability gains offered by today's managed-code environments.

Several managed-code environments exist, the two most popular being J2ME and the .NET Compact Framework. The rest of this book describes the most important aspects of mobile device applications and runtimes and teaches the software engineering concepts that will enable you to build great mobile applications. The .NET Compact Framework is used to demonstrate these concepts with many examples. Regardless of language or runtime choice, the general principals discussed are applicable to all mobile device development whether using native code or managed-code environments.

I hope you enjoy the book and have fun experimenting and learning what great opportunities mobile devices have to offer for developing innovative software!

CHAPTER 2

Characteristics of Mobile Applications

Intelligence is quickness to apprehend as distinct from ability, which is capacity to act wisely on the thing apprehended.

—A. N. Whitehead (1861–1947, British mathematician and philosopher) (Encarta 2004, Quotations)

Introduction

Mobile applications are different from their desktop counterparts, and it is worth spending some time and space exploring what makes them special. To be successful in mobile application development, it is important to have both a keen understanding of what mobile devices really are and how they differ from desktop and laptop computers that users also interact with.

This chapter is intended to set the context and get you "thinking mobility." Getting into the habit of thinking from a device perspective is important because it will have an enormous effect on how you go about designing your applications. To build great mobile applications, it is important to understand what key characteristics define great mobile applications. This chapter answers the questions "How does mobile application use differ from desktop use?" and "What are the most important characteristics of good mobile applications?"

Armed with this understanding, it will be possible for you to focus on the engineering challenges that matter most for mobile device software development.

Usage Patterns

Perhaps the most critical difference between mobile device applications and desktop applications is the way in which people use them. Picture yourself at your computer desktop; what are you doing? If you are like most people, you are doing one of three things: browsing the Web, working on documents (word processing, spreadsheets, pictures, photographs, and so on), or communicating (e-mail, instant messaging, and so forth). These tend to be long-time duration and exploratory activities and the user will periodically switch between these activities midstream. If you are a developer (and the odds are pretty good you are if you are reading this book!), you can add software development to this list, which is absolutely a long-time duration and exploratory activity. If you are a player of computer games, you will know that many of the most interesting games for desktop computers are long-term and exploratory games allowing users to explore and interact with complex virtual worlds.

People who use both desktop applications and mobile device applications tend to use the two in different but complementary ways. While working with a mobile device, the user's activities tend to be short session length interrupt-driven or interrupt-causing interactions. The user is typically either responding to being interrupted or using the device to make an immediate request of some other person or process. Today's typical mobile phone is a great example of this. When you place a phone call or send an SMS text message, you are interrupting someone; when you get a phone call or an SMS message, you are being interrupted. This same usage model carries over to all kinds of mobile device applications. Successful mobile applications must be as natural and intuitive as making or receiving a phone call or SMS message.

Mobile device applications tend also to be more focused on enabling a few specific features very well as opposed to offering the general-purpose exploratory environment that successful desktop applications do. Because mobile devices are often operated using a single hand or by tapping a small screen with a stylus, it is important that users of the device be able to quickly discover and navigate to the information and features they want. The ability to quickly navigate to a small set of key features is an important aspect of a great mobile device experience.

Long-Duration vs. Short-Duration Activities

People using desktop computers tend to do so for long sessions. Working for an hour at a time is not unusual, and several-hour sessions are not atypical. In these sessions people mold and develop ideas over time and tend to do a great deal of iterating and revising. Because of this, startup time is not as important as giving the users the rich features they may need while exploring and working with their information.

Laptop computers tend to share many of the same usage patterns as desktops, but it is possible to see some mobile device characteristics emerging. Speeding up startup time (or wakeup time) and getting users back to the activities they were doing when they last shut down is an increasing priority. However, the usage patterns of laptops are still much more desktop oriented than they are mobile device oriented, and part of this is simply due to the relative physical size of the devices. Users can do an awful lot of things on a mobile phone in the time it would take them to get their laptop out of their bag, open the lid, start up the computer, get to the application they want to work with, and get online if required. This is very different from the "take it out of your pocket and use it right away" model that mobile phones or PDAs offer.

When using mobile devices, the same people's activities tend to be short term, ranging from several seconds to several minutes. Activities such as making a phone call, checking an appointment schedule, or entering or reading instant messages are all done using frequent but short-duration sessions. Even playing games tends to be a short-term activity on mobile devices. People playing games on mobile devices usually play for relatively short periods of time when they are in between activities. The games are intended to allow the user to pass extra time pleasurably while waiting for a train, sitting at an airport, or waiting to meet someone at the mall. Because of this focus on short-session usage and immediacy, mobile devices are usually in an "always on" or "instant on" state, where the time for users to access the device is on par with the time it takes for them to take the device out of their pocket.

It is important to note that although session time tends to be short, the underlying data the user works with is often long term. In the case of a mobile game, users may want to pick up where they left off the last time they played. For productivity applications, this trend is even more pronounced, with a classic example being the address book on a mobile phone (which must always be available). A common task when speaking to someone on the phone or in person is checking a personal appointment calendar and booking a follow-up meeting with the person. The user has a need to be able to quickly access the device, navigate to the person's contact information, create a new schedule item, and then resume the conversation without further delay. The underlying data is long term and durable, but the application usage pattern is short term and immediate.

Exploratory vs. Focused Activities

Desktop and laptop computers offer a very rich platform for exploring information. The large-screen real estate available enables the display of a great deal of peripheral information that may be of interest to the user. The keyboard and mouse offer a rich way to navigate through that information in a random-access manner. This enables the user to jump rapidly to any of the information visible on the large screen, flip through several layers of windows that currently may be open, quickly enter and revise relatively large amounts of data in a short time, or "drag and drop" to move information around various documents. These are all exploratory mechanisms for working with information.

Browsing the Web on a desktop computer is a great example of this kind of exploratory experience. Common high-bandwidth network access offers the possibility of downloading large amounts of information locally. This allows more information to be downloaded than the user has immediate need for, just in case the user will find it of peripheral interest. The user is commonly presented with a rich downloaded document to explore with many areas of interest to potentially branch off to. During this exploration, users commonly branch out into other documents and often have several browser windows open simultaneously so that they can switch between them to find the information they are looking for. Anyone who has used the Web to find a lowest-cost airfare is familiar with this experience. Multiple browser windows to different travel sites are open, and different arrival and departure dates are priced. Data is often copy/pasted from browsers into e-mail or other documents. Faced with a rich Web page with a great deal of information and many links, the user's next specific action is very difficult to predict. Will the user click a link? Will the user type a new address into the Web browser access bar? Will the user copy/paste some information from a Web page into a document? Will the user start an e-mail or instant message session? The possibilities are almost endless, and because of this the user typically works in an exploratory mode.

Similar exploratory usage patterns exist for rich client applications on personal computers such as e-mail applications, spreadsheets, and content-creation applications such as word processors and paint programs as well as for development tools. Users "task switch" often and in random-access ways to get to the information they need from different sources and integrate it for their own use. A person typing into a word processing document will continually iterate over the text, making improvements to the content and layout, revising the text, and navigating the document in a random-access manner. Users may switch to another application to grab some relevant information and copy it into the document they are working with. Spreadsheets offer an even more exploratory user interface by giving the user a huge tabular space in which to enter, modify, and analyze data; to draw charts; and to ask what-if questions. Development tools are also immensely exploratory and enable developers to quickly navigate around exploring their code and user interface design, browsing definitions, performing code transformations, and seeking reference materials relevant to the tasks they are trying to accomplish. Debugging code is by definition an act of exploring, experimentation, and analysis.

The best desktop applications enable users to explore information in a very free-form way. Conversely, great mobile applications enable the same users to zero in on specific information and services as quickly and as efficiently as possible with little or no navigation.

The same users deal with local documents differently on mobile devices than they do on desktop computers. It is often useful to be able to view and make small modifications to desktop-created word processing documents and spreadsheets on mobile devices, but these documents are almost never created and authored on devices. It is safe to assume that 90 percent of the content creation for these documents will happen on desktops and that devices will be used primarily for reading these documents.

In addition to applications used to surf the Internet and work with documents, there are also custom applications. Many kinds of custom applications exist on the desktop—line-of-business applications, communications applications, analytical applications, data-entry and tracking applications, and so on. All of these applications have mobile device variants. The same "explore vs. focus" difference discussed previously exists between desktop and mobile applications. To be useful, the mobile applications should offer a focused experience to the same person who may use a more exploratory version of the desktop application. Think of mobile applications as offering a different view on the same data and processes as a desktop application. The data and processes are the same as the desktop, but the view is transformed and focused into a way that offers instant access to the key elements that the user may need while mobile.

A common mistake developers make when trying to bring a desktop application to a device is trying to bring down the whole application verbatim and shoehorn it into a device. This never works satisfactorily because of the usage differences between desktops and mobile devices discussed here.

A second common mistake is to take a desktop application and user interface and start slicing pieces out of it until it runs on the device. Related to this are efforts to port pieces of a larger desktop user interface to a device by breaking the large interface into a series of nested dialogs that can be displayed on the device's screen. Doing this will usually result in an awkward and less-functional desktop application, not a well-honed mobile device application. The fundamental question that needs to be asked is "What is the view of the data and processes that will be most useful for people using mobile devices?" From the answer to this question, you can start constructing the user interface from the ground up.

It is essential to think about the scenarios that users need to accomplish when mobile and to specifically optimize these tasks so that they work better than they do on the desktop. It is equally important to consider what parts of the application are not critical for mobile usage. These parts of the application should be de-emphasized or eliminated. Your mobile application should serve to behave as a kind of fish-eye lens for the users' needs, allowing a broad view but specifically zeroing on the most important tasks they want to accomplish.

A More In-Depth Look into Mobile Web Browsers

A mobile Web browser is an interesting example of a common rich client application running on a mobile device. Because of this, it is useful to examine how mobile Web browsers differ from their desktop counterparts. This will give some good metaphors to think about how other desktop applications may manifest themselves as mobile device applications and what design changes may be required to make the mobile experience a good one.

Many mobile devices now offer Internet browsers, but these browsers are very different in their usage models from desktop browsers. Although technologically similar (they both render HTML for display), their interaction with users is significantly different. Desktop browsers are designed to access the widest array of Web sites and to download and display complex documents. Mobile Internet browsers are designed to access mobile Web sites and download and distill documents to their essential information. Mobile browsers tend to work in one of two ways: (1) They download content specifically intended for mobile devices that is simpler in layout, has smaller-sized photos and images, and is designed to be read in a smaller window; or (2) they download generic Web-content and attempt to distill it down to its essence and display that to users.

Building a Great Web Experience for a Mobile Device Requires Cooperation Between the Device and Server

It is worth noting that trying to distill generic HTML pages into a good viewable experience for a mobile device is a complex problem. Given the huge variety of layout possible with HTML and the mixing of core information with peripheral content and advertising, it is challenging to pull out what the essential information is and fit that onto a mobile device screen.

Instead of putting all the burden onto the device, a better result can often be achieved by tackling the problem on the server. Often, popular Web sites such as MSNBC or the BBC offer separate mobile device versions of their content. These two sites take different approaches to solving this problem that are worth understanding:

- http://www.msnbc.com/news/MobileChannel/mmc.asp—This Web site automatically adjusts its response to the capabilities of the browser that makes the request. Results differ significantly when accessing the Web site from a desktop browser or a mobile device browser.

- http://news.bbc.co.uk/text_only.stm—This BBC Web site offers a Web view with low-resolution pictures and limited formatting that can be displayed effectively on mobile devices.

The goal of displaying HTML content effectively on a mobile device can be achieved much more effectively if the server is willing to meet the device half way and provide a simplified view of the data. Solving mobile device application challenges by building additional targeted server services is a good idea not just for Web applications but for all applications that access data on servers. If there is work you can do on a server to simplify design challenges faced by mobile devices, it often makes sense to do this.

In addition, although the address bar is prominently displayed and used in desktop browsers, it is often hidden and is much less used on mobile devices. Due to the smaller screen sizes and more limited input mechanisms, the increased time it would take to type a URL into a device and the space that the address bar takes up on the screen, the concept of an address bar is much less useful on a mobile device. Adding to this is the fact that much generic Web content will not render acceptably on mobile devices. All of this greatly lowers the utility of completely random-access navigation to Web addresses.

None of this should leave you with the impression that Web browsing for mobile devices is not useful or interesting; it is both! Many good mobile Web applications offer the user a lot of utility when accessed from devices. With the advent of server-side Web application technologies such as the ASP.NET Mobile Controls, it is now easy for Web developers to build "mobile views" to their existing Web content. Web browsing for mobile applications is a "killer application," but it is a different "killer application" from its desktop relative.

Form Factor

The need to fit comfortably into one's pocket is a key defining characteristic of most mobile devices. This physical constraint is the basis for the mobile device's utility; if it fits in your pocket, it is mobile. Some additional important form-factor considerations are as follows:

- *The ability to be used in crowded and noisy spaces*—This is a reason why speech input is not always a great idea even if it is technically possible. It is also important that a mobile device not be disturbing to those around it (a reason why voice response is not always a great idea). A train full of people arguing with their mobile devices is not a pleasant social environment. Think of having a silent mode or headphones if sound is required for your mobile application.
- *Single- or two-handed operation*—Many devices are intended to be operated by one hand. Most mobile phones meet this criterion. Some are intended to be held in one hand and operated with another. Most PDAs fall into this category. Laptops generally require two hands and a flat surface for efficient usage. Your mobile application should follow whatever paradigm the device imposes on usage; that is, don't build an application that requires two-handed use to get anything useful done if it's going to run on a mobile phone that people typically operate with one hand. This is an important aspect for the usability testing of your application. Another important consideration is the physical environment in which a handheld application is being used. A touch-screen display offers a rich environment for navigating applications, but all too often application designers build and test the user interfaces either running on a desktop-based device emulator or sitting at their desks. This results in user interfaces that are far too small for real-world usage. The real world is full of bumps, jitters, vibrations, and people who want to use their devices while walking down the street or by pressing the screen with their fingers rather than the stylus. Paradoxically, for real-world usage, touch-screen input on small mobile devices often requires larger user interface controls than stationary applications being used on personal computers. It is important to understand whether your application needs to be "one-hand friendly," real-world two-hand "stylus friendly," or "finger friendly" when used with a touch screen while the user is mobile.

■ *No power cords or communications cables for long periods of time—* To be effective mobile devices, the devices need to be able to oper- ate untethered for long periods of time. A good rule of thumb is that the devices and the applications running on them should not require being connected to wired power or communication sources more than once a day. How often your application requires the device to be running at full power and how often your application needs to be connected to online data are important design considerations.

These form-factor considerations should strongly influence your design. Engineering creativity is required to solve form-factor problems as well as to adapt software design to different form factors.

T9, a Great Example of a Smart Engineering Solution to a Mobile Device Constraint

T9 is a way to allow for rapid one-handed text entry on mobile phones that have the standard 12-key phone number pads. Prior to T9, users entering sentences of text into a mobile phone needed to tap in each letter by laboriously hitting the 1 through 9 keys up to 4 times to get the correct letter. Table 2.1 shows the num- ber of key presses necessary with and without T9 to type the simple text "text message."

Table 2.1 Mobile Phone Key Presses Necessary to Type a "Text Message"

Desired Letter	Key Taps Before T9	Key Taps with T9
T	8, = t	8, = t
E	3,3, = d, e	3, = e
X	9,9, = w, x	9, = x
T	8,= t	8,= t
<space>	1,= space	1,= space
M	6,= m	6,= m
E	3,= d, e	3,= e
S	7,7,7,7= p, q, r, s	7,= s
S	7,7,7,7= p, q, r, s	7,= s
A	2,= a	2,= a

Table 2.1 Mobile Phone Key Presses Necessary to Type a "Text Message"

Desired Letter	Key Taps Before T9	Key Taps with T9
G	4,= g	4,= g
E	3,3 = d, e	3 = e
Total Taps:	21	12

Twelve taps compared to 21 taps represents a savings of more than 40 percent in key presses. In practice, the T9 time savings is even greater because you avoid confirmation delays incurred when you want to enter two sequential letters represented by the same numeric key.

For example, both *r* and *s* are represented by the number 7 on the keypad. If you want to spell *cars*, you must wait for a second after you enter *r* to allow the input software to realize you are done with that letter and move the insert point to the next letter to be entered. Anyone who has ever tried both ways for a few days will never go back to the pre-T9 way of entering short text.

How does it work? Statistics! When you enter the keys 8, 3, 9, the software looks in its dictionary and determines that the only likely words you could be typing are either *vex* or *text*, so these are the two options it gives you. When you enter the final key 8, the software finds that only one stored word in its dictionary meets this key combination, *text*, and that word is chosen for you. By maintaining a dictionary of words and key combinations in your local language, the software is able to greatly increase your efficiency in writing short messages. If you need to go outside of the words available in the dictionary, you can enter the unknown words via the old input mechanism.

Is this suitable for writing the novel *War and Peace* on your mobile phone? No, of course not; but it is perfectly suitable for typing the sentence "Just finished reading *War and Peace*—long book!" and sending it to your friend.

T9 is a great example of "thinking mobile" and solving a problem specific to entering typical information onto mobile devices. We can learn from this creative idea. The key message is "Don't solve the generic problem; solve the specific problem your users face and optimize, optimize, optimize."

Reliability Requirements

With regard to reliability requirements, mobile devices paradoxically resemble servers more than they do desktops. The reasons for this are as follows:

- *Much like servers, mobile devices and their applications are often left running 24 hours a day, 7 days a week.* Cell phones and PDAs are often left running all the time or have standby modes that ensure that when they start up they come up in a state that closely resembles the one they were last used in. Although desktop computers are also increasingly left on all the time, users still reboot them, log on and off occasionally, and start and shut down applications fairly frequently; this causes improperly held system resources to periodically get flushed. In contrast, because the applications on mobile devices are meant to be "instant access," the applications are often left running in a background state so that they do not need to incur startup delays and users can pick up where they left off with the applications. For these reasons, devices resemble servers in that they need to sit ready to provide instant services for their clients.
- *Much like servers, mobile device applications have to deal effectively with unexpected failures.* Mobile devices operate in a demanding environment. Communications failures occur often and midstream. Users think nothing of popping the battery out of the back of a mobile phone midstream if they are running low on power or think the device is behaving in an awkward way. The operating system itself may shut down a background mobile application if it is running low on resources. Worse still, devices get lost, are stolen, are dropped into puddles, and suffer all means of cruel and unusual punishment at the hands of their users. Even with this, users are devastated when their mobile phone disappears or stops working and they realize that they had important and hard-to-replace information on it. For all these reasons, mobile applications, like mission-critical servers, need to make sure that the important data and state they are managing is held in longer-term storage that can survive the application unexpectedly vanishing or failing. Mobile application developers need to think like mission-critical server application developers and ensure that data important to users is stored safely and in a form that can be recovered if data corruption occurs due to sudden failure. Developers should also consider enabling appropriate backup measures to allow automatic off-device archives that enable users to recover from catastrophic loss of important

information; users rarely back up their own important data even though the need to do so should be obvious.

- *Much like servers, mobile device operating systems and applications often do not use memory paging files.* Your desktop computer probably has a large paging file set up by default that enables it to swap out memory not being used to a file on disk. This file is called a memory paging file or a swap file. If new memory is requested by an application because it is starting up or because it has additional memory needs and the system is running low on physical memory, the operating system will swap out pages of memory that have not recently been used to a file on disk. If the paged-out memory is later accessed, it is swapped back into memory and other pages are swapped out as needed. In this way your desktop computer can function as if it has a much larger amount of RAM than it actually does. This is intended to enable users to run many applications simultaneously while keeping the one in the foreground as responsive as possible. It also allows leaked memory to be relatively harmlessly swapped out to disk on the grounds that the application that is leaking memory will probably be shut down before its leak becomes so large that it consumes all of the page file memory. Servers tend not to use this strategy because they are designed for maximum throughput. A server wants to keep everything in physical memory where it can be accessed quickly. Devices tend not to use page files because they do not have huge disk drives onto which they can quickly swap in and out pages of memory. Having this capacity on a device would be prohibitive from expense, size, speed, and power-consumption perspectives. You may object that "in theory memory could be swapped to some kind of flash memory on a device"; however, this is not practical because writing to flash is not quick and is not intended to be done over and over again in rapid succession.

- *Many mobile devices serve other critical purposes while running foreground applications.* If a mobile phone ceases to work as a mobile phone because your application crashes, drastically slows down in responsiveness, blocks the user interface, or otherwise misbehaves, the end user will not be very happy. Most mobile operating systems have levels of protection to guard the critical functions, but your application is certainly capable of making the device less useful for its other functions if it misbehaves. In server terms, this would be known as a "denial-of-service" problem. Like servers, many devices need to manage a series of critical services that must be available for users at all times.

For these reasons, it is important that your mobile device application be able to run reliably and efficiently over long periods of time.

Important Characteristics of Mobile Applications

This chapter has spent a fair amount of time and space comparing and contrasting mobile devices and their applications with their desktop and server counterparts. It is now appropriate to specifically list the things that define great mobile applications.

Startup Time

Quick startup time is an important characteristic of mobile applications. Because users tend to use mobile devices frequently and for short durations, the ability to quickly start up a mobile application is imperative. It may be undesirable to sit at a desk staring at a word processor, encyclopedia, or development tool splash screen for 6 seconds as it starts up, but this is a minor annoyance compared to the overall time you will spend using the application. For a mobile device application that the user wants to use for 20 seconds to check or update some small piece of information, 6 seconds is an outrageously long time to wait. A good rule of thumb is that the user's session time with an application must be much longer than any startup time he or she endures. Desktop applications have long session times, so users are willing to suffer larger startup times. Mobile applications have short session times, so proportionately shorter startup times are required. Startup time is important for desktop applications, but it is critical for mobile devices because people use them intermittently and for short durations.

Responsiveness

A mobile device looks like a small mechanical tool that fits in your pocket, and people expect it to behave that way. When people tap it, push a button, or do anything physical to it, they expect a physical response. If they do not get an immediate response, they will become impatient and try again. This can cause problems when the second tap, click, or poke is processed by your application or another application that errantly gets the second click. Therefore, it is of utmost importance that users receive some type of acknowledgment immediately upon performing an action on a device.

The best kind of acknowledgment is the completion of the requested action; nothing tops that. The second best response is an acknowledgment that the request has been received and is being processed in the background, leaving the application ready to take another request. The third best response is to acknowledge the request and show something like a wait cursor to let users know their request is being worked on; the application is not responsive, but users receive some indication that work has been initiated and is being done on their behalf. The worst response is to do nothing and leave users wondering whether their action was registered. As with some other characteristics we will explore, this requirement is not unique to mobile devices, but it does have a special relevance because of the way people work with devices and expect them to work for them.

Focused Purpose

Focused purpose is another characteristic of a successful mobile application. The application must have a clearly defined set of things it does very well; it must do them with a minimum number of clicks, taps, or other user gestures; and it must do them quickly. The importance to mobile devices of focused purpose is often exemplified by having special buttons on the devices that are assigned to specific tasks (for example, a button to jump right to the stored contacts database, a button to view schedules, or a button to read in a bar code number and send it to a specific application).

Your mobile application should strive to identify which common tasks it is going to make as easy as absolutely possible. This is true for high-level application features as well as low-level tasks that are commonly performed by users working with your application. If your mobile application needs to enable users to enter dates quickly, for example, make sure that choosing dates is as easy (and quick) as possible and measure the effectiveness of this process. If your mobile application needs to enable users to choose locations on regional street maps to give them directions on how to get somewhere, make sure the user's experience in doing this is as quick as possible.

A common error in building mobile applications it to write as little code as possible with the intention of keeping the application as small as possible. This is a noble goal but should not be done at the expense of user productivity. Spend the time to write the extra code to make sure your application has a focused purpose and enables users to achieve their goals as quickly as possible.

Customized Interactions with Off-Device Information Sources

It is important to understand that building a great mobile application is not just a matter of getting the code that runs on the device right. Thought must also be given to the off-device software that the mobile application interacts with. Information sources that expose services to mobile devices should be given proper consideration in the application's design to ensure that they are returning information in a way that is appropriate for mobile devices. A good example of this is e-mail services for mobile devices. Rich e-mail applications require server- and client-side software. The client accesses the server to get information about incoming messages and then downloads the relevant content to the local devices. Because mobile devices tend to utilize network connections that are intermittent in availability, lower bandwidth, and often more expensive than those personal computers use, the e-mail server services for mobile devices should be tailored to meet these constraints. This typically means providing server facilities to limit the size of content being downloaded or specifying filters to identify the information that is truly useful to a mobile user. A server-side service originally designed for desktop access may need to be extended to effectively support mobile scenarios. In addition, configuration mechanisms must be designed to run on servers, desktops, or the mobile devices themselves that enable users to specify their information needs and tune the information filters to suit their requirements. Design for mobile applications often extends well beyond the physical boundaries of the devices themselves.

Consistency of Experience

Because mobile devices are compact and self-contained, users naturally view the whole device as a single unified experience. Each mobile device has its own gestalt. Typically, successful mobile applications do not appear so much as discrete applications but rather as natural feature extensions of the mobile device's experience. For this reason, following style guidelines for each specific device you are building mobile applications for is important. How a user starts, stops, navigates through the features of a mobile device, and answers common prompts are very specific and learned behaviors unique to the target device. Users adapt unconsciously to a mobile device's user interface metaphors, and deviations from these patterns become very uncomfortable. Consistency of experience is important for desktop applications as well, but because desktop applications offer such rich experiences there are often multiple ways to accomplish a given task (such as keystrokes, mouse clicks, menus, and toolbars). For mobile applications, there is often only one way to accomplish a given task, and the user gets implicitly trained on how to do this. It is far better to have four different versions of your device application, each tuned to the user interface metaphors of specific devices, than it is to have one general application that does not integrate well into any of the target devices.

Computer Architecture Differences

In terms of architecture, desktop and laptop computers are like large houses in the countryside. Mobile devices are like apartments and condominiums in the city. Both serve specific needs and pose specific restrictions on how they can most effectively be used.

Houses tend to be relatively large and have lots of storage space. Some storage space is close at hand, whereas some other space is harder to get to. In a house, the stuff you do not use very often is stored in the attic or the basement, and now and then you have to go look for it when you need it.

Apartments and condominiums, on the other hand, tend to have very little storage space. Things you need close at hand are kept there. Less frequently used things are discarded. Rather than own things you use infrequently, it is often easier just to rent them as needed.

The same holds true for mobile devices. Both the available memory as well as the long-term storage is geared toward keeping around what you use often. Less frequently used data should be pushed onto servers to be accessed when needed.

On a desktop computer, RAM and long-term storage space are separated. On devices, your RAM is often used both as working application RAM as well as mid- and long-term storage. Flash storage devices are also increasingly being used for longer-term storage, and the bulk of this storage space is often in the form of removable memory cards.

Some Very Quick Math to Prove a Point About Memory Sizes

A rich mobile device today may have 64MB of RAM. This RAM is often partitioned between program RAM and virtual file system. Let's assume that 32MB of this RAM goes to the file system to hold all the long-term data you work with (things such as photos, documents, music, and other information). This leaves 32MB for the operating system and applications to share. Assume that five applications are running simultaneously (not uncommon), all are using roughly equal amounts of RAM, and that the operating system further uses resources equal to an application. This leaves a ration of 5 to 6MB of RAM for each application to use. This size is considerable but by no means infinite. A few big digital photographs brought into memory could consume most of this RAM. Many mobile devices have considerably less RAM to work with and may be asked to run more applications simultaneously. The RAM available on the device sets the absolute limit and is non-negotiable. If you use up the available physical memory, things will not be moved to a page file on hard disk as it would on the desktop. Most likely you will run out of memory and your application will crash.

A few megabytes of working space is pretty good when used effectively in the same way that a one-bedroom apartment in Manhattan can offer a nice amount of space so long as you do not try to fill it with too much stuff. Keep piling more stuff in and you will reach a critical point where nothing else will fit and you can only navigate around the apartment with extreme difficulty. With enough stuff in it, your apartment will become unusable. So it is with mobile devices.

Summary

Mobile devices differ significantly from desktop computers and laptops. Because of this, applications for mobile devices differ from desktop applications in significant ways. Desktop applications tend to get used in long sessions, and great desktop applications offer the user an exploratory environment for the information they work with. Mobile device applications tend to be used in short spurts, frequently, but for short session durations. Because of this, great mobile device applications offer a focused and efficient experience for accomplishing specific tasks rather than a general exploratory environment.

Quick startup time, responsiveness, and focused purpose are the hallmarks of good mobile application design. All these things amount to a highly productive user experience when using mobile devices. Keep these goals in mind when designing, building, and testing your mobile device application.

Architecturally, mobile devices differ from desktop and laptop computers in that most mobile devices do not have a hard drive and often use the available RAM for both program execution and file storage. Increasingly, mobile devices can use flash memory for long-term file storage. Flash offers good long-term storage capability but is typically not used as an extension of program RAM the way desktop computers offer a disk-based paging file for virtual RAM extension. This means that efficient memory management is more important for mobile devices than it is for desktops because execution RAM is a more limited resource.

With regard to the need for reliability, mobile devices have more in common with servers than they do with desktop computers. Like servers, the available RAM drives the overall performance of the system, and devices are often left on for weeks or months at a time without rebooting unless the user detects that things have gone drastically wrong. Ensuring that your applications efficiently manage their resources and particularly that they do not leak memory will have a significant impact on the overall performance of the device and the satisfaction of end users. Managed-code runtime environments can be a great aid in this effort.

A useful metaphor is to think of personal computers as being analogous to big houses in the countryside with lots of available storage space. Mobile devices are analogous to apartments in a metropolis, small and efficient. Both can offer comfortable living environments with their own advantages, but to live effectively accommodations must be made to meet the physical realities of the space available.

CHAPTER 3

Design of the .NET Compact Framework

Design is the conscious effort to impose meaningful order.

—Victor Papanek (Austrian-born U.S. designer, teacher, and writer,
1925-1998) (Encarta 2004, Quotations)

Introduction

This chapter provides a conceptual explanation of how the .NET Compact Framework and other managed code runtimes work. Developers building managed-code applications for mobile devices will benefit from having a good model in their heads that explains how their application runs in a managed-code environment. Native code developers will benefit by understanding some of the design strategies used by managed-code runtimes to achieve good performance and space efficiency on mobile devices.

Fundamentally, there are three kinds of software most developers build:

- *Applications*—An application represents a computer program that an end user interacts with. It is something that gets run to serve specific end-user needs or provide services to end users. Application design decisions are based on their utility to the end user. For the purpose of this book, "applications" should be considered graphical applications with rich user interfaces.
- *Reusable components*—Reusable components represent "chunky" pieces of code that developers can use to more quickly compose applications. Design decisions for building components are made with the intent of making the component easily reusable by developers building applications. Technologically, components fall in between applications and frameworks with regard to the level of design formality. Reusable

components can either be graphical or "headless," meaning that they lack user interface code. Components tend to be designed to contain a few large primary classes along with smaller classes that support the use of the larger ones. A graphical charting control is a good example of a reusable component. Many different applications can take advantage of a single well-designed charting control. A charting control would likely have one main "chart" class and possibly several smaller peripheral classes that represent chart characteristics such as the data displayed in the chart, information about the chart's axis, and color characteristics of lines on the chart.

- *Frameworks*—Frameworks are formalized, rigorously designed and organized trees of objects. The goal of a framework is to serve as the substrate on top of which applications and components can be built. A great deal of the effort of building a framework goes into thinking about how to logically organize the trees of objects that a framework contains to make sure they represent a consistent whole. This effort is made because frameworks exist to solve problems for the largest number of developers. Frameworks usually consist of a large number of small to mid-sized classes that developers use over and over again to aid them in solving programming problems. Although the line between what is a framework and what is a component is a bit fuzzy, components tend to meet specific application needs, whereas frameworks are more general-purpose sets of design tools. The .NET Compact Framework is an example of a framework.

Actually, the .NET Compact Framework is a bit more than just a framework. It is both a *programming framework* for use by developers building mobile applications, components, and higher-level frameworks as well as an execution engine that can take compiled applications and run them in a managed execution environment. This execution engine is also commonly referred to as a *runtime*.

Because the .NET Compact Framework was itself a mobile device software-development project, it is worth understanding the goals and philosophy that governed its design. An understanding of the answers to the following questions will be useful for both developers and software architects:

- *What kinds of features were chosen and what design decisions were made when designing the .NET Compact Framework?* While sharing many similarities, different mobile device runtimes also have important differences that are based on the usage scenarios that have governed their design. Mobile device runtimes are optimized for small size and efficient execution, but each runtime technology has identified areas in which size and resources have been judiciously traded off for rich functionality. This knowledge will be useful for developers and architects who need to decide what features they need from the mobile runtime they choose to develop on top of whether this is to be the .NET Compact Framework, J2ME, or any other mobile runtime environment.

- *Specifically, how is the .NET Compact Framework architected?* This will be of interest to developers and architects who want to build frameworks on top of managed runtimes by helping them understand what the key aspects of design for mobile device frameworks are.
- *What characteristics are important to maximize the performance of applications, components, and frameworks built on top of the .NET Compact Framework?* This is important to anyone writing code that utilizes a managed runtime such as the .NET Compact Framework.

Designing the .NET Compact Framework

Every successful engineering effort needs an underlying set of goals to guide its design. It would be pleasing but incorrect to say that the design goals of the .NET Compact Framework sprung out of one mind complete from the start. The design goals for the .NET Compact Framework evolved through the spirited arguments and passionately held beliefs of the core members of the tools and runtime team. Some held that achieving absolute minimum size was the most important. Some thought cross-platform capability sat at the top of the list. Some thought building enterprise data-centric applications for the Pocket PC was the key to success in the marketplace. These ideas were explored and weighed against one another and as early as possible tried out with a target audience of developers through a series of early hands-on labs. With external developers building real mobile applications on our early bits in these labs, we learned an incredible amount about what was important, compelling, and necessary for mobile device runtimes. This feedback guided us through the first half of our multiyear development process, and we are grateful for the invaluable real-world input that our early adopters gave us. Using this feedback we were able to refine, iterate, and distill the design principals that were to guide the project to completion. The goals agreed upon, the second half of the development process was about putting these into practice, refining them when necessary, and iterating on the product to balance the competing design requirements of size, performance, and features. The end result, the .NET Compact Framework v1.1, we feel very good about. This process of iterative design is extremely important for mobile devices for the simple reason that devices represent a less-understood domain than either desktop or server development does. Mobile devices as flexible application platforms are relatively new, and people are feeling their way around in the early light of a new day; iteration guided by feedback is essential. The subject of how to adopt an iterative design process is a recurrent theme throughout this book.

In approximate order of importance, the following were the key goals in the design of the first version of the .NET Compact Framework:

1. *To be a binary compatible, standards-implementing, subset of the desktop and server .NET Framework.* A great deal of engineering effort went into design of the desktop and server .NET Framework, and it would be foolish to not leverage these efforts. In addition, the core of this work has been submitted to and approved by standards bodies (ECMA-334 and ECMA-335, ISO/IEC 23270 (C#), ISO/IEC 23271 (CLI), and ISO/IEC 23272), including the binary format for compiled applications (IL), the C# programming language, and the base class libraries of the programming framework. It was an explicit goal of the .NET Compact Framework to implement these standards and with that make use of the existing .NET language compilers. The ability to use the highly tested and already proven C# and VB.NET compilers to build applications for the .NET Compact Framework as well as the ability to leverage a large number of design, testing, and debugging tools already available for desktop and server development was a significant engineering efficiency and reliability improvement above building a new and custom implementation of these.

2. *Cross-platform capability.* Although the first implementations of the .NET Compact Framework are for Pocket PC, Windows CE, and the Microsoft Smartphone operating systems, the .NET Compact Framework itself was designed to be able to be ported to other platforms if and when a compelling case exists to do so. One example of the practical implications of this design decision is the fact that all calls from the .NET Compact Framework that touch the underlying operating system are made through a single interface known as "the PAL" (platform abstraction layer). Doing so ensured a clear design understanding of underlying operating system dependencies and makes porting the runtime and libraries to another operating system a well-understood task. This is not to say that porting

to any operating system would be trivial, only that this was thought of in the design of the .NET Compact Framework. For example, some operating systems may not inherently support operating system functionality that the PAL maps to, requiring the PAL for that platform to implement things such as threading, memory management, graphics, or other functionality missing from the target operating system. This can be a significant task, but it is a well-understood and tested process that was accounted for in the design process of the .NET Compact Framework.

3. *Rich client capability, including support for drawing and forms, being a Web services client, and having a rich data-access model.* We came to the conclusion that to be compelling a device runtime had to meet a few key criteria for application builders: It had to allow the building of rich user interfaces with the modern controls that developers expect (for example, grids, list views, and tree views). It had to allow applications to consume Web services as easily as desktop .NET applications could (that is, trivially). It had to provide a rich, modern, and extensible model for dealing with database data (ADO.NET). Support for all of these was implemented in the object library of the .NET Compact Framework.

4. *Small on-device memory and storage footprint.* Our on-device footprint had to be smaller than 2MB of storage in order to become a practical option for getting into mass-market devices' ROM images. Being adopted into the common ROM image of mass-market devices was seen as important to being an integral part of the mobile devices' platform. To aid in adoption, it was also important to be able to be installed into the RAM file systems of existing devices while leaving plenty of room for applications and data. Both goals required a sub-2MB footprint on devices. In addition, the .NET Compact Framework needed to be able to operate in highly RAM-constrained environments. These goals are significantly different from the desktop and server .NET Framework, which runs in a comparatively unconstrained environment and prioritizes the goal of maximum total performance throughput higher than absolute size efficiency.

5. *Prove support for at least two .NET languages, C# and Visual Basic .NET.* Although in theory any programming language that targeted the .NET Compact Framework's (ECMA and ISO) standardized subset of IL byte codes and set of programming libraries should be able to compile to run on the .NET Compact Framework, this needed to be proven by an actual multilanguage implementation. We chose C# and Visual Basic .NET because they are the most popular

.NET languages. As with the desktop/server implementation, this meant including a version of the Microsoft.VisualBasic.DLL runtime library in the .NET Compact Framework.

6. *Be a suitable replacement for native code for most kinds of business, scientific, productivity, and entertainment applications.* It was important that desktop and server developers felt comfortable and syntactically unconstrained when developing on the .NET Compact Framework. If this goal was not achieved, the platform would not attract the large number of desktop and server developers to the platform that we hoped to. This lesson had been learned from previous device runtime efforts that had not achieved "critical mass." Both Microsoft's Embedded Visual Basic and others' efforts historically fell short because they lacked key features developers commonly use when building desktop and sever software or use in native code development for devices. We believed any successful successor to native code development needed support for the following:

- *Floating-point mathematics, trigonometric, and transcendental functions*—Coming from a desktop and server perspective, these seem like obvious things to include, but from a device perspective it was by no means clear at the outset. For size, cost, and power-consumption reasons, many mobile device processors do not have built-in support for floating-point mathematics. Instead, this functionality is provided by software libraries running on top of the processors. We came to the conclusion that although most algorithms are integer based, for applications of any real-world complexity there are almost always cases where some kind of decimal mathematics is required. Looking at what was required to do financial calculations (for example, interest payments or drawing graphs), scientific calculations, or even calculations in games led us to the belief that floating-point math support was a requirement for building a successful mobile device managed-code successor to native code.

- *All of the basic mechanics of the programming languages and commonly used programming libraries*—We could not remove any modern object-oriented language features such as inheritance or structured exception handling nor could we do without commonly used low-level libraries such as those for file I/O streams. Developers simply expected these to be there as part of the core programming experience, and if they were not there the experience of programming felt hamstrung. Developers needed to feel comfortable and empowered.

7. *Allow access to underlying operating system when necessary.* We realized that as much as cross-platform portability was an important goal, developers should not be limited to only the features we thought to include. We would strive to provide a suitable subset of the desktop .NET Framework to build the kinds of applications developers said they wanted, but there were inevitably going to be cases where developers would need to go outside the bounds of the functionality we provided. It was no good enabling developers to build 90 percent of their mobile device application in managed code if they were stuck because a critical 10 percent was missing. Therefore a suitable way to allow calls into native code was deemed essential to allow developers to work around functionality that was missing in the .NET Compact Framework. Four examples: Presently the explicit management of network connections, the ability to dial the phone, the playing of sounds, and the accessing of cryptography APIs require calls to native code (or calls to third-party libraries that wrap calls to native code); not everyone needs this functionality, but those who do would sorely miss it if they could not call into native code to get to it.

Why Was the First Release of the .NET Compact Framework Version 1.1 and Not Version 1.0?

The astute reader will have noticed that the first release of the .NET Compact Framework is referred to as version 1.1, not version 1.0. There is a good reason for this.

The first release of the .NET Compact Framework was designed to be compatible with and ship at the same time as the version 1.1 of the desktop and server .NET Framework. Version 1.0 of the .NET Framework shipped in 2002 with Visual Studio .NET 2002. Version 1.1 of the .NET Framework and the .NET Compact Framework shipped with Visual Studio .NET 2003. As the version numbers imply, version 1.1 is a minor release and update to the functionality in version 1.0.

For binary compatibility and logistical reasons, it was decided to synchronize version numbers between the .NET Framework and the .NET Compact Framework. This means that the .NET Compact Framework version 1.1 can be considered a binary compatible subset of the functionality present in the desktop and server release of the .NET Framework version 1.1.

We apologize for any confusion.

Desktop Subset

In designing the .NET Compact Framework, we knew that we needed to end up with a compatible subset of the desktop .NET Framework that met developers' needs. How to define this subset was the subject of significant debate. Was it best to take the desktop .NET Framework and start removing the pieces that we did not need, or should we design from the ground up starting from nothing and adding only what was proven necessary? Unable to resolve this philosophical question, we resolved to do both and see which approach proved the more workable. This was a costly effort both in terms of time and resources, but in the end I believe it was the only way to solve this debate. A top-down approach allowed us to identify the key areas of richness we wanted to support, and a bottom-up approach gave us a very good idea of how small our minimal implementation could be and what our size and performance budget was to add features. (For the record, I was on the losing side of the debate, having originally advocated a top-down approach to building the programming libraries. The top-down model proved useful in understanding what we wanted to build but could not give us the performance we needed. The bottom-up approach was the only way to ensure we achieved this goal.)

In the end the choice became very clear. The only way to achieve maximum performance and meet our size goals was to start from scratch and build from the ground up, adding each type, class, method, or property only as needed and justified. Even through this process we ended up with more framework than most people predicted in the outset, but the result was a clean and optimized solution. I believe there is a general lesson to be learned here: When designing a subset of a desktop or server framework, component, or application, it can be useful to early prototype by taking the desktop or server component and removing pieces to get a sense of what you want; however, when it comes to actual implementation, building from the bottom up will give you a much cleaner and well-understood implementation. Think top down, build bottom up, and measure at every step of the way.

Managed Code and Native Code

For most applications, the size of the application's code is significantly smaller than the size of the runtime and operating system code running below it. This is particularly true for graphical user interface applications, where the application developer deals with higher-level abstractions while a great deal of code executes in libraries below to deliver the user interface. This means that a well-designed and highly performing runtime is essential. There are two ways to approach the design of a managed code runtime:

1. Implement as much of the runtime and programming libraries in native code as possible and then build a thin managed-code interface to expose it to application and component developers. This has the potential benefit of maximum performance but the downside of complexity and potentially lower reliability because the runtime is not taking advantage of its own managed code execution capabilities.
2. Implement only what is absolutely necessary in native code and implement all other functionality in managed code. This has the potential benefit of increased portability, better reliability, and a forced dedication to getting the highest performance possible out of the managed-code execution engine because all code possible will be utilizing it.

Whenever possible, functionality in the .NET Compact Framework was implemented in managed code; only about 20 percent to 30 percent of the total size of the .NET Compact Framework is due to native code. All the programming libraries were written as managed code. Only the execution engine itself and a small part of the graphics subsystem are written in native code.

Using managed code for all the programming libraries allows them to be loaded, compiled, and memory managed just like any other libraries. Figure 3.1 shows a split between native code and managed code in the logical pieces of the .NET Compact Framework.

Schematic of .NET Compact Framework

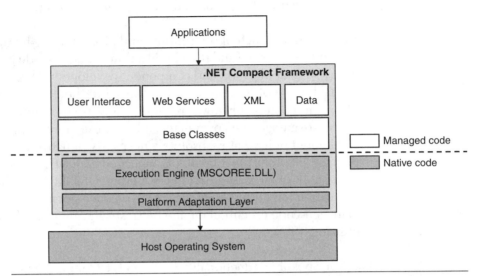

Figure 3.1 Native and managed code components of the .NET Compact Framework.

The Execution Engine

The .NET Compact Framework execution engine is the low-level code that deals with loading, JIT compiling, executing managed code, as well as managing memory. It gets to do all the grunt work that makes managed code work.

The execution engine is written in C/C++ and compiled down into the native processor's instruction set. Additionally, the execution engine has the burden of translating the .NET Compact Framework and end-user applications into an executable format at runtime. This is known as JIT compilation ("just-in-time" compilation). The execution engine also handles any transitions from managed code to native code, such as the calling of native code APIs in the underlying operating system; this is known as thunking.

Because the execution engine handles all the low-level interactions with the operating system, it takes on a large design and testing burden to ensure that it is as reliable as possible.

The Managed-Code Libraries

The managed-code libraries of the .NET Compact Framework are the programmatic part that developers interact with. As with the desktop .NET Framework, the .NET Compact Framework libraries are factored into a series of DLL files. The libraries are present at design time on desktop computers and also installed on the target devices for runtime use. These DLLs have design time filenames such as System.DLL, System.Windows.Forms.DLL, and System.Xml.DLL. The on-device filenames may differ due to naming and versioning needs on the target devices. During compilation, the managed-code libraries are used the same way header files are used by C/C++ or type libraries are used by older (VB6 and earlier) Visual Basic code to give knowledge of the interfaces and types being used by the code being compiled. The fact that these files share the same *.DLL file extension as C/C++ native code libraries is for familiar file-naming purposes only; the binary content is very different, and they could just as easily be named with other file extensions. The fact that the .NET Compact Framework filenames also generally match the filenames of desktop .NET Framework assemblies is also for the user's convenience only. In fact they could be refactored into more files or combined into a single file if necessary. A future implementation on a non-Windows platform may choose to do this if it is beneficial to do so. Your application generally does not need to worry about this implementation detail because it is the runtime's task to find, load, and manage common libraries present on a device.

From a programmatic perspective, each of these DLLs exposes a set of hierarchical namespaces to the developer containing classes and types. Example namespaces containing classes and types are System.*, System.Xml.*, System.Data.*, System.Drawing.*, and so on. There is a many-to-many relationship between DLLs and namespaces; a DLL can contribute to multiple namespaces (for example, Foo.DLL can contain types in both MyNamespace.* and SomeOtherNameSpace.SomethingElse.* if it wants), and multiple DLLs can contribute to the same namespaces (for example, Foo.DLL and Bar.DLL can both contribute types to MyNamespace.* and SomeOtherNameSpace.SomethingElse.* if they want). When an application is compiled, the compiler is told the set of files it should look into to find classes and types the user is trying to use in his application; these are commonly known as references. If a type/method/property is not found in the developer's code or the referenced libraries, a compilation error is generated. Additionally, if multiple versions of types are found in different DLLs, an ambiguous type compilation error is generated.

Other than at compile time when the compiler is given a list of files to look into for referenced classes, developers need not worry about which classes reside in which files. Instead, developers should think only of the logical hierarchy of namespaces they are using and generally not worry about which of the referenced files contains any specific type.

The Base Class Libraries

The base classes are the nuts and bolts of programming. They include the common types and functionality that developers use to implement most data-processing algorithms. The base classes include the following:

- All the core types such as integers, strings, floating point, date/time, arrays and collections.
- File I/O, streams, sockets networking.
- The capability to look up and bind to the types, methods, properties in assemblies at runtime. This is known as reflection.
- The capability to work with culture/locale-specific information. This is known as globalization.

The functionality above along with additional base classes is encapsulated in the following hierarchical namespaces:

System.*

System.Collections.*

System.ComponentModel.*

System.Diagnostics.Globalization.*

System.IO.*

System.Net.Sockets.*

System.Security.*

System.Text.*

System.Threading.*

User Interface Libraries

The user interface libraries were created with two goals in mind: (1) to enable developers to build rich enterprise applications using modern high-level user interface controls such as Buttons, PictureBoxes, ListViews, TreeViews, TabControls, and so on; and (2) to enable developers to perform low-level drawing operations on mobile devices using rich bitmap operations with the ability to draw two-dimensional objects such as lines, polygons, text, and images.

This functionality is offered in two hierarchical namespaces:

- *System.Drawing.* * —Two-dimensional drawing capability
- *System.Windows.* *—User interface controls and supporting functionality

Web Services Client Libraries

Web services are a standards-based way to communicate between applications running on different platforms. In a nutshell, a Web service server is a Web server that exposes programmatic interfaces to applications that can be accessed using XML as the language of conversation. The syntax of this XML conversation is SOAP, which stands for Simple Object Access Protocol. A Web service client is an application that can call to make SOAP requests of Web service servers and interpret the SOAP responses sent back. To describe the interfaces being exposed, Web service servers return WSDL documents on request. WSDL stands for Web Service Description Language, and like SOAP it is a syntax built on top of XML. WSDL describes the programmatic interface the Web service exposes; SOAP is used to make requests of those interfaces.

A key feature of the desktop and server .NET Framework as well as the Visual Studio .NET development tool is the easy ability to create and consume Web services. Visual Studio .NET is capable of parsing a server-generated WSDL document and generating a set of easy-to-use client proxy classes that enable developers to access the Web service. Because of these proxy classes, calling a Web service is conceptually as easy as creating an object and calling a method on it.

It was a specific design goal of the .NET Compact Framework to support a rich enough set of classes, properties, and methods to compile these Visual Studio .NET autogenerated client proxy classes. This goal was successfully met, and mobile device applications can just as easily be Web service clients as their desktop and server counterparts.

This functionality is present in the System.Net.* namespace.

XML Libraries

Why is XML so important? To understand this, it is necessary to understand the pros and cons of the two basic ways to exchange data between applications, namely via binary formats and via text formats.

Binary data exchange demands a strict contract between all parties on how to format and interpret data. Binary formats require careful planning for their version management by all parties using the formats. This reduces flexibility; a change to a binary format that all parties do not agree to will break applications that use that data. In compensation for this drawback, binary data offers the potential for the most compact representation. This brings with it savings in size and increased processing speed.

Text files have traditionally offered the opposite proposition: interoperability through a looser contract and more verbose encoding format. For many uses, XML has replaced the traditional text file as the way to store and exchange simple data. XML files are text files but they are text files that include some definition of their structure. This allows them to be easily processed in standard ways and allows for better reuse. Developers choose text formats because they are easier to work with—they allow the exchange of data in a format that is more forgiving to schema changes and versioning needs. XML takes text storage to a new level.

XML offers a useful middle ground between too much structure and too little. This semistructured storage is a substantial improvement over generic text files. Data is stored in a hierarchical text format using tags to provide hints as to the data contained. For example, font information may be stored via the text `<Font> xxx </Font>`, which allows an application interpreting the text to easily discern what this data item is about. Applications working with XML data can choose only the text portions they are interested in or understand. XML is thus an important incremental improvement over previous text formats such as *.INI files, PropertyBags, and HTML text because it provides both increased structure and flexibility.

Because XML has become such a popular medium of information exchange, XML support is important for any modern programming framework. Without it each developer would be left to write his or her own set of functions for parsing text files and extracting or writing the data he or she needs. This solution is fraught with inefficiency and has great potential for introducing unneeded bugs into applications. Because most developers are building applications and not XML parsers, a custom implementation will usually do only what is minimally required and is almost always not tested exhaustively. Moreover, a custom implementation will almost always trade off maximum performance for lower development time. In summary, custom implementations tend to be less reliable and less efficient than a well-engineered solution intended for broad reuse.

It is therefore highly preferable to use prebuilt and rigorously tested XML libraries for reading and writing XML data. These have the benefit of being designed, built, and tested by a group of people whose main goal was to build the fastest and most reliable XML engine they knew how to.

The .NET Compact Framework offers a two-layered approach for working with XML:

- *Forward only XML readers and writers*—The XmlReader and Xml-Writer classes serve the need for maximum performance, forward only, noncached XML reading and writing. The goal of these readers and writers is to maintain as little state as necessary while reading or writing XML from and to streams. For developers working with larger-sized XML documents and needing the maximum performance, these will be the option of choice.
- *XML DOM (Document Object Model)*—The XmlDocument class is used to represent an in-memory tree of objects describing an XML document. The XmlDocument and its associated classes represent a Document Object Model intended to allow easy access to members of the represented XML tree. XML is read in by the forward-only XmlReader discussed above and used to build a representative XML tree in memory. Similarly, an XML tree can be written out to a stream; this uses the XmlWriter to accomplish the task. Developers working with small to moderate-size XML documents or wanting minimum complexity when working with XML will choose the Xml-Document class.

Conceptually, this functionality can be thought of as being present in the System.Xml.* namespace.

Data Libraries

Modern databases store data in sets of related tables. The .NET Framework offers an object model called ADO.NET to work with this kind of relational data. ADO.NET gives the developer classes to manage a set of related relational tables in memory along with classes to provide views onto this data. Data managed using ADO.NET is referred to as being in a DataSet.

What's the Difference Between ADO and ADO.NET?

Microsoft has in the past 10 to 15 years offered various object libraries for data access, each building improvements on the model that came before it. Before the managed-code ADO.NET concept, there was ADO, which stood for Active Data Objects and was primarily intended to enable Visual Basic developers to work with database information. These previous models (and their many and confusing three-letter acronyms such as DAO, RDO, and ADO, and each of their different version numbers—mea culpa for any naming confusion!) have been supplanted by ADO.NET.

Whereas previous data technologies such as ADO offered RowSets, each of which represented a single table of data with cursors to identify the current row, ADO.NET offers DataSets, which represent sets of related tables in memory with object references between the tables.

ADO.NET represents data as an in-memory graph of tables to be navigated using object-oriented mechanisms and not as a single table with a cursor to iterate through the rows. In ADO.NET, the concept of a current-row cursor does not exist because the data is explicitly separated from any database connection that would require a cursor.

ADO.NET uses DataReaders to interface ADO.NET DataSets with underlying data sources. A DataReader represents a forward-only way to read data from a data source. These DataReaders are internally used to populate ADO.NET DataSets.

Developers work with relational DataSets in memory and can do a number of things with that data, including the following:

- *Persist changes to databases*—A DataAdapter class exists to interface between ADO.NET DataSets and databases. DataAdapter classes take the list of additions, updates, and deletes made to a DataSet and apply the appropriate logic to propagate them to the underlying database. Typically this is done by executing SQL statements or calling stored procedures that work on the database.
- *Persist as XML*—DataSets can serialize themselves into XML to be stored to a file and later reloaded.
- *Send to another tier*—Because DataSets, including information about the changes made to them, can easily be persisted as XML, they can easily be passed between computing tiers via Web service calls.
- *Local use*—DataSets can be used as a powerful abstraction for working with relational data in memory. If this data is treated as read-only, changes made to it locally are not propagated back to any server or long-term storage.

Factoring of Useful Design and Debugging Information into Optional Components

Managed code can contain a great deal of information useful for developers debugging their frameworks, components, and applications. An example of this kind of value-adding data is the text descriptions of exceptions that can occur during code execution. It is one thing to get an error message such as "Unknown exception occurred" or "Exception System.IO.SomeRandomException was thrown" and quite another to get a detailed human-readable error message describing what went wrong and what the probable cause was. This data is helpful to have when testing and debugging, but storing all the error strings for a large programming framework such as the .NET Compact Framework can take up a large amount of space and be prohibitively expensive for mobile devices.

The desktop .NET Framework simply includes this kind of rich exception information along with other resources. Not only is this information available in English, it is localized into all the principal languages that Visual Studio is localized into; this means that end users can be presented rich diagnostic information in their own language when appropriate. To allow access to this information programmatically, each managed code exception has a .Message property that allows programmatic access to this text.

Having rich debug strings is certainly a benefit; however, this benefit comes at a size cost. By definition, verbose text descriptions take up space. Even more space is taken up when this text is localized. Hence a design constraint is raised; compact size and rich textual error information are conflicting design goals.

The .NET Compact Framework solves this problem by cleaving this information into separate satellite components that are not a core part of the .NET Compact Framework. These satellite components can be installed on top of .NET Compact Framework as needed or desired. The file containing this information is called System.SR.dll and it is about 91KB in size. Additional versions of this file exist for other localized languages. Presently 10 localized language versions of this file exist, amounting to more than 900KB of data, which is a sizable fraction of the .NET Compact Framework's size. Therefore, removing these strings from the .NET Compact Framework resulted in a significant size savings.

Devices with the .NET Compact Framework installed on them in RAM or ROM will typically not have these satellite files installed; instead, they are optionally installed as needed or desired. The Visual Studio .NET development environment will automatically install them at debug time because developers will almost always want these present.

At runtime when an exception is thrown the .NET Compact Framework looks to see whether the appropriate language-exception string file is present on the device. If it is, the file is accessed and the appropriate exception description is loaded. Failing this, the .NET Compact Framework looks to see whether a language-invariant (English) exception string resource file is present. If it is, the text is loaded. Failing this, default text is displayed that is not specific to the error (although the exception's programmatic name may give some idea as to what the error was).

Through the mechanism of using optional satellite components, a good balance was achieved in the .NET Compact Framework of needing to be as small as possible but still provide developers with rich debug information.

A similar design strategy is employed where components benefit from extra design-time information that is not needed at runtime. When building custom controls, it is possible to build separate design and runtime versions of the components with the design-time versions containing additional meta data that is interpreted by the development tool to provide a richer design-time experience.

For your designs, you might want to consider similar models of having optional resource files or having separate design-time versions of your components if significant size savings can be achieved.

SQL CE / SQL Connectors

Another optional component that can be installed on top of the .NET Compact Framework is the ability to communicate with specific databases. When the .NET Compact Framework version 1.1 shipped, parallel to it shipped optional .NET Compact Framework components for accessing local SQL CE databases and remote SQL Server databases. These are very useful for building applications that work with these databases but are not themselves a core part of the .NET Compact Framework. Similar components exist for accessing other third-party databases.

Items Not in the First Version of the .NET Compact Framework

Security Checks

The concept of *evidence-based permissions* was central in the design of the Common Language Runtime, which serves as the basis for both the desktop .NET Framework and the .NET Compact Framework. This concept is also commonly referred to as *code-access security.*

Code-access security offers the ability to define and administer policy that assigns code-execution rights based on evidence provided by the code in question. Evidence can consist of things such as a cryptographic signature verifying the publisher of the component, the strong name of the component itself, the location where the component is installed in the local file system, or the URL from which the component was downloaded. Based on the evidence supplied and the local policy on the machine running the code, specific permissions can be granted to code. Examples of possible permission levels include the following:

- *Full trust*—The code runs with full trust on the system and can do anything a native application could.
- *Restricted access to the file system*—File I/O can be forbidden or restricted to certain directories based on the evidence a component provides.
- *Restricted access to user interface*—The ability to bring up user interfaces can be permitted or denied components.
- *Network access*—The ability to access the network can be permitted or denied components.
- *Native code access*—The ability to call into native code can be permitted or denied components.

These and many more permissions are available and can be set as policies on the desktop and server .NET Framework. Much literature and documentation exists on this topic.

The .NET Compact Framework was designed with the ability to support this policy-based security model. In the first release of the .NET Compact Framework, however, the policy is simply defined as "all code has full trust." This means that applications targeting the .NET Compact Framework v1.1 running on devices run with the same set of permissions as native code does on the device.

The decision to pin the security permissions at "run at full trust" for the first release of the .NET Compact Framework was made for pragmatic reasons. Based on discussions with early adopters, it was apparent that the first wave of compelling mobile applications for devices would generally consist of applications that were explicitly installed by a user or an administrator on the devices and not downloaded and run on-the-fly. These kinds of applications were essentially replacing traditional native code applications for the devices, and because of this a similar permission model was appropriate. Given an infinite amount of time to design, build, test, and refine our security policy based on customer feedback, we would have built a more sophisticated model in the first version. However, after much discussion, it was apparent that this was not a requirement for applications to be successful in our first version. Because of this, the building of a sophisticated security policy engine was deferred to a following release in favor of the other feature work that went into the first version. It was a tough decision, but looking back on it we believe we made the right choice. It is worth noting that on some mass-market devices such as some smart phones there exist on-device security policies that require native code applications to have approved cryptographic signatures; managed-code applications are subject to the same policies on these devices.

Moving forward, it will be desirable to enable a security model that supports downloading code on-the-fly and assigning permissions based on evidence supplied by the code. For this reason, it is likely that future versions of the .NET Compact Framework will have several graded levels of trust and permissions, ranging from evidence-based "full trust" to very limited capabilities for lower-trust code. In addition, different kinds of mobile devices will likely have different policies set on them. Some devices will have policy set by end users, some by administrators, some by hardware manufacturers, and some by network operators who host the devices. The code-access security model is built to support this.

Multimedia

Mutimedia support was another area we chose not to explicitly support in the first version of the .NET Compact Framework. This means that developers wanting to do things such as play sounds or show videos will have to call native code to do this. As above, if we had had an infinite amount of time and space to develop, test, and refine these concepts, they would have been supported in the first release of the .NET Compact Framework. The practical feedback we got from our early adopters was that this was not a success-limiting factor for the kinds of applications people needed to build presently. Future versions of the .NET Compact Framework are likely to add richer multimedia support. Looking back this has also seemed to be a correct decision.

How Code Is Executed and Run

When a managed code application is first started up, several steps occur to load, verify, and start code execution. When the managed-code application is up and running, the managed-code runtime continues to play an important role in loading new classes, JIT compiling code when necessary and managing the memory of the application. It is useful to have a good conceptual understanding of how this happens. The process of starting up and running an application can be explained in the six steps described here:

1. *A managed application is loaded.* The binary header of the application indicates to the operating system that it is not a native application. Instead of simply starting to execute instructions, the .NET Compact Framework execution engine is loaded and told to get the application running.
2. *The execution engine finds the class with the "main" entry point for it to execute.* This is a class with a function signature matching `static void Main()`. If a type with this signature is found, the class is loaded and the "main" procedure is attempted to be run (Steps 3 and 4).
3. *The class is loaded.* Information about the class is loaded and verified to make certain that it is a consistent and well-formed class definition. All methods (that is, code-execution entry points) in the class are marked as "uncompiled."
4. *The execution engine attempts to run the specified procedure.* If the procedure already has compiled code associated with it, the code is run.
5. *If the execution engine discovers that the property or method it is about to run has not been compiled, it gets compiled on demand.* The class information for the method is loaded. The code contained is verified to ensure that it contains safe, legal and well-formed IL instructions and then it is JIT compiled. If the method references other types that have not yet been loaded, the class or type definitions are loaded as needed. Note: The methods inside these classes are not compiled until needed; this is the meaning of JIT (just in time).

6. *The now-compiled method is executed.* Any type or object allocations required are requested from the execution engine. Any method calls to classes bring us back to Step 5.

This all sounds like a lot of work but in reality it happens very quickly.

What's a "Type"?

Note: Any data that a programmer can work with is a "type." Another way of saying this is that all data types and classes are types. Everything is a type, including integers, decimals, other scalars, strings, and classes. Any "thing" you can pass around in code is an instance of a type. Classes are special types in that they contain not just data but also code and support object-oriented behaviors such as inheritance.

Note: As classes and other types have their definitions loaded into memory and get verified and compiled, this data goes into allocated memory just like other data that developers allocate in their application. Example: If you create an ArrayList object:

```
System.Collections.ArrayList aList = new System.Collections.ArrayList();
```

You are doing several things:

1. The code above is represented in your application as IL. This IL gets JIT complied at runtime right before it is first run. The code is placed into allocated memory.

2. When the code gets JITed, the execution engine looks to see whether it has the information for the type System.Collections.ArrayList loaded into memory; if not, memory for this type definition is allocated and it is loaded into memory and associated with the class ArrayList.

3. When the actual code above is run, a constructor for the ArrayList object needs to be run. If this code has not been loaded and JITed yet, memory gets allocated and the constructor's code gets JITed. The code is loaded, verified, and JITed, and the memory for this constructor's code is associated with the ArrayList class' constructor.

The same holds true for any type that gets loaded or method that gets called; if the work has not been done before to load it, it will get loaded and compiled as needed, and the memory used to do that is associated with the type.

This memory allocation and tracking is important. As you will see below, code and class definition data, just like objects, can get garbage collected.

Memory Management and Garbage Collection

When running through all of its normal execution paths, your code will cause type definitions to get loaded into memory, code to get compiled and executed and objects to get allocated and discarded. The .NET Compact Framework was designed to provide the best balance between startup performance, steady-state performance, and the need to continue executing code even in highly memory-constrained environments. To do this, the class loader, JIT engine, memory allocator, and garbage collector work together.

As your code is running, it will likely be creating new objects and discarding these objects periodically. To handle the need for object allocation and cleanup efficiently, the .NET Compact Framework uses garbage collection. Most modern managed-code environments use some form of garbage collection.

A garbage collector fundamentally is designed to do two things: (1) reclaim memory that is no longer being used; and (2) compact the pieces of memory being used so that the largest blocks of continuous memory are available for new allocations. This solves a common problem called memory fragmentation. Memory fragmentation is similar in concept to disk fragmentation. If no reorganization of storage takes place periodically, after a time the storage area becomes disorganized with small free and occupied storage spaces scattered; these are fragments. Think of this as entropy applied to disk and memory storage; active work is required to reverse these entopic effects. The result of disk fragmentation is slow access times because lots of hopping around the disk is required to read a file. Fragmentation in memory is even worse because object allocation requires a continuous block of memory of sufficient size for the object's data. After a large number of allocations and releases of different-sized chunks of memory, the free pieces of memory are too small and scattered to allow the larger allocation sizes required by objects. Compacting all the memory that is currently in use but scattered can create large blocks of free memory that can efficiently be used for new object allocations.

Reclamation of memory is a relatively straightforward process. Execution is temporarily suspended and the set of live objects (objects that can be reached directly and indirectly by your code) is traced down and recursively marked. The rest of the objects in memory, because they are no longer reachable by live code, remain unmarked and so can be identified as garbage objects and can be reclaimed. This kind of garbage collection is known as "mark and sweep." Typically this operation is fairly quick.

The ability to compact the objects in memory is an advanced benefit of managed-code execution. Unlike native code, all known references to your objects are known to the execution engine. This allows objects to be moved around in memory when it becomes useful to do so. The manager of the memory (the execution engine) keeps track of which objects are where and can move them around when it needs to. In this way, a set of managed objects scattered around in memory can be compacted.

The .NET Compact Framework, with its JIT compiler, memory manager, and garbage collector, also has one additional trick up its sleeve: the capability to garbage collect JITed code. Normally this is not a desirable thing to do, but under special circumstances it can prove very valuable. If the execution engine has gone to the effort of JIT compiling the managed code to native instructions in order to achieve maximum execution performance, throwing out the JITed code seems wasteful because it will need to re-JIT the code the next time it needs to execute. It is, however, beneficial to be able to do this under two circumstances:

1. When the application has JITed and run a lot of code that will not need to be executed again any time soon. A common case for this is when an application runs in different stages. Code that executes in the beginning of the application to set things up may never need to be run again. If memory is needed, it makes sense to reclaim the memory that holds this code.

2. When the set of live objects in memory is so large that the application execution will fail if more memory cannot be found for additional object allocations that need to occur during the normal execution of the application's algorithms. In this case, the execution engine must be willing to throw out and periodically recompile code the application needs just so the application can keep running. If the alternative is the application halting execution because there is no memory left, throwing out JITed code is the only solution, even if it means wasting time recompiling code later.

Memory Management and Garbage Collection Walkthrough

It is useful to understand how the execution engine interacts with your application's code and objects during execution. The following set of schematic diagrams walk through the memory management that occurs during different application execution stages.

Available application memory being used by Live Objects, Dead Objects, Types, and Classes in different states of compilation

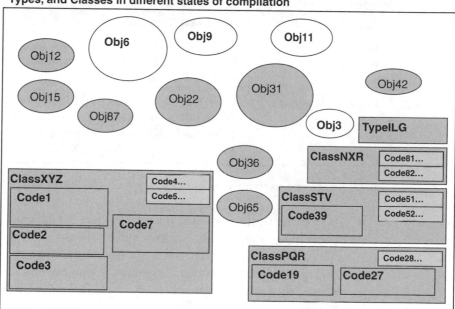

Figure 3.2 A simple schematic representing the state of an application's memory while running.

Table 3.1 Key to Interpreting Figure 3.2, Figure 3.3, and Beyond

Figure	Definition
Dark gray ovals	Objects currently in use (for example, Obj12 in Figure 3.2).
White ovals	Dead objects. These are garbage objects that can no longer be reached by the application and can be reclaimed for additional memory (for example, Obj6 in Figure 3.2).
Dark gray rectangles	Class and type definitions that have been loaded into memory because the types have been accessed by running code.
Interior rectangles	Code inside classes. (All code is inside classes.)

continues

Table 3.1 Key to Interpreting Figure 3.2, Figure 3.3, and Beyond *(continued)*

Figure	Definition
Dark gray interior rectangles	Code that has been JITed because the method has been called at least once (for example, Code1 inside ClassXYZ in Figure 3.2).
Light gray interior rectangles	Code that has yet to be JITed. These rectangles are smaller than the JITed code rectangles because un-JITed methods take very little space in memory (for example, Code4 inside ClassXYZ in Figure 3.2).

Things to observe in the schematic above include the following:

- The size of any item in the schematic is meant to give an idea of relative memory usage. Larger classes and types use more memory than smaller types because they contain more "stuff." Objects of different types use different amounts of memory. Dead objects use up memory until they are garbage collected. Un-JITed methods take up very little space.
- All of the definitions for the types and classes your application is using are loaded into memory. Different types and classes take up different amounts of memory.
- A class' methods that have been called at least once have been JIT compiled. Example: ClassXYZ has Code1, Code2, Code3, and Code7 JIT compiled.
- Classes' methods that have not been called yet are not yet compiled and therefore do not take up much memory. Example: ClassXYZ has two methods, Code4 and Code5 that exist in pre-JITed state. If they are called, they will be JIT compiled and memory will be allocated to store the compiled code.
- Objects are instances of types and classes and take up memory.
- "Live objects" are objects that can be reached by your code either directly through global and static variables, variables on the stack, or through these variables.
- "Dead objects" are objects that can no longer be reached by your code but have not yet been reclaimed by the execution engine. These are represented as Obj3, Obj6, Obj9, and Obj11 in Figure 3.2. Until they are cleaned up, they take up memory just like live objects and JITed code.

As your application goes about creating and discarding objects and other heap-allocated types, eventually it will hit a point where no additional objects can be created without cleaning up the dead objects. At this point, the execution engine will force a garbage collection. Figure 3.3 shows the application's memory state right before garbage collection.

When a garbage collection occurs, the live objects can also be compacted. It is often possible to free up a good deal of continuous memory for the creation of new objects by removing the dead objects from memory and compacting live objects. Figure 3.4 shows the application's memory state right after garbage collection and compaction.

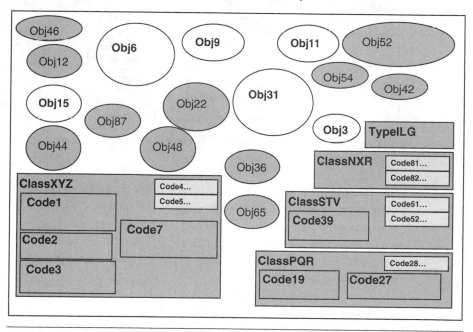

No room for next object we want to create! Cleanup is needed!

Figure 3.3 Application memory state right before garbage collection.

Garbage Collection: Get rid of dead objects and compact memory

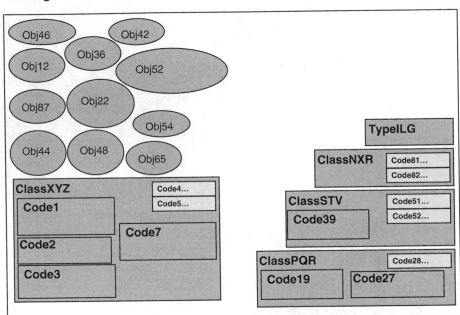

Figure 3.4 Dead objects garbage collected and memory compacted.

In normal steady-state execution, objects are periodically created and discarded. The execution engine does a garbage collection and memory compaction when needed to free up memory required for new objects. Figure 3.5 shows a typical application's memory state with a mix of live and dead objects, JITed and un-JITed code, and some spare memory to allocate new objects in.

In well-performing applications, there exists ample memory for the creation and discarding of the objects, and garbage collection does not need to occur very often. The amount of space recovered when garbage collection occurs is sufficient to let the application continue to create and discard all the objects it needs for a good while. Figure 3.6 shows a typical application's memory state right after a periodic garbage collection.

Normal steady-state operation: Periodic garbage collections solve memory needs

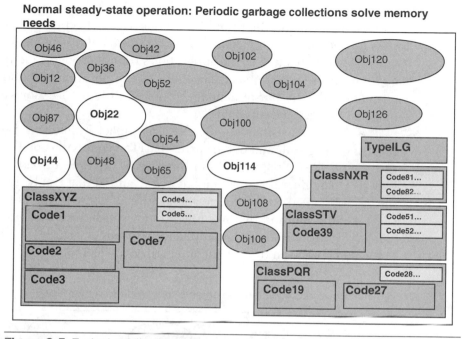

Figure 3.5 Typical application memory state for steady-state execution.

Normal steady-state operation: Periodic garbage collections solve memory needs

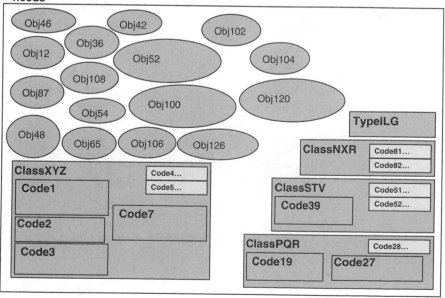

Figure 3.6 Typical application memory state for steady-state execution right after garbage collection.

In some cases, the large number of live objects being used makes it impossible for a simple "mark and sweep" garbage collection of discarded objects to free up enough memory to allow the execution engine to create the new objects demanded by the application's running code. If memory cannot be found for required object allocations, the application execution must be terminated due to "out-of-memory" problems. Figure 3.7 shows an application that has reached this point.

To address this situation, the .NET Compact Framework is capable of releasing a large amount of the currently JITed code. All code that is not executing on the stack (or stacks in the case of multiple threads) can be released. Doing this allows memory to be reclaimed that can be used to meet the application's demands for new objects or the new JITing of new code in the case of a method that has never been run before but has now been called. Figure 3.8 shows the application's memory state after previously JITed code has been thrown out and garbage collected.

A challenge occurs when live objects use up all free memory

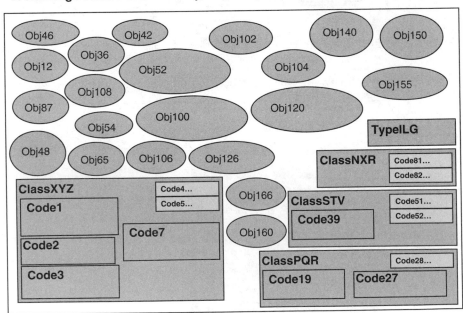

Figure 3.7 Live objects crowding all of the available memory.

All JITed code that can be thrown out is, and objects are compacted, creating room for new objects

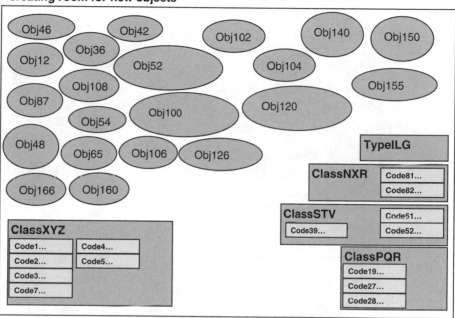

Figure 3.8 Previously JITed code is thrown out, and the memory the methods' JITed code previously took up has been reclaimed.

The discarding of JITed code is a drastic step because some of this code will need to be re-JITed, but it can be a very effective strategy if a significant amount of code that was previously JITed is no longer required for execution. This is often the case when a significant amount of "startup" code was run to set things up or if the application is partitioned into logical blocks that do not all need to execute at the same time. Figure 3.9 shows the application's memory state shortly after tossing out all the JITed code it can. Methods are re-JITed as they are called and new objects can be allocated as needed.

Severe performance problems will occur if the application continues to allocate more and more objects and not discard them. This will cause a condition where the only thing that can be kept in memory is all of the live objects and the code that is immediately executing on the application's stack (or "stacks" if there are multiple threads). In this case common code is continually JITed and discarded because only a small portion of the system's memory is available to hold the JITed code. At this point the system is in constant churn; this is commonly referred to as "thrashing" because

Code that is needed is re-JITed, new objects are created, old objects are discarded. Object Garbage collections works as normal

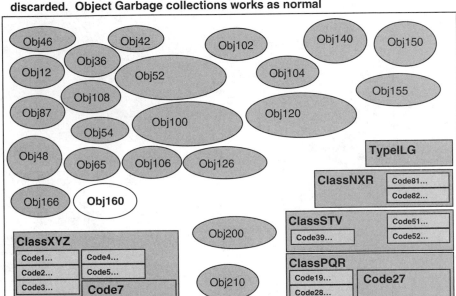

Figure 3.9 Methods get re-JITed as they are called, new objects are allocated, and discarded objects become garbage.

the application and run-time are inefficiently struggling just to keep incrementally running the next piece of code. As the application asymptotically approaches this state application performance will decline drastically. This is a state to be avoided! Figure 3.10 shows an application caught in such as state.

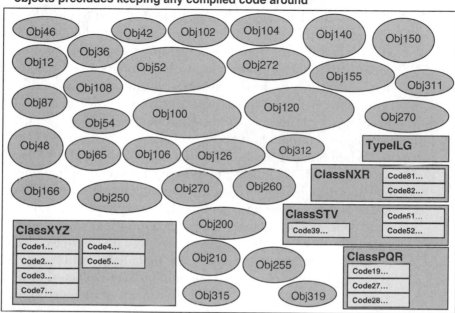

Figure 3.10 Severe memory pressure. Live objects take up all available memory, even after all possible JITed code has been discarded.

Summary

The .NET Compact Framework is a rich managed-code runtime for mobile devices suitable for building a wide range of applications, components, and frameworks. It was designed from the ground up for use in resource-constrained devices but with the specific design goal of being a binary-compatible subset of the desktop and server .NET Framework. As with other modern managed-code runtimes, the .NET Compact Framework consists of a native code execution engine and a managed-code set of class libraries that run on top of it. Design strategies specifically tailored for mobile and embedded devices were employed to both provide a rich subset of desktop .NET Framework functionality and to meet size and performance goals for mobile devices.

The class libraries that ship as part of the .NET Compact Framework version 1.1 can be thought of as consisting of five logical blocks: (1) user interface and graphics support, (2) XML support, (3) Web services client support, (4) data-access support, and underpinning all these, (5) base class libraries. The base class libraries were designed to give desktop developers a very comfortable and empowered feeling when writing code for devices; all the basic features developers expect should be there. The combination of these libraries gives developers a rich palette of functionality with which to design business-, productivity-, scientific-, and entertainment-oriented applications. Future versions of the .NET Compact Framework are likely to add support for code-access security models as well as for multimedia support.

When building applications that run on managed runtimes, particularly on mobile devices, it is useful to have a good conceptual understanding of how the runtime is managing the application's memory and execution. The .NET Compact Framework offers JIT compilation of code as well as garbage collection of memory the application uses. Under normal execution circumstances, only object memory needs to be garbage collected and compacted periodically. In cases of severe memory pressure, code that has been JIT compiled can be thrown out and garbage collected as well to reclaim needed space. Just as it is possible to run out of memory in native code applications, it is possible to cause severe memory pressure in managed-code environments as well. This results when an application uses up all available memory through object allocations. In these kinds of circumstances, application performance will decline drastically as the managed code garbage collector struggles to reclaim a dwindling amount of memory. The application will be forced to fail if the necessary memory allocations cannot be made. Memory pressure is a situation to be avoided, and the subsequent chapters in this book will spend a significant amount of time discussing how to design algorithms and build applications that efficiently work with device resources such as garbage-collected memory.

Managed-code runtimes such as the .NET Compact Framework offer developers great advantages when building mobile device applications. The productivity and reliability of managed-code environments and the presence of rich class libraries and components for code reuse are compelling. However, developers still need to have a good conceptual understanding of how memory and code execution is being handled to make the most of these advances in mobile application platforms. This knowledge coupled with device-specific design and engineering skills will enable you to build great mobile applications.

CHAPTER 4

How to Be Successful Developing Mobile Applications

From the Merriam-Webster Dictionary:

Main Entry: **meth·od·ol·o·gy**

Pronunciation: "me-thə-'dä-lə-jE

Function: noun

Inflected Form(s): plural **-gies**

Etymology: New Latin methodologia, from Latin methodus + -logia -logy

Date: 1800

1: *A body of methods, rules, and postulates employed by a discipline: a particular procedure or set of procedures.*

2: *The analysis of the principles or procedures of inquiry in a particular field.*

(www.m-w.com, 2004)

Introduction

This chapter is specifically about defining a software development methodology for use when designing and building mobile applications.

Developing software poses two kinds of difficulties for developers, architects, and managers. There are those difficulties that are truly inherent to software development, and difficulties that are transient, reflecting the immaturity of the development tools and technologies available at the present time.

In the past 10 to 15 years, desktop and server application development have gone through a huge transformation in solving the "transient" problems of software development. Today's development tools are incomparably more productive than they were even a decade ago. This is particularly true in the areas of user interface design and debugging. This same transformation is now underway for mobile development. Many of the design and debugging enhancements for desktop and server development are now available for mobile devices, making this part of mobile software development much easier and more accessible to a wider range of developers than just a few years ago. The productivity of writing software has gone up. Because of this, more software development projects now are feasible (some of which would have otherwise been unreasonable to undertake). Mobile software development projects that only a few years ago would have been unjustifiable due to cost and complexity concerns are now quite feasible because of the advances in programming tools and technologies.

But as with desktop and server development, there is a huge gulf between "being able to write code" and "being able to build great applications." The latter challenge represents the inherent difficulties of modern software development. It is one thing to be able to sit down, write, and debug code and quite another to knit all the code into a well-performing, reliable, and flexible application.

The way to successfully navigate the inherent difficulties present in software development is through good methodologies. In short, a methodology is a set of guiding principles to get you to a successful end. Many of the methodologies for writing desktop and server applications apply equally well to mobile device software development, but special emphasis must be placed on the challenges that are unique or accentuated when building mobile device applications.

This chapter is divided into two halves. The first half of the chapter discusses overall development methodologies, adding specific mobile device notes where appropriate. The second half of the chapter specifically lays out a software development methodology for mobile application development. The goal of the earlier sections of this chapter is to get you specifically thinking about the importance of methodologies in software development, and the latter portions of the chapter lay out a concrete software development methodology to follow in mobile software development.

Inherent and Transient Difficulties in Software Engineering

NOTE: The software engineering book *The Mythical Man Month* does an excellent job of exploring and discussing this topic. It is highly recommended reading for those looking for a good grounding in general software development methodologies.

Transient Difficulties and the Tools That Solve Them

Some of the challenges facing software developers can rightfully be described as "transient difficulties." These are problems that improved development tools can mitigate. Debugging is a great example of a transient difficulty. Over the years, huge advances have been made in improving developers' abilities to debug their applications as they run. This has moved debugging from a laborious task that was done separately with paper and pencil, low-level tools such as disassemblers, and debug-print statements along with brilliantly tuned intuitions to something that is now a very natural and interactive part of any modern development tool. Few developers using modern development tools today even think of debugging as a separate activity distinct from designing and writing their code. It is now all part of the natural process of software development, and developers switch smoothly from one activity to another. Not long ago this was definitely not the case, and certainly not for software running on devices. Once formidable, the difficulty of debugging code has today been greatly reduced. It was a transient difficulty, and better technology has addressed it.

Inherent Difficulties and the Methodologies That Address Them

The second class of software development challenges comprises those challenges that are best described as "inherently difficult." These kinds of challenges are at the heart of software engineering. Better development tools themselves will not solve these kinds of problems. Instead, these problems require a good *methodology* to guide the engineering effort and ensure that software projects succeed despite the challenges.

A good example of an inherently complex challenge is algorithm design. Modern object-oriented development languages have made code encapsulation and organization much easier but they have not made algorithm design easy or automatic. Writing good algorithms is certainly aided by the richer set of base classes that modern programming frameworks offer, but designing fundamentally new algorithms is still hard work and will probably remain so for the foreseeable future. This is because algorithms are inherently purpose specific in nature and there is no general way known to translate your intent into the best possible algorithm; this can only be done in an automated way if the scope of the problem being solved is narrowed down greatly and specific tools are built for the task. The same holds true for writing multithreaded code. Better tools, programming languages, and libraries can help, and the problem can be solved for many well-bounded cases; however, a good general-purpose machine for breaking up generic problems into parallel pieces eludes us. It appears to be an inherently hard problem that requires careful deign and good methodology.

Modern programming languages and graphical design surfaces can make developers more expressive, but they do not take away the need for good algorithmic design skills. These skills are needed to build the critical systems that drive the behavior and efficiency of software. The best that modern programming technology has achieved is allowing for the packaging of complex algorithms into reusable components and frameworks and the modeling of interactions between these components. This allows commonly used critical systems to be designed by experts and reused by generalists. Modeling technologies such as UML (Unified Modeling Language) and graphical design surfaces can make component design simpler and communication clearer between component authors and clients, but they do not remove the core complexity of good algorithm design. Tools will continue to get better to reduce the transient difficulties, but core challenges will remain.

Components have great utility because they allow the reuse of hard work, but they do not make the hard work of designing the algorithms any easier. Component-oriented design is a *methodology* that has emerged to help software engineers address one of the most vexing problems facing software development. It is a software development methodology that advises developers and architects to separate their problems into discrete and layered components.

Critical components and algorithms are identified and get the most expert design, coding, and testing. Higher-level generally less-rigorously tested code uses these components to provide essential functionality to the applications being developed. Componentization succeeds as a methodology because it allows the partitioning of applications. It allows engineers, architects, and managers to identify and concentrate on the most difficult algorithmic challenges. Like any methodology, componentization can be overused and misused. If everything possible is made into a separate component under the mistaken belief that the more components a project is broken into the better the engineering, the result will be overly complex interfaces between a myriad of different components. Modeling tools may help visualize this, but a complicated mess is still a complicated mess. Too many unnecessary components blurs the sharp focus that componentization is intended to place on ensuring the excellence of critical pieces. Methodologies must be applied wisely and with explicit goals in mind. A methodology is only useful if it can be measured against goals to ensure that its benefits are being realized.

Two Good Cases for a Component-Based Methodology

Working with XML and working with cryptography are two areas where componentization has effectively solved complex problems and significantly reduced the complexity of working with these technologies.

XML parsing is a technical challenge where having a methodology of component reuse makes good sense. Very few developers write their own XML parsers for their applications for the sole reason that it is a difficult job to design and implement a great performing, highly robust, and general-purpose XML parser. If everyone who wanted to use XML in their application had to write their own XML parser, all kinds of small bugs and inconsistencies would be produced. This would defeat the interoperability promise that XML is founded on. Other than as an academic exercise in algorithm design (and it is a great exercise), writing your own XML parser is a fool's errand; you will never get it done as well as the people whose sole job it is to write and test one. Instead of having a software development process where everyone writes his or her own specific XML parsing routines, there is a design methodology that recommends using prebuilt and tested general-purpose components. Several native code and managed-code XML parsers have been created with very rigorous algorithmic design and testing processes. These few components are reused by the many application developers who want to use XML. This is a methodological approach to solving the inherently difficult problem of building a robust XML parser.

Another great example where a methodology of reuse is favored over custom implementation is cryptography. Design of cryptographic algorithms is a complex and specialized art form. Conflicting with this specialist drive is the fact that every day the cryptographic functionality becomes more important to developers building common applications. It has been demonstrated that a great way to build an insecure application is to write your own cryptographic algorithms. Unless you are doing cryptographic research, building your own cryptographic systems is highly discouraged by good software engineering practice. Designing, implementing, and maintaining a cryptographic system that is secure, robust, and fast is very hard work. It would be foolish and error prone for everyone who needed cryptographic functionality to write his own cryptographic systems into his applications. So here we have another clear inherent difficulty in algorithm design that better tools do not solve for us. It is addressed not by throwing one's hands up in the air and saying, "Well, it's hard and that's it," but by coming up with a software development methodology for componentization of common difficult algorithmic problems coupled with a methodology that makes certain all members of the project team use these components in a consistent way.

A further benefit of using an off-the-shelf component methodology to address these kinds of problems is reduced maintenance burdens. When flaws are found in these components (which they inevitably will be), they can be centrally fixed instead of having the same kinds of problems pop up across multiple software implementations.

Any mobile software development project of sufficient complexity will need a good set of methodologies that address the inherent difficulties present in mobile software development. There needs to be a process for identifying the difficult problems and making sure they are getting addressed in the best way possible. Componentization addresses one specific type of software development challenge. Along with appropriate componentization, other complementary methodologies will be required to address additional challenges such as ensuring the necessary application performance, designing good mobile device user interfaces, and building robust mobile communications. Knowing how to spot what the inherent difficulties are and how to go about addressing them is the hallmark of a good development lead.

To sum up, there are problems that development tools can help us with, and these problems will get easier every year as tools advance. In contrast to these transiently difficult problems, there are also inherently difficult problems that can be solved only by having the right software engineering approaches. This means having a methodology that makes sure that the most important problems do not get addressed in an ad hoc manner but rather get the full attention and deep consideration they require.

A Few Software Development Approaches Through the Years

Every successive generation of computing has had its own challenges and corresponding methodologies for success. These methodologies have been, and continue to be, based on both the available state-of-the-art in development tools as well as the specific kinds of solutions being developed.

Initially, computing resources such as memory, registers, and processing cycles were very scarce, so writing the most compact and efficient algorithms was imperative. This is still a goal to strive for, but it is now balanced by the great long-term benefits of writing serviceable and reusable code. Today the goal is not to write the most efficient code but rather to write the most efficient code that is understandable, reliable, and maintainable.

Batch Computing

In the era of batch computing (that is, before interactive software), the algorithm was the king. It was possible and indeed essential to specify the inputs into the system as well as the outputs expected from the system before starting coding. Because the usage model was based on input -> processing -> output, a great deal of time was spent working on the core algorithm and the avoidance of unnecessary space or storage usage was a paramount design goal. This model has great merit and today is still the ideal to strive for in designing individual procedures that process information in a batch mode (for example, in sorting algorithm design). Individual functions can be designed this way but not complex and user interactive systems. This was the era of the "flowchart."

Stateless Server Processing

When building reliable server applications that respond to requests, the Holy Grail is to be "stateless." Your code gets a request, processes it, and then returns the results without any need to maintain state in between successive requests. This is very similar to batch processing in using the input -> processing -> output model. Complex modern Web applications of course do maintain state in between successive requests (for example, shopping carts on Amazon), and this is best achieved by managing the state in a very central encapsulated way so that as much code as possible runs in a stateless way.

Event-Driven Interactive Computing

Event-driven computing represents the computing model where an application is a long-standing conversation with an end user. Code is run to respond to user actions and requests; the application reacts to what the user does. In contrast to a batch application, an interactive application does not have a fixed termination time but keeps on processing new events triggered by the user until the user decides his or her session is over. This programming model is commonly called "event driven" because discrete events are generated based on user actions that the developer's application responds to (for example, mouse click events, list selection events, and window close events). A clean state management model is essential for building good event-driven interactive applications.

Development Is an Iterative Process, but It Does Have Rules

Few people today advocate the use of flowcharts to map out the functional behavior of applications. For one thing, the flowcharts would be immense. Today's model of event-driven programming, rich user interfaces, and the widespread availability of rapid application development tools make the concept of a flowchart mapping out all of an application's algorithms and user interactions seem quaint. Specific key algorithms can be mapped out in this detail if required, but by and large a higher-level approach is called for.

On the flip side, there is the ad hoc approach of "just sit down and start cranking out code until the application is done." Tempting as it is, this reckless programming approach is equally flawed and usually results in a messy ball of code that performs poorly, is riddled with bugs, cannot be maintained, and must ultimately be thrown out and be rewritten. These kinds of applications often appear hacked together or kluged for the simple reason that they are. All design decisions tend to become tactical answers to the question "How do I solve the specific problem I am facing right now?" with little thought given to the overall effect to the system at large both in terms of system behavior as well as code complexity.

In contrast to the ad hoc approach described above, one school of thought states, "Spec out the application in full detail before you write a line of code." Some projects with many developers may require this level of detailed coordination, but these projects also require the discipline to keep their specifications current if they are to remain meaningful through the development process. They also require a detailed level of foreknowledge about the end behavior of the application that is often not realistic to know ahead of time. Although admirable, the "spec everything to infinite detail" approach is usually not appropriate in modern development, particularly of first version products, because things will be learned and requirements will change as the product gets developed. This is especially true for mobile device applications, which may require field testing to understand how people will use them in the real world. It is important that a level of flexibility be part of the design process to accommodate learning and challenges that emerge through the development process. There should be a specification, but it should start flexible and move toward greater specificity as the product matures toward its completion.

It is important to pick a realistic level of process that you and your team can adhere to. Even if you are working as an individual, there is a level of self-discipline that it is beneficial to hold yourself to. Smaller projects, as mobile device applications tend to be, should adopt an approach that members can benefit from and buy into. Having too much plan breeds inflexibility when changes are needed. An overly rigorous and inflexible specification or plan will simply get abandoned. On the other hand, having no plan or too little process will result in a wandering product definition that will drift either into crises or mediocrity. There is a happy medium that is dependent on the size, scope, and maturity of the product you are developing. It is important to assess the size of the project and from there draw up a realistic process that will get you there.

Several great books exist on the subject of software development processes, so the remarks here are brief. The rules I have personally found to be essential in mobile software development are as follows:

- *Have a development methodology.* A methodology is a plan for how you will go about designing and writing code. The rest of this chapter is devoted to developing a methodology for mobile applications.
- *Have an explicit project plan contained in one central document.* Every project can benefit from having one master document that

everyone has agreed to adhere to. A template for such a project plan is defined below.

- *Plan on iterating*. Changes will be required, and unforeseen problems will arise. Mobile devices are not closed systems, and successfully interacting with the user and the world at large is a complex process; you will learn as you go along. It is best to admit this and incorporate it into your planning process.

The Project-Description Document

For all software development projects beyond the most trivial, it is important to have a single "live document" that states (1) the project requirements and what the product will do when it is finished, (2) The design philosophy, (3) the architecture of the application, (4) current status of the effort, and (5) the plan that will bring the product from its present state to a successful conclusion. Large products may have additional subsidiary documents, but there should always be a key top-level document that states the essential goals, status, and plan. This document needs to be a living document that all team members agree represents the effort.

The single live document that drives the development process should be broken into the following sections:

- *The goals*—This section of the document clearly states what the finished product will do and what the philosophy behind the project is.
- *The status*—This section of the document accurately describes the status of the project at the present time. It is part of the logistical plan for the project and states where the project is along the path to reaching its goals. It should state which milestone the project development effort is working toward and what items remain to exit the current milestone successfully. Also stated should be a list of the biggest risks or unknowns that need to get resolved.
- *The application's architecture and relevant state diagrams*—This information is the technical side of the plan. For mobile device applications, this should include the appropriate state diagrams that describe the discrete states that the application can be put into and how these relate to the memory and resources that will be kept in memory. (You will read much more on this later in the book.) This live design text represents the contract that all the development team members agree to adhere to in their implementation. If you are the sole developer, this document represents a way of keeping yourself honest; anyone who has ever built a large project by himself

or herself will appreciate the temptation of cutting corners to get a feature working at the expense of good design. It is much harder to cut corners when you have an explicit contract defined that you need to state your proposed shortcuts in. This section should not be overly long or overly complex for the reason that it will be discarded if its use is onerous. It should state what is needed to keep the design organized and, importantly, it needs to be kept current with any agreed-upon design changes.

- *The development plan with discrete milestones identified*—Even more than a schedule, a measured plan is needed that states the discrete milestones that your project will pass through to get to completion. By definition milestones are your way to track progress toward a defined final goal. Each milestone represents a resting point where you can stop to consider your progress, clean up code that has been left in a messy state, and adjust designs as necessary. The goals may change as your project progresses, and you may need to adjust milestones; this is fine. The architecture may change as your design evolves, and revised state models may be required; this is also fine. The user interface will almost certainly need to be revamped a few times. Achieving a prestated milestone (or failing to achieve one) is the surest way to measure your progress as well as to reflect on how your future path to the finish line needs to be adjusted. Milestones are your friend.

Plan on Iterating

You will learn things as you go along. Despite your best efforts at foresight, unexpected challenges will arise. You will hit performance problems and you will probably not get the user interface right the first time. Increased experience with mobile development means that you will hopefully make fewer mistakes in future development efforts, but you will almost certainly make some mistakes. Plan on design iterations during individual milestones and especially at the end of development milestones when you take stock of where the project is and what key problems have emerged. The iterative nature of modern software development raises the importance of having a design document that is kept current and a methodology that gives you a good capacity for iteration.

None of the Details Matter If the Big Picture Is Not Right

This statement is obvious and is often forgotten in the process of getting a mobile application's code written. Developers get lost in the code and forget about what the application is about. On desktop and Web applications, this most often manifests itself in awkward and unintuitive user interfaces and key missing functions. The application works but never works quite right, and the end user must jump through hoops to learn, navigate, and get use out of the application. The result of forgetting about the big picture is that the application being developed will lack clarity of purpose.

Because mobile device applications have a more focused usage model and a constrained user interface, a lack of clarity of purpose will be worse for these devices. It is harder and more frustrating for the end user to work around poor design in a mobile device application. An application can become a nightmare to navigate, performance problems quickly become aggravating, and the user is left frustrated. Because their size matches other common handheld devices (watches, phones, Swiss army knives, music players, screwdrivers, and so on), mobile devices leave the user with the impression that they should behave crisply and intuitively. Mobile applications need to be tractable to a user without the need for instructions. Almost everyone has had a confusing experience with a digital watch or remote control with too many or poorly laid-out buttons. Clarity of purpose is important.

For this reason, it is important that you clearly state the goals of the application in your main design document. These goals may change over time, but everyone should be working toward the same agreed-to set. If there is a required change of focus, everyone must change focus and a design document with an explicit goals section helps this happen. No matter how much code you write, if your application does not clearly meet the stated goals you have not succeeded.

Solve Problems in the Right Order; Go Back If You Need To

Everything is important, but some things are more important than others. In the mathematical analysis of functions, there are first-order effects, second-order effects, third-order effects, ..., nth-order effects. The lower the order, the more effect the term has on the behavior of the system; higher-order effects can often be discarded. So it is with mobile application development; you cannot concentrate on everything, so learn to concentrate on the things that matter most.

Below are listed steps that show how to approach the most significant aspects of your mobile application's design. They are listed in order. As you make changes and iterate on your design, it is important to revisit the lower-order steps to make sure that the changes you make to solve specific problems do not cause unacceptable regressions. For example, it is possible to solve a communications problem in a way that affects the way users interact with data in the user interface; this may or may not be appropriate. If you change the communications model of your mobile application, it is important to examine how these changes affect the fundamental aspects that drive the end user's perception of your application.

Step 0: Before You Start, Decide On the Scope of Your Application

This is Step 0 because it really precedes the design and development work. Before you start drawing up plans and building software, you need to have a fundamental idea about what the result is going to be.

A desktop application is like a wide-angle lens in that it typically shows a great deal of information and enables the user to explore a wide space. In contrast, a mobile application is like a magnifying glass or zoom lens. It enables the user to quickly zoom in on specific details, to enter and access a narrower range of data quickly, or to make decisions on a real-time basis. Mobile applications tend to represent a focused subset of the scenarios possible in a comparable desktop application. It is important to be specific about what scenarios your mobile application is going to zoom in on.

Before starting the real application development, decide what your application is going to do and what it is not going to do. If you are creating the mobile version of a desktop application, define the subset of functionality that the user will be able to access quickly and in a mobile way. If you are building a new application that does not have a desktop analogue, write down the key scenarios users will perform with the application and how they will experience them through a mobile device. Drawing pictures or creating prototypes often proves helpful in fleshing out these scenarios. If there is a specific group of end users in mind, spend time with them and have them work with the mock-up applications to get you feedback.

The Right Subset of Features Governs Everything Else

If you clearly identify the key scenarios and features of your mobile application, it will guide the rest of your development. Having an explicit statement of how end users will use your application and a detailed understanding of the experience they should have will be invaluable in guiding the performance tuning as well as the design of the user interface, communications system, and memory model.

If you do not specify the top scenarios and features, you will end up with a hodgepodge of features mixed into an application. Because the primary functions of the application have not been listed or prioritized, the user interface will not be optimized to perform the key tasks properly. For example, if entering dates is a key thing the user will need to do, you should optimize the user interface to make this as fast and reliable as possible. Conversely, if dates are rarely required to be entered, an unoptimized user interface for date entry may be acceptable and design and development resources should be expended elsewhere. Unless the most important scenarios are identified, listed, and agreed upon by the development team, the application's performance will not be tuned for these and features may well be cut that are important to the end user.

To set up for success, write down the key requirements and features and make it the first section of your design document.

Examples of Good and Poor Scenario Specification

Poor Example	Good Example
Banking Application "Make the Web functionality of MyBankFoo's Web banking available online and offline for users with mobile devices." *This example does not specify what the most important functionality is. Is it the ability to check one's balance? Bill payment? Transition history? Transfers? Point-of-purchase transactions? Getting car loans and mortgages? What are the main things the user will need to do from a mobile device?*	**Banking Application** "1. Users should be able to access their bank balance from a mobile phone using one hand and in fewer than five clicks. 2. The user should be able to pay for and confirm purchases from vending machines using the device's infrared port in fewer than three clicks." *We have identified the two key scenarios we want to enable.*

Survey Taking
"Replace using paper and clipboard for taking public surveys and manually keying in results."
What kinds of questions will be asked? When will the data be synchronized?

Survey Taking
"The application should enable users to collect public survey information onto a Pocket PC. Questions will be asked as multiple choice or simple numeric input and will be cached locally and sent to a server when the device is placed into a PC cradle. Up to 20 questions can be asked in a survey, and the results of up to 1,000 survey responses need to be stored on the device. No manual text entry will be required."
We have specified what kinds of questions the application needs to handle and we have specified how the device will be synchronized. (Importantly, when drawing up the list of scenarios, we don't care specifically how results are stored locally or what the specific synchronization mechanism is as long as the scenarios work—this will be important to our implementation but the end user does not care.) We have also specified what the application need not do well (that is, deal with free-form text).

Inventory Tracking
"A version of the desktop inventory tracking system will be made available for on- and offline mobile devices."

Porting a desktop or web-application's full functionality will almost never result in a satisfactory outcome.

Inventory Tracking
"The application is intended for use inside a warehouse with intermittent access to a Wi-Fi network.
"Inventory tracking information for up to 5,000 products must be stored for offline use on the device.
"Item IDs can be scanned in via a bar code reader.
"Items can be added and deducted from inventory. Devices will synchronize using the Wi-Fi network when prompted by the user.
"Live, up-to-date access to a back-end database is required on demand.
"Key scenario: Scan in a box, specify whether the item is being added or deducted from inventory by clicking a button. Scan in a purchase order number from a form to associate with an inventory item.
"Key requirement: If bar code scanning does not work, the user must be able to quickly key in the numbers manually using touch screen and stylus. Failure of bar code scanning should be logged for performance and reliability tracking purposes."
We have specified what the key requirements are as well as the main scenario in which the application will be used.

Game/Learning Application

"Build a mobile device application that teaches users foreign language vocabulary."

What kind of dictionary capacity is required? What will the basic user experience be?

Game/Learning Application

"The application is a game that will test user's foreign language vocabulary skills.

"Users will be given multiple-choice questions on vocabulary that they can answer by clicking the screen.

"Up to 1,000 different vocabulary words can be stored on the device.

"Example sentences of all words must be stored on the device as well."

These are reasonable expectations for a learning game. We'll need to explore more about how the game will work, but we have the high-level input/output model defined and the data capacity specified.

Travel Application

"Store and manage all of the user's travel information and make it available offline on a mobile phone."

This is not specific enough about what the application will do or how the user will use the application.

Travel Application

"The user will be able to access e-ticket airplane reservations stored on the device. Reservation number, flight number, flight time, and airport information will be available on his mobile phone and will be able to be navigated to within three clicks. This information is intended to be quickly called up and handed to a worker at a check-in desk."

Step 1: Start with Performance, Stay with Performance

After identifying the key features and scenarios for your application, your main concern should be the end user's experience when using your mobile application. This means designing and coding for performance and responsiveness.

- You should define general responsiveness metrics for your application. For example: "Bringing up a dialog should never take more than 0.5 seconds" or "A visual response to clicking a control should appear instantaneously" or "Expanding tree-view nodes should never take longer than 0.15 seconds." These are all good metrics to strive for.
- You should define specific metrics for your key scenarios. For example: "Loading inventory data should never stall the user interface for more than 0.2 seconds without bringing up a wait cursor" or "In no case should loading inventory data take more than 3 seconds."

Test your assumptions in real-life usage scenarios. Even without real data or code in place, it is easy to put wait states into your application's skeletal user interface to test the effects of delays when the user performs common tasks. It is important to get a good feel for what is an acceptable wait time and what is unacceptable. Applications should always strive to offer immediate acknowledgement that an action is underway, even if the action cannot be completed immediately. Work can also be pushed to background threads if the work will take a long or indeterminate amount of time.

As you are developing your application, use realistic sizes of data that reflect or exceed the likely usage by end users. A very common mistake developers make is using a small sample of data during development only to find out that the application performs terribly when used with actual amounts of real-world data. The sooner you can move to testing with real-world data, the sooner these problems will surface and the better the chance you can address and mitigate performance problems.

Follow a performance driven development methodology at every stage of development. If performance goals are not being met stop coding and revist the design of the preceding levels!

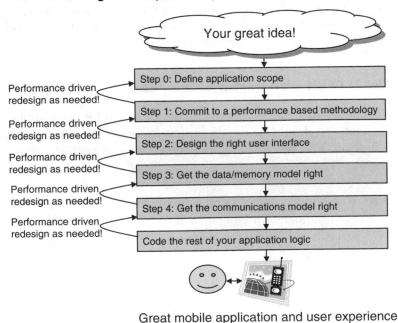

Great mobile application and user experience

Figure 4.1 A performance-driven methodology.

Figure 4.1 shows a flowchart for mobile application development. If you hit a performance problem, *stop*! To restate this, when you hit a performance problem in your design and development, *stop adding new code immediately*! All too often, developers will continue coding, wanting to reach "code complete," with the promise of fixing performance problems afterward. This strategy is risky at best! It is rarely successful in desktop and server development and is usually quite painful; the results will be worse on devices. The reason for this is that performance problems are often not the result of a discrete algorithm that can simply be tuned or optimized without effects on other parts of the system. Until you can diagnose the problem in detail and prove that an alternative solution will fix it, you really have no idea how much redesign may be required to address the issue. You might get lucky, but luck has a way of running out pretty quickly for engineers who depend on it.

In many cases, performance problems are systematic and application wide. Some systematic causes of poor performance are the ways data is moved into and out of memory, the number of resources held in memory at any given time, or the way the user interface draws and updates information on the screen. These kinds of performance problems are usually caused by fundamental design choices that can only be satisfactorily addressed early in the design and development process. The cost of moving on to "code compete" and later needing to re-architect your data-access strategy, redesign your memory usage model, or move work onto a background thread to speed up user interface responsiveness is huge. Even if you get late design changes to application code working, you will end up with messy spaghetti code. Real performance is built from the ground up.

Count on the fact that your application will continue to get bigger and more complex as you go along. You will write more code, create more objects, and have more components fighting for a finite pool of resources. If your mobile application has performance problems you do not address when they arise, they will get worse, not better, as your code base continues to grow. Moreover, as you add more code, additional dependencies will be introduced into the data model, the memory usage model, the user interface model, the communications model, and other logic you have written. You will be painting yourself into a corner.

A common, plausible, but deeply mistaken rationalization is, "I need to get all the code written before I can understand which parts of my application need to get tuned." This is badly flawed because it assumes that the separate parts of your application are somehow not interdependent. After you have written all of your application's code, you will have introduced a great many explicit and implicit dependencies between different systems and will very likely only be able to make incremental improvements without radical redesign. Even if you have taken pains to try to encapsulate your application design, this will inevitably be the case. More code equals more interdependencies; try to avoid this through good design, but also count on it being a fact of life. The time to address performance problems is when the code base is still fluid and open to re-architecture. The best time to do this is when the code is first written.

When a performance problem arises, stop and assess the situation and find out what is going on. Is the user interface being updated in an inefficient way? Is your application holding too much data in memory so that the garbage collector is constantly running? Is the processing you are doing of inherently long duration and a good candidate to be moved to a background thread so it can run asynchronously to the user interface? Are you working with a large amount of data using a higher-level stateful object model when a lower-level stateless programming model would be better? Identify the root causes of the problem and re-architect your code to fix these before writing more code that will depend on the assumptions you have made.

The result of adhering to a disciplined and performance-focused development process is that your application's code, data, and memory usage models will stay lean and the user interface design will stay clean and efficient.

Good Performance Allows a Good User Experience (Bad Performance Means None of the Subsequent Steps Will Matter)

If you build a beautiful and intuitive mobile user interface, a clean and robust communications model, and a nice object-oriented data model but your application behaves poorly, end users will be frustrated. The very nature of mobile devices means that end users expect responsiveness. People carry them in their pockets and expect on-demand usage.

It is important to understand that all performance is subjective. The user does not care how long it took to get the data, he only cares how long it appeared to take and what happened in the interval. This can be used to your advantage when designing applications. Long-duration operations are not necessarily bad as long as the application behaves in a way that makes users feel like they are in control and the application is responsive. The proof of performance is in real users' perceptions.

Make the user's perception of performance your mobile application's primary development goal. It should come even before user interface design because important aspects of user interface design will be dictated by performance needs. For example, assume your application has a user-requested operation that will take 20 seconds to complete. Because 20 seconds is a long time for a user interface to remain unresponsive, your mobile application should probably push this work into a background thread so that the user interface remains interactive while the request is being processed. If this is the case, you may want to devote a portion of the user interface real estate to giving your users status information on the ongoing operation so that they know the request is underway and is progressing.

An Example of a Performance-Dictated User Interface

Both ActiveSync and Internet Explorer for Pocket PCs and smart phones offer user interface elements dedicated to keeping the end user informed of asynchronous requests that they have initiated. These keep the user interface responsive and the user engaged.

ActiveSync may need to initiate a phone call or other high-latency data connection to synchronize calendar information with a back-end Exchange. When it does so, the device's user interface shows a label that contains the current state of the communications attempt. The label shows text such as "Dialing phone ...," "Connecting to server," "Synchronizing schedule," "Downloaded 12 of 20," and so on. This simple user interface notification element offers no absolute performance gain, but it does keep users assured that progress is being made on their behalf and thus discourages users from aborting the request out of frustration.

Pocket Internet Explorer may also need to establish data connections, look up the IP addresses of URLs, and other tasks when downloading a Web page. When performing these latency-prone tasks, the browser window's caption is updated with text describing the communication's state. In addition, an animated Windows flag is displayed when Web content is being downloaded. Both actions keep the user informed that progress is being made.

In both cases, the user interface is kept responsive and users are offered the option to cancel the operation if they want to. Offering the option to cancel makes users feel empowered, and showing incremental progress makes them less likely to cancel. Certainly it would be best if these tasks could be made to happen instantaneously, but when this is not possible keeping the user interface responsive and keeping the user informed of progress is a good second best.

Step 2: Design the Right User Interface

As discussed above, before commencing a mobile application's design it is important to identify the key scenarios and features that define the scope of the application. Following this committing to a performance-oriented development process will ensure you do not code yourself into a corner. If you

Commit to having a user interface experience that performs well. Redesign as required to achieve this goal.

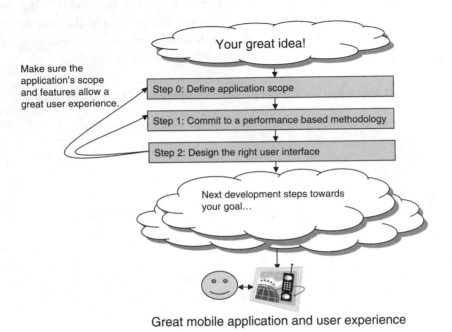

Figure 4.2 Performance-driven user interface development.

cannot make the scenarios and features you have chosen perform well, it is back to the drawing board.

Designing the right user interface is the next on the stack of importance. Just as good performance is tailored to human perceptions, good user interface design is specific to the device being targeted. The optimum user interface for one class of mobile devices will not be the best user interface for another class. It pays to get specific.

Be prepared to iterate on the user interface's design—particularly if you are new to mobile device user interface design or if you are working with a new class of device that has a form factor different from other devices you have developed for in the past. As you gain experience working with a given device class, the user interface design process will become faster but you will still find the need to iterate to get things to look and feel right.

It is always a good design practice to separate your application logic from your presentation logic so that changes in user interface design do not ripple and cause the need for modifications to your application logic. This is doubly true for device design. If you can abstract your application logic from your presentation logic, you will be in a strong position to both (1) iterate and improve the user interface design for the device you are presently targeting, and (2) port the application to new classes of devices quickly. Today's handheld PDA application can easily be tomorrow's smart phone application if the user interface code is not woven deeply into the core of the application logic. Keeping application logic and user interface logic cleanly separated will pay great dividends both in code maintainability and code portability.

A Good User Interface Means Happy Users (A Bad User Interface Means Growing Frustration Daily)

The keys to user interface design are end-user productivity and responsiveness. It is important that the primary scenarios of a mobile application can be accomplished quickly by users. For example, if calendar dates need to be entered frequently by end users, this should be made as quick, simple, and as predictive as possible. Alternately, if users commonly need to be able to select an item from a large list of related items, the quickest way may not be to place all the items in a single ListBox but rather to design a custom graphical user interface that helps guide users as quickly as possible to the right item. A list of car parts may benefit from a graphic of a car that the user can tap on. Similarly, a medical application may benefit from a human body graphic that users can select body locations on. The correct user interface is dependent on the task at hand and the specific device on which the application is being run. This is why the "write once, run anywhere" user interface concept tends to fall short on devices. "Write once, run anywhere" approaches are just not focused enough to provide a great experience on a broad set of devices that have different display and input capabilities.

Closely related to productivity is responsiveness. The user interface for a mobile device must respond crisply. This is not to say that the user cannot be left waiting; this is sometimes unavoidable. However, the user should never be left guessing whether the action they just requested is underway or if they need to try again. A sluggishly behaving handheld device can be a frustrating thing to use because there is a great psychological expectation that things will happen when you push buttons, tap screens, or otherwise interact with something that fits in your hand.

Step 3: Get Your Data and Memory Model Right

Your mobile application's data and memory models determine how the objects and resources that are currently held in memory are managed. Conversely,

Commit to making your application's data and memory models perform well. If you experience performance problems revisit previous design steps.

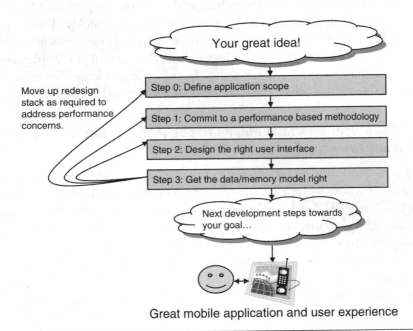

Move up redesign stack as required to address performance concerns.

Your great idea!

Step 0: Define application scope

Step 1: Commit to a performance based methodology

Step 2: Design the right user interface

Step 3: Get the data/memory model right

Next development steps towards your goal…

Great mobile application and user experience

Figure 4.3 Performance-driven data and memory model design.

these models also determine how your application discards data and resources to allow space to be reclaimed for application usage. Mobile devices differ markedly from their desktop counterparts in the need for efficient data and memory management.

Mobile devices have traded large memory pools and memory paging files for small size and low power consumption. The application running on a mobile device is no longer living in a large mansion but in a stylish condominium. The sport utility vehicle that your desktop applications are used to driving around in has been traded in for a motorcycle. Thinking of your application as living in a much smaller physical space is a good analogy to keep in mind as you are designing your mobile application's data and memory model.

To a large extent, desktop application programmers, other than those dealing with huge in-memory resources (for example, complex painting programs often work with huge matrices of data), tend not to think about memory models. For this reason, desktop applications tend not to do much systematic and proactive housecleaning with the data and resources they hold in memory. Whatever data is needed is eventually loaded into memory and very little is proactively discarded. Data and resources are kept loaded in memory out of laziness or just in case they may be needed by the user. If your application has gone to the trouble of downloading some data or images from a network resource, why not keep them around just in case the user wants to access them again? To a large extent this makes sense for desktop applications; in-memory data that is not used is eventually paged out of physical memory and onto the hard drive, and it is much quicker to page this data back in than it is to go to the network again and re-request it. The application has a huge house to work in, and unused things just get moved into the attic somewhere.

As discussed earlier in this book, the situation is markedly different for mobile devices. Given the finite-sized memory available and the dearth of secondary storage to page memory out to, developers must be mindful of the memory and resources they are using. It is imperative that mobile application developers have an explicit model that decides how much to keep in memory and when to discard things to be garbage collected. On devices, it is often the right strategy to discard data from memory or explicitly place it onto a flash storage card and reacquire the data into memory as needed.

A Good Data Model Means Good Performance and Flexible Design (A Bad Data Model Means Locked-In Bad Performance)

If there is a specific art to building great mobile applications, this is an important part of it. Being a good memory and resource manager means three things: (1) the learned ability to cleverly keep what is vital and immediately useful in memory, (2) finding ways to cache important data on the device but out of active memory, and (3) relegating the rest of the data to storage off the device. If you can acquire the ability to do these three things, you will be well along the road to designing great performing applications that users love to use.

Step 4: Get Your Communications and Input/Output Models Right

Your communications and input/output models determine the way in which your application communicates with resources outside of its process. These can be either resources local to your device, such as on-device files and local databases, or resources residing external to your physical device, such as those accessed via sockets-based communication, files on servers, Web services, and remote databases. How your application communicates with both local and remote resources will have a great effect on users' perception of

Commit to having your application's communications model perform well for the user. If your communications design causes bad user performance perceptions revisit previous design steps to fix this user perception.

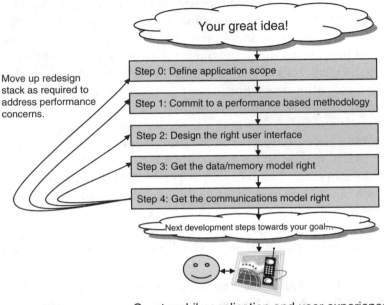

Figure 4.4 Performance-driven communications design.

your application and so ranks high on the list of things to incorporate into your development methodology.

Working with Resources Local to Your Device

Almost any application that maintains long-term information for the user does so by storing and retrieving information locally on the device. The most important considerations for working with device local data are data format and the level of programming abstraction used to work with that data.

Data Format

Choosing the format to store your data in is generally a balance between efficiency and convenience. Any given data can be stored in binary files, plain-text files, XML text files, or in the structured tables of a local database. Efficiency means minimizing size and maximizing performance. Convenience means maximizing developer productivity, code maintainability, minimizing the testing burden, enabling data interoperability between applications, and maintaining flexibility for augmenting the data format in the future.

Binary storage formats offer the greatest possibilities for both size reduction and performance. For this reason, dense data such as images are most often stored in binary formats. So specialized are the needs for storing image data that several popular image formats are available that each offer trade-offs with size, performance, and fidelity. Each binary image format is geared toward a specific set of needs. Beyond images, any data can be stored in a binary format. However, binary data is hard to work with; if you are creating your own binary formats, both data versioning and interoperability with other applications will be problematic.

Text storage formats offer the greatest ease of use and interoperability potential because they are readily decipherable. However, text files are verbose compared to their binary counterparts. XML is even more verbose than simple text because it adds schema information to the text data. This added schema meta data greatly increases versioning and interoperability flexibility, but at the expense of using more space. In addition, XML requires more processing to parse in and write out compared to simple comma- or tab-separated data in text files. Flexibility has a cost. This cost can be reduced by using intelligent implementation strategies, but it cannot be eliminated.

Databases offer the highest amount of data organization but bring with them the overhead of a database engine.

Levels of Programming Model Abstraction

Programming models for working with stored data usually are available in several layers. For example, when working with files in the .NET Compact Framework, the following increasing levels of abstraction are offered:

- Binary streams
- Text streams
- XML forward-only readers and writers
- XML Document Object Model (DOM)

Each of these layers offers an increasing level of abstraction to make working with data easier, but does so with increased overhead. Sometimes this overhead is negligible and well worth the developer productivity and robustness that high-level pretested APIs provide. Other times, particularly when working with large amounts of data, the higher-level abstractions introduce added memory and processing requirements that are unacceptable. In these cases, developers should go one level lower in the API stack and try to solve their problems using a lower-level API that has lower overhead. It is important to understand the overhead associated with each increasing level of abstraction.

Choosing the Right Storage Format and Programming Model

Which data format to use for your data is entirely dependent on the goals of your application; there is no universal right answer. A common mistake developers make when approaching mobile device development is to assume that because resources are more limited they should jump right to the lowest level of abstraction and use binary files and stream-based file I/O. In some cases, this may indeed be required, but in most cases it is just taking on unnecessary work that will require additional testing and probably yield an inferior and inflexible result. A general rule of thumb is that you should use the highest level of abstraction that you can afford size and performance wise. For relatively small amounts of data, it is foolish to invent your own binary format because XML is a fantastic choice for moderate storage needs. XML is easy to work with, is robust for versioning needs, and good higher-level APIs exist to make programming easy. Similarly, if a binary format is truly needed, such as for the storage of large image data, there is great benefit in using an already existing and well-proven format if one exists. Because there are several well-proven image formats, it would generally be a waste to invent your own. Reuse and utilize existing components and formats whenever possible; invent your own only when you have proven that higher-level approaches will not work.

Working with Resources External to Your Device

Other than simple games and basic productivity applications such as calculators, most interesting mobile device applications have some interaction with data that is off of the device. This data may be in a database that is replicated onto the device. It may be an on-device address book that is synchronized with an e-mail server. It may be images or music that are downloaded from the Web, from a desktop PC, or "beamed over" from another device. SMS messages arrive on mobile phones and are sent by them. XML data is pushed to and pulled from Web services. Data may be accessed over a Wi-Fi network, transferred via a flash memory card plugged into a device, sent over a GPRS mobile phone connection, beamed via infrared, or just plain sent over an Ethernet cable plugged into a device. In short, there is a great variety in the types of data that can be communicated and the means by which it can be transferred.

Having decided the set of key scenarios your mobile application is going to enable, having dedicated yourself to be performance driven in your development, having prototyped the user interface that will enable the user to interact with the application, consideration must then be given to the communications model.

Of greatest importance to defining the communications model is to look at the scenarios you have defined and determine what communication is required to enable these scenarios. Some key questions to ask include the following:

- Is a connection to live data required all the time or only intermittently?
- How much data needs to be moved around? This may affect your other choices.
- How will data be moved back and forth? Via a wireless network connection? A cradle to PC connection? A flash memory storage card?
- What is the cost structure for the communication? Whereas Wi-Fi on an intranet costs nothing, mobile network usage is usually billed by metering the size of the data transferred.

Performance and Reliability

You should assume that mobile network communication will fail often and at the most inconvenient time for users. Even if the device is plugged into a network directly with a cable, it is appropriate to take a defensive approach and assume that the server will go down; the cable will get cut; proxy servers, NATs, routers, and firewalls will randomly conspire against you; and that little gremlins sit in the hardware and will attack your data packets with tiny hammers to prevent them from getting to their destination. A healthy dose of skepticism bordering on paranoia will be rewarded. Assume anything that will make you design defensively and deal robustly with the reality of intermittent communications failures and unexpected problems.

Most everyone has seen desktop and server applications occasionally stall because a needed network resource was unavailable. Usually the application in question either hangs or sits stuck for what seems an interminable amount of time before it finally times out and returns control to the user. In mobile devices, the situation is invariably worse. Trains go into tunnels and elevator doors shut blocking previously available signals without warning the running mobile application. Phone calls get interrupted between cell towers, Wi-Fi base stations get unplugged, and sometimes things just plain go wrong for reasons that often remain unfathomable.

Hopefully I have made some progress in convincing you that defensive coding is in order. The ways to facilitate this are as follows:

- Perform all network-oriented operations in an asynchronous way that allows the user interface to remain responsive and enables users to cancel the request and move on with their work.
- Wrap all network access routines in try/catch blocks (that is, structured exception handing). Assume that all of these catch blocks will get run occasionally, and simulate this situation in your application's design and testing to see how your error handling code responds. It is appropriate that an exception should get thrown when a network connection intermittently fails; it is equally appropriate that your code should catch these intermittent exceptions and deal robustly with them on the user's behalf.

Accessing networked resources makes mobile applications vastly more powerful, but also inherently introduces elements that are outside your control into the application. It is fundamental that your mobile application deal robustly with the very real likelihood that any external access will fail unexpectedly or will take an unacceptable amount of time to complete. Dealing with these situations gracefully will go a long way into making your mobile application look and work great. Your end users will thank you or at the least will not curse your name when "the network goes down."

Levels of Abstraction in the Programming Model

As with local device data, several layers of abstraction exist for working with networked resources. For example, the .NET Compact Framework offers the following layers of APIs for working with networked data:

- Sockets with streams
- HTTP request/response
- SOAP engine

Each of these levels of increasing abstraction offers successively more convenience and the robustness of pretested infrastructure. As with device local communication, you should choose the highest level of abstraction that you can afford and only move to lower levels of abstraction when you prove that the higher levels cannot be adapted to meet your needs. Using lower-level programming models means more explicit control over what is going on and the maximum flexibility, but this comes at the cost of complexity, interoperability, and the need for more dedicated testing. Know also that even the lowest levels of abstraction will not give you full control; your mobile application will always have to deal with network failure, and often this can be more complicated when working with lower levels of abstraction. There is a reason why developers have moved from assembly language to higher-level languages for all but the most specific low-level tasks, and this same line of reasoning should apply to your choice of communications programming model. More abstract is almost always better.

Go Back to Steps 0, 1, 2, and 3 As Necessary

Modern development is an iterative process. This is particularly true for mobile device development. Based on your level of skill and experience, you will

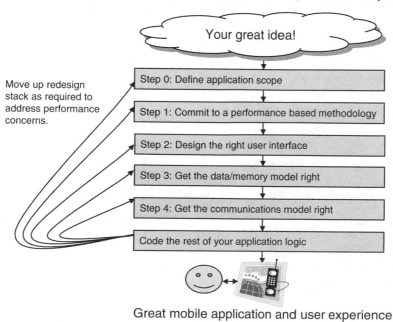

Great mobile application and user experience

Figure 4.5 Revisit your previous deign as needed to address performance concerns.

make the best initial decisions you can and you will revise them as needed. Experience with mobile development will make your initial decisions better, but it will not make them perfect. There will always be one more unanticipated design problem lurking that will force you to reevaluate your design and make tweaks or in many cases radical changes. Much of the rest of this book focuses on giving you the knowledge and insights necessary to make the best possible initial design decisions while giving you the engineering skills that allow you to leave the door open to revising designs as needed.

An important part of good mobile software design is finding ways to discover the design problems that will inevitably crop up as early as possible and also designing your code in a modular and flexible enough way that it can accommodate needed redesign without becoming hopelessly tangled.

When designing and testing your communications model, you may uncover core problems in your design. You may discover that too much memory is being utilized, meaning that too much user data is being held in memory at one time, or the data is being held in an inefficient way. If you change the data model, it will likely have effects on the communications model that controls how data is brought into and out of longer-term storage. Data model and communications model changes may in turn necessitate design changes in the user interface. These changes may need to account for the fact that the amount of data in memory at any given time is different than previously assumed or that the way in which the data needs to be retrieved must be done differently than assumed to ensure a responsive user interface. Finally, in doing all of this learning, you may discover that some of the design objectives of the application must change. Alternatively, you may discover additional design objectives that have emerged through the use and testing of your application. Modern application development is iterative. Because mobile devices are brave new world to explore, expect to iterate more.

With all of these interrelationships between design stages, it is easy to get lost somewhere in the middle and just write a lot of spaghetti code to tie it all together and make patch-up design changes as required. You should avoid this temptation and use your own defined product milestones to keep the design process honest. Make it an explicit exit criterion for each milestone to rationalize your design. When exiting a development milestone, you should answer the following questions:

- Are the key scenarios and features originally specified still valid or do they need to be redefined?
- Does the user interface cleanly represent the scenarios and enable users to perform the most common actions with a minimum number of manual steps? Is the user interface highly responsive to the user?

Is the user interface appropriate for the form factor of the device you are targeting?

- Is the underlying data model for bringing objects into memory and discarding objects sound? Will it scale to the real-world data your users will use? Is it stable over time as the user brings the application through all of the possible states, requests additional data, or runs the application for weeks at a time?

- Does the mobile application's communication model meet your needs? Are you using the highest level of abstraction that you can in your APIs and file formats?

All of your design decisions need to be grounded in a fundamentally performance-oriented design philosophy. If your application is not meeting performance requirements at any point in its design, *stop coding! Stop coding! Stop coding!* And immediately work to understand what the performance bottlenecks are and resolve them before moving on. This is important at any stage of the design but should be mandatory at the end of any of the coding milestones you set. As your application development proceeds toward its completion, design changes should become less frequent and will become harder to make because of inherent interdependencies between code modules that have been written. Plan on lots of early iteration and early design changes and fewer and fewer changes as your design moves through different milestones and the code becomes more mature.

Step 5: Packaging Your Application for Installation

For mobile devices, packaging and installation is often referred to as *provisioning*. This step should be listed under the category heading of "last but certainly not least" because like the other steps it will require iteration to get it right. Thought must be given to what pieces need to be deployed for your application to run on its target devices, how users will accomplish this, and how the application will be updated in the future. Here are a few important design questions for thinking about your mobile application's provisioning strategy:

- *What gets deployed with your application*? Is the application a single binary executable file or does the application have additional data files that get installed with it such as images, text files, database files? Should and can any of these files be folded into the application's binary file as resources to simplify deployment? Does the application

require other runtime libraries or components to be installed with it
onto the device?

- *How does the application get deployed onto a device?* Is the application installed directly onto a device via a networked connection? Is the application installed via a desktop PC with the device tethered to it via a cable? Is the application installed onto a device via a storage card that is inserted into the device? Is the application beamed from one device onto another via an IrDA port, facilitating peer-to-peer distribution?

- *Who will be deploying the application?* Will it be end users? Are the end users familiar with the target devices and their installation procedures? Will corporations be deploying the application on their employees' devices? Will the application be deployed by a mobile telephone operator or downloaded from the Web?

- *How will the application be versioned?* Will the application itself periodically check for new versions from a network location? Will a server scan devices to see whether they need a new version installed? Will new versions be installed when the device is placed into a cradle?

- *Are there security implications?* In any widely deployed application, there are always security implications that need to be considered. Does the application need to get signed? Does the data that the application works with need to be secured in some way? What happens to the data on a device if the device is lost or stolen?

Due to the large variety of mobile devices and networking models for devices, there is no single right answer. The best solution will depend on the type of the device, how it connects with the network, what the desired user experience is, and what the policies the network operators that may control access to the device may have.

A provisioning plan for your application should be written down on paper and added to your application's scenarios list. It is also highly desirable to place the development and testing of real-world packaging and install into an early development milestone for your application. Modern development environments do a great job of installing your application right onto the device for testing, but end users will usually not be using your development tool to install their application. Practical experience has shown that end-user deployment is always an issue.

Summary

It is an often-quoted and time-honored maxim that "a mediocre plan well executed is far superior to an excellent and detailed plan which sits unimplemented." So it is with modern software development. It does no good to have a rigorous plan and development methodology if it is too inflexible to adapt to the reality of iterative learning. "Different development projects require different levels of rigor and experience" is the best guide to understanding how much formality the development process can both bare and benefit from. Then there is dealing with the unexpected. As you develop and test your mobile solution, things will invariably happen that will force you to change your plans in some significant way. Count on it and have a process that can handle it. So in chronological order:

1. *Have a development methodology and stick to it.* In this chapter, I have presented one and elaborate on it more in the following chapters. It is a good methodology for mobile device development. If you find your needs differ, modify the methodology, but do have a methodology.
2. *Have a single top document that defines your goals and tracks your progress.* The level of formality of this document will depend on your organization. If you are a single developer working alone, the document may simply track the high-level goals and scenarios, your milestones to get there, and track undone items that need to be addressed; it need not be more than a few pages long. If you are a larger organization, this document may represent a formal contract between you and other organizations that tracks in detail what is being delivered, the design decisions being made, and detailed milestones and status along the way. Have a document that you can live with and keep "live." Make it a single document that represents the goals of your project and honestly tracks your progress.
3. Define *milestones with well-specified exit criteria.* This is the best way to keep yourself and other members of the development team honest. A set of clearly defined milestones that tracks your progress to completing the application and meeting the defined goals is an invaluable asset whether you are working alone or in a large organization. The value of milestones can simply not be overstated. If you are unsure how many milestones to use, I recommend starting with five. If you cannot break up your project into five measurable steps, it is either so trivial it can be completed in a day or two or you are just not trying. Five milestones represent a reasonable number to start with

and allows for a reasonable level of granularity in your development progress. For larger projects, you may find it desirable to break these milestones into smaller sub-milestones; for smaller projects you may get away with four, but try not to go smaller than that. These milestones serve three important functions: (1) They allow you to honestly measure your progress to a known goal, (2) they allow you to reassess your goals and future milestones and incorporate whatever learning you have done along the way, and (3) milestone exits define a formal time for review, code cleanup, and any rationalization of the design that needs to take place. Without milestones and end-of-milestone cleanup, there is a strong tendency for coding to occur without interruption and for all coding decisions to become tactical fixes. This results in an unmaintainable spaghetti mess. You may or may not set dates to your milestones; the larger the group the more important target dates become. The most important thing is that everyone needs to cross the current milestone finish line together before moving to the next milestone. Milestones are your friend, use them!

4. *Be guided by performance.* For mobile device applications, usability is king, and your mobile application's performance will have an overwhelming effect on its usability. As your development progresses, unresolved performance problems will only get worse; this is an absolute truism. The constrained memory and resource models on mobile devices are a significant difference from the more elastic model present on desktops. Set strict rules about your applications' performance and responsiveness and hold your development process to them. Tie solving performance problems to milestone exit criteria. Performance will be the final arbiter of what your mobile device application is capable of achieving. The silver lining to this dark cloud handing over your development process is that good mobile device performance is achievable. It is achievable through good design, disciplined process, and creative problem solving. Developers operating in a "desktop mindset" may hit a performance problem and just assume that devices are not capable of doing what they want to achieve. By and large this is a failure of imagination on the developer's part. Through good user interface design, having an explicit data and memory model, and good communications model design, there is little modern mobile device applications are not capable of.

CHAPTER 5

Our Friend, the State Machine

state ['stAt]

Function: noun

Usage: often attributive

Etymology: Middle English stat, from Old French & Latin; Old French estat, from Latin status, from stare to stand — more at STAND

Date: 13th century

1a: *mode or condition of being <a state of readiness>* ***b*** *(1) : condition of mind or temperament <in a highly nervous state> (2) : a condition of abnormal tension or excitement*

2a: *a condition or stage in the physical being of something*

(www.m-w.com, 2004)

ma·chine [m& shEn]

n (plural ma·chines)

1. mechanical engineering mechanical device: a device with moving parts, often powered by electricity, used to perform a task, especially one that would otherwise be done by hand

a washing machine

(Encarta 2004, Dictionary)

Introduction

The state machine is a very useful concept for structuring applications. The well-considered use of state machines will aid in keeping both user interface logic and application logic organized and maintainable. This will result in code that has both increased flexibility and robustness, not just for mobile applications but for all application development. Because mobile applications need to manage screen real estate and system resources efficiently and deterministically, state machines are particularly useful in mobile software development. State machines can be used to manage what sets of resources are being kept in memory at any given time as well as what user interface elements are occupying different areas of a mobile device's screen. For these kinds of tasks, state machines are ideal.

This chapter introduces and explores the uses of state machines and explains how they can be used to help you write efficient and robust mobile applications.

What Is a State Machine?

Anyone who has taken courses in digital logic design will be intimately familiar with the concept of a "state machine." This book uses a simplified version of this state machine definition. If you are not yet familiar with state machines, the concept is relatively simple and you probably already intuitively understand how state machines work.

The "state" of your application can be defined as the aggregate of all of its variables. The values of all of an application's variables give it a unique state that will only be changed when some external event causes a change. Examples of these kinds of state-changing events are events such as a user pressing a key, a button being clicked, an event firing due to an incoming message, or even a timer event. At any given moment, your application is in a certain state. It will enter a new state when something perturbs that state. The state that your application is currently in plus the new input are used to determine the next state.

A state machine is a formal structuring of this reality. Instead of using all of the application variables as a broad definition of the application's state, a state machine creates a single variable and defines it as the holder of some important aspect of the application's state. This variable is usually a global or class-level integer enumeration (for example, int m_myApplicationState;) with a defined set of valid states. The great strength of the state machine approach is that it enables you to come up with an explicit definition of valid states for some aspect of your application and enforce proper behaviors as an application moves from one state to another. An application can have more than one state machine with each separate state machine governing some useful set of behaviors that need to be structured. An application without any state machines is really just an application with a great many state machines; each application-level variable effectively is its own state machine and all kinds of code can access and modify this state. State machines are used to take a set of related variables or behaviors and organize them in a logical and maintainable way. State machines = organized behavior.

Figure 5.1 shows a state machine schematic for a multiple-choice vocabulary teaching game. This example is used several times in this chapter. The application's behavior has been broken down into a few logical states. These logical states exist whether or not we choose to define them in a state machine. The state machine is just a formal definition of how the application operates. It enables us to think crisply about the different states the application can move through as the user interacts with it.

Another way of viewing the different states of the application is by building a state transition table. This table lists the discrete states that the application can exist in and shows which state transitions are possible. Table 5.1 shows the list of states and transitions for our application.

State Machine for simple multiple choice game

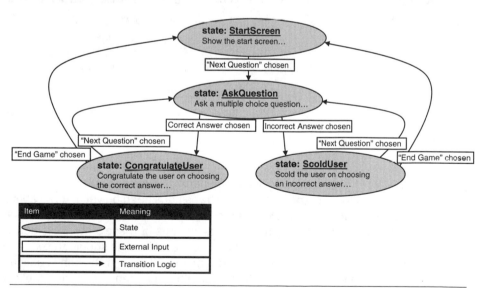

Figure 5.1 A state machine for a simple multiple-choice vocabulary game.

Table 5.1 State Transitions for the Multiple-Choice Vocabulary Game

State	External Input	Next State
StartScreen	"Next Question" chosen by user	AskQuestion
StartScreen	"Correct Answer" chosen by user	*Illegal state transition!*
StartScreen	"Incorrect Answer" chosen by user	*Illegal state transition!*
StartScreen	"End Game" chosen by user	*Illegal state transition!*
AskQuestion	"Next Question" chosen by user	*Illegal state transition!*
AskQuestion	"Correct Answer" chosen by user	CongratulateUser
AskQuestion	"Incorrect Answer" chosen by user	ScoldUser
AskQuestion	"End Game" chosen by user	*Illegal state transition!*
CongratulateUser	"Next Question" chosen by user	AskQuestion
CongratulateUser	"Correct Answer" chosen by user	*Illegal state transition!*
CongratulateUser	"Incorrect Answer" chosen by user	*Illegal state transition!*
CongratulateUser	"End Game" chosen by user	StartScreen
ScoldUser	"Next Question" chosen by user	AskQuestion
ScoldUser	"Correct Answer" chosen by user	*Illegal state transition!*
ScoldUser	"Incorrect Answer" chosen by user	*Illegal state transition!*
ScoldUser	"End Game" chosen by user	StartScreen

NOTE: I have chosen to list all the permutations of State and External Inputs above to illustrate that not all state transitions need be valid. Rows above with the Next State marked as "Illegal state transition" are not permissible in our application. If the application somehow gets into one of these state transitions, some of the application logic is faulty. The state machine logic should throw an exception or at least raise a debugger assert if an invalid state transition is encountered. Identifying illegal state transitions can aid you in debugging your applications.

Listing 5.1 realizes in code the state machine defined above. The code should bear a close resemblance to the state transitions defined in Table 5.1 and Figure 5.1. In the function below, you will notice that the code for each of the state transitions has a commented-out function call. This function call represents work to do for the state transition and is commented out to allow the code below to compile as a self-contained unit; the implementation of the function calls is left to you. It is a useful design pattern to define your state transitions as a switch/case statement block. Each "case" statement represents a state transition and should call a function to perform any work necessary to accomplish the state transition. This kind of centralization and encapsulation of state management is the most powerful thing about state machines; you have a central place where all of the important application transitions are defined and processed.

Listing 5.1 Sample Code for State Machine for Multiple-Choice Game

```
class MyStateMachineClass
{
  private enum GameState
  {
    StartScreen,
    AskQuestion,
    CongratulateUser,
    ScoldUser
  }
  private GameState m_CurrentGameState;

  //----------------------------------------------
  //The state machine that drives our user interface
  //and manages other application state based on the
  //mode the user is currently in
  //----------------------------------------------
  private void StateChangeForGame(GameState  newGameUIState)
  {
    //See which state the application is being brought into
    switch(newGameUIState)
    {
      case GameState.StartScreen:
        //If we are coming from a state that does not allow
        //transition to this state, throw an exception
        if ((m_CurrentGameState != GameState.CongratulateUser)
          && (m_CurrentGameState != GameState.ScoldUser))
        {
          throw new System.Exception("Illegal State Change!");
        }
```

```
//UNDONE: Place code here to
// 1. Hide, Show, Move UI controls into place
// 2. Set up whatever variables/game state needed
//    for this mode
//
// SetUpGameStateForStartScreen();
break;

case GameState.AskQuestion:
  //If we are coming from a state that does not allow
  //transition to this state, throw an exception
  if ((m_CurrentGameState != GameState.StartScreen)
    && (m_CurrentGameState != GameState.CongratulateUser)
    && (m_CurrentGameState != GameState.ScoldUser))
  {
    throw new System.Exception("Illegal State Change!");
  }

  //UNDONE: Place code here to
  // 1. Hide, Show, Move UI controls into place
  // 2. Set up whatever variables/game state needed
  //    for this mode
  //
  // SetUpGameStateForAskQuestion();
  break;

case GameState.CongratulateUser:
  //If we are coming from a state that does not allow
  //transition to this state, throw an exception
  if (m_CurrentGameState != GameState.AskQuestion)
  {
    throw new System.Exception("Illegal State Change!");
  }

  //UNDONE: Place code here to
  // 1. Hide, Show, Move UI controls into place
  // 2. Set up whatever variables/game state needed
  //    for this mode
  //
  // SetUpGameStateForCongratulateUser();
  break;

case GameState.ScoldUser:
  //If we are coming from a state that does not allow
```

```
      //transition to this state, throw an exception
      if (m_CurrentGameState != GameState.AskQuestion)
      {
        throw new System.Exception("Illegal State Change!");
      }

      //UNDONE: Place code here to
      // 1. Hide, Show, Move UI controls into place
      // 2. Set up whatever variables/game state needed
      //    for this mode
      //
      // SetUpGameStateForScoldUser();
      break;

    default:
      throw new System.Exception("Unknown state!");
  }

  //Store the new requested state as our current state
  m_CurrentGameState = newGameUIState;
  }
} //End class
```

Implicit vs. Explicit State Machines

Whether or not you plan for it, your code will inherently be state driven. For example, developers often change the enabled or visible property of a control to false (for example, `TextBox1.Visible = false;`) when the application is in a state where the control is not valid for user interaction. There are two approaches to writing this kind of code:

Approach 1: An Ad Hoc, Decentralized, and Implicit Approach to State Management (Bad Design)

Many applications that grow gradually more complex exhibit this kind of ad hoc design. Aspects of the application's state are changed in many different locations. State data is held in properties such as the Visible, Enabled, Size, or Position properties of controls. Variables that hold key state data are changed in-line by whatever code needs to have it happen, and the loading or discarding of application data happens in a distributed and ad hoc way. This results in a tug-of-war between different parts of the application as each new function does whatever it needs to do to get its work done without regard to the rest of the application. The most common example of this is having event code that responds to a user interface event such as clicking a button containing in-line code that changes the state of the application. Listing 5.2 contains code that could typically be found inside an application's form class that follows this ad hoc approach. Both code for the form1 "load event" and the button1 "click event" make changes that affect the overall state of the form.

Listing 5.2 Application State Being Changed Implicitly (Bad Design)

```
//Code that gets run when the form is loaded
private void Form1_Load(object sender, System.EventArgs e)
{
  textBox1.Visible = true;
  listBox1.Visible = false;
}


string m_someImportantInfo;

//The user has clicked the button and wants to move on to the
//next step in this application. Hide the text box and show
//list box in its place.
private void button1_Click(object sender, System.EventArgs e)
{
  m_someImportantInfo = textBox1.Text;
  textBox1.Visible = false;
  listBox1.Visible = true;
}
```

Approach 2: A Planned, Centralized, and Explicit Approach to State Management (Good Design)

In contrast to ad hoc state management is explicit state management. With this approach, all state changes happen through a central function. Event code that needs to change some aspect of the application's state does so through a single function that all other code that also needs to change the application's state also calls and defers to for state transition logic. Listing 5.3 shows an example of this approach.

Listing 5.3 Application State Being Changed Explicitly (Good Design)

```
string m_someImportantInfo;
//Define the states the application can be in
enum MyStates
{
  step1,
  step2
}


//The central function that is called
//whenever the application state needs
//to be changed
void ChangeApplicationState(MyStates newState)
{
  switch (newState)
  {

  case MyStates.step1:
    textBox1.Visible = true;
    listBox1.Visible = false;
    break;
  case MyStates.step2:
    m_someImportantInfo = textBox1.Text;
    textBox1.Visible = false;
    listBox1.Visible = true;
    break;


  }
}


//The user has clicked the button and wants to move on to the
//next step in this application. Hide the text box and show
//list box in its place.
private void button1_Click(object sender, System.EventArgs e)
{
      //Call a central function to change the state
  ChangeApplicationState(MyStates.step2);
}

//Code that gets run when the form is loaded
private void Form1_Load(object sender, System.EventArgs e)
{
      //Call a central function to change the state
  ChangeApplicationState(MyStates.step1);
}
```

The code above performs the same tasks as the previous example but does so in a well-encapsulated way. Each user interface element's event handling code does not directly modify the user interface's state but instead calls a central state-management function to perform the necessary work. This process scales well as our application grows and changes. If we need to change some aspect of the way our user interface works, our application has a central function that does this. As we add additional controls or additional application states, we have a central and well-understood way to incorporate these additions into our programming model.

Wait! I'm Writing a Mobile Application. Isn't My Code Supposed to Be Smaller Than Desktop Code?

In brief, "No." Your code does not need to be smaller than desktop code; your code needs to be better! It is a common mistake and excuse of developers writing mobile application code to assume that they should try to cram as much code into any given function and to perform every action possible in-line as opposed to calling helper functions. This is throwing out good design principles. Let's call this tendency "optimizing with a microscope."

The highest-order optimizations are achieved at the macro level, not the micro level. Good encapsulated design gives you far better ability to find and make these macro optimizations. Having a central set of functions that manage your application's state will enable you to better understand the structure of your application and thus optimize it. Getting great performance involves iterating, analyzing, and changing your original design assumptions when they prove inadequate. A centralized state approach will prove much more valuable in helping you do this than an ad hoc approach that distributes your application's state management.

There are indeed cases when you will want to optimize specific algorithms and bring code out of separate function calls and make it in-line. These are cases where the code is run very frequently, such as in tight loops that do heavy-duty processing work on large sets of data. When required these situations can be systematically identified and addressed. This is not the case for application-level state machines that are called when the application goes from one discrete mode of operation or user interface display into another; these changes don't happen many times a second or occur repeatedly inside tight loops.

Finally, it is much easier to take encapsulated code and move it in-line into calling functions than it is to take a bunch of random code and try to derive a manageable encapsulation. Anyone who has tried to reverse engineer someone else's spaghetti code will attest to this!

For these reasons, good code design is at least as important for mobile device software as it is for desktops. Good code organization will help you build great mobile applications, and using state machines can help you achieve good organization in your code.

Whether or not you realize it, a significant portion your application's code relates to managing its state. You are in the state machine business anyway and can either choose to approach it explicitly or not choose it and end up with an implicit model. Approaching state explicitly has significant benefits, not the least of which is that it will force you into a mindset where you think more crisply about the way your application operates.

Much early application development and prototyping work tends to happen informally. This should not discourage you from using state machines. On the contrary, state machines can be of great value here as well. As you can see from above, the extra code in using a state machine approach is minimal. It is very easy to add new states, delete states, and rename states to meet changing definitions as you work out an idea. I find state machines particularly useful in designing mobile application user interfaces because it gives me a central place to play around with control positioning and resizing logic. Even in ad hoc development, a state machine approach can save time and give you flexibility in exploring your ideas.

How Many State Machines Should Be in Any Given Application?

Hopefully by now you have been convinced of the propriety of using state machines as a central part of your mobile application's design. As in any aspect of design, there are top-level guidelines and important implementation details. Designing the proper kinds of state machines is a bit of an art form that improves with experience. A state machine should be "an abstraction of one or more variables that can take only a set of finite values, each of which map to a useful discrete state." These variables should somehow correlate to different states that an application or class can be in. As in the code example above, it is useful to define an explicit enumeration that names and lists the valid set of states you want managed by a specific state machine.

Sometimes it is useful to have multiple state machines inside the same application. A state machine that manages cached data that was retrieved from a database may be used in addition to a separate state machine that manages graphical objects such as pens and brushes that are cached for use in common drawing. A third state machine may manage the running of tasks on background threads. Although all of these state machines could be combined into a single combined "über state machine," because there is little or no correlation in the states the separate machines manage the combined state machine would simply be the sum of all the permutations possible, and not of any added use. Similarly, it is possible to err at the other extreme and rather than build one useful central state machine you end up with dozens of little state machines each managing single application variables. The key here is *correlation*. It is appropriate and useful to use a state machine to manage a set of variables, objects, and resources if they somehow correlate to one another.

Below are some descriptions of useful state machines to use in your design.

The User Interface State Machine

User interfaces represent one of the most obvious areas where state machines are of great use. The behavior of controls sharing a form often correlate; some controls are shown and hidden at the same time; some controls are always hidden when other controls are visible; some controls are repositioned when other controls are shown, and so on. Each form you design should have a state machine associated with it that drives its visual behavior. If the form itself contains multiple subpages that users can flip through, such as tabbed dialogs or multistep wizards, it probably makes sense for each of these subpages to have a state machine of its own.

A form's user interface state is particularly important for mobile devices because screen real estate is a scarce commodity that needs to be properly managed. As the user navigates between different application states, user interface elements need to be shown and hidden or resized and moved around to make sure the appropriate information is available for the user in each state that the application can be in. Different parts of the application naturally vie for screen space, and if the logic to show, hide, or reposition controls is distributed in your application's logic a mess will result. There needs to be a central arbitrator for managing screen real estate and a state machine is great for this.

Figure 5.2 shows the user interface states for our Pocket PC vocabulary learning game. The top of the screen is devoted to the game's play field. The character moves around the play field and collects objects when the user answers vocabulary questions correctly. In the diagram are shown four states of the application along with arrows indicating the possible transitions between user interface states.

As you can see, each state has certain information that it wants to display to the user and certain input that it wants to allow in response. On a large desktop screen, this might not be a big challenge; given the limited real estate available on a mobile device, however, we need to be as efficient as possible in our use of it. A text box is used to display questions and answers and supplemental text is also painted directly to the playfield bitmap

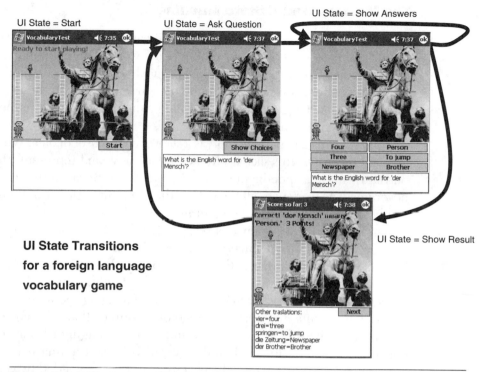

Figure 5.2 Different user interface states in a multiple-choice game.

above it. Various buttons are displayed to the users, enabling them to make selections and move the application onto the next state. In this example, four distinct user interface states were required.

State machines also prove very useful in experimenting and refining the user interface. Various different positionings and sizings were able to be tested quickly by simply changing the layout code managed by the state machine. For instance, originally the text display area was located above the play field, but usage testing indicated that it would work better if positioned below, so it was moved and retested in various different configurations. Additionally, the size of the text box used to display general information to the user in different application states was experimented with to find an optimum configuration balancing utility and aesthetics. Although a state machine is not explicitly necessary to do this user interface reorganization it makes it much easier. Having all the code that controls the visibility, sizing, and positioning of controls in one place makes this kind of iterative design much quicker and more comprehensible than trying to manage layout changes that are scattered in many different places in an application's logic.

The Memory Model State Machine

Most applications keep some kind of significant state in memory. Word processors keep a model of the document being worked on in memory. Spreadsheets keep the tabular data of the spreadsheet they are working with in memory. Games keep state relating to the current play field the user is playing on. The language vocabulary teaching game previously described keeps part of a dictionary in memory.

Often the data kept in memory is a slice of a larger set of data. When working with databases, this slice is often called a "view" and represents the full or partial result of a specific query on the database. Because the user almost never needs to work with all the data at the same time, significant efficiencies can be achieved by only keeping in memory what the user currently needs. The user wants the experience of being able to work with all the data, but this does not mean all the data needs to be loaded in memory simultaneously.

As with user interfaces, there are two ways to manage this data, either explicitly or implicitly. As noted earlier in this book, many desktop applications tend to take a very casual approach to managing the memory they are using. This results in a wasteful usage of resources that is somewhat compensated for by the large memory and memory paging files available on desktop computers. For mobile devices, it will result in unacceptably poor performance as unnecessary objects crowd out space needed by your application to run efficiently. Taking a more proactive and explicit approach to managing memory usage in mobile device applications is highly advisable.

When designing your mobile application's memory model, it is important to ask yourself the following questions:

- How much data needs to be loaded at any given time for use by the user?
- When and under what circumstances should loaded data be discarded? In answering this question, you should be aggressive. If data is not immediately useable by the user there should be a model for discarding it.
- What is the right format for storing the data in memory? For small amounts of data, it may make sense to choose the most convenient format from a programmatic perspective. For larger amounts of data, such as for a large number of rows retrieved from a database, coming up with a memory and computationally optimized format for storing the data is imperative. There should also be a model that allows the most relevant pieces of data to be kept in memory and the rest flushed out.

■ Is there data that it makes sense to permanently cache in memory? There is no point in being overly aggressive in throwing out an object as soon as you are done with an immediate need for it if the application will need to reload or re-create it moments later. Memory is a resource to be wisely used neither wastefully nor in a miserly way. There is no gain in being memory wise and processor foolish.

If you are dealing with several different types of data or system resources, you may need a state machine for each. In the example above of a vocabulary learning game, there are several kinds of data and resources that must me managed in memory efficiently:

■ *Vocabulary words*—The dictionary we use for the game may contain thousands or tens of thousands of potential vocabulary words each with definitions and usage examples. We could try to load all these into memory at once, but this would almost certainly be wasteful. What we want is for the user of the application to have an experience that is comparable to having all the words loaded into memory at once while we intelligently swap words in and out as the game progresses. The software design challenge is to come up with a flexible state machine and supporting set of algorithms that provide this experience. Our memory management algorithms should provide that a fixed number of random words are loaded into memory and that these words are used for a while and then thrown out in favor of a new set of words. The design should also be scalable so that we can specify the number of words loaded into memory and tune this number as we learn more about the user's needs as well as the target device's available capacity to hold this data in memory. Because we are likely to hold a significant number of vocabulary words, their associated definitions, and other related information in memory, perhaps a hundred items at a time, it is also worth thinking about the most efficient way to store and access this data in memory.

■ *Game board data*—Because our game is a graphical, each level of the game board will have some resources and state associated with it. All bitmaps and objects holding state relating to pieces on the game board take up memory. It is likely we will want a state machine that keeps the data for one game board level in memory at any given time and discards the data as soon as it is no longer needed such as when the data for another level is loaded.

■ *Globally cached graphics objects*—Our graphical game is going to be doing a lot of common and repetitive drawing tasks. Rather than continually creating and discarding commonly used pens, brushes, and bitmaps, it may make sense to have a state model that allows these very commonly used resources to be kept in memory as long as repetitive drawing tasks need to occur. When the game's state switches to a mode where these resources are not required, they can be discarded.

The Background Processing State Machine

There will be portions of your mobile application that require potentially long-duration processing or network access; any processing operation that can potentially take more than 0.5 seconds to complete falls into the grouping of "long-duration activities." A few examples include the following:

- *Recursive or iterative computations that explore lots of options*— Search algorithms, data-analysis algorithms, and games with artificial intelligence fall into this camp. A search of an optimum next chess move can explore many thousands of possible moves to varying degrees of depth. These operations can take a significant amount of time.
- *Large loads or saves of data*—Loading several hundred pieces of information from an XML file or database can take a while.
- *Networked operations*—Almost anything that happens over a network is susceptible to potential latency and communications problems.

For these kinds of operations, you will want to consider running them asynchronously to your application's user interface thread. For any asynchronous operation, a state machine allowing the user interface thread to communicate with the background thread and gain necessary information about the processing's progress is important. The user interface thread will want to be able to periodically query the state of the background operation and will want to give the user the option of aborting the operation. Conversely, the background processing thread will want the ability to update the user interface thread on its progress as well as get a notification if the foreground thread wants it to abort processing. A state-machine-driven processing model is an excellent way of meeting these objectives.

Following is an example that shows using a state machine to drive a potentially long-running background calculation. The calculation finds the next biggest prime number after a specified integer. The code can either be run synchronously for debugging purposes or asynchronously so that the user interface does not get blocked when the processing is occurring. Figure 5.3 shows the simple state machine that is used to allow the background processing thread to communicate its status. The state machine also allows the user interface thread to request that the background processing be terminated.

State-machine for background prime number finder

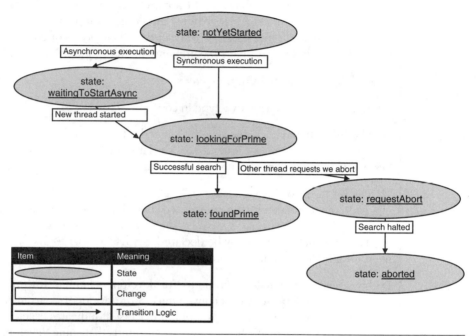

Figure 5.3 A state machine for a background processing algorithm that calculates prime numbers.

Coding Style: Goto Statements and Full Namespace Paths

It is worth taking a few moments to explain two of the coding style decisions that were made for the code listed in this book.

The use of the "goto" statement in code:

It is a matter of some debate whether the use of goto statements represents good or poor design. The goto statement is somewhat contentious because it causes a jump in execution that does not follow conditional (if/then) or loop constructs.

I am of the camp of people who believe that goto statements represent good programming design as long as:

(1) They are forward only in direction.

(2) They aid the readability of the code in question.

Goto statements only represent poor design if they make the flow of execution unclear. Allowing goto statements in multiple directions is an example of this because it allows control to bounce around up and down a function and makes the logic potentially hard to follow; most everyone is against this kind of usage. Allowing goto statements in a forward-only direction is simple to follow and in some cases can be a more natural construct than using loops or conditional statements. It is in these cases that I recommend and use goto.

The use of full paths in namespaces:

There are two ways to specify a type in code:

(1) The full path name can be specified in code. For example, `System.Threading.Thread newThread;` declares a variable newThread of type System.Threading.Thread. This is verbose but simple.

(2) The C# `using` or Visual Basic .NET `Imports` keyword can be used at the top of a code file to indicate that a namespace should be assumed. For example, if a C# code file contains `using System.Threading;` at its top, a System.Threading.Thread variable can simply be declared as `Thread newThread;` without the need for a full path name.

Both ways are functionally equivalent. For developers familiar with the namespaces, the latter can be a convenience. For developers learning a namespace, the former is the most helpful because it indicates exactly where each class or type logically belongs. On the grounds that some developers reading this book may not yet be fully familiar with the .NET namespaces, I have chosen to use the lengthier syntax.

Note: An assembly must be referenced before its classes and types can be used in your code. It is important to understand that the `using` and `Imports` keywords are only a syntactic convenience; they do not cause an assembly reference to be made. For the compiler to be aware of the types in an assembly, you must specifically make a reference to the assembly. In Visual Studio .NET, the list of referenced assemblies is listed in the TreeView control in the Solution Explorer window. New projects typically have a default set of common references preconfigured.

Listing 5.4 Code for the Background Thread Prime Number Calculator

```
using System;
public class FindNextPrimeNumber
{
  //States we can be in.
  public enum ProcessingState
  {
    notYetStarted,
    waitingToStartAsync,
    lookingForPrime,
    foundPrime,
    requestAbort,
    aborted
  }

  int m_startTickCount;
  int m_endTickCount;
  long m_startPoint;
  long m_NextHighestPrime;
  ProcessingState m_processingState;

  //---------------------------------------------------
  //A very simple state machine.
  //---------------------------------------------------
  public void setProcessingState(ProcessingState nextState)
  {
    //---------------------------------------------------
    //Some very simple protective code to make sure
    //we can't enter another state if we have either
    //Successfully finished, or successfully aborted
    //---------------------------------------------------
    if   ((m_processingState == ProcessingState.aborted)
      ||  (m_processingState == ProcessingState.foundPrime))
    {
      return;
    }

    //Allow the state change
    lock(this)
    {
    m_processingState = nextState;
    }
  }
}
```

```
public ProcessingState getProcessingState()
{
  ProcessingState currentState;
  //Thread saftey
  lock(this)
  {
    currentState = m_processingState;
  }
  return currentState;
}

public int getTickCountDelta()
{
  if (getProcessingState() == ProcessingState.lookingForPrime)
  {
    throw new Exception(
      "Still looking for prime! No final time calculated");
  }

  return m_endTickCount - m_startTickCount;
}

//-------------------------------------------------
//Returns the prime
//-------------------------------------------------
public long getPrime()
{
  if (getProcessingState() != ProcessingState.foundPrime)
  {
    throw new Exception("Prime number not calculated yet!");
  }

  return m_NextHighestPrime;
}

//Class constructor
public FindNextPrimeNumber(long startPoint)
{
  setProcessingState(ProcessingState.notYetStarted);
  m_startPoint = startPoint;
}

//-----------------------------------------------------------
//Creates a new worker thread that will call
```

```
// "findNextHighestPrime()"
//----------------------------------------------------------
public void findNextHighestPrime_Async()
{
  System.Threading.ThreadStart threadStart;
  threadStart =
    new System.Threading.ThreadStart(findNextHighestPrime);

  System.Threading.Thread newThread;
  newThread = new System.Threading.Thread(threadStart);

  //Set our processing state to say that we are looking
  setProcessingState(ProcessingState.waitingToStartAsync);
  newThread.Start();
}


//----------------------------------------------------------
//This is the main worker function. This synchronously starts
//looking for the next prime number and does not exit until
//either:
// (a) The next prime is found
// (b) An external thread to this thread tells us to abort
//----------------------------------------------------------
public void findNextHighestPrime()
{
  //If we've been told to abort, don't even start looking
  if(getProcessingState() == ProcessingState.requestAbort)
  {
    goto finished_looking;
  }

  //Set our processing state to say that we are looking
  setProcessingState(ProcessingState.lookingForPrime);

  m_startTickCount = System.Environment.TickCount;
  long currentItem;
  //See if it's odd
  if ((m_startPoint & 1) == 1)
  {
    //It's odd, start at the next odd number
    currentItem = m_startPoint + 2;
  }
  else
  {
```

```
      //It's even, start at the next odd number
      currentItem = m_startPoint + 1;
  }


  //Look for the prime item.
  while(getProcessingState()  ==
        ProcessingState.lookingForPrime)
  {

    //If we found the prime item, return it
    if(isItemPrime(currentItem) == true)
    {
      m_NextHighestPrime =  currentItem;
      //Update our state
      setProcessingState(ProcessingState.foundPrime);
    }

    currentItem = currentItem  + 2;
  }

finished_looking:
      //Exit. At this point we have either been
      //Told to abort the search by another thread, or
      //we have found and recorded the next highest prime number

      //Record the time
      m_endTickCount = System.Environment.TickCount;

  //If an abort was requested, note that we have aborted
  //the process.
  if (getProcessingState() == ProcessingState.requestAbort)
  {
    setProcessingState(ProcessingState.aborted);
  }
} //End function

//Helper function that looks to see if a specific item
//is a prime number.
private bool isItemPrime(long potentialPrime)
{
  //If it's even, it's not prime
  if ((potentialPrime & 1) == 0)
  {
    return false;
```

```
}

//We want to look up until just past the square root
//of the item
long end_point_of_search;
end_point_of_search =
   (long) System.Math.Sqrt(potentialPrime) + 1;

long current_test_item = 3;
while(current_test_item <= end_point_of_search )
{
   //--------------------------------
   //Check to make sure we have not been asked to abort!
   //--------------------------------
   if (getProcessingState() !=
         ProcessingState.lookingForPrime)
   {
      return false;
   }

   //If the item is divisible without remainder,
   //it is not prime
   if(potentialPrime % current_test_item == 0)
   {
      return false;
   }

   //advance by two
   current_test_item  = current_test_item  + 2;
}

//The item is prime
return true;
}
} //end class
```

Listing 5.5 contains code that can be placed in a form to test the background processing algorithm above.

Listing 5.5 Test Code to Call the Background Thread Prime Number Calculator Above

```
//-----------------------------------------------------------
//Code to process the click event of Button1 on the form
//
//Call the prime number function on this thread!
//(This will block the thread)
//-----------------------------------------------------------
private void button1_Click(object sender, System.EventArgs e)
{
  long testItem;
  testItem = System.Convert.ToInt64("123456789012345");

  FindNextPrimeNumber nextPrimeFinder;
  nextPrimeFinder = new FindNextPrimeNumber(testItem);

  nextPrimeFinder.findNextHighestPrime();

  long nextHighestPrime;
  nextHighestPrime = nextPrimeFinder.getPrime();

  System.Windows.Forms.MessageBox.Show(
    System.Convert.ToString(nextHighestPrime));

    //How long did the calculation take?
  int calculation_time;
  calculation_time = nextPrimeFinder.getTickCountDelta();
  System.Windows.Forms.MessageBox.Show(
    System.Convert.ToString(calculation_time) + " ms");
}


//-----------------------------------------------------------
//Code to process the click event of Button2 on the form
//
//Call the prime number function on another thread!
//(This will not
//block this thread)
//We will use a state machine to track the progress
//-----------------------------------------------------------
private void button2_Click(object sender, System.EventArgs e)
{
  long testItem;
  testItem = System.Convert.ToInt64("123456789012345");
```

```
FindNextPrimeNumber nextPrimeFinder;
nextPrimeFinder = new FindNextPrimeNumber(testItem);

//---------------------------------
//Do the processing on another thread
//---------------------------------
nextPrimeFinder.findNextHighestPrime_Async();

//Go in a loop and wait until we either find the result
//or it is aborted
while((nextPrimeFinder.getProcessingState() !=
    FindNextPrimeNumber.ProcessingState.foundPrime)
  &&
  (nextPrimeFinder.getProcessingState() !=
    FindNextPrimeNumber.ProcessingState.aborted))
{
    //TEST CODE ONLY:
    //Show a message box, allow the user to dismiss it
    //This will help pass the time!
System.Windows.Forms.MessageBox.Show("Still Looking...Hit OK");

    //We could abort the search by calling:
    //nextPrimeFinder.setProcessingState(
    //   FindNextPrimeNumber.ProcessingState.requestAbort);

}

//If we aborted the search, exit gracefully
if (nextPrimeFinder.getProcessingState() ==
FindNextPrimeNumber.ProcessingState.aborted)
{
  System.Windows.Forms.MessageBox.Show("Search was aborted!");
  return;
}

long nextHighestPrime;
nextHighestPrime = nextPrimeFinder.getPrime();

System.Windows.Forms.MessageBox.Show(
  System.Convert.ToString(nextHighestPrime));

//How long did the calculation take?
int calculation_time;
```

```
calculation_time = nextPrimeFinder.getTickCountDelta();
System.Windows.Forms.MessageBox.Show(
  System.Convert.ToString(calculation_time) + " ms");
}
```

The sample number I passed in (123456789012345) took about 10 to 20 seconds to run on my Pocket PC emulator. Add or remove digits to your sample number to increase or decrease the processing time. (Longer numbers will typically take longer to run.)

NOTE: To keep the sample simple, I've purposefully put very few rules into the state transition function. In a real implementation, I would suggest putting more rules such as only allowing valid transitions and throwing exceptions in unexpected cases. Having strict rules on state transitions is very useful for ferreting out unexpected bugs due to code running on more than one thread. Things can get tricky and good rules, asserts, and exceptions will go a long way in helping you find subtle bugs that will cause you hours of frustration later.

State Machines Inside Games

State machines are extremely useful in action games where different game characters need to move around the screen and perform actions in different modes. Each character may have different modes of motion—for example: facingLeft, facingRight, runningLeft, runningRight, climbingLadder, and falling. Using a state machine for each game character with well-defined rules for what the characters behaviors can be in each state and which state transitions are allowable is a very useful way to build complex behavior into both computer-controlled and user-controlled characters.

Summary

As an idea, the state machine is a remarkably useful and durable concept. State machines enable developers to build well-organized and flexible applications. Because mobile device development is inherently an iterative and exploratory process, using state machines where appropriate will serve you well by allowing your application to adapt as you learn and refine your design. In areas such as user interface management, resource and memory management, and background processing, state machines enable you to design clean, understandable, and well-functioning code. Take the time and explicitly draw out the right state models in your applications instead of letting them form in a distributed and implicit way. State machine design is a good practice in server, desktop, and mobile device software design. Because mobile devices demand efficient screen real estate, memory, processing power, and other resource usage, a good state machine–based design is especially beneficial for devices. This little bit of extra design discipline will pay for itself over and over again as you prototype, design, build, maintain, and extend your mobile applications.

CHAPTER 6

Step 0: Before You Start, Decide on the Scope of Your Application

Rube Goldberg (1883–1970) was a cartoonist who drew images of fantastically complicated mechanical devices that accomplished everyday tasks. The devices would have all kinds of fascinating levers, pulleys, springs, and instructions. It is worth carefully studying the intricacies of his machines and then endeavoring never to build anything like them inside a mobile device. Keep it simple and focused!

—Ivo Salmre
(for Rube Goldberg machines, see http://www.rube-goldberg.com/)

Introduction

This chapter is called "Step 0" because in a book that is primarily about how to go about building mobile device applications some thought must first be given to the question, "What is the mobile application going to do?" It is important to always have an appropriate set of end goals for the application being developed; these define the scope of the application. Goals may change as you learn more about your target device's capabilities and limitations and new or clarified requirements emerge through the testing of your application, but there always needs to be a destination that your application development is traveling toward. Without scope and goals, your mobile application will flounder in a sea of mediocre features. It is far better to identify the few important things mobile device users need from your application and to do them exceedingly well than it is to try to cram everything into a single all-purpose application.

The purpose of this short chapter is to help you properly scope your mobile application's design. For a mobile application to be successful, it is important that the application have a specific focus. Productive mobile device applications tend to be used in short spurts to get data, modify data, or request services. Having the correct scope of features enables users to quickly get to the information and services they need. A mobile application that has a large number of forms that the user can navigate through and explore for 20 minutes probably lacks the proper focus; 20 seconds should be the timeframe you are thinking about. This also holds true for mobile entertainment applications as well; a great mobile game must be easy to use, quick to start, and be able to be played in short spurts.

Standalone or Part of a Larger System?

A basic question to be answered is how your mobile device application relates to other applications. A mobile application can be a standalone application, a part of a suite of focused on-device applications, or the portable part of a larger distributed system.

Standalone Applications

A simple game or calculation program may be a standalone application. Standalone applications interact with no other applications and only provide users with a fixed set of quickly accessible features. If this is the case, your application will be relatively simple to scope. Even in this case some refinement may be required. For example, a calculator that enables you to quickly add, subtract, divide, and multiply numbers will have a significantly different focus than an algebraic equation solver and graphing calculator. These applications are likely to have significantly different user interfaces and navigation models. Users will have different things they want to accomplish in 20 seconds with each application, and this requires a different design focus. Even in small standalone applications, proper scope is important.

Suites of Related Applications on a Device

Most interesting applications interact with other systems. In some cases, instead of having a single large multifaceted application you may want to have a set of applications on the same device that share data in an on-device database. Each application can have its own focus and concentrate on excelling at achieving its goals. In cases where a suite of applications is being constructed to work on shared data, it is important to outline exactly what each application does and does not do. A good example of this partitioning on the desktop is the relationship between the members of an office suite. An office suite typically contains software for word processing, software for calculating (spreadsheets), software for presentations, and software for communications. These interact in many ways and can share data and common components, but rarely is there confusion as to which software application should be used for any given task. Some people may think that the individual office applications themselves may be too complicated and lack focus, but imagine what would happen if they were all combined into one "super application." It would be a mess. Small and focused is beautiful.

If you have discrete tasks that need to be performed on a mobile device, it often makes sense to break these up into separate applications instead of building one giant kitchen sink, salad maker, and barbecue of an application. These compound-purpose applications are difficult to navigate and hard to maintain. It needs to be obvious to the end user what tool to use for any given task. In cases where there is confusion of purpose between applications in a suite, it is usually the product of incomplete or incremental design where a new set of needed capabilities are identified and addressed in an ad hoc way by modifying existing applications rather than thinking about the features systematically. If a new "killer scenario" emerges during your mobile application development, ask yourself whether this scenario should be grafted onto the existing application or realized cleanly in a separate application. It is easy to merge applications together but difficult to tease interwoven code apart. When in doubt, start it as a separate application and remember the 20-second rule: Users should be able to take the mobile device out of their pocket and easily navigate to their desired information in 20 seconds of unhurried device operation.

Device Applications That Interact with Desktop or Server Applications

Many device applications interact with off-device resources such as data present on a desktop computer, available on a corporate server, or exposed as an Internet service. There are two important things to keep in mind when defining the scope of mobile applications that are part of larger systems:

1. *Identify the key set of on-device scenarios.* Usage scenarios for desktop and Web applications differ significantly from mobile device usage scenarios. For this reason, it rarely makes sense to take the set of features in a desktop or Web application and transfer them to mobile

devices. It is important to ask these questions: What are the things that the users of this application will need to do quickly when mobile? What are the key things that users need to find or accomplish quickly that will compel them to take the device out of their pocket? The answer to these questions will define your mobile application's usage scenarios.

2. *Identify whether the device will interact with desktop data or server data*. For large applications, often copies of data are scattered everywhere. Data may live on a number of servers, data may live on desktops, and data may live on devices. It is important to have a clear vision of what data your mobile application will interact with. When given the choice between interacting with data on a server and data on a desktop, the correct answer is almost always to interact with server-based data. There are two reasons for this: (1) The data on the desktop is usually a local cached copy of the server data and will be less current, and (2) although desktop computers may not always be accessible, servers are designed for accessibility. Usually when a decision is made to have a mobile device synchronize with desktop-based data rather than server data the decision is done for short-term tactical reasons rather than for well-considered strategic reasons. Typical of short-term rationalizations are statements such as "Because I can't get permission to access the server data from a device, I'll just build a model that synchronizes with a desktop copy of that data" or "The server data is too complex to deal with, but the data on the desktop is all stored in a simple format so I'll just synchronize with that data." These urges should be resisted. If the data truly does live on the server, you should synchronize with that data even if you need to build an intermediary server solution to support accessing the data. Having a clean architecture for interacting with other tiers of your application will pay rich dividends in reliability and development time. Short-term tactical solutions tend quickly to turn into long-term maintenance nightmares. Understanding the scope of your mobile application requires being able to draw a clear diagram that shows the interactions your mobile data has with off-device systems.

Do Not Port Your Desktop Application! Think Devices!

Mobile device applications may share information sources and broad purpose with desktop applications, but beyond this the two classes of applications have little in common. Mobile applications should be designed for mobile devices from the start and not ported by removing pieces of a desktop application until it fits onto a device. For this reason, it is important to decide the scope of the mobile application and then design from the ground up.

Mobile Software Usage Patterns vs. Desktop Software

A myth that is worth dispelling is that mobile devices will replace personal computers; there seems to be no practical evidence to support this. As noted in the early chapters of this book, people use mobile devices in qualitatively different ways than they use desktop computers. To be successful in creating great mobile applications, think of mobile devices as augmenting existing software with new mobile behaviors as well as creating entirely new classes of software rather than replacing existing desktop or Web software.

Desktop and laptop computers do many things well, namely providing a rich random-access exploratory way of working with different sources of data. It is not uncommon during a session with a desktop or laptop computer to pull information together from several different sources and use applications in an ad hoc way. Think of working with a word processor, doing e-mail, shopping for airline tickets on the Web, or programming with a software development tool. All of these are rich exploratory activities that often involve long sessions at the computer. The user tends to work in an ad hoc way with different applications and data sources, often switching contexts between them. Good mobile device software, on the other hand, provides the user with a focused, task-centric ability to zoom in on needed information during short usage sessions. Think of the frustration of trying to look up an address on a badly designed mobile device address book. The user wants to quickly make a phone call. The last thing the user wants is to randomly explore data; 10 seconds is a frustratingly long time to fiddle with buttons and navigate user interface when trying to initiate a phone call. Mobile devices are about portability, about always being on, and about quick access to information and services in situations where a desktop or laptop computer is simply not the right paradigm.

When designing your mobile device application, it is important to specifically consider the usage patterns and specific circumstances of the people who are going to be using the software. Is the application going to be used in a delivery truck right after a package delivery is made? Will the application need to be simple enough to be used by people while walking down crowded streets or will people use it while sitting down in someone's office and looking up complex data? Is the application going to be used during a flight, where communications will need to be cached until connectivity is available?

Is the application going to be part of a package, where the same person uses the desktop and mobile device software, or will the people using desktop computers and mobile devices be separate and united only by the data they work with? What is the level of experience the target user has with using other computers and applications? Will the user interface need to be simplified to take user inexperience into account? It is important to map out what the scenarios are for the mobile device part of your system and how the users will expect to use them. This will not only help you determine the right features and user interface for your mobile application but may also help you choose the right target hardware for your mobile solution. If your application requires a certain kind of user interface, this may have a strong effect on the hardware and form factors you choose for your application.

Surfing the Web on a Mobile Device Is Different

I have heard an oft-quoted estimate that in only a few years there will be more mobile devices hooked up to the Internet than desktop computers. Possibly so, but it is incorrect to assume that these devices will use the Internet in the same way that desktop users do. It is worth understanding why this is so.

As pointed out earlier in the book, one of the first things you may notice when using a mobile device Web browser is that the address bar is often hidden by default. This seems a crippling omission from a desktop perspective, but is not so on mobile devices. The reason for this is twofold: (1) It is usually not easy to type a long URL into a mobile device quickly, and given that Web site names demand letter-to-letter accuracy, T9 text entry is not particularly useful in speeding this up; and (2) most general Web content does not display well on mobile devices due to image sizes and screen layout demands.

For this reason mobile Web browsing works by storing a list of the most useful mobile sites and making sure that the links from these starting points also point to useful mobile device content.

It is for this reason that work is proceeding to define a top-level domain on the Internet specifically for mobile device content (for example, .mobile rather than .com). Mobile devices are going to be very important participants in the Internet world, but not in the same way as desktop browsers are today. This is something to be excited about because it means more mobile-specific Web innovations to come rather than a rehashing of the same desktop ideas repackaged for mobile devices.

Steps to Define the Scope of Your Mobile Application

The following is a list of steps you should follow when determining the scope of your mobile application:

1. *Write down the mobile device scenarios.* There is no substitute for actually committing your list of user scenarios to writing. The more specific the scenarios, the better. Define who the mobile applications user will be. Define what devices they will be carrying with them. Define when and where they will use the mobile application. Define the tasks they will accomplish with the mobile software. Define the session length and frequency of their interaction with the device. Getting all of this down in writing will sharpen your thinking and also enable you to get specific feedback from team members, potential application users, and other relevant parties. Equally importantly, state the things that the mobile application is not intended to accomplish. This will define the bounds and scope of your mobile application.

2. *Decide what part of the system goes onto devices.* It is valuable to decide on a preliminary partitioning of your application into server, device, and desktop portions if appropriate. This will give you a good understanding of what the processing, storage, and communications needs will be for your mobile device.

3. *Do initial prototyping.* With todays RAD design tools, it is relatively simple to build a simple prototype that resembles what you have in mind. This is an excellent thing to do. Having a prototype put together and running on a device will give you a good understanding of the capabilities and limitations of your chosen hardware and expose design issues you may not have thought of. Having a prototype running will also enable you to get feedback on the usage scenarios you have defined.

4. *Consider whether the user interface developed in your prototype is appropriate for your target device.* Building a prototype application should give you a clear understanding of how the mobile application will present its data and interact with the user. Not every application is appropriate for every device. The prototype should demonstrate how the scenarios you have defined will look and work on physical device hardware. Based on this feedback, you may need to modify your scenarios, your user interface paradigm, or your choice of target mobile device.

5. *Consider the data implications of your prototype.* Your prototype application should give you a better understanding of the kind of data your application will work with and under what circumstances this data will be sent or received. You should be able to make a determination of whether a local database is required and what kind of local storage may be required. As with the user interface, the data needs of your application may force you to reconsider your selected target hardware based on database availability or storage requirements.

6. *Consider whether the connectivity implications of your prototype are feasible for your target device.* Think critically about the communications and connectivity needs of your mobile application. Is high-speed network access required? Is broad mobile roaming a requirement? Are syncing and network connectivity through a desktop or laptop sufficient for your needs?

7. *Proceed with the software design!* Armed with a good list of user scenarios, an initial idea of what the correct partitioning of your application should be, and valuable feedback based on building a mock-up of your application, you are in a good position to proceed with the software design of your mobile application.

Each of us should reserve the right to wake up smarter tomorrow than we are today. It is important to have a plan in mind when you set forth on your mobile application's development. It is also important to understand that in the course of your application's development you will learn things that will force you to reevaluate and adjust your plan. Having a vision and concrete scenarios to give scope to it is important. Without these you will end up with a washing machine that makes terrible coffee, bakes lousy bread, and does a bad job with the dishes. You must have a clear understanding of what your mobile application is, and as importantly is not, intended to accomplish. If the plan needs to be modified, modify it, but by all means have a definite scope and scenarios defined for your mobile application.

CHAPTER 7

Step 1: Start with Performance; Stay with Performance

per·form·ance [pr fáʊrmns] *working effectiveness: the effectiveness of the way something or somebody does his or her job*

(Encarta 2004, Dictionary)

The very best way to stay on course is to never get off course. If you've just stepped off the path, stop, and step back on the path.

—The author of this chapter

Introduction

As indicated by the dictionary definition above, performance is not just speed, it is effectiveness. Things need to perform effectively to be considered useful. Your mobile application's performance will be the first and main criteria by which users will judge its quality and usefulness. Although great performance will not guarantee the success of your mobile application, the lack of acceptable performance will surely doom your efforts to failure.

Economics teaches us that excess capital creates the ability for investment and growth. Fundamentally, performance represents the excess capital that you have to invest in your mobile application's growth and development. If you have great performance, you can add features, try out new models, and extend the scope of your application. The excess capital created by your surplus of acceptable performance allows you this freedom. If your mobile application has poor performance, you are painting yourself into a corner and are doing the coding equivalent of living paycheck to paycheck. If the performance is poor or barely acceptable, you will struggle to scrape by with your existing features and you will spend all your time just keeping things barely working, making patches and hacks to just stay mediocre. There is no single thing you have more control over and no single thing that developers tend to get wrong through inattention, lack of planning, and lack of discipline. Performance counts!

Finally, all performance is subjective. It does no good to argue to someone that their application performs acceptably when they say that it feels sluggish. This is like telling someone test driving an old station wagon that the car really has the horsepower and transmission to be a sports car and they should just look at the vehicle's specs. If it feels sluggish, it is sluggish. Great performance is not about the speed of the individual pieces, it is the perceived behavior of the integrated whole.

The Importance of a Disciplined Approach

Thomas Edison, no slouch himself at building useful devices, is reported to have explained, "Genius is 1 percent inspiration and 99 percent perspiration." Achieving good performance is 80 percent discipline and 20 percent creativity. Discipline in your development process will allow you to find your performance problems and prevent you from ignoring or deferring them. Ignoring performance problems will be tempting; fixing performance problems does not add features and is not perceived of as sexy design work. Nevertheless, addressing performance in a methodical way is critically important if you are going to succeed in the mobile development work you undertake. Disciplined work will allow you to both uncover performance problems early as well as find solutions to them before they get ingrained in your design. Many of these problems can be solved by adapting the ideas presented here and found in further research by you. In cases where no useful precedent exists, the occasional burst of creative genius may allow you to see a new solution that no one has thought of yet and allow you to break new ground in your design. The most important thing is having a disciplined approach that forces you to confront the performance problems that will inevitably come up and keep at them until they are solved. When testing out filaments for his light bulb, Thomas Edison went through hundreds of test filament materials before he settled on the one that provided the best combination of incandescence and longevity. So it is with performance: It is all about testing and learning what works. As Mr. Edison showed, focus, persistence, and creativity pay great rewards.

Define the User Scenarios That Count

You should have a list of what the key user experience scenarios are. Some of these may be general in nature, such as the following:

- The user will never be left waiting for more than 0.5 seconds without some kind of visual notification that things are happening.
- The user will never be left waiting for more than 4 seconds without the ability to abort a long duration operation.

Some scenarios will be very specific:

- Starting a new game of chess should not take more than 1 second.
- Accessing a customer's order information should not take longer than 3 seconds.

Write down the scenarios in your main design document. Whether you are working alone or in a group, it is always useful to have a written reminder of what the experience of using your application is supposed to be. This list may change over time to reflect things you learn in testing your application, but the value of having the key scenarios explicitly listed in one place is worth the effort.

Use Software Development Milestones with Performance-Driven Exit Criteria

Having concrete milestones to measure your progress toward completing your application is a proven mechanism for building and shipping great software. Without milestones to measure your progress against defined metrics, you are just wandering toward your goal, sometimes making progress, sometimes moving askew, and sometimes regressing. Milestones are both a way of marking and celebrating the progress toward your goals as well as preventing difficult but necessary decisions from being indefinitely deferred.

To be effective, milestones should define the user scenarios that must work at the exit of the milestone, the features that must be "code complete," and set specific performance metrics that must be met in order to exit the milestone. Getting to a milestone is usually relatively easy; it is the point where your development team writes (or you write, if you are working alone) the necessary code to make the things work that you have outlined in your milestone's goal list. The real work is successfully "exiting the milestone"; this is where disagreements, contention, and poor compromises can arise. The basic code may be written to enable a scenario, but does this really meet the spirit of the milestone? Is the code cobbled together and full of so many hacks that it cannot really be considered code complete and is the performance "good enough to ship"? These are the key questions that need to be answered. This is the point where real leadership and discipline need to be applied to make sure the project is truly on track to exit the milestone and move another big step toward successful completion.

A Few Words on Meeting Development Milestones

It is important to ensure that a project does not limp across a milestone but rather strides across it confidently and with team members proud and in agreement of what was accomplished. There will be a temptation to put off performance goals because "they are not really features"; don't do it! Experience has shown over and over again that it is far better to cross a milestone confidently but behind schedule than it is to limp through the milestone because the goals have been compromised.

Making a milestone's goals easier to achieve does nothing to bring the end goal closer. When faced with a schedule crisis, you only have three choices:

1. Cut product features to allow concentration on the remaining features. If you are going to end up cutting a feature, cut it early and concentrate on doing an excellent job with the remaining features. Cutting features late can be very painful for the people who were working on the code, for the end users who expected the features, and for the rest of the product, which may have dependencies on the feature. Because cutting features is difficult, it must be done correctly, as early as possible, and with leadership.

2. Extending the schedule to something more realistic based on the facts you now have at hand. You will learn things as you go along that will enable you to better adjust the schedules. If the milestone's schedule needs to be moved out along with the rest of the product's schedule, do it decisively and realistically. The end result needs to be a new schedule that people believe in.

3. Finding ways to level the workload among members of the team. It is almost never effective mid-cycle to bring additional members who are not familiar with the work already going on onto a development team. However, it may be possible to better distribute the work among members of the team. As with the two previous points, realism, promptness, and decisiveness are important to making workload decisions. It is better to have one painful workload-leveling exercise than a continuous series of them.

From a performance perspective, exit criteria for milestones are critical for the simple reason that the performance of an application usually cannot be made significantly better later in the application's development cycle without drastic redesign. The common excuse of "We've got to hit code complete, we'll tackle performance in an upcoming milestone" simply does not pass muster. Addressing performance concerns invariably becomes more difficult later in the software development cycle because as more code gets written interdependencies pile up and the necessary design changes become more difficult to make. When someone says, "We'll investigate and fix the performance problems later in the product cycle," what they are really saying is, "We don't understand the performance problems we have now and can't prove that we can fix them later. What we are building right now is a prototype that we might end up shipping anyway; we'll probably rewrite a huge part of the application when we build it for real."

Have specific and realistic performance exit criteria for your milestones. It is far better to delay exiting a project milestone than it is to crawl over the finish line with a limping application. Addressing performance problems in the milestones where the underperforming code was written will allow the maximum amount of creativity to be applied to solving the problems while options are still open to do creative things. The performance exit criteria should cover two areas: end-user responsiveness and absolute performance of critical algorithms.

Consider End-User Responsiveness

The user interface of your mobile application must remain responsive to people using the device it is running on. If your application exhibits stalls that leave the user waiting without any feedback, make explicit decisions about how these conditions will be handled.

- Can the stalls be removed or sped up through better design?
- Can the stalls be handled by bringing up splash screens or wait cursors that let the user know activity is going on?
- Can the work be moved to a background thread to keep the user interface responsive?

Consider the Absolute Performance of Critical Algorithms

There will be some key algorithms that your application uses that have a disproportionate effect on the experience users perceive. These are algorithms that do things central to the application. They may do things like load data from a database, parse files, compute graphs for display on the device, or construct reports to show the user. For example, if it takes three minutes to draw a chart based on data the user has gathered, this is too long, even if the user interface remains responsive during the wait. For these key algorithms, care and creativity must be used to ensure an acceptable user experience.

Some questions to ask when analyzing critical algorithms include the following:

- Can the algorithms be speeded up by tuning or redesign?
- Can the algorithms' execution needs be predicted and front loaded before the user demands them so that the user perceives a better experience?
- Can any of the heavy lifting be done off of the device by a server?
- Can things be precalculated or predrawn at design time to remove or reduce the need for any runtime computation?

To sum up on milestones and performance goals: Having performance-driven exit criteria for your milestones and making them a disciplined part of your development process will make certain that your software development project stays on track.

Perform Code Reviews

Having performance-oriented code reviews of the application code being written is a great way to improve your code quality. Although design by committee is not a great strategy for building algorithms, peer review of code is a proven method of improving code quality. Code reviews offer two benefits:

1. *Identification of improvements to algorithms*—Both the act of preparing for a code review and the review itself help identify ways to write better performing algorithm code and design more responsive user interfaces.
2. *Sharing of skills, lessons learned, and increased code familiarity*—If the code being reviewed demonstrates some particularly novel approach to solving a difficult performance problem, this is a good learning tool for everyone participating in the code review. In addition, everyone will benefit from a deeper shared understanding of how the application's component pieces function.

To get the most out of a code peer review, it is important to have consistent coding standards that members of the group adhere to. Using common mechanisms for implementing state machines, resource caches, and user interface code will go a long way in bringing all the members of the team to a common understanding and allow best practices to be adopted and common mistakes to be quickly spotted and fixed.

It is recommendable to develop a list of standard guidelines that outline how code is to be written in your projects. This can be as simple as annotating a sample source file to show coding conventions or it can be a comprehensive design guide. What degree of specification is most appropriate depends on your organization's capabilities and needs. If no existing standards or guidelines exist, it is worth putting some together. Start simple, borrow liberally from existing published guidelines, and make sure the document is useful and used by members of your team. Consistency is its own reward.

Define Your Application's Memory Model

Because mobile applications run in constrained memory environments, it is valuable to specify and maintain an explicit model that describes out how memory will be used and managed by your application. In today's higher-level, object-oriented and garbage-collected computing environments, this usually does not require keeping specific track of how individual chunks of memory get allocated, although this is important in lower-level programming for things such as device drivers. Instead, it is important that your mobile applications have a defined model for what is kept in memory and for how long. As part of the design process, answer the following questions:

- *What global resources will be cached in memory?* Some things are useful to cache. Some things are wasteful to hold on to. Be crisp in your thinking about both.
- *How much application data will be loaded into memory at any given time?* Most applications deal with sizable amounts of data, only some of which needs to be loaded at any given time.
- *Under what circumstances will loaded data and resources be discarded?* Having a housecleaning model for getting rid of data and resources that are no longer needed is important to make room for other data and resources.

As a developer you have a choice to either manage these important aspects explicitly or have them implicitly grow until the application becomes unwieldy. These considerations were discussed in the earlier chapter on the usage of state machines to manage an application's memory model. If you have not read this yet, it is worth going back and reviewing this material. This will also be the focus of the upcoming chapter dedicated to performance and memory management.

Measure Often and Incrementally

Find ways to measure the important characteristics of your application. Measurement is the key to gaining the feedback that will guide your performance-tuning work. Algorithm execution durations and user interface responsiveness can be measured. Numbers of object allocations and memory usage can be measured. When you identify a performance problem, spend time thinking about what the most useful pieces of data you can get are and how to gather that data. A few suggestions in order of decreasing preference:

1. *Use code instrumentation.* With only a little bit of effort, it is possible to add code to measure things in your application. This process is called instrumentation. If you can gather sufficient information through the simple instrumentation of your code, you will be in a good position to optimize your designs. Gathering timing information is usually easy to do; sample code is provided later in this chapter. Additionally, it is often possible to make native operating system calls to get higher-resolution timing data if it is necessary. Comparing different algorithms based on information gleaned from code instrumentation is often very enlightening.

2. *Consider automated testing and logging of performance metrics.* When possible, it is useful to have automated tests that can be run to log performance metrics for key scenarios. If it is possible to instrument your code and generate consistent metrics that are measured and stored from build to build, this will be a great aid in tracking down performance problems when they occur. If consistent build-to-build metrics are available to compare a mobile application's performance in completing key tasks, it will be possible to quickly pinpoint when regressions occur. Quick detection of problems is the easiest way to isolate and identify the design changes that were responsible for any performance regressions.

3. *Use runtime-generated metrics and device profiling tools.* Some managed code-execution environments offer the ability to get metrics from the managed-code runtime. These runtime metrics measure things such as code execution times, numbers of object allocations, and numbers of garbage collections. This information

can be useful in tuning specific algorithms and finding cases where unexpected object allocations are occurring. The best strategy for doing this kind of analysis is to isolate the code you are trying to analyze as much as possible. If you can place the specific code you want to analyze in a separate project and run it to gather the metrics, you can get accurate and actionable data on the algorithm's performance characteristics. This kind of analysis is helpful in comparing the efficiency of different algorithms. If advanced runtime profiling hooks and analysis tools are available, these can also offer great insight into where the processing time is being spent. Note: See the section below titled "Getting Profiling Information from the .NET Compact Framework" for a description on how to get basic profiling metrics from the .NET Compact Framework.

4. *Use algorithm metrics from desktop/server profiling tools.* Some terrific managed-code profiling tools exist for desktop and server runtime environments. The state-of-the-art in profiling tools for desktop and server code are presently considerably ahead of the state-of-the-art for devices; this is likely to remain the case for some time to come. Partially this is due to the greater maturity of the desktop and server markets, and partially this is due to the fact that desktop and server runtimes have larger memory budgets to support all kinds of profiling hooks. Expect device runtimes to mature and gain richer profiling capabilities but still lag their desktop and server counterparts. Desktop and server analysis tools can give in-depth views as to which functions are using the bulk of the processing time and where potential inefficiencies lie in your code. Additionally, today's profiling tools often integrate into standard development environments, making analysis much easier. Running your device code in a desktop or server environment will let you view how it performs on these platforms and may give you some insight into how they behave on devices. Note: Keep in mind that desktop, server, and device JIT, exception handling, and garbage-collection strategies are likely to vary significantly. Desktops and servers have much greater memory capacities than mobile devices, and different microprocessors excel at different kinds of calculations. Using desktop or server profiling results may bring useful insights, but some of the code's performance characteristics will differ when run on devices. Device performance will differ particularly if the code makes extensive use of file I/O, networking, or graphics because these will vary greatly on different hardware and operating systems. Desktop and server profiling tools are helpful to improve your intuition and understand where object allocations are occurring but the final proof is always on the device.

5. *Use memory-usage data from the device operating system and device native code profiling tools.* It is often possible to make native operating system calls to get higher-resolution timing data and memory-usage data. It is also possible to use native code profiling tools to get code execution statistics. If you are building a native code application or component, this is exactly the data you want; go forth and measure. If you are trying to get information about a managed-code application, this can be tricky. When getting application or system memory-usage data from the operating system, be aware that a managed runtime's behavior may only roughly correlate to system memory usage. Because of things such as periodic garbage collections, your memory-usage chart is likely to exhibit a saw-tooth wave pattern as discarded objects build up and then are periodically freed by the garbage collector. This information can still be useful if you are trying to look for long-term memory leaks. Alternatively, you can preemptively call the garbage collector before taking a memory sample—only do this during testing; manually triggering the garbage collector during normal application execution will almost always detrimentally affect the application's performance. Regardless, getting memory-usage data from the operating system directly may require native operating system calls and some tinkering. If you can get the data you need from the managed runtime, all the better.

Of these strategies, code instrumentation will give you the quickest and most valuable first-order results. When gathering metrics to analyze your performance, start with simple instrumentation and move on from there if needed.

Getting Profiling Information from the .NET Compact Framework

The .NET Compact Framework version 1.1 has a mechanism built in to it that allows the generation of "quick and dirty" execution metrics on managed-code applications it runs. It works at a granular application level by outputting a text file at the end of an application's execution. The text file contains data such as the following:

- The total execution time

- The number of objects allocated during code execution

- The number of garbage collections during code execution

- The number of exceptions thrown (Exceptions can be expensive if thrown often and needlessly inside loops.)

Because the metrics generated are application level, this kind of data works best if you are trying to compare two different algorithms or tune a single algorithm. The algorithms to be tested should each be isolated into their own executable files. The executables should have as little else in them as possible to guarantee that the algorithm being tested produces the bulk of execution activities. If appropriate, remove any forms or other application logic that can force unwanted components to get loaded, JITed, and run.

For technical instructions on how to enable the generation of these runtime metrics, refer to the article titled "Developing Well-Performing .NET Compact Framework Applications" at `http://msdn.microsoft.com`.

As of this writing, the article could be found at the URL `http://msdn.microsoft.com/library/default.asp?url=/library/en-us/dnnetcomp/html/netcfperf.asp`.

This article also contains many interesting performance comparisons for accessing functionality in different ways and is well worth a read.

A Measurement Tool You Can Use

Because designing for performance is an exploratory art, it is useful to have a few handy tools at your side to help you take quick measurements. The sample code below is intended to give a tool you can use to instrument your code.

The code in Listing 7.1 can be used easily and is small enough to include as part of your mobile application with little overhead. It is intended to be a general-purpose performance probe to enable you to take quick spot measurements of code-execution times. This will give a quick idea of how long code execution takes and enable you to identify trouble spots and areas where new design strategies may be needed. The code is also useful as a way to quickly compare two different approaches to see which is superior for your needs. For example, if it takes three seconds for you to set up your user interface and fill the data in a TreeView control, you might consider changing your algorithm to only fill in the top-level nodes and defer the filling of the child nodes until they are needed. The final proof is in the measurement and the end user's experience.

Listing 7.1 Performance Sampling Code to Instrument Your Code With

```csharp
using System;

internal class PerformanceSampling
{
  //Arbitrary number, but 8 seems like enough samplers for
  //most uses.
  const int NUMBER_SAMPLERS = 8;

  static  string [] m_perfSamplesNames =
                    new string[NUMBER_SAMPLERS];

  static  int [] m_perfSamplesStartTicks =
                    new int[NUMBER_SAMPLERS];

  static  int [] m_perfSamplesDuration =
                    new int[NUMBER_SAMPLERS];

  //Take a start tick count for a sample
  internal static void StartSample(int sampleIndex,
                                   string sampleName)
  {
    m_perfSamplesNames[sampleIndex] = sampleName;

    m_perfSamplesStartTicks[sampleIndex] =
      System.Environment.TickCount;
  }

  //Take a start tick count for a sample
  internal static void StopSample(int sampleIndex)
  {
    int stopTickCount = System.Environment.TickCount;

    //The counter resets itself every 24.9 days
    //(which is about 2 billion ms)
    //we'll account for this unlikely possibility
    if (stopTickCount >= m_perfSamplesStartTicks[sampleIndex])
    {
      //In almost all cases we will run this code.
      m_perfSamplesDuration[sampleIndex] =
          stopTickCount - m_perfSamplesStartTicks[sampleIndex];
    }
    else
```

```
        {
            //We have wrapped back around to zero and should account
            //for this
            m_perfSamplesDuration[sampleIndex] =
                stopTickCount +
                (int.MaxValue - m_perfSamplesStartTicks[sampleIndex])
                + 1;
        }

    }

    //Return the length of a sample we have taken
    //(length in milliseconds)
    internal static int GetSampleDuration(int sampleIndex)
    {
        return m_perfSamplesDuration[sampleIndex];
    }

    //Returns the number of seconds that have elapsed
    //during the sample period
    internal static string GetSampleDurationText(int sampleIndex)
    {
        return m_perfSamplesNames[sampleIndex] + ": " +
            System.Convert.ToString(
                (m_perfSamplesDuration[sampleIndex] / (double) 1000.0)
            ) + " seconds.";
    }
}
```

NOTE: The .NET Framework documentation claims that the interval of the .TickCount property cannot be less than 500 ms (0.5 seconds). In practice, I have found the resolution to be quite a bit better than this (under 100 ms, or 0.1 seconds). You will have to do your own experimentation. If you find you need a higher-resolution counter, you can modify the code above to make calls into the native code operating system and access lower-level system counters. For most cases, the code above should suffice, and its simplicity makes it very attractive to use when quick measurements are required.

Listing 7.2 Test Code Showing Use of Timing Instrumentation Code Above

```
private void button1_Click(object sender, System.EventArgs e)
{
  const int TEST_SAMPLE_INDEX = 2; //Choose any valid index
  //Start sampling
  PerformanceSampling.StartSample(TEST_SAMPLE_INDEX,
    "TestSample");
  //Show the message box
  System.Windows.Forms.MessageBox.Show(
    "Hit OK to finish Sample");

  //Stop sampling
  PerformanceSampling.StopSample(TEST_SAMPLE_INDEX);
  //Show the results
  System.Windows.Forms.MessageBox.Show(
    PerformanceSampling.GetSampleDurationText(
    TEST_SAMPLE_INDEX));
}
```

Tips for Getting Good Measurements Results

1. As a rule of thumb, the longer the duration of the event you are measuring, the lower the margin of error. So if you are comparing two algorithms that take around 0.5 seconds to run, consider running them 10 times in a row and dividing the result by 10.

2. Repeat any experiment several times and make sure you are getting reasonably similar results.

3. When comparing two algorithms head to head, consider running each algorithm several times and throwing out the first measurement of each if it differs significantly from the other measurements. The first time your application runs code, it may force dependent libraries to be loaded and compiled. If both algorithms have similar dependencies, the first measurement will take the hit of loading and JITing this code. This JIT time should usually not be included in your comparative measurements.

4. For best results when comparing two different algorithms, restart the application between tests. Restarting the application will flush out all precompiled and cached code and give you a common starting point for each test.

As with almost any timing measurement, there are no perfect measurements, there are only good-enough measurements. It is only important to make your measurement much larger than the noise level that will always be present. No matter what you are trying to measure, there are always ways to tune your technique to get the results you need.

Test with Real Data Sizes

A common mistake developers make is to design and test their algorithm using smaller than real-world data. Real-world data can take longer to load and save and, as importantly, can take up more valuable application memory space and dramatically slow down the overall performance of a mobile application. Some typical examples where developers may develop and test with smaller sizes of data than end users will encounter include the following:

- An application that uses a database is tested with 20 rows of sample data when in production 200 or 2,000 rows will be used.
- An XML text file needs to be parsed as part of the application. A 15KB file is used instead of the 300KB file that will be used in production.
- An application dealing with digital photographs is being designed. Photographs are downloaded from a Web server and cached locally on the device. During development, four sample 200KB pictures are used rather than the 800KB (or larger) digital photographs that are normally taken by digital cameras.

The mistakes shown in the examples above are understandable. When designing an application, data formats often change and it is much easier to remake a file with 10 rows of data than one with 200. It is also much easier to run and test applications when you do not need to wait for all the data to load at startup time. Sadly, the end users will not have this luxury; they will need to deal with real data sizes. Therefore it is important to move to real-world data or simulated data of a representative size early in a mobile application's design and development process.

Because there is a tendency to continue to work with small-sized test data as long as possible, it is easy to forget to switch to real data until too late in the development process. Often real data is only used in the field tests of a near-complete application. By this time, all kinds of dependencies will have built up in between code modules, and implicit capacity assumptions will have been made in the mobile application's design. It will be painful if not impossible to untangle these dependencies and change the application's underlying data and memory models to account for real-world data sizes. To ensure that you move to real-world representative data sizes, make it an exit criteria for the milestone in which the code dealing with the data is written. Specifically, make it a milestone exit criterion to have switched to using real data sizes in your daily development and testing. Acceptable performance with real-world data should be a criterion to successfully exit every milestone.

Stress Test Your Application

Popular and useful applications have a way of growing beyond their original intended uses and capacities. People commonly use and abuse all kinds of equipment beyond stated tolerances. Your application should expect this to occur. It is advisable to do some simple stress testing to see how your application scales when that data it works with grows to the following:

- *20% bigger file/data size than the design specified*—This represents basic growing room for your application. Your application should be able to handle this with no problem.
- *50% bigger file/data size than the design specified*—This represents plausible overuse of your application. Does the performance degrade gracefully or do dire effects occur?
- *100% bigger file/data size than the design specified*—Major overuse.
- *200% bigger file/data size than the design specified*—True stress testing.

Ideally your application should be able to gracefully manage these increased data sizes. If you have a good memory model that ensures only the proper amount of state is kept in memory, the user may not even notice any degradation. More realistically, your application will experience some kind of reduced performance when working with larger data sizes and the operative question becomes "What is the acceptable range?" It is important to understand in what range the application's performance is linear and at what point it will start to encounter exponential performance reductions.

If your application starts to fall over at any of these stress points, you should consider placing safeguards in your application that guard against these conditions. For example, you could write checks in your code that explicitly disallow working with data sizes larger than allowed for acceptable performance. Alternatively, your mobile application could warn users that loading larger amounts of data will cause significant performance deterioration and give them an estimation of the effects of their requests to work with larger sizes of data.

Your design document should both state what the expected maximum data size is and what should happen when the user attempts to exceed capacity thresholds.

Never Put Off Performance Work (It Will Always Get Worse!)

I have stated this before and I will almost certainly state it again several times in this book: Do *not* put off performance work! Putting off performance work is like putting off fixing difficult bugs; it almost never pays off. It is easy to convince yourself to defer this work. Let me help out with a few common excuses I like to use:

- *I'm working towards code complete. After code complete, I'll have a better idea of how the whole application works and be able to tune it then*. Wrong. After you hit code complete, you will have a very difficult time reengineering parts of your application due to explicit or implicit assumptions you have made in your algorithms. The more code you write, the harder it is to change it. If you hit a performance problem that will affect the user's experience with your application, you should figure out how to fix it while the code is still malleable.
- *No need to worry about code efficiency now, I'll just use whatever coding techniques I'm most familiar with and take a few shortcuts. Later I'll find the slow algorithms and figure out how to rewrite them properly*. Wrong again. If you are writing needlessly wasteful code, you should be fixing this before you write your algorithms. This is particularly true for code that will perform many string operations or algorithms that allocate objects in loops. It is often not harder to use the efficient string handling or object allocation techniques (more on this later); it just requires a little more investigation up front to find out what the efficient techniques are for the programming system you are using. There are two important steps to writing code that performs well: (1) Choose the right algorithm that meets your needs. (2) Code the algorithm using the efficient techniques available to you. Writing needlessly poor-quality code with the idea of fixing it up later is like trying to rapidly paint a house by splashing paint on all the walls: You can get 80 percent of the house painted quickly, but you will end up painting it all again before you are done.

  Note: It is important to note that this does not mean that you should spend endless hours handcrafting each and every algorithm; this is equally bad and can produce unmaintainable code that is needlessly micro-optimized. Some parts of your application matter a great deal more than others, and you need to assess and measure what is important and concentrate your special efforts there. What it does mean is that it is worth understanding what the efficient coding mechanisms are for working with strings, arrays, collections, object and type allocations, sorting algorithms, common data types and operations, and getting into the habit of writing good-quality code (or at least not arbitrarily bad-quality code!) Always take the time to write good-quality code and then measure the different parts of your application to find out what the most critical systems are to ensuring great performance. After you have done this basic good design work, you can then spend your valuable time optimizing the most important parts further.

- *Performance is just a matter of tuning the algorithms I have already written.* Wrong a third time. Although good gains can be found sometimes by fixing individual algorithms, other times fundamental redesign is required. Unless you write terrible-quality code, the greatest performance gains may come not from optimizing the algorithms you have written, but in restructuring your application's data model and user interface in fundamental ways that allow it to perform drastically better. It is important to know when to revisit your fundamental designs and look for creative alternatives.

  Some performance problems may be based, not so much on how you process data, but rather on how much data you need to process at any given time. No heavy lifting will be required of your algorithms if you are working with smaller amounts of data or data that is already presorted or organized in the way that the application needs it. These kinds of fundamental optimizations can be at the very heart of your application's data model, state machines, and user-interaction model. After you have built a great deal of code on top of these models, you may be able to tune the code in the core algorithms to get some incremental gains, but you will have a difficult time making fundamental changes to the way your application relates to the data. Great application performance is systematic and based on an efficient overall design, not just isolated in individual processing algorithms.

- *Better performance is just not possible. I have reached the limit of what can be done with my application and we'll just have to live with the slow performance.* Dead wrong. Better performance is always possible; it may just require a radical rethink. You may need to change how your application works. You may need to move code off the device and onto a server (or the other way around). You may need to precalculate things at design time, build optimized lookup tables, and place them into your code. You may need to split your single application into three smaller applications. There are almost an endless number of ways to "cheat the clock" and find ways to raise your application's performance. Although it is true that there are often fastest-possible algorithms for accomplishing any single task, your application is almost never a single algorithm or task. Your application is a user experience. If you cannot find a way to get acceptable performance and are confident that the performance metrics you are using are the right ones, it is time to think more creatively. To quote and old truism, "Necessity is the mother of invention." Often the greatest insights are made when faced with these kinds of challenges, because they force you to think about the true nature of the problem you are trying to solve. Poor performance is generally due to a failure in imagining a creative solution to a problem that has not been thought of before. Stand on your head for a while and dwell on it or do whatever it is you do when you need to think creatively. Something will pop up.

Tackling performance problems as they arise enables you to confidently move forward to the next stage of your application's development. If something goes drastically wrong with performance down the road, you can backtrack to a known point where the performance was good and work from there. Fixing performance problems along the way is a lot like clipping into a safety line when you are climbing and reach a new point in your progression upward; you can only fall so far past the point you last clipped in. If you do not take the time to consolidate your gains, you can fall all the way to the bottom and that can hurt a lot. Do not go climbing recklessly ahead with your application's development without stabilizing your application's performance.

Defining Performance Objectives

It is hard to reach objectives you do not specifically set because you will never know when you have crossed the finish line. Paradoxically, it can also be said that it is easy to meet ambiguous objectives because almost anything can be rationalized as being "good enough." Depending on your disposition, you can easily fall into one of these traps and either end up over-optimizing areas that do not really matter or ignoring areas that matter critically. Most likely you will land in both of these camps occasionally, choosing to optimize the easy things or areas that present intriguing problems to explore while deferring unpleasant decisions that do not promise easy resolution or seem to be full of nothing but grunt work.

If you are working in a team, matters can get further complicated by the fact that different people will have different beliefs as to what constitutes "acceptable performance." Often these beliefs will be influenced by perceptions about what additional work will be required to fix the problems, who will need to do the work, and whose fault it is that things went wrong. It is comforting to think that we make cold, well-measured, and impartial judgments based on objective facts, but a great deal of evidence in human nature says otherwise. We are all influenced not just by our senses but also by our thoughts about how difficult, fun, challenging, or tedious fixing the problems facing us may be.

The best way to deal with performance objectives is to write them down in your design document. List them explicitly and attach numbers to them. Update them based on what you learn as necessary, but keep track of the changes you make. Having specific stated goals and being explicitly aware of how, when, and why they change through the development cycle is the best way to keep yourself and your team true to these goals.

All Performance Is Subjective

Performance is whatever the end user experiences. If the experience seems sluggish, it is sluggish. If it seems snappy, it is snappy. Because we are building mobile applications for people and not for machines with stopwatches, the art of measuring performance is in coming up with the right metrics to accurately measure the user experience. When in doubt, the final determination as to whether the performance of a mobile application is good enough can be achieved by testing it on real end users and getting their feedback. It does no good to try to explain to an end user why your mobile application really does perform well despite what they think. All performance is subjective.

Instant User Responsiveness

A car with great performance feels responsive; every action provides some immediate feedback to the driver that tells him that the right things are happening. On mobile devices this feedback is most often visual. Sometimes feedback can be provided through auditory or tactile means, as in the case of audibly confirming a button that has been pressed or vibrating a phone to signal an event's occurrence. Regardless of the method of responsiveness, it is critical to give end users rapid acknowledgement that their command has been received and that work is underway to do their bidding.

Responsiveness and Home Electronics Remote Controls

Different kinds of devices give different kinds of feedback. A hallmark of a well-considered device design is prompt, unmistakable, and useful user feedback.

As a thought experiment, consider your television's remote control. Several kinds of feedback are often given by a good remote control. First, the buttons are usually physically pressable; anyone who has tried a remote control that does not have discrete physical buttons will recognize the feeling of uncertainty that occurs when pressing one of these "soft buttons." Second, a remote control often lights up in response to pressing a button, indicating that the control has received and is attempting to respond to your input. Third, a television set usually directly responds visually to receiving a remote control's command by bringing up a visual volume bar, showing a number, or showing another visual confirmation. If any of these responses were delayed by more than 0.5 seconds, the remote control would feel sluggish due to the lack of feedback. This is referred to as response latency and will immediately make users feel they have an inferior product. It is not that the user demands that the results of the commands sent occur immediately (although this is always nice); it is the simple act of immediate acknowledgment that makes an overwhelming difference between a poor and a good experience.

Consider this in your application design. Good feedback often requires a little extra code and polishing work on your application but makes a huge difference to the end user's experience and perception of your application's quality.

Have stated goals for always acknowledging a user's commands even if they cannot be processed immediately. Usually any latency of more than 0.5 seconds in acknowledging an end user's command will cause frustration. When there is response latency, it will often cause the user to try the command again, which may create more frustration if the second command toggles the application into an undesired state or is otherwise processed in an unintended way.

A good human analogy is your experience when waiting in line. When you get to the front of a line, you want to be acknowledged by the person serving you. If you are ignored for any length of time, your anxiety goes up quickly. Even if you are asked to wait for a few moments, being acknowledged is far superior to not getting any response from the person serving you. Do not let your application ignore the user even for a short time.

An Example Showing Different Levels of User Responsiveness

Below is a code example showing three different levels of user responsiveness corresponding to clicking three buttons. Each button performs an equivalent four seconds of simulated work. In each case, the user interface is unresponsive for the duration of the work, but the user experience varies greatly between the different cases. This example shows that small things can make a big difference with regard to user perceptions of performance and responsiveness. The following are the three experiences offered by the three different buttons on the sample application:

1. *Bad experience*—In this case, the user interface simply locks up for the duration of the work. The user is not told why, is not given any indication for how long the user interface will stay unresponsive, and is not told when the application has become responsive again. This is very frustrating for end users because they have to guess when they can click again. Clicks made while the application is unresponsive are queued up and processed when the application becomes responsive again. This may cause undesirable actions if the user starts poking at the application to see whether it has returned to responsiveness. This example shows thoughtlessly bad design.

2. *Better experience*—In this case, the user interface displays a "wait cursor" for the duration of the unresponsiveness. This gives users an indication that the application is presently not responsive and also lets them know when the application becomes responsive again by the disappearance of the wait cursor. With only minimal effort, the user experience has been improved significantly.

3. *Even better experience*—In this case, users not only get a wait cursor to tell them when the application is unresponsive, but also get text displayed that explains what is going on. This is more satisfactory for users because they become an informed participant in the process and are given text to read while the work is being done. If there are updates along the way during the work, the user can be kept informed. Keeping users informed goes a long way toward keeping them satisfied. This takes a bit more work than the second example, but if we can give users incremental updates and make them participants in the process it is worth the effort.

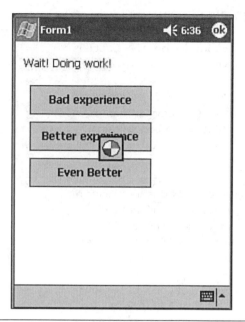

Figure 7.1 Responsiveness example.

Listing 7.3 is intended to be placed into a Pocket PC Form class. Perform the following steps to create and run the sample:

1. Start a new C#, Pocket PC project using Visual Studio .NET (2003 or later).
2. Place a label control and three button controls onto the Pocket PC form's design surface (as shown above in Figure 7.1).
3. Double-click a blank part of the form designer; this will create and hook up the `Form1_Load` event sink shown below. Enter the code shown below in this procedure.
4. Double-click Button1 on the form; this will create and hook up the `button1_Click` event sink shown below. Enter the code shown below into this procedure.
5. Do the same for Button2 and Button3, and type in their code.
6. Press F5 to run the application either on the Pocket PC emulator or a real Pocket PC device. (Press Ctrl+F5 to start without attaching the debugger if you want.)

Listing 7.3 Three Different Levels of User Responsiveness

```csharp
//Place captions on the buttons
private void Form1_Load(object sender, System.EventArgs e)
{
button1.Text = "Bad experience";
button2.Text = "Better experience";
button3.Text = "Even Better";
}


//----------------------------------------
//Example of a bad experience:
//    - No visual indication is given when work is started
//    - No visual indication is given when work is ended
//    - User interface is unresponsive during work
//    - End user is left to guess when the task completes
//----------------------------------------
private void button1_Click(object sender, System.EventArgs e)
{
   //Simulate work by pausing for 4 seconds

   System.Threading.Thread.Sleep(4000);
}


//----------------------------------------
//Example of a better experience:
//    + A visual indication is given when work is started
//      (wait cursor appears)
//    + A visual indication is given when work is ended
//      (wait cursor disappears)
//    - User interface is unresponsive during work
//    + End user knows when task is completed and UI is responsive
//      again
//----------------------------------------
private void button2_Click(object sender, System.EventArgs e)
{
   System.Windows.Forms.Cursor.Current =
     System.Windows.Forms.Cursors.WaitCursor;

   //Simulate work by pausing for 4 seconds
   System.Threading.Thread.Sleep(4000);

   System.Windows.Forms.Cursor.Current =
     System.Windows.Forms.Cursors.Default;
}
```

```
//----------------------------------------
//Example of an even better experience:
//    + A visual indication is given when work is started
//       (wait cursor appears)
//    + Additional text is displayed telling the user what is
//       going on
//    + A visual indication is given when work is ended
//       (wait cursor disappears)
//    - User interface is unresponsive during work
//    + End user knows when task is completed and UI is responsive
//       again
//    + Text tells user what happened
//----------------------------------------
private void button3_Click(object sender, System.EventArgs e)
{
  //Give user text that explains what is going on
  label1.Text = "Wait! Doing work!";
  //Force the UI to update the text
  //(otherwise it will wait until it processes the repaint
  //message, this may be after we exit this function)
  label1.Update();

  //Show wait cursor
  System.Windows.Forms.Cursor.Current =
    System.Windows.Forms.Cursors.WaitCursor;

  //Simulate work by pausing for 2.8 seconds
  System.Threading.Thread.Sleep(2800);

  //Optional Incremental status update
  label1.Text = "Wait! Almost done!";
  label1.Update();

  //Simulate work by pausing for 1.2 seconds
  System.Threading.Thread.Sleep(1200);


  //Give text indication that we are done
 //(Update whenever UI normally updates)
  label1.Text = "Success!";
  //Get rid of the wait cursor
  System.Windows.Forms.Cursor.Current =
  System.Windows.Forms.Cursors.Default;
}
```

It would, of course, be best if the user interface never became unresponsive, but for relatively short delays or cases where work has to be done synchronously there are a great many simple cosmetic things that can be done to keep the user's satisfaction high and anxiety low.

Maximum Wait Cursor Times

There are limits to how long a user can be kept waiting when the user interface is unresponsive. Having a wait cursor display and giving periodic updates to the user can extend this time, but there is still a fundamental point after which users will become annoyed and frustrated by the fact that their application is unresponsive. This time is probably around five seconds in all cases and about a second or two for frequently accessed functionality.

You should specify in your design document not only how you will go about reducing the end user's frustration with wait states but also what the maximum delay tolerances are. Longer delays than these thresholds mean that redesign has to be considered. Stating these goals explicitly ensures that end users gets a consistent experience throughout their use of your mobile application.

Maximum Data Load/Save Times, Startup Times, and Shutdown Times

Often when long-duration tasks are required, they can be pushed to a background thread and can happen without the user being aware of their duration. Background operations are said to occur "asynchronously." However, in some situations specific work is required to be completed before the application can proceed. Common situations where this can occur include the following:

- *Loading of documents*—If the purpose of the application is to work on a document, it may need to be loaded fully before the application can continue.
- *Exiting the application and saving loaded data*—If the user needs to know that the data was successfully saved, this must happen synchronously with the application shutting down.
- *Startup of the application and initialization of data*—As with loading a document, there may be startup information that needs to be loaded and processed before the application can meaningfully proceed.

Delays, even for unavoidable tasks, can be frustrating to the user. In some cases, splash screens, wait cursors, or progress bars can mitigate the user's frustration, but they can only go so far. A 30-second startup time is still a 30-second startup time, and that's going to annoy users of mobile devices who only have 20 seconds of work they want to perform before they put the device back in their pocket. As described in the section above, you should explicitly specify what the maximum delays are that the user can incur in these cases. If your application exceeds these tolerances, you need to make design changes. Are you really loading the minimum amount of data needed to start up? Can the startup data be cached or stored in a format that is quicker to load? If there is network data you require on startup, can this be cached locally? There are all kinds of creative solutions that can be explored for speeding up application performance at these key points, and sometimes you need to rethink previous design assumptions to get the performance your users will expect from an instant-access mobile device.

The Cost of Runtime Exceptions

Modern runtime environments offer structured exception handling that allows code to deal with exceptional circumstances robustly. Programmers can catch exceptions thrown by lower-level framework code and can also throw and catch their own exceptions. Structured exception handling is a great robustness feature that allows managed-code frameworks, components, and applications to clean up after unforeseen failures and resume normal execution. When an exception is raised, the runtime takes control and starts walking the stack upward looking for an appropriate handler to catch the exception being thrown. It is more important that things unwind properly than that the exception gets handled as quickly as normally executing code. The common result of this is that throwing and handling exceptions is moderately expensive from a performance perspective.

For good application performance, your code should avoid conditions where exceptions are being frequently thrown in the normal course of an application's execution. Rather than writing code that causes exceptions to be thrown and caught during the normal execution of your algorithms, your mobile application code should aggressively seek to avoid circumstances that would cause an exception to be raised during normal code execution. When designing your own algorithms for maximum performance, avoid writing code that causes exceptions to be raised unless truly exceptional circumstances occur. It should normally be possible to run your entire application without a single exception being raised.

If you are finding that your application's code is commonly handling framework-raised exceptions or raising and handling its own exceptions, examine and redesign your code to avoid these exceptional circumstances.

Structured exception handling is a powerful capability of object-oriented programming but must be used properly. Along with things such as object allocation and garbage collection, structured exceptions can make programming simpler and robust when used properly, but can cause significant performance problems when misused.

An Example Comparing Equivalent Algorithms That Do and Do Not Throw Exceptions

Listing 7.4 is a sample application that compares two algorithms performing equivalent work but with significantly different performance characteristics. One algorithm adds two numbers together and returns the sum as well as a Boolean value that specifies whether the result is positive or negative. The other algorithm also adds two numbers together and returns the result but raises an exception if the result is negative. As you might expect, the algorithm that throws an exception as part of its normal execution runs drastically slower in comparison to the non–exception-throwing loop. Although in an absolute sense both algorithms run quite quickly and perform 10,000 iterations in fewer than 2.5 seconds, one algorithm performs more than 350 times faster than the other algorithm; for tight loop computations, this difference can be crucial.

Table 7.1 shows the results of running the test on a physical Pocket PC device without the debugger hooked up. As you can see, the algorithm that runs without throwing and catching exceptions runs several hundred times faster. Our example used a very simple algorithm along with a simple mechanism for throwing and catching exceptions; relatively little cleanup and unwinding was required by the runtime to deal with the exception. Because of the simplicity of the work being done, the effects of throwing an exception are very pronounced. Results for different kinds of algorithms will vary depending on the complexity of the algorithm as well as the work required to handle thrown exceptions; however, one thing should be clear: Frequently thrown exceptions can be expensive, and their unnecessary use should be avoided under normal code-execution conditions.

Table 7.1 Comparative Performance of a Simple Algorithm with and without Exceptions

# Iterations	No Exception Thrown (sec)	Exception Thrown (sec)	x Times Faster Without Exception
10,000	0.006	2.202	367 times faster
10,000	0.006	2.201	367 times faster
100,000	0.061	22.716	372 times faster
100,000	0.055	22.834	415 times faster
100,000	0.055	22.995	418 times faster

Figure 7.2 shows the sample application running in a Pocket PC emulator.

NOTE: It is worth noting that because exception handling is a core runtime and debugging feature of the .NET Compact Framework and Visual Studio .NET, the application's performance can vary greatly under two conditions:

1. The performance of code that throws exceptions can be vastly impeded if the debugger is attached to the program while it is running. This is because the development environment is made aware of exceptions that are thrown even if they are caught by the application's code. This means that running algorithms that throw lots of exceptions will be very slow if the debugger is attached! Something to think about in your design and development; throwing lots of exceptions can slow down development. The behavior of the development environment should generally not force you to change the way you write code; but in this case, it should be an added incentive to avoid having lots of exceptions thrown inside loops of frequently run code.

2. The performance of handling exceptions will vary significantly between emulators and physical devices. For the most accurate measurements of how throwing and handling exceptions will affect your application, it is recommended that you run the tests on a physical device without the debugger attached to measure the effects accurately.

Figure 7.2 Sample application comparing exception and nonexception algorithms.

The code in Listing 7.4 belongs inside a Form in a Pocket PC project. Do the following to build and run the application:

1. Start Visual Studio .NET (2003 or later) and create a C# Smart Device Application.
2. Choose Pocket PC as the target platform. (A project will be created for you and Pocket PC Form designer will appear.)
3. Add the following controls to the form. See Figure 7.2 for an indication on how to lay out the controls on the form.
   - A TextBox, rename it **textBoxNumberAttempts**.
   - A Button, rename it **buttonRunNoExceptionCode**.
   - A Button, rename it **buttonRunExceptionCode**.
   - A ListBox, keep it named **listBox1**.
4. For each of the Button controls above, double-click the Button in the Form designer. In the event handler function generated and hooked up for you, enter the `button<ButtonName>_Click` code listed below.
5. Enter the rest of the code listed below.

6. Set the MinimizeBox property of the form to false. At runtime this will give the form an OK box at the top right that makes it easy to close the form and exit the application; this is very useful for repeated testing.
7. Add a new class to the project and call it **PerformanceSampling**, delete the previous contents in the class file, and enter in the code listed in Listing 7.1.
8. Run the application on a physical device or an emulator using F5. Use Ctrl+F5 if you want to run the sample without the debugger attached—this is recommended for this sample because exceptions are handled much more slowly with the debugger attached.

Listing 7.4 Performance Comparison Between Exception-Throwing Algorithm and Non–Exception-Throwing Algorithm

```
//===========================================================
//Note: This sample uses the PerformanceSampling class
//          defined earlier in this chapter. Make sure this
//          class is included in your project.
//===========================================================
//TEST FUNCTION:
//
//Attempt to add 'n1' and 'n2' together and return the result
// in 'n3'
//
// return:
//    TRUE: If the result is positive
//    FALSE: If the result is negative
//===========================================================
bool returnFalseIfLessThanZero_Add2Numbers(int n1, int n2,
                                    out int n3)
{
  n3 = n1 + n2;

  //Is the item less than 0?
  if(n3 < 0)
  {
    return false;
  }
  return true;
}
```

```
//==========================================================
//TEST FUNCTION:
//
//Attempt to add 'n1' and 'n2' together and return the result
// in 'n3'
//
//This function THROWS AN EXCEPTION if 'n3' is less than 0.
//Otherwise TRUE is returned
//==========================================================
bool exceptionIfLessThanZero_Add2Numbers(int n1, int n2,
                   out int n3)
{
  n3 = n1 + n2;

  //Is the item less than 0?
  if(n3 < 0)
  {
    throw new Exception("Less than 0!");
  }
  return true;
}



//==========================================================
//Calls a simple function a large number of times and
//measures the total execution time.
//
//The function called DOES NOT raise an exception
//==========================================================
private void buttonRunNoExceptionCode_Click(object sender,
                                System.EventArgs e)
{
const int TEST_NUMBER = 0;
int numberIterations;
numberIterations =
  System.Convert.ToInt32(textBoxNumberAttempts.Text);

//Show the number of iterations we are going to perform
listBox1.Items.Add("=>" + numberIterations.ToString() +
                      " Iterations");

int count_SumLessThanZero;
int dataOut;


//----------------------------------------------------------
//Start the performance timer
```

```
//------------------------------------------------------------
PerformanceSampling.StartSample(TEST_NUMBER, "No Exception");
//------------------------------------------------------------
//Run the loop that calls the function
//------------------------------------------------------------
count_SumLessThanZero = 0;
bool sumGreaterThanZero;
for(int i = 0; i < numberIterations; i++)
{
  //=======================
  //Call the test function!
  //=======================
  sumGreaterThanZero =
    returnFalseIfLessThanZero_Add2Numbers(-2, -3, out dataOut);

  if(sumGreaterThanZero == false)
  {
    count_SumLessThanZero++;
  }
} //end of loop


//------------------------------------------------------------
//Stop the performance timer
//------------------------------------------------------------
PerformanceSampling.StopSample(TEST_NUMBER);


//------------------------------------------------------------
//Output the results to the user
//------------------------------------------------------------
if(count_SumLessThanZero == numberIterations)
{
  System.Windows.Forms.MessageBox.Show("Test Passed");
  listBox1.Items.Add(
    PerformanceSampling.GetSampleDurationText(TEST_NUMBER));
}
else
{
  System.Windows.Forms.MessageBox.Show(
      "Something is wrong with the test");
}

} //end of function


//============================================================
```

```csharp
//Calls a simple function a large number of times and
//measures the total execution time.
//
//The function called DOES raise an exception
//==========================================================
private void buttonRunExceptionCode_Click(object sender,
                        System.EventArgs e)
{
const int TEST_NUMBER = 1;

//Get the # of iterations
int numberIterations;
numberIterations =
  System.Convert.ToInt32(textBoxNumberAttempts.Text);

//Show the number of iterations we are going to perform
listBox1.Items.Add("=>" + numberIterations.ToString() +
                        " Iterations");

int count_SumLessThanZero;
int dataOut;

//-----------------------------------------------------------
//Start the performance timer
//-----------------------------------------------------------
PerformanceSampling.StartSample(TEST_NUMBER ,
                                "Catch Exception");

//-----------------------------------------------------------
//Run the loop that calls the function
//-----------------------------------------------------------
count_SumLessThanZero = 0;
bool sumGreaterThanZero;
for(int i = 0; i < numberIterations; i++)
{
  try
  {
  //=======================
  //Call the test function!
  //=======================
  sumGreaterThanZero =
    exceptionIfLessThanZero_Add2Numbers(-2, -3, out dataOut);
  }
  catch
```

```
    {
      count_SumLessThanZero++;
    }

  } //end of loop

  //------------------------------------------------------------
  //Stop the performance timer
  //------------------------------------------------------------
  PerformanceSampling.StopSample(TEST_NUMBER);

  //------------------------------------------------------------
  //Output the results to the user
  //------------------------------------------------------------
  if(count_SumLessThanZero == numberIterations)
  {
    System.Windows.Forms.MessageBox.Show("Test Passed");
    listBox1.Items.Add(
      PerformanceSampling.GetSampleDurationText(TEST_NUMBER));
  }
  else
  {
    System.Windows.Forms.MessageBox.Show(
        "Something is wrong with the test");
  }

} //End of function
```

Summary

Good performance along with good user interface design is what gives your mobile application elegance. Having good performance also enables you to expend development capital on extending the functionality of your application. When you have good performance, you have the freedom to move your application in new and exciting directions. If your mobile application has struggling performance, it is similar to having a poor-quality roof over your head; you will spend all your time running from spot to spot patching things until you finally decide the whole roof needs to be replaced; this is not an enviable position to be in. Good performance happens by choice and through disciplined execution, poor performance happens by default. Explicitly choose good performance and make it the top goal of your mobile development efforts.

Interdependencies between different modules will creep in as you write code and develop your application. The more code you write, the more the application solidifies and leaves you with less freedom to make radical changes to the system. Great performance often requires radical redesign, and the best time to fix performance problems is right when they are created. There are two ways to ensure this: (1) Have firm performance goals tied to each of your development milestones and do not declare success and exit a milestone until the stated performance goals have been met. (2) Measure and analyze your performance as you go along.

All performance is subjective. If your application feels slow, unresponsive, or sluggish, it is. Pay careful attention to the details of what makes the subjective experience of using your application good or bad. For this reason, it is good to prototype and test ideas on real people using real devices. People using mobile devices demand feedback from their devices. Without device feedback in response to their requests, users quickly become anxious. Keep minimizing user anxiety at the top of your mind. Do not leave users guessing whether something is happening; let them know promptly that good things are going on inside the device to service their requests.

Finally, be creative. Almost all problems are solvable given enough hard work and creativity. If you have hit what seems to be a fundamental performance limit in your algorithms, perhaps it is time to review what the core purpose of your application is and consider whether there are novel ways of achieving that goal. Great ideas come from solving problems that at first seem intractable. Thinking creatively about performance can be both fun and rewarding.

CHAPTER 8

Performance and Memory Management

"A man should keep his little brain attic stocked with all the furniture that he is likely to use, and the rest he can put away in the lumber room of his library, where he can get it if he wants it."

—Arthur Conan Doyle (Encarta 2004, Quotations)

Defining Your Application Memory Model

As the author of the Sherlock Holmes stories indicates in the preceding quote, there is a need to partition what resources you can fit close at hand and what you need to place into longer-term storage. For mobile devices this means having a good memory model.

The most important thing about a memory model is having one. It is all too easy to allow the memory utilization of applications you are developing to grow incrementally, organically, and in a casual and unplanned way. For desktop applications, this results in confusing code that is often hard to maintain and upgrade and in applications that do not perform as reliably or efficiently as they are capable of. For mobile device applications, a sloppy memory model will result in applications hitting a "performance wall" that makes them perform unacceptably. When you get into this situation, it is usually hard to fix the problems without large-scale redesign. Having a well-defined memory utilization model for your applications avoids this morass and enhances design flexibility.

It is useful to think of application memory utilization on two levels:

1. *Macro "application-level" memory management*—This refers to the application-level data and resources your application maintains while it is running. This data is generally long-lived with the data having scope outside of specific functions. Having a good model for manag-

ing how much of this data is in memory at a given time and when to throw out data and resources your application does not need for immediate use is essential for building mobile applications that perform well. Having too much long-lived state will crowd out memory that could otherwise be used for caching JITed code or as working memory for your functions and will force a managed application's garbage collector to run often and inefficiently.

2. *Micro "algorithm-level" memory allocation*—Functions allocate temporary memory to execute the instructions specified by your algorithms. Whether this is done efficiently or inefficiently is determined by your algorithm implementation strategy. For example, when writing code that will be executed in loops, it is important to write this code in as resource efficient a way as possible so as not to incur unnecessary overhead in execution. Paying close attention to the memory allocation efficiency of the algorithms you create can have a dramatic effect on the overall performance of your application.

Desktop applications that hold a large memory working set (working set = memory in use) will typically push more and more data into a disk-based paging file. This results in rarely used data being pushed out of memory and helps mitigate wasteful macro application-level memory management. The result is relatively linear application performance over a wide range of memory usage. In addition, desktop managed-code systems are capable of sophisticated garbage-collection mechanisms that can partially offset the inefficiencies of wasteful algorithms. This helps performance at a micro level. Desktop applications still suffer from poor memory management, but the effects are dampened by the large computing environment.

Mobile devices have smaller RAM budgets, and they generally do not in order to have huge secondary storage mechanisms for paging in and out memory quickly. Further, to run on the more resource-constrained systems, mobile device runtime garbage collectors are often simpler. This means that sloppy memory management will have a disproportionate effect on mobile device applications both at macro and micro levels. Mobile devices are far less tolerant of poor memory management.

Both desktop and mobile device application development will benefit greatly from well-thought-out memory management, but on mobile devices this kind of planning is imperative. Without well-thought-out memory management, a desktop application will tend to become increasingly more clunky and sluggish. In contrast, a mobile device application without good macro and micro memory management strategies will quickly cross a threshold where it becomes too painful for users to use.

Macro "Application Level" Memory Management

Figure 8.1 shows schematically how an application's performance will degrade with increasing use of memory. As you can see, a desktop application has a much wider range of memory usage in which its performance behavior remains fairly good. Past a memory usage threshold performance starts to degrade markedly as memory starts getting swapped in and out of a page file and the garbage collector makes more frequent efforts to free up and compact memory; still the performance degrades much less rapidly than on a mobile device. In contrast, mobile devices have a smaller range of memory usage in which good performance is maintained. Past a critical threshold a mobile application's performance will degrade drastically as the garbage collector runs almost continually to try to recover ever-decreasing amounts of free memory. The diagram conveys that there is a comfortable range of memory utilization where application will perform well. As long as memory consumption stays below this critical threshold, all is generally well. However, if the critical memory usage

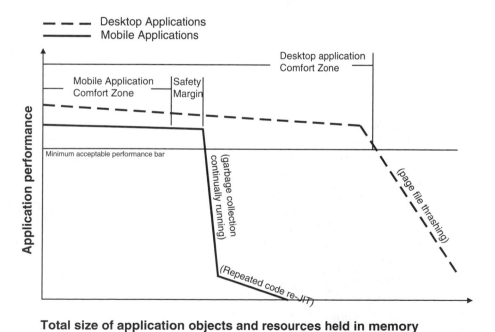

Application performance based on memory consumption

Total size of application objects and resources held in memory

Figure 8.1 Application performance trends with increased memory consumption.

threshold is crossed, the application's performance will deteriorate rapidly as the garbage collector is forced to run ever more frequently and invasively try to recover memory for your application's usage.

I'm Writing Native Code. Is This Still an Issue for Me?

Unlike managed-code runtimes (.NET Compact Framework, Java, and so on), native code development does not use garbage collection. However, this does not mean that you are off the hook if you are writing native code; on the contrary, the design burden is often greater! On desktop computers, native code applications benefit implicitly from the operating system's ability to page memory in and out of RAM and onto a disk-based page file. This results in sluggish but still functioning applications. If your mobile device application memory usage exceeds available memory capacity, your application will just run out of memory and fail. This means that for native code development for mobile devices the onus is on the developer to preemptively avoid these low-memory situations. Additionally, native code algorithms that needlessly allocate and free memory because of inefficient design will have to contend with memory-fragmentation issues that also decrease application performance. Whereas managed-code runtimes can compact memory during garbage collection to decrease memory fragmentation, native code has no such built-in facility. The bottom line is that you still need to design carefully and do your own memory management.

As a mobile application designer, your job is *not* to find a way to utilize all the free memory and push the application right up to but not beyond the threshold where performance will deteriorate rapidly. Instead, you should aim to maintain a safe margin of free memory so that your application can continue to run efficiently over a wide rage of situations. The reason for this is that your application is typically not in full control of all the memory on the device; memory is shared by the operating system and different applications the user may be running. If any application allocates and holds unnecessary memory, all of the applications' performances will suffer. Take no more than you need, and give back what you do not need close at hand.

As with other aspects of mobile device design, coming up with the right memory model to meet your needs is a matter of experimentation and experience. You will have to experiment with different approaches and tune your model based on the resources available on your mobile device and the requirements of your application. Learning to engineer in the kind of flexibility that gives you the capacity for experimentation is important to successful mobile application development.

> ## Won't This Problem Just Go Away with the "Next Generation" of Mobile Devices?
>
> Extra memory costs money, generates heat, consumes power, and takes up additional space. All of these factors will improve over time, but they will not vanish. Even with the predictions of Moore's law continuing to provide us with successive generations of more powerful computing at lower costs there will be a strong incentive to keep mobile devices cheap, small, and running a long time on a single battery charge.
>
> Most mobile devices today already have an ample amount of memory to perform a wide variety of tasks, but this memory needs to be used with prudence. All too often, poor desktop design habits are brought to devices. This results in undisciplined memory allocation in algorithms and poor memory management that keeps resources in memory when they are no longer useful.
>
> Earlier in this book, an analogy was made comparing today's desktop computers to large houses in the country and mobile devices to smart-looking but small apartments in the city. This mental image of "finite size" is an important one to keep in mind. You can accomplish almost everything you want on a mobile device, but you cannot do it all at once or keep everything in memory at the same time. You need a well-classified set of rules about how to bring things into your apartment and when to throw things out.
>
> Future mobile devices will be more powerful and have more memory, but more will also be asked of them. Good memory management strategies will still be essential for building great applications for these devices.

It is wasteful to keep things you do not need in memory because these things take up room that could better be used by the active parts of your application. On the other hand, throwing everything out the moment you do not need it immediately is equally foolish.

A metaphor: If you live in a small apartment and find you need a stapler to staple your papers together, you go to the store and buy a stapler. This takes time and resources—not a lot, but enough. If you throw the stapler out as soon as you do not immediately need it, you have slightly more space in your apartment (after you've taken out the garbage containing the discarded stapler) but no stapler. The next time you need to staple things together, you need to take the time and expense of going back to the store and buying another stapler. To do this would be foolish; if there is a reasonable chance you will need a stapler in the upcoming year or two, you keep it around. However, if you can guarantee that you will never need a stapler again (perhaps you have decided to use paper clips from now on), you should throw it out no matter how little room it takes up. Who needs the clutter of useless objects?

There is a reasonable balance that needs to be found. Because a stapler is a pretty useful thing, not too big, and used fairly often, you keep it around. What about a large steam-cleaning machine for carpets? You could go out and buy one, spend a lot of resources to get it, and then keep it around; if you live in small place and do not steam clean your carpets too often, however, this would not be the wisest solution. Instead you go and rent one, do your work, and then get rid of it. Some things you plan to keep and some things you get rid of when you are done with them.

The tricky part comes when objects fall somewhere in between. These objects are not individually too big or expensive, each takes up only a moderate amount of space, and they are potentially useful at some point in the future. These are like clothes you almost never wear. These are items that you should throw out but keep around just in case you change your mind. Keeping a few of them around is no problem, but so many things fall into this category that you can easily fill your whole apartment with moderately useful objects and leave no room for other things you use more often. You can end up with an apartment full of clothes you rarely wear and boxes of stuff you almost never use. This is okay if you have a giant house with lots of storage, but an absolute mess when you are living in an apartment. Desktop = big house. Mobile device = apartment.

Clearly there are rules about what should be kept around and what should be thrown out. Thankfully these rules are generally based on common sense and just need to be applied systematically. That is what having an explicit application memory model is about: applying common sense in a disciplined way to keep your mobile application running efficiently.

As with any kind of engineering problem, a fundamental tension needs to be solved by a balanced solution. The reluctance to dispose of an object you may use again at some time in the future must be balanced with the benefits of having working room for your application to perform well in.

What kind of information belongs in your macro memory model? It is helpful to sort the application data and resources you work with into two top-level buckets: (1) the objects and resources that your application needs to efficiently run, and (2) the actual user information that your application is working with.

1. *Necessary application overhead*—This includes the resources your application needs to keep the user interface and other aspects of your application going. Examples are open connections to databases, open files, threads, graphics, and user interface objects such as

brushes, pens, controls on forms, and the forms themselves. These are all incidental to the data that the user is actually working with but are vital to the application actually interacting with the user or with external sources of information.

2. *User data*—This is actual data the user is interested in working with. It is the portion of that data that is being held in memory as opposed to being stored in some database or file on the device or externally. For example, if a mobile application is intended to let the user navigate the streets of London, the user data is the information about the streets of the city that is presently loaded into memory. If the application tracks inventory, the user data is the loaded inventory data. If the application is a chess game, the user data is the in-memory representation of the state of the chessboard.

Here again the concept of state machines will be handy. Consider having two top-level state machines for your application, one to manage each kind of data listed above. It is useful to separate of your application's overhead data from the user's data and to have a different machine that manages each.

Is a Bitmap "User" Data or "Application Overhead" Data?

Because bitmap data represents images loaded into memory and ready for use in an application's graphics, it can take up a significant amount of space. Bitmap data for large images can be costly to keep in memory so managing when it comes into memory and when it is discarded is worth giving some thought to.

Some kinds of bitmaps are user data. For example, if your application is a real estate application that loads photos of houses into memory, each house photo is unique and corresponds to the user data associated with a given property. Just like the street location of a house or the price of a house, it is data that is loaded per data item. The same would go for medical images that belong to patient records; each image is associated with user data.

Some kinds of bitmaps are "application overhead." Bitmaps used to make fancy-looking buttons, cached background images, and the predrawn pieces of a graphical chart are all application overhead because they are not specifically associated with the data the user is working with. A generic bitmap of a human body that can be used by a medical application to indicate locations of injuries would fall into the same camp. These are common resources not specific to any user data. They are generic resources that depend on the mode the application is in. Some forms may use these bitmaps and others may not; the image data can be loaded or discarded based on the mode of the application and is not dependent on the set of data the user is working with.

Some kinds of bitmaps could fall into either camp. If you have a real estate application that can show three kinds of floor-plan bitmaps based on the user's loaded data or if your medial application has six different body-type images corresponding to different patients' sex, size, and weight, these could be considered either application overhead or user data. Similarly, if your game has bitmaps for all the characters on the screen but these bitmaps are changed to look different as the user advances to different levels, the bitmaps represent cases where a credible argument can be made for them either being user data or application overhead. In these cases, you will have to choose to place the resources in the memory model that makes the most sense for your application. Put these kinds of images into whichever memory management bucket best meets your needs.

Managing an Application's "Overhead" Data

As noted previously, "application overhead" is data that the user does not directly interact with and so it is not "user data." It represents the resources needed for the application to function effectively so users can see and manipulate their data. Managing the objects and resources that your application needs to run effectively can usually be done by means of a simple state machine. As your application goes through different states, different resources are useful to have around. When entering a new state, needed resources can be created and stored in application memory. Similarly, when exiting an application state, resources not immediately needed in the next state can be discarded and the space they use can be returned to the free memory pool. Often these states correspond to user forms that are currently displayed or tabs on a form that the user flips through and brings to the foreground. When designing your application's state model, it is often useful to identify discrete user interface modes and use them as the basis for building your state model.

Let's take a look at a simple database-oriented application. This application stores and works with medical data for patients. The data is stored in a database and is loaded on a per-patient basis with password security required to load or save a patient's data. This kind of an application could be broken up into five different discrete states where the user is presented with different user interfaces for accomplishing tasks. These states are as follows:

1. *Loading data from database*—This screen enables the device's user to authenticate access to the database and load a specific patient's data. Application overhead required includes the following:
   - Database connections
   - A form that shows the database logon user interface

2. *Saving data to database*—This screen enables the user to authenticate access to the database and save a specific patient's data. Application overhead required includes the following:
   - Database connections
   - A form that shows the database logon user interface to the user
3. *Main screen of application*—This screen displays a patient's case history that has been loaded from the database and enables the device's user to view and navigate this data. Application overhead required includes the following:
   - The form for the main screen
   - Common bitmaps that are being used in the user interface
4. *Details screen for working with and editing specific data*—This screen is displayed when the user needs to edit the details of some of the patient's data or enter new data. Application overhead required includes the following:
   - The form for editing a loaded record
   - Custom controls on the form that allow for specific data-entry needs (for example, a custom control with validating logic for entering blood pressure data or a custom control for editing medication dosage information)
- *Charting screen for displaying sets of data points*—This screen is for displaying graphical information relating to some aspect of the patient's medical history. For example, charts could be drawn that show blood pressure over time or blood white cell counts to monitor infections. Application overhead required includes the following:
   - Graphics pens and brushes used for drawing chart data
   - Font objects used for drawing labels on a chart
   - Cached background bitmaps
   - An offscreen bitmap for drawing the graph image onto before copying it onto the screen

Some of these states share common resources. For example, a black graphics pen resource for drawing lines or an appropriately sized font or bitmap image may be useful in several of the states above. The need for a database connection is shared by two of the states listed above. Also some objects may not be required by each of the states but may be very time-consuming to create; you may want to test the performance behavior of caching these kinds of objects.

You can easily create a state machine to manage these kinds of resources. All that needs to be done when entering a new state is to determine which objects it is necessary to create if they are not already in existence and which objects should be released if they have been allocated in a previous state. Having all of this logic managed by a single state machine rather than distributed throughout your application makes this information very easy to maintain. A state machine also makes it easy to experiment with different optimizations and tune your application's performance.

Using IDisposable and Freeing Expensive Nonmanaged Resources in the .NET Framework

When an object is no longer needed, your application code should discard it by removing any variable references that point to the object. When the garbage collector is next run (usually based on the need to allocate memory for the application), the memory is reclaimed when the runtime discovers that no live references exist to the object. This generally works well but means that the cleanup of objects can be deferred indefinitely if no pressing need causes a garbage collection to occur. Because we do not know when a given object is going to be garbage collected, the memory lifetime of the object is said to be "nondeterministic." Nondeterministic cleanup is a common challenge for garbage-collected memory management systems. It is generally not a good idea to write application logic that runs when the object's finalizer (destructor) is run because your application does not have explicit control on when the code will be run.

Problems can arise when the discarded managed object also represents an "expensive unmanaged resource," such as a database connection, a file handle, or a graphics resource of some sort. Until the object gets cleaned up by the garbage collection, the unmanaged resource it represents is still held. This can be costly to system performance both for the client device as well as for any server resources the client may be holding.

To address this problem, the .NET Framework has a design pattern that allows code to explicitly release the underlying resource held by an object. Objects that represent expensive resources all have a `Dispose()` method. This method is defined in the IDisposable interface; classes that support deterministic reclamation of their resources implement this interface and thus have the `Dispose()` method as part of their class.

If an object has a `Dispose()` method, you should always call it when your application has finished its use of the object. `Dispose()` should be called when you are about to remove any variable references to it and leave it for the garbage collector to clean up. This will guarantee that the expensive resource that the object represents is immediately released. As with other aspects of memory management, it is a good idea to do this in desktop applications but vital that it be done in mobile device applications because there are fewer resources (such as operating system handles) to go around!

Similarly, if you are designing a class that represents an expensive resource, you should implement the IDisposable interface to allow code that uses the class to deterministically release the resources the class holds. Review the .NET Framework documentation on `IDisposable.Dispose()` for details on how to implement this properly.

Note: C# has added a special keyword to its language that can aid in calling `.Dispose()` when the scope of a resource's usage is bounded within a block of code in a function. Instead of needing to explicitly call `.Dispose()`, the variable can be declared with the `using` keyword. For example:

```
using(System.Drawing.Graphics myGfx = System.Drawing.Graphics.
FromImage(myImage))
{
  //Do work with myGfx...
} //myGfx.Dispose() is automatically called here...
```

When declared this way, `Dispose()` is automatically called when the variable goes out of scope. The `using` keyword can be a nice convenience when the lifetime of a resource is well defined within a block of code.

Managing the Amount of User Data in Memory

User data represents the actual data the application's user is viewing or manipulating. Managing the amount and lifetime of user data kept in memory can be more complex than managing application overhead data because the kinds of data that can be held in memory can vary based on the structure and purpose of your application. The user data held by a chess game is different in structure from user data that holds the medical history of a patient. A chess board's state can be held in a predetermined size array of integer values. A patient's medical history may have no defined size boundary; it may consist of sets of measurements, text notes, images, links to additional data, and almost a limitless amount of related information.

Managing the state of a chessboard is usually a matter of deciding when to load the array of data into memory, when to save it, and when to discard the data. This can be handled by a fairly simple state machine designed for the task.

Managing the memory used to hold the complex medical records of patients can be considerably more complex. These records can be of arbitrary size, and this probably means you will need to come up with a windowing model for this data where the device's user is given a partial view onto the full set of data but not all of the data needs to be kept in memory at one time. The mobile device's user is given the illusion that all the data is kept in memory when in actuality data is swapped in and out as needed. This can be a simple machine, but it can also be a very sophisticated machine depending on the kinds of data managed and the resources available to manage that data.

For management of potentially complex user data, a good approach is to build a well-encapsulated class that manages the state that is kept in memory at any given time. This class is in charge of loading new data and discarding old data when it is no longer needed. It manages the outside world's access to the user data and creates the illusion of infinite memory capacity. Other application code accessing the data from outside the encapsulation class should not need to have any knowledge of the internal state of this user data management class. Having a specific class tasked managing all of the user's data allows you a great deal of design flexibility. Some benefits of this approach are as follows:

- *The ability to automatically manage the amount of loaded data*—If you are finding that your application is thrashing under memory pressure, you can narrow the size of the window of data that is kept in memory at any time without needing to redesign your whole application. Because nothing outside of the class is aware of what is being cached in memory and what needs to be reloaded, you have more design flexibility to tune this algorithm.
- *The ability to have different implementations for different device classes*—If you are targeting multiple classes of devices, you can tune for each device's memory and storage limitations. A mobile phone and a PDA may have different memory characteristics or different abilities to load data on demand. These device differences may require you to approach data caching differently. Having this logic in one well-defined place enables you to do this much more easily.

Using a Load-on-Demand Model

There are two basic strategies for allocating objects:

1. *When entering a new application state, create all the objects that may be needed by that state.* This has the virtue of simplicity. When your application enters a state, simply call a function that ensures all of the needed objects are available and in a ready-to-use state. If you are sure that the all objects you create will be needed by the application in the immediate future, this is a fine strategy. The problem with this strategy is that as your application evolves and your design changes it is easy to end up with a lot of excess baggage. Old objects

that are not actually needed but are created and loaded anyway are a waste of valuable resources. Be careful when you decide to batch-create a set of objects because your application may evolve to the point where you are creating unused overhead and you will pay a performance tax for this.

2. *Defer the creation of any object until a proven need for it arises.* This model is a slightly more complex to design but ends up being more efficient in many cases because you only create objects when they are needed. This model is often deferred to as a using a "class factory," "resource dispenser," or "lazy loading."

The code sample in Listing 8.1 shows two ways of doing deferred creation and caching of globally used graphical resources. There are two modes of object creation:

1. *Batch creation of grouped resources*—The following code creates an array list that holds four bitmaps. These bitmaps represent frames of an animated image; as such they are all loaded together and placed into an indexed array that can be easily accessed. Program code needing access to this collection of images would call `GraphicsGlobals.PlayerBitmapsCollection();`. If the array of bitmaps is already loaded into memory, the function returns the cached object without delay. Otherwise, the individual bitmap resources are loaded into the array list and returned. When the application enters a state where these in-memory bitmaps are not needed, the application's code can call `GraphicsGlobals.g_PlayerBitmapsCollection_CleanUp();` to release the bitmap resources and the array list. The system resources for the bitmaps will be freed immediately and the managed memory for these objects will be reclaimed as necessary during garbage collection.

2. *Individual creation of drawing resources*—For resources whose usages are not lumped together like the bitmap images above, it is often useful to create a caching access function to control access to the resource. The first time the function to request a resource is called (for example, `GraphicsGlobals.g_GetBlackPen();`), the function creates the instance of the resource. Subsequent calls return the cached instance. For commonly used resources, this is often much more efficient than continually creating and destroying instances of the resource each time it is needed by some separate piece of code. In the following code, I have made the assumption that all of these

resources should be released at the same time and written a function (GraphicsGlobals.g_CleanUpDrawingResources();) that frees any of the cached resources that are created. When the application enters a state where these resources are not needed, this function should be called.

Some Common Sense About Caching

If you are going to be using the same resource repeatedly inside a function, it is not efficient to call the caching access function (or property) each time you need the resource. In these cases, it is better to call the function once and store it in a local variable for the duration of its required use. You get the benefit of using a globally cached resource rather than needing to create and destroy the resource in your function as well the efficiency of not needing to make unnecessary function calls inside your algorithm. Common sense should dictate when this is a good approach.

Listing 8.1 Ways of Deferred Loading, Caching, and Releasing Graphics Resources

```
using system;

public class GraphicsGlobals
{
private static   System.Drawing.Bitmap   s_Player_Bitmap1;
private static   System.Drawing.Bitmap   s_Player_Bitmap2;
private static   System.Drawing.Bitmap   s_Player_Bitmap3;
private static   System.Drawing.Bitmap   s_Player_Bitmap4;
private static   System.Collections.ArrayList s_colPlayerBitmaps;

  //-------------------------------------------------
  //Releases all the resources
  //-------------------------------------------------
  public static void g_PlayerBitmapsCollection_CleanUp()
  {
    //If we don't have any bitmaps loaded, there is nothing to clean up
    if(s_colPlayerBitmaps == null) { return;}

    //Tell each of these objects to free up
    //whatever nonmanaged resources they are
    //holding.
    s_Player_Bitmap1.Dispose();   s_Player_Bitmap2.Dispose();
    s_Player_Bitmap3.Dispose();   s_Player_Bitmap4.Dispose();
```

```
    //Clear each of these variables, so they do not keep
    //the objects in memory
    s_Player_Bitmap1 = null;  s_Player_Bitmap2 = null;
    s_Player_Bitmap3 = null;  s_Player_Bitmap4 = null;

    //Get rid of the array list
    s_colPlayerBitmaps = null;
}

//Function: Returns Collection of Bitmaps
public static System.Collections.ArrayList
  g_PlayerBitmapsCollection()
{
  //----------------------------------------------------
  //If we have already loaded these, just return them
  //----------------------------------------------------
  if(s_colPlayerBitmaps != null) {return s_colPlayerBitmaps;}

  //Load the bitmaps as resources from our executable binary
  System.Reflection.Assembly thisAssembly =
    System.Reflection.Assembly.GetExecutingAssembly();

  System.Reflection.AssemblyName thisAssemblyName =
    thisAssembly.GetName();

  string assemblyName = thisAssemblyName.Name;

  //Load the bitmaps
  s_Player_Bitmap1 = new System.Drawing.Bitmap(
    thisAssembly.GetManifestResourceStream(assemblyName
    + ".Hank_RightRun1.bmp"));

  s_Player_Bitmap2 = new System.Drawing.Bitmap(
    thisAssembly.GetManifestResourceStream(assemblyName +
    ".Hank_RightRun2.bmp"));

  s_Player_Bitmap3 = new System.Drawing.Bitmap(
    thisAssembly.GetManifestResourceStream(assemblyName +
    ".Hank_LeftRun1.bmp"));

  s_Player_Bitmap4 = new System.Drawing.Bitmap(
    thisAssembly.GetManifestResourceStream(assemblyName +
    ".Hank_LeftRun2.bmp"));
```

```
  //Add them to the collection
  s_colPlayerBitmaps = new System.Collections.ArrayList();
  s_colPlayerBitmaps.Add(s_Player_Bitmap1);
  s_colPlayerBitmaps.Add(s_Player_Bitmap2);

  s_colPlayerBitmaps.Add(s_Player_Bitmap3);
  s_colPlayerBitmaps.Add(s_Player_Bitmap4);

  //Return the collection
  return s_colPlayerBitmaps;
}

private static System.Drawing.Pen s_blackPen;
private static System.Drawing.Pen s_whitePen;
private static System.Drawing.Imaging.ImageAttributes
  s_ImageAttribute;

private static System.Drawing.Font s_boldFont;

//---------------------------------------
//Called to release any drawing resources we
//may have cached
//---------------------------------------
private static void g_CleanUpDrawingResources()
{
  //Clean up the black pen, if we've got one
  if(s_blackPen != null)
  {s_blackPen.Dispose(); s_blackPen = null;}

  //Clean up the white pen, if we've got one
  if(s_whitePen != null)
  {s_whitePen.Dispose(); s_whitePen = null;}

  //Clean up the ImageAttribute, if we've got one
  //Note: This type does not have a Dispose() method
  //because all of its data is managed-data
  if(s_ImageAttribute != null)
  {s_ImageAttribute = null;}

  //Clean up the bold font, if we've got one
  if(s_boldFont != null)
  {s_boldFont.Dispose(); s_boldFont = null;}
}
```

```
//-------------------------------------
//This function allows us access to the
//cached black pen
//-------------------------------------
private static System.Drawing.Pen g_GetBlackPen()
{
  //If the pen does not exist yet, create it
  if(s_blackPen == null)
  {
    s_blackPen = new System.Drawing.Pen(
      System.Drawing.Color.Black);
  }

  //Return the black pen
  return s_blackPen;
}


//-------------------------------------
//This function allows us access to the
//cached white pen
//-------------------------------------
private static System.Drawing.Pen g_GetWhitePen()
{
  //If the pen does not exist yet, create it
  if(s_whitePen == null)
  {s_whitePen  = new System.Drawing.Pen(
     System.Drawing.Color.White);}

  //Return the white pen
  return s_whitePen;
}


//-------------------------------------
//This function allows us access to the
//cached bold font
//-------------------------------------
private static System.Drawing.Font g_GetBoldFont()
{
  //If the pen does not exist yet, create it
  if(s_boldFont == null)
  {
    s_boldFont  = new System.Drawing.Font(
      System.Drawing.FontFamily.GenericSerif,
      10, System.Drawing.FontStyle.Bold);
  }
```

```
      //Return the bold font
      return s_boldFont;
  }


  //------------------------------------------------
  //This function allows us access to the
  //cached imageAttributes we use for bitmaps
  //with transparency
  //------------------------------------------------
  private static System.Drawing.Imaging.ImageAttributes
    g_GetTransparencyImageAttribute()
  {
    //If it does not exist, create it
    if(s_ImageAttribute == null)
    {
      //Create an image attribute
      s_ImageAttribute =
        new System.Drawing.Imaging.ImageAttributes();

      s_ImageAttribute.SetColorKey(System.Drawing.Color.White,
        System.Drawing.Color.White);
    }


    //Return it
    return s_ImageAttribute;
  }
} //End class
```

Micro "Algorithm-Level" Memory Management

Modern programming languages, class libraries and managed runtimes greatly enhance the productivity of writing code. However by abstracting the programmer from the need to think about the low-level memory allocations that their algorithms are making they also make it easy to write inefficient code. There are two kinds of inefficiencies that can occur when writing algorithms:

1. *Unnecessary computation inefficiencies*—These kinds of inefficiencies occur when the algorithm you have designed performs more calculations or loop iterations to produce a result that could have been

achieved using a more efficient algorithm. The classic example is sorting arrays of data. Sometimes you may have a choice between sorting algorithms that may in special cases be "Order N" (meaning they take linearly more time to sort more items), "Order N∗Log(N)" (meaning they do not scale linearly with more items but are still better than exponential) and algorithms that are "Order N^2" (meaning they take exponentially more time to sort more items). Infinitely many other orders of calculation exist (for example, "N^3"). The right algorithm to choose depends on the amount of data you are working with, the memory you have available, and other factors such as the state of the data you are working with. Specific strategies such as preprocessing data before sending it down to a device, or keeping the data in a specific in-memory relational format, may be able to increase algorithmic performance significantly. A great deal of classical computer science literature exists describing efficient algorithm design and measurement, and this book does not attempt to cover this topic. Suffice it to say that the more data you need to process, the more important your choice of computational algorithm is. When it is important, carefully consider your algorithm design and look at the research out there on the topic. Often many people have treaded the same ground already and you can leverage their learning.

2. *Unnecessary memory-allocation inefficiencies*—After you have chosen an algorithmic strategy, your code's performance will be drastically affected by how efficiently you implement that algorithm. More than anything, this involves trying to avoid unnecessary memory allocations and particularly allocations that take place inside loops. This section of the book focuses on this topic.

   You should have as a goal "zero memory allocations" inside loops you write. There are cases where this may be unavoidable, such as when building a tree of objects that requires the allocation of new nodes to place onto the tree. In many other cases, there are often great efficiencies that can be achieved by carefully examining the need for each object allocation and looking for alternatives. What is generally avoidable is the allocation and discarding of objects inside algorithmic loops.

Write Environmental Algorithms: Don't Litter!

Just like in the physical world, litter is garbage that is needlessly generated and discarded. Litter is usually the product of carelessness and sloppiness. It is the creating of a long-term problem based on short-term convenience.

Creating unnecessary garbage in your algorithms in the form of temporary objects that are not really necessary slows your application down in two ways:

1. *Directly*—Every time you create an object memory needs to be allocated and initialized before it can be used. This is a direct and up-front cost that your algorithm will pay.
2. *Indirectly*—After the object is discarded, it becomes garbage. This garbage piles up in your application until there is so much of it that it must be cleaned up before more memory can be allocated for new objects. This is, of course, known as garbage collection. This garbage collection takes time, and if there is enough garbage piled up it will cause a noticeable stall in your application's operation. The more you litter, the quicker the garbage piles up and the more often time needs to be spent cleaning it up!

In all of your programming, you should seek to create as little litter as possible. There is nothing wrong with instantiating an object if it is going to serve some indispensable need for you; if the object is short-lived and the task can be easily accomplished without the object, however, you are just creating litter. Don't be a litterbug.

"Value Types" and the .NET Framework

For local variables inside functions, it is often efficient to use value types rather than objects when you want to encapsulate some simple data. A value type is just a convenient way to group together a bunch of related data rather than passing it around as individual variables.

Value types are more lightweight than objects but can be "boxed" inside objects and passed around like them when needed. Value types can be useful and can aid performance (versus using objects), but because they look, and in many ways act like objects and can get "boxed" inside shell objects, be careful when you use them to make sure you are not accidentally introducing overhead and creating unneeded garbage. A good rule of thumb is to test your algorithms using both individual variables (for example, basic types such as int, string, double) and value types to compare the performance to make sure it is similar.

Read the .NET Framework reference information for "value types" and for the C# "struct" for more information.

An example of declaring a value type and declaring a class:

```
//NOTE: IN VB.NET this would be a 'type' not a 'struct'
//This is a value type
struct  MyRect_Type
{
  public int x;
  public int y;
}

   //This is a class
class  MyRect_Class
{
  public int x;
  public int y;
}

//Some sample code
class  TestClass
   {
   public void foo()
   {
   //Must be allocated as an object
   MyRect_Class myRectClass = new MyRect_Class();
   myRectClass.x = 1;
   myRectClass.y = 2;
   //Allocates a new object
   myRectClass = new MyRect_Class();

   //Can be declared like a scalar type
   MyRect_Type myRectType;
   myRectType.x = 1;
   myRectType.y = 2;
   //Clears the values of the type but does not allocate an object!
   myRectType = new MyRect_Type();
   }
}
```

Write Environmental Algorithms: Reduce, Reuse, and Recycle

Following is an example showing several different implementations of the same basic algorithm. The purpose of the algorithm is to process an array of strings. Each string in the array consists of three parts separated by an underscore character (for example, big_shaggy_dog). The algorithm is designed to look at each item in the array and find out if its center part is blue (for example, my_blue_car). If the center segment is blue, it will be replaced with orange (for example, my_blue_car becomes my_orange_car).

Each of these algorithms also uses a helper class to make it easy to dissect the string and get to the data in each of the three segments. The first algorithm (Listing 8.3, Listing 8.4) shows a reasonable first approach, and the next two algorithms (Listing 8.5, Listing 8.6 and Listing 8.7, Listing 8.8) show optimizations made to improve on the original tactic. The optimizations are designed to directly improve the performance of the algorithm as well as to decrease the amount of litter each algorithm produces.

Listing 8.2 Common Code Used in All Test Cases Below

```
//Number of times we want to repeat the test
const int LOOP_SIZE = 8000;
//-----------------------------------------------------
//This function resets the contents of our test
//array, so we can run the test algorithm
//over and over
//-----------------------------------------------------
private void ResetTestArray(ref string [] testArray)
{
  if (testArray == null)
  {
    testArray  = new string[6];
  }

  testArray[0] = "big_blue_duck";
  testArray[1] = "small_yellow_horse";
  testArray[2] = "wide_blue_cow";
  testArray[3] = "tall_green_zepplin";
  testArray[4] = "short_blue_train";
  testArray[5] = "short_purple_dinosaur";
}
```

Listing 8.3 A Test Case Showing Wasteful Allocations (A Typical First Implementation of a Function)

Note: This sample uses the PerformanceSampling class defined earlier in this book.

```
private void button2_Click(object sender, System.EventArgs e)
{
  //Run the garbage collector so we know we're starting
  //from a clean slate for our test.
  //ONLY CALL DURING TESTING! Calling the GC manually will slow
  //down overall application throughput!
  System.GC.Collect();
  string [] testArray = null;


  //-------------------------------------------------
  //Go through the items in the array and
  //look for ones where the middle word is
  //'blue'. Replace the 'blue' with 'orange'
  //-------------------------------------------------

  //Start the stopwatch for our test!
  PerformanceSampling.StartSample(0, "WastefulWorkerClass");
  WastefulWorkerClass workerClass1;

  int outerLoop;
  for (outerLoop = 0; outerLoop < LOOP_SIZE; outerLoop++)
  {
    //Set up the data in the array we want to do our test on
    ResetTestArray(ref testArray);

    int topIndex = testArray.Length - 1;
    for(int idx = 0; idx <= topIndex; idx++)
    {
      //-----------------------------------
      //Create an instance of a helper class
      //that dissects our string into three pieces
      //
      //This is wasteful!
      //-----------------------------------
      workerClass1 = new WastefulWorkerClass(testArray[idx]);

      //If the middle word is "blue", make it "orange"
      if(workerClass1.MiddleSegment == "blue")
      {
```

```
        //Replace the middle item
        workerClass1.MiddleSegment = "orange";
        //Replace the word
        testArray[idx] = workerClass1.getWholeString();
      }

  } //end inner for
}//end outer for
//Get the time we completed our test
PerformanceSampling.StopSample(0);
System.Windows.Forms.MessageBox.Show(
   PerformanceSampling.GetSampleDurationText(0));
}
```

Listing 8.4 The Worker Class for Our First Test Case

```
using System;

public class WastefulWorkerClass
{
  private string m_beginning_segment;
  public string BeginSegment
  {
    get { return m_beginning_segment;}
    set { m_beginning_segment = value;}
  }


  private string m_middle_segment;
  public string MiddleSegment
  {
    get{return m_middle_segment;}
    set{m_middle_segment = value;}
  }

  private string m_end_segment;
  public string EndSegment
  {
    get{return m_end_segment;}
    set{m_end_segment = value;}
  }

  public WastefulWorkerClass(string in_word)
```

```
{
  int index_segment1;

  //Look for a "_" in the string
  index_segment1 = in_word.IndexOf("_",0);

  //If there is no "_", the first segment is the whole thing
  if(index_segment1 == -1)
  {
    m_beginning_segment = in_word;
    m_middle_segment = "";
    m_end_segment = "";
    return;
  }

    //If there is a "_", split it
  else
  {
    //If the "_" is the first char, the first segment is ""
    if(index_segment1 == 0)
    {
      m_beginning_segment = "";
    }
    else
    {
      //The first segment
      m_beginning_segment  = in_word.Substring(0, index_segment1);
    }

    //Find the 2nd "_"
    int index_segment2;
    index_segment2 = in_word.IndexOf("_", index_segment1 + 1);

    //2nd "_" does not exist
    if(index_segment2 == -1)
    {
      m_middle_segment = "";
      m_end_segment = in_word.Substring(index_segment1 + 1);
      return;
    }

    //Set the end segment
    m_middle_segment = in_word.Substring(index_segment1 + 1,
                        index_segment2 - index_segment1 -1);
```

```
        m_end_segment = in_word.Substring(index_segment2 + 1);


    }
}

//Returns the whole 3 segments joined by "-"s
public string getWholeString()
{

    return m_beginning_segment + "_" + m_middle_segment + "_" +
        m_end_segment;

}

} //end class
```

Reuse Allocated Objects Whenever Possible

Creating an instance of a helper class in each iteration of the processing loop is wasteful. Even though the object is relatively small because it has few data members, it still has overhead. In addition, each time a new object instance is created, an old object instance is discarded. This creates garbage that will have to be collected later. We can easily remove this wasteful object allocation.

Listing 8.5 A Test Case Showing Slightly Reduced Object Allocations (A Typical Refinement of a First Function Implementation)

This sample uses the PerformanceSampling class defined earlier in this book.

```
private void button3_Click(object sender, System.EventArgs e)
{
    //Run the garbage collector so we start from a "clean"
    //state for our test
    //ONLY CALL DURING TESTING! Calling the GC manually will slow
    //down overall application throughput!
    System.GC.Collect();

    string [] testArray = null;

    //-------------------------------------------
    //Go through the items in the array and
    //look for ones where the middle word is
    //'blue'. Replace the 'blue' with 'orange'
```

```
//----------------------------------------------

//Start the stopwatch!
PerformanceSampling.StartSample(1, "LessWasteful");

//------------------------------------------------
//LESS WASTEFUL: Allocate the object before we get in the
//loop
//------------------------------------------------
LessWastefulWorkerClass workerClass1;
workerClass1 = new LessWastefulWorkerClass();

int outerLoop;
for (outerLoop = 0; outerLoop < LOOP_SIZE; outerLoop++)
{
  //Set up the data in the array we want to do our test on
  ResetTestArray(ref testArray);
  int topIndex = testArray.Length - 1;

  for(int idx = 0; idx <= topIndex; idx++)
  {
    //----------------------------------------------------
    //Instead of reallocating the object, let's just reuse
    //it
    //----------------------------------------------------
    //workerClass1 = new WastefulWorkerClass(
    //                    testArray[topIndex]);
    workerClass1.ReuseClass(testArray[idx]);

    //If the middle word is "blue", make it "orange"
    if(workerClass1.MiddleSegment == "blue")
    {
      //Replace the middle item
      workerClass1.MiddleSegment = "orange";
      //Replace the word
      testArray[idx ] = workerClass1.getWholeString();
    }
  }
}

//Stop the stopwatch!
PerformanceSampling.StopSample(1);
System.Windows.Forms.MessageBox.Show(
  PerformanceSampling.GetSampleDurationText(1));
}
```

Listing 8.6 The Worker Class for Our Second Test Case

```csharp
using System;

public class LessWastefulWorkerClass
{
  private string m_beginning_segment;
  public string BeginSegment
  {
    get {return m_beginning_segment;}
    set {m_beginning_segment = value;}
  }


  private string m_middle_segment;
  public string MiddleSegment
  {
    get { return m_middle_segment;}
    set { m_middle_segment = value;}
  }

  private string m_end_segment;
  public string EndSegment
  {
    get {return m_end_segment;}
    set {m_end_segment = value;}
  }

  public void ReuseClass(string in_word)
  {
    //-----------------------------------------
    //To reuse the class, clear all the internal state
    //-----------------------------------------
    m_beginning_segment  = "";
    m_middle_segment  = "";
    m_end_segment  = "";

    int index_segment1;

    //Look for a "_" in the string
    index_segment1 = in_word.IndexOf("_",0);

    //If there is no "_", the first segment is the whole thing
    if(index_segment1 == -1)
```

```
    {
      m_beginning_segment = in_word;
      return;
    }

      //If there is a "_", split it
    else
    {
      if(index_segment1 == 0)
      {
      }
      else
      {
        m_beginning_segment  = in_word.Substring(0,
                                  index_segment1);
      }

      int index_segment2;
      index_segment2 = in_word.IndexOf("_", index_segment1 + 1);

      if(index_segment2 == -1)
      {
        m_end_segment = in_word.Substring(index_segment1 + 1);
        return;
      }

      //Set the end segment
      m_middle_segment = in_word.Substring(index_segment1 + 1,
                           index_segment2 - index_segment1 -1);
      m_end_segment = in_word.Substring(index_segment2 + 1);

    }
  }

  public string getWholeString()
  {
    return m_beginning_segment + "_" + m_middle_segment + "_" +
                                  m_end_segment;
  }
}
```

> ### *There Is Room for Further Improvements in the Preceding Code*
>
> The approach above still demonstrates significant waste because we are continually allocating and discarding strings. If we were to code for maximum performance, we would look to eliminate the creation of any unnecessary string objects.

Reduce Unnecessary Object Allocations

Notice that in the algorithm above, we are often computing a lot of values that we do not need. Specifically, we are generating at least three new strings in each iteration of the loop, one for the first segment of the original sting, one for the middle segment, and one for the end segment. For example, the string big_blue_boat is dissected into three different strings: big, blue, boat. These strings take time to create and will need to be cleaned up later as well.

The algorithm checks only the middle segment of a string to see whether it matches a specific value (blue). As long as the value does not match, no other processing is needed. This means that most of the time we are wastefully allocating strings for the beginning and end segments even though these are only used by the algorithm if it puts the whole string back together again from the pieces. What if instead of creating new strings out of pieces of the old string in each iteration of the loop we just store the character index values that tell us where the underscores (_) are in the string? We can store this data in integer values, which should be much less expensive than allocating new strings. If we do this, we can use the original string and the index values to do a string comparison starting at the first underscore and going to the second underscore (for example, _blue_ in the example above). Only in the case where we find a match will we need to do any additional string creation to replace the middle segment. In most cases, we will be much better off and will not need to do any object or string allocation. Only in the case where we find a match in the middle segment will we need to do additional string operations, and in any case we will only need to do as many as we were going to do previously anyway. In no case should we be worse off.

Listing 8.7 A Test Case Showing Significantly Reduced Object Allocations (Typical of Doing Significant Algorithm Optimizations on the First Implementation)

This sample uses the PerformanceSampling class defined earlier in this book.

```
private void button5_Click(object sender, System.EventArgs e)
{
  //Run the garbage collector, so we start from a
  //clean slate for our test
  //ONLY CALL DURING TESTING! Calling the GC manually will slow
  //down overall application throughput!
  System.GC.Collect();

  string [] testArray = null;

  //--------------------------------------------
  //Go through the items in the array and
  //look for ones where the middle word is
  //'blue'. Replace the 'blue' with 'orange'
  //--------------------------------------------

  //Start the stopwatch for the test
  PerformanceSampling.StartSample(2, "DeferredObjects");

  //------------------------------------------------
  //LESS WASTEFUL: Allocate the object before we get in the
  //loop
  //------------------------------------------------
  LessAllocationsWorkerClass workerClass1;
  workerClass1 = new LessAllocationsWorkerClass();

  int outerLoop;
  for (outerLoop = 0; outerLoop < LOOP_SIZE; outerLoop++)
  {
    //Set up the data in the array we want to do our test on
    ResetTestArray(ref testArray);
    int topIndex = testArray.Length - 1;

    for(int idx = 0; idx <= topIndex; idx++)
    {
      //--------------------------------------------------------
      //Less Wasteful:
      //Instead of reallocating the object, let's just reuse it
```

```
            //Also: The implementation does NOT create additional
            //strings
            //------------------------------------------------------
            //workerClass1 = new WastefulWorkerClass(
            //                   testArray[topIndex]);
            workerClass1.ReuseClass(testArray[idx]);


            //If the middle word is "blue", make it "orange"
            //-------------------------------------------------
            //Less Wasteful:
            //This compare does not need to create any additional
            //strings
            //-------------------------------------------------
            if(workerClass1.CompareMiddleSegment("blue") == 0)
            {
              //Replace the middle item
              workerClass1.MiddleSegment = "orange";
              //Replace the word
              testArray[idx ] = workerClass1.getWholeString();
            }
          }
        }
      //Stop the stopwatch!
      PerformanceSampling.StopSample(2);
      System.Windows.Forms.MessageBox.Show(
              PerformanceSampling.GetSampleDurationText(2));
}
```

Listing 8.8 The Worker Class for Our Third Test Case

```
using System;

public class LessAllocationsWorkerClass
{
  public string MiddleSegment
  {
    set
    {
      m_middleSegmentNew = value;
    }
  }
```

```
private string m_middleSegmentNew;
private int m_index_1st_undscore;
private int m_index_2nd_undscore;
private string m_stringIn;

public void ReuseClass(string in_word)
{

  //----------------------------------------
  //To reuse the class, clear all the internal state
  //----------------------------------------
  m_index_1st_undscore  = -1;
  m_index_2nd_undscore  = -1;
  m_middleSegmentNew = null;
  m_stringIn  = in_word;   //This does not make a string copy


  //Look for a "_" in the string
  m_index_1st_undscore   = in_word.IndexOf("_",0);

  //If there is no "_", the first segment is the whole thing
  if(m_index_1st_undscore == -1)
  {
    return;
  }
  //Look for the 2nd "_";
  m_index_2nd_undscore   = in_word.IndexOf("_",
                          m_index_1st_undscore + 1);
}


public int CompareMiddleSegment(string compareTo)
{
  //If there is no 2nd underscore, there is no middle
  if(m_index_2nd_undscore < 0)
  {
    //If we are comparing to an empty string, then this is a
    //match
    if((compareTo == null) || (compareTo == ""))
    {return 0;}

    return -1;
  }

  //Compare the middle segment to the 1st and second segments
```

```
    return System.String.Compare(m_stringIn,
      m_index_1st_undscore + 1,
      compareTo,
      0,
      m_index_2nd_undscore - m_index_1st_undscore -1);
  }


  public string getWholeString()
  {

    //If we've been given no new middle segment, return the
    //original
    if (m_middleSegmentNew == null)
    {
      return m_stringIn;
    }

    //Build the return string
    return m_stringIn.Substring(0,m_index_1st_undscore + 1) +
      m_middleSegmentNew + m_stringIn.Substring(
            m_index_2nd_undscore,
            m_stringIn.Length - m_index_2nd_undscore);


  }
}
```

Analysis of the Successive Optimizations Done Above

There are usually significant savings to be achieved in tuning your application's algorithms. The most important thing to do is to measure the performance gains your tuning is intended to accomplish. Some performance "improvements" you make might inadvertently hurt performance because of memory allocations you were not aware of or perhaps for other reasons. In developing the code example above, I had several situations where I thought changes might improve results, but upon measurement and deeper consideration learned that the changes were detrimental. Always measure and compare your performance!

It is also important to test on the actual hardware you intend to run on to see what the "on-device" experience is. Using an emulator can be very useful for code design and basic tuning, but the results may differ on the physical hardware due to processor differences, memory differences, and other factors. Some code may run faster on physical devices and some may run slower. The final proof is always on the actual hardware end users will use. For the same reason, it is important to run code with and without the debugger attached to measure performance. An attached debugger can dramatically slow down algorithm performance in some cases.

The results of the three different algorithms tested above were as follows.

Table 8.1 Test Case Results for 8,000 Loop Iterations Running in Pocket PC Emulator (Results in Seconds)

Trial #	Wasteful Allocations	Slightly Reduced Allocations	Significantly Reduced Allocations
1	12.65	12.2	8.925
2	12.775	12.35	8.55
3	12.575	12.25	8.225
4	12.625	12.525	8.575
Average	**12.65625**	**12.33125**	**8.56875**
% time savings vs. test baseline	0%	2.57%	32.30%

Table 8.2 Test Case Results for 2,000 Loop Iterations Running on Physical Pocket PC Device (Results in Seconds)

Trial #	Wasteful Allocations	Slightly Reduced Allocations	Significantly Reduced Allocations
1	30.609	30.151	20.484
2	30.538	30.016	20.362
3	30.517	30.195	20.377
4	30.457	30.316	20.429
Average	**30.53025**	**30.1695**	**20.413**
% Time savings vs. test baseline	0%	1.18%	33.14%

Analysis of test results above:

- *The first optimization, reusing an object instead of reallocating it, improved performance only marginally.* Probably this is because the object itself was small in size and held little data. In retrospect, this may not be too surprising. Given that this was an easy optimization to make involving only a few lines of code, it is worth keeping. An additional benefit not reflected in the numbers above is that by removing an object allocation from a loop with high iterations we should be reducing the "object littering" of our application considerably. This should result in the garbage collector needing to run less often and give our application better overall performance. The optimization did not have a great direct impact on the execution speed but it did no harm and reduced our littering considerably.
- *The second optimization we did, removing several string object allocations and replacing them with string indexes instead, had a significant impact on performance.* The algorithm's overall performance was directly improved by more than one third by making a few changes to how our helper class was designed and deferring any string object creation until absolutely necessary. Not only does this result in direct performance improvements, but as above we have greatly reduced the amount of garbage our algorithm produces. This will mean fewer overall garbage collections and a smoother and faster running application.
- *The ratios of performance improvement were reasonably similar for emulator and physical Pocket PC devices, but the absolute performance differed drastically for the algorithm.* In this case (string allocations), optimizations produced similar improvements on the emulator and on physical devices, but the best performing algorithm ran at about 934 iterations/second on the emulator and at 122 iterations/second on the physical device. This made the emulator about 7.6 times faster than a physical device for this kind of algorithm. If this is a critical algorithm and we are going to run it on thousands of pieces of data, we need to make sure the on-device user experience is good. This may require us to use background threads to do data processing or may require us to work with smaller sets of data at any given time. The only way to get real-world measurements is to run on real-world devices with real-world data.

Pay Special Attention to String Usage in Your Algorithms

Strings are special and unique data types in their ubiquity and utility in building software. Strings often represent human-readable text and just as often convey machine data such as database query strings. In short, strings are everywhere and byte for byte may be the most commonly used and abused data type in many applications. Modern programming languages make it very easy to work with strings, to create them, to split them, to copy them, and to append them. Consider the following simple statements:

```
string str1 = "foo"; //Allocates a string object
string str2 = "bar"; //Allocates a string object
string str3 = str1 + str2; //Allocates a string object
string str3 = str3 + str3; //Allocates a string object
```

Each statement is allocating data and creating types in memory, and we haven't even called any functions yet! Strings are used so casually by developers that they are very easy to abuse. Unoptimized string handling is one of the largest causes of poor performance and also one of the easiest to prevent. A few facts and rules of thumb follow. (These facts are based on the .NET Framework/.NET Compact Framework. Other runtimes tend to follow similar rules. Check your specific language/runtime reference guide for specific details.)

- *Strings are immutable.* This fancy word *immutable* simply means that the text data for a string cannot be changed in memory. Any code operation that you may think is changing the data in the string is actually creating a new string. Immutability has some very nice characteristics. For example, because the string data itself is static, multiple variables can point to the same data; this makes assigning one string variable to another a shallow "pointer" copy and not a deep copy of the underlying data. The downside of immutability is the inability to make any changes to the data. If you want to change the data, add to the data, or truncate the data, the change will be reflected in a new copy of the string.
- *When string data is no longer referenced by any "live" variables, it is garbage.* Example:

```
string  str1 = "foo"; //"foo" is static data compiled into your
                //application binary
```

```
string str2 = str1 + str1; //you have just created a new string that
                           //is the concatenation of two strings

str2 = "bar";   //Since no other variables point to the data str2
                //used to point to, it is now garbage and will
                //have to be cleaned up.
```

- *When you want to reference some subset of a string, it is often far more efficient to do so using integer indexes into the string.* Because strings are data in an array of characters, it is easy to get to the data using integer indexes. There exist plenty of functions to enable you to seek out and look at data inside strings with indexes (just not change that data!).
- *When you are building a new string in a loop, strongly consider using a StringBuilder object.* All kinds of strings are built out of other variables processed in loops. A typical example of dynamic string creation would be a loop that generated a text report with each line containing the following data:

```
//Inefficient code inside loop...
{
myString = myString +"CustomerID: " +
System.Convert.ToString(customer[idx].id) + ", Name: "  +
System.Convert.ToString(customer[idx].name);
}
```

Instead of concatenating the strings together and creating a new string in each iteration of the loop, a StringBuilder class could be used to build the report. The StringBuilder is a class that is very useful for working with a dynamically sized array of characters to build strings. It enables you to efficiently add onto this array, to change the contents or length of the array, and, importantly, to create a new string based on the char array. Learn to use the StringBuilder class because it is the key to writing efficient algorithms that generate string data.

- *Measure the performance of your algorithm.* When writing a string-processing algorithm, test its speed! Try a few different approaches. You will quickly learn what is efficient and what is not.

An Example That Shows How to Build Strings Efficiently

Listing 8.9 has two similar string-processing algorithms that produce identical computational results. Both increment a counter and at each increment append the string representation of the counter to a growing piece of text. Both run the same amount of iterations, and both algorithms are of similar complexity to write. Yet one of the algorithms is vastly better performing than the other.

Listing 8.9 Comparing String Usage to StringBuilder in Algorithms

This sample uses the PerformanceSampling class defined earlier in this book.

```csharp
const int COUNT_UNTIL = 300;
const int LOOP_ITERATIONS = 40;


//-------------------------------------------------------
//NOT VERY EFFICIENT!
//
//Use regular strings to simulate building a typical set of
//strings
//-------------------------------------------------------
private void button1_Click(object sender, System.EventArgs e)
{
  //Do a garbage collection before we start running, to start
  //us from a clean state.
  //ONLY CALL DURING TESTING! Calling the GC manually will slow
  //down overall application throughput!
  System.GC.Collect();
  int numberToStore = 0;

  PerformanceSampling.StartSample(0, "StringAllocaitons");
  string total_result = "";
  for (int outer_loop = 0; outer_loop < LOOP_ITERATIONS;
       outer_loop++)
  {
    //Clear out the old result
    total_result = "";

    //Count up to 'x_counter' and append the test of each count
    //to our working string
    for(int x_counter = 0; x_counter < COUNT_UNTIL; x_counter++)
```

```
        {
          total_result = total_result + numberToStore.ToString()
                        + ", ";

          //Advance the counter
          numberToStore ++;
        }
      }
      PerformanceSampling.StopSample(0);

      //Display the length of the string
      System.Windows.Forms.MessageBox.Show("String Length: " +
                          total_result.Length.ToString());

      //Display string
      System.Windows.Forms.MessageBox.Show("String : " +
                          total_result);


      //Display the time it took to run
      System.Windows.Forms.MessageBox.Show(
            PerformanceSampling.GetSampleDurationText(0));
    }


    //---------------------------------------------------------
    //MUCH MORE EFFICIENT!
    //
    //Use the string builder to simulate building a fairly typical
    //set of strings
    //---------------------------------------------------------
    private void button2_Click(object sender, System.EventArgs e)
    {
      //Do a garbage collection before we start running, to start
      //us from a clean state.
      //ONLY CALL DURING TESTING! Calling the GC manually will slow
      //down overall application throughput!
      System.GC.Collect();
      System.Text.StringBuilder sb =
            new System.Text.StringBuilder();

      string total_result = "";
      int numberToStore = 0;

      PerformanceSampling.StartSample(1, "StringBuilder");
```

```
for (int outer_loop = 0; outer_loop < LOOP_ITERATIONS;
     outer_loop++)
{
  //Clear the string builder (not creating a new SB object)
  sb.Length = 0;
  //Clear out our old result string
  total_result = "";

  //Count up to 'x_counter' and append the test of each count
  //to our working string
  for(int x_counter = 0; x_counter < COUNT_UNTIL; x_counter++)
  {
    sb.Append(numberToStore );
    sb.Append(", ");

    //Advance the counter
    numberToStore ++;
  }
  //Pretend we're doing something with the string...
  total_result = sb.ToString();
}

PerformanceSampling.StopSample(1);

//Display the length of the string
System.Windows.Forms.MessageBox.Show("String Length: "
              + total_result.Length.ToString());

//Display string
System.Windows.Forms.MessageBox.Show("String : "
              + total_result);

//Display the time it took to run
System.Windows.Forms.MessageBox.Show(
      PerformanceSampling.GetSampleDurationText(1));
}
```

Table 8.3 Comparison Results for 40 × 300 Loop Iterations Running in Emulator (Results in Seconds)

Trial #	Wasteful String Allocations	Using StringBuilder
1	25.475	0.85
2	25.225	0.925
3	24.5	0.875
Average	25.07	0.88
% Time savings vs. baseline test	0%	96.5%

Table 8.4 Comparison Results for 40 × 300 Loop Iterations Running on Physical Pocket PC (Results in Seconds)

Trial #	Wasteful String Allocations	Using StringBuilder
1	22.502	6.257
2	22.34	6.346
3	22.378	6.35
Average	22.41	6.32
% Time savings vs. baseline test	0%	71.8%

Analysis of results above:

■ *When constructing strings out of multiple segments, the StringBuilder can be vastly more efficient than working with individual immutable strings.* String concatenations and other modifications inside loops can be very expensive operations causing a great deal of object allocation and discarding. In contrast, the StringBuilder treats the data not as an immutable string but rather as a mutable array of characters and manages its size efficiently, growing the array size in sizable chunks when necessary. An immutable string object is allocated when the application requests one by calling the ToString() method. The StringBuilder class can be used to great effect in processing text.

- *Loops that create new strings generate a great deal of garbage.* Depending on the available amount of free memory, the garbage collector may run during the algorithm's execution if needed. It may run several times, and in memory-constrained situations it may run almost continually. This results in increasingly bad performance as memory pressure mounts. Even after exiting the algorithm, there will be a lot of garbage left around that needs to be cleaned up. Everything you allocate and discard eventually has to be looked at and cleaned up.

- *Sometimes a physical mobile device can out perform an emulator on a much faster machine.* In the string-allocation case above, we see that the physical Pocket PC actually outperformed my laptop running an emulator. However, in the StringBuilder case the Pocket PC did not perform as fast as the emulator. In both cases, the StringBuilder solution greatly outperformed the string-allocation method, but the ratios were not the same for the emulator and physical device tests. As a rule of thumb, when comparing algorithms what is faster on a PC is usually faster on a mobile device; if accurate performance assessment is important, however, it is always useful to test the performance on the physical hardware.

Summary

When managing memory in your mobile application it is important to think both at a macro/application level and also at the micro/algorithm level. At the macro level, it is important to have a memory model that does not use up too much of your device's memory yet at the same time enables you to keep the data and resources that your application uses frequently close at hand. A state machine approach can be very useful for doing this for application resources. For your application's user data, consider designing a specific class whose job it is to manage the amount of application data that is kept in memory at any given time. This class serves as an encapsulated machine that knows how to bring new user data in when needed as well as shuttle old data out when it is unnecessarily taking up room. For any object that has a `Dispose()` method, be sure to call it when you are through with the object; this will preemptively release any nonmanaged resources held by the object and increase the overall throughput of the system.

At an algorithmic level, it is important not just to pick the right kind of algorithm for the data you are processing but also to implement the algorithm efficiently. You should strive to implement algorithms with as few object allocations as possible; this is especially true for code that runs in loops. Strings are of particular concern because they are so commonly used and it is very easy to write code that allocates and releases strings implicitly and wastefully. For strings algorithms, two valuable approaches are (1) using indexes to refer to data inside strings instead of extracting the substrings out as new strings and (2) using a StringBuilder (or your runtime environment's equivalent) for the construction of strings. You must be wary of creating and throwing away objects in your algorithms because the allocation and initialization takes time and the objects eventually turn into garbage that must be cleaned up by the runtime. Creating litter means creating a downstream need to clean it up, and this will reduce your application's overall performance. Objects are useful concepts but can be expensive when misused; design your algorithms accordingly.

Your mobile device application's execution environment behaves much like a small apartment. If you do not have too many items lying around, living there can be a joy. Bring too many things into your apartment and it becomes difficult to move around and get things done. If in the course of your daily activities you generate a lot of trash, you are going to spend a good amount of your time walking in and out of your apartment bringing the trash out and tidying up. Cleaning up litter takes time away from what you really want to do. At the macro living level, strive for an elegant but sparse apartment with all the important things you need close at hand but nothing else causing clutter. At the micro level try not to generate too much trash!

CHAPTER 9

Performance and Multithreading

Time the devourer of everything.

—Ovid (43 BC – 17 AD), Roman poet (Encarta 2004, Quotations)

Introduction: When and How to Use Background Threads

Because devices are used frequently but for small amounts of time, users demand highly responsive experiences when using mobile software. Put simply, users do not want to waste time waiting for an application to respond to them. When used properly, a background thread can aid foreground responsiveness. The ability to create and use background threads is a powerful feature for building sophisticated mobile applications. This power brings with it both good and bad news.

First the bad news: Take it as a rule with very few exceptions, extra threads will not make your code run faster. In an absolute sense, additional threads will almost always make your code run slower. This is because you are giving the operating system one more stream of execution that it needs to manage and periodically switch control in and out of. This switching between execution streams has a performance penalty.

More bad news: Using background threads increases the complexity of your application significantly and has the potential to produce timing-related bugs. Timing-related bugs are notoriously difficult to track down. When first experimenting with threads, it is easy to see them as the answer to every problem regardless of actual need. As soon as developers master the basics of background threading, there is an inclination to become a bit "thread happy" and find reason after reason to create and utilize background threads. This tendency to overuse threads is even more pronounced when working on a project as a group; everyone has a task for which they would like their own isolated background thread in which to do their work free of the need to share execution with any other code. This sounds like a workable idea until all the pieces of code are run together and the application now has seven threads running concurrently doing all kinds of fascinating but unnecessary things. Extra threads that are not absolutely necessary drag down performance and increase an application's complexity. For good mobile application performance, developers working in groups need to find a way to efficiently distribute or queue tasks among a very limited number of threads.

Now the good news: Background threads can be used to great positive effect. What multiple threads enable you to do is to have more than one parallel stream of execution going on in your application. The microprocessor grants each thread slices of time to run in and some time is also spent switching between the threads. Although the total number of program instructions executed by the parallel threads is somewhat lower than what a single thread would achieve if it had all the time slices to itself, the two threads get to perform separate tasks concurrently. Sometimes this is a very useful thing.

An additional thread or two can make your application more responsive to the user by performing tasks in the background while keeping the foreground user interface responsive. A good analogy to consider is that of a hotel front desk. To run a hotel that is responsive to guests' needs, you always want to have someone manning the front desk. Any time, day or night, a guest may walk up to the front desk with a request or query, and there needs to be someone free to take the request without delay. This front desk clerk is your user interface. Whenever there is a task that needs to be performed that will take some time, the front desk clerk defers this work to someone else to perform so that they can remain responsive to guests with new requests. The other workers represent tasks occurring via background threading. No extra work is free. In a hotel it costs extra money to employ more workers and keep the person manning the front desk free to handle new requests. On a mobile device, you pay out of your overall application's performance budget. There is a fixed amount of processing power your application has and it must be partitioned wisely between foreground, background tasks and system time spent switching between the two.

If there are long-running algorithms that need to be completed to arrive at an analytical answer, a background thread is a good candidate for performing this work. For example, when algorithmically choosing the next move in chess game, it can take some significant time to compare alternatives; a background thread is a great place to do this work. If an application's user is 90 percent likely to request a particular photo or chunk of data imminently and its loading takes several seconds or requires accessing a networked resource, doing this work preemptively on a background thread can produce a stunningly good user experience. There are plenty of good reasons for your application to use a background thread to meet specific user interface responsiveness needs. A background thread can be used reactively to run a long-duration algorithm in response to a user request or preemptively to fetch data or perform calculations in anticipation of a user's needs.

Multitasking and Multithreading in Modern Operating Systems

Today's modern multitasking operating systems allow a microprocessor to be used as a shared resource. The microprocessor's time gets spilt between different tasks, all of which get to pretend that they are sole owners of this resource. This is known as *multitasking* and the tasks being performed are known as *processes*. There are probably several tasks already running concurrently on your mobile device at any given time. This number is probably more than you would guess. Some of these tasks are serving low-level needs that you would not consider "applications," and some are running as familiar application software. The operating system occasionally interrupts a task in the middle of what it is doing and passes control over to another waiting process or thread. This works well because most of the time applications are not doing much; they are usually waiting for external input to handle. In contrast, if each application process used all its allotted processing time to calculate Pi to its infinite lengths, the overall system performance would suffer greatly. Multitasking works because the microprocessor is an underutilized resource most of the time.

The subject of how to fairly divide time between different processes and threads is a deeply specialized topic that would fill its own book. Suffice it to say that processor time is divided reasonably fairly between the different tasks that vie for it.

Switching control between different processes involves what is commonly referred as a *context switch*. Because each application process gets to pretend that it is in sole ownership of the microprocessor, all kinds of data needs to get swapped in and out when execution control gets handed from one process to another. Microprocessor registers need to get their values swapped out, the program counter needs to get swapped out, virtual memory pointers need to get moved around, and if there is a pipeline of instructions queued up or a memory cache associated with the microprocessor, these too need to be dealt with. Context switches are not cheap. The more processes your device has or the smaller the time slice size that gets allotted to each process when it is its turn to run, the larger the percentage of total time that gets spent switching from one process to another.

Because operating system process context switches are so expensive, most modern operating systems support multithreading as a more light-weight form of multitasking. Multithreading enables you to support multiple threads of execution inside a single process. Switching execution context between different threads is generally less expensive than switching process contexts. But switching thread contexts is not free either. Some overhead is required to change the execution address, swap out register values, and perform other necessary bookkeeping to keep things running smoothly.

Allowing multiple streams of execution inside the same application's memory space greatly raises the potential complexity of the application's code by throwing out time determinacy of execution. If two threads are trying to access the same areas of memory at roughly the same time, unintuitive and complex situations can arise. This is true with native C/C++ code and also true when working with managed code. To deal with this, the concepts of locks, mutexes, semaphores, and critical sections exist; these enable you to create sections of code that are not re-entrant. This is similar to a multilane highway having a section where traffic merges down into a single lane. Again, a fairly large book could be devoted to detailing the intricacies and pitfalls of parallel code execution.

In the end, all the different processes and threads compete for the single microprocessor's time (or in the case of a multiprocessor system, for a pool of processors' time). Each process has at least one thread and many may have several. The operating system will do its best to give each process and its threads a fair share of execution time (note: "fair" does not mean "equal") while trying to minimize the costs of context switches between them.

Being able to create the illusion of parallel processing on a single processor machine is a powerful concept, but it does not come for free. Use, but use with care.

What About Hardware That Supports Multiple Microprocessors?

Many servers and some desktop computers contain multiple microprocessors. Additionally "multicore" microprocessors are becoming more common; these have multiple processing units contained on a single chip and have many of the same advantages as having several physically separate processors. Having multiple processors allows for the possibility of true parallel execution of code.

It is not inconceivable that in the future this trend will come to mobile devices. Although cost and power consumption concerns are inhibitors to having multiple physical central processing units in a mobile device, multicore processors mitigate many of these concerns. However, effective utilization of multiple processors requires dedicated support from the operating system—this is not a trivial task. Multi-microprocessor support has not been a priority for most mobile device operating systems to-date; rather these operating systems tend to focus on compactness and efficiency instead of coordinating parallel execution on multiple processors.

Nevertheless the question gets asked, "If a computing device has multiple microprocessors, should my application use multiple threads to speed things up?" The answer here is the same as when designing for a single processor device: "Probably not. Only use multiple threads when it is beneficial to have things happen asynchronously." Even on a multiprocessor system with an operating system that supports parallel execution having an application run multiple threads is no guarantee of better performance. The reason for this is twofold:

1. In addition to your application, the operating system is almost always running other processes as well as taking care of operating system housecleaning and accounting tasks such as managing low-level device drivers and scheduling. This means that your application cannot usually count on having all of the processors on the device assigned to its threads at any given time. Introducing an additional process or thread simply creates "another mouth to feed" for an operating system that is already splitting its processing resources between many different tasks. Without specific agreement from the operating system to dedicate a processor to a specific thread of execution, your application is just creating another demand on the available processing resources.

2. In practice it is very difficult to design good parallel-execution algorithms. Breaking problems into parallel executable tracks and efficiently coordinating these activities is challenging and is the subject of continued research. If multiple threads are working to solve parts of the same problem, there is a significant risk that they will get in one another's way by requesting access to the same memory or wanting to use some resource that does not allow parallel access.

Parallel execution works best when the parallel tasks being executed do not interfere with one another. This is why servers often benefit from multiple processors; servers are often serving many independent and nonconflicting client requests. Servers with multiple processors can often respond in parallel to simultaneous requests from different clients. The parallel tasks they are asked to perform are often read-only in nature or are modifying data that does not overlap. Both of these tasks can respond well to parallel execution. Applications running on these servers often have pools of threads (commonly known as *thread pools*) that are dispatched to respond to incoming requests.

> Applications with rich client user interfaces usually do not fall into the "easy parallel division of work" camp because the application is generally used to allow a single user to work on a set of related data and user interface elements. The job of a desktop application is generally to respond as well as possible to its single user, not to serve many users vying for its time on independent and parallel tasks.
>
> If there is application work that will benefit from being run asynchronously, it can make sense to have multiple threads whether or not the device has multiple microprocessors. The basic question is whether the benefits of asynchronous execution are worth the costs of added complexity in your application. On a client computing device, multiple processors, if present, are just extra hands to help speed up the overall performance of the machine. For rich client computing, it almost never makes sense to view these processors as dedicated resources that get assigned to various parts of your application.

When to Use Background Threads

In general your application should have one main thread. The application's user interface should be driven by this thread, and when all the active windows are closed the application should terminate. Terminating the application usually requires telling any running background threads to shut down and then with no application windows open to keep the main thread alive its execution can end. (At this point, the `main()` function of the application is exited and control is handed back to the runtime and operating system to do any final cleanup.) Having multiple threads managing their own user interface windows greatly complicates this model and should be avoided.

Occasionally some action a user requests will require a significant amount or indeterminate amount of time to complete. If the time required to complete a needed task is only a few seconds, you may choose to pop up a wait cursor and perform the operation synchronously on the user interface's thread. If the time required is longer or indeterminate in length, pushing the work onto a background thread is an appropriate solution. There are two ways to do this:

1. *Create a new thread*. In this model, a new thread is started and a function is specified as its entry point. The function runs and when it exits the thread terminates.
2. *Have a background thread waiting for work*. In this model, a background thread or pool of threads is created in advance and waits for work to perform. Typically the background threads sit sleeping either

blocked and waiting for some action to wake them or periodically waking up based on a timer to look for work. A woken-up thread performs the requested work and then goes back to sleep to wait for additional requests to wake it again.

NOTE: The desktop .NET Framework has built-in support background thread pools. This model uses "asynchronous delegates" to push work onto a waiting thread pool. General-purpose asynchronous delegates are not supported in version 1.1 of the .NET Compact Framework.

A C/C++ programmer would think of a delegate as similar to "a function pointer." A LISP programmer would think of a delegate as similar to "a closure." A delegate enables you to specify a binding to a specific object's method and to call that method later without the need to refer to either the object or the specific method's name. The .NET Compact Framework supports delegates.

Asynchronous delegates give the ability to asynchronously execute the method that a delegate is bound to using a thread on a background thread pool. This thread pool is managed by the runtime. Async delegates are a nice abstraction because they free the developer from needing to design and test their own thread pooling mechanisms. Because the .NET Compact Framework was designed to run on resource-constrained devices, it was a design decision in version 1.1 not to implement the cross-thread communication for parameter passing required for generic async delegates. If you want to maintain a thread pool using the .NET Compact Framework and perform background work on managed threads, you can do so by explicitly calling the `System.Threading.ThreadPool.QueueUserWorkItem()` method.

Instead of generic asynchronous delegate support, the .NET Compact Framework has built-in support for performing some of the most commonly requested tasks asynchronously. For tasks such as making asynchronous HTTP requests for data from a Web server, the .NET Compact Framework's async support matches that of the desktop .NET Framework. In addition, the System.Threading.Timer class is supported for running timer delegates on background threads. (These threads are managed by the runtime.) So although the .NET Compact Framework version 1.1 does not support general-purpose asynchronous delegates, it has specifically implemented asynchronous calling support for the most common tasks.

Creating a new thread to do background processing or using built-in thread pool support are significantly easier than designing and managing your own custom thread pool. These are the approaches I recommend starting off with when background processing is needed. The only downside to explicitly creating a new thread to run a background task is the extra overhead in creating and destroying threads on demand. In most cases, this effect should be negligible, and the simplicity of design makes the choice attractive. Only when you have proven that the "create a thread only when needed" approach does not meet your needs should you look to using a custom thread pool approach. Start simple and only take on complexity when the need proves itself.

Design Guidelines for Using Threads in Your Mobile Application

Have One Main Thread for Your User Interface

As noted earlier in the chapter, you should think of your main thread as acting like the front desk receptionist at a good hotel. The most important priority for the front desk is to be available and responsive to needs of customers. When asked to do something, the front desk person may perform the task himself if the task is quick. Longer-duration tasks are shuttled off to other hotel employees so that the front desk can remain responsive. A similar model should be applied to your application design with the front desk representing your application's user interface and other hotel employees representing background threads.

Design Your User Interface for Maximum Responsiveness

Foremost in your design goals should be to ensure that your application's user interface remains responsive and interactive with the user. This means avoiding long stalls in the user interface's operation as well as keeping the user informed and feeling part of background tasks whenever possible and appropriate.

Start Off with a Single-Threaded Application Design

Because additional threads greatly increase the complexity of your application, additional threads should only be added when a proven need arises. Avoid being "thread happy."

Consider Using a Wait Cursor Approach Instead of Multithreading for Simple Cases

Wait cursors are the poor man's version of multithreading, but the approach has much to recommend it, most of all simplicity. Instead of doing work in the background asynchronously, displaying a wait cursor is a polite way to tell users to wait because the application is doing work on their behalf.

When you have identified locations where latency occurs, consider using a wait cursor to indicate to the user that work is being done and that they will be notified when their interaction with the application can resume. Your first line of defense in ensuring a good user interface is simply making the user aware when the interface is going to be unresponsive for a few moments. Displaying a wait cursor is a good way to inform users that work is being done on their behalf and that the work should be completed shortly.

Consider Using a Background Thread If the Latency Is Long or Indeterminate

A wait cursor approach is not appropriate if either (1) the length of the task to be performed is long enough to frustrate the user, or (2) the duration of the task is unknown or unbounded, such as when accessing an off device resource. In these two cases, consider a background thread approach.

Design Threading Code for Simplicity and Document for Safety

Thread safety is tricky stuff. Without careful attention to how member variables are being read and written, your application can end up reading a variable on one thread that is in the middle of being written by another thread; the "atomicity" of most in-memory data operations is *not* guaranteed because it takes several microprocessor instructions to write most data types. The fact that these issues are timing dependent and do not occur often makes them very difficult to track down, reproduce, and debug. Even when variable access can be guaranteed to be atomic, without attention to how a class' member functions are called you can end up in a situation where data gets corrupted or program logic behaves in an unexpected way because related data is modified concurrently by algorithms running on different threads; imagine two threads inserting and deleting to the same linked list at the same time. To deal with these situations robustly, it is necessary to define "critical sections" in your code; these ensure that only one stream of execution can concurrently run any code tied to the same semaphore object. (This is done in C# using the lock(*object*) statement and in Visual Basic using SyncLock(*object*)—see the MSDN language reference for these two statements for more details.) To complicate matters further, code can also "deadlock" if two threads currently in different critical sections try to call code that needs to enter a critical section currently "owned" by the other thread; both threads' execution will halt at the entrance to the other's critical sections. For this reason, as well as for performance concerns, overly liberal use of critical sections can cause its own problems.

You could try to make all your classes' properties and methods thread-safe; however, ensuring this would be exceedingly difficult and wasteful from a performance and design perspective. You would end up with many different critical sections throughout your application's code along a myriad of objects for the critical sections' use as semaphores. This kind of code is extremely difficult to design and test and can suffer unnecessary performance overhead due to thread-safety checks and unnecessarily serialized execution. Neither the .NET Framework nor the .NET Compact Framework attempts to do this; instead they both take a documentation approach and explicitly declare which operations are thread-safe and which are not. Developers are expected to read the documentation and use the classes, properties, and methods accordingly. A class with a method that is not thread-safe should not have that method called from different threads concurrently. Instead, either two different instances of the class should be created or the calling of the non-thread-safe method should be serialized by placing it into a critical section in your application's code. What is necessary and thread-safe is exposed that way, what is not is documented.

You should take a similar approach in your own design. Make the surface area of classes, functions, and properties that need to be accessed by multiple threads as small as possible and state these explicitly in your code. Critical section locks should only be declared and used when multithreaded access is absolutely required and concurrent execution or data-access problems in your code are identified that cannot be easily fixed by improved design. Design, code review and test these special classes and functions rigorously and document your classes, properties, and methods accordingly. If accessing a type, property, or method is not thread-safe or you have doubts as to whether it can be concurrently accessed safely from different threads, document this in your code. For example:

```
// THIS <VARIABLE/PROPERTY/METHOD> IS NOT INTENDED TO BE
// ACCESSED FROM MULTIPLE THREADS!!!
// The expected use of this method is by the
// <foreground/background> thread to...
```

Identifying what the critical parts of your code are that need to be thread-safe and explicitly stating which pieces are either not thread-safe or have not been designed with thread-safety in mind allows you to concentrate your design efforts on those pieces that truly need to be accessed concurrently by multiple threads. Explicit documentation will also help ensure that the code remains robust as it is evolved and maintained in the future.

Consider Cases Where Work Can Preemptively Be Done

Some user requests take a while to process. For example, a significant amount of data may have to be loaded or calculated, network requests may need to be made, or complex images may need to be rendered to respond to an upcoming user request. If this work stalls the application, the device's user will get frustrated waiting for it. It would be good to avoid this frustration when possible. If your application can with sufficient probability predict its user's next actions and has enough information to know what heavy processing or high-latency work will be required to react to them, it is worth considering preemptively doing this work on a background thread in anticipation of the user's next actions. By analogy, if you are running a restaurant and every morning the same person comes in at 8 a.m. and impatiently orders two fried eggs, a blueberry muffin, a bowl of cereal, and a cup of coffee, it is worth considering having these ready and waiting for the impatient customer. Even if one out of a hundred days the customer does not show up, it is still worth the effort if it greatly increases the customer's satisfaction on a majority of days he does show up. By having an on-demand service ready for demanding customers, you are providing a unique and valuable service for them.

Preemptively doing work based on a request the user has not yet made is a good way to eliminate or significantly lower the length of annoying stalls a user will face when using your mobile application. When done well, this kind of approach can significantly raise users' perceptions of the quality of your mobile application, because it provides the instant-gratification experience that users seek when using mobile devices.

As with the earlier warning about not becoming "thread happy," it is important to prove the need for preemptive processing in your application before embarking on designing these kinds of systems. Preemptive processing can add application complexity and should only be used if the payoff in user experience justifies it. The best way to prove this is by getting accurate time measurements for the delays users will face as well as testing out the predicted results of preemptive processing.

Predicting User Needs in Advance

Doing predictive work on behalf of the user can be tricky but can also be used to great effect. When it is done well, users almost never appreciate the hard work that is being done to meet their needs; things just seem to work smoothly.

A good example is the picture viewer in Windows XP. This viewer pops up when you double-click a photo in a file-explorer window. The photo to be viewed is loaded and displayed. Unbeknownst to the user, the next photo in the directory gets loaded in the background while the first one is displayed. When the user does the most common next action (clicks the Next Image button in the photo viewer), the next photo will probably pop up without visible delay. This is no small feat for today's large digital photographs, which can take a significant amount of time to load, decompress, and size properly for display.

This next image lookahead appears to be forward only. If you click the Previous Image button, you are likely to see the text "Generating preview" appear for a moment as the photo is loaded on demand. Moving in reverse is not as common an action as moving forward, so it is not optimized for. Because digital images can take significant memory resources, it is generally not feasible today to pre-load a large number of images in case a user may want to view any of them. Similarly, if you click the Next Image button repeatedly and quickly you will see the same "Generating preview" text pop up as the photo you requested gets loaded on demand; you are getting ahead of the lookahead feature's ability to load the photo. Most people look at a photo for a second or two before moving on to the next photo, so this is the scenario that is optimized for.

The picture viewer is wisely optimizing for two facts:

1. When people look at photos, most of the time they move sequentially forward through the list of photos.

2. When people look at a photo, they often look at it for long enough for the system to load the next photo in the background.

Whether or not the picture viewer is using a background thread to accomplish this task (I don't know), it is demonstrating a good use of asynchronous processing to give the user an optimized experience for their most common action. This is smart thinking!

Sample Code You Can Use — Using a Background Thread to Accomplish a Single Task

The code in Listing 9.1 is a class that enables you to manage the execution of a task on a background thread. It uses a state machine to keep track of its progress in getting set up, starting a new thread, running code on the thread, and exiting the thread when finished.

The sample also offers the ability for the main thread to request that the background operation be aborted. Calling the `m_threadExecute.setProcessingState(ThreadExecuteTask.ProcessingState.requestAbort)` method from another thread signals to the background processing thread that a request to abort has been made of it. It is up to the code running on the background processing thread to periodically check for this state and to abort if possible. The state machine for `ThreadExecuteTask` is shown in Figure 9.1.

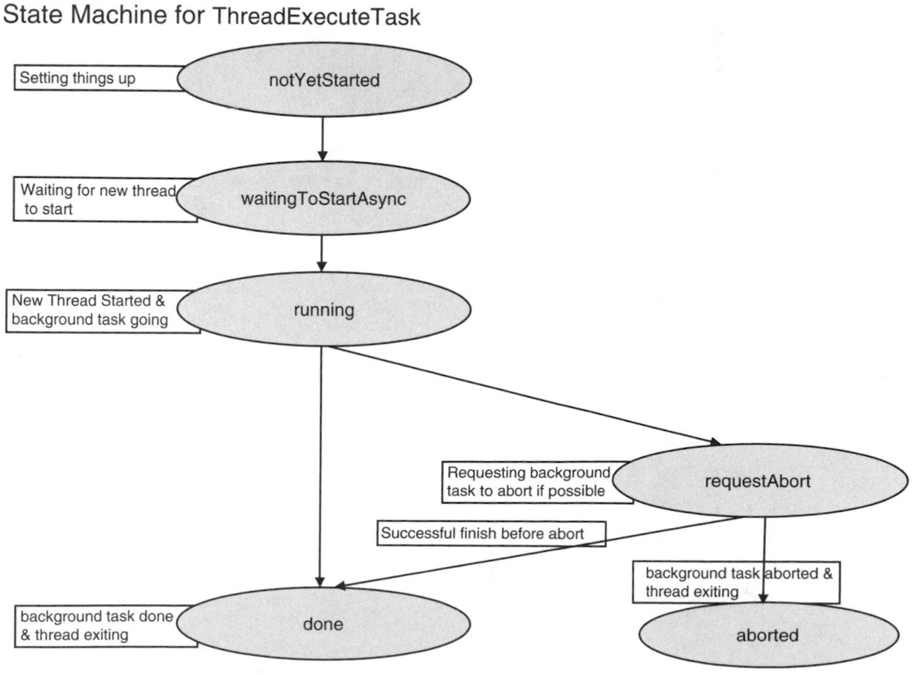

Figure 9.1 State machine for single task executing on a background thread.

Listing 9.1 Code to Manage Single Task Execution on a Background Thread

```csharp
using System;
public class ThreadExecuteTask
{
  //States we can be in.
  public enum ProcessingState
  {
    //----------------
    //Initial state
    //----------------
    //Not doing anything interesting yet
    notYetStarted,

    //----------------
    //Working states
    //----------------
    //We are waiting for the background thread to start
    waitingToStartAsync,

    //Code is running in the background thread
    running,

    //Requesting that the calculation be aborted
    requestAbort,

    //----------------
    //Final states
    //----------------

    //Final State: We have successfully completed background
    //execution
    done,

    //Final State: We have aborted the background execution
    //before finishing
    aborted
  }

  ProcessingState m_processingState;

  public delegate void
      ExecuteMeOnAnotherThread(ThreadExecuteTask checkForAborts);
```

```
private ExecuteMeOnAnotherThread m_CallFunction;
private object m_useForStateMachineLock;


public  ThreadExecuteTask
          (ExecuteMeOnAnotherThread functionToCall)
{
  //Create an object we can use for a lock for the
  //state-machine transition function
  m_useForStateMachineLock = new Object();

  //Mark our execution as ready to start
  m_processingState = ProcessingState.notYetStarted;

  //Store the function we are supposed to call on the new
  //thread
  m_CallFunction = functionToCall;

  //----------------------------------------------------
  //Create a new thread and have it start executing on:
  // this.ThreadStartPoint()
  //----------------------------------------------------
  System.Threading.ThreadStart threadStart;
  threadStart =
    new System.Threading.ThreadStart(ThreadStartPoint);

  System.Threading.Thread newThread;
  newThread = new System.Threading.Thread(threadStart);

  //Mark our execution as ready to start (for determinism,
  //it is important to do this before we start the thread!)
  setProcessingState(ProcessingState.waitingToStartAsync);

  //Tell the OS to start our new thread async.
  newThread.Start();
  //Return control to the caller on this thread
}

//----------------------------------------------------
//This function is the entry point that is called on the
//new thread
//----------------------------------------------------
private void ThreadStartPoint()
{
```

```
//Set the processing state to indicate we are running on
//a new thread!
setProcessingState(ProcessingState.running);

//Run the user's code, and pass in a pointer to our class
//so that code can occasionally call to see if an abort has
//been requested
m_CallFunction(this);

//If we didn't abort, change the execution state to indicate
//success
if(m_processingState != ProcessingState.aborted)
{
  //Mark our execution as done
  setProcessingState(ProcessingState.done);
}

//Exit the thread...
}

//-------------------------------------------------
//The state machine.
//-------------------------------------------------
public void setProcessingState(ProcessingState nextState)
{
  //We should only allow one thread of execution to try
  //to modify the state at any given time.
  lock(m_useForStateMachineLock)
  {
    //If we are entering the state we are already in,
    //do nothing.
    if (m_processingState == nextState)
    {
      return;
    }

    //-------------------------------------------------
    //Some very simple protective code to make sure
    //we can't enter another state if we have either
    //Successfully finished, or Successfully aborted
    //-------------------------------------------------

    if   ((m_processingState == ProcessingState.aborted)
      ||  (m_processingState == ProcessingState.done))
```

```
  {
    return;
  }

  //Make sure the state transition is valid
  switch(nextState)
  {
    case ProcessingState.notYetStarted:
      throw new Exception
        ("Cannot enter 'notYetStarted' state");

    case ProcessingState.waitingToStartAsync:
      if(m_processingState != ProcessingState.notYetStarted)
      {throw new Exception("Invalid state transition");}
      break;

    case ProcessingState.running:
      if(m_processingState !=
         ProcessingState.waitingToStartAsync)
      {throw new Exception("Invalid state transition");}

      break;

    case ProcessingState.done:
      //We can complete work only if we have been running.
      //It is also possible that the user requested an
      //abort, but we finished the work before aborting
      if((m_processingState != ProcessingState.running) &&
         (m_processingState != ProcessingState.requestAbort)
        )
      {throw new Exception("Invalid state transition");}

      break;

    case ProcessingState.aborted:
      if(m_processingState != ProcessingState.requestAbort)
      {throw new Exception("Invalid state transition");}

      break;
  }

  //Allow the state change
  m_processingState = nextState;
}
```

```
    }

    public ProcessingState State
    {
      get
      {
        ProcessingState currentState;
        //Prevents simultaneous read/write of state
        lock(m_useForStateMachineLock)
        {
          currentState = m_processingState;
        }
        return currentState;
      }
    }
} // End class
```

Listing 9.2 shows simulated work that can be done in a background thread. A message box is shown when the code starts to run on a background thread. Simulating the work is a series of one-third-second delays in between which the worker code checks to see whether another thread has requested it to abort its processing.

Listing 9.2 Test Example for Work To Be Done on a Background Thread

```
using System;
//------------------------------------------------------------
//Test code we will use to try background thread execution
//------------------------------------------------------------
public class Test1
{
  public int m_loopX;

  //------------------------------------------------------------
  //The function that gets called on a background thread
  //
  // [in] threadExecute: The class managing our thread's
  //                     execution. We can check this to see if
  //                     we should abort our calculation.
  //------------------------------------------------------------
  public void ThreadEntryPoint(ThreadExecuteTask threadExecute)
```

```
        {
            //This message box will be shown in the context of the thread
            //it is running in
            System.Windows.Forms.MessageBox.Show("In TEST");

            //-------------------------------
            //60 times
            //-------------------------------
            for (m_loopX = 0; m_loopX < 60; m_loopX++)
            {
                //If an abort has been requested, we should quit
                if(threadExecute.State ==
                    ThreadExecuteTask.ProcessingState.requestAbort)
                {
                    threadExecute.setProcessingState(
                        ThreadExecuteTask.ProcessingState.aborted);
                    return;
                }

                //Simulate work: Wait 1/3 second
                System.Threading.Thread.Sleep(333);
            }
        }
    }
} //End Class
```

Listing 9.3 contains code that can be run from the main user interface thread to initiate and control background processing. This code snippet is not a standalone class and should be placed inside a form and have the button click events hooked up to buttons on the form.

Listing 9.3 Code to Test and Run the Sample Code Above

```
//The class that will manage our new thread's execution
private ThreadExecuteTask m_threadExecute;
//The class with the method we want to run async
Test1 m_testMe;

//-------------------------------------------------------
//This code needs to be run before the other code because
//it starts the background execution!
//
```

```csharp
//Create a new thread and get the execution going
//------------------------------------------------------
private void buttonStartAsyncExecution_Click(
                    object sender, System.EventArgs e)
{
  //Create an instance of the class we
  //want to call a method on, in another thread
  m_testMe = new Test1();

  //Package the class' method entry point up in a delegate
  ThreadExecuteTask.ExecuteMeOnAnotherThread delegateCallCode;
  delegateCallCode =
    new ThreadExecuteTask.ExecuteMeOnAnotherThread(
                          m_testMe.ThreadEntryPoint);

  //Tell the thread to get going!
  m_threadExecute = new ThreadExecuteTask(delegateCallCode);

}

//Check the status of our execution
private void buttonCheckStatus_Click(object sender,
                                  System.EventArgs e)
{
  //Ask the thread management class what state it's in
  System.Windows.Forms.MessageBox.Show(
          m_threadExecute.State.ToString());

  //Ask the class with the method running on the thread how it's
progressing
  System.Windows.Forms.MessageBox.Show(
                    m_testMe.m_loopX.ToString());
}

//Cause an illegal state transition (will raise an exception)
private void buttonCauseException_Click(object sender,
                                  System.EventArgs e)
{
  m_threadExecute.setProcessingState(
        ThreadExecuteTask.ProcessingState.notYetStarted);
}

//Request the async code to abort its work
private void buttonAbort_Click(object sender, System.EventArgs e)
```

```
{
  m_threadExecute.setProcessingState(
      ThreadExecuteTask.ProcessingState.requestAbort);
}
```

Threads and User Interface

A question that occasionally gets asked is, "Should I use multiple user interface threads?" The answer is almost certainly "No." In almost no cases does it make sense for different parts of a user interface to be driven by different threads. This is particularly true for mobile devices where the application user interfaces are usually full screen windows.

Usually windows are tied to a thread that owns them; this is true for Windows CE, Pocket PC, and the Microsoft Smartphone OS (as well as for desktop operating systems such as Windows XP and earlier versions). Each window has a thread it belongs to and gets commands from. Multiple windows can be owned by the same thread. The thread serves as the "message pump" to the windows and sends them messages when the window needs to be painted, when a key is tapped, when the button is clicked, and so forth.

Although it is possible to have an application with a user interface running on multiple different threads (for example, one thread per top-level window), it is almost never a good idea. It will make your application structure much messier and will not make it run faster. If you find yourself needing more than one thread for your user interface, ask yourself what it is that you are really trying to accomplish and whether it could be done using one main user interface thread and multiple background worker threads; this is a much cleaner model.

More often than not, the intent of having multiple threads with user interface associated with each is driven by a desire to keep the user informed of the progress of tasks occurring on different background threads. It is far better to have a single foreground interface thread poll for this data periodically using a timer than it is to have multiple threads driving multiple windows on the screen. Designing your background tasks as classes with state machines makes this data easy to collect from the user interface thread. This is yet another good reason to use a state machine approach.

Even if your windowing model is not tied to any specific threads, it is generally a good idea to have one thread of execution that "takes care of the user interface."

> ### On the .NET Compact Framework, Do Not Access User Interface Controls from Threads That They Do Not Belong To
>
> Neither the desktop .NET Framework nor the .NET Compact Framework supports accessing most of the properties and methods of user interface elements from threads that they do not belong to. Although the code will compile the execution, results will not be predictable. To allow calling from in between threads, the .NET Framework and .NET Compact framework support a method called `Control.Invoke()`. The .NET Compact Framework v1.1 only supports using the `Control.Invoke()` mechanism to call functions with no parameters. See the MSDN documentation for this method for more information.
>
> A reasonable and easy way to communicate data between a background thread and a user interface thread is to have code running on the user interface thread periodically poll an object you have specifically designed to manage background execution to see whether there is data waiting for the user interface. Doing this is generally easier than delving into the intricacies of cross-thread method invocation.
>
> A second approach is to use a callback delegate that points to a function on your application's form. A function (without parameters, see above) in your form's class can be designated and this function can be called via the form's `Invoke()` method. This call to `Invoke()` will cause the function to be executed on the user interface's thread. The function can then retrieve whatever data it needs to and update the user interface accordingly. The upside of this approach is that the foreground thread does not need to poll and receives updates immediately when the background work is done. The downside of this approach is that it creates a (hopefully short) synchronous linkage between the foreground and background threads execution. When the delegate is executed on the background thread, the background thread's execution is paused, the execution context is switched to the foreground thread, and then the delegate is run. This prevents the background thread from moving on to other queued work. Only when the delegate's execution is complete is the background thread able to resume execution.

An Example Using Background Processing with Foreground Thread User Interface Updates

For this example, we will return to the "prime number" example introduced in Chapter 5, "Our Friend, the State Machine," and make some significant modifications and improvements. This time we will build a smart phone application that computes large prime numbers. The application will stay dynamic while a large number of calculations occur on a background thread. The application enables the user to abort the background thread if desired.

Importantly, the application will also give the user a good understanding of the progress that is being made on his behalf by the application. This progress report is intended to keep the user satisfied that the background task is proceeding well.

This application can also easily be adapted to run on a Pocket PC. The choice of Microsoft Smartphone was simply for variety.

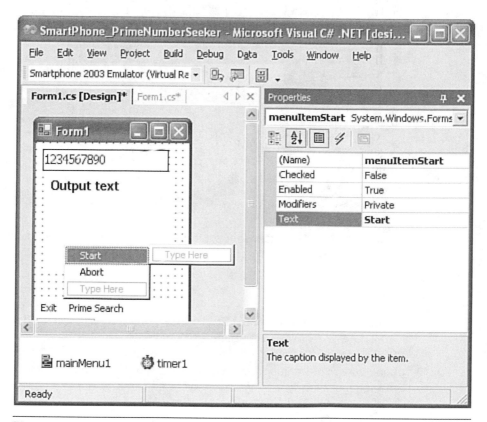

Figure 9.2 The Visual Studio development environment showing the Smartphone's user interface being designed.

Application before starting test

Application during test

Application after test run

Figure 9.3 Runtime screenshots of the Smartphone emulator running the prime number calculation.

NOTE: If you are using Visual Studio .NET 2003, you will need to download and install the SDK for Windows Mobile 2003-based Smartphones. Visual Studio .NET 2003 shipped with Pocket PC development support "in the box," but not Smartphone development support. Because the Software Development Kit for the Smartphone shipped after Visual Studio .NET 2003, it must be downloaded and installed on top of Visual Studio .NET. The SDK is freely downloadable from Microsoft's Web site (see Appendix A, "Additional Resources for the .NET Compact Framework"). The SDK includes the necessary components for Smartphone user interface design as well as a Smartphone emulator that lets you run the applications without needing a physical Smartphone.

Do the following to build and run the application:

1. Start Visual Studio .NET (2003 or later) and create a C# Smart Device Application.
2. Choose Smartphone as the target platform. (A project will be created for you, and a Smartphone form designer will appear.)

3. Using Figure 9.2 above as a layout model, add the following controls to the form:
   - A TextBox (textBox1); set its Text property to a large text string (for example, 12345678901234).
   - A Label (label1); resize the Label so it takes up most of the form's display area. It will need to display text that is several lines long.
   - A Timer control (timer1).

4. Select the MainMenu component at the bottom of the form's designer window and add the following menu subitems:
   - On the left-side menu (where it says Type Here), change the menu text to read **Exit**. Using the Properties window, rename the menu item from menuItem1 to **menuItemExit**.
   - To the right of the Exit menu you just added (where it says Type Here), change the menu text to be **Prime Search**. Note: Use Figure 9.2 above as a guide if needed.
   - Above of the Prime Search menu you just added (where it says Type Here), change the menu text to be **Start**. Using the Properties window, rename the menu item from menuItem2 to **menuItemStart**. Note: Use Figure 9.2 above as a guide if needed.
   - Below of the Start menu you just added (where it says Type Here), change the menu text to be **Abort**. Using the Properties window, rename the menu item from menuItem2 to **menuItemAbort**. Note: Use Figure 9.2 above as a guide if needed.

5. Add a new class to the project. Name it **FindNextPrimeNumber.cs**. Replace the contents in the class' code editor with the code in Listing 9.5.

6. Go back to the Form1.cs [Design] window and double-click the menu item Exit. This will auto-generate a function called `void menuItemExit_Click()` for you and bring you to it in the code editor. Enter the code in Listing 9.4 for this function.

7. Go back to the Form1.cs [Design] window and double-click the menu item Start. This will autogenerate a function called `private void menuItemStart_Click()` for you and bring you to it in the code editor. Enter the code in Listing 9.4 for this function.

8. Go back to the Form1.cs [Design] window and double-click the menu item Abort. This will autogenerate a function called `private void menuItemAbort_Click()` for you and bring you to it in the code editor. Enter the code in Listing 9.4 for this function.

9. Go back to the Form1.cs [Design] window and double-click timer1 control at the bottom of the designer. This will autogenerate a

function called `private void timer1_Tick()` for you. Enter the code in Listing 9.4 for this function.

10. Enter the rest of the code listed in Listing 9.4 into the Form1.cs class.

11. Press F5 to compile and deploy the application to the Smartphone emulator.

When the application is running, you can press the phone button to bring up the Prime Search menu and then press the 1 key to select the Start submenu item. This sets the background search running. As the search runs, the timer1 control should generate a timer event several times a second that triggers the user interface to update the status text displayed on the form. These dynamic updates several times a second keep users informed that progress is being made on their request. The search continues until a prime number is found or the user selects the Abort menu item by selecting the Prime Search menu and pressing 2. To lengthen the time searches take, place a larger number into the text box on the form before starting a search. The number 12345678901234 runs for more than 20 seconds in my emulator. Presently, the following code does not prevent a new search from being started while an old one is still running. A good additional feature to add to the application below would be to check for this condition and to abort an existing search if it were already running. It is also worth looking at the code in Listing 9.5 to see how the `lock` keyword works to ensure that critical sections of code that are not thread-safe are not entered concurrently by different threads.

Listing 9.4 Code That Goes into the Smartphone Form1.cs class

```
//-------------------------------------------------------
//All this code belongs inside a Form1.cs class
//-------------------------------------------------------

//The object that will do our background calculation
FindNextPrimeNumber m_findNextPrimeNumber;
//-------------------------------------------------------
//Update the status text.
//-------------------------------------------------------
void setCalculationStatusText(string text)
{
    label1.Text = text;
```

```
}

//-------------------------------------------------------
//Menu item for "Exiting" the application
//-------------------------------------------------------
private void menuItemExit_Click(object sender,
                                System.EventArgs e)
{
  this.Close();
}


//-------------------------------------------------------
//Menu item for starting the background calculation
//-------------------------------------------------------
private void menuItemStart_Click(object sender,
  System.EventArgs e)
{
  //What number do we want to start looking at
  long startNumber = System.Convert.ToInt64(textBox1.Text);
  //Set up the background calculation
  m_findNextPrimeNumber = new FindNextPrimeNumber(startNumber);

  //Start the background processing running.
  m_findNextPrimeNumber.findNextHighestPrime_Async();

  //Set up the timer that will track the calculation
  timer1.Interval = 400; //400 ms
  timer1.Enabled = true;
}


//-------------------------------------------------------
//Menu item for "Aborting" a calculation under progress
//-------------------------------------------------------
private void menuItemAbort_Click(object sender,
                                 System.EventArgs e)
{
  //If we are not doing a calculation, do nothing.
  if(m_findNextPrimeNumber == null) return;

  //Set the thread up to abort
  m_findNextPrimeNumber.setProcessingState(
    FindNextPrimeNumber.ProcessingState.requestAbort);

  //Let the user instantly know we are getting
```

```csharp
      //ready to abort...
      setCalculationStatusText("Waiting to abort..");
  }


  //----------------------------------------------------------
  //This timer gets called on the UI thread and allows
  //us to keep track of progress on our background
  //calculation
  //----------------------------------------------------------
  private void timer1_Tick(object sender, System.EventArgs e)
  {
    //If we get called and we have no prime number
    //we are looking for, turn off the timer
    if (m_findNextPrimeNumber == null)
    {
      timer1.Enabled = false;
      return;
    }


    //---------------------------------------------
    //If we've been aborted, throw out the prime seeker
    //and turn off the timer
    //---------------------------------------------
    if (m_findNextPrimeNumber.getProcessingState ==
      FindNextPrimeNumber.ProcessingState.aborted)
    {
      timer1.Enabled = false;
      m_findNextPrimeNumber = null;
      setCalculationStatusText("Prime search aborted");
      return;
    }


    //---------------------------------------------
    //Did we find the right answer?
    //---------------------------------------------
    if (m_findNextPrimeNumber.getProcessingState ==
      FindNextPrimeNumber.ProcessingState.foundPrime)
    {
      timer1.Enabled = false;

      //Show the result
      setCalculationStatusText("Found! Next Prime = " +
        m_findNextPrimeNumber.getPrime().ToString());
```

```
      m_findNextPrimeNumber = null;

      return;
   }


   //--------------------------------------------
   //The calculation is progressing. Give the
   //user an idea of the progress being made.
   //--------------------------------------------
   //Get the two output values
   long numberCalculationsToFar;
   long currentItem;
   m_findNextPrimeNumber.getExecutionProgressInfo(
      out numberCalculationsToFar, out currentItem);
   setCalculationStatusText("In progress. Looking at: " +
      currentItem.ToString() + ". " +
      numberCalculationsToFar.ToString() +
      " calculations done for you so far!");
}
```

Listing 9.5 Code for the FindNextPrimeNumber.cs Class

```
using System;
public class FindNextPrimeNumber
{
//States we can be in.
public enum ProcessingState
{
   notYetStarted,
   waitingToStartAsync,
   lookingForPrime,
   foundPrime,
   requestAbort,
   aborted
}

long m_startPoint;
long m_NextHighestPrime;

//How many items have been searched?
long m_comparisonsSoFar;
//What is the current item we are doing a prime search for?
```

```csharp
long m_CurrentNumberBeingExamined;
//Called to get an update on how the calculation is progressing
public void getExecutionProgressInfo(
                out long numberCalculationsSoFar,
                out long currentItemBeingLookedAt)
{

  //NOTE: We are using this thread lock to make sure that
  //we are not reading these values while they are in the
  //middle of being written out. Because m_comparisonsSoFar
  //and m_CurrentNumberBeingExamined may be
  //accessed from multiple threads, any read or write
  //operation to them needs to be synchronized with "lock" to
  //ensure that reads and writes are "atomic".
  lock(this)
  {
    numberCalculationsSoFar = m_comparisonsSoFar;
    currentItemBeingLookedAt = m_CurrentNumberBeingExamined;
  }

}

ProcessingState m_processingState;
//-----------------------------------------------
//A very simple state machine.
//-----------------------------------------------
public void setProcessingState(ProcessingState nextState)
{
  //-----------------------------------------------
  //Some very simple protective code to make sure
  //we can't enter another state if we have either
  //Successfully finished, or Successfully aborted
  //-----------------------------------------------

  if   ((m_processingState == ProcessingState.aborted)
    || (m_processingState == ProcessingState.foundPrime))
  {
    return;
  }

  //Allow the state change
  m_processingState = nextState;
}
```

```csharp
public ProcessingState getProcessingState
{
  get {return m_processingState;}
}


//-------------------------------------------------
//Returns the prime
//-------------------------------------------------
public long getPrime()
{
  if (m_processingState != ProcessingState.foundPrime)
  {
    throw new Exception("Prime number not calculated yet!");
  }
  return m_NextHighestPrime;

}


//Class constructor
public FindNextPrimeNumber(long startPoint)
{
  setProcessingState(ProcessingState.notYetStarted);
  m_startPoint = startPoint;
}


//-----------------------------------------------------------
//Creates a new worker thread that will call
// "findNextHighestPrime()"
//-----------------------------------------------------------
public void findNextHighestPrime_Async()
{
  System.Threading.ThreadStart threadStart;
  threadStart =
    new System.Threading.ThreadStart(findNextHighestPrime);

  System.Threading.Thread newThread;
  newThread = new System.Threading.Thread(threadStart);

  //Set our processing state to say that we are looking
  setProcessingState(ProcessingState.waitingToStartAsync);
  newThread.Start();
}
```

```
//-------------------------------------------------------------
//This is the main worker function. This synchronously starts
//looking for the next prime number and does not exit until
//either:
// (a) The next prime is found
// (b) An external thread to this thread tells us to abort
//-------------------------------------------------------------
public void findNextHighestPrime()
{
  //If we've been told to abort, don't even start looking
  if(m_processingState == ProcessingState.requestAbort)
  {
    goto finished_looking;
  }

  //Set our processing state to say that we are looking
  setProcessingState(ProcessingState.lookingForPrime);

  long currentItem;
  //See if it's odd
  if ((m_startPoint & 1) == 1)
  {
    //It's odd, start at the next odd number
    currentItem = m_startPoint + 2;
  }
  else
  {
    //It's even, start at the next odd number
    currentItem = m_startPoint + 1;
  }

  //Look for the prime item.
  while(m_processingState  == ProcessingState.lookingForPrime)
  {
    //If we found the prime item, return it
    if(isItemPrime(currentItem) == true)
    {
      m_NextHighestPrime =  currentItem;
      //Update our state
      setProcessingState(ProcessingState.foundPrime);
    }

    currentItem = currentItem  + 2;
  }
```

```
    finished_looking:
      //Exit. At this point we have either been
      //Told to abort the search by another thread, or
      //we have found and recorded the next highest prime number

      //If an abort was requested, note that we have aborted
      //the process.
      if (m_processingState == ProcessingState.requestAbort)
      {
        setProcessingState(ProcessingState.aborted);
      }
}


//Helper function that looks to see if a specific item
//is a prime number.
private bool isItemPrime(long potentialPrime)
{
  //If it's even, it's not prime
  if ((potentialPrime & 1) == 0)
  {
    return false;
  }

  //We want to look up until just past the square root
  //of the item
  long end_point_of_search;
  end_point_of_search = (long) System.Math.Sqrt(potentialPrime) + 1;

  long current_test_item = 3;
  while(current_test_item <= end_point_of_search )
  {
    //----------------------------------
    //Check to make sure we have not been asked to abort!
    //----------------------------------
    if (m_processingState != ProcessingState.lookingForPrime)
    {
      return false;
    }

    //If the item is divisible without remainder,
    //it is not prime
    if(potentialPrime % current_test_item == 0)
    {
      return false;
```

```
    }

    //advance by two
    current_test_item  = current_test_item  + 2;
    //----------------------------------------------------
    //Up the count of items we have examined
    //----------------------------------------------------
    //NOTE: We are using this thread lock to make sure that
    //we are not reading these values while they are in the
    //middle of being written out. Because m_comparisonsSoFar
    //and m_CurrentNumberBeingExamined may be
    //accessed from multiple threads, any read or write
    //operation to them needs to be synchronized with "lock" to
    //ensure that reads and writes are "atomic".
    lock(this)
    {
      m_CurrentNumberBeingExamined = potentialPrime;
      m_comparisonsSoFar++;
    }
  }

  //The item is prime
  return true;
} //End function
} //End class
```

Summary

Background threads can be useful in improving the end user's experience with your mobile application by increasing the responsiveness of the user interface, but only if used properly. Use background threads sparingly, specifically, and only when they solve a real application responsiveness problem that cannot be solved in the foreground thread. It is best to approach your application's design using a single-threaded model and only add background processing when the need proves itself.

Great care is warranted when writing background threading code and designing classes that need to be accessed from multiple threads. It is very useful to document your application's code to explicitly indicate which pieces are going to be accessed by multiple threads and as importantly which are not. Keep the number of classes, functions, properties, and member variables that need to be shared between multiple threads as small as possible and apply rigorous design, review, testing, and documentation efforts to these parts.

As with other aspects of design, using state machines can be beneficial when approaching asynchronous processing. State machines are a great way to manage background execution. A state machine allows for communication between different threads. They enable background threads to advertise their processing progress as well as allow other threads to request things from the background thread such as requesting the aborting of the background work. Encapsulating a background task in a class is a good abstraction and allows you to think of the background task as a logical entity with defined inputs and outputs.

In almost all cases, it is a good idea to have only one thread that drives the user interface; this is the main thread of your application. The user interface thread can periodically poll background tasks to see how they are progressing and relay this information to the user as appropriate. Alternatively, background threads can push this information to the user interface thread via a cross-thread communications mechanism such as the .NET Compact Frameworks `Control.Invoke()` mechanism.

Threads are a very useful but sophisticated concept. Like any advanced technique, there is a tendency to over-apply the use of threading. Unnecessary threads slow down overall application performance and overly complex threading models make code hard to maintain and debug. Use threads only when a proven need exists and then use them in the simplest manner possible. Following these simple guidelines will allow you to get the benefits of multithreading while avoiding the many potential pitfalls of concurrent streams of code execution.

CHAPTER 10

Performance and XML

Introduction: Working with XML

XML is rapidly becoming the text format of choice for storing and passing around data. It is more useful than generic text files because of two important concepts: (1) hierarchy—data can easily be stored with parent and child relationships, and (2) semistructuredness—XML allows a great deal of flexibility in the amount of structure that is applied to the data being passed around. XML data can be tightly bound to a specific schema (the schema can also be specified as an XML document) or it can be passed around willy-nilly with no formal guidelines describing what the document contains.

XML bears a close resemblance to another popular information encoding, HTML. HTML stands for HyperText Markup Language, which is a fancy way of saying "text tags that describe how a document looks." Similarly XML stands for eXtensible Markup Language, which is a fancy way of saying "text tags that describe data." XML is a product of things learned through the evolution of HTML, and both derive from an older more abstract format called SGML. HTML's semistructured and hierarchical text format has proven in usage to be more flexible than many preexisting binary formats. Popular adoption of HTML and then XML has shown that trading the compactness of binary formats for the flexibility, extensibility, and portability of text formats is often a good bargain. The tag and attribute syntax used by HTML to describe layout and content was seen by developers to be a powerful and extensible model for describing data. A downside of HTML has also emerged as a result of it rapid evolution; because the format has evolved organically over the years, the syntax has many irregularities that would not have been allowed into the language if it had been designed in a planned way. Because of the evolved complexity of the format, browsers also tend to be tolerant of documents that are "less than well formed," meaning that they tolerate errors in document syntax and do their best to present the document to the user anyway. This makes the proper parsing of HTML more difficult than it needs to be. XML borrows the text format approach and the tag and attribute syntax of HTML but maintains a normalized syntax suitable for use by generic parsing engines. XML parsers usually also insist that the documents are well formed and complete; strict adherence to XML document syntax rules greatly increases interoperability. This makes commonly available XML parsers suitable for a wide variety of uses.

Like HTML, XML has succeeded because people have agreed to use it to exchange information between different systems. The importance of broad adoption is hard to overstate. When a format gains popular adoption, network effects ensue and the technology quickly dominates. In recent years, XML has rapidly grown in adoption and now is used as the base format for many higher-level communications formats, including SOAP (Simple Object Access Protocol, the basis for Web services), WSDL (Web Service Description Language), XSL (eXtensible Schema Language), RSS (Really Simple Syndication, a mechanism for distributing content), and many other formats. Some of these XML formats are generic and some uses are specific to an industry's or a company's technology. When designing a new data-storage or data-interchange format today, the question is often not so much "Should XML be used?" but "What level of abstraction on top of XML should be used?" Most likely your connected mobile device applications will use XML to meet some kind of communication, storage, or data-interchange need. You may need to consume another system's XML formatted data, or you may need to design your own XML formats for others to use. Different approaches to working with XML at successively higher levels of abstraction exist. Each of these has its own advantages and disadvantages. For these reasons, it is important to know how to work with XML in the most appropriate way to meet your needs.

XML is very useful, but it is important to acknowledge that XML is not a panacea for every data-interchange need. XML offers flexibility but at the expense of being very verbose. Both XML and binary data exchange formats should be considered and the right one chosen based on the amount of data that needs to be exchanged and the nature of the communications networks your mobile application is using. When it is feasible to use XML, it offers great flexibility and is a preferred choice. However, XML is not the right solution for exchanging large amounts of data over lower-bandwidth connections. This is important to keep in mind as you design your mobile application's data communications model.

As long as data sizes and transfer times can be managed properly, XML can be great way to pass data between individual mobile devices, between a mobile device and a desktop computer, or between mobile devices and servers. Choosing to use XML as the way to store and pass around data is only the first in a series of decisions. Equally important are the lower-level mechanics of how your application will read in and write out the XML. As with many software engineering decisions, there are no universal right choices but rather trade-offs that need to be balanced to achieve developer productivity, code maintainability, and end-user performance. This chapter provides an overview of these basic design decisions.

To XML or Not to XML?

With all the momentum behind XML, it is easy to assume that it should be used to meet all data-exchange and storage needs. This is not the case. XML is powerful because it is flexible, but it is wasteful in size. If a relatively small amount of data is to be exchanged, XML is an excellent choice. For example, if 20 rows of rich database data need to be downloaded, the XML file may approach 20KB in size, whereas a binary implementation for transmitting that data may be able to squeeze the data into 2KB or perhaps an even smaller size. The time difference in downloading 20KB of data versus downloading 2KB of data is usually negligible compared to the time spent establishing a connection with a server, passing necessary credentials, and doing other setup work for communication. In either case, the absolute user wait time for transferring the data is relatively small, so the difference in storage size is not an overwhelming design factor in choosing a storage format. For relatively small amounts of data, the use of XML is justified because of the benefits of having a flexible data-interchange format. However, what if the data were 10 times larger and the design question was between transferring 200KB of XML data or 20KB of binary data? At this point, the user's wait time for data transfer between the device and server would start becoming significant, and measurements would need to be taken to weigh the impact of each implementation.

The speed of the communications network being used by your mobile application is an important factor to consider. Wi-Fi speeds may make the transfer time a nonissue for some data, and GPRS mobile phone networks may make transfer time and cost important factors to consider. If the size of the data to be transferred was another order of magnitude larger and the question was between transferring 2MB of XML data and 200KB of binary data, the choice of data format would be very significant because connection latency times would likely be dwarfed by the actual time spent transferring the data. Add on top of this the probable fact that parsing the XML data will take longer than parsing binary data that is optimized for reloading.

For small amounts of data, the use of XML is usually a clear choice. As the data sizes get larger, significant design consideration and real-world measurement and testing must be done to ensure that the benefits of XML usage are greater than the communications and processing overhead that is incurred. Like any verbose format, XML documents can be compressed before transmission and decompressed after to reduce transfer size, but this is additional processing work and binds the client and server to a common compression format; it can be done but is not a panacea. It is important to make a knowledgeable decision based on clearly elaborated facts and an assessment of the end user's experience. In some cases it may make sense to use XML for communication between servers but then perform binary communication between servers and devices. Each situation is unique and based on the user's needs, the nature of the communications networks being used, and the engineering costs associated with binary and XML-based communication. Experiment, measure often, and choose wisely.

Comparing XML to Other Text Formats

A great deal of literature exists describing XML and a full exploration of the subject is well beyond the scope of this book. Nevertheless, it is useful to present a very brief overview of how XML compares to other text-based formats. This will be done by way of example.

A Few Different Ways to Store Data as Text

Assume that our application has a need to store some user data. This user data consists of three items: an ID number, a name, and an address. Our application needs to store this data for its own use and may also want to pass the data to other applications. Three common ways to store this data as text are XML, comma-delimited values, and as values in an INI file.

Storing the data as XML

Like HTML, XML stores data as text surrounded by tags that add context to the data being passed in:

```
<UserInfo>
    <UserID> 12 </UserID>
    <UserName> Bob </UserName>
    <UserAddress> Someplace, Somewhere </UserName>
</UserInfo>
```

It is worth noting that the same data could also be stored as XML using tag attributes, for example:

```
<UserInfo UserID="12" UserName="Bob" UserAddress="Someplace,
Somewhere"> </UserInfo>
```

If appropriate, some combination of attributes and subtags can be used. Which XML format is most appropriate depends on the specific usage of the XML. Attributes can be simpler, but tags are more flexible because they can have attributes and subtags.

Storing the Data as a Comma-Delimited File

Historically, this kind of data was often stored as comma-delimited data:

```
12, Bob, "SomePlace, Somewhere"
```

Storing the Data in an INI File

INI files have also been a popular way to store data in the past. An INI file stores data as a set of name/value pairs:

```
[UserInfo]
UserID=12
UserName=Bob
UserAddress=Someplace, Somewhere
```

Other common formats exist as well such as PropertyBags, which sit somewhere between XML and INI files in terms of structure and flexibility and were popular with Visual Basic 5 and 6 developers. What XML does above and beyond many previous formats is lend additional structure to the data. This structure allows for hierarchical data that is not order dependent. It is a bit more verbose than many other text formats, but it is much more flexible. This flexibility makes it easy to version, maintain, and pass data between different systems.

XML Data Is Hierarchical

The hierarchical nature of XML is important to understand. Think of your XML document as a tree of objects, with each object potentially having additional child objects. To show this, our XML example above can be modified to show some more hierarchy:

```
<UserInfo>
    <UserID> 12 </UserID>"
    <Name>
        <FirstName>  Ivo  </FirstName>
        <LastName>  Salmre </LastName>
    </Name>
    <Address>
        <Street>10 SomeStreet</Street>
        <City>Seattle</City>
        <State>WA</State>
    </Address>
</UserInfo>
```

Here we have made Name and Address subnodes of UserInfo.

Other XML Features

There is much more to XML, including standardized schema, typed data, and validation possibilities. The examples above are only the most trivial examples of XML fragments. Good documentation exists describing the intricacies of XML both in the .NET Framework documentation as well as generically on the Web. This book and its samples focus on the practicalities of using XML on mobile devices and is not in any way an exhaustive study of XML usage.

In practical usage, most XML data exchange falls somewhere in between the extremes of rigorous structure and free-form data. What level of rigor to apply to data formats is a choice left up to both the sender and the consumer of the data. A computing node generating XML may make it adhere to rigorously defined schema or it may simply choose an XML encoding that is convenient for it. Similarly, a computing device consuming XML can choose to verify its contents to ensure it conforms to an expected schema or it can assume the data is correctly formatted and attempt to parse the results. Because tasks such as schema verification can be computationally expensive, when required they are often best done by a server before data is sent onto a device.

Different Ways to Work with XML

Due to its utility and popular adoption XML has quickly matured. With this maturation, programming models have arisen that make XML easier to work with. As a general rule, whenever more specialized XML APIs exist, you should avoid working with XML using generic file I/O APIs. Higher-level APIs have the benefit of greatly increasing developer productivity as well as pushing the design and testing burden onto someone else who's sole job it has been to build a great XML parser. If you write your own XML parser, you will be spending a lot of time solving a problem that has already been well addressed by others on lots of different platforms; it is better to concentrate your efforts in areas where you can add unique value.

Despite the fact that existing well-tested and performance-tuned APIs exist, there are still important design decisions to make when using XML. The most important programming decision you will make is what level of API abstraction to use. Will you choose to work with low-level, forward-only XML APIs, or will you work with higher-level random-access XML APIs that expose the XML as an in-memory tree. There are three fundamental approaches for working with XML data:

1. *Roll your own "optimized" parser from scratch.* It is almost never worth doing this if predeveloped and tested approaches exist. This approach is strongly discouraged because the payoff almost never matches the effort required and the long-term maintenance burden incurred.

2. *Use a high-level, general-purpose and random-access XML parsing DOM.* DOM stands for Document Object Model, and it is a way of working with XML data as an in-memory tree. High-level APIs for working with XML result in highly reliable and maintainable code. For smaller XML documents, documents that require constant random access to all parts of the XML document tree, or XML documents that need to be fully re-persisted to files, this approach is a great one.

3. *Use a low-level forward-only reading/writing XML API.* Low-level APIs offer maximum performance but put additional burden on the programmer. These APIs are forward only and allow the XML tree to be read in or written out as a stream of XML elements without storing the whole XML document in memory. On mobile devices where memory is precious and particularly when working with larger sized or read-only data this is the only reasonable approach to achieve acceptable performance. It represents a very good middle ground between using high-level APIs and the roll-your-own approach. This is the right way to go if the high-level APIs require too much processing or memory overhead to meet your needs.

The first approach (step 1) is not recommended because it is a low-developer-productivity and high-maintenance approach. The second two of these approaches are examined and contrasted below.

A Simple Example Using Both the XML DOM and the XML Reader/Writer

Below we compare the use of the higher-level XML DOM with the lower-level forward-only XML reader/writer when working with some simple XML. The XML produced and consumed in both cases is identical. It is important to note that the data used in this example is trivially small and either approach will yield acceptable performance. Real performance differences arise as the size of the data increases. To think about this conceptually picture the UserInfo data node below repeated a hundred or a thousand times. If desired, build a data file to represent this and test your algorithms on it to contrast the approaches.

Example: XML File Contents

```
<AllMyData>
  <UserInfo>
    <UserID>14</UserID>
    <Name>
      <FirstName>Ivo</FirstName>
      <LastName>Salmre</LastName>
    </Name>
  </UserInfo>
</AllMyData>
```

It is worth noting that I have chosen to not use UserInfo as the top-level node, but rather to have one more node on top of this. This is a good design practice because XML allows only one top-level "root node." If we made UserInfo the root node, it would have limited the flexibility of storing other top-level information in the file without redoing the design. Using a generic root-level node allows the freedom to add other nodes below it as our needs expand. For example, in addition to UserInfo, I may want to add nodes for ServerInfo or ApplicationInfo that store important information that is not user specific. Additionally, I may have more than one user and may want a UserInfo node for each. The data structure above supports including multiple

UserInfo sections one after another; this would not have been possible if UserData was the root node of the document.

XML DOM

The XML DOM (Document Object Model) works with XML data in memory represented as a tree of objects. Each XML element is represented using an in-memory object. The XML DOM approach can be thought of as "highly stateful" in that all the data necessary to re-create the XML document is loaded in as state when an XML document is read in. XML trees can be created in memory and then serialized to files or over network streams. Similarly, any XML content in the file system or XML received over any data stream can be used to populate an in-memory XML DOM tree.

Having an in-memory tree of objects is a very convenient way of working with data that is of moderate size and needs only incremental updates. A 20KB file of XML can fairly rapidly be loaded into memory, worked on as a tree of objects, and saved back to the file system. As long as your data is relatively small in size, the XML DOM is a great way to create XML, work with it in memory, and output XML to a file or network stream.

The utility of the DOM approach is bounded both by how much memory you have available to hold the parser-generated object tree and by how much processing power is available to parse the whole tree of XML data. The downside of the XML DOM approach is that it is monolithic; the whole XML file or stream is parsed and placed into memory before you get to access any of it. If your application only needs to work with a small amount of the data present in a large file, you are incurring a great overhead to access that data.

Reasons to use an XML DOM approach:

- *The XML DOM is a simple and powerful programming model*. Having an in-memory tree representing an XML document makes it easy to work with data in a random-access way.
- *The XML DOM is great for small and moderate amounts of data*. As long as a file is reasonably small, its contents will not take up too much memory.
- *The XML DOM is the best choice if you need to work with and potentially modify all of the XML data while it is in memory*. The XML DOM is a powerful tool if your application needs to work with the XML data in a random-access way and the data needs to be re-persisted to a file or stream.

Reasons to avoid using an XML DOM approach:

- *The XML DOM programming model forces all XML data to be parsed and loaded into an in-memory tree before it can be accessed.* Building a large in-memory tree of the whole document is very wasteful if your application only needs access to a small amount of the XML data inside.
- *Using the XML DOM will result in increasingly poor performance as the size of the XML increases.* Because, for large files, many objects will be created in limited device memory, this can potentially cause severe memory pressure. Additionally, all created objects will eventually need to be garbage collected, which will incur a downstream cleanup cost for your application.
- *The XML DOM is a poor choice if you only need to use the data in a read-only way.* The DOM incurs overhead but makes it easy to write the XML data back out. If you are only using the data in a read-only way or plan to write it out in a different format, you are paying a performance penalty without getting much gain.

Listing 10.1 below contains sample code for reading and writing the XML data shown above using the XML DOM.

Listing 10.1 Using the XML DOM to Save and Load Data from a File

```
using System;

//------------------------------------------------
//Shows saving and loading data using the
//XML Document Object Model
//------------------------------------------------
public class SaveAndLoadXML_UseDOM
{
  //XML Tags we will use in our document
  const string XML_ROOT_TAG = "AllMyData";
  const string XML_USERINFO_TAG = "UserInfo";
  const string XML_USERID_TAG = "UserID";
  const string XML_NAMEINFO_TAG = "Name";
  const string XML_FIRSTNAME_TAG = "FirstName";
  const string XML_LASTNAME_TAG = "LastName";

  //-------------------------------------------------------
  //Loads the state of the user
  //
```

```csharp
// [in] fileName:   The name of the file we are saving to
// [out] userId:    UserID we have loaded
// [out] firstName: User's FirstName we have loaded
// [out] lastName:  User's LastName we have loaded
//----------------------------------------------------------
public static void XML_LoadUserInfo(string fileName,
  out int userId, out string firstName, out string lastName)
{
  //Start out with null values
  userId = 0;
  firstName = "";
  lastName = "";
  //Assume we have not loaded the user data
  bool gotUserInfoData = false;

  System.Xml.XmlDocument xmlDocument =
    new System.Xml.XmlDocument();

  xmlDocument.Load(fileName);

  //Grab the root node
  System.Xml.XmlElement rootElement;
  rootElement =
    (System.Xml.XmlElement) xmlDocument.ChildNodes[0];

  //Make sure the root node matches our expected text
  //Otherwise, this could just be some random other XML file
  if (rootElement.Name != XML_ROOT_TAG)
  {
    throw new Exception("Root node not of expected type!");
  }

  //-----------------------------------------
  //A simple machine that iterates through all the nodes
  //-----------------------------------------
  foreach(System.Xml.XmlElement childOf_RootNode in
    rootElement.ChildNodes)
  {

    //If it's a UserInfo node, we want to look inside it
    if(childOf_RootNode.Name == XML_USERINFO_TAG)
    {
      gotUserInfoData  = true; //We found the user data
```

```csharp
//-----------------------------------
//Load each of the subitems
//-----------------------------------
foreach(System.Xml.XmlElement child_UserDataNode in
  childOf_RootNode.ChildNodes)
{
  //UserID
  if(child_UserDataNode.Name == XML_USERID_TAG)
  {
    userId= System.Convert.ToInt32(
      child_UserDataNode.InnerText);
  }
    //UserName
  else if(child_UserDataNode.Name == XML_NAMEINFO_TAG)
  {
    foreach(System.Xml.XmlElement child_Name in
      child_UserDataNode.ChildNodes)
    {
      //FirstName
      if(child_Name.Name == XML_FIRSTNAME_TAG)
      {
        firstName = child_Name.InnerText;
      }
        //LastName
      else if(child_Name.Name == XML_LASTNAME_TAG)
      {
        lastName = child_Name.InnerText;
      }

    } //End of UserName parsing loop
  } //"End if" for "is UserName?"

}//End of UserInfo parsing loop
} //"End if" for "is UserInfo"?

}//End of root node parsing loop

if (gotUserInfoData == false)
{
  throw new Exception("User data not found in XML!");
}

}
```

```csharp
//-----------------------------------------------------------
//Saves the state of the user
//
// [in] fileName:  The name of the file we are saving to
// [in] userId:    UserID we want to save
// [in] firstName: User's FirstName we want to save
// [in] lastName:  User's LastName we want to save
//-----------------------------------------------------------
public static void XML_SaveUserInfo(string fileName,
  int userId, string firstName, string lastName)
{

  System.Xml.XmlDocument xmlDocument =
    new System.Xml.XmlDocument();

  //-----------------------------------------------------------
  //Add the top-level document element
  //-----------------------------------------------------------
  System.Xml.XmlElement rootNodeForDocument;
  rootNodeForDocument = xmlDocument.CreateElement(
    XML_ROOT_TAG);
  xmlDocument.AppendChild(rootNodeForDocument);

  //-----------------------------------------------------------
  //Add the data for the user info
  //-----------------------------------------------------------
  System.Xml.XmlElement topNodeForUserData;
  topNodeForUserData = xmlDocument.CreateElement(
    XML_USERINFO_TAG);
  rootNodeForDocument.AppendChild(topNodeForUserData);


  //-----------------------------------------------------------
  //Add the UserID value to our document
  //-----------------------------------------------------------
  //Create a sub-node for the namespace info
  System.Xml.XmlElement subNodeForUserID;
  subNodeForUserID =
    xmlDocument.CreateElement(XML_USERID_TAG);
  subNodeForUserID.InnerText =
    System.Convert.ToString(userId);
  //Attach the UserID sub-node to the top level node
  topNodeForUserData.AppendChild(subNodeForUserID);
```

```
//-----------------------------------------------------------
//Add all the NameInfo values to our document
//-----------------------------------------------------------
//Create a sub-node for the namespace info
System.Xml.XmlElement subNodeForNameInfo;
subNodeForNameInfo = xmlDocument.CreateElement(
  XML_NAMEINFO_TAG);
//FirstName
System.Xml.XmlElement subNodeFirstName;
subNodeFirstName = xmlDocument.CreateElement(
  XML_FIRSTNAME_TAG);
subNodeFirstName.InnerText = firstName;

//LastName
System.Xml.XmlElement subNodeLastName;
subNodeLastName = xmlDocument.CreateElement(
  XML_LASTNAME_TAG);
subNodeLastName.InnerText = lastName;

//Attach the first and last name subnodes to the NameInfo
//parent note
subNodeForNameInfo.AppendChild(subNodeFirstName);
subNodeForNameInfo.AppendChild(subNodeLastName);

//Attach the NameInfo subnode (with its children too) to
//the top-level node
topNodeForUserData.AppendChild(subNodeForNameInfo);


//-----------------------------------------------------------
//Save the document
//-----------------------------------------------------------
try
{
  xmlDocument.Save(fileName);
}
catch (System.Exception ex)
{
  System.Windows.Forms.MessageBox.Show(
    "Error occurred saving XML document - " + ex.Message);
}
} //End of function
} //End of class
```

Listing 10.2 Calling the XML Save and Load Code

```
private void button1_Click(object sender, System.EventArgs e)
{
  const string FILENAME = "TestFileName.XML";

  //Save using the XML DOM
  SaveAndLoadXML_UseDOM.XML_SaveUserInfo(FILENAME, 14, "Ivo",
                                         "Salmre");
  //Save using the forward only XMLWriter
  //SaveAndLoadXML_UseReaderWriter.XML_SaveUserInfo(FILENAME,
  //                                  18, "Ivo", "Salmre");

  int userID;
  string firstName;
  string lastName;

  //Load using the XML DOM
  SaveAndLoadXML_UseDOM.XML_LoadUserInfo(FILENAME, out userID,
                                out firstName, out lastName);

  //Load using the forward only XML Reader
  //SaveAndLoadXML_UseReaderWriter.XML_LoadUserInfo(FILENAME,
  //          out userID, out firstName, out lastName);

  System.Windows.Forms.MessageBox.Show("Done! " +
    userID.ToString() + ", " + lastName + ", " + firstName);
}
```

XML Forward-Only Reader/Writer

In contrast to the highly stateful and random-access-capable XML DOM approach are the forward-only XMLReader and XMLWriter. These are minimally stateful in that they only maintain the minimum amount of state necessary to be able to read and write XML data and do not try to build or work with an in-memory tree of XML data. These are referred to as forward-only models because they provide a programmatic cursor that points to the current location in the XML file and work with data at that point; the cursor can be moved forward but not backward. The XMLReader has a lot of advanced features, but it basically allows applications to cursor through the nodes of an XML document. When reading in XML, the XMLReader reads in only one node and its associated attributes at any given time; think of this as akin to reading in one line of text at a time from a normal text file. When the developer is done looking at that node and its attributes, it commands the XMLReader to move onward to the next element, at which point the XMLReader discards any state it is holding pertaining to the contents of the current node. Forward-only access is a necessary trait for having the highest performance and lowest overhead.

It is worth pointing out that the XML DOM is built on top of the forward-only XMLReader and XMLWriter classes. The XML DOM uses the forward-only XMLReader to parse the XML and builds an in-memory tree of the data it reads in. When writing out XML, the DOM iterates over its in-memory XML tree and pushes all of the nodes out through an XMLWriter to output them to a stream or file. By inference, anything possible with the XML DOM is possible with the XML reader and writer. The XML DOM does as efficient of a job as possible for being a stateful, general-purpose and random-access XML parser.

The gains in using the XMLReader and XMLWriter instead of the XML DOM stem from optimizing for the fact that your application either does not need general-purpose parsing or that you can do with less in-memory state because you do not need to write out the full XML tree that you read in. If you do not need all the rich functionality of the XML DOM, the XMLReader and XMLWriter can allow you to get better performance by working at a lower level of abstraction.

How Do the XMLReader and XMLWriter Differ from SAX?

The .NET Framework and .NET Compact Framework implement a cursor-based approach where the end developer's algorithms tell the XMLReader how to move forward and parse the next elements of XML data, but this is not the only forward-only approach to working with XML. Another popular approach to forward-only processing of XML data is the SAX (Simple API for XML) model. Whereas the XMLReader uses a cursor-based approach where the programmer chooses how and when to move the cursor forward, the SAX model is an event-based model where a parsing engine runs through the XML document (also in a forward-only way) and generates events that end developers code can process to examine the XML as it is being parsed. The XML reader model is "pull based," where application code pulls the next piece of XML it wants to work with. The SAX model is "push based," where pieces of XML are pushed to events that application code handles. They both serve the same purpose, namely to facilitate high-speed, low-overhead parsing of XML. Choosing between SAX and XML readers/writers is a matter of preference and availability on the platform you are working on. The recommendations in this section apply to both forward-only models.

Reasons to Use a Forward-Only XML Approach

■ *Forward only models like the XMLReader offer the fastest reliable way to read XML, even from huge files.* The state maintained by the framework while parsing XML is the minimum required. This state does not grow with the length of XML that has been parsed, so there is potentially no limit to the size of the XML document you can search through for data you want to extract. The only long-term state generated are the objects your application decides to create based on its parsing needs.

■ *Forward-only models such as the XMLWriter offer a fast and simple way for writing well-formed XML.* The code for writing out XML using the XMLWriter is fast and simple to understand. Even for complex XML documents, your code to navigate your own internal data structures is likely to be more complex than the code that writes out the XML. Using the XMLWriter is much easier than writing your own custom code to write out XML tags. There are few, if any, reasons not to use the XMLWriter instead of designing your own custom code to write out XML tags.

■ *Forward-only models are great for extracting specific data or writing short streams of XML data.* If you are looking to extract specific data from an XML document and know where that data sits in the data hierarchy of the file, using the XMLReader and your own state machine to navigate to the data is relatively straightforward. Similarly, if you know ahead of time what the format of the XML you need to write out needs to be, working with the XMLWriter is straightforward.

Reasons to Avoid a Forward-Only XML Approach

■ *Forward-only models do not support random access to document elements.* You get one shot to do something with the data as you are reading it in. If your algorithm needs to dynamically cross-reference between different parts of the XML document or make related changes to different parts, you will have to write some pretty complex and stateful code to do this. Because the XML DOM maintains an in-memory tree, it is easy to walk this tree to search and make changes.

■ *Forward-only models require significant work to reconstruct an entire tree structure.* If you want to write out the same XML you read in, you will be duplicating a good portion of the XML DOM's functionality to do this. XML readers are great for allowing you to pull out specific pieces of data. XML writers are great for allowing your application to quickly output specific pieces of XML. If you need to read in an XML document and make significant changes to portions of it before writing it back out, the DOM is your friend.

- *Forward-only models offer a more complex programming model for navigating and searching complex documents.* Writing generic parsing code that works with arbitrary XML hierarchies can be complex. You will need to have sophisticated state that lets you know where in the document's hierarchy you are in order to find the information you are looking for. For example, if you are looking for the <Name> tag that is inside a specific <Customer> tag and your XML document has <Name> tags that correspond to <Customer>, <Employee>, and <Vendor> objects that may exist at different depths of the XML tree, you will need to write code to keep track of where in the document you are presently looking to distinguish between these cases in order to guarantee you are accessing the correct information. If your document follows a single well-defined schema this may not be too bad. On the other hand, if your document may be in one of several schemas, the problem becomes algorithmically complex. In cases where the XML document may be of significant complexity, consider doing the processing on a server where both more processing power exists and more powerful APIs for searching XML documents also exist (for example, XPATH for document queries).

Below is sample code for reading and writing the XML data shown above using the forward-only XML reader/writer. Of specific interest may be the state machine used in the XMLReader to track document location; note how even for this simple XML document this code is not trivial. Comparatively, the code for outputting XML documents using the XMLWriter is very simple.

Listing 10.3 Using the Forward-Only XML Reader/Writers to Save and Load XML Data from a File

```
using System;
public class SaveAndLoadXML_UseReaderWriter
{
    //XML Tags we will use in our document
    const string XML_ROOT_TAG = "AllMyData";
    const string XML_USERINFO_TAG = "UserInfo";
```

```
const string XML_USERID_TAG = "UserID";
const string XML_NAMEINFO_TAG = "Name";
const string XML_FIRSTNAME_TAG = "FirstName";
const string XML_LASTNAME_TAG = "LastName";

//The set of states we are tracking as we read in data
private enum ReadLocation
{
  inAllMyData,
  inUserInfo,
  inUserID,
  inName,
  inFirstName,
  inLastName,
}


//----------------------------------------------------------
//Saves the state of the user
//
// [in] fileName: The name of the file we are saving to
// [in] userId:    UserID we have loaded
// [in] firstName: User's FirstName we have loaded
// [in] lastName:  User's LastName we have loaded
//----------------------------------------------------------
public static void XML_SaveUserInfo(string fileName,
  int userId, string firstName, string lastName)
{
  System.Xml.XmlTextWriter xmlTextWriter;
  xmlTextWriter = new System.Xml.XmlTextWriter(fileName,
    System.Text.Encoding.Default);

  //Write out the contents of the document!
  //<Root>
  xmlTextWriter.WriteStartElement(XML_ROOT_TAG);

  //<Root>
  xmlTextWriter.WriteStartElement(XML_USERINFO_TAG);
  //<Root><UserID>

  //<Root><UserInfo>
  xmlTextWriter.WriteStartElement(XML_NAMEINFO_TAG);
  //<Root><UserInfo><Name>
  xmlTextWriter.WriteStartElement(XML_FIRSTNAME_TAG);
  //<Root><UserInfo><Name><FirstName>
```

```
xmlTextWriter.WriteString(firstName); //Value being written
xmlTextWriter.WriteEndElement(); //Close first name
//<Root><UserInfo><Name>
xmlTextWriter.WriteStartElement(XML_LASTNAME_TAG);
//<Root><UserInfo><Name><LastName>
xmlTextWriter.WriteString(lastName); //Value being written
xmlTextWriter.WriteEndElement(); //Close last name
//<Root><UserInfo><Name>
xmlTextWriter.WriteEndElement(); //Close Name
//<Root><UserInfo>

//<Root><UserInfo>
xmlTextWriter.WriteStartElement(XML_USERID_TAG);
//<Root><UserInfo><UserID>

//Value being written
xmlTextWriter.WriteString(userId.ToString());
xmlTextWriter.WriteEndElement(); //Close UserID
//<Root><UserInfo>

xmlTextWriter.WriteEndElement(); //Close UserInfo
//<Root>

xmlTextWriter.WriteEndElement(); //Close Document
//

xmlTextWriter.Close();
}


//---------------------------------------------------------
//Loads the state of the user
//
// [in] fileName:   The name of the file we are saving to
// [out] userId:    UserID we have loaded
// [out] firstName: User's FirstName we have loaded
// [out] lastName:  User's LastName we have loaded
//---------------------------------------------------------
public static void XML_LoadUserInfo(string fileName,
  out int userId, out string firstName, out string lastName)
{
  ReadLocation currentReadLocation;

  //Start out with null values
  userId = 0;
```

```
firstName = "";
lastName = "";


System.Xml.XmlTextReader xmlReader =
  new System.Xml.XmlTextReader(fileName);

xmlReader.WhitespaceHandling =
  System.Xml.WhitespaceHandling.None;

bool readSuccess;

readSuccess = xmlReader.Read();
if(readSuccess == false)
{
  throw new System.Exception("No XML data to read!");
}

//Make sure we recognize the root tag.
if(xmlReader.Name != XML_ROOT_TAG)
{
  throw new System.Exception(
    "Root tag different from expected!");
}

//Note where we are in the document
currentReadLocation = ReadLocation.inAllMyData;

//-----------------------------------------------
//Loop through our document and read what we need
//-----------------------------------------------
while(readSuccess)
{

  switch(xmlReader.NodeType)
  {
      //Called when we enter a new Element
    case System.Xml.XmlNodeType.Element:
    {
      string nodeName = xmlReader.Name;

      LoadHelper_NewElementEncountered(nodeName,
        ref currentReadLocation);
      break;
    }
```

```
//----------------------------------------------------
//Here's where we can actually extract some text and
//get the data we are trying to load
//----------------------------------------------------
case System.Xml.XmlNodeType.Text:
{

    switch(currentReadLocation)
    {
      case ReadLocation.inFirstName:
      { firstName = xmlReader.Value; break; }

      case ReadLocation.inLastName:
      { lastName = xmlReader.Value;break; }

      case ReadLocation.inUserID:
      {
        userId = System.Convert.ToInt32(xmlReader.Value);
        break;
      }

    }
    break;
}


    //----------------------------------------------------
    //Gets called when we have encountered the end of
    //an element
    //
    //We may want to switch our state based on what node
    //we are exiting to indicate that we are going back
    //to that node's parent
    //----------------------------------------------------
case System.Xml.XmlNodeType.EndElement:
{
    bool continueParsing;
    continueParsing = LoadHelper_EndElementEncountered(
      ref currentReadLocation);

    if(continueParsing == false)
    { goto finished_reading_wanted_data; }
    break;
}
```

```
      default:
      {
        //There is no harm in having other XML node types, but
        //using our sample XML, we should note this occurrence
        //code...
        System.Windows.Forms.MessageBox.Show(
          "Unexpected XML type encountered" + xmlReader.Name);
        break;
      }

    } //End of Case statement-based current type of XML
    //element the parser is on.

    //Go to the next node
    readSuccess = xmlReader.Read();
  }

  //If we made it to this point without exiting the UserInfo
  //XML tag, something went wrong with the XML data we were
  //reading.
  throw new Exception("Could not find UserInfo in XML!");

  finished_reading_wanted_data:
    //Close the file, we're done with it!
    xmlReader.Close();
}


//-----------------------------------------------------
//Helper logic that decides what state we should enter
//when we encounter an exit tag.
//-----------------------------------------------------
private static bool LoadHelper_EndElementEncountered(
  ref ReadLocation currentReadLocation)
{
  switch(currentReadLocation)
  {
      //If we are leaving the Name node, we are going back
      //up to the UserInfo
    case ReadLocation.inName:
    { currentReadLocation = ReadLocation.inUserInfo; break; }

      //If we are leaving the FirstName node, we are going
      //back up to the Name node
```

```
      case ReadLocation.inFirstName:
      { currentReadLocation = ReadLocation.inName; break; }


        //If we are leaving the LastName node, we are going back
        //up to the Name node
      case ReadLocation.inLastName:
      { currentReadLocation = ReadLocation.inName; break; }


        //If we are leaving the UserID node, we are going back
        //up to the UserInfo node
      case ReadLocation.inUserID:
      { currentReadLocation = ReadLocation.inUserInfo; break; }


        //If we are leaving the UserInfo node, we have just
        //finished reading in the UserID, FirstName,
        //and LastName.
        //
        //We can exit the loop, as we have all the information
        //we want!
      case ReadLocation.inUserInfo:
      {
        return false;   //We should stop parsing
      }
    }

  return true; //Continue parsing
}

private static void LoadHelper_NewElementEncountered(
  string nodeName, ref ReadLocation currentReadLocation)
{
  //----------------------------------------------------------
  //We have entered a new element!
  //
  //What state we can enter is dependent on what state we are
  //presently in
  //----------------------------------------------------------
  switch (currentReadLocation)
  {
      //If we're in the "AllMyData" Node, here are the nodes
      //we can enter
    case (ReadLocation.inAllMyData):
    {
      if (nodeName == XML_USERINFO_TAG)
```

```
            {
                currentReadLocation = ReadLocation.inUserInfo;
            }
            break;
        }

            //If we're in the UserInfo node, here are the nodes
            //we can enter
        case (ReadLocation.inUserInfo):
        {
            if (nodeName == XML_USERID_TAG)
            {
                currentReadLocation = ReadLocation.inUserID;
            }
            else if (nodeName == XML_NAMEINFO_TAG)
            {
                currentReadLocation = ReadLocation.inName;
            }
            break;
        }


            //If we're in the Name node, here are the nodes
            //we can enter
        case (ReadLocation.inName):
        {
            if (nodeName == XML_FIRSTNAME_TAG)
            {
                currentReadLocation = ReadLocation.inFirstName;
            }
            else if (nodeName == XML_LASTNAME_TAG)
            {
                currentReadLocation = ReadLocation.inLastName;
            }
            break;
        }
    }
  } //End function
} //End Class
```

Improving Performance by Offloading Work to Others

A great deal of thinking goes into how to build the fastest possible implementation of an algorithm. Often not enough thought goes into considering
whether the work being done is appropriate at all on a mobile device. In
many cases, work can either be done ahead of time before the data goes
onto a mobile device or can be offloaded to a server and done on demand.
Because of their higher memory capacities, more powerful processors, and
larger storage capacities, servers can both do valuable preprocessing and
on-demand work that can be of benefit to mobile applications.

The right time to do server processing on XML data is before it ever
comes onto a device. If a mobile application is going to benefit from having
data presorted, presearched, or pretransformed, doing this work on the
server before sending the data down to a device can pay real performance
dividends. This is an area well worth spending creative energies on.

Avoid Doing Complex Data Transformations on the Device

It is often useful to turn XML data into some kind of user-viewable data.
Populating a ListBox or ListView control with data from an XML document
is a simple example. Generating HTML from XML data is a more complex
example. In each case, some kind of transformation is performed on the
XML to achieve a human-readable result. Transformations are often complex and processor intensive. Find a way to do as much of the required
transformation work as possible on a server before sending the data down to
a device. The more heavy lifting that can be done before data comes onto a
device, the lighter the workload will be on the device.

If you are reading data from a database that needs to be transformed in
some way, consider having an intermediary Web service on the server that
performs the transformations before sending the data down to a device.

Avoid Doing Complex Data Searches on the Device

Searching data for specific requested information is another fundamental
pattern in applications. Most applications that work with data do some kind
of searching, filtering, or sorting. This searching can range from very simple
searches to complex data mining. As with XML transformations, any work
that can be done to presearch, preorganize or prefilter the data into more
easily accessible forms before bringing it down to the mobile device will aid
in making your mobile application perform well. If you are downloading

XML documents from a server that will need to be queried for information, consider doing the search ahead of time on the server and only downloading the results; this will save device processing time as well as reduce the amount of data that needs to be downloaded.

Consider Removing Unnecessary Information Before Data Is Sent to a Device

Unnecessary information sent to a device takes extra time both to transmit and to parse on the device. If you are dealing with XML documents that contain lots of information that will not be useful on the device, it is worth considering processing the document on a server to remove the extra information. In this way, a server can separate the wheat from the chaff and only send information down to the device that will be of use.

When Not to Offload Work onto a Server

As important as understanding when work can be offloaded to servers is understanding cases where it is not efficient to do so. There is much fanciful talk about using distributed computing to push all kinds work onto other devices waiting on a network. This is a nice idea in concept but very difficult to do in practice. It is usually not worthwhile to push a large amount of data up from a device and onto a server for immediate processing. Unless the data to be processed is very dense and the analysis required is intense, the time, inconvenience, connection reliability requirements, and potential bandwidth costs of moving the data back and forth across a network is not warranted. A case where pushing data from a device to a server for immediate processing may be useful is complex image analysis where data such as aerial photographs or medical images acquired by a high-resolution camera need computationally intensive algorithmic analysis. In these cases, the size of the data being round-tripped to the server is trivial compared to the processing needing to be performed; in these cases, the latency of sending the data is outweighed by the speed gains of processing the data on a more powerful machine. The time required to process the data on the device must be weighed against the latency of sending the data to a server, the time to process the data on a server, and the very real possibility that the server may not be available to the mobile device when needed. Pushing data from a mobile device to a server is usually not worthwhile for XML documents; the size to data ratio is not high, and the analysis that needs to be done is usually not complex enough. Additionally, the requirement to be online to have the analysis performed makes the model of round-tripping data to a server for processing unattractive for mobile device applications.

Why Are XSLT and XPath Not Supported in Version 1.1 of the .NET Compact Framework?

When designing the .NET Compact Framework, two main design constraints needed to be balanced. The need to minimize the size of the .NET Compact Framework (a less than 2MB device footprint was the goal) was balanced with the desire to give developers as much functionality as possible. In meeting this balance, the utility and appropriateness of features was carefully weighed against the additional size that the features would add to the .NET Compact Framework. This resulted in the decision not to support XPath and XSLT in the first release of the .NET Compact Framework.

XPath is query language useful for searching XML documents. It is a powerful concept, but it is complex and requires significant computational power to use effectively. XSLT is technology for transforming a tree of XML into a new document based on specified rules; it is often used to turn XML data into HTML user interface documents. It also requires significant computational power to work effectively.

Both of these features are clearly useful and desirable to have in the developer's toolset, but are they appropriate for mobile device applications running on resource-constrained devices? Supporting XSLT and XPath would have added size to the .NET Compact Framework and also given developers functionality that would not have performed well for many tasks that the functionality would be used for. For these reasons, it was decided not to include XPath and XSLT support in version 1.1 of the .NET Compact Framework.

Future versions of the .NET Compact Framework may well add support for these features; XPath support in particular has been a requested feature. Developers are advised, however, to think long and hard about what computational burdens they are taking on when they use highly value-adding but computationally demanding libraries. There is a tendency to assume that features built in to a framework will perform well under all circumstances; this is incorrect. Just as this chapter recommends that developers choose carefully between the convenience of a stateful XML DOM approach and a more complex but far less-stateful forward-only XMLReader/XMLWriter approach, the same advice applies for any higher-level stateful or computationally demanding library. Use it if it is appropriate, but be aware of the cost and always measure the results.

Summary

XML is an extremely useful data format both for storing application-specific data and for information interchange between applications. It offers a nice compromise between the simplicity and freedom of text files and rigor of databases. XML use will doubtless continue to grow on servers, desktops, and mobile devices.

An important top-level decision to make is whether to use XML or binary data formats for any given communications task. XML offers great benefits, but these come at the expense of additional size and processing requirements on devices. For many uses, this overhead is justified by the benefits, and good design practices can ensure acceptable device performance. However, for data of large-enough size or when working with lower-bandwidth connections, binary alternatives should also be considered. The best thing to do is to measure the effects of using binary and XML-based communication in real-world situations and make a design decision based on achieving acceptable end-user performance. If good performance cannot be achieved by designing and tuning an efficient XML implementation, binary alternatives or changes in the communications model may need to be considered.

When working with XML, it is important to consider the size of the data being processed as well as the specific purpose it is being put to. For small XML documents (for example, 20KB), it is often convenient to use an XML DOM approach where the entire XML tree is loaded into memory. The XML DOM offers random access to the document data and the easy ability to write the document back out. A significant disadvantage of the XML DOM is that it loads all of the XML data into memory at once and is therefore highly stateful. This disadvantage can become critical when working with larger documents.

Forward-only XML libraries offer a good lower-level alternative appropriate for working with larger amounts of XML. The .NET Compact Framework offers the XMLReader and XMLWriter, and other frameworks may offer the SAX model for forward-only access to XML. These allow for maximum performance because they are not stateful and therefore do not need to build an in-memory tree of the data that represents the document. The XMLReader can be complex to work with if the document is complex; a state machine approach can be useful in keeping track of your position in the document's hierarchy. The XMLWriter is very easy to use for writing out XML data. Using a forward-only model may be the only reasonable approach on mobile devices when working with large amounts of XML data.

Look for ways to preprocess XML data before bringing it down to a mobile device. Although it is usually not useful to round-trip data up to a server for processing, it can be very useful to preprocess XML information before bringing it down to a device. The goal of preprocessing is to transform the data into a form that is efficient to consume on devices.

Chances are very good if your application stores, interchanges data, or connects to networked information sources you will end up using XML in some way or another. The advantages of a standardized text format are overwhelmingly compelling for many uses. That said, after you decide to use XML you have a great deal of additional latitude in how your application will work with it. The partition of work between servers and mobile devices, the level of abstraction and statefulness of the APIs you use, and the processing model used for working with the XML will have a large effect on the performance your end users experience. It is important to understand the options you have, what the relative strengths of these options are, and to experiment to find the right XML approach for your application.

CHAPTER 11

Graphics and User Interface Performance

Mr. Braddock: "Well would you mind telling me what these last four years of hard work was for?"

Benjamin Braddock: "You got me ...."

—The Graduate (1967)

Elaine Robinson: "I don't want you to go anywhere until you have a definite plan."

—The Graduate (1967)

Introduction

The Graduate is undoubtedly one if the best movies of all time, but what does it have to do with mobile application user interface development?

It would be a waste to spend a great deal of time designing and tuning your application's processing algorithms and its data-access and memory models but neglect to pay sufficient attention to the code that interacts directly with the operating system to provide the user experience. This chapter is about getting the right user interface development plan together, one that ensures that the user's mobile device experience is a crisp and visually pleasurable one. You need a definite plan.

The most visible aspect of an application's performance is its user interface. How quickly the application responds to user commands and the speed with which repetitive drawing tasks are done has an enormous effect on the perception of the quality of your application. Sluggish performance, user interface flicker, and any stalls that occur during what the user expects to be smooth operations will result in a negative assessment of the quality of your application. Because mobile devices are often held and operated in people's hands and used like mechanical tools, there is an even greater expectation of responsiveness than with desktop computers; a pocket watch does not have flicker or periodic states of unresponsiveness nor does a street map or a pocket notepad. Many developers have needlessly mired their application in bad user interface performance; an application that appears sluggish is simply not a good application. Good user interface performance on mobile devices is achievable but is a matter of meticulous attention to detail. What is needed is a strategy for ensuring that the right problems are addressed so that the result is a responsive user interface and good user experience.

Mobile device applications pose a seeming paradox to performance-minded developers. On one hand, end users expect a device that is operated while being held in their hand to behave like a physical gadget and give immediate responses to their actions. On the other hand, mobile devices have fewer computational resources than their desktop brethren with which to generate the desired effect of immediate response. The seeming paradox of higher expectations and lower processing power is resolved by the fact that the user interface devices present are smaller than desktop computers and that the devices themselves are typically running fewer processes in parallel than today's desktop computers. Excellent performance and responsiveness are indeed possible for mobile applications. Nevertheless, well-considered approaches to designing user interface algorithms are important to ensure a highly responsive experience for users.

As with memory management and other aspects of performance, good engineering practices for mobile software design are not unique to mobile devices. Learning to design and write great-performing mobile device user interface code will make your desktop applications perform significantly better as well. Desktop environments today are so powerful that many developers simply ignore thinking about performance when designing their user interfaces. This results in unnecessarily sluggish user interface behavior. Comparing a user interface that was designed with performance as a top-level goal with a user interface where performance was a secondary or tertiary consideration will immediately show you the difference between the two approaches. The first application looks and feels fast and has no flicker when things update, no random pauses, and no overall sluggishness; it feels like a sleek machine. The second application feels a bit sluggish; it probably has some flicker as controls such as list boxes are updated, and occasionally stutters; it is like a car in general need of a tune-up. Even if the underlying functionality is identical, a user interface's responsiveness and the visual smoothness of an application has a great effect on the perception of its quality. This is true for desktops and doubly true for mobile devices. Compare two mobile phones, one with crisp behavior and one that is a bit sluggish and you will immediately notice the difference. Regardless of the features and underlying quality of the applications, the snappy-performing phone will feel more solid and reliable.

Writing user interfaces that perform well can be broken into three areas of consideration:

- *Design strategies for writing user interface code that performs.* Most modern programming frameworks have higher-level abstractions for driving the user interface. A framework manages windows and dialogs as well as the controls that live inside them. The developer writes code that responds to events generated by the user interacting with these user interface elements. Because of the higher-level abstractions used, it is easy to forget that each programmatic action requested of the user interface has a potentially significant cost. There are often good ways and bad ways to write this code. Optimizing the design of this high-level code is important to make user interfaces run with "snappy" performance.
- *Design strategies for writing graphics code that performs.* Whereas user interface code works with higher-level abstractions such as controls and windows, graphics code works with bitmaps and lower-level rendering abstractions. Graphics code is the code that does the low-level drawing and image manipulation. Graphics code often performs lots of small actions inside a loop or is called by event handling code to paint or repaint pictures that are used by higher-level user interface code. Whether you are doing page-flipping animation for a game, drawing bar charts for a business application, or writing the rendering code for a custom control, there are important ways to maximize your graphics throughput.
- *Choosing appropriate bitmap formats and sizes.* Both high-level user interface code as well as lower-level graphics code often work with images. Many formats and usage choices exist for this data, each optimized for a different purpose. Choosing the right image strategy for your needs will give you the right size and performance balance.

Performance Design Strategies for User Interface Code

User interface code is complex because it is the boundary where your code interacts with both the operating system and the end user. Your user interface literally sits in between and brokers requests connecting the user and the operating system. As an application designer, you face myriad choices:

- Which standard or custom controls should be used to display data and interact with the user?
- Does it make sense to build your own custom controls or extend the behavior of existing controls to meet special needs?
- What strategies should be used for populating user interface elements that hold a lot of data? Controls containing lists or trees of data are of particular importance.
- Which control events should be responded to? When should this response be suppressed?
- Is there a way to reduce the number of events that get fired when common or repetitive tasks occur?
- Is it necessary to force the immediate update or repainting of a control for short-term user experience gain at the cost of longer-term performance?

Because of all these dimensions of choices, the possible code implementations to solve a specific user interface need are almost endless. This is liberating but at the same time it also allows the possibility of haphazard and inefficient design. It is as if you went to the furniture store to buy a new couch and they handed you several bags of parts, more than you need for any single couch, and gave you no instructions but instead sent you off to create your own couch. Maybe you end up with a great-looking and sturdy couch, or maybe you end up with something less structurally sound that resembles the primitive shelter building efforts of early man. Without instructions, a strategy and good construction guidelines, odds are you will end up with the latter. With a good design plan, you will get the former. As with our fictitious couch, after you put enough pieces together, it becomes hard to take them all apart again and revise your design. If you want to avoid a substandard result or the need to start again from scratch, you need some design strategies to guide you and ensure your application's user interface development stays on the right path.

Below are covered some of the main design strategies for performance-oriented user interface design.

Use the Built-In Performance Features

If the mobile application runtime you are using has specific features to help build well-performing user interface code, you should use them. Moreover, you should actively review the list of events, properties, and methods for the controls you use and look for specific performance-oriented features. This seems obvious but is very often overlooked. The best way to learn about the performance-oriented features of a user interface framework is to examine members of its window, form, or control classes. It is also useful to examine the overloaded versions of methods that exist to perform common tasks to see whether there are methods that enable you to perform operations in a batched mode rather than by calling a method over and over again in a loop. As you would expect, batched mode operations are typically faster. This review usually only takes a few minutes, and you may be surprised at what you discover; lots of poor interface code is simply the result of using inefficient properties or methods to get things done or not calling methods that suspend user interface actions when updates are being performed.

.NET Compact Framework—Performance Using TreeViews and ListViews

The TreeView and ListView controls are both useful for displaying sets of related data in user interfaces. Because these controls work with sets, there is often a need to add or remove items in bulk from the controls. To achieve this efficiently, both controls offer methods to improve performance.

- **.BeginUpdate() / .EndUpdate()**—Both of these methods exist on the Tree-View and ListView controls. They serve to suspend and resume the redrawing of a control. Calling `BeginUpdate()` tells the control not to redraw automatically each time an item is added or removed. `EndUpdate()` tells the control that it can update its display again. Unnecessary drawing can be very taxing to the performance of your application. If your application is adding or removing multiple items from controls, it is a good idea to surround the code that adds or removes the items with calls to `BeginUpdate()` and `EndUpdate()`.

- **.AddRange()**—The TreeView control's nodes collection contains an `AddRange()` method (for example, `treeView1.Nodes.AddRange()`) that enables you to bulk add a set of tree nodes into the TreeView control. Using this batch mode is preferable to iteratively adding each node.

The performance and user interface smoothness benefits of using these built-in efficiency mechanisms can be substantial. When doing a lot of work with any control, it is a good idea to scan its list of properties and methods to see whether any specific members exist to aid in improving performance.

Example: Performance Differences in Varying Approaches for Working with a TreeView Control

This code in Listing 11.1 measures the efficiency of populating a .NET Compact Framework TreeView control using three different techniques. To build the sample, use Visual Studio .NET to create a new C# mobile device project and select the Pocket PC as your target platform. Onto the blank Form designer, add a TreeView control and five buttons as shown in Figure 11.1.

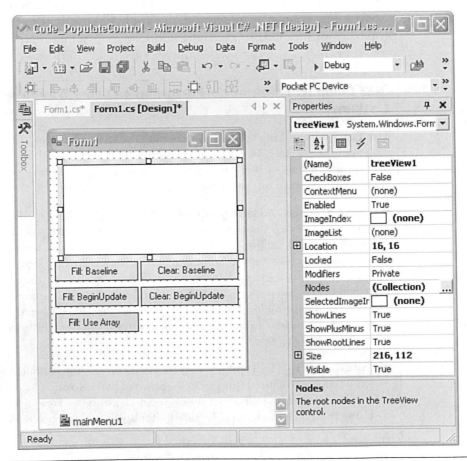

Figure 11.1 The Visual Studio .NET Form Designer with TreeView and Button controls.

> ### Visual Studio .NET Will Add and Wire Up a Blank Event Handler for You
>
> All you need to do is double-click the button in the Visual Studio .NET Form designer. The name of the function added will be the name of the control (for example, button1) + _Click. Visual Studio will (1) create the event handler function for you, (2) write code into the Form's InitializeComponent() function to hook up the click event handler it just created, and (3) bring you into the code editor to write the code that goes into the event handler. If you want to change the name of the button, do so by changing the Name property in the Properties window (the right-side window in Figure 11.1). It is helpful to do this before you double-click the button to create and wire up the event handler because when the event handler function is created it uses the current control name. If the control name is changed after the event handler function is created, the event handler will still be hooked up properly, but its name will not match the new name of the control. Fixing this so the control name and event function name match will require manual steps by you; it's not hard, but it is extra work.

The code in Listing 11.1 consists of a set of click event handlers for the various buttons on your form. The actual function names you use will be based on the names you give your button controls. I have the used the following button control names in my code: UnOptimizedFill, UnOptimized-Clear, UseBeginEndUpdateForFill, UseBeginEndUpdateForClear, FillArrayBeforeAttachingToTree. If you use the default button names Visual Studio .NET gives, you will have button1, button2, button3, button4, and button5 rather than the event handler function names that will change accordingly. In either case, it is easiest to double-click each of the buttons in the Visual Studio .NET Form designer to create and hook up the empty event handlers and then enter the event handling code listed inside the function definitions created for you.

Listing 11.1 Populating and Clearing a TreeView Control Using Alternative Strategies

```
//-----------------------------------------------------------
//Note #1: This sample uses the "PerformanceSampling" class
//         defined earlier in this book. Make sure this class
//         is included in your project.
//Note #2: This code need to be inserted into a Form class that
//         has a TreeView control and buttons hooked up to the
//         xxx_Click functions below.
//-----------------------------------------------------------
```

```csharp
//Number of items to place into the tree view
const int NUMBER_ITEMS = 800;

//-------------------------------------------
//Code for: "Fill: Baseline" Button
//
//"Unoptimized" Approach to filling a TreeView
//-------------------------------------------
private void UnOptimizedFill_Click(
                        object sender, System.EventArgs e)
{
  //To make sure we're testing the same thing, make sure
  //the array is clear
   if (treeView1.Nodes.Count > 0)
   {
     treeView1.BeginUpdate();
     treeView1.Nodes.Clear();
     treeView1.EndUpdate();
     treeView1.Update();
    }
  //For more consistent measurement, Collect the garbage
  //before running
  System.GC.Collect();

  //Start the test timer
  PerformanceSampling.StartSample(0, "TreeViewPopulate");

  //Fill the TreeView
  for(int i = 0; i < NUMBER_ITEMS ; i++)
  {
     treeView1.Nodes.Add("TreeItem" + i.ToString());
  }

  //Stop the test timer & and show the results
  PerformanceSampling.StopSample(0);
  System.Windows.Forms.MessageBox.Show(
             PerformanceSampling.GetSampleDurationText(0));
}


//-------------------------------------------
//Code for: "Clear: Baseline" Button
//
//"Unoptimized" Approach to filling a TreeView
//-------------------------------------------
```

```csharp
private void UnOptimizedClear_Click(
                            object sender, System.EventArgs e)
{
    //For more consistent measurement, Collect the garbage
    // before running
    System.GC.Collect();

    //Start the test timer
    PerformanceSampling.StartSample(1, "TreeViewClear");
    treeView1.Nodes.Clear();

    PerformanceSampling.StopSample(1);
    System.Windows.Forms.MessageBox.Show(
                PerformanceSampling.GetSampleDurationText(1));

}


//---------------------------------------------
//Code for: "Fill: BeginUpdate" Button
//
//"Using BeginUpdate()" Approach
//---------------------------------------------
private void UseBeginEndUpdateForFill_Click(
                            object sender, System.EventArgs e)
{

    //To make sure we're testing the same thing, make sure
    //the array is clear
    if (treeView1.Nodes.Count > 0)
    {
        treeView1.BeginUpdate();
        treeView1.Nodes.Clear();
        treeView1.EndUpdate();
        treeView1.Update();
    }
    //For more consistent measurement, Collect the garbage
    // before running
    System.GC.Collect();

    //Start the test timer
    PerformanceSampling.StartSample(2,
                            "Populate - Use BeginUpdate");

    //Fill the TreeView
```

```
    treeView1.BeginUpdate();
    for(int i = 0; i < NUMBER_ITEMS ; i++)
    {
        treeView1.Nodes.Add("TreeItem" + i.ToString());
    }
    treeView1.EndUpdate();

    //Stop the test timer & and show the results
    PerformanceSampling.StopSample(2);
    System.Windows.Forms.MessageBox.Show(
                PerformanceSampling.GetSampleDurationText(2));


}


//---------------------------------------------
//Code for: "Clear: BeginUpdate" Button
//
//"Using BeginUpdate()" Approach
//---------------------------------------------
private void UseBeginEndUpdateForClear_Click(
                        object sender, System.EventArgs e)
{
    //For more consistent measurement, Collect the garbage
    //before running
    System.GC.Collect();

    //Start the test timer
    PerformanceSampling.StartSample(3, "Clear - Use BeginUpdate");

    treeView1.BeginUpdate();
    treeView1.Nodes.Clear();
    treeView1.EndUpdate();

    //Stop the test timer & and show the results
    PerformanceSampling.StopSample(3);
    System.Windows.Forms.MessageBox.Show(
                PerformanceSampling.GetSampleDurationText(3));


}


//---------------------------------------------
//Code for: "Fill: Use Array" Button
//
//"Using Array" Approach
```

```
//---------------------------------------------
private void FillArrayBeforeAttachingToTree_Click(
                    object sender, System.EventArgs e)
{
    //To make sure we're testing the same thing, make sure
    // the array is clear
    if (treeView1.Nodes.Count > 0)
    {
        treeView1.BeginUpdate();
        treeView1.Nodes.Clear();
        treeView1.EndUpdate();
        treeView1.Update();
    }
    //For more consistent measurement, Collect the garbage before
    // running
    System.GC.Collect();

    //Start the test timer
    PerformanceSampling.StartSample(4, "Populate - Use Array");

    //Allocate space for our array of tree nodes
    System.Windows.Forms.TreeNode [] newTreeNodes =
        new System.Windows.Forms.TreeNode[NUMBER_ITEMS];

    //Fill up the array
    for(int i = 0; i < NUMBER_ITEMS ; i++)
    {
        newTreeNodes[i] =
         new System.Windows.Forms.TreeNode(
         "TreeItem" + i.ToString());
    }

    //Connect the array to the TreeView
    treeView1.BeginUpdate();
    treeView1.Nodes.AddRange(newTreeNodes);
    treeView1.EndUpdate();

    //Stop the test timer and show the results
    PerformanceSampling.StopSample(4);
    System.Windows.Forms.MessageBox.Show(
                PerformanceSampling.GetSampleDurationText(4));
}
```

The results of various approaches to adding and removing items from the TreeView control are listed in Table 11.1 and Table 11.2.

Table 11.1 Physical Pocket PC—Adding 800 Items (Results in Seconds)

Trial #	Unoptimized	Using BeginUpdate()	Using Array
1	40.785	12.484	10.388
2	40.533	12.322	10.419
3	40.878	13.343	11.686
Average	**40.732**	**12.716**	**10.831**
% Time savings vs. baseline test	Baseline (0%)	68.78%	73.41%

As can be seen from the numbers in Table 11.1, using the `BeginUpdate()` and `EndUpdate()` methods surrounding the code that adds items to the TreeView control resulted in a time savings of about two thirds (68.78 percent). Additionally, the visual experience was more appealing because the end user suffers less control redraw flicker during the update. Using the `AddRange()` method ("Using Array" column) to populate the TreeView saved the application an additional 6 percent of overhead over using `BeginUpdate()/EndUpdate()`; this is also notable.

It was surprising to discover that not only did `BeginUpdate()/EndUpdate()` greatly increase the speed of adding items to the TreeView control, it also had a large impact on the speed of removing items. Table 11.2 compares the different approaches for removing items from the TreeView.

Table 11.2 Clearing 800 Items (Results in Seconds)

Trial #	Unoptimized	Using BeginUpdate()
1	18.791	8.656
2	15.91	8.964
3	16.821	8.516
Average	**17.174**	**8.712**
% Time savings vs. baseline test	Baseline (0%)	49.27%

As can be seen from Table 11.2, a time savings of almost 50 percent was achieved by just surrounding the code that removes items from the Tree-View with calls to `BeginUpdate()` and `EndUpdate()`.

The lessons learned from these measurements are threefold:

1. It is important to seek out the built-in performance improving mechanisms present in the user interface framework you are using.
2. It is wrong to assume that conceptually simple operations such as "clear all the items out of the control" will automatically run quickly and cannot be speeded up.
3. It is always worth taking the time to measure the speed of various approaches to find the most optimum way to accomplish a user interface task.

Test with the Actual Number of Elements You Will Display in Your Application

A common design mistake encountered when writing user interface code is to design and test with smaller sets of data than will actually be encountered in the mobile application's deployment. An algorithm that works fine retrieving 20 items from a database and populating a user interface with them may or may not work well with 200 items. If you are using smaller sets of data for your testing, you are leaving the door open for nasty surprises later in the development or deployment cycle when the real-world data comes in. It is far better to discover these kinds of performance issues earlier when creative design strategies can be explored for mitigating them; late design changes will always be harder to implement, riskier to application stability, and usually produce less-satisfying results.

Another common mistake is using different data sources during the design of an application. For example, using a local database or text file during design as stop gap until the real data becomes available on the remote server the mobile application will actually have to access. Most often these kinds of issues occur either when the real databases and data are not yet available for use at application design time or when the data is sensitive and live data is not available to the application designers for testing purposes. Similar kinds of performance shocks can occur when data sources are switched. As above it is best test early with real-world conditions.

In any case, it is important to specify the capacity, location, and access mechanism for the data your application will display in its user interface. Do this early in the design process and test with data of this size, location, and access mechanism. If your application is intended to work with a large variety of data sizes, test with the largest capacity. It is highly recommended to give yourself some performance buffer and test with data capacities that exceed your design specification by a reasonable amount and see how the application's performance is affected. If your data can be pulled from different sources, test the performance using each data-access mechanism. If your application will need to access the data via a dialup or lower-bandwidth connection, test it under these conditions. Not only should the application run correctly in these situations, it is also important that your application remain visually attractive and behave responsively throughout any prolonged user interface update. Doing these things will keep your design process focused on the real-world performance you will need to achieve. There simply is not a substitute for working with same data in the same way that your end users will.

Procrastination Is Good! Defer, Defer, Defer...

Many applications serve to give the user a condensed view onto a large amount of dynamic data. The data may be stored locally in a file or database, or pulled dynamically down from a network as needed.

For example, a mobile application for real estate agents may give a view onto hundreds or thousands of properties and organize them in a hierarchy navigable by the application's user via a mobile phone or a PDA. A first-iteration design to achieve this goal might typically load all the skeletal information about available house listings into memory and enable the user to navigate the hierarchy and find potential properties. When a specific property is selected the application would then load details such as photos, floor plans, street maps, and the market status for the property on demand.

For the top-down navigation of housing choices, a TreeView control can offer rich hierarchical view on the possible property listings. For instance, a TreeView control could be used to offer three top-level nodes, each representing a different pivot of the data based on a probable decision process that an end user might use to navigate the data. Below are three examples of listing hierarchies that the application's users might want:

- *Navigation 1*—Start with the neighborhood, and then look at price groupings to determine which units to show. TreeView hierarchy: Neighborhoods->Price->ListOfUnits.
- *Navigation 2*—Start with the price groupings, and then look at house types and finally the neighborhood to arrive at the list of units to

show. TreeView hierarchy: Price->HouseType-> Neighborhood->ListOfUnits.

- Navigation 3: Start with the type of house, and then look at price ranges and then the neighborhoods. TreeView hierarchy: House-Type->Price->Neighborhood->ListOfUnits.

Figure 11.2 shows what this TreeView navigation might look like. Three top-level nodes Neighborhood, Price, and HouseType exist. Each parent node has subnodes enabling users to drill down through the hierarchy and finally arrive at the set of houses they want to look at.

Although a tree is a potentially useful metaphor for enabling house selection based on hierarchical categories, there is a potential problem; the tree can grow quite large even for a moderate amount of data. A simple hierarchy of 10 neighborhoods * 4 house types in each * 4 price groupings in each * 6 houses meeting each criteria = 960 leaf nodes in our tree. This number would be further multiplied by the number of top-level navigations we want to support.

960 for Neighborhoods->House Type ->Price ->ListOfUnits

960 for Price->Neighborhoods->HouseType->ListOfUnits

960 for HouseType->Price->Neighborhood->ListOfUnits

Figure 11.2 A simple example of what TreeView real estate navigation could look like.

If we populate the TreeView in advance of the application user's navigation, we will end up creating and populating a huge number of tree nodes, most of which users will never navigate to in any given application usage session. Creating all these TreeView members takes time, and the TreeView item nodes themselves consume system resources. Holding thousands of TreeView items in memory would have a detrimental effect on our mobile application's performance. Unless we think the user is going to visit each of these nodes individually and repeatedly, we can achieve better performance by using a more sophisticated approach. What we would like to do is keep the TreeView user interface metaphor but avoid creating hundreds or thousands of unvisited TreeView items. A way to accomplish this is to create the needed TreeView nodes only when it becomes clear that the user will access them. This can be done by using some clever code to (1) populate the TreeView control only up until the point where it has been expanded to, and (2) handle the event that indicates a node of the TreeView control is about to be expanded and needs to be populated with valid data. Doing this can save the mobile application the time and resources required to fill a huge amount of nodes and will result in a better end user experience.

More sophisticated approaches such as looking ahead one level deep in the TreeView and prepopulating the nodes are also possible; this could potentially provide the user an even richer experience. The richness of the approach you choose to use to intelligently defer work is bounded only by the work required to design and implement your concepts.

.NET Compact Framework—Not All Supported Event Handlers Are Exposed by the Visual Studio .NET Designer

The .NET Compact Framework supports a subset of the desktop .NET Framework's control events. It is worth noting that just because an event signature is defined in the .NET Compact Framework is no guarantee that the event is fired at runtime. There may have been specific compatibility and object inheritance reasons that the event definition for a control needed to be included but is not triggered by the .NET Compact Framework at runtime. The proof is wiring the event up and seeing whether it fires at runtime. Further complicating this situation is the fact that not all of the events supported by the .NET Compact Framework are exposed by the Visual Studio .NET graphical design environment. There are supported events that are not listed in the C# events list in the property sheet or the Visual Basic .NET event drop-down box in the code editor.

An event that is exposed by the design environment should be supported by the .NET Compact Framework, but there are additional events that are supported but not exposed by Visual Studio .NET. The reason for this is project coordination: the design time team and the runtime team were not perfectly in sync! (Expect this to get better with future iterations.) The most common events are exposed but some more specialized events may require you to hook them up by hand. This is not hard to do, but it requires a little bit of specialized knowledge about how event handlers are hooked up.

If you want to use an event that is supported by the .NET Compact Framework but not exposed by the Visual Studio .NET design environment, you will need to manually insert one line of code into the InitializeComponent() function of the form containing the control. You will find the InitializeComponent() function in the normally hidden or collapsed "Windows Form Designer–Generated Code" section in the class' code editor.

The code snippet shows how to add a BeforeExpand event handler for a Tree-View control:

```
#region Windows Form Designer generated code
private void InitializeComponent()
{
....a bunch of code for other controls…
//
// treeView1
//
this.treeView1.ImageIndex = -1;
this.treeView1.Location = new System.Drawing.Point(72, 48);
this.treeView1.Name = "treeView1";
this.treeView1.SelectedImageIndex = -1;
this.treeView1.Size = new System.Drawing.Size(168, 176);
this.treeView1.TabIndex = 0;
//HERE IS THE 1 LINE OF CODE YOU NEED TO WRITE TO HOOK UP THE EVENT
this.treeView1.BeforeExpand += new System.Windows.Forms.
TreeViewCancelEventHandler(this.TreeView1BeforeExpand);
... a bunch of code for other controls
}
```

The code above hooks up an event handler for the BeforeExpand event of the treeView1 control. The event handler must have a specific function signature. In this case, it is as follows:

```
private void TreeView1BeforeExpand(object sender,
System.Windows.Forms.TreeViewCancelEventArgs e)
{
}
```

A good way to have both of these code snippets autogenerated for you is to use a desktop Windows Application project. The Visual Studio .NET desktop projects support graphically creating and hooking up all supported event handlers. This code can be copy/pasted into the appropriate parts of your .NET Compact Framework application.

A slightly modified variant of the strategy above is also worth considering. Because the form designer automatically inserts and deletes code inside the `InitializeComponent()` function, there is a chance it could step on top of your custom-added code. To avoid this, you may want to create your own function (for example, `MyInitializeComponent()`) to place your custom initialization code into and call this function in the form's constructor code right after the call to `InitializeComponent()`. Doing this will ensure that the form's designer does not accidentally delete your code.

Example: On-Demand Population of a TreeView Control

Figure 11.3 shows a simple application consisting of a TreeView control (treeview1) and a Button (button1). Clicking the button at runtime sets up or resets the state of the TreeView control. After the TreeView control has been set up by clicking the button, it offers three top-level nodes that can be dynamically populated. The nodes are Neighborhoods, Prices and House-Types. To keep the code size small and the sample simple, only the code to dynamically populate the Neighborhoods node is included in the Listing 11.2. Clicking the other nodes will bring up a MessageBox the first time they are clicked to show where the dynamic TreeView population should occur and you are free to add your own code here.

Listing 11.2 contains the code that needs to be inserted into a Form class for this example. To create the sample, follow these steps:

1. Start a new Smart Device project in Visual Studio .NET and select the Pocket PC as the target platform.
2. Add a TreeView control and a Button control to the Form designer.
3. Double-click the Button in the Form designer; this will create and wire up the `button1_Click` event handler below.
4. Enter the `Button1_Click` code listed below to populate the TreeView.
5. Enter the rest of the code listed below including the constants defined above the `button1_Click` event handler.
6. Hand wire in the event handler for the TreeView's `BeforeExpand` event, as described in the section above.
7. Compile and run the example.

Figure 11.3 Pocket PC emulator with an application that dynamically populates a TreeView control.

Listing 11.2 Dynamic Population of TreeView Control

```
//Dummy text to put in the placeholder child nodes
const string dummy_node = "_dummynode";
//Tag we will use to indicate a node
const string node_needToBePopulated = "_populateMe";
//Text we will use for our top-level nodes
const string nodeText_Neighborhoods = "Neighborhoods";
const string nodeText_Prices = "Prices";
const string nodeText_HouseType = "HouseTypes";


//------------------------------------------------------------
//Click event handler for our button
//
//Sets up our TreeView to show incremental filling of the
//tree
//------------------------------------------------------------
```

```
private void button1_Click(object sender, System.EventArgs e)
{
  TreeNode tnNewNode;

  //Turn off UI updates before we fill in the tree
  treeView1.BeginUpdate();
  //Throw out any old data
  treeView1.Nodes.Clear();
  //---------------------------
  //"Neighborhoods" node
  //---------------------------
  //Add the top-level "Neighborhoods" node.
  tnNewNode = treeView1.Nodes.Add("Neighborhoods");

  //Set a tag on the node that indicates that we will
  //dynamically fill in the node
  tnNewNode.Tag = node_needToBePopulated ;
  //This dummy child node only exists so that the node has
  //at least one child node and therefore the tree node is
  //expandable.
  tnNewNode.Nodes.Add(dummy_node);

  //---------------------------
  //"Price" node
  //---------------------------
  tnNewNode = treeView1.Nodes.Add("Price");

  //Set a tag on the node that indicates that we will
  //dynamically fill in the node
  tnNewNode.Tag = node_needToBePopulated ;

  //This dummy child node only exists so that the node has
  //at least one child node and therefore the tree node is
  //expandable.
  tnNewNode.Nodes.Add(dummy_node);

  //---------------------------
  //"HouseType" node
  //---------------------------
  tnNewNode = treeView1.Nodes.Add("HouseType");

  //Set a tag on the node that indicates that we will
  //dynamically fill in the node
```

```
    tnNewNode.Tag = node_needToBePopulated ;

    //This dummy child node only exists so that the node has
    //at least one child node and therefore the tree node is
    //expandable.
    tnNewNode.Nodes.Add(dummy_node );

    //Resume the UI updates
    treeView1.EndUpdate();
}


//----------------------------------------------------
//BeforeExpand event handler for our TreeView
//NOTE: This event handler will have to be hooked up
//      by hand in the Form's "InitializeComponent()"
//      function.
//
//Called when a user asks to expand a node that has at least
//one child node. This is called before the node's children
//are shown and gives us a chance to dynamically populate the
//TreeView control.
//----------------------------------------------------
private void TreeView1BeforeExpand
(object sender, System.Windows.Forms.TreeViewCancelEventArgs e)
{
    //Get the node that is about to be expanded
    System.Windows.Forms.TreeNode tnExpanding;
    tnExpanding = e.Node;

    //If the node is not marked "need to be populated" the
    //node is fine "as is."
    if(tnExpanding.Tag != (object) node_needToBePopulated)
    {
        return; //Allow things to continue without hindrance
    }


    //----------------------------------------------------
    //Dynamic tree population required.
    //We know the node needs to be populated, figure out which
    //node it is
    //----------------------------------------------------
    if(tnExpanding.Text == nodeText_Neighborhoods)
    {
        PopulateTreeViewNeighborhoods(tnExpanding);
```

```
      return; //done adding items!
    }
    else
    {
      //Check other possibilities for tree nodes we need to add.
      System.Windows.Forms.MessageBox.Show(
        "UN-DONE: Add code to dynamically populate this node");

      //Remove the tag from the node so we don't run this
      //code again
      tnExpanding.Tag = "";
    }
}


//----------------------------------------------------------
//This function is called to dynamically add child nodes
//To the "Neighborhood" Node
//----------------------------------------------------------
void PopulateTreeViewNeighborhoods(TreeNode tnAddTo)
{
  TreeView tvControl;
  tvControl = tnAddTo.TreeView;

  tvControl.BeginUpdate();
  //Clear the dummy subnode we have in there
  tnAddTo.Nodes.Clear();

  //Declare four nodes we want to make children
  //of the node that was passed in.
  TreeNode [] newNeighborhoodNodes;
  newNeighborhoodNodes = new TreeNode[4];
  newNeighborhoodNodes[0] = new TreeNode("Capitol Hill");
  newNeighborhoodNodes[1] = new TreeNode("Chelsea");
  newNeighborhoodNodes[2] = new TreeNode("Downtown");
  newNeighborhoodNodes[3] = new TreeNode("South Bay");
  //Add the child nodes to the tree view
  tnAddTo.Nodes.AddRange(newNeighborhoodNodes);

  tvControl.EndUpdate();
}
```

The code above shows how, with some cleverness and only a bit of additional code, complex user interface population can be deferred until the user has a need for the data. Whether working with the .NET Compact Framework or other device runtimes, learning how to defer the population of expansive user interface elements is a powerful technique.

Keep a Careful Eye on Event-Driven Code

A large portion of modern user interface code consists of code that responds to framework-generated events. Knowing which events to handle, how often the events are triggered, and when to avoid responding to events is important for designing user interface code that performs well.

A common situation that causes poor application performance is mistakenly handling events generated by code believing that the events are user generated.

Example: Showing the TextBox "Changed" Event Being Triggered When the .Text Property Is Set

Listing 11.3 contains the code that needs to be inserted into a Form class for this example. To create the sample, follow these steps:

1. Start a new Smart Device project in Visual Studio .NET, selecting the Pocket PC as the target platform.
2. Add a TextBox, Label, ListBox, and Button to the Form.
3. Double-click the Button in the Form designer; this will create and wire up the `button1_Click` event handler below. Enter the code in Listing 11.3 to respond to this event.
4. Double-click the TextBox in the Form designer; this will create and wire up the `textbox1_ TextChanged` event handler below. Enter the code in Listing 11.3 to respond to this event.
5. Compile and run the example.
6. Type text into the text box and note that each key press runs the `textbox1_TextChanged()` event code below.
7. Click the Button and note that it also triggers the `textbox1_TextChanged()` event code below.

NOTE: Programmatically setting the text property of the TextBox actually triggers the `TextChanged` event twice when running on the .NET Compact Framework Version 1.1.

Running the same code on the desktop triggers the event only once. It is likely that in the future releases the .NET Compact Framework behavior will be changed to match the desktop .NET Framework behavior (only one event triggering). Events can be tricky stuff. Keep an eye on how and when events fire.

Listing 11.3 Programmatic TextBox Update Causes Event Code to Be Run

```
int m_eventTriggerCount;
private void textBox1_TextChanged(object sender, System.EventArgs e)
{
m_eventTriggerCount++;
//Update a label to show the # of events
label1.Text = "Events: #" + m_eventTriggerCount.ToString();
//List each of the events
listBox1.Items.Add(m_eventTriggerCount.ToString() + textBox1.Text);
}

private void button1_Click(object sender, System.EventArgs e)
{
  //This triggers a TextChanged event
  //same as if the user typed in text
  textBox1.Text = "Hello World";
}
```

Listing 11.3 shows that programmatically setting the Text property of a TextBox fires the same event code as a user typing in text. Depending on your assumptions, this may or may not be what you expected. Often people write code to populate user interfaces after retrieving data from some external source. RadioButton and CheckBox buttons have their Checked properties set, TextBox values are filled, ListBox and ComboBox contents are filled, and so on. It is often assumed that this setup work does not trigger user interface events. Usually the intent is not to want these events to be triggered as the user interface is just being set up for the user to use. Very often the only time an application's programmer wants the application's event handler code to be run is when an external event occurs such as a timer ticking, a user clicking a button, or a user entering text into a control.

Avoiding Getting Caught Off-Guard by Events

Event code is tricky because it is not possible to tell by inspection when an application's event handling code will be called. Examining an application's source code shows clearly when calls are made to runtime libraries and to other application code, but does not indicate when the runtime triggers application events. For this reason, most developers simply make assumptions about when events are triggered and do not check these assumptions closely. In addition, as an application grows in user features and correspondingly in internal complexity more event handling and event generating user interface code gets written; this code may have subtle interactions that are not apparent by inspection. For example, code that responds to selecting an item in a ListBox may run code that causes an update to a CheckBox's and a TextBox's properties. For example:

```
textboxUserName.Text = selectedRecord.Username;
checkboxDeliverPackageToHomeAddress.Checked =
selectedRecord.DeliverToHome;
```

This code seems simple, but if events are hooked up to the TextBox or CheckBox controls they may be triggered and may run application code meant only to process end-user actions. This code may in turn change other user interface elements and cause a cascade of events unexpected by the application's developer.

Here are three good ways to help ensure that your application does not get caught off-guard with events:

1. *Instrument application code during development.* Counting the number of times an event gets fired is a low-overhead activity; it only requires incrementing an integer. It can also be diagnostically useful to keep an ordered list of events that occur and examine these. This instrumentation can be conditionally compiled into your application. It is a good idea to periodically audit your application's behavior throughout the development cycle and examine what a highly instrumented version tells you. Instrumentation is easy and remarkably effective.

2. *Have a clear state model for when events should run code and when they should immediately exit.* A common case where event code is unintentionally run is when the application's user interface is being

populated with data. In these cases, the desire is simply to push data into the user interface and not to respond to events triggered by this push. An easy way to deal with this is to set a Form-level flag that states "the application is doing user interface updates now, event handlers should exit without processing." Each event handler should in its first line of code check the state of this flag and if it is set, exit without further processing.

3. *Periodically place breakpoints in each of the applications event handlers and walk through the sequence of events that execute.* Periodically it is useful to single step through the set of events that fire in your user interface and see what processing is going on and in what order. You may find event cascades that are inadvertently being caused when the user interface is updated by application code; you may also find redundant processing you are doing that is costly. Event code that causes multiple redundant reads from or updates to a database is a good example of code that should be discovered and eliminated.

Event-driven code is a wonderfully useful concept, but like any abstraction it comes at a cost of reduced low-level understanding of what is going on. Unless you understand the sequence and frequency of events that are causing your application's code to run, you cannot truly say that you understand the behavior of your application. This can cause not only performance problems but also reliability problems. It is well worth spending the time to get a firm and detailed understanding of where and when the events in your application are firing.

Figure 11.4 and Listing 11.4 show a sample application that demonstrates both instrumentation and using a state model to prevent user interface event code from running when programmatic updates to the application's user interface are occurring. To create the sample, follow these steps:

1. Start a new Smart Device project in Visual Studio .NET, selecting the Pocket PC as the target platform.
2. Add a TextBox, RadioButton, ListBox, and Button control to the Form (see Figure 11.4 for how this should look).
3. Double-click the Button1 in the Form designer. This will create and wire up the `button1_Click` event handler below. Enter the code below in Listing 11.4 to respond to this event.
4. Double-click the TextBox in the Form designer. This will create and wire up the `textbox1_TextChanged` event handler below. Enter the code below in Listing 11.4 to respond to this event.

5. Double-click the RadioButton1 in the Form designer. This will create and wire up the `radioButton1_Click` event handler below. Enter the code in Listing 11.4 to respond to this event.

6. Rename the second button from button2 to **buttonShowEventLog** and double-click the Button in the Form designer. This will create and wire up the `buttonShowEventLog_Click` event handler below. Enter the code in Listing 11.4 to respond to this event.

7. Enter the rest of the code below including the `#if` and `#endif` statements and the class-level variables.

8. To the very top of the Form's class file, add the statement `#define EVENTINSTRUMENTATION`. This will enable the conditionally compiled code.

9. Compile and run the example. Click Button1, type in the TextBox, and click the ShowEventLog button to see the list of instrumented events that have been triggered.

10. Stop the application's execution and uncomment the line `m_userInterfaceUpdateOccuring = true;` in the `Button1_Click` event handler and then re-run the application. Observe that this flag, when set to true, had prevented the unwanted application code from running when the event handlers were triggered by programmatic access to the properties of the controls.

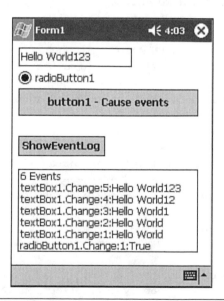

Figure 11.4 Pocket PC showing an application with event-logging instrumentation.

Listing 11.4 Using a State Model for Updates and Instrumentation to Better Understand and Control Event Processing

```
//-----------------------------------------------------------
//Place this #define statement at the top
//of the class if event logging is desired
//#define EVENTINSTRUMENTATION
//-----------------------------------------------------------


//-----------------------------------------------------------
//A flag that tells control event handlers if they should
//exit without doing any work
//-----------------------------------------------------------
bool m_userInterfaceUpdateOccuring;

//Counters for event occurrences
private int m_radioButton1ChangeEventCount;
private int m_textBox1ChangeEventCount;


//-----------------------------------------------------------
//Code we only want to include if we are running in an
//instrumented mode. This code has relatively high execution
//overhead and we only want to compile it in and run it if
//we are doing diagnostics.
//-----------------------------------------------------------
#if EVENTINSTRUMENTATION
private System.Collections.ArrayList m_instrumentedEventLog;
//-----------------------------------------------------------
//Logs the occurrence of an event into an array we can inspect
//
//Note: No attempt is made to keep the size of the
//      logging array bounded, so the longer the application
//      runs the larger this array will become
//-----------------------------------------------------------
private void instrumented_logEventOccurrence(string eventData)
{
    //Create the event log if it has not already been created
    if (m_instrumentedEventLog == null)
    {
      m_instrumentedEventLog =
                new System.Collections.ArrayList();
    }
```

```
    //Log the event
    m_instrumentedEventLog.Add(eventData);
}


//------------------------------------------------------------
//Show the list of events that have occurred
//Note: This implementation is pretty crude.
//       You may want instead to show the events
//       list in a separate dialog that pops up for the
//       purpose.
//------------------------------------------------------------
private void instrumentation_ShowEventLog()
{
  System.Windows.Forms.ListBox.ObjectCollection listItems;
  listItems = listBoxEventLog.Items;

  //Clear the items in the list
  listItems.Clear();
  //If there are no events, exit
  if (m_instrumentedEventLog == null)
  {
    listItems.Add("0 Events");
    return;
  }

  //At the top of the list show the total of events we
  //have counted
  listItems.Add(m_instrumentedEventLog.Count.ToString() +
                " Events");
  //List the items in reverse order, so the most recent are
  //displayed first
  string logItem;
  for(int listIdx = m_instrumentedEventLog.Count - 1;
      listIdx >= 0; listIdx--)
  {
    logItem = (string) m_instrumentedEventLog[listIdx];
    listItems.Add(logItem);
  }
}
#endif


//------------------------------------------------------------
//RadioButton1 Changed event
//------------------------------------------------------------
```

```
private void radioButton1_CheckedChanged
                            (object sender, System.EventArgs e)
{
  //If our application is updating the data in the
  //user interface we do not want to treat this as
  //a user triggered event. If this is the case,
  //exit and do nothing.
  if(m_userInterfaceUpdateOccuring == true)
  {return;}

  //Count the number of times this event has been called
  m_radioButton1ChangeEventCount++;

#if EVENTINSTRUMENTATION
  //Log the occurrence of the event
instrumented_logEventOccurrence("radioButton1.Change:" + //event
    m_radioButton1ChangeEventCount.ToString() + ":" + //#times
    radioButton1.Checked.ToString()); //value
#endif

}

//-------------------------------------------------------------
//Button1 click event
//Simulates a case where code updates the user interface
//potentially causing event code to be run
//-------------------------------------------------------------
private void button1_Click(object sender, System.EventArgs e)
{
  //Indicate that we do not want the event handlers
  //to process events right now because we are updating
  //the user interface.

  //m_userInterfaceUpdateOccuring   = true;

  radioButton1.Checked = true;
  textBox1.Text = "Hello World";

  //We are done updating the user interface
  m_userInterfaceUpdateOccuring   = false;
}

//-------------------------------------------------------------
//TextBox changed event handler
//-------------------------------------------------------------
```

```
private void textBox1_TextChanged
                            (object sender, System.EventArgs e)
{
  //If our application is updating the data in the
  //user interface we do not want to treat this as
  //a user triggered event. If this is the case,
  //exit and do nothing.
  if(m_userInterfaceUpdateOccuring == true)
  {return;}

  //Count the number of times we execute this event
  m_textBox1ChangeEventCount++;

#if EVENTINSTRUMENTATION
  //Log the occurrence of the event
  instrumented_logEventOccurrence("textBox1.Change:" + //Event
    m_textBox1ChangeEventCount.ToString() + ":" +  //# times
    textBox1.Text.ToString()); //Value
#endif
}

private void buttonShowEventLog_Click
                (object sender, System.EventArgs e)
{
#if EVENTINSTRUMENTATION
  instrumentation_ShowEventLog();
#endif
}
```

Never Leave the User Guessing

Responsiveness is a significant aspect of performance. It is always best to have no delays in the user interface's interactions with the user, but in some cases this may not be possible. When work must be done that forces the end user to wait, extra effort should be applied to make sure that the wait is as comfortable as possible. Think of it as similar to designing a nice comfortable room in your doctor's office. It would be great if you did not need to wait at all, but this seems not to be possible. (If you know of an exception, let me know!) It would be a much worse experience if there were no receptionist to acknowledge your arrival, if you were never told how long you will need to wait, if the surroundings were uncomfortable, and if there were nothing to look at or read to pass the time. Having a fish tank in the room to look at while you wait is an aesthetically nice distraction. Having the receptionist acknowledge your arrival goes a long way as well. The experience is even better if the receptionist tells you how long the wait will be and offers you today's newspaper and a beverage of your choice to keep you comfortable. (Again, if you know of a doctor's office where this occurs, let me know.)

It is frustrating for end users to wait and not know how long a task will take to complete. Having a mobile device pour you a nice cup of coffee and engage you in interesting conversation is probably too much to hope for, but clearly there are simple things that can be done to improve the waiting experience in mobile applications. Progress bars and wait cursors serve no computational purpose yet they are important ways to inform users and make them a participant in the process. Chapter 7, "Step 1: Start with Performance, Stay with Performance," outlines several different levels of user responsiveness and offers an example that shows them. To review this and offer some more detail, the different levels of end-user experience when waiting for a mobile application are as follows:

- *The worst experience: No responsiveness.* An application that becomes unresponsive and does not offer users any indications that work is being done on their behalf looks an awful lot like an application that has crashed or locked up. The end user anxiety level will quickly climb and they will start attempting to click buttons or tap on the screen to get the application to respond in some way. This leaves a series of random unintended events for your application to process when it returns control back to the user interface. After a short while, the user will probably try to close the application, switch to another application, or yank out the battery of the device to try to reset it if the former strategies do not yield acceptable responses. (Mobile phones make this very easy to do.) Making this situation worse is having a mobile application that does not give the user any visual indication when the work is complete. Assuming users have patiently waited and did not push any buttons or yank out the battery while the application was stalled, how are they supposed to know when the application is responsive again? In all cases, avoid having a user interface that looks like it should be responding to requests but is not.
- *A better experience: Showing a wait cursor while the application is unresponsive.* A wait cursor serves two important purposes. First, it lets end users know work is being done on their behalf, and second, it lets them know when the work is completed so they can resume using the application. Given that showing a wait cursor is usually a trivial task, there is really no excuse not to at least do this small bit of

responsiveness work. Any action that takes more than a few tenths of a second is a user interface stall that the user will notice and there is little reason not to let them know that work is being done on their behalf. A wait cursor will buy you a few seconds of grace and patience from the device's user, but if the work is going to take more than a few seconds you should look at having a more informative progress indicator in addition to the wait cursor. Additionally, if almost every action the user does results in a wait cursor length delay, you should look more at optimizations and background processing for your mobile application's design; delays are fine for some things but not for almost everything.

■ *An even better experience: Showing the user a progress bar or displaying progress text that indicates what is going on.* If the action the user needs to wait for will take more than a few seconds, consider having an updating progress bar or progress text that informs the user of progress that is occurring, the percent of work remaining or an updating estimate of the time remaining to completion. Showing a wait cursor does not prevent you from displaying text that informs the user of the progress of the work. You may want to display some text on the form behind the wait cursor that tells the user what is being done on their behalf. Any information you can give the user that indicates progress is useful. Informative text can be particularly useful in keeping users feeling like they are part of the process. For example, an algorithm that downloads information from a server might display the following incremental progress updates: "Locating server," "Found server, logging in," "Downloading information (10%)," "Downloading information (60%)," "Done!" This kind of information makes the user feel involved in the process. Note the importance of telling them that the action has completed successfully. Further, if there are problems during the download, users may be able to glean information from the progress text that can be used to resolve the problem.

When writing code that periodically updates the user on the progress of a long-running task, you may need to explicitly make the control draw itself. Unless explicitly called to update, forms and controls usually only queue up messages that request they be redrawn; unforced updates occur when the system has spare time to process them. Because your computational work may be occurring on the same thread as the user interface, the work being done will not allow the queued messages to be processed until control is handed back to the user interface. To solve this the .NET Compact Framework supports an `Update()` method on each control. When this method is called, the control is repainted immediately. Listing 11.5 shows a simple work algorithm that periodically updates the text in a Label control to show progress. Unless a call to `label1.Update()` is made when the Label's text is updated, the new text will not display to the user until after the work is complete.

■ *A better experience yet: Giving the user progress information and the ability to cancel the operation.* Some tasks may take a significant amount of time, and the user may want to cancel them before they complete. A synchronization task with a server might unexpectedly take several minutes, and the mobile device's user may decide that they need to enter an elevator or go underground to a subway where there is no network access. Alternatively, the end user of the mobile device may need to get to information in another part of the application quickly and cannot wait for the task currently underway to complete. If a task is going to take a long time and is going to block the user interface, it is good design to offer the user the ability to cancel the action being performed on his behalf. This can be done by having your algorithm periodically poll for a flag that is set if the user presses a cancel button. As the chapter on background threading explained, a state machine governing the background task's status is a good way to implement this.

If the long-running task is being performed on the foreground (user interface) thread, offering the user the ability to cancel is more complicated but still possible. As with updating the user interface during heavy processing, responding to user requests such as clicking a cancel button cannot happen unless the thread's user interface messages are being processed. The .NET Compact Framework offers a solution to this and other mobile device frameworks are likely to have a similar concept. Making a call to the static method `System.Windows.Forms.Application.DoEvents()` forces all the queued up messages on the thread to be processed before execution continues. This means that user interface painting messages will be processed and this also includes processing queued-up button click and key press messages. If you call `DoEvents()` on a reasonably frequent bases (a few times a second), you can keep the application's user interface responsive to user requests while performing the processing task at hand.

Calling `DoEvents()` to process a thread's queued-up user interface messages seems like a wonderful cure-all, but it is not. Extreme *caution must be used* when calling `DoEvents()` because subtle and highly undesirable effects can arise. Because `DoEvents()` processes all messages before returning control to the code that called it, things such as timer event handlers can get called and running event handlers can be re-entered as well. It is possible to end up with multiple nested calls into the event handlers for user interface elements and timers if `DoEvents()` is called inside an event and a new event message has been queued up before the first one is completed. If you are going to use `DoEvents()`, you must write your application's event handling code very defensively. Putting checks at the top of your event handlers to exit the function if it is being re-entered is highly recommended. Before entering a block of code that will perform a long-duration task and will call `DoEvents()` in the middle of it, be sure to set the Enabled property of any controls that should not be allowed to generate events to false; this will disable the user from being able to click them and queue up events. There are almost no cases where re-entrant events are desirable; the code gets very confusing to understand and debug. Given the choice between using `DoEvents()` and creating a background thread to do processing, I would almost always choose a well-designed background threading solution. As complicated as multiple threads are to conceptualize, their execution model is usually simpler and more predictable than the mixture of framework and application code that can get called when using `DoEvents()`. None of this is specific to mobile devices; the same issues exist on the desktop but given the user's demand for responsiveness in mobile devices it is worth drawing out this issue specifically. Nevertheless `DoEvents()` can occasionally be useful and I describe it here along with the warning *caveat emptor* (let the buyer beware!). If you buy the `DoEvents()` ticket, you will take the ride with all of its ups and downs.

- *The best experience: Find a way to perform the task in a way that does not block the user.* If your mobile application can push work onto a background thread, enabling users to continue with other tasks and give them a notification when the task is complete, you have achieved the Holy Grail of responsiveness. Doing this requires a great deal of thought about what the user interaction model is for pushing work onto a background thread. Thought must be given to how to keep the user notified of progress and in control of the background processing without being too intrusive to the foreground user interface experience. A good desktop application example of this would be Microsoft Word's support for printing a document in the background while enabling the user to continue to edit the live document in the foreground. It is a useful feature and looks simple, but there is significant design behind it to make it work.

Listing 11.5 Calling a Control's Update() Method to Show Progress Text

```
//-------------------------------------------------
//This code belongs in a Form containing a single
//Button (button1) and a Label (label1)
//-------------------------------------------------
private void button1_Click(object sender, System.EventArgs e)
{
  //Show a wait cursor
  System.Windows.Forms.Cursor.Current =
          System.Windows.Forms.Cursors.WaitCursor;

  string testString;
  for(int loop3 = 0; loop3 < 100; loop3 = loop3 + 10)
  {
    label1.Text = loop3.ToString() + "% Done...";
    //!!!!!!!!!!!!!!!!!!!!!!!!!!!!!!!!!!!!!!!!!!!!!!!!!
    //Uncomment the line below to show progress updates!
    //!!!!!!!!!!!!!!!!!!!!!!!!!!!!!!!!!!!!!!!!!!!!!!!!!
    //label1.Update();
    testString = "";

    for(int loop2 = 0; loop2 < 1000; loop2++)
    {
      testString  = testString  + "test";
    }
  }
    label1.Text = "Done!";

  //Remove the wait cursor
  System.Windows.Forms.Cursor.Current =
          System.Windows.Forms.Cursors.Default;
}
```

Choosing Appropriate Bitmap Formats and Sizes

Working with bitmap images is common both for low-level graphics work as well as high-level user interface design. Most user interface frameworks offer some notion of a PictureBox control that can display bitmaps, and lower-level graphics libraries deal mainly with bitmap-level operations. Many kinds of interesting applications work with bitmap images, such as street maps, medical images, real estate photos, and play fields for games to name only a few. When working with bitmap data, it is important to think of both the file representation of an image as well as the in-memory storage of image data. Several different file formats exist for storing and streaming bitmap data, each with specific strengths and weaknesses. Regardless of the file format used, the in-memory representation of bitmaps is usually as a matrix in memory corresponding to the pixel dimensions of the image; it is a noncompressed format suitable for quick use with the graphics hardware and the underlying operating system.

Size Does Matter

The first question to ask when looking at bitmap data for mobile devices is what are the physical pixel dimensions of the images you are proposing to bring down to the devices and load into memory?

To keep the math simple, let's assume we are dealing with square-shaped bitmaps. A 1-megapixel image would translate to 1,000 pixels × 1,000 pixels. This resolution is far larger than the screens of most mobile devices and until recently larger than most desktop screens (1024 × 768 is only 786,432 pixels). Even inexpensive digital cameras today take photographs in excess of 2 megapixels, 4 megapixel cameras are not uncommon, and the pixel count keeps climbing every year.

Physical displays with many pixels consume more power than lower-resolution screens, cost more, take up more space, and are more fragile. In addition, a larger screen means larger amounts of device memory and processing power devoted to graphics. Doubtless over time, mobile device screens will continue to get more pixels but there are good reasons to believe that the resolution will continue to lag both digital camera output and desktop display resolutions. Even assuming a large mobile device display of 500 × 500 pixels, it will contain only 250,000 pixels. This is one fourth of a 1-megapixel image and only one sixteenth of a 4-megapixel image. To approach this from another direction, to fit a 4-megapixel image on 240 × 320 Pocket PC display (76,800 pixels) would require throwing out a staggering 98 percent of the pixels in the image. Similarly, a 2-megapixel image would require throwing out 96 percent of the pixels to fit on the same Pocket PC screen, and a 1-megapixel would contain a 92 percent excess of pixels.

Why does this matter? Several reasons:

- *Download size*—If your application does not need the extra pixels, what is the point in downloading them? Downloading larger files takes more time and often costs more money. Mobile device Web applications specifically cater to reduced screen sizes by having lower-resolution images. This makes sense for rich on-device applications as well.
- *On-device storage size*—If your mobile device application downloads a large image, you will need to store it somewhere. This typically means either storing it in a RAM-based file system or in flash storage. In either case, unnecessarily large images require extra read and write time and use up space that could either be used for more images or other data. Would you rather have a single 4-megapixel image on your device or dozens of screen-sized images?
- *In-memory representation*—This is perhaps the most significant aspect to consider. If your mobile application loads a 4-megapixel image into memory, it is creating an in-memory bitmap with 4 million pixels. How often do you declare and use an integer array of 4 million items in your application? That is an awful lot of limited availability program memory to use and almost certainly significantly larger than your loaded code and all other application state. Regardless of the efficiency of the file compression used an in-memory bitmap is just that, a mapping of image bits into memory. Further, if you are using an image file format that requires mathematically complex algorithms to achieve high compression ratios, this math will need to be done to uncompress the images as well, meaning that this will cost your application dearly in performance. Having large bitmaps loaded into memory is a great way to use up all the free memory on a device and either drive the performance of your mobile application right into the ground or cause your application to fail because it has run out of memory.

The moral of the story here should be clear: It does not make sense to use images with pixel counts larger than your device's screen size. These images will be slow to transfer, will need a lot of memory to store and load into memory, and will need to be transformed down into a size that fits on the mobile device's screen regardless. Paying attention to your mobile device's available screen size and choosing image sizes that relate to the space you have to work with makes the most sense. If your application will have a PictureBox that is 120 × 120 pixels, use an image of that size.

Most real-world images are far larger than mobile devices can deal with effectively. How should this disparity be addressed? This is a good opportunity for doing processing off-device to make the on-device experience better. If your images are static images that are known at design time, shrink them down into the actual device resolutions you will be displaying. If your application is dealing with dynamic images, use a server to do the image resizing. A server could dynamically load and resize a large image to a device-sized image if need be but it is far more efficient and scalable to do this work once and cache the results on the server for future use. Because the device-sized images are small, it only requires a trivial amount of extra server storage space to store them along side full-sized images. The easiest time to do this work is when the images are uploaded to a server.

If you try to load large-resolution images into a mobile device application, you will create severe memory pressure. Avoid doing this because end users will see no benefit from images that are larger than their device's screen resolution. Instead, make sure that the digital images that do go onto devices are of a resolution that matches the screen real estate they will be displayed on. This will perform much better.

Getting the File Size Down: Compression vs. Resolution

There are three ways to reduce the file size of a digital image:

1. *Reduce the resolution.* This consists of shrinking the actual number of pixels in an image. If you go into Windows XP's Paint program, load a photograph, choose the Image->Stretch/Skew menu item and "stretch" the image to be 50 percent of its original width, you are reducing the number of pixels by half. Stretch it to 50 percent of its height next and you have removed another half of the image's original resolution. Your image is now 25 percent of the number of pixels of the original (50 percent * 50 percent = 25 percent). Less pixel data to store means lower total size.

2. *Choose the right file format.* Various common file formats differ in their ability to compress different images. Some are good with photographs (lots of colors, few sharp lines); others are good with computer-drawn graphics (sharp lines, fewer colors). Some do no compression at all. Choosing the right format will give you the best-quality image at the lowest size.

   Some image formats also allow you to choose the color depth that images are stored with. The color depth represents the number of bits used to describe the image. If fewer colors are required, a smaller color depth may be able to be chosen to reduce the file size.

3. *Increase the compression.* Lossy compression algorithms often allow you to choose the amount of loss you are willing to accept to hit the size goal you want.

The best way to meet your file size goals is to start with the image's resolution. Shrink the image down to the right dimensions for your device; this way you are getting rid of unneeded data. Second, choose the right file format that yields the best image at the lowest size and minimum color depth. Third, if you are using a lossy compression method, play with the compression settings.

So Many File Formats, So Little Time

There are many file formats available for digital images. Each has benefits and limitations. Here are descriptions of some of the most common formats that are often supported on mobile devices.

.JPG/.JPEG Files (Joint Photographic Experts Group)

True to their name, JPEG files excel at storing photographic and real-world images. JPEG is a variably lossy compression format meaning that you can generally achieve great size-compression benefits by accepting a bit of distortion to the image. All the JPEG photographs you take with common digital cameras use lossy compression. This is why you can fit a stunning looking 3-megapixel image into a 600KB file. More-sophisticated painting programs will let you set the JPEG compression ratio and enable you to explicitly trade off fidelity for size reduction. Often you can get very good looking photographs at very reasonable sizes. A Pocket PC screen resolution-sized photograph may compress down to below 20KB and still look great using JPEG file formats.

Because JPEG is meant to work with real-world images, it will usually not yield the best results for computer-generated raster images such as text on screen snapshots, sharp lines, and sharp color transitions. For these kinds of images, you will generally want to choose a nonlossy format.

*.PNG (Portable Network Graphics)

PNG is a relative newcomer to file formats but is fast gaining acceptance as an excellent file format for images. The effort to create the PNG format arose as a response to some intellectual property rights issues with the *.GIF format. PNG files offer excellent nonlossy compression for digital images. If your platform supports *.PNG images and you need nonlossy compression, this is the format for you. The *.PNG format offers better compression than *.GIF in many cases and is a better choice if both are available.

*.GIF (Graphics Interchange Format)

Think of the GIF format as the popular predecessor to PNG. GIF files offer nonlossy compression as well but are limited to using 256 colors. Because of this limitation, the GIF format is not appropriate for storing photographic images. *.GIF files were heavily used in Web pages in the early years of popular Internet usage and for this reason still have a wide following.

*.BMP (Bitmap Files)

Bitmap files are noncompressed image data. They store data in a format similar to the in-memory bitmap format. Other than not requiring much work to decompress, there are no particular advantages of using *.BMP files other than wide availability.

In developing applications for the .NET Compact Framework, *.JPG files are most appropriate for photo images, and *.PNG files are most appropriate for bitmap images that require complete fidelity. A common scenario for requiring complete pixel fidelity is if a particular image will be used by defining one pixel color as transparent. Transparency regions can be used in complex drawing operations involving other images that "show through" them—more on this later in the book in Chapter 13, "Step 2: Design the Right User Interface."

What to Do If the Mobile Device Is the Source of the High-Resolution Image

Many mobile phones today come with digital cameras capable of taking photographs. Some of these images may be in excess of 1 megapixel (for example, 1,000 × 1,000 pixels), and doubtless this trend will continue upward. Like photographs taken by digital cameras, the images are of far higher resolution than the devices are capable of usefully displaying on their screens; the images are intended for viewing on larger-screened devices (desktop computers) or for printing. It is very wasteful to load and keep a bitmap of this size in memory, but because of latency and connectivity issues it does not make sense to send the picture to a server to be reduced and sent back down to the device either. The solution to work with a large resolution image and still efficiently manage memory on the device is as follows:

1. Load the high-resolution image into memory. Note: If the image is large enough, this may not actually be possible—in which case, a smaller resolution image must somehow be created before even it can be loaded, possibly when the image itself is acquired. A lower resolution image can be saved along with the full-sized image.
2. Immediately make a reduced-sized copy of the image in memory that compresses the image into the dimensions it will be displayed in. This will create an in-memory bitmap image with a much lower pixel count.
3. Dispose and release the original high-resolution bitmap as soon as possible.

If your runtime framework supports saving images, it may make sense to save and cache the reduced size image for future use so that your mobile application does not need to go through the temporary memory and processor usage spike of loading the large image. The important thing is to keep the steady-state amount of memory your mobile application is using down to a minimum, and this means not keeping any extra pixel data in memory that you cannot display. For digital photographs, this can save megabytes of program memory and on mobile devices this will have a significant impact on the performance of your application.

Different Managed Runtime Approaches to User Interface

There are two ways for a managed runtime to integrate into a host device's graphics and user interface model. The runtime can utilize preexisting user interface libraries supported by the operating system or it can bring its own libraries with it to do this work.

The .NET Compact Framework running on Windows CE, Pocket PC, and Smartphone devices defers to the operating system to render and manage the majority of its user interface controls. What this means is that a .NET Compact Framework Window corresponds to a Windows CE Window. A .NET Compact Framework ListView control corresponds to a Windows CE ListView control, a .NET Compact Framework Button corresponds to a Windows CE Button, and so on. This is beneficial for several reasons:

1. *Performance.* The operating system folks have spent a lot of time designing and tuning their user interface controls. It would be difficult to get this level of performance in a custom implementation that hand drew all of these windows and controls and managed their interactions with the user.

2. *Look and feel.* The .NET Compact Framework controls have the same behavioral characteristics as the underlying Windows controls. A user interface implementation is made up of many small decisions such as "Exactly how are the pixels drawn to render the control?" "What happens when you select a block of text and press the back-arrow key? Or type a letter? Or double-click a word?" It is very difficult to exactly duplicate the underlying look and feel of a user interface and humans are very adept at sensing subtle differences.

3. *Size.* Re-implementing the code to draw and manage controls that are already in the operating system takes extra space in the framework. By deferring to existing operating system implementations, a considerable amount of space can be saved.

Although most controls in the .NET Compact Framework running on a Pocket PC, Smartphone, or Windows CE device delegate down to the operating system this does not mean that it is not possible to create entirely new controls using the framework. It is possible to implement a graphical control "from scratch" in the .NET Compact Framework, and this is done in cases where no underlying operating system control exists. This can be done by end developers and is done in the .NET Compact Framework for controls such as the GridControl.

Not all managed runtimes take this approach. Some get only a drawing space from the underlying operating system and draw and manage all the controls by themselves. The benefit of this approach is the potential for a common look and feel regardless of the device an application is running on. The downsides of a custom user interface implementation are extra size and processing overhead and risking not matching the look and feel of the underlying operating system. It is a trade-off.

If the .NET Compact Framework is ported to another platform (it was designed with this ability in mind) it would either need to utilize the underlying operating system's user interface capabilities or bring along its own implementation of these controls in native or managed code libraries. Varying mobile device operating systems differ greatly in their built-in support for user interface controls, so the work required and the design strategy depend highly on the target operating system.

Design Strategies for Graphics Code That Performs

It is appropriate to think of graphics code separately from higher-level user interface code. User interface code generally uses higher-level abstractions offered by the operating system or the programming framework. Concepts such as Button controls, ListBoxes, ListViews, Panels, and Grid controls are examples of these abstractions. At the lowest-level controls are implemented as a series of drawing instructions and low-level interactions with the operating system and users. Application developers almost never have to deal with the controls at this low-level of abstraction. Typically, when using user interface controls, the developer relies on the fact that the underlying graphics needed to draw and maintain the controls are done in an optimized way; the developer's goal is to use the controls in as efficient a way as possible at a high level. In contrast, when working with graphics the developer needs to specifically think of the low-level painting tasks that need to be done and how to accomplish them most efficiently.

From a level of abstraction point of view, higher-level user interface code is analogous to doing network communications using HTTP requests and responses; graphics code is analogous to working with sockets or even packet-level communications. As with networking, whenever possible it is better to use the higher-level abstractions. The higher-level abstractions are easy to use, efficient for most tasks, and well tested. Working efficiently with lower-level frameworks such as graphics libraries requires a more detailed understanding and management of what is going on and careful consideration of what efficiencies can be achieved across the application. Graphics code looks and acts differently than user interface code.

Because the end goal of low-level graphics work is to provide parts of a rich user interface, low-level graphics code and higher-level user interface code must interact at some point. The graphics you create will almost certainly coexist alongside higher-level user interface components such as Buttons, Menus, and ListView controls. Only rarely does it make sense for the entire user interface to be driven by low-level graphics code, for the simple reason that it is usually not useful for an application to do things such as manually paint controls and deal with lower-level user interactions. Instead it is much more efficient for application developers to use predeveloped and proven libraries for user interface needs and only use graphics functions to drive those parts of the user interface that have extraordinary needs. For this there needs to be well-defined models for how to mix higher-level user interface code with lower-level graphics code.

A 4-Minute Tutorial on .NET Compact Framework Graphics

The .NET Framework and .NET Compact Framework documentation have extensive information on graphics that is worth reading. Here are the very basics.

The System.Drawing.Graphics object is the workhorse of .NET graphics. If you are familiar with native code Windows development, think of this as the object-oriented version of the hDC (the Device Context). To draw anything (for example, shapes, lines, text, bitmaps) onto a bitmap surface, your code calls a method on a Graphics object to do it. Equally importantly, if you create a Graphics object, be sure to Dispose() of it when you are done with it because it takes up valuable system resources. You should have a good reason for keeping around any Graphics objects you have.

If you are passed a Graphics object instead of creating one, you are usually being lent the object by the caller. In these cases, it is typically not your code's job to Dispose() of the object; problems will occur if you call Dispose() on an object that still needs to be used by other code. The most common case for this is when writing a Paint handler for a custom control or hooking into a Paint handler for a Form or Control. In these cases, your function gets a Graphics object passed into it to do any drawing you need done.

Pens, Brushes, Fonts, and Bitmaps also need to be created. These objects do not belong to any Graphics object; the same objects can be used with different Graphics objects. These objects also need to have Dispose() called on them when your code is done with them. It can be very useful and efficient, however, for your mobile application to keep around globally the Pens, Brushes, Fonts, or Bitmaps you use frequently. Smart caching strategies can significantly improve performance.

An ImageAttributes class is used to specify drawing attributes for rendering bitmaps. It is passed into some overloads of Graphics.DrawImage() and allows your application to set a transparency color for a bitmap being copied onto another surface. Using ImageAttributes on the .NET Compact Framework allows your code to designate one color in a bitmap to be a transparent color; this means that your code can render nonrectangular images onto bitmaps. This proves very useful for writing games. As with the other classes, ImageAtributes objects should get Dispose() called on them during their cleanup.

Ways to Integrate Graphics with User Interface Code

There are several ways to integrate low-level graphics code and higher-level user interface code. It is important to choose the right one for the task your application is trying to accomplish. Three of the most common ways for graphics code and user interface code it interact are as follows:

1. Displaying bitmap images in a PictureBox
2. Painting to a Form
3. Implementing a custom control

Each of these are described and demonstrated below.

Displaying Bitmap Images in a PictureBox

Drawing graphics onto an offscreen bitmap and displaying that bitmap in a PictureBox control on a form is one of the easiest and most powerful ways to leverage custom-drawn graphics. For almost all business graphics you want to draw, and even for many games, this is an excellent approach because of its simplicity.

To utilize this approach, your application simply creates a Bitmap object and its corresponding Graphics object and then uses the Graphics object to draw everything it wants to onto the bitmap before assigning the bitmap to the PictureBox control's Image property. The PictureBox control takes care of the rest. It makes sure the onscreen image is updated and it handles all repaints necessary; if part or all of the PictureBox gets obscured by another control or window temporarily, the PictureBox handles repainting itself when it becomes unobscured. The PictureBox makes sure that it is displaying an image identical to that of the bitmap; no additional application logic is required to facilitate this.

Because of its simplicity, this approach is excellent for displaying graphical data that does not change second to second. It is also reasonably efficient because the PictureBox knows when it needs to redraw itself. PictureBox controls can also expose some events that your application code can hook into (for example, Click), which enables you to add some interactivity to them as well, further raising the utility of this approach.

Figure 11.5 shows an application consisting of a Button and a PictureBox. Pressing the Button creates an offscreen bitmap, draws an ellipse and some text to it, and assigns the bitmap to the PictureBox. Listing 11.6 shows the code to place into button1's click event to do this. Perform the following steps to build and run the application:

1. Start a new Smart Device project in Visual Studio .NET and select the Pocket PC as the target platform.
2. Add a PictureBox and Button control to the Form. (See Figure 11.5 for how this should look; the PictureBox will be blank at design time.)

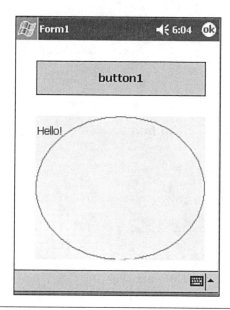

Figure 11.5 Drawing into an offscreen bitmap and sending it to a picture box.

3. Double-click Button1 in the Form designer. This will create and wire up the `button1_Click` event handler below. Enter the code in Listing 11.6 to respond to this event.

4. Compile and run the example. Click Button1.

The PictureBox approach is recommended as the first strategy to try when there is a need to display graphical data. If it meets your application's needs, great! Only when this approach proves itself inadequate should you look to the other more complicated approaches.

Listing 11.6 Drawing into an Offscreen Bitmap and Sending It to a Picture Box

```
//------------------------------------------------------------
//Draw into a bitmap. Send the bitmap to a PictureBox
//------------------------------------------------------------
private void button1_Click(object sender, System.EventArgs e)
{
  //Create a new bitmap
  System.Drawing.Bitmap myBitmap;
  myBitmap = new System.Drawing.Bitmap(pictureBox1.Width,
                                 pictureBox1.Height);
```

```
//-------------------------------------------------------
//Create a graphics object so we can draw in the bitmap
//-------------------------------------------------------
System.Drawing.Graphics myGfx;
myGfx = System.Drawing.Graphics.FromImage(myBitmap);

//Paint our bitmap all yellow
myGfx.Clear(System.Drawing.Color.Yellow);

//Create a pen
System.Drawing.Pen myPen;
myPen = new System.Drawing.Pen(System.Drawing.Color.Blue);

//-------------------------------------------------------
//Draw an ellipse
//-------------------------------------------------------
myGfx.DrawEllipse(myPen, 0,0,myBitmap.Width - 1,
                myBitmap.Height -1);

//Create a solid brush
System.Drawing.Brush myBrush;

//-------------------------------------------------------
//Draw the text with the brush
//-------------------------------------------------------
myBrush = new System.Drawing.SolidBrush(
                        System.Drawing.Color.Black);
//Note: We are using the Font object from the Form
myGfx.DrawString("Hello!", this.Font, myBrush, 2, 10);

//-------------------------------------------------------
//Important! Clean up after ourselves
//-------------------------------------------------------
myGfx.Dispose();
myPen.Dispose();
myBrush.Dispose();

//-------------------------------------------------------
//Tell the picture box that it should display the
//bitmap we just created and drew on.
//-------------------------------------------------------
pictureBox1.Image = myBitmap;
}
```

Painting to a Form

There are two ways to paint to a form:

1. Create a Graphics object for it and use that object to do your painting.
2. Hook into the OnPaint() function for the form and get handed a Graphics object to draw with.

Creating a Graphics object for a form and drawing onto it is generally of limited use because any drawing you make is volatile. The form will be perfectly happy to let your application draw everything it wants onto its surface, but will not keep track of anything that you have drawn. This means that the next time something causes the form to be repainted everything your code has painted will disappear. Therefore, this method is not suitable for graphics that you want to hold on the screen for any length of time. For example, this is a poor way to draw a chart for the user to view on their mobile device because your application is not in control of when all or parts the picture it has drawn will be overwritten. However, this drawing method can be useful in cases where you are continually redrawing the whole onscreen image, such as in an action game. If the image is redrawn several times a second, it does not matter if it is volatile.

Listing 11.7 demonstrates this kind of drawing. To build and run the application, follow these steps:

1. Start a new Smart Device project in Visual Studio .NET and select the Pocket PC as the target platform.
2. Add a Button control to the form.
3. Double-click the Button1 in the Form designer. This will create and wire up the button1_Click event handler shown. Enter the code in Listing 11.7 to respond to this event.
4. Compile and run the example. Click Button1.

Listing 11.7 Creating a Graphics Object for a Form

```
//------------------------------------------------------------
//Creates a Graphics object for a form and draws onto it
//------------------------------------------------------------
private void button1_Click(object sender, System.EventArgs e)
{
  //Create a Graphics object for the form
```

```
System.Drawing.Graphics myGfx;
myGfx = this.CreateGraphics();

//Create a Brush
System.Drawing.Brush myBrush;
myBrush = new System.Drawing.SolidBrush(
                         System.Drawing.Color.DarkGreen);

//Fill the rectangle
myGfx.FillRectangle(myBrush,4,2,60,20);

//-------------------------------------
//Important: Clean up!
//-------------------------------------
myBrush.Dispose();
myGfx.Dispose();
}
```

Hooking into the Paint requests for a form is the way to get involved in the low-level drawing mechanics of that form. When the operating system needs help in restoring the way the user interface looks, it requests that windows and controls repaint themselves. Think of the operating system as a museum curator looking after each piece of art your application has created. For simple maintenance, it may be able to do the work itself, but for more complex tasks it is going to need to call the original artist in to restore the work to its pristine condition. The operating system is in charge of determining when it needs your application to redraw parts of its user interface; however, you can tell the operating system that your form or control needs to be redrawn by calling its `Invalidate()` function.

Paint functions are intended to be called by the operating system when your application needs to have "touch up" work done on it. If you have a reasonably static graphical image that you want to redraw only when necessary, hooking into the Paint function is a good way to do this. However, you should consider whether using a PictureBox control to display your information would also meet your needs; with the PictureBox approach, you do not need to deal with any low-level repaint requests.

Listing 11.8 contains an example Paint function implementation that draws a rectangle and a piece of text onto the form when paint requests are made if it. This paint function should be placed inside a form's code. There are three experiments worth trying with this code to give you a better idea of how and when the operating system calls the paint function:

- *Place a button on the form that calls this.Update().* Note that this typically does not cause the OnPaint function to be called. Calls to `Update()` only request that the form or control be repainted if there are regions that are invalid.
- *Place a button on the form that calls this.Invalidate().* This does cause the OnPaint requests to get queued up and handled as soon as the operating system has time to do it, which is usually very quickly. Calling `this.Invalidate(); this.Update();` will cause a repaint to immediately occur.
- *Place a button on the form that displays a MessageBox control.* Move the message box around above the Form and see what causes `OnPaint()` to be called. In my experiments moving the MessageBox over the colored rectangle did not cause `OnPaint()` to get called (the operating system seemed to take care of this repainting without needing our application's help), but moving the MessageBox over the printed text did cause `OnPaint()` to get called. Hence, it appears that the operating system is capable of performing rudimentary repaints for you without needing to call `OnPaint()` for everything.

The key thing to understand about hooking into Paint functions is that you are not in control of when they get called. You can force them to happen by declaring an area invalidated, but you cannot control external factors that may cause Paint requests. For this reason, it is extremely important that the painting operations occur as quickly and with as little overhead as possible. Slow repainting will make your application look and behave very sluggishly.

Listing 11.8 Hooking into the Paint Function for a Form

```
//Brushes we want to cache, so we don't need to create/dispose them
//all the time
System.Drawing.Brush m_brushBlue;
System.Drawing.Brush m_brushYellow;
//Just for fun, let's count the number of times we are called
int m_paintCount;
//------------------------------------------------------------
//We are overriding our base classes Paint event. This means
//every time the form gets called to paint itself, this
//function will get called.
//------------------------------------------------------------
protected override void OnPaint(PaintEventArgs e)
{
```

```
//IMPORTANT: Call the base class and allow it to do its
//paint work
base.OnPaint(e);

//Up the count of the number of times we have been called
m_paintCount = m_paintCount + 1;

//------------------------------------------------------------
//Important:
//Instead of creating a graphics object, we are being lent one
//for the duration of this call. This means that it is not
//our job to .Dispose() of the object
//------------------------------------------------------------
System.Drawing.Graphics myGfx;
myGfx = e.Graphics;

//------------------------------------------------------------
//Because this painting needs to occur quickly, let's cache the
//brushes so we don't need to create/dispose them every time
//we are called
//------------------------------------------------------------
if(m_brushBlue == null)
{
   m_brushBlue = new System.Drawing.SolidBrush(
                               System.Drawing.Color.Blue);
}
if(m_brushYellow == null)
{
   m_brushYellow = new System.Drawing.SolidBrush(
                               System.Drawing.Color.Yellow);
}

//------------------------------------------------------------
//Do the drawing
//------------------------------------------------------------
myGfx.FillRectangle(m_brushBlue, 2,2, 100, 100);
myGfx.DrawString("PaintCount: " + m_paintCount.ToString(),
                               this.Font, m_brushYellow,3,3);

   //Exit: Nothing we want to call .Dispose() on.
}
```

Event Handlers or Function Overrides?

There is a second way to hook into Paint requests. The example above uses an inheritance approach to hook into Paint requests for a form. It is also possible to use an event handler to handle Paint requests. This works almost exactly the same way hooking up a "Click" event handler; a function is registered to receive the event requests. If an event handler were used instead of overriding the `OnPaint()` method, the code above would need to be changed in three ways:

1. The method name and signature should change to match that needed for a Paint event handler (for example, `protected void PaintEventHandler (object sender, PaintEventArgs e)` instead of `protected override void OnPaint(PaintEventArgs e)`).

2. The call to `base.OnPaint(e)` should be removed because it is not the responsibility of an event handler to call this. In fact, the base implementation of `base.OnPaint(e)` is what calls any registered event handlers.

3. Code needs to be added to the Form's `InitializeComponent` function to hook up the new event handler. (For example, add `this.Paint += new System.Windows.Forms.PaintEventHandler(this.PaintEventHandler)` to the end of the code in `InitialzeComponent()`.)

Whether you use event handling or inheritance is a matter of preference. For low-level work such as hooking into Paint processing, I prefer the inheritance approach because I find it easier to understand. For higher-level events such as Click events, I prefer the event handler approach because the form designer generates this code for me when I double-click the control in the designer.

Implementing a Custom Control

Encapsulating graphics code into a custom control is a good way to package up graphics functionality in a way that can be reused. Implementing a custom control is very similar to overriding the Paint function of a form. It is a low-level approach for manually rendering and maintaining a user interface component.

Custom controls are useful if you want to build an interactive experience for users working with graphical data. If you need a chart that dynamically changes and updates as the user clicks different portions of it or a grid that pivots data as users work with it, a custom control may be the best choice. If all you are doing is outputting graphical data that the user will look at in a read-only way, creating a custom control is unneeded complexity. As with hooking into the `OnPaint()` function as shown above, it is worth considering whether a PictureBox can meet your needs before jumping into a low-level custom control implementation. If your goal is to produce good looking read-only charts, a class that creates an offscreen bitmap and then displays it in a PictureBox control is sufficient for the task. If you decide later that what your application really needs is an interactive custom control experience, the same class you used to create the static chart image is a good place to start for building your custom control. Start simple and only move to lower-level paradigms when higher-level alternatives prove insufficient. Using this approach you will get the job done faster and will do so with fewer low-level debugging headaches.

There are good reasons to build custom controls and the main one is interactivity. The advantages of implementing a custom control are that it gets the ability to respond to low-level events such as mouse movements over the screen area it is in charge of and it gets full control of painting in the region owned by the control. In cases where you want to be able to draw on-screen highlights dynamically, having a custom control implementation can make a lot of sense. Custom controls can also create their own events that the rest of the application can hook into and respond to.

The case of a bar-chart control may illustrate the power of custom controls. Most controls have a Click event to let the application know that a part of the control has been clicked. In a bar-chart control, it may be desirable not just to let the application's developer know that the bar-chart has been clicked, but additionally to indicate which bar-chart column, if any, was selected by the user. To enable this, a bar-chart custom control could create a ColumnClick event that is triggered whenever the area of a chart column it is displaying gets clicked. This event could give the application's developer specific information on which bar-chart column has been clicked so they could write code to respond to this event. The control could also offer the device's users visual feedback such as highlighting the selected column to let them know that their selection has been registered.

Custom controls can be powerful abstractions to use in your application development, but it is important not to invent unnecessary reasons to use them. If high interactivity is required with the end user and/or detailed custom events are useful for application developers to have exposed to them, a custom control solution is worth considering.

Listing 11.9 and Listing 11.10 show a very simple implementation of a custom control in the .NET Compact Framework. Listing 11.9 shows the code for the control itself, and Listing 11.10 shows the code that is used to dynamically create the control instance, place it into a form, and hook up an event handler to the control. Figure 11.6 shows an image of a Pocket PC running an application that uses this basic custom control.

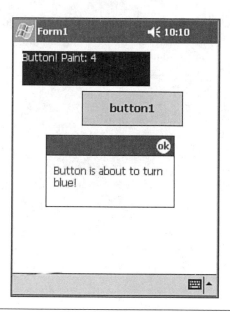

Figure 11.6 MessageBox shown in response to the custom control's event being triggered.

NOTE: It Is Possible to Make Custom Controls Visible at Design Time

For the sake of simplicity, this example dynamically creates a custom control at runtime. Additional pieces are needed to expose the control to developers at design time, to make it appear like the standard controls available in the form designer. This is a subject beyond the scope of this book, but is covered in the .NET Compact Framework documentation.

To build and run the application, follow these steps:

1. Start a new Smart Device project in Visual Studio .NET and select the Pocket PC as the target platform.
2. Add a new class to the project; call it **myButton**. Into the class' code editor, enter the code in Listing 11.9.
3. Go to the form designer for Form1. Add a button to the form. Double-click the button to go to the code editor and enter the code listed in the `button1_click()` event handler in Listing 11.10.
4. Above the `button1_click()` event handler, enter the rest of the code in Listing 11.10.
5. Compile and run the example. Click Button1.

Listing 11.9 A Simple Custom Control That Changes Colors and Fires a Custom Event

```
//A very simple custom control
public class myButton : System.Windows.Forms.Control
{
//--------------------------------------------------------
//Objects we need for drawing
//--------------------------------------------------------
System.Drawing.Brush m_RectangleBrush;
System.Drawing.Brush m_TextBrush;
System.Drawing.Color m_RectangleColor;


//--------------------------------------------------------
//The event we want to expose. This is a public delegate.
//--------------------------------------------------------
public event System.EventHandler EventButtonTurningBlue;

//The constructor
public myButton() : base()
{
  //NOTE: We should write a "Dispose()" function and
  //destructor that clean up these objects

  //Create the brushes we will need
  m_RectangleColor = System.Drawing.Color.Black;

  m_RectangleBrush = new System.Drawing.SolidBrush(
                        m_RectangleColor);

  m_TextBrush = new System.Drawing.SolidBrush(
                        System.Drawing.Color.White);
}



//--------------------------------------------------------
//Internal response to being clicked is to cycle
//through three different button colors
//--------------------------------------------------------
protected override void OnClick(System.EventArgs e)
{
  //--------------------------------------------------
  //Important: Call the base implementation. This
  //will allow any event handlers hooked up to this
  //control to be called
  //--------------------------------------------------
```

```
base.OnClick(e);

//----------------------------------------------------------
//Select our new brush color based on the last brush color
//----------------------------------------------------------
if (m_RectangleColor == System.Drawing.Color.Black)
{
  m_RectangleColor = System.Drawing.Color.Blue;

  //!!!!!!!!!!!!!!!!!!!!!!!!!!!!!!!!!!!!!!!!!!!!!!!!!!!!!!
  //Trigger an event!
  //!!!!!!!!!!!!!!!!!!!!!!!!!!!!!!!!!!!!!!!!!!!!!!!!!!!!!!
  if(EventButtonTurningBlue!= null)
  {
    //Call the event, pass no event arguments
    EventButtonTurningBlue(this, null);
  }
}
else if (m_RectangleColor == System.Drawing.Color.Blue)
{
  m_RectangleColor = System.Drawing.Color.Red;
}
else
{
  m_RectangleColor = System.Drawing.Color.Black;
  }

//--------------------------------------------------
//Release the old brush
//--------------------------------------------------
m_RectangleBrush.Dispose();

//----------------------------------------------------------
//Create the new brush we want to draw the background with
//----------------------------------------------------------
m_RectangleBrush =
  new System.Drawing.SolidBrush(m_RectangleColor);

//----------------------------------------------------------
//Tell the operating system that our control needs to be
//redrawn as soon as reasonable
//----------------------------------------------------------
this.Invalidate();
}
```

```
//------------------------------------------------------------
//Just for fun; let's count how many times we get painted
//------------------------------------------------------------
int m_paintCount;
protected override void OnPaint(
                    System.Windows.Forms.PaintEventArgs e)
{
    //----------------------------------------------------------
    //IMPORTANT: Call the base class and allow it to do its
    //paint work
    //----------------------------------------------------------
    base.OnPaint(e);

    //Up the count of the number of times we have been called
    m_paintCount = m_paintCount + 1;

    //----------------------------------------------------------
    //Important:
    //Instead of creating a graphics object, we are being lent one
    //for the duration of this call. This means that it is not
    //our job to .Dispose() of the object
    //----------------------------------------------------------
    System.Drawing.Graphics myGfx;
    myGfx = e.Graphics;

    //Draw the rectangle
    myGfx.FillRectangle(m_RectangleBrush, 0,0,
                    this.Width, this.Height);
    //Draw the text
    myGfx.DrawString("Button! Paint: " + m_paintCount.ToString(),
                    this.Parent.Font, m_TextBrush,0,0);
} //end function
} //end class
```

Listing 11.10 Code to Place Inside a Form to Create an Instance of the Custom Control

```
//--------------------------------------------------
//This code will get hooked up as our event handler
//--------------------------------------------------
private void CallWhenButtonTurningBlue(object sender,
                                    System.EventArgs e)
{
```

```
        System.Windows.Forms.MessageBox.Show(
                              "Button is about to turn blue!");
}


//Our new button
myButton m_newControl;


//------------------------------------------------------
//This function is to be hooked up to the click event
//of Button1
//------------------------------------------------------
private void button1_Click(object sender, System.EventArgs e)
{
   //------------------------------------------------------
   //To keep things simple, allow only one instance of
   //the control.
   //------------------------------------------------------
   if(m_newControl != null) {return;}

   //Create an instance of our button
   m_newControl = new myButton();
   //Tell it where it should be located inside its parent
   m_newControl.Bounds = new Rectangle(10, 10, 150, 40);

   //------------------------------------
   //Connect up an event handler
   //------------------------------------
   m_newControl.EventButtonTurningBlue  +=
       new System.EventHandler(this.CallWhenButtonTurningBlue);

   //Add it to the list of controls in this form.
   //This will make it visible
   this.Controls.Add(m_newControl);
}
```

Think About Where You Are Doing Your Drawing, Onscreen or Offscreen

Good-looking graphics are as much an art as engineering; this means that technique and planning are equally important. Drawing a single rectangle on a screen or a single piece of text will run quickly enough. Drawing a complex chart or a game board "on-the-fly" onto the visible screen area will likely result in a shoddy user experience. Consider the case of a complex chart that takes 1.5 seconds to draw. This amount of time is well above the minimum human threshold of awareness, and human eyesight can discern quite a few discrete events that go on during this time span. If drawing a chart consists of drawing a background image, drawing and labeling the axis of the chart, drawing lines on the chart, placing dots where actual data points are, and generating a key table that identifies each data set by line color, this can result in a very messy visual build if done in front of the user. The result is even worse if the graphics being produced are for an action game; in this case, the user will experience a great deal of flicker as things get moved around and painted onto the screen.

A second reason for not drawing in sight of the user is that the user interface bitmap space is usually volatile. Unlike an offscreen bitmap that your code owns to itself, onscreen real estate is a resource shared by all the running applications' windows and controls and the operating system. Most operating systems do not maintain whatever images you may draw onto the surface of the user interface. This means that you will lose any images you drew onto the user interface if another application dialog comes up in front of the window your code was drawing to.

It is far more aesthetically pleasing and less error prone to draw to an offscreen buffer and then copy the results into the foreground when your drawing is complete. This kind of solution is also more portable and easier to design, maintain, and debug. Instead of needing to learn the intricacies of the operating system's painting model, your application can own as much of the drawing as possible in its own well-understood environment and interface specifically with the user interface only when it is done. An offscreen drawing approach is almost always the best way to go for graphical operations of any complexity, even if you need to bring up a wait cursor while the image is rendering.

As discussed in the previous sections, the .NET Compact Framework has two good ways to move an offscreen drawing into the user interface. The first is using a PictureBox control and setting its Image property to the bitmap you have just completed drawing (for example, pictureBox1.Image = myNewBitmap).

The second way is to get a Graphics object for the user interface element it is drawing into (usually a Form object) and to call `Graphics.DrawImage()` to do the image transfer:

```
//Get a graphics object for the form
System.Drawing.Graphics gfx;
gfx = this.CreateGraphics();
```

```
//Draw the bitmap into the graphics starting at
//destination coordinate x=10, y=15);
gfx.DrawImage(myBitmap, 10,15);
```

It is specifically worth noting that there are several overloads available for `Graphics.DrawImage()`. The one listed above is the simplest and fastest; it just takes the bits in one bitmap and copies them into another. Other overloads allow more complex abilities that enable things such as drawing only a specified region of the source image into the destination image, stretching or compacting the image being copied and using a transparency mask to allow see-through regions in an image. Each of these performs some kind of a transformation when copying the image from the source to the destination. In general, the more complex a transformation your code wants to perform during the image copy, the more costly it will be performance wise.

One of the best things you can do to maintain good performance is to make the source and destination bitmaps match as closely as possible. If it is possible make sure that the image transfer is a 1:1 bit copy and that the pixels are not being stretched or compressed. Use transparency masks only when they make sense. Although not an issue when using the .NET Compact Framework, other runtime frameworks may offer a choice in the number of colors used in an image or the bit depth used to maintain this information. Matching this information in the source and destination bitmaps can improve performance significantly. The overall goal is to get rid of any impedance mismatches between source and destination so that the image transfer operation resembles a direct memory-copy operation as much as possible. Direct memory copies are generally optimized for performance on all platforms.

Define Your Rendering Process

Sophisticated drawings tend to grow organically in their complexity. An initial prototype is built to do graphing. Onto this prototype is added the ability not just to graph but also label the graph axis. Marker points are added to designate where the data points lie and where the connecting lines are. Support for displaying multiple data sets simultaneously is added. A key table is added to identify the different data sets. Support for multiple colors is added. The ability to draw on top of a background image is added. Chart titles are added. Suddenly a huge pile of code exists that does the graphing. Each graphing piece is worried only about its own work, and little thought has been given to overall efficiency. Game code can suffer the same feature creep as new features get added and piled on top of the list of things that need to be done to render a game board.

For this reason, it is important to spend time and rationalize the rendering process you are using. Doing so will help you get the most performance out of your system as well as give you added flexibility to add new features. It should be a milestone task to review any changes to your rendering model and to rationalize them into a system tuned for maximum overall throughput. Doing this work is not hard; it just requires that you write down in order what steps are being taken and what resources are being used at each step.

Consider the following example.

Unrationalized Chart-Graphing Pipeline

1. Create blank bitmap (150 × 150 pixels).
2. Copy background image into blank bitmap. (Background image is 150 × 150 pixels, straight copy.)
3. Draw graph axis. (Red Pen, Blue Pen, Yellow Pen are created and disposed.)
4. Calculate number of ticks on each axis.
5. Draw line of each tick.
6. Draw text for each tick. (White Brush is created and disposed, 8-point Font is created and disposed.)
7. Draw data for each data set we are graphing. (Red Pen, Orange Pen, Yellow Pen, Green Pen are created and disposed.)
8. Draw a line between each point.
9. Draw a square at each point.
10. Draw title onto chart. (White brush created and destroyed.)
11. Draw key chart to identify data sets.
12. Draw box. (White pen created and disposed.)
13. Draw sample lines for each data set. (Red Pen, Orange Pen, Yellow Pen, Green Pen created and disposed.)
14. Label text for each data set. (Red Brush, Orange Brush, Yellow Brush, Green Brush created and disposed, 8-point Font created and disposed.)

In looking at the model above, we can see that we are creating and disposing of a lot of identical pens, brushes, and fonts. Without much hard work, this model can be rationalized to require fewer resource allocations.

Consider this more rationalized chart-graphing pipeline.

Resource Creation

1. If not already allocated, create a bitmap (150 × 150 pixels).
2. Create needed Pens: Red, Orange, Yellow, Green, Blue.
3. Create needed Brushes: White, Red, Orange, Yellow, Green.
4. Create needed Fonts: 8 point.
5. Clear bitmap.
6. Copy background image into bitmap.
7. Draw graph axis.
8. Calculate number of ticks on each axis.
9. Draw line of each tick.
10. Draw text for each tick.
11. Draw data for each data set we are graphing.
12. Draw a line between each point.
13. Draw a square at each point.
14. Draw title onto chart.
15. Draw key chart to identify data sets.
16. Draw box.
17. Draw sample lines for each data set.
18. Label text for each data set.
19. Release Pens, Brushes, Fonts.

Just getting all the pieces laid out in order can often identify areas for improvement. If you cannot state in a few simple steps what your application's rendering process is, it is a good sign that the model needs to be looked at and rationalized.

Procrastination Is Bad, Precalculate Everything Possible

When designing higher-level user interface code, it is a good strategy to try to defer work for as long as possible; populating controls with a large amount of data that a user may never view can be a waste of processing time. Deferring work is a good strategy because the data being populated into the user interface controls is dynamic, and the potential amount of data is often large enough that populating the user interface with it would be wasteful. If the information was bounded in size and known in advance, it would make a great deal of sense to try to precalculate or pre-initialize the data ahead of time. This is often the case with graphical data.

Graphics work is often made up of many small repetitive tasks strung together one after another. As such, it is a good candidate for using prefabricated pieces. Any drawing that can be done in advance will save time. This is doubly true if the work can be done at design time before the application ever runs. If it is possible to examine the steps of your application's rendering process and remove steps that can be done outside of your rendering process, your application's performance will benefit.

Let's take a look at two common cases to illustrate this point.

Example 1: Pre-Rendering for a Business Chart

Figure 11.7 shows a fairly rich image that displays (fictitious) data in a bar chart. The chart attempts to visually show the relative growth rates of different economies over a period of time. To aid the user in visually comprehending the data, it was decided to show each country's data in columns painted with the country's currency symbol. Further, the chart has a background image; in this case, a smooth gradient going from dark to light; this could in theory be any background image.

The first approach to drawing the chart would probably be starting with a blank bitmap. Into this bitmap would be drawn the background gradient, the axis of the chart, the title of the chart, the tick marks on both of the axes, labels for the tick marks and for the columns, the solid color for each column's bar chart, the currency symbols overlaid on top of the bar chart columns, and the exact values of percentages printed on top of the columns. This is a lot of drawing to do. Given that we know that we are trying to draw a bar chart that displays per-country economic data, we can make several optimizations to greatly cut down the processing needed to render the graph.

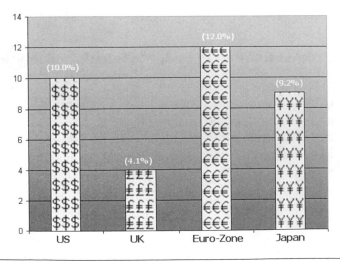

Figure 11.7 Graph showing growth rates for different countries.

The first optimization we can do is to determine everything that will be the same in each graph we draw and to turn this into our predrawn background. Figure 11.8 shows this. Into the background bitmap we have elected to predraw the background color gradient, the vertical lines and part of the title of the graph. We have elected not to draw the following data into the background image: the bar-chart columns themselves, the names and positions of the countries on the chart, the number labels for each tick on the vertical axis, the text on top of the columns, and the columns themselves. All of this needs to be dynamically generated at runtime.

An important decision to make is whether we want to draw this background bitmap once every time we run the application or if we want to create it at design time, compile it as a resource into our application, and simply load the bitmap. If the bitmap is truly static or if we only need a few different kinds of bitmaps, it probably makes sense to design it on the desktop and include it as a binary resource in our application. An added benefit of doing this work at design time is that we can have a graphic artist design it for us and make it as aesthetically pleasing as possible. Regardless, either way we will save a great deal of processing time because each time the chart needs to be rendered a complicated part of it has already been predrawn and cached for our application's needs.

Figure 11.8 Predrawn background for graph.

There are optimizations to be found when rendering the chart data as well. Assuming that the text to be displayed is truly dynamic, this will need to be calculated and drawn by the graphics text rendering framework. This still leaves the nontrivial matter of rendering our decorated bar-chart columns.

As we planned to in our original implementation, we could draw the rectangles for each column and then print text on top of them, but this is needlessly time-consuming. There is also the matter of partially rendered lines of text. It may or may not be easy to get the framework to render 38 percent of the height of a $$$ or 76 percent of the height of a €€€. We could discard this feature altogether because it is too complicated but this would be a shame because the markings on the columns make it very easy to identify which column corresponds to which country and therefore reduces the chances for user error. We want the bells and whistles but we do not want to pay for them.

As a first-order optimization, we could create bitmap image of one line of each currency symbol—that is, a 30 × 10 pixel image of $$$—and all the other currencies. This would probably be quick to copy on top of our background image, and we could write a loop to do this as many times as we need to and clip off the top copy at the right point to meet the correct column height. In fact, we can do even better than this. Why not just have predrawn bitmaps available already that represent the maximum height of each column that we want to draw? There could be four predrawn columns, one for the US, one for Japan, one for the UK, and one for the EU. When our application needed to draw any of these columns, it would simply use one of these bitmaps and copy part of it onto our drawing surface. The vertical extent of the bitmap that we choose to copy will vary with the height of the column we need to draw on our chart. As with the background image, if we can generate the images at design time it is possible to have graphic designers help in getting the images to look as good as possible. Figure 11.9 shows these predrawn columns.

How much extra memory would this approach take? Assume that our chart columns can be up to 180 pixels tall and each column is 32 pixels wide. Further, let's assume 4 bytes of color data for each pixel. That means 180 × 32 × 4 bytes = 23,040 bytes, or 22.5KB of in-memory bitmap space. This may or may not be prohibitive for us. How big is this relative to other things we have in memory? Assuming the background image is about 200 × 200 pixels, this gives us 200 × 200 × 4 = 156.25KB. We will also need another bitmap of the same size to copy both the background and foreground data into for our final graph image; that brings us up to 312.5KB overhead for the background image and the drawing space; not small, but certainly manageable on most mobile devices. All four column bitmaps would still only

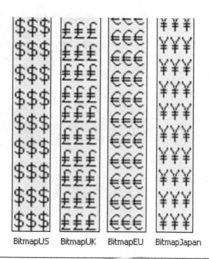

Figure 11.9 Predrawn bar chart for decorated columns.

add up to 22.5 * 4 = 90KB, which is significantly smaller than the background image and the blank bitmap we will need to put all of the images together on. Investing 90KB of memory space to save us the need to do many different memory copies of smaller images or avoiding the need to manually try to draw the text on top of the bar-chart columns is probably a very good optimization.

Example 2: Pre-Rendering for an Action Game

It is interesting to observe that the optimizations for rendering in an action game have a strong resemblance to those used in rendering our chart. Figure 11.10 shows an image of an action game I wrote for the .NET Compact Framework to demonstrate graphics concepts.

NOTE: Those Interested in the Source Code to This Sample Application Can Find It Online

The application was written in VB.NET and is called HankTheCaveMan. This application demonstrates many of the graphics concepts discussed in this chapter. The full source code for the application is available for download on the community code sharing site www.gotdotnet.com along with myriad different samples and information.

Figure 11.10 Action game written for the .NET Compact Framework.

There are three layers of images that need to be rendered onto the screen.

1. *Background picture*—The game has a static photograph used as a background image.
2. *Static foreground*—These are all the items that are in the foreground that do not change from frame to frame. These are the floors and ladders on the game field. They are an important part of the foreground and change from level to level, but they do not change from frame to frame when rendering the game.
3. *Dynamic foreground*—These are all the active elements on the screen that may change from frame to frame. They include the caveman, the cavewoman, the two boulders, the bird, and the four animated torches on the screen. These kinds of graphical elements are commonly referred to as "sprites." Also in the dynamic foreground are the energy bar on the upper left of the play field and the Score/Bonus counter on the upper right. All of these elements are represented programmatically by objects in a collection.

Preceding the rendering loop is the loading of the background image and the drawing of the play field floors and ladders onto it. These are combined in memory and held as our background image. The floors and ladder do not change from frame to frame, so there is no point in rendering them along with every frame. Because we already need to have a background image loaded, we take no additional size hit for drawing our static play field onto it.

The basics of the rendering engine are simple. Every active element on the screen has an object associated with it that holds its position on the play field as well as instructions on how to render it. The rendering loop holds a destination bitmap. This destination bitmap is the same size as the background image. A Graphics object for the destination bitmap has been created and is maintained throughout the application's lifetime. All the Fonts, Brushes, and Pens needed for drawing are also kept globally so that any image rending code that needs them can access them without the need to allocate its own drawing resources.

When a frame is rendered, the background image is first copied into the destination bitmap. After this, each of the objects in the render collection is asked to render itself onto the destination bitmap. Some of these objects are text objects; these call `Graphics.DrawString()` to draw their text onto the destination bitmap. One of the other nontext objects is a rectangle "energy bar"; this is drawn as two rectangles, an outer border and an inner filled rectangle. The rest of the objects are multiframe bitmap images, meaning that they have several bitmaps that can represent the different possible states of the sprite; this allows the objects to be animated by flipping through the images.

Hank (the caveman) has 8 images associated with him; 2 for running left, 2 for running right, 2 for climbing, 2 facing forward. Each sprite has an internal state machine that keeps track of which image to display when it is rendered. The images are small; Hank's images are 21 × 35 pixels, rounding up to the nearest 4 (probable alignment in memory) this gives us 24 × 36 = 864 pixels. 864 pixels × 4 bytes/pixel = about 3.5KB per image. Loading all of Hank's 8 images into memory should take somewhere on the order of 28KB of memory, which is pretty manageable.

Each of these small sprites is rendered using the same background transparency mask when they are copied onto the background image. This means that one of the colors of the sprite's bitmap is designated as transparent and allows the background image to show through when it is copied onto it. This is not as fast as a straight memory copy of opaque rectangular images but produces a much nicer result by allowing images to appear as nonrectangular.

As noted above, this game-rendering model has a great deal in common with our chart-drawing scheme. The game does as much pre-rendering as possible outside of our rendering loop. It is also using predrawn images wherever possible. The game's rendering loop only does a simple bitmap copy of the background image, draws a handful of small sprites with background transparency bitmaps, draws a small amount of text, and draws a few simple rectangles. As long as the game does not allocate memory or otherwise waste time inside the rendering loop, this can all occur very quickly.

Cache Commonly Used Resources

Often when writing graphical processing code your application will use the same resources over and over again. Common classes that get reused are Bitmaps, Pens, Brushes, and Fonts. It is wasteful to keep loading or creating the same resources over and over; unnecessary processing time is spent either reloading a resource from storage or re-requesting it from the operating system. Having equivalent resources loaded in memory at the same time is wasteful as well; for instance, multiple copies of the same bitmap image are wasteful to have around when a single loaded copy could be shared. Finally, disposing of resources further taxes system performance. To avoid these performance taxes, there are cases where it is useful for your application to have an application global resource dispenser that takes care of loading, caching, and disposing of commonly used resources.

Listing 11.11 shows an example with three approaches to loading and maintaining resources in memory.

- *Approach 1 is a latch-based approach*—Any code that needs a common resource calls a static property on the GraphicsGlobals class to get it. If the resource is already loaded, it is returned to the requester. If the resource has not yet been loaded, it is created, cached, and then returned to the user. This approach as two advantages. (1) The requester need not be concerned about any initialization code; the request will always return a valid object. (2) The managed resource can be freed if the application concludes that it will not be needed for a while; if needed, the next request will re-create it. The only disadvantage of this approach is the slight overhead of going through a property accessor function whenever the resource is requested; this overhead is typically negligible.
- *Approach 2 is a batch-based approach*. When a group of resources have similar usage patterns and lifetimes, they can be initialized in bulk. Code that wants to make use of these global resources can di-

rectly access the variables, but it must be sure that they have been initialized before they are used. These resources should also be released and have `Dispose()` called on them when the application gets to a state when the resources will not be utilized for a while.

- *Approach 3 is a collection-based approach.* When a group of resources are always used together, such as the bitmap frames of an animated image, it can make sense to load them together and return them as an array or collection of resources. If the resources are expensive to load or take up significant memory, it may be useful to keep a copy of them cached centrally so that duplicate creations of the same resources do not occur. As above, it is important to have a strategy to release and `Dispose()` of these resources when they are no longer needed.

Listing 11.11 Three Useful Ways to Cache Graphical Resources

```
using System;
using System.Drawing;

internal class GraphicsGlobals
{
  //=========================================================
  //Approach 1: Create the resource on demand
  //             and keep cached afterward.
  //
  //External code gets access view the public properties, but
  //the variable itself is internal to the class
  //=========================================================
  private static Pen s_bluePen;
  public static Pen globalBluePen
  {
  get
  {
      //If we have not created a
      if(s_bluePen == null)
      {
        s_bluePen  = new System.Drawing.Pen(
                          System.Drawing.Color.Blue);
      }
      return s_bluePen;
  }
  } //End property
```

```
//===========================================================
//Approach 2:
//Globally load and cache a bunch of commonly
//used Pens, ImageAttributes, Fonts, and Brushes
//
//External code gets access to the public members,
//no accessor functions needed.
//===========================================================
public static Pen g_blackPen;
public static Pen g_whitePen;
public static System.Drawing.Imaging.ImageAttributes
            g_ImageAttribute;
private static bool s_alreadyInitialized;
public static Font g_boldFont;
public static Font g_smallTextFont;
public static Brush g_greenBrush;
public static Brush g_yellowBrush;
public static Brush g_redBrush;
public static Brush g_blackBrush;


//===========================================================
//Needs to be called before anyone accesses the globals above
//===========================================================
public static void InitializeGlobals()
{
  if (s_alreadyInitialized == true) {return;}
  g_blackPen = new System.Drawing.Pen(Color.Black);
  g_whitePen = new System.Drawing.Pen(Color.White);
  g_ImageAttribute = new
          System.Drawing.Imaging.ImageAttributes();
  g_ImageAttribute.SetColorKey(Color.White, Color.White);
  g_boldFont = new Font(FontFamily.GenericSerif,
                      10, FontStyle.Bold);
  g_smallTextFont = new Font(FontFamily.GenericSansSerif,
                      8, FontStyle.Regular);

  g_blackBrush = new SolidBrush(System.Drawing.Color.Black);
  g_greenBrush = new SolidBrush(
                        System.Drawing.Color.LightGreen);
  g_yellowBrush = new SolidBrush(System.Drawing.Color.Yellow);
  g_redBrush = new SolidBrush(System.Drawing.Color.Red);


  s_alreadyInitialized = true;
```

```
}

//========================================================
//Approach 3: Return an array of related resources.
//            Cache the resources locally so that multiple
//            requests do not load duplicate (wasteful)
//            versions
//
//========================================================
private static  Bitmap  m_CaveMan_Bitmap1;
private static  Bitmap  m_CaveMan_Bitmap2;
private static  Bitmap  m_CaveMan_Bitmap3;
private static  Bitmap  m_CaveMan_Bitmap4;
private static  System.Collections.ArrayList
                   m_colCaveManBitmaps;


//--------------------------------------------------------
//Create and load an array of images for a sprite
//--------------------------------------------------------
public static System.Collections.ArrayList
                      g_CaveManPictureCollection()
{
  //Only load the bitmaps if we do not have them loaded yet
  if (m_CaveMan_Bitmap1 == null)
  {
    //--------------------------------------------------------
    //Load the bitmaps. These bitmaps are stored as embedded
    //resources in our binary application
    //
    //Loading the images from external files would be similar
    //but slightly simpler (we could just specify the file
    //name in the bitmaps constructor).
    //--------------------------------------------------------
    //Get a reference to our binary assembly
    System.Reflection.Assembly thisAssembly =
            System.Reflection.Assembly.GetExecutingAssembly();

    //Get the name of the assembly
    System.Reflection.AssemblyName thisAssemblyName =
                                    thisAssembly.GetName();
    string assemblyName = thisAssemblyName.Name;

    //Load the bitmaps as binary streams from our assembly
    m_CaveMan_Bitmap1 = new System.Drawing.Bitmap(
```

```
            thisAssembly.GetManifestResourceStream(
            assemblyName + ".Hank_RightRun1.bmp"));

        m_CaveMan_Bitmap2 = new System.Drawing.Bitmap(
            thisAssembly.GetManifestResourceStream(
            assemblyName + ".Hank_RightRun2.bmp"));

        m_CaveMan_Bitmap3 = new System.Drawing.Bitmap(
            thisAssembly.GetManifestResourceStream(
            assemblyName + ".Hank_LeftRun1.bmp"));

        m_CaveMan_Bitmap4 = new System.Drawing.Bitmap(
            thisAssembly.GetManifestResourceStream(
            assemblyName + ".Hank_LeftRun2.bmp"));

        //Add them to the collection
        m_colCaveManBitmaps = new System.Collections.ArrayList();
        m_colCaveManBitmaps.Add(m_CaveMan_Bitmap1);
        m_colCaveManBitmaps.Add(m_CaveMan_Bitmap2);
        m_colCaveManBitmaps.Add(m_CaveMan_Bitmap3);
        m_colCaveManBitmaps.Add(m_CaveMan_Bitmap4);
    }

    //Return the collection
    return m_colCaveManBitmaps;
  }
} //End class
```

Find Ways to Avoid Object Allocations for Repeated or Continuous Drawing

Unnecessary object allocation and destruction is one of the most common causes of poorly performing graphics code. Graphics code often runs inside loops or is called often. Further, graphics objects are relatively expensive, using both significant amounts of memory as well as system resources. If your mobile device application is allocating and freeing memory each time it is called to render graphics, you will create memory pressure and this will lead to frequent garbage collections and stalls in your application's performance. It is therefore important keep a close eye out for any kinds of object allocations that may be occurring inside your graphics rendering code. This particularly applies to objects associated with graphics resources but is also true for any other objects (for example, collections, arrays, strings) that may be present in your graphics rendering code.

A few examples of things to look out for:

- *Bitmap objects*—There are often cases when it is useful to have a Bitmap object that is used as a temporary holding space for an image or part of an image your application is building. If your mobile device application needs temporary space to do drawing in, this is fine; but avoid creating and disposing of multiple bitmaps in your drawing cycles. It is usually much better to have one scratchpad space that is used over and over again as a common resource than it is to go through the expense of continually creating and disposing temporary bitmaps. The scratchpad bitmap should be of the dimensions of the largest scratchpad space you need in your routines (but no larger). If the scratchpad space needs to be cleared before drawing to it this is easy and fast to do with a call to `Graphics.Clear()`. Also, as shown in the sample code above, it is worth loading and caching commonly used bitmaps in memory. Make sure only one instance of each bitmap is loaded at any given time. If your application has multiple copies of identical bitmap resources loaded, it is wasting a lot of memory.
- *Graphics objects*—If you are going to do continuous drawing into a bitmap, such as drawing frame after frame of game board, it is probably worth caching the Graphics objects of the offscreen bitmap as well as the onscreen destination for the drawing. Doing so will prevent you from needing to continually allocate and free these objects. In your drawing cycle, you should never have to allocate the Graphics object for a bitmap or form more than once; ideally you should avoid needing to allocate and dispose of them at all. The same holds true for any other bitmaps that you are drawing to; cache their Graphics objects instead of continually recreating them. Keep in mind that a Graphics object is only needed for bitmaps that you are drawing into; if a bitmap is used only as a source of image information, you should not need a Graphics object for it at all.
- *Fonts, Brushes, Pens, ImageAttributes*—A common and understandable mistake that developers make is overly aggressively managing resource lifetimes at a micro level without looking at their usage at a macro level. A graphics image you are drawing may consist of 30 discrete drawing steps where lines are drawn, ellipses are filled, text is printed, and bitmaps are copied. Each of these operations uses some combination of Pens, Fonts, Brushes, and, if you are using transparency masks, ImageAttributes. The situation is made more critical on

mobile devices because unlike the desktop .NET Framework, the .NET Compact Framework does not have static versions of the basic Brushes and Pens; for example System.Drawing.Pens.Blue and System.Drawing.Brushes.DarkOrange exist on the desktop .NET Framework but must be allocated on the .NET Compact Framework. The solution to this challenge it to create your own global set of Pens and Brushes that you will use throughout for your application's drawing needs. You should review the code in your application's drawing cycles and keep a careful eye out for the repeated creation of identical resources and remove these redundancies. The Fonts, Brushes, Pens, and ImageAttributes you need should either only be allocated once in the drawing cycle or be cached globally when continual drawing is needed by your application.

■ *Value types that get cast to objects (a.k.a. "boxed" into objects)*—The most common value type used in graphics code is the System.Drawing.Rectangle structure. Working with value types is normally very efficient because they can be allocated on the stack (and not on the global memory heap as objects are). However value types can also be treated as objects and placed into arrays or collections or passed any place that accepts an object type. Keep a careful eye on your use of value types to make certain that you are not continually allocating and releasing memory implicitly through their "boxing" and "unboxing" into objects.

The need to avoid continual object allocations in your application's graphics code must be balanced with the need to manage your mobile device application's global memory usage. If only certain parts of your application make use of graphics functionality, consider disposing of these resources when your application enters a state where the graphics resources are not of imminent use. Using a state machine and defining which graphics resources can be released when leaving a specific application state is a good design practice.

Summary

Writing code to ensure a user interface's responsiveness will not make your application's algorithms perform faster. It will not speed your application's march to "feature complete." It may even add complexity to your mobile device application's code. The only reason to do responsiveness coding and performance tuning is to offer the end user a more comfortable experience; but isn't this the point? If you want the end user to have a high-quality impression of your mobile application, you must spend time on fit and finish issues such as responsiveness. As with other aspects of performance, this work cannot be back loaded to the tail end of your development process. At the end of your design process, you may be able to apply some Band-Aids such as showing wait cursors at points where your application's user interface stalls, but this is like putting a nice coat of paint on a house that is shoddily constructed; it is better than nothing, but it is not much. Keep responsiveness in the top of your mind and make it an exit criterion for every development milestone. The right time to fix responsiveness problems is when they are created and before they have cemented themselves into your application.

Good user interface performance comes from actively managing the end user's experience with your mobile device application. As the user navigates thorough the application's functionality, your mobile application's goal should be to ensure a responsive and anxiety-free experience. User interfaces cause complicated interactions between your application's code and the runtime libraries the application is built on top of. Controls are created and populated into forms, events are triggered, and many levels of interaction are possible between your code and that of the framework. Good performance is achieved by utilizing the performance-oriented features in the framework, by structuring the application's user interface code to keep the user a participant when long-duration tasks occur, and by aggressively measuring and instrumenting your user interface code to get a clear understanding of what goes on under the hood of your user interface.

Examine the properties and methods of the controls you use. Often there are specific features put into controls to allow for performance optimizations. Keep a close eye on the events that your application is responding to. It is specifically worth understanding and experimentally verifying when each of the events you are responding to gets triggered. Events seem simple and understandable by inspection of code, but they are an area where you, as the application developer, have given up control to the system. The operating system and user interface framework determine when your event handling code is going to run; this could occur more often than you anticipate or could occur in unexpected ways when message processing occurs by the system. Subtle interactions between events, properties, and methods of controls can arise that you may not be aware of. Extra and unneeded execution of user interface events is a source of both performance problems and complexity. Be specifically mindful of cases where events can be re-entrant.

When working with bitmaps, size does matter. Today's high-resolution digital images take up an enormous amount of space both on disk and especially in memory. Digital photographs and also desktop-generated bitmaps can provide images of a resolution far beyond what mobile devices are capable of displaying. Be acutely aware of the screen size of the devices you are working with and the size of the bitmaps you are bringing down to the devices; they should be of a similar magnitude. For images of any significant size, it is a good idea to use a compressive data format. JPEG is recommended for images that can tolerate lossy compression, and PNG files are recommend for images where exact fidelity is required. Be aware that regardless of the efficiency of the compression algorithms you are using, once a bitmap image is loaded into memory it takes up a size governed by its dimensions and not by its compressed file size.

Graphics work should be thought of separately from higher-level user interface coding and optimized in its own right. Optimizing graphics drawing code requires different techniques than tuning higher-level user interface code; it is a specialized art. Because graphics images your mobile application generates are usually indented to coexist with higher-level user interface elements, some thought must be given to how your graphics code will interface with the user interface; there are several different models for this. It is a good idea to use the highest-level of abstraction appropriate for this interaction. If you are generating static images, creating an in-memory bitmap and assigning that bitmap to the Image property of a PictureBox is a good and conceptually simple way to go. If continual updates of an image are required, consider having the application draw the image offscreen and copying frames onto the surface of a form periodically like a movie projector. Building a custom control is a good way to go if you require high user interactivity within the graphics you have drawn, such as in a graph that allows the user to visually drill into specific parts of the data drawn on it. Custom controls can also generate custom events for your application to hook into. Each of these user interface integration strategies is appropriate for a specific kind of interaction; it is important to be explicit about what the goals of graphics in your mobile application are and to choose the appropriate strategy to achieve these goals.

When working with graphics code it is important to have a systemic view of how your mobile application will accomplish its rendering. It is important not to be "penny wise and pound foolish" with resources. If there are Bitmaps, Graphics objects, Pens, Brushes, Fonts, or ImageAttributes, you will need throughout your drawing, you will need to come up with a system for creating and caching these resources. Prebuilt bitmaps can take up valuable memory but they are extremely useful in speeding up drawing; using them judiciously will result in a rich and well-performing application. Take care not to have two identical resources loaded at the same time, this is just wasteful. Think also about whether your application can be separated into different states, which states need which graphical resources, and when cached resources should be disposed of because they are not needed in the near term.

Rich graphical experiences are possible on mobile devices and can add a great deal to the overall experience users have with your mobile application. It is important to think creatively, analytically, and systematically when building your graphical experience. The creativity of an artist to see what is possible, the problem-solving analytics of an engineer, and the shrewd eye for wasteful practices of an accountant are required to build a great-performing and rich graphical experience. Working with graphics on mobile devices can be challenging and fun; make sure you keep a close eye on performance, and then the sky is the limit!

CHAPTER 12

Performance Summary

Performance Summary

Congratulations! You have made it to the end of the performance part of the book. If you have read all the way up to here, you should have a very good grounding on the most important aspects of designing mobile application code that performs well. You will be in a position to explore the creative possibilities that mobile devices offer. Because performance is a multifaceted topic, it has been approached in the previous chapters by drilling into details of the specific areas and layers of design that most influence a mobile application's performance. The discussion started with an overview of performance from a design philosophy and process perspective. We then moved on to looking at how various areas of common mobile application functionality can be made to perform poorly or well depending on design choices and looked at specific strategies to ensure good performance in those domains. It is now time to round out the performance discussion by integrating the different discussion threads back together into a set of concluding thoughts and best practices.

Performance and Memory Management Summary

How you manage memory in your mobile application both at macro and micro levels will have an overwhelming effect on what you will be able to achieve in your mobile development efforts. In designing your mobile application's memory-usage model and writing your algorithms, it is important to be mindful of what you are driving the garbage collector to do in response to your decisions. Although you are not in explicit control of the garbage collector it has a strong influence on the overall performance of managed-code applications. Native code developers will have similar kinds of issues but will need to manage their memory themselves. Full garbage collections are expensive; the runtime needs to go through all the live top-level objects and trace down the tree of subobjects to find all the objects still in use so that the remaining garbage objects can be reclaimed. Each garbage collection has a fixed minimum cost based on the number of objects that need to be looked at; repeating the operation often will cause a significant drag on your application.

How often the garbage collector runs is directly determined by how quickly your code creates memory pressure in your application. Two things combine to create memory pressure in applications: (1) the total amount of application state you maintain, which means any forms, global objects, user data, and any objects contained inside global parent objects; and (2) the temporary objects you create and destroy through the running of your algorithms. The memory-usage pattern of your application will resemble a saw-tooth wave. The height of the saw tooth is determined by how much working space you leave for your algorithms to use—that is, the space not taken up by your steady-state allocated memory. The upward slope of the saw tooth is determined by how efficient your algorithms are with their object allocations. The more frugal your algorithms are in new object allocation, the more gradual the slope of the saw tooth. Eventually the memory usage will cross a threshold and garbage collection will be triggered to clean up all unused objects.

Figures 12.1, 12.2, 12.3, and 12.4 describe four basic patterns of memory usage.

Figure 12.1 shows the memory usage and garbage-collection pattern for a worst-case scenario with high steady-state memory usage and wasteful algorithms. In this case, the mobile application's steady-state memory usage is using up most of the available memory on the system. This leaves little room for the constant object allocations and disposals that occur when running inefficient algorithms. It is important to remember that the space used up by an object is not available for immediate reuse when the object is thrown away; the memory must be garbage collected to reclaim it for working use. The constant allocation and discarding of objects creates a very steep memory-usage curve. Because there is little room for doing these allocations, very frequent garbage collections occur, each with its own processing overhead. The result is poor performance because the garbage collector is forced to run almost continually just to keep the application limping along.

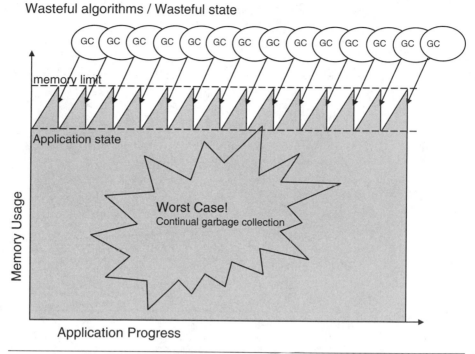

Wasteful algorithms / Wasteful state

Figure 12.1 The worst case: excessive application state and wasteful algorithms.

Figure 12.2 shows an intermediate case of performance. In this memory-usage pattern, the application still has algorithms that make wasteful object allocations, but the steady-state memory usage is much lower. This means that even though the line tracing continual object allocation and discarding is steep, there is much more working room than in the preceding example for the garbage to pile up. The result is that less-frequent garbage collections need to occur. This results in significantly better performance than in the case above.

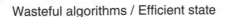

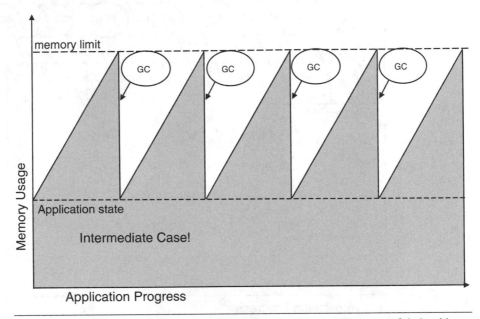

Figure 12.2 An intermediate case: efficient application state but wasteful algorithms.

Figure 12.3 shows another intermediate model of memory management that is the reverse of the case above. This diagram shows a memory-usage pattern where the steady-state memory usage of the applications is high, representing lots of globally held objects or system data, but the application's algorithmic memory usage is efficient. Although there is not a large amount of working memory for use, the fact that running algorithms are not wastefully allocating objects prevents the need for the garbage collector to run continually.

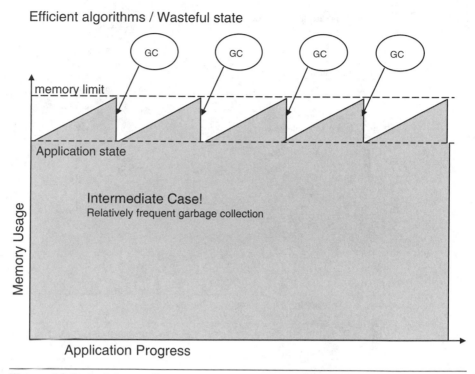

Figure 12.3 An intermediate case: excessive application state but economical algorithms.

Figure 12.4 shows the best case for memory utilization. The number of steady-state objects held by the application is limited so that there is plenty of working room for algorithms to run. At the same time, the algorithms are not overly wasteful in creating temporary objects. The result is very infrequent garbage collections; this means good performance and few application stalls.

The memory-usage model shown in Figure 12.4 is what you should strive for in your mobile applications. The application should maintain what is necessary in application state for the user's data but do so as efficiently as possible. It should also hold in memory those resources that would commonly need to be created and destroyed during the steady-state operation of your application.

Good memory management is keeping things balanced and making effective utilization of the memory that your application has to work with. It makes no sense to keep the global state as small as possible if your application needs to continually create and destroy the same temporary objects to

Efficient algorithms / Efficient state

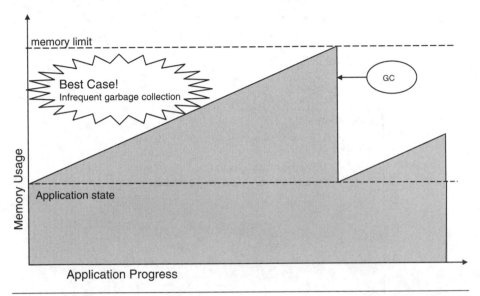

Figure 12.4 The best case: efficient application state and economical algorithms.

meet its normal running needs. Nor does it make sense to keep so much global state that your application's memory does not have room to effectively run its algorithms without the garbage collector continually cleaning up. What is required is a good balance.

Performance and Multithreading

As a general rule, multiple threads will not make your mobile application run faster. Another rule of thumb is that managing parallel threads of execution will make your application code more complex and more difficult to understand, maintain, and debug. For these reasons, it is important to not become "thread happy" and continually invent new uses for threads when they are not absolutely required.

There are, however, very good reasons to use background threading in your mobile applications. The most compelling use of threads is to keep your mobile device application responsive to the user when long-duration or indeterminate-duration tasks need to occur. A long-duration task is usually something that requires significant calculation or algorithmic processing to be performed. An indeterminate-duration activity is anything that requires access to resources that are outside your immediate control. (For example, when accessing any information across a network, it is virtually impossible to predict the latencies that may occur.) For these kinds of activities, asynchronous execution is a great choice.

The simplest and most effective model for multithreading is to have one main thread that interacts with the user and to have background threads to perform asynchronous tasks. The main foreground thread can periodically poll to see whether background tasks have been completed or whether there is intermediate progress information that the user should be made aware of. These background-processing threads can either be created on demand or can exist in a pool waiting for work to do. Creating the threads on demand is conceptually simpler than building a thread pool manager. When prebuilt infrastructure for managing background execution does not exist, creating threads on demand is the way I recommend approaching background threading for mobile device applications. Frameworks may include built-in functionality for performing common tasks asynchronously, so make sure to look for this before you go off and create your own threading model; there is no sense in reinventing the wheel if a well-designed and tested wheel already exists.

Performance and API Abstraction Levels

It is important to work at the right level of abstraction. Higher levels of API abstraction offer a simplified, convenient, and well-tested programming model, but often at the expense of added overhead. Lower-level APIs offer the possibility of the greatest control of performance but do so at the cost of added complexity in your code. Networking code and XML parsing are two examples of framework functionality where multiple layers of abstraction exist for the application developer to choose from. Your application should always use the highest level of abstraction that is appropriate for the tasks it is trying to accomplish.

The case of working with XML is an instructive example. In theory, developers could achieve the absolute maximum performance by working directly at a file I/O stream level to parse the data they needed. However, this would be a foolish, error prone, and thankless task if well-designed and proven higher-level APIs exist to do the work without incurring a significant performance penalty. Ideally, developers would like to use the XML Document Object Model (DOM) to load and save their data as an XML tree. If the XML data being worked on is of moderate size, this is a great model. Developers must remember, however, that the XML DOM is a stateful API; when it loads XML into memory, it actually creates an in-memory tree of objects representing the XML document. For a large-enough XML file, this in-memory tree will cause severe memory pressure. In contrast, the XML DOM itself is built on top of stateless and forward-only XMLReader and XMLWriter classes; these classes parse or generate XML data in a minimally stateful way. The XMLReader and XMLWriter keep only enough data around to allow them to continue parsing or streaming the XML; they neither generate nor use an in-memory tree of the data. When working with larger XML documents on mobile devices with limited memory resources, the stateless forward-only model is the right way to go. This is true even with the greater programming burden that the lower-level APIs place on the application developer to manage the XML parsing process. Choosing the right level of API abstractions requires understanding how much data is going to be moved and what the overhead is that is associated with higher-level abstractions.

Performance with User Interface and Graphics

User interface and graphics are where end users will get their first and deepest impressions of your application. An application that looks sharp and appears responsive is sharp and responsive. There are almost an endless number of ways to present data and interact with the user, so the design choices are broad. This can be both empowering and daunting; some guidance is in order. When populating the user interface, it is important to consider what data a user is likely to need and to not spend time populating controls with large lists or trees of data that the user is unlikely to navigate to; this would be a waste of time and system resources. Instead it is worth spending the time to design user interfaces that enable users to navigate to the data they want and to defer populating unnecessary user interface elements until needed. A good deal of experimentation can be required to get this model right; be prepared to iterate on your design.

Careful investigation should be done to understand how the user interface interacts with your mobile application's code. It is of particular importance to understand how the user interface framework invokes your application's event handling code. It is often impossible to tell by code inspection alone what events will be fired when and how the event handling code interacts with properties and methods your application may call. Instrumenting your code and periodically spending time auditing when user interface event handlers are being called can be a good way to gain a firm understanding of the interactions between your code and the user interface framework.

In-memory bitmaps and stored images are an area where graphics and user interface code interact. It is often useful to use stored images in your application either as part of the user interface or as application data. When using images, it is important to check the dimensions of the images to make sure that the dimensions are of the same general size as your user interface; images with larger dimensions than needed take up extra memory to store and use significantly more system memory when loaded. Separately it is also worth taking a look at the image storage formats being used to make sure that the most efficient format is being used for the task at hand. *.JPG files are typically most useful for photographic images and *.PNC files are typically most useful for computer-drawn graphics.

Graphics code is code that does custom drawing. It is useful for presenting rich custom images to users and also for implementing highly interactive custom controls. There are often several ways to integrate graphics code into your user interface ranging from very simple (for example, displaying drawn images in PictureBox controls) to complex (for example, creating a custom control). As with choosing the right API abstractions described previously, it is important to choose the right model for graphics integration in your application; use the simplest model appropriate.

There are great optimizations possible in graphics drawing code. To recognize and achieve these benefits, you must think of your mobile application's drawing tasks holistically. Graphics code often consists of many small steps chained together or run in loops. To achieve maximum graphics performance, your application design process should (1) look for areas where graphics work can be done ahead of time, such as predrawing parts of an image whenever possible; or (2) seek to minimize the number of redundant allocations of objects and system resources. If common Pens, Brushes, bitmap working spaces, or other resources are used more than once, they should be created and cached.

Look For and Pay Attention to Performance Warning Signs

You ignore performance problems at your peril. Turning a blind eye and not looking for potential performance problems in your mobile device application's design is a sure way to invite problems down the road. Performance problems are best addressed when they are created, and it is at this point when they are easiest to diagnose. More than on a desktop application, your mobile application consists of a series of interlocking and interdependent systems that need to share the same finite system resources. Because the pool of available memory is smaller and the concept of swapping out infrequently used memory to a disk paging file does not exist for mobile devices, any one wasteful element of your application can cause large-scale performance problems for the whole application. For instance, maintaining large bitmaps in memory will directly take away from memory that may be needed to store a tree of XML data or compiled function code. It is easy to diagnose cases where your application simply runs out of memory. It is far more difficult to diagnose the source of a problem when your application is becoming slowly starved of memory and the garbage collector is forced to run more and more frequently just to keep the application running.

The interdependence of the parts of your application means that both integrated and component-level analysis is required. Each individual component part of your application (the code that deals with loading and saving data, the code the deals with graphics, the code that deals with network I/O, and so on) should be reviewed to understand the state that it demands and the kinds of temporary allocations it makes when it is running; obviously, smaller is better. As soon as possible, these components need to be integrated together into your application to see how the system performs as a whole. The data used to test the application must be of a similar size to the real-world data your mobile application will use.

When performance problems arise, it is important to diagnose and deal with them promptly. The more code that gets written and integrated into your application, the harder it will be to discover and fix the parts of your application that are responsible for performance problems. Some runtimes can give you profiling data such as the number of objects allocated, the number of garbage collections performed, and other useful memory-usage metrics to help you understand the root causes of performance problems in your application. Instrumenting your code with diagnostic measurements is another useful method for pulling out comparative performance data. Finally, isolating portions of your application and looking at the algorithms and memory-usage characteristics of individual parts in detail can prove helpful.

When performance problems exist, it is extremely important to not continue to add features and code to your mobile application in the false belief that performance can be addressed in the future. You should only add code and features to your mobile device application when you have the extra performance capacity to support those features. If you find you are hitting a performance wall, you need to find ways to economize application state and algorithmic object churn before adding additional resource-consuming pieces to your application. Extra performance capacity is the currency you have to spend on new features; if you are in debt, find a way to get out of debt before spending more.

Conclusion and Best Practices

Writing great mobile device applications is a matter of balancing competing design goals, coming up with clever mechanisms to avoid doing unnecessary work, and most importantly keeping a disciplined performance-minded approach in your development. The following are a summary of some of the best practices to help with this:

- *Make a conscious and proactive decision to manage your mobile application's memory.* Do not allow your mobile device application's memory model to come about as a matter of passive or arbitrary design. Make an explicit statement of what is to be kept in memory and when it will be discarded.
- *Define discrete application states and identify the resources that are required in each state.* A state machine approach can be very useful in implementing this kind of memory management. Your mobile device application should maintain a specific list of states and state transition behaviors that enable you to tune your application's memory usage.
- *Do not be afraid to cache commonly used resources.* It should be a goal to keep your application's steady-state memory usage as low as possible, but this should not be done at the expense of throwing out useful objects. If you continually have to re-create and dispose of critical objects, these objects should be cached instead to avoid this memory churn. Consider having a resource dispenser class that is in charge of allocating, caching, freeing, and handing out resources to the rest of your application. This dispenser class can separate the dispensing of resources from their allocation and destruction. If you have a central resource dispenser, the rest of your application code does not need to worry about allocation and disposal strategies and your resource dispenser can be tuned to your application's needs in its different states.
- *Use the wait cursor and give feedback to users for any task that takes more than an instant.* For any task that takes more than half a second, a wait cursor should be used. For any task that takes more than

a couple of seconds or takes an indeterminate amount of time, users should be given additional updates indicating what progress is being made on their behalf.

■ *Develop and test with real-world data sizes and connectivity models.* It is important to test your mobile device application in a similar environment to the one that end users will experience. This means both using data sizes that end users will expect to work with as well as using connectivity models (for example, connection speed and latency) users will experience. If your application has capacity thresholds above which performance starts deteriorating significantly, consider explicitly disallowing the application to reach these states; you do your application's users no favors by allowing them to get into poorly performing states.

■ *Be mindful of dimensions of bitmaps you use.* Common digital images today are significantly larger than can be usefully displayed on mobile device screens. It is time wasteful to move these images over networks, space wasteful to store them on mobile devices, and extremely memory wasteful to load them into memory. An extra 0.5MB of image data loaded into memory is equivalent to hundreds or thousands of nonimage data items held in memory; 500KB of pixels is approximately 500,000 integers worth of data. Whenever possible, reduce image dimensions down to the target device's display capacity before downloading them. If this is not possible and high-resolution images need to be loaded into memory, consider immediately making smaller-resolution copies in memory and releasing the large-sized original so that your application does not hold huge amounts of unnecessary memory.

■ *Look for ways to preprocess data.* This is true for graphics code, XML code, and any other significant code that needs to be executed. The more you can precalculate and put into an easy-to-consume format, the less processing time you spend at runtime.

Good performance is essential to building high-quality mobile applications. The necessary performance can be achieved by creative and disciplined design. The guidelines and design strategies outlined in the preceding chapters should serve as a good beginning in helping you approach performance challenges in a creative and well-considered way.

CHAPTER 13

Step 2: Design the Right User Interface

"The ability to simplify means to eliminate the unnecessary so that the necessary may speak."

—Hans Hofmann (1880–1966), German-born U.S. painter and teacher
(Encarta 2004, Quotations)

Think Devices!

Next to your mobile application's performance, the application's user interface will most determine the quality of experience users have with your application. Having an intuitive, responsive, reliable, and good-looking user interface makes a big difference. As with other creative endeavors, designing a good mobile application user interface requires both creativity and discipline.

Creativity is required to find novel solutions that enable you to present your application's functionality on the relatively small canvas offered by mobile devices. Desktop displays are becoming enormous in both physical dimensions and effective resolution. Mobile devices are bounded by their environment; they must be easily carried around by users and used unobtrusively so that others in the surrounding environment are not disturbed. Conveying the information and interactivity you want to deliver is an exercise in both distillation and creative organization of information. In addition to the challenges of fitting the needed information onto a mobile device screen, there are human and social factors to keep in mind. Think of how frequently today a mobile phone's ringing interrupts the flow of a conversation or meeting, or disturbs others in public areas. Think of what would happen if everyone in a room tried to talk on their mobile phones at once; the result would be an incomprehensible cacophony. (Sadly, this is no longer a theoretical problem!) Think of what would happen if everyone in a crowded elevator or subway needed both hands to access their schedule, business, or personal information stored on a mobile phone; elbows would be everywhere and tempers would flare. It is easy to work with one hand in a crowded space, much harder to work with two. Both the information that needs to be conveyed as well as the context in which the application is being used should have a significant impact on how the user interface is designed. These are problems that need to be solved creatively.

Discipline is required to maintain consistency in user interface design. One of the hallmarks of a poorly designed mobile device user interface is inconsistency of experience through the flow of the application. Forcing the user to change focus to different parts of the screen or press different physical buttons to travel in a straight line through the application's user interface is bewildering to users. As with many other aspects of mobile device design this problem is not unique to mobile devices but is exacerbated by the fact that devices offer a constrained and concentrated view to users; this makes awkward navigation harder to work around for people using the application. Keeping a disciplined approach that ensures consistent and simple navigation through your application is important.

Discipline is also required in the realization of the user interface code to ensure that the application's code stays flexible and open to experimentation and refinement. User interface code has a way of becoming messy and tangled. Successive small tactical changes piled upon one another, each to solve an immediate problem, have a way of making the code base fragile and resistant to change. Discipline is required to keep the user interface code from becoming a single system of intricate and interlocking systems. Instead the goal should be to define and realize the user interface as a robust set of discrete states. The implementation of each user interface state should be insulated enough from other states as to allow iteration on its design without destabilizing the other states. As recommended earlier in this book, an adherence to a state machine approach when defining and implementing a mobile device's user interface can pay rich dividends when experimenting with, refining, and maintaining user interface code. A disciplined coding approach does not decrease flexibility, it increases it.

Mobile device user interfaces are fun. They can be challenging and they require new ways of thinking and problem solving. For developers coming from the design perspective of desktop- or Web browser-based applications, mobile device user interfaces offer unique challenges that must be mastered. As the mobile application's designer, you must get your head into the mindset of mobile device thinking.

One Size Does Not Fit All

Only a few years ago, the concept of "write once, run anywhere" was all the rage; we were all going to write applications that seamlessly ran on different desktop operating systems, transferred down to our cell phones, and ran on our wristwatches without modification. Presently this concept seems about as useful as the concept of a "universal shoe"; substandard in all cases, if at all possible.

Think about how ridiculous it would be to have one universal shoe that was meant to be worn on feet of any size and used for all purposes. The same shoe for the foot of a child aged six as for a grown adult and for all activities ranging from ice climbing to ballroom dancing. I have tried to dance in ski boots and can attest to the fact that it does not quite work—whether I can dance even given suitable footwear is still a matter of some debate and a question beyond the scope of this book. In any case, the concept of the universality of a user interface is broken for two reasons: (1) Devices come in different sizes and shapes, and (2) different device classes are used for different optimized purposes.

The fact that devices come in different sizes and form factors has a great practical impact on the utility of any given user interface on a particular device. For example, a smart phone user interface is typically significantly narrower than a Pocket PC's. Both of these are vastly narrower than a tablet computer form factor. These differences are not arbitrary, they have a lot to do with how the devices are meant to be carried (for example, pants pocket, jacket pocket, backpack, or briefcase) and under what circumstances they are intended to be used. The dimensions of the device's screen will have a significant influence on the information layout you choose. Importantly, input mechanisms differ from device to device as well. Devices such as smart phones have an extended 12-key telephone keypad and no concept of a screen pointer, whereas PDA devices tend to have touch screens as their primary input mechanism. Some devices use a touch screen for input, whereas other devices forego a touch screen in favor of a rugged read-only display that is more durable and will not break when placed in your backpack with a set of keys and crammed under an airplane seat for takeoff. Still other devices have a full keyboard and a stylus to allow work while standing or sitting at a desk. The variety of different sizes and input mechanisms is large, and it is virtually impossible to come up with a generic user interface model that works well for all of them. Runtime models that attempt to dynamically adapt a user interface based on the abilities of the target device generally result in a low quality of experience because they cannot discern what the most important aspects of the application user interface are and how best to express these richly on the target devices they are run on.

Each class of device has an optimized set of purposes and usage models it was designed for. Mobile phones are used primarily for making phone calls, viewing previously entered information, and entering small amounts of information consisting usually of sentence or two of text or simple numeric input. Pocket PC types of interfaces can offer a much larger display capability for exploring information, but because most do not come with a built-in keypad they are not suitable for entering free-form text. A Pocket PC Phone may be reasonably used for making phone calls, but if its user is using it only as a phone he has probably chosen the wrong device for his needs. Tablet computer form-factor devices may often be used while standing because they allow free-form entry of information with a stylus, but typing is difficult in this position. Laptops are well suited for typing in or exploring information but not for making quick phone calls or instantaneously retrieving information. This is because of their longer boot-up time as well as because of the way they are carried; you cannot take a full laptop out of your breast pocket, turn it on, and dial a number in eight seconds; nor can a laptop stay on indefinitely to receive phone calls, due to battery-life considerations. It is important to match your application's user interface to the overall gestalt of the device it is running on.

Although universal application portability is not possible in a useful sense, reuse and synergy are possible between device classes. Often core application logic can be shared between different implementations that are customized for target mobile devices. It may make sense to abstract common application logic into binary components that are shared by different device-specific implementations or it may be more efficient just to reuse the same source code in the different device projects; the choice is yours. In contrast to core application logic, user interface code is another matter. To have a rich device experience, you should plan on having a customized user interface for each device class you intend your application to run on. Plan on having customized implementations tuned to the physical strengths and constraints of the devices being targeted, tuned to the usage models for those devices and conforming to the navigation metaphors offered by each of the specific device models. There is no such thing as a one-size-fits-all "universal shoe," and software is more complex than footwear. Plan to specialize!

One Hand or Two?

An important characteristic for your mobile application is determining whether it is intended to be operated using one hand or two hands. Usually this choice is coupled with the choice of mobile device hardware for your application.

For example, if the application is intended to be run on a smart phone, your application will have to keep one-handed operation in mind as a specific design and testing goal. The flip side of this decision process is if your application usage scenarios require one-handed operation you should choose a device that is centered on a one-handed usage paradigm. Single-handed operation means input of information and application navigation using the same hand that holds the device.

Minimizing the number of times users will need to switch buttons as they navigate through the application is important for successful one-handed operation. For example, if your application presents the user with a five-step process, it should be possible to navigate this user interface by pressing a single physical button five times if the user desires the default values. Having to switch buttons requires the user to switch his or her visual attention from the screen to the physical buttons on the phone. It is remarkably distracting, breaks the user's stream of thought, and increases input error. Picking the right default values so all the user has to do is affirm them is also important to increasing usability. Reducing the number of button clicks required to accomplish a common task to an absolute minimum is also important; it reduces the possibility of error and reduces the amount of time users spend accomplishing the short tasks they typically perform with mobile devices. When the overall session time with a mobile application is around 20 seconds, shaving off a few seconds by having a lean and efficient navigation model makes a big difference.

Good single-handed usage design requires paying close attention to the navigation metaphors present on the target mobile phone. For example, the tab-dialog metaphor is usually not used for single-handed application navigation because there is not enough space to display all of the tabs on most single-handed devices. There is also no good way to navigate different tabs on a single-handed, non–touch screen display; to use tab controls a device is typically held with one hand and its screen is tapped with a stylus in the other hand. Instead of using tab controls for navigation, smart phone user interfaces that are intended for single-handed navigation between multiple screens often display choices as a series of lists and have a button that navigates the application back to the previous screen. Forward navigation works by pressing number keys representing numbered list choices, and backward navigation works by pressing the back key. Users will become confused and frustrated if the device-specific navigation metaphors do not work as expected in your application.

Another significant factor in application navigation is how users view the device as a whole. When using a smart phone, users tend to view the whole device as "one application" more than they do on Pocket PCs or Tablet PCs. On smart phones, there is much less of a concept of starting applications or switching to applications; instead the user perceives only navigating to different screens on the device. This blurring of application boundaries makes adhering to common navigation models even more important. As a general rule, the smaller the device, the more the user will think of it as a single application and expect consistent navigation through the entire device.

In contrast to the smart phone, a Pocket PC is designed for two-handed operation. One hand holds the device, and the other is used to navigate and make decisions. If your application is intended to run on a Pocket PC type of device with a touch screen and stylus for input, you will want to design for optimal usage of the form factor's input and output mechanisms. As noted previously, the choice of device may be dictated by the user experience you need to enable with your application.

When working with touch-screen based devices, there is a need for careful consideration of the layout of user interface elements. It is important to ensure that users working with stylus in hand do not obscure important parts of the screen as their hand hovers over the device to make selections; this problem does not exist in smart phones because one-handed operation ensures that the screen is always in view. In contrast to smart phone user interfaces, the tab control metaphor is often a very good user interface model for Pocket PC applications because the screen has ample space to display tabs for navigation and the touch screen allows for quick navigation between the tabs.

You should decide whether your application is one handed or two handed. Sometimes the choice of hardware is predetermined; other times the choice is part of the software design. Regardless, after a target device is chosen, your choice of single- or two-handed operation is also chosen. It is important to make this decision explicit and to enforce it in your user interface design and testing process.

Smaller Screen Real Estate and the Increased Importance of Navigation

As noted earlier in this book, mobile device applications are used frequently but in short spurts; contrast this with desktop application session times, which tend to be much longer. Because the session length for mobile applications tends to be short, users need to be able to navigate more quickly to the information they want to access. Generally speaking, the smaller the device, the shorter the session times and the higher the requirement for quick navigation.

Applications running on small screens require navigation to display information that a large screen can display at a glance. Table 13.1 contrasts a desktop display, a Pocket PC-sized display and a Smartphone display. Most desktop displays today will easily exceed 1024 × 768 pixels, offering a large amount of screen real estate to show information to users.

Table 13.1 Relative Screen Areas of Different Devices

Device Type	Typical Resolution	Number Pixels	Relative Size
Desktop/laptop	1024 × 768	786,432	100%
Pocket PC	240 × 320	76,800	9.77%
Smart phone	176 × 220	38,720	4.92%

A typical Pocket PC display has less than 10 percent of the screen area of a low- to mid-resolution desktop or laptop display. A smart phone has 5 percent of this resolution. This is not as dire as it seems for three reasons:

1. Desktop displays tend to use more buttons, bigger pictures, and more screen real estate to convey information than their mobile device brethren. There tend to be more controls on any given information screen, and groups of controls tend to be spaced farther apart from one another.
2. Devices offer a more concentrated experience and forgo many of the general-purpose features present in desktop applications in favor of focusing in on what users want in mobile scenarios.
3. In reality, a human being can only concentrate on a small part of a large screen at once. This means that the amount of information a person is usually working with at any given time is relatively small. It only appears that we see the whole screen fully at any given moment; in reality, our eyes are constantly glancing around to take in different parts

as needed. It does mean, however, that navigation between screens of information will be a more common task on mobile applications.

A useful metaphor is to think of your application as a work of writing and to consider how this would be reflected on different devices:

- A desktop application screen is capable of expressing several related paragraphs of information. Each paragraph explores a different idea and is represented on a part of the screen with its user interface controls being analogous to the sentences within a paragraph. Although users cannot take in all of the different paragraphs of information simultaneously, they can easily and often subconsciously switch their visual attention from one "paragraph" to another.
- By analogy, a Pocket PC application screen is capable of conveying a single paragraph of information at any given moment. The paragraph is broken into six to eight sentences, each being analogous to controls laid out on the screen. Navigation between different paragraphs is accomplished by tabs at the bottom of the screen. When designing a Pocket PC-sized user interface, it is important to divide your functionality into logical paragraphs, understand which paragraphs are most essential and should be presented first, and understand how the user will navigate between the paragraphs using the tab control. Ideally, the user can, at a glance, see the detailed contents of one paragraph of information and the outline of what all the other paragraphs contain. The user must make a conscious decision to switch between different "paragraphs" of information, usually by selecting a TabControl tab on the bottom of the device's touch screen.
- A smart phone application's screen is analogous to conveying several sentences of information at any given time, perhaps one to four sentences. This is enough information to express a short paragraph, but often it is necessary to break up a larger "paragraph-sized" concept into two related screens of information. The navigation metaphor is either one dimensional, moving forward or backward through the application's screens, or explicitly list based. The user interface switches between one of two modes:

    Details mode—The user can see a short "paragraph's" worth of information that allows navigation forward or backward to the adjoining paragraphs. This is a typical application screen on a smart phone.

    Outline mode—The user is presented with an outline list of paragraphs to choose from that can be navigated to. This is a list navigation screen on a smart phone.

The smart phone user interface size does not support displaying both the outline and the detail at the same time. When designing a smart-phone-sized user interface, it is important to think hard about the individual sentence-level concepts you want to convey, which sentences need to be on the screen at the same time, which sentences are most important and should be listed first, how to navigate between the different screens, and when to offer outline views.

Lists or Tabs?

Lists and TabViews represent two common user interface navigation metaphors for mobile devices each with their own strengths.

Smart phones use lists to present multiple simultaneous navigation choices. By definition the list is a one-dimensional series of choices. Lists are a good user interface metaphor for devices with relatively small and narrow screens, particularly if the devices have numeric keypads that can map physical numbered buttons to choices on the screen. A user can relatively quickly navigate lists by viewing the options on the screen and pressing buttons. Quickly users will remember the key combinations for navigating a shallow series of lists that represent common tasks. This kind of navigation works a lot like a voice menu on a telephone, but is faster because it is visual rather than auditory; users have to keep pressing keys to navigate menus until they end up where they want. It is important to keep the lists predictable and relatively shallow.

In contrast to the smart phone's one-dimensional model where the user navigates menus to get to interesting screens, Pocket PC-type devices have enough screen real estate to display both one page of interesting user interface and navigation options at the same time. It is for this reason that Pocket PC applications often use tab controls to display an application's user interface. When using tab controls, you are effectively reusing the same screen real estate over again for each tab. This can lead to a lot of controls and event handlers inside a class with a lot of confusing and interrelated code. A useful way of managing this complexity is to create a new class file for each tab on the tab control and have any event handlers for controls on the tab call into the class to do the required processing; this creates a helpful encapsulation that keeps the tabs insulated from one another. Figure 13.1 shows a tab control interface for navigating the functionality in a Pocket PC scientific calculator; each tab offers a related chunk of functionality and users can navigate between different tabs easily as their needs dictate.

A tab for input of complex formulas...

A tab for rich graphing functionality...

A tab for maintaining calculation history...

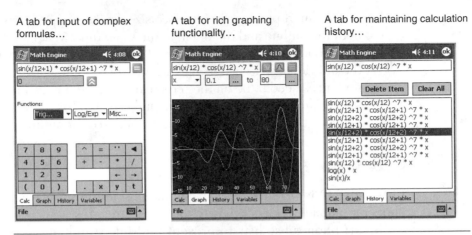

Figure 13.1 Tab controls allow a great deal of functionality to be exposed in logical chunks.

Mobile Phone User Interfaces and the Importance of Consistent Click-Through

When working with mobile-phone-sized user interfaces, it is important to ensure that navigation does not require the user to switch buttons to accomplish common tasks. It is extremely distracting to be navigating a user interface with a button on the upper-left side of the phone and abruptly need to find and press a button on the upper-right side to continue the natural flow of the application; this is particularly true when the application is being held and operated in a single hand. This simple concept of one-button navigation cannot be overemphasized because it is so often disregarded resulting in a needlessly awkward and frustrating user experience. Smart-phone-type user interfaces often follow a straight line, one-dimensional navigation with one main button meaning "Okay, go forward" and another meaning "No, go backward." Pay careful attention to the specifics of the navigation model on the mobile phone your mobile application is targeting; design and test aggressively to ensure that your application follows this model.

Touch Screens and the Importance of Big Buttons

A common mistake in building touch screen user interfaces is to make controls too small. The practical consequence of this is that users have a hard time pressing the right buttons or entering accurate data when using the mobile device application. This causes a great deal of user frustration because users feel they are not coordinated enough to use your user interface. Do not make your users feel clumsy! Several reasons contribute to small user interface control problems:

- *Design and testing using a software emulator*—When running in a desktop-based emulator, it is easy to see where the mouse pointer is and exactly where clicking will occur on the device's screen. It is significantly easier to accurately operate small user interface controls using a mouse on an emulator than it is using a stylus on a physical device.

- *Display and touch screen parallax and calibration inaccuracies*—The touch screen's surface usually sits some small but not insignificant distance above the physical display elements. Depending on the angle the device is held at by users and the angle of the stylus they are holding, parallax inaccuracies can occur between where users think they are clicking and where the click is registered. Different devices exhibit this problem to different degrees, and ruggedized devices that go to extra lengths to protect their screens will tend to have an even more pronounced parallax effect. Inaccuracies can also be introduced if the touch screen has not been calibrated accurately enough. This means that the stylus is less accurate than you may think.

- *Real-world usage*—It may be possible to click a small button accurately in your office, but what if you were on a bus, in a taxi, walking down the street, or sitting in a train? Using mobile devices in the real-world subjects the user to all kinds of distractions, vibrations, and short but sudden accelerations that make working with small controls on a touch screen more difficult.

- A *desire to "fit it all on one screen"*—Trying to fit too much information onto a single screen means creating a crowded environment and shrinking controls. The higher the density of controls, the greater the probability they will be inaccurately selected.

- *Reliance on built-in software input mechanisms*—Devices such as the Pocket PC offer a pop-up software keyboard that the user can type into. This is a useful feature, but it is a general-purpose feature and because of this it has a lot of keys it needs to display in a small space. If you have more specific needs, you should optimize the user interface's input mechanisms.

Figure 13.2 shows the same application using the software keyboard (a.k.a. SIP or software input panel) and a custom set of buttons for common inputs. Although the software keyboard offers a fairly good general purpose mechanism for typing in letters, numbers and symbols, a dedicated set of

Application showing inefficient
use of software keyboard

Application showing purpose
dedicated input user interface

Dropdown lists further sumplify
input of common data

  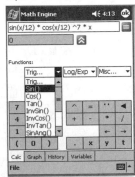

Figure 13.2 Comparing different kinds of user interface input mechanisms.

larger user interface controls designed specifically for scientific calculator usage offers a more accurate and easier-to-use interface. The generic software keyboard is valuable for limited general-purpose input, but it can and should be improved upon for more task-specific input. When designing a touch screen user interface, you should make the controls as big and purpose dedicated as practically possible.

Optimize for Common Data Entry

Whenever possible, it is a good idea to help the user fill in common input quickly and accurately. Because mobile device users rarely have a full-sized keyboard with which to input data, extra effort is warranted in helping them. A great example of this is a date picker. One way to input a date is to require the user to manually type it in letter by letter (for example, January 6, 2006, or 6/1/2006; this is time-consuming and prone to input errors as well as internationalization issues due to varying date formats. A better way is to give the user list boxes for day, month, and year and save them the need to type the data in. A better way still is a pop-up control or dialog that displays a calendar that they can quickly pick from to fill in the date field. (Note: Given the common need to enter dates, it is likely that future versions of the .NET Compact Framework will add a calendar control, but the general problem of rapid input of complex data remains.)

A mistake that is sometimes made when designing user interfaces for mobile devices is to try to save screen and program space by using TextBox controls for complex data input; this forces the user to manually type in the complex data such as dates. This kind of "efficiency" is a Pyrrhic victory at best; screen real estate and program size used for saving the user time and increasing accuracy is space and effort well spent.

Figure 13.2 demonstrates this concept by having both buttons and drop-down list boxes to help the user enter data into a scientific calculator. Instead of requiring the user to hunt-and-peck the letters sin () for a trigonometric function, he or she can simply select the function from a drop-down list box. Common variable names x, y, and t are represented as buttons on form along with other common mathematical symbols. Complex mathematical formula input with this interface is much faster than manual entry via a generic onscreen keyboard. Further optimizations to this user interface are doubtless possible.

Ensure That Redundant Manual Input Exists for Automated Input Mechanisms

Special-purpose mobile applications often use custom hardware to accelerate data input. A good example of this is a bar code scanner plugged into a mobile device to allow for the quick entry of bar code data attached to physical objects. If a mobile application has to interact with the physical world, having a bar code scanner or even speech-recognition support are both potential ways to raise the usability of the application and the productivity of its user. When possible and valuable, these kinds of real-world input mechanisms should be explored and used. There is, however, a danger in relying on them exclusively. Physical bar code labels or readers may become dirty or damaged, and speech recognition may have to deal with noisy environments and day-to-day voice irregularities that diminish their accuracy. For these reasons, it is important to always have a manual fallback that allows the application's input to be manually keyed in when more automated mechanisms fail. For the same reason that supermarket checkout counters allow the cashier to manually enter the bar code number of an item if the scanner repeatedly fails, your state-of-the-art mobile application should have a dedicated user interface that allows fast entry of manual data when automated input mechanisms fail. An application that works great 90 percent of the time and is worthless 10 percent of the time is not a good or reliable mobile application; an application that works great 90 percent of the time and has a decent manual workaround for the remaining 10 percent is.

Emulator and Physical Device Testing

Software emulators are wonderful things. They enable you to quickly design, test, and debug your application without needing to worry about setting up physical devices, switching your attention from the computer to the device, or many of the other hassles that working with an additional piece of hardware implies. Software emulators are even great for demonstrating your application; their images can easily be projected onto a large display, and it is possible to travel with many different emulator images stored on your laptop, saving you from carrying a tangle of wires and a suitcase full of electronics. (Airport security loves this.) However, what emulators are not good for is testing the performance of your application or testing the usability of your mobile device application's user interface. For this you need to test your application on physical device hardware. Despite your best efforts it is impossible to faithfully test the usability of your application using an emulator. Here are a few reasons why this is so:

- *Emulators are not physically held.* Most mobile devices are operated by holding them in your hand and either operating them with your thumb (one handed) or with your other hand. This simply cannot be done with an image on a screen.
- *The desktop/laptop mouse and keyboard allow you to cheat.* Typing letters into a text box using a keyboard is not the same as using a 12-key telephone keypad to enter data. Clicking with a mouse is not the same as pressing on a touch screen.
- *The size of your hand is not represented on a computer screen.* User interface layout cannot be properly gauged when using an emulator because the mouse cursor is small and does not obscure the screen when you hover over a button. The mouse cursor is not physically connected to anything. In contrast, a touch screen stylus is large and is physically connected to your even larger hand; it does obscure a large portion of the screen when you reach over the screen to press a button.
- *Desktop and laptop pointing is more accurate than device pointing.* Laptop screens offer a flat surface that displays the pointer on the same screen enabling you to physically see where you are about to press. A mobile device with a touch screen does not display a mouse pointer. Where the "click" occurs when you tap on the screen will be approximately where the user thinks it should be, but will be affected by such things as parallax that is dependent on the user's angle to the screen, the physical separation between the touch screen and the display elements, and the calibration of the touch screen. In practice this means that there is a physical limit to the size that a user interface element can be before users keep missing it when they tap on the screen.

■ *An emulator can easily be reset and is not used for other purposes in between testing your application.* An emulated smart phone is not the same phone you are taking phone calls on and keeping your appointment calendar on. The fact that your physical device is often not single purpose but instead has other functions that the user will rely on it for is important. You will need to make sure that your application behaves well when the device is being run 24 hours a day and 7 days a week as well as understand what the effects of other device applications are on your application. This kind of real-world usage cannot be accurately simulated.

Keeping the points listed above in mind when designing your mobile device application is important but is not a substitute for testing on actual hardware. Fundamentally, the only way to really test the user interface of your mobile application is to test it on the hardware on which it will be running.

Figure 13.3 shows an example of how user interface usability can differ on an emulator versus on a physical device. The example shown is a foreign-language vocabulary teaching game where an animated character moves around the screen based on a user's correct or incorrect answers to multiple-choice questions. When using a device emulator to design and test the application, all appears well; the choices are laid out neatly on the screen and navigation is simple. Testing on a physical device, however, reveals some significant usability issues. As a user moves his or her hand over the screen to select an item, it obscures the question as well as the game's play field. This means the question cannot be viewed while the user is selecting between various answer options. In addition, it means that a user must move his or her hand away from the screen to see the results of the choice they have made; if they do not move their hand quickly enough, they will miss the game play that occurs on the screen and thus some of the enjoyment of the application. Clearly this is not an optimal situation, but this only becomes obvious when testing on a physical device, because on an emulator screen running on a PC the screen is not blocked by the user's physical hand.

Figure 13.4 shows two possibilities for improvements to our handheld application's user interface. Both possibilities give users a better view of the play field as they make selections while holding the device in their hand. At first glance, the screen on the right seems superior because it allows the viewing of the question while selecting from the options; in real-world usage, however, this may prove not to be the most important factor. Issues such as where users rest their hand between choices and the overall physical balance of the device while held in a user's hand are important factors that

What you see on the emulator...   What you get on a physical device...

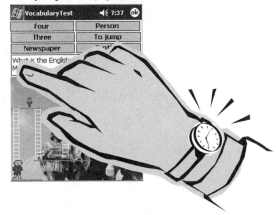

Figure 13.3 Contrasting user interface usability on an emulator vs. physical device.

A few alternate screen layouts that make more sense on a physical device...

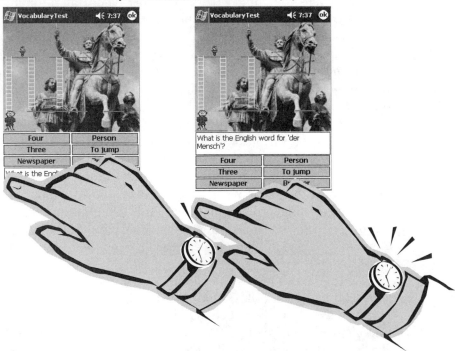

Figure 13.4 More usable alternative screen layouts based on physical device testing.

will determine the optimum design. In this case, after a fair amount of testing I selected the view on the left for just these reasons.

The use of software-based device emulation can greatly speed up development and debugging and should be used whenever convenient, but this does not obviate the need for continual usability testing on physical devices. You will be continually surprised at what you discover when testing the application on real mobile devices.

Design Your Mobile User Interface Code to Allow for Easy Testing and Iteration

User interface design is an iterative process. You should be prepared to revise your user interface several times during the application's development and testing process as you learn things about how the application is getting used. If your mobile application's user interface code is tightly coupled with its application logic, it will be very difficult to do this; user interface changes require laboriously searching through the application logic and finding all parts that affect the user interface. This makes behavioral changes very difficult. In highly interdependent user interface code, bugs introduced by user interface changes are difficult to track down and robustly eliminate because they are scattered rather than concentrated and well encapsulated.

It is highly beneficial to design your application logic to be decoupled from the user interface. The two should interact only through a small and well-defined set of interfaces. As Figure 13.5 shows, this can be accomplished by using two mechanisms.

1. *Using a state machine to manage controls*—A state machine is perfect for managing the user interface needs of a mobile device application. The mobile application's screen is a scarce and valuable resource and it needs to be managed effectively. It must be utilized effectively as the user navigates through the different states of your application. Having a state machine that shows, hides, and repositions controls as needed on the screen is a very effective way to do this. Having all of the user interface modes abstracted into a single state machine allows you the maximum flexibility in changing the on-screen display model without needing to search through and modify a lot of code distributed throughout the different functions and event handlers of your user interface.

2. *Using indirect functions to update the user interface*—There are two ways to go about modifying information displayed on the mobile device's screen: (1) directly and in-line (for example, `Label1.Text = newText`), or (2) indirectly (for example, `UpdateDownload StatusText(newText);`). The advantage of the indirect approach is that it allows your code to decouple the actual control you use from the update you want to make. The indirect function `Update-DownloadStatusText(newText);` might update `Label1` today, but tomorrow you might decide that what we really want to do is paint this text onto a bitmap that is being displayed or show it as scrolling text on a ticker on the screen. Figure 13.5 shows an arrow coming down from the user interface to the UI Update Functions block as well as up from the application's logic. The arrow coming down from the user interface represents display update code that is run as a result of handling events generated by the user interface. For example, a common response to clicking a button may be to update the text in a label or list box. Instead of performing this update inside the button's event handler, it is far more flexible to call a generic `UpdateXXXXXXX();)` function to do the work. Having an intermediary function removes the tight coupling between the two controls and allows the control implementations to be switched as needed. In your mobile application's user interface design, you want to avoid tight coupling both in between the application logic and the user interface controls as well as in between the individual controls that are part of the user interface. A single level of indirection avoids tight coupling.

Not only does using state machine and indirect functions to update user interface controls enable you to easily iterate on your mobile application's presentation layer design, it also allows for much better portability of your application between device classes. A tight coupling between user interface code and application logic makes it very laborious to port an application to another form factor, which requires different user interface controls and layout. Conversely, a well-defined set of functions that manages the interactions between your application logic and the presentation layer makes it much easier to adapt your application from one device class to another. This is an important consideration if you want the flexibility of supporting new device types in the future. As discussed earlier in this chapter the concept of "write once, run anywhere" does not work particularly well for allowing a single binary application to provide a rich experience on different classes of devices, but this does not mean that you cannot design your mobile application to make portability easy. You can and you should.

User Interface

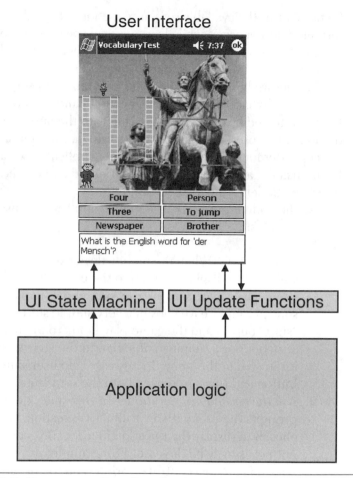

Figure 13.5 Clean separation of application logic and user interface.

A State Model for User Interface Layout and Management

A fairly simple example is useful in demonstrating the utility of a state-machine-driven user interface. This example will show the benefits of the state machine approach for evolving user interface design. Continuing with the scenario described in Figures 13.3, 13.4, and 13.5, the code will implement the main parts of the user interface for a foreign-language vocabulary teaching game for the Pocket PC. As the application's user answers multiple-choice vocabulary questions, action will occur on a play field section of the screen reflecting correct and incorrect choices. The play field will use about

60 percent of the available screen real estate; its goal is to keep the user entertained and engaged while learning new vocabulary words. To keep things simple, for now the application's user interface code will represent the play field as a yellow rectangle bitmap displayed in a picture box. You may want to fill this picture box instead with a loaded bitmap image to supply a more realistic view of what the play field will contain and see how the play field's visibility is affected by the user interacting with the application. This application demonstrates user interface concepts using a multiple-choice game, but the concepts demonstrated here are equally applicable for applications ranging from business applications to action-oriented games; the state machine user interface model is remarkably versatile.

As shown in Figure 13.6, the mobile application's user interface has four different states:

1. *Start screen*—When the mobile device application is first started, we will want to display a screen to the users that welcomes them to the game, gives necessary instructions, and allows them an easy way to start playing. I have chosen a very simple start screen showing only a "start" button and the game play field. You may want to add text instructions or a running animation to the start screen to get the user interested in the game. In any case, the user simply clicks the "start" button and they are moved onto the next state.

2. *Ask the vocabulary question*—In this state, the mobile application prompts the user with a vocabulary question. In our code we have chosen to display the question in a TextBox control, but this need not necessarily be the case. For example, the question could be displayed in a Label control or printed on top of the play field bitmap if it makes sense to do so. If our device supports speech synthesis, we may even want to audibly ask the question. We have chosen to use a read-only text box because it meets our needs and enables us to easily display a potentially larger amount of information using text box scrollbars if necessary. In addition to displaying the question, the application gives the user two options for answering it. Users can choose a Challenge Me! option if they believe they know the answer or a Can't Think of It option if they want more hints; the two choices can also have different game-scoring possibilities. To keep things simple in the sample code, our implementation treats both of these choices the same and moves them to the next state regardless of what they choose; you may choose to add code to differentiate the choices or just remove one of the buttons if you choose not to. Our mobile application implementation has chosen to present these

options using Button controls, but as above this need not necessarily be the case; radio buttons or a list box could just as easily be used to display the options if either metaphor were more appropriate for the device we are targeting. The right user interface metaphor depends on the nature of the application as well as the kind of device it is running on.

3. *Present the user with the multiple-choice answers*—In this application state, our mobile device game presents the user with multiple-choice options to answer the question. For the Pocket PC user interface, we have again chosen to use Button controls; for a smart phone interface, a numbered list box would probably be most appropriate. In this state, we have also chosen to dynamically reduce the size of the Text-Box control to fit all of the button choices onto the screen. Users are allowed to guess answers until they get the right one. If the wrong answer is selected, we have chosen to gray-out (set the Enabled property to false) the wrong choice. Our application logic may also want to display text that explains what the incorrect word really means. Because there is little room in our reduced-sized text box for this kind of information, we may want to draw the text onto the top of the play field bitmap; this implementation is again left to the reader.

4. *Present users with a final assessment of their performance on the question and wait for them to request the next question*—This application state allows the game the opportunity to review users' choices with them and reinforce their learning. Because the vocabulary question is complete, we no longer need to display the question or have space dedicated to allowing the user to select multiple-choice answers. Because of this, the application has hidden all the buttons used to display multiple-choice answers and has used the extra space to enlarge the text box area. Having a large text box area allows us ample room to display text that recaps the learning of the question. For instance, we could display all of the multiple-choice words along with their translations; we could also display an example sentence showing the use of the correct word.

The code in Listing 13.1 demonstrates several useful concepts for building flexible mobile device user interfaces. When designing this user interface, I started with the idea of positioning the user interface elements above the game play field. Knowing that getting the user interface right is a matter of real-world testing and iteration, it is desirable to write the code in a centralized and abstract way so that it can easily be modified without requiring complex and scattered changes in the user interface or application logic. It is for

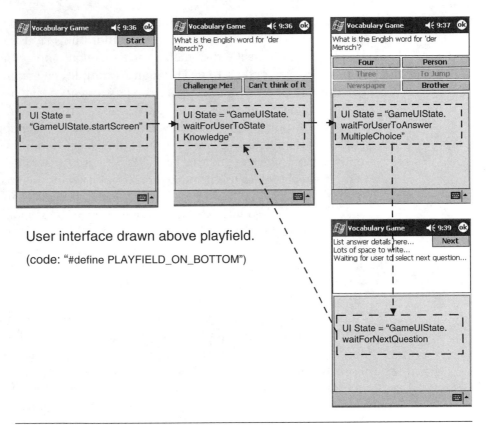

User interface drawn above playfield.

(code: "#define PLAYFIELD_ON_BOTTOM")

Figure 13.6 User interface displayed on top of form.

this reason that I have chosen to place the bulk of the dynamic layout code into a state machine function called StateChangeForGameUI(). Any changes in control resizing and positioning will be driven by this code. If we need to make tweaks or even radical changes to the layout, we know all of the work happens here; this means less work tracking down complex and distributed layout logic and more robust application operation. Having the user interface layout responsibility concentrated in one function (the state machine) makes it easy to experiment with different user interface layout possibilities without destabilizing the rest of the user interface code or application logic.

Figure 13.6 and Figure 13.7 display two possible configurations for our mobile vocabulary teaching game. It is important to note that in going from one layout model to the other not only have the user interface controls been moved around on the screen but elements have also been reordered in relation to one another. In Figure 13.6, the text box is positioned and dynamically resized above the other elements on the screen. In Figure 13.7, the text box is positioned and dynamically resized below any other buttons that are on the screen. Because in both cases the text box anchors itself differently to the controls surrounding it, this requires different application logic to be run. Other control positioning and reordering would also be easily possible; because the positioning code has been cleanly abstracted and centralized into our state machine, we can run whatever user interface logic we need to in order to get the onscreen positioning as we like it. The rest of the application and user interface logic are not affected by our experimentation.

Equally important is that we have built abstracted functions to deal with updating our user interface contents. All the user interface content-updating code is either in our state machine or in dedicated functions used for the task; no user interface content is updated directly in the event handling code for our controls. This combination of abstraction and centralization makes it easy to reconfigure our user interface to use different controls as needed. This is important not just for getting the right look and feel on any given device class, but is also useful for porting the application to different device classes. For instance, our mobile application would probably use a different set of controls for user input and output if ported to a smart phone. Because the smart phone does not have a touch screen, buttons are not the best choice for answering multiple-choice questions; a list box would be better. The code in Listing 13.1 could easily be adapted to use a list box instead of buttons for the multiple-choice inputs. Other user interface changes would also be required but because our application logic and our user interface code are well encapsulated and the interaction between application logic and user interface code is centralized in a known set of functions the porting work would not be difficult. Good encapsulation, abstraction, and centralization would allow us to provide a great user experience on another class of device much more easily than if the code were decentralized and not state machine based.

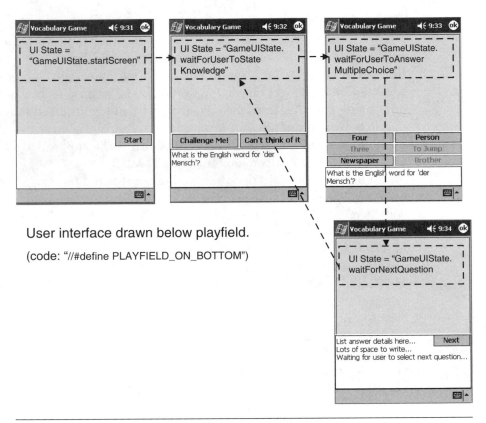

User interface drawn below playfield.

(code: "//#define PLAYFIELD_ON_BOTTOM")

Figure 13.7 User interface displayed on bottom of form.

Sample Code Showing Two Different Layout Models for the Same Application

The code in Listing 13.1 belongs inside a form in a Pocket PC project. Do the following to build and run the application:

1. Start Visual Studio .NET (2003 or later) and create a C# "Smart Device Application"

2. Choose Pocket PC as the target platform. (A project will be created for you and Pocket PC Form designer will appear.)

3. Add the following controls to the form. Note: Don't worry about the size or position of these controls; put them wherever it is easiest to work with them on the screen. The controls will be dynamically resized and positioned at runtime by the user interface code below.

- A TextBox, rename it **textBoxAskQuestion**, set its MultiLine property true, and set its ReadOnly property true.
- A PictureBox, rename it **pictureBoxGameBoard**.
- A Button, rename it **buttonShowAnswers_AdvancedVersion**.
- A Button, rename it **buttonShowAnswers_SimpleVersion**.
- A Button, rename it **buttonAskQuestion**.
- A Button, rename it **buttonAnswer0**.
- A Button, rename it **buttonAnswer1**.
- A Button, rename it **buttonAnswer2**.
- A Button, rename it **buttonAnswer3**.
- A Button, rename it **buttonAnswer4**.
- A Button, rename it **buttonAnswer5**.

4. Double-click a blank region of the Form designer, and in the event handler function generated and hooked up for you, enter the `Form_Load` code listed below.

5. For each of the Button controls above, double-click the Button in the Form designer. In the event handler function generated and hooked up for you, enter the `button<ButtonName>_Click` code listed below.

6. Enter the rest of the code listed below.

7. Set the MinimizeBox property of the form to false. At runtime this will give the form an OK box at the top right that makes it easy to close the form and exit the application. This is very useful for repeated testing.

8. At the top of the form's code file, as the first line in the file, enter the text **#define PLAYFIELD_ON_BOTTOM**.

9. Run the application both with the `#define` `PLAYFIELD_ON_BOTTOM` conditional compile directive in place and also with it commented out (that is, `//#define` `PLAYFIELD_ON_BOTTOM`) and observe the different layout models. Try them both out on a physical device and decide which model works best in terms of user look and feel and the visibility of the play field.

10. Try your own modifications to the layout. Possibly it makes sense to have some user interface elements above the play field and some below. Maybe some of the elements should be on top of the play field or to the right or left of it. Making modifications to the state machine code should enable you to easily test and refine these concepts.

Listing 13.1 Use of State Machine to Experiment with Two Different UI layouts

```
//------------------------------------------------------------
//The state machine that drives showing hand hiding buttons
//------------------------------------------------------------
private enum GameUIState
{
  startScreen = 1,
  waitForNextQuestion = 2,
  waitForUserToStateKnowledge = 4,
  waitForUserToAnswerMultipleChoice = 8
}
//Current state of game
private GameUIState m_GameUIState;


//============================================================
//State machine used for driving the user interface
//============================================================
private void StateChangeForGameUI(GameUIState newGameUIState)
{
  m_GameUIState = newGameUIState;
  switch(newGameUIState)
  {
    case GameUIState.startScreen:
      buttonAskQuestion.Visible = true;
      buttonAskQuestion.Text = "Start";

      //Hide the text box
      textBoxAskQuestion.Visible = false;

      SetAnswerButtonVisibility(false);
      SetDifficultyButtonVisibility(false);

      break;

    case GameUIState.waitForNextQuestion:
      setQuestionText("List answer details here... \r\n" +
        "Lots of space to write...\r\n"+
        "Waiting for user to select next question...");
      textBoxAskQuestion.Visible = true;

      buttonAskQuestion.Text = "Next";
      buttonAskQuestion.Visible = true;
      //Make sure the button is displayed on top
```

```
        buttonAskQuestion.BringToFront();

        SetAnswerButtonVisibility(false);
        SetDifficultyButtonVisibility(false);

#if PLAYFIELD_ON_BOTTOM //PLAYFIELD is below user controls
    textBoxAskQuestion.Height = pictureBoxGameBoard.Top - 2;
#else //PLAYFIELD is above user controls

        textBoxAskQuestion.Top = pictureBoxGameBoard.Top +
          pictureBoxGameBoard.Height + 2;
        textBoxAskQuestion.Height = this.Height -
          textBoxAskQuestion.Top;
#endif
        break;

        case GameUIState.waitForUserToStateKnowledge:

        SetTextForVocabularyQuestion();
        textBoxAskQuestion.Visible = true;
        buttonAskQuestion.Visible = false;
        SetAnswerButtonVisibility(false);
        SetDifficultyButtonVisibility(true);

#if PLAYFIELD_ON_BOTTOM //PLAYFIELD is below user controls
    textBoxAskQuestion.Height =
                buttonShowAnswers_AdvancedVersion.Top - 2;
#else //PLAYFIELD is above user controls

        textBoxAskQuestion.Top =
          buttonShowAnswers_AdvancedVersion.Top +
          buttonShowAnswers_AdvancedVersion.Height + 2;

        textBoxAskQuestion.Height = this.Height -
          textBoxAskQuestion.Top;
#endif

        break;
    case GameUIState.waitForUserToAnswerMultipleChoice:
        buttonAskQuestion.Visible = false;
        SetDifficultyButtonVisibility(false);
        //Enable the buttons so they can be clicked by the user
        SetAnswerButtonEnabled(true);
        SetAnswerButtonVisibility(true);
```

```
#if PLAYFIELD_ON_BOTTOM //PLAYFIELD is below user controls
      textBoxAskQuestion.Height = buttonAnswer0.Top - 2;
#else //PLAYFIELD is above user controls
      //Position the text box to make good use of the screen
      textBoxAskQuestion.Top = buttonAnswer5.Top +
        buttonAnswer5.Height + 2;
      textBoxAskQuestion.Height = this.Height -
        textBoxAskQuestion.Top;
#endif
    break;
  }
}


//===============================================================
//Sets up the static layout of our user interface.
//These are all the items whose positions will remain fixed
//The user interface state machine will make changes to other
//properties
//===============================================================
private void SetStartControlPositionAndState()
{
  pictureBoxGameBoard.Width = 240;
  pictureBoxGameBoard.Height = 176;

  //Set the size of the multiple-choice answer buttons
  const int answerButtons_dx = 117;
  const int answerButtons_dy = 18;

  buttonAnswer0.Width = answerButtons_dx;
  buttonAnswer0.Height = answerButtons_dy;
  buttonAnswer1.Size = buttonAnswer0.Size;
  buttonAnswer2.Size = buttonAnswer0.Size;
  buttonAnswer3.Size = buttonAnswer0.Size;
  buttonAnswer4.Size = buttonAnswer0.Size;
  buttonAnswer5.Size = buttonAnswer0.Size;

  buttonShowAnswers_AdvancedVersion.Width = answerButtons_dx;
  buttonShowAnswers_AdvancedVersion.Height = 24;
  buttonShowAnswers_SimpleVersion.Size =
    buttonShowAnswers_AdvancedVersion.Size;

  //Pixels between adjacent buttons
  const int dx_betweenButtons = 3;
  const int dy_betweenButtons = 2;

  const int answerbuttons_beginX = 3;
```

```
//Make a background image for our bitmap, so we can see it
//in our testing
System.Drawing.Bitmap gameBoard;
gameBoard = new System.Drawing.Bitmap(
     pictureBoxGameBoard.Width, pictureBoxGameBoard.Height);

System.Drawing.Graphics gameboard_gfx;
gameboard_gfx = System.Drawing.Graphics.FromImage(gameBoard);
gameboard_gfx.Clear(System.Drawing.Color.Yellow);
System.Drawing.Pen myPen = new System.Drawing.Pen(
     System.Drawing.Color.Blue);
gameboard_gfx.DrawRectangle(myPen, 2,2, gameBoard.Width-4,
                           gameBoard.Height-6);
myPen.Dispose();
gameboard_gfx.Dispose();
pictureBoxGameBoard.Image = gameBoard;

//Position the text box that contains the questions we ask
//as well as detailed answers to users
textBoxAskQuestion.Left = 0;
textBoxAskQuestion.Width = 240;

buttonAskQuestion.Width = 64;
buttonAskQuestion.Height = 20;

#if PLAYFIELD_ON_BOTTOM //PLAYFIELD is below user controls
  const int answerbuttons_beginY = 42;
  const int showanswers_beginY = 77;
  //-------------------------------------------
  //Set up the "Easy" or "Hard" option buttons for the game
  //-------------------------------------------
  buttonShowAnswers_AdvancedVersion.Top = showanswers_beginY;
  buttonShowAnswers_SimpleVersion.Top = showanswers_beginY;

  //-------------------------------------------
  //Set up the multiple-choice answers
  //-------------------------------------------
  //Set the control that the others will line up based on
  buttonAnswer0.Top = answerbuttons_beginY;

  //Place Picture Box below the controls
  pictureBoxGameBoard.Top =
    (answerButtons_dy + dy_betweenButtons) * 3 +
    answerbuttons_beginY;
```

```
   buttonAskQuestion.Top = 0;
   buttonAskQuestion.Left = 174;

   textBoxAskQuestion.Top = 0;
#else //PLAYFIELD is above user controls
   const int answerbuttons_beginY = 174;

   //------------------------------------------------------
   //Set up the "Easy" or "Hard" option buttons for the game
   //------------------------------------------------------
   buttonShowAnswers_AdvancedVersion.Top = answerbuttons_beginY;
   buttonShowAnswers_SimpleVersion.Top = answerbuttons_beginY;

   //------------------------------------------------
   //Set up the multiple-choice answers
   //------------------------------------------------
   //Set the control that the others will line up based on
   buttonAnswer0.Top = answerbuttons_beginY;

   pictureBoxGameBoard.Top = 0;

   buttonAskQuestion.Top = answerbuttons_beginY;
   buttonAskQuestion.Left = 174;
#endif

   buttonShowAnswers_AdvancedVersion.Left = answerbuttons_beginX;
   buttonShowAnswers_SimpleVersion.Left =
       buttonShowAnswers_AdvancedVersion.Left +
       answerButtons_dx + dx_betweenButtons;

   pictureBoxGameBoard.Left = 0;
   pictureBoxGameBoard.Width = 240;
   pictureBoxGameBoard.Height = 172;


   buttonAnswer0.Left = answerbuttons_beginX;

   buttonAnswer1.Left = buttonAnswer0.Left + answerButtons_dx +
                        dx_betweenButtons;
   buttonAnswer1.Top = buttonAnswer0.Top;

   //next row
   buttonAnswer2.Left = buttonAnswer0.Left;
   buttonAnswer2.Top = buttonAnswer0.Top + answerButtons_dy +
                        dy_betweenButtons;
```

```
buttonAnswer3.Left = buttonAnswer2.Left + answerButtons_dx +
                     dx_betweenButtons;
buttonAnswer3.Top = buttonAnswer2.Top;

//next row
buttonAnswer4.Left = buttonAnswer2.Left;
buttonAnswer4.Top = buttonAnswer2.Top + answerButtons_dy +
                    dy_betweenButtons;

buttonAnswer5.Left = buttonAnswer4.Left + answerButtons_dx +
                     dx_betweenButtons;
buttonAnswer5.Top = buttonAnswer4.Top;
}


//------------------------------------------------------------
//A helper function that allows us to set the visibility
//state of the buttons that show vocabulary answers
//------------------------------------------------------------
private void SetAnswerButtonVisibility(bool visibleState)
{
  buttonAnswer0.Visible = visibleState;
  buttonAnswer1.Visible = visibleState;
  buttonAnswer2.Visible = visibleState;
  buttonAnswer3.Visible = visibleState;
  buttonAnswer4.Visible = visibleState;
  buttonAnswer5.Visible = visibleState;
}


//------------------------------------------------------------
//A helper function called to set the visibility state of some
//controls
//------------------------------------------------------------
private void SetDifficultyButtonVisibility(bool visibleState)
{
  buttonShowAnswers_AdvancedVersion.Visible = visibleState;
  buttonShowAnswers_SimpleVersion.Visible = visibleState;
}


//------------------------------------------------------------
//A helper function that allows us to set the visibility
//of the buttons that show vocabulary answers
//------------------------------------------------------------
private void SetAnswerButtonEnabled(bool enabledState)
{
```

```
  buttonAnswer0.Enabled = enabledState;
  buttonAnswer1.Enabled = enabledState;
  buttonAnswer2.Enabled = enabledState;
  buttonAnswer3.Enabled = enabledState;
  buttonAnswer4.Enabled = enabledState;
  buttonAnswer5.Enabled = enabledState;
}


//------------------------------------------------------------
//Sets the text in the text box and buttons necessary
//to ask a question.
//
//In a real implementation, this function would look up
//the vocabulary questions dynamically
//------------------------------------------------------------
private void SetTextForVocabularyQuestion()
{
  setQuestionText(
    "What is the English word for 'der Mensch'?");

  buttonAnswer0.Text = "Four";
  buttonAnswer1.Text = "Person";
  buttonAnswer2.Text = "Three";
  buttonAnswer3.Text = "To Jump";
  buttonAnswer4.Text = "Newspaper";
  buttonAnswer5.Text = "Brother";
}
//Called to evaluate a user selected a multiple-choice answer
private void evaluateMultipleChoiceAnswer(Button buttonClicked,
  int selection)
{
  //Note: In the nonprototype implementation, the correct
  //answer would be a dynamic value, not always "button #1"

  //If the user did not select the correct answer, disable
  //the button they pressed
  if(selection != 1)
  {
    //The answer selected was not the correct one
    buttonClicked.Enabled = false;
  }
  else
  {
    //They got the right answer, move on with the game
```

```
        StateChangeForGameUI(GameUIState.waitForNextQuestion);
    }
}


//Abstracts setting the question text
void setQuestionText(string textIn)
{ textBoxAskQuestion.Text  = textIn; }


//-------------------------------------------------------------
//EVENT HANDLER: User wants to see next question
//-------------------------------------------------------------
private void buttonAskQuestion_Click(object sender,
                                        System.EventArgs e)
{

    SetTextForVocabularyQuestion();
    StateChangeForGameUI(GameUIState.waitForUserToStateKnowledge);
}


//-------------------------------------------------------------
//EVENT HANDLER:
//User wants to answer the question displayed and what's
//the hardest list of options possible to challenge him/her
//-------------------------------------------------------------
private void buttonShowAnswers_AdvancedVersion_Click(
                        object sender, System.EventArgs e)
{
  //Set the state of the game to show the multiple-choice
  //options
  StateChangeForGameUI(
            GameUIState.waitForUserToAnswerMultipleChoice);
}


//-------------------------------------------------------------
//EVENT HANDLER:
//User wants to answer the question displayed and what's
//the simplest list of options possible to challenge him/her
//-------------------------------------------------------------
private void buttonShowAnswers_SimpleVersion_Click(
                        object sender, System.EventArgs e)
{
  //Set the state of the game to show the multiple-choice
  //options
  StateChangeForGameUI(
            GameUIState.waitForUserToAnswerMultipleChoice);
```

```
}

//EVENT HANDLER: A multiple-choice answer button was clicked
private void buttonAnswer0_Click(
                        object sender, System.EventArgs e)
{
   evaluateMultipleChoiceAnswer(buttonAnswer0, 0);
}

//EVENT HANDLER: A multiple-choice answer button was clicked
private void buttonAnswer1_Click(
                        object sender, System.EventArgs e)
{
   evaluateMultipleChoiceAnswer(buttonAnswer1, 1);
}

//EVENT HANDLER: A multiple-choice answer button was clicked
private void buttonAnswer2_Click(
                        object sender, System.EventArgs e)
{
   evaluateMultipleChoiceAnswer(buttonAnswer2, 2);
}

//EVENT HANDLER: A multiple-choice answer button was clicked
private void buttonAnswer3_Click(
                        object sender, System.EventArgs e)
{
   evaluateMultipleChoiceAnswer(buttonAnswer3, 3);
}

//EVENT HANDLER: A multiple-choice answer button was clicked
private void buttonAnswer4_Click(
                        object sender, System.EventArgs e)
{
   evaluateMultipleChoiceAnswer(buttonAnswer4, 4);
}

//EVENT HANDLER: A multiple-choice answer button was clicked
private void buttonAnswer5_Click(
                        object sender, System.EventArgs e)
{
   evaluateMultipleChoiceAnswer(buttonAnswer5, 5);
}
```

```
//-----------------------------------------------------------
//EVENT HANDLER: Called when form is loaded
//-----------------------------------------------------------
private void Form1_Load(object sender, System.EventArgs e)
{
    //Set the static properties of our visual interface
    SetStartControlPositionAndState();
    //Set the dynamic properties based on the state we're entering
    StateChangeForGameUI(GameUIState.startScreen);
}
```

Layout of Controls

For mobile device applications, the layout of the user interface is important both for ease of use by the end user as well as to allow your application to present all the information that it needs to. It is almost never a good idea to take a desktop user interface and bring it down to a mobile device; I have never seen this work in practice. The screen resolution and usage model of a desktop application is radically different from that of a mobile device, and trying to cram a desktop user interface and application usage model into a device form factor is a recipe for failure. At best you will end up with a mediocre and awkward application. A far better approach is to consider, prioritize, and explicitly list the desktop scenarios that will need to be able to be performed on a mobile device along with the unique mobility scenarios you want to enable and then build an application user interface that specifically meets these needs. The same holds true for taking a mobile device application that runs on one form factor and bringing it to another; rarely does it make sense to bring over the user interface verbatim. Even if most of the application logic can be brought over unchanged, it is worth explicitly listing the key scenarios and the device-specific usage models and then designing the user interface from the ground up to meet these needs.

Real Estate Is Expensive

The smaller the device screen, the more attention must be paid to its efficient usage. Good screen real estate management is not about figuring out how to cram as many controls onto a mobile device screen as possible at any given time; almost the opposite in fact.

   Mobile device real estate is limited enough that you could not fit most of the typical controls in a desktop application onto a mobile device screen even if you reduced the fonts to a minimum, shrunk down the controls as small as they could go, and lined them up as tightly as possible as if your user interface layout were a game of Tetris. Clearly, a different approach is required. The best mobile device interfaces are not busy with detail on the screen, they are sparse and elegant; paradoxically, they look as if they have room to spare. Instead of thinking about how to fit all the controls onto the mobile device's screen at once, it is worthwhile to approach the problem from the other direction and ask, "What is the absolute minimum information and controls that need to be on the screen to enable the user to take the next step?" Consider the following questions when designing the layout of your mobile device application's user interface:

- *What is the minimum set of information that needs to be displayed and the minimum set of controls required for navigation?* Can this set be reduced further by splitting the present screen into two or more smaller user interface states that can be displayed separately?
- *When moving from one user interface state to another should controls be resized?* Often times it can be desirable to shrink or grow the size of a user interface element to show or hide more detailed information as screen real estate allows.
- *Would a custom control be a more efficient way to display the information now being shown by several controls?* This decision must be weighed carefully. Creating a purpose-specific custom control can be a good way to efficiently use user interface real estate but must be weighed against two balancing factors: (1) The development cost of creating a custom control is much higher than that of using preexisting, pretested, controls, and (2) the usability issues of creating a new user interface metaphor. The end user already knows how to use the existing controls and will have to learn any new visual concepts you introduce. Still, in some cases the work is justified and can yield impressive results.

Location, Location, Location

Not all screen areas are equal. Placing controls in the top, bottom, left, right, or middle of your mobile device screen will result in different usability characteristics. These usability characteristics often vary from device class to device class. For example, Pocket PC controls that take text input should be placed at the top of the screen because there is a pop-up software keyboard called a SIP (software input panel) that is shown at the bottom of the screen to enable text entry. Two things should govern the location of the controls you place onto your user interface:

1. *The style and usage guidelines for the mobile device you are targeting*—Most programmable mobile devices have style guidelines for layout of user interface. These are important both to ensure that your application behaves well with the input methods present on the device (for example, buttons, touch screen, pop-up keyboard) as well as to ensure that users get a consistent look and feel between applications they are using. If you have not read the style guidelines for the device you are targeting, it is highly worth giving them a read through. This information is far better than any generic layout advice that could be given. Note: The fact that different device classes have different style guidelines is another reason why "write once, run anywhere" models tend to fail. It is just too difficult a problem to build a single user interface framework that correctly and automatically adapts to different devices style guidelines.

2. *Usability testing on real devices*—The final arbiter of your user interface's usability is a real user using it on a real device (that is, not an emulator). Because mobile devices are used in handheld situations such as outdoors, on trains, in airplanes, or in crowded elevators, there is simply no substitute for testing out the application on the real physical hardware it is going to be running on and in realistic environments.

Pick the Right Controls for the Right Devices

Along with following the correct style and layout guidelines for a given mobile device, it is important to choose the correct set of user controls for the devices you are targeting. A mobile runtime framework may support a range of user interface controls. Only some of these are appropriate for use on any given mobile device. For example, because smart phones do not have touch screens or mouse pointers for random-access navigation controls such as tab views, generic buttons and radio buttons are not particularly useful user interface metaphors for these devices. Instead list boxes and menus are far more appropriate controls for use on smart phones. In general, the smaller the device, the more specific are the requirements for controls that can be used.

When to use Different Forms and When to Swap Controls Around

There are two ways to facilitate navigation in your user interface: (1) Bring up new forms in response to user actions, and (2) show and hide controls on a single form. Both of these are mechanisms for showing a new screen full of information to the user.

There is nothing wrong with storing and managing multiple screens' worth of information in a single form and showing and hiding controls as needed. You should keep multiple screens' worth of user interface on one form if they represent related concepts and you may want to tune the relationships between them. Moving information from one "screen" to another is easier to do if they are managed in the same class.

You should separate functionality into different forms if the functionality is truly separate and there is little chance that you will want to swap the user interface elements between the two forms as you tune your user interface. This eliminates unnecessary clutter.

If your target mobile device has a large enough screen, tab controls are a middle case that allows you an in-between compromise. Usually each tab in a tab control should be thought of conceptually as a different form. The great advantage of using a tab control is that you do not have to do the showing and hiding of each screen of information manually; it is handled by the framework. Consider placing the event handling code for each tab's contents into separate class. This will give you a nice encapsulation that keeps your code from getting too messy.

Advanced User Interfaces with the .NET Compact Framework

The .NET Compact Framework offers some advanced features that will be of interest to developers. Because these concepts are specific to the .NET Compact Framework, they are specifically drawn out in this section. Other mobile device runtime frameworks may have similar concepts, so this may be worth reading even if you are using one of these.

Dynamic Creation of Controls

It can be useful to be able to dynamically create controls at runtime. As shown in Figure 13.8 and Listing 13.2, this is a simple thing to do with the .NET Compact Framework. Dynamic controls are useful to use for several reasons:

- *When form load time is lagging*—When there are a lot of controls on a form or the controls are sufficiently heavyweight, it can take a significant amount of processing to initialize them. All controls you lay out on your design surface are initialized when the form is created and loaded. This initialization takes place in the function called

`InitializeComponent();` the contents of this function are managed by the form's designer; you can examine the contents of this function if you want. If you want to speed up the form's load time, you may want to defer the creation of a control until it is needed. Note: You may also choose to take the autogenerated code in the `InitializeComponent()` function and attempt to hand-optimize it. If you do this, you should place your own code into a separately named function so that it does not get accidentally overwritten by the development tool. You should also be aware that the Form designer may no longer be available to help you design your form. As with any optimization, be sure to measure rigorously to make sure you are getting the optimizations you expect!

- *When the number of controls you will need is unknown at design time*—For example, if your mobile application needs an array of RadioButton controls whose number is based on the number of items returned from a database query, you will need to create this array at runtime when the number of needed controls is determined.

- *When no design-time implementation exists for the control you want to use*—For the .NET Compact Framework, it can be a significant challenge to create design-time instances of custom controls; often this can take more development time than the runtime versions of the controls. If you are creating a custom control for your own development use, it may not be worth the trouble of creating a design-time version of it just so it can appear in the Form designer. Instead you can save the unneeded development effort and just create the control at runtime.

There are three things you need to do after you create an instance of a dynamic control to make it work:

1. *Initialize the control.* You should set the size and position of the control and any other properties that need to be set before you display the control.

2. *Hook up any events you want to handle.* Most controls are only useful when code is hooked up to handle events they can generate. For any events you want to hook up, there are several steps to take:
   a. You will need a function that is the event sink (that is, gets called when the event is triggered).
   b. You will need to create an event handler (a.k.a. a delegate with the right function signature) that points to your event sink function.

c. You will need to register this event handler with the control.

This may sound complicated, but in practice it is usually simple and can be accomplished in one line of code. For example, in this code, a., b., and c. occur:

```
newButton.Click += new System.EventHandler
(this.ClickHandlerForButtons);
```

They are:

a. `this.ClickHandlerForButtons` is the event sink function.

b. `new System.EventHandler()` is the delegate that points to the event sink.

c. `newButton.Click +=...` adds the event handler to the list of event handlers that get called when the event gets fired.

Looking in a Form's `InitializeComponent()` function can be a good place to copy event handler registration code from. It is important to note that a single function can be an event sink for an arbitrary number of different events. This is very useful for working with arrays of controls because the events for multiple controls can be mapped to a single function.

3. *Set the parent property of the new control to the form it needs to be displayed on.* This final step really creates and hosts the control on the form. As long as the control's parent property points to null, the control is not on the form.

Dynamic Control Creation Example

Figure 13.8 and Listing 13.2 show a sample application that dynamically creates Button controls and hooks up Click event handlers to these controls. The example can easily be adapted to dynamically create any kind of control you want.

The code in Listing 13.2 belongs inside a form in a Pocket PC project. Do the following to build and run the application:

1. Start Visual Studio .NET (2003 or later) and create a C# Smart Device Application.

2. Choose Pocket PC as the target platform. (A project will be created for you and Pocket PC Form designer will appear.)

3. Add a Button control to the form and rename it **buttonCreateNewButtons**.

4. Double-click the button you just added to the Form designer. The code window will pop up with a function skeleton for `private void buttonCreateNewButtons_Click(object sender,`

Application before creation of any dynamic controls...

Application after the creation of 6 dynamic controls...

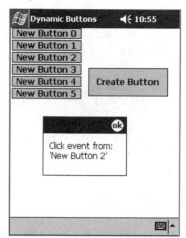

Figure 13.8 Dynamic creation of controls at runtime.

System.EventArgs e). Enter in the code listed below for this function.

5. Into the code window, enter in the rest of the code listed below, both the code above and below the listing of the function you just entered.

6. Set the MinimizeBox property of the form to false. At runtime this will give the form an OK box at the top-right corner that makes it easy to close the form and exit the application. This is very useful for repeated testing.

7. Run the application. You should observe that each time you click the buttonCreateNewButtons button, a new button is added to the form (as shown in Figure 13.8). Clicking any of the new buttons should trigger the event handler code listed below and show a message box that shows the text of the control that was clicked.

Listing 13.2 Dynamic Creation of Controls on a Form at Runtime

```
//----------------------------------------------------------------

//Counter for the number of button controls we create
//----------------------------------------------------------------

private int m_nextNewButtonIndex;
```

```csharp
//----------------------------------------------------------------
//EVENT HANDLER: Click event handler for the button we have
//                on our form.
//
//This function creates a new button, attaches it to our
//form and hooks up a "Click" event handler for it
//----------------------------------------------------------------
private void buttonCreateNewButtons_Click(object sender,
                                          System.EventArgs e)
{
    //Eventually we will start creating new buttons off the
    //bottom of the screen, so lets stop at 8
    if (m_nextNewButtonIndex > 8)
    {
      return;
    }


    //-----------------------------------------------------------
    //Create the button (not yet attached to our form)
    //set its location, size, and text
    //-----------------------------------------------------------
    const int newButtonHeight = 15;
    System.Windows.Forms.Button newButton;
    newButton = new System.Windows.Forms.Button();
    newButton.Width = 100;
    newButton.Height = newButtonHeight;
    newButton.Left = 2;
    newButton.Top = (newButtonHeight + 2) * m_nextNewButtonIndex ;
    newButton.Text = "New Button " +
                     m_nextNewButtonIndex.ToString();


    //-----------------------------------------------------------
    //Attach an event handler to the "Click" event of this
    //control.
    //-----------------------------------------------------------
    newButton.Click += new System.EventHandler
                         (this.ClickHandlerForButtons);


    //-----------------------------------------------------------
    //Attach this button to the form. This will actually
    //Create the button on the form!
    //-----------------------------------------------------------
    newButton.Parent = this;
```

```
  //Increment our counter for the next button we create
  m_nextNewButtonIndex++;
}


//----------------------------------------------------------
//Event handler we will dynamically hook up to our new
//buttons
//----------------------------------------------------------
private void ClickHandlerForButtons(object sender,
                                     System.EventArgs e)
{
  Button buttonCausingEvent;
  buttonCausingEvent = (System.Windows.Forms.Button) sender;

  //Bring up a message box announcing that we have received
  //the event
  System.Windows.Forms.MessageBox.Show(
    "Click event from: \n\r'" + buttonCausingEvent.Text + "'");
}
```

Custom Controls and Overriding Behaviors in Existing Controls

The .NET Compact Framework allows two kinds of control inheritance: (1) building a custom control from scratch, and (2) overriding the nonpainting/nonrendering behaviors of existing System.Windows.Forms.* controls.

First a few words on what the .NET Compact Framework (version 1.1) does not support: Unlike the desktop .NET Framework, the .NET Compact Framework does not allow developers to override the visual characteristics of how the standard controls are drawn. (For example, you cannot inherit from a Button, TreeView, TextBox, or other standard control and override how it is painted.) This is for internal performance reasons.

A developer wanting a control with a custom look on the .NET Compact Framework will have to derive from the base Control class (System.Windows.Forms.Control), which does allow for the custom rendering of a control. This is most useful for controls that produce completely new user interactions (for example, a charting control) rather than controls that give modified behaviors for existing controls. A basic example for creating a custom rendering control from scratch is shown in Chapter 11, "Graphics and User Interface Performance"; this would be a good place to start if you want to create your own custom rendering control.

Although the .NET Compact Framework does not support overriding the rendering behavior of its internal controls it does support overriding the functional behavior of these controls. There are two ways to extend the internal controls: (1) adding additional methods, properties, and events that expose higher-level value-added functionality; and (2) overriding existing properties and methods to supply a more purpose-dedicated experience. A good example showing both of these characteristics is creating a filtered TextBox control that only accepts certain formats of input. The sample code in Listing 13.3 and Listing 13.4 does this.

Filtered Text Box Example

When input needs to meet specific formatting rules, it is often useful to create a custom control that explicitly forces the input to meet this criteria. A common example in the United States is the need to enter a Social Security number. Social Security numbers come in the format of ###-##-####, three digits separated by a dash, followed by two digits separated by a dash, and finally four more digits. There are many additional other text-input formats it may be useful to enforce, another example being postal codes (Zip codes). Different countries use different formats, some numeric and some alphanumeric; for example, both Canadian and United Kingdom postal codes consist of both numbers and letters. In all of these cases, if precise input is required, a filtering TextBox control can be a valuable asset. It would also be useful for this control to have a property that tells developers whether the text currently entered meets the definition of valid and complete input. Our sample code will do both filtering and validation.

Figure 13.9 shows the test application at runtime. The button on the form is pressed to create an instance of the filtering TextBox control. Typing into the text box causes the filtering and formatting code in our `SocialSecurityTextBox` class to get run. Two functions are called in this class:

1. The first function that is called is the overridden `SocialSecurity-TextBox.OnKeyPress()` method. This gives us a chance to intercept and prefilter the key press events that come in. In our case, because we do not want any letters to be input, we will filter these out if the user tries to enter them. By not passing them on to the base class implementation of `OnKeyPress()`, we are preventing the text box from ever seeing these key presses. We could do much more filtering and do things such as disallowing any additional numeric input if the user tries to enter more digits after the end of the number, but for the example let's keep things simple. It is worth noting that care

Application prior to entering all necessary digits…

Application after entering all necessary digits…

Figure 13.9 Dynamic creation of controls at runtime.

should be taken in filtering key events so as not to be overly restrictive and filter out useful key press events such as the backspace character that is used to delete text.

2. The second function that is called is the overridden `Social-SecurityTextBox.OnTextChanged()` method. This is called when the contents of the Text property change, such as when a key press has been registered. Here we take the opportunity to apply our formatting code and force any text that has been entered into meeting our defined format. We keep only the numbers that have been entered and make sure that there is a dash (-) separating the third and forth digit and the fifth and sixth digit. Care must be taken here as well because if we update the Text property of the text box inside the `OnTextChanged` method this will cause our `OnTextChanged` method to be called recursively. We do not want to get into a complicated situation here, so we check for this case at the beginning of the function and exit doing nothing if this occurs. Next we check the length of our processed text; if it is 11 characters, we have a full Social Security number, if not, we do not. We update our internal state to indicate this. Finally we call our text box base class' `OnTextChanged()` method; this causes any event handlers that are listening for `TextChange` events to get called.

The code in Listing 13.3 is a standalone class and can be entered as is. The code in Listing 13.4 belongs inside a form in a Pocket PC project. Do the following to build and run the application:

1. Start Visual Studio .NET (2003 or later) and create a C# Smart Device Application.
2. Choose Pocket PC as the target platform. (A project will be created for you and Pocket PC Form designer will appear.)
3. Add a Button control to the form. (It will be named button1.)
4. Add a Label control to the form. (It will be named label1.)
5. Add a new class to the project. Name the class **SocialSecurityText-Box**, delete all preexisting code that is shown in the text editor for this class, and enter the code in Listing 13.3.
6. Go back to Form1's designer.
7. Double-click the button you added to the Form designer. The code window will pop up with a function skeleton for `private void button1_Click(object sender, System.EventArgs e)`. Enter in the code listed in Listing 13.4 for this function.
8. Into the code window, enter in the rest of the code listed below, both the code above and below the listing of function you just entered.
9. Set the MinimizeBox property of the form to false. At runtime this will give the form an OK box at the top-right corner that makes it easy to close the form and exit the application. This is very useful for repeated testing.
10. Run the application. You should observe that when you click the button1 button, a new text box is added to the top of the form. The text box enables you to type only numbers into it and formats the numbers into the template ###-##-####. As you type, the label on the screen is updated to tell you whether you have entered all the numbers required.

This example could easily be updated to support other input formats. In addition, support for custom events could be added; for instance, our inherited TextBox control could raise an event when all the necessary data to meet an input template was entered.

Listing 13.3 A Filtering Text Box That Takes the Format ###-##-####

```
using System;
//------------------------------------------------------------
//This class is a control derived from the TextBox control.
//It uses all the drawing behavior of the TextBox, but adds
//a filter on the text box contents ensuring that only text
//that meets the format:
// ###-##-####
//can be entered. This matches the format of Social Security
//numbers used in the United States.
//------------------------------------------------------------
public class SocialSecurityTextBox :
                              System.Windows.Forms.TextBox
{
private bool m_inputIsFullValidEntry;


//------------------------------------------------------------
//Indicates whether we have a full
//Social Security number
//------------------------------------------------------------
public bool IsFullValidInput
{get {return m_inputIsFullValidEntry;}}

//A string builder we will use often
System.Text.StringBuilder m_sb;
//The maximum length of our processed string
const int SSNumberLength = 11;


//------------------------------------------------------------
//Constructor
//------------------------------------------------------------
public SocialSecurityTextBox()
{
  //Allocate our string builder and give us a few extra
  //characters of room to work in by default
    m_sb = new System.Text.StringBuilder(SSNumberLength + 5);
    m_inputIsFullValidEntry = false;
}


//------------------------------------------------------------
//Format incoming text to make sure it is in the format:
//
// SS Format :  ###-##-####
```

```
// char index:  01234567890
//
// [in] inString        : Text we want to format
// [in/out] selectionStart: Current insert point in the text,
//                          this will get moved if it needs to
//                          based on appends or deletes we make
//------------------------------------------------------------
private string formatText_NNN_NN_NNNN(string inString,
                                      ref int selectionStart)
{
   const int firstDashIndex = 3;
   const int secondDashIndex = 6;

   //Clear out the old data, and place the input string into
   //the string builder so we can work on it.
   m_sb.Length = 0;
   m_sb.Append(inString);


   //---------------------------------------------------
   //Go through each character in the string up until
   //we reach the maximum length of our formatted text
   //---------------------------------------------------
   int currentCharIndex;
   currentCharIndex = 0;
   while((currentCharIndex < m_sb.Length) &&
         (currentCharIndex < SSNumberLength))
   {
       char currentChar;
       currentChar = m_sb[currentCharIndex];
     if((currentCharIndex == firstDashIndex) ||
        (currentCharIndex == secondDashIndex))
       //-------------------------------------------------------
       //The character needs to be a "-"
       //-------------------------------------------------------
       {
         if(currentChar != '-')
         {
           //Insert a dash
           m_sb.Insert(currentCharIndex, "-");

           //If we added a character before the insert point,
           //advance the insert point
           if(currentCharIndex <= selectionStart)
           {
```

```
                selectionStart++;
              }
            }
            //This character is fine now, advance to the next char
            currentCharIndex++;
          }
          else
          //-------------------------------------------------------
          //The character needs to be a digit
          //-------------------------------------------------------
          {
            if(System.Char.IsDigit(currentChar) == false)
            {
              //Remove a character
              m_sb.Remove(currentCharIndex,1);
              //If we removed a character before the insert point,
              //retreat the insert point
              if(currentCharIndex < selectionStart)
              {
                selectionStart--;
              }

              //Don't advance the char count, we need to look at
              //the character that took the place of the one we
              //have removed
            }
            else
            {
              //The character is a digit, all is well.
              currentCharIndex++;
            }
          }
        }
    }

    //If we are over the length, truncate it
    if(m_sb.Length > SSNumberLength)
    {
      m_sb.Length = SSNumberLength;
    }

    //Return our new string
    return m_sb.ToString();
}
```

```csharp
bool m_in_OnChangeFunction;
protected override void OnTextChanged(EventArgs e)
{
    //-------------------------------------------------------
    //If we change the .Text property, we will get called
    //re-entrantly. In this case we want to do nothing, and
    //just exit the function without passing on the event
    //to anyone else.
    //-------------------------------------------------------
    if(m_in_OnChangeFunction == true)
    {
        return;
    }

    //Note that we are now in the OnChanged function
    //so we can detect re-entrancy (see code above)
    m_in_OnChangeFunction = true;

    //Get the current .Text property
    string oldText = this.Text;
    //Get the current SelectionStart Index
    int selectionStart = this.SelectionStart;
    //Format the string so it meets our needs
    string newText = formatText_NNN_NN_NNNN(oldText,
                                ref selectionStart);

    //If the text differs from the original, update the
    //.Text property
    if (System.String.Compare(oldText, newText ) != 0)
    {
        //This will cause us to get called re-entrantly
        this.Text = newText;
        //Update the location of the insert point
        this.SelectionStart = selectionStart;
    }

    //Because we have just forced the text entry into the
    //right format; if the length matches the length of
    //the Social Security number, we know that it is in
    //the format ###-##-####.
    if (this.Text.Length == SSNumberLength)
    {
        //Yes, we have a full Social Security number
        m_inputIsFullValidEntry = true;
```

```
      }
      else
      {
         //No, we do note have a full Social Security number yet
         m_inputIsFullValidEntry = false;
      }

      //Call our base class and let anyone who wants
      //to know that the text has changed get called
      base.OnTextChanged(e);

      //Note that we are exiting our code now and want to turn
      //off the re-entrancy check.
      m_in_OnChangeFunction = false;
   }

   protected override void OnKeyPress(
                      System.Windows.Forms.KeyPressEventArgs e)
   {
      //Because we know we don't want any letters in our input,
      //just ingore them if we detect them.
      char keyPressed = e.KeyChar;
      if(System.Char.IsLetter(keyPressed))
      {
         //Tell the system we have handled the event
         e.Handled = true;
         return;
      }
   //Process the key press as normal
   base.OnKeyPress (e);
   } //End function
   } //End class
```

Listing 13.4 Code in Form to Create the Custom TextBox Control

```
//----------------------------------------------------------
//The variable to hold our new TextBox control
//----------------------------------------------------------
SocialSecurityTextBox m_filteredTextBox;


//----------------------------------------------------------
//EVENT HANDLER: Create an instance of our custom control
//               and place it onto the form
//----------------------------------------------------------
```

```csharp
private void button1_Click(object sender, System.EventArgs e)
{
  //Create, position and host the control
  m_filteredTextBox = new SocialSecurityTextBox();
  m_filteredTextBox.Bounds =
        new System.Drawing.Rectangle(2,2,160, 20);

  //Hook up the event handler
  m_filteredTextBox.TextChanged +=
        new EventHandler(this.textBox_TextChanged);

  //Set the parent
  m_filteredTextBox.Parent = this;

  //Select the control
  m_filteredTextBox.Focus();

  //Disable this button so a second SocialSecurityTextBox does
  //not get created on top of this one
  button1.Enabled = false;
}


//-----------------------------------------------------------
//EVENT HANDLER: This gets dynamically hooked up when the control
//                  is created
//-----------------------------------------------------------
private void textBox_TextChanged(object sender,
                                        System.EventArgs e)
{
  if (m_filteredTextBox.IsFullValidInput == true)
  {
    label1.Text = "FULL SOCIAL SECURITY NUMBER!!!";
  }
  else
  {
    label1.Text = "Not full input yet...";
  }
}
```

Using Transparent Bitmap Regions

Bitmaps with transparency masks are useful for many reasons. When writing a game, developers can use bitmaps with transparent regions to draw and move nonrectangular images around the screen play field. In mapping applications, bitmaps with transparency masks can be used to draw images on top of maps generated by other sources; drawing a location marker onto a map is a good example. Finally, the ability to integrate nonrectangular bitmaps onto other graphics is useful for creating good-looking user interfaces and business graphics.

Bitmaps are essentially two-dimensional arrays of integers with each integer representing the color of a pixel at a specific location. For this reason, bitmaps are by their very nature rectangular. A nonrectangular image can be represented in a rectangular bitmap by declaring one color as the background color and filling the pixels outside the contained nonrectangular image with this color. Having a regular rectangular array of data has many advantages, not the least of which is the ability to easily copy a part of one image onto a part of another image; only very simple algorithms are required to do this if the regions are rectangular. The result of copying a rectangular portion of one bitmap onto another is simply one rectangle of image information replacing another; this is useful in many cases, but only allows the drawing of rectangular regions. This means that rectangular bitmaps containing nonrectangular images with a single background color are copied as opaque rectangles, foreground and background, to the destination. The result is not visually appealing. An alternative to doing this is to take a background image and hand-draw onto it all of the nonrectangular images, either using drawing functions (for example, .DrawLine(), .FillCircle()) or by setting the pixel data directly one pixel at a time. Both of these can produce good visual results, but are slow to perform and complex to write. What is needed is a way to copy one bitmap onto another but not copy over the background color. Figure 13.10 shows a simple game bitmap image; the bitmap is rectangular, but the image we want to draw is not. To be able to draw this image without its rectangular background, the function that copies over the bitmap needs to be told not to copy over pixels of our background color. In the .NET Compact Framework, this is done via the ImageAttributes class.

The ImageAttributes class has a SetColorKey() method that allows your code to set a masking color. This ImageAttributes class can then be passed as a parameter to one of the Graphics.DrawImage() function overloads; only one of the function overloads supports taking in this parameter. This DrawImage() function takes as parameters the source bitmap for the image we want to copy, the dimensions and location to copy to

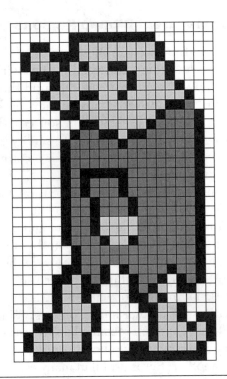

Figure 13.10 A sample bitmap image with nonrectangular foreground and one-color background.

and from, and an ImageAttributes object that specifies what color mask will define transparency in the source image. All of the source image pixel information is then copied over onto the destination bitmap except for pixels matching the mask color specified in the ImageAttributes object. Source image pixels that are the same color as the mask are left uncopied. This allows the preexisting pixels in the destination image to "show through" the transparent regions in the bitmap we are copying. This copy operation is not quite as fast as a simple rectangular image copy, but it runs fairly quickly, making it an attractive option for working with non-rectangular images. When repeated or frequent drawing is required, it is a good idea to globally cache an ImageAttributes object that can be used in all your application's bitmap drawing code that deals with irregular shapes with transparent backgrounds; this saves the need to continually allocate and discard the ImageAttributes objects and reduces garbage buildup in your application's memory.

Using Bitmaps with Transparent Regions Example

Figure 13.11 shows an example of using transparent regions to meet advanced drawing needs. The first of the screenshots in Figure 13.11 shows the background image being drawn. In this case, the background image consists of black text drawn onto a white background. The second screenshot shows another image, a graphic consisting of a blue background with a yellow rectangle drawn on top of it along with two yellow ellipses. The third screenshot shows the second image drawn on top of the first image but with yellow defined as transparent. The result is that when the second image is copied onto the first, any pixels that are yellow in color are not copied over, leaving the original pixels in the destination bitmap showing through.

The code in Listing 13.5 enables you to build the application shown in Figure 13.11. To build the application, do the following:

1. Start Visual Studio .NET (2003 or later) and create a C# Smart Device Application.
2. Choose Pocket PC as the target platform. (A project will be created for you and Pocket PC Form designer will appear.)
3. Add Button control to the form designer (it will be named button1), and rename it to **buttonDrawBackground**.
4. Double-click the button in the designer and fill in the code for `buttonDrawBackground_Click()` in the listing below.
5. Add a Button control to the Form designer and rename it to **buttonDrawForeground**.
6. Double-click the button in the designer and fill in the code for `buttonDrawForeground_Click()` in the listing below.

Application showing only background image…

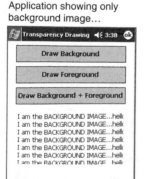

Application showing only foreground image…

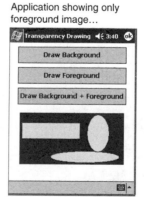

Foreground image drawn on top of background, using transparency…

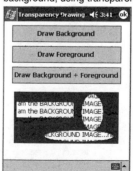

Figure 13.11 Application showing drawing using transparent background.

7. Add a Button control to the Form designer and rename it to **buttonDrawBackgroundPlusForeground**.

8. Double-click the button in the designer and fill in the code for `buttonDrawBackgroundPlusForeground _Click()` in the listing below.

9. Enter all of the remaining code in the listing below.

10. Go back to the form's designer.

11. Set the MinimizeBox property of the form to false. At runtime this will give the form an OK box at the top-right corner that makes it easy to close the form and exit the application. This is very useful for repeated testing.

12. Run the application; you should be able to reproduce the images in Figure 13.11.

More Fun with Transparent Bitmaps

The choice of yellow as the transparency color is completely arbitrary. It would be just as easy to choose blue as the transparency color and allow everything in the foreground bitmap that was yellow to be copied over and everything that was blue to be treated as transparent. It would also be simple to reverse the background and foreground bitmaps and make the yellow and blue rectangles and ellipses be the background and the black and white text the foreground; in this case, we would need to choose either black or white as our transparency color, and the text or its background would be made a transparent depending on our decision. Transparencies are a powerful concept and can be used to great effect with all kinds of bitmap images.

Listing 13.5 Code in Form to Demonstrate the Use of Transparencies

```
//-----------------------------------------------------------
//Dimensions for our bitmaps and the onscreen PictureBox
//-----------------------------------------------------------
const int bitmap_dx = 200;
const int bitmap_dy = 100;


//-----------------------------------------------------------
//Creates and draws the background image
//-----------------------------------------------------------
System.Drawing.Bitmap m_backgroundBitmap;
void CreateBackground()
{
   if(m_backgroundBitmap == null)
   {
```

```csharp
        m_backgroundBitmap = new Bitmap(bitmap_dx, bitmap_dy);
    }
    //Make the bitmap white
    System.Drawing.Graphics gfx;
    gfx = System.Drawing.Graphics.FromImage(m_backgroundBitmap);
    gfx.Clear(System.Drawing.Color.White);

    //Draw a bunch of text in black
    System.Drawing.Brush myBrush;
    myBrush = new System.Drawing.SolidBrush(
                            System.Drawing.Color.Black);

    for(int y = 0; y < bitmap_dy; y = y + 15)
    {
      gfx.DrawString("I am the BACKGROUND IMAGE...hello",
                  this.Font, myBrush, 0, y);
    }

    //Clean up
    myBrush.Dispose();
    gfx.Dispose();
}


//-------------------------------------------------------
//Creates and draws the foreground image
//-------------------------------------------------------
System.Drawing.Bitmap m_foregroundBitmap;
void CreateForeground()
{
  if(m_foregroundBitmap == null)
  {
    m_foregroundBitmap = new Bitmap(bitmap_dx, bitmap_dy);
  }
  //Make the whole bitmap blue
  System.Drawing.Graphics gfx;
  gfx = System.Drawing.Graphics.FromImage(m_foregroundBitmap);
  gfx.Clear(System.Drawing.Color.Blue);

  //Draw some shapes in yellow
  System.Drawing.Brush yellowBrush;
  yellowBrush = new System.Drawing.SolidBrush(
                            System.Drawing.Color.Yellow);
  gfx.FillEllipse(yellowBrush, 130, 4, 40, 70);
  gfx.FillRectangle(yellowBrush, 5, 20, 110, 30);
```

```
  gfx.FillEllipse(yellowBrush, 60, 75, 130, 20);

  //Clean up
  yellowBrush.Dispose();
  gfx.Dispose();
}


//----------------------------------------------------------
//Sets the size and left hand location of the PictureBox
//----------------------------------------------------------
private void SetPictureBoxDimensions()
{
  pictureBox1.Width = bitmap_dx;
  pictureBox1.Height = bitmap_dy;
  pictureBox1.Left = 20;
}


//----------------------------------------------------------
//EVENT HANDLER: Display the BACKGROUND image in the PictureBox
//----------------------------------------------------------
private void buttonDrawBackground_Click(object sender,
                                        System.EventArgs e)
{
    SetPictureBoxDimensions();
    CreateBackground();
    pictureBox1.Image = m_backgroundBitmap;
}


//----------------------------------------------------------
//EVENT HANDLER: Display the FOREGROUND image in the PictureBox
//----------------------------------------------------------
private void buttonDrawForeground_Click(object sender,
                                        System.EventArgs e)
{
  SetPictureBoxDimensions();
  CreateForeground();
  pictureBox1.Image = m_foregroundBitmap;

}


//----------------------------------------------------------
//EVENT HANDLER: Overlay the FOREGROUND image ON TOP OF the
//               BACKGROUND image. Use a TRANSPARENCY MASK
//               so that the color YELLOW in the FOREGROUND
```

```csharp
//                   image becomes transparent and shows the
//                   contents of the BACKGROUND IMAGE
//-----------------------------------------------------------
private void buttonDrawBackgroundPlusForeground_Click(
                            object sender, System.EventArgs e)
{
  SetPictureBoxDimensions();
  CreateForeground();
  CreateBackground();
  //Get the graphics of the BACKGROUND image because that
  //is what we are going to draw on top of.
  System.Drawing.Graphics gfx;
  gfx = System.Drawing.Graphics.FromImage(m_backgroundBitmap);

  //-------------------------------------------------------
  //Create an ImageAttributes class. This class allows us
  //to set the TRANSPARANCY COLOR for our draw operation
  //-------------------------------------------------------
  System.Drawing.Imaging.ImageAttributes trasparencyInfo =
              new System.Drawing.Imaging.ImageAttributes();
  //-------------------------------------------------------
  //Set the transparency color
  //-------------------------------------------------------
  trasparencyInfo.SetColorKey(System.Drawing.Color.Yellow,
                              System.Drawing.Color.Yellow);

  //Set our drawing rectangle
  System.Drawing.Rectangle rect =
              new System.Drawing.Rectangle(0,0,
                    m_backgroundBitmap.Width,
                    m_backgroundBitmap.Height);

  //-------------------------------------------------------
  //Draw the FOREGROUND on top of the BACKGROUND bitmap and
  //use the Transparency Color in the ImageAttributes to
  //give us a transparent window onto the background
  //-------------------------------------------------------
  gfx.DrawImage(m_foregroundBitmap,
              rect,
              0,0,
              m_foregroundBitmap.Width,
              m_foregroundBitmap.Height,
              System.Drawing.GraphicsUnit.Pixel,
              trasparencyInfo);
```

```
//Cleanup
gfx.Dispose();

//Show the results in the bitmap
pictureBox1.Image = m_backgroundBitmap;
}
```

Embedding Images as Resources in Your Application

Many applications make use of bitmap images to present a rich user interface to users. Custom buttons with images painted on them, graphics images used in drawing, logo images, or other background images all can improve the visual aesthetics of mobile device applications. Games often make extensive use of predrawn images rather than drawing complex images from scratch. For these reasons, it is often useful to have images packaged with your application's binary code. These images are then automatically deployed along with the application; this is much more robust than needing to manage the deployment of a set of image files along with your application. There is no size penalty for embedding images in your application versus deploying them as separate files; in both cases, they are binary image streams that your application accesses as needed.

To use binary resources embedded in your application, two things are needed:

1. The images must be compiled into your application. This can be specified at design time in the development environment.
2. Your application must know how to locate the resources at runtime. Binary resources embedded in compiled .NET assemblies are addressed using syntax similar to file paths, specifying where the resource is located inside the loaded assemblies of your application at runtime.

Both of these are described next.

How to Embed an Image in Your Application

It is relatively straightforward to use Visual Studio .NET to compile binary resources into your application.

1. Start Visual Studio .NET.
2. Create a C# Smart Device Application project.

3. Choose the menu Project->Add Existing Item.
4. In the Add Existing Item dialog, change the Files of Type filter setting to show Image Files.
5. Locate the image file you want to add and choose it. (Note: I strongly suggest choosing an image file that is smaller than 300KB; otherwise you will be building a giant image file into your application that is probably significantly bigger than the application itself; large-resolution bitmaps may cause the device to run out of memory when loaded at runtime.) For the sake of this example, let's assume you chose a file called MyImage.PNG.
6. In the Visual Studio .NET Solution Explorer window, select the image file you have just added (MyImage.PNG), right-click it, and select the Properties menu item.
7. In the Properties window, look at the Build Action property. By default it is set to Content; this means that the file will be copied down to the device alongside the application when it is deployed.
8. Change the Build Action property to be Embedded Resource; this means that the binary contents of MyImage.PNG will be built in to the application's executable image every time the application is compiled.

The Names of Embedded Resources are Case Sensitive

Regardless of whether your programming language is case sensitive (C# is, VB.NET is not), embedded resource names are. Pay careful attention to the case of the letters in the filenames of the files you make embedded resources; your application will need to use the exact same casing to locate the resource streams at runtime. If the resource stream you are trying to find cannot be found because the name does not match exactly, an exception will be thrown by the runtime. This is a common mistake and can be very frustrating to track down if you do not know to look for case-sensitivity problems.

How to Access an Embedded Image in Your Application

The code in Listing 13.6 shows how to load a bitmap image from an embedded resource stream in your application. As above, we are using the image filename MyImage.PNG as our example image. The code should be placed inside a form with a Button and a PictureBox control. As with previous examples, the `button1_click` event should be wired to the button1 control by double-clicking the button in the designer to generate the function outline.

Listing 13.6 Code in Form to Demonstrate the Loading of Embedded Resources

```
System.Drawing.Bitmap m_myBitmapImage;
//-------------------------------------------
//Loads an image that is stored as a binary
//resource inside our assembly
//-------------------------------------------
public void LoadImageFromResource()
{
  //If we have already loaded the bitmap
  //no point in doing it again.
  if(m_myBitmapImage != null)
  {return;}

  //---------------------------------------------------
  //Get a reference to our application's binary assembly
  //---------------------------------------------------
  System.Reflection.Assembly thisAssembly =
    System.Reflection.Assembly.GetExecutingAssembly();

  //-----------------------------------------
  //Get the name of the assembly
  //-----------------------------------------
  System.Reflection.AssemblyName thisAssemblyName =
                              thisAssembly.GetName();
  string assemblyName = thisAssemblyName.Name;

  //-------------------------------------------------------
  //Stream the image in from our assembly and create an
  //in-memory bitmap
  //
  //NOTE: The ResourceStream name is CASE SENSITIVE,
  //      be sure the image name matches EXACTLY with
  //      file name of the image file you add to the project
  //-------------------------------------------------------
  m_myBitmapImage = new System.Drawing.Bitmap(
    thisAssembly.GetManifestResourceStream(
                        assemblyName + ".MyImage.PNG"));

}

//-------------------------------------------------------
//Load the image and display it in a picture box
//-------------------------------------------------------
```

```
private void button1_Click(object sender, System.EventArgs e)
{
    LoadImageFromResource();
    pictureBox1.Image = m_myBitmapImage;
}
```

Image Storage Formats and Bitmap Transparencies

When using bitmaps in your application, it is important to think about the image formats you are using. For tiny bitmaps (for example, 8 × 8 pixels), the image compression does not matter much because the images are small anyway. For larger bitmaps, it may be possible to save a considerable amount of space by using lossy (for example, *.JPG) or nonlossy (for example, *.PNG) image-compression formats versus using noncompressed (for example, *.BMP) formats. An uncompressed screen-sized background image can add a lot of size to your application. Care must be taken in choosing storage formats for images that are going to have one color in the image treated as transparent at runtime; in these cases, only nonlossy compression should be used. Lossy compression can often yield higher-storage efficiency, but this is gained by giving up control of the color of each individual pixel in the image; you are getting an approximate image. A bitmap image that has transparent regions needs to be able to exactly specify the color of each pixel.

Summary

Building a great mobile device user interface can be a challenging and engrossing design problem. First, you must either adapt your design idea to the usage patterns and form factor of the selected target device or choose the appropriate mobile device type that meets your design goals. Devices differ significantly from desktop and laptop computers in their user interface capabilities and user-usage patterns. Different classes of devices also significantly differ from one another. Choosing a one-size-fits-all approach to developing a mobile device user interface intended to run on different classes of devices guarantees a poor fit for everyone. Choose your target devices and optimize your mobile user interface design for each of them to provide the best possible experience.

It is important to come to an explicit design decision as to whether your application's user interface will be driven by one-handed or two-handed usage. Often this decision is dictated by the hardware you choose to target; for example, touch screens are two handed and phone keypads are usually one handed. Make an explicit written statement in your design document about the one- or two-handedness of the application and enforce this design decision throughout your design and development. When designing one-handed user interfaces consistent and simple "click through" is important; do not make the user switch from one button to another when running down common navigation paths in the application. The user should not have to shift his or her vision from device to keypad while navigating your application; this is distracting and breaks the flow of his thought.

The size of the screen being targeted by your mobile device application will have a big impact on your design. Smaller screens tend to use list-oriented user interfaces; larger screens with touch pads or mouse pointers can often benefit from a tab-dialog metaphor for navigation between screens. Divide your mobile application's functionality into purpose-focused screens. Think carefully about the information you want to display on each screen and how navigation between screens is facilitated. Desktop applications tend to display several paragraphs of information simultaneously. Pocket PC-type applications tend to display one paragraph of information simultaneously with tab links to other paragraphs. Smartphones display list outlines that enable the user to drill into and view each chunk of information separately.

Because mobile devices tend not to have full-sized keyboards, rapid entry of text is not a strength of most mobile devices. For this reason, when text data needs to be entered, it is useful to spend design time optimizing the user's productivity in entering common types of information. Often specialized user interfaces with larger buttons or customized user interfaces can aid the user in entering specific data such as dates, numbers, currency, addresses, or any other data that is not free-form text. External devices such as bar code scanners and speech- and visual-recognition systems can be a good way to speed up the input of specific data, but your mobile application should always give the user a manual way to key-in this information if the external input system fails, as inevitably it occasionally will.

Software emulators for mobile devices are extremely useful in speeding up development, but they are no substitute for usability testing using real devices. An emulator image running on a laptop is not sufficient for testing a handheld mobile application's usability. Navigation, input, balance, comfort, and data visibility while working with the device are issues that can be accurately assessed only when running on physical hardware.

When writing the code for your mobile device's user interface, it is important to structure your code in such a way that it will be easy to iterate on the user interface's design. Getting a mobile device user interface design correct will require several successive iterations on the layout and navigation of your application. Your mobile application's code will require flexibility to accommodate these changes. Centralizing the user interface management code in a state machine and using wrapper methods to insulate one control's event handling from another's updating are good ways to ensure flexibility in your design. It is fundamentally important to avoid distributing responsibility for managing your user interface; the more you can centralize the code that drives your user interface, the easier it will be to modify that code when the need arises to do so. Using helper classes to group together related user interface functions, such as all the event handlers for controls on a given display tab, also helps insulate user interface code from other code. Having a clean abstracted interface between your application logic and presentation layer logic is extremely important to maintain design flexibility. An added benefit to building well-encapsulated user interface code is that it will be much easier to port your mobile device application to other classes of devices.

The .NET Compact Framework offers some advanced user interface functionality that can be useful when building rich mobile device user interfaces. The .NET Compact Framework enables developers to create two kinds of custom controls: (1) custom controls that implement their own visual display characteristics from scratch and derive from System.Windows.Forms.Control, and (2) custom controls that implement behaviors on top of existing controls by deriving from and extending nonabstract controls such as the System.Windows.Forms.TextBox control. Both types of custom controls are useful. The ability to dynamically create controls at runtime can be very useful; building a design-time version of a .NET Compact Framework control can be a laborious task, and unless you are in the market of selling custom controls you may want to forego this step and just create custom control instances dynamically at runtime.

The ability to define transparency colors in bitmap copy operations allows your application to create rich graphical displays useful in entertainment, productivity, and scientific applications. The System.Drawing.Imaging.ImageAttributes class is the key to drawing with transparencies when using the .NET Compact Framework; it allows your code to set the color key that will be treated as transparent when copying a source bitmap onto a destination bitmap. Transparency regions can be useful when working with all kinds of bitmap images, from text and shapes dynamically drawn onto bitmaps to predrawn images loaded at runtime. Bitmap images used by your application can be stored as part of your application's binary image; doing this makes it easier to deploy your application by reducing the number of files your application is dependent upon.

User interface design for mobile applications is both challenging and rewarding and can be a lot of fun. It requires a great deal of creativity to distil what the essential information is that needs to be presented to users and what the right application navigation metaphors should be. It is exciting to experiment, and you will learn rapidly as you try out different concepts. As emphasized in the earlier sections of this book, the perception of good performance by the user is essential to building a good mobile device user experience. If you keep performance top of mind, design your user interfaces with creativity, and write your code with disciplined flexibility built in, you will have a great experience working and experimenting with mobile user interface design.

CHAPTER 14

Step 3: Get Your Data Access Model Right

The author of this book asserts that just as there are few funny jokes about librarians, there are no pithy quotes about databases or data access. The subject is just too utilitarian. The author challenges the reader to prove him wrong.

—Ivo Salmre

Introduction to Mobile Application Data Access

After deciding on the scope of your application, committing to a performance-minded development methodology, and coming up with a user interface model for your mobile application, it is important to get the data access model for your application right.

Your mobile application's data access model defines how the application deals with its longer-term information retrieval and storage needs. As discussed earlier in the book, memory models determine how your application manages data and resources in memory; similarly your mobile device application will need a data access model that determines how it moves data in and out of longer-term storage.

Almost all meaningful applications work with data that has a long lifetime. This data can be either in a structured database on the server or device, or stored in a less-formal way in individually managed files. Scientific, business, and productivity applications center on entering, manipulating, analyzing, and displaying data. Rich games also work with data and often persist it between sessions. As a general rule, the more complex and useful an application, the more long-lived data it works with.

An important data access difference between mobile device applications and their desktop and server counterparts is that a mobile device will likely only have an intermittent connection to any off-device database servers. For a desktop application, not being able to access a server usually indicates an abnormal condition that needs to be dealt with. For a mobile device application, lack of access to a server indicates the usual state of affairs; times of connectivity are special either because they occur intermittently or because they are expensive. This factor can make managing data, giving dynamic views onto it, and allowing the user to make changes to it challenging. Data has both an in-memory and a long-term storage lifetime; both of these need to be considered in your mobile application's design. Your mobile application's data model represents the state that must be managed to provide the end user a useful experience when using your application.

A common misstep developers take is bringing unaltered desktop and server data access models to devices without thorough consideration of the memory utilization consequences of those models. This is an easy and understandable mistake; the programming models syntactically look very similar, and often desktop or server code can quickly be ported to run on devices. However, bringing a desktop or server data access strategy into a mobile device application rarely results in a satisfactory experience. The reason for this can be described in three words, "in-memory state." Higher abstraction is often achieved by creating additional layers of objects. Both the creation and disposal of these objects causes memory pressure and takes processing time.

More than on desktop applications, the data access model chosen for devices bumps right into the mobile application's memory-management model. This can result in serious performance consequences if there is not room for both. Just as when working with XML data, there are low-level stateless APIs and higher-level value-adding but stateful programming models. Higher-level data access models can save the developer coding time but at the cost of requiring a significant amount of in-memory state. If this state is truly needed and utilized by the mobile application and the size of data being managed in memory can be kept small, the use of highly stateful data access strategies is justified. Conversely, if the amount of data that needs to be kept in memory is large or the added features of the higher-level programming model are not needed, the developer is misusing valuable mobile device memory. Often the same data can be held in memory much more efficiently by using a set of types dedicated to the specific data being managed rather than using a general-purpose data access programming model. Wasted memory will impact the mobile application's performance adversely and profoundly; it will either immediately cause performance problems or prevent you from adding additional functionality later because you do not have the performance budget to support the new features. Keep things as lean and mean as possible.

When first implementing data access strategies on mobile devices, desktop and server developers commonly conclude that mobile devices simply are not capable of providing the performance they need. This is almost never the case. What needs to be done is that the data access requirements for the mobile application need to be considered carefully, and a data model must be designed that is tailored to meet these requirements. For example, if the data is largely read-only, efficiencies can be gained by storing the data in memory using a custom data-format optimized for size and rapid searches and not for managing updates; this might provide only fractional application performance increases on the desktop, but on a mobile device the differences can be large.

Choosing the Right Abstractions for In-Memory Storage of Data

Data returned from a database query or read in from a file must be held in memory so that it can be viewed and manipulated. There are two basic ways to work with this data in memory:

1. *Use a general-purpose abstract model.* Many programming frameworks offer an abstract model for working with data returned from databases. ADO.NET is the model supported by the .NET Compact Framework, and its use is described later in this chapter; other frameworks have different models. An abstract model has the virtue of being very flexible. Data that is returned from a database is stored in generic tables and rows of objects. Each row contains fields corresponding to column definitions. The grid of rows and columns forms a table. Tables can be grouped together in sets with additional tables describing the relationships between the columns in different tables. When you do a generic query of a database and do not know in advance what kind of data you are going to get back, storing it in this kind of abstract format is a necessity. Today's advanced data access models can also track changes made to the data locally. These changes can later be rejected, committed, or otherwise reconciled with the data in the database. In addition, the various data access frameworks can aid in the execution of transactions and can offer flexible views onto the data locally. Generic data-binding models also

exist to allow the binding of data in the tables to user interface elements. These general-purpose data access programming models are flexible, can respond robustly to changes in the database formats, and offer abstractions for looking at the types of the data being worked with at runtime. This flexibility comes at the cost of additional objects. These objects are used to contain meta data (meta data = information about the information), hold relationships between the various data elements, and track changes to the data. When using these higher-level in-memory data access technologies, your application is effectively creating an in-memory database of the data; this is powerful but can be expensive in computational and memory requirements.

2. *Use a custom model tailored to your data.* In contrast to the abstract model for working with data is the bare-bones approach of building a custom implementation that contains only what is required to hold and use the data. When using a custom data access strategy, your mobile application dispenses with the abstractions offered by an in-memory database of generic rows, columns, tables, and relationships and chooses to store the data in the most efficient format possible for the problem being solved. Usually this means an array of simple types that contain the data. In this custom-built model, your application loses a lot of the flexibility of a general-purpose approach and takes on the burden of keeping track of updates and managing data relationships. The benefit is that the application can potentially save a significant amount of in-memory state by using only what is absolutely required. If the data being worked with can easily be represented in a single table and does not have complicated interrelationships, a custom tailored format can be a great choice.

The most appropriate model to choose is determined by the size and complexity of the data being used. Building your own data model is a fool's errand if your data has many interrelationships that need to be managed and represented in the mobile application's memory. On the other hand, if your data consists of a few simple fields in a single database table and the data is read-only, it is equally foolish to choose a complex and stateful data model when a simple array of data would accomplish the desired end. It is likely your mobile application's data needs will fall somewhere in between these extremes, and you will have to try out different models and choose the most appropriate for your needs. As described above, this choice is similar to the technology decision mobile application developers need to make when working with XML data. The developer must choose between potential design and implementation simplicity versus runtime efficiency.

Choosing the Right Long-Term Storage Model for Data

The long-term storage model for your data describes where information goes when your application goes away. Even mobile devices that are on all the time and keep applications running in the background will need a safe and structured place to store data that has a long lifetime. A common example of this on mobile phones is the PIM (Personal Information Manager). A user who places his address book onto a phone expects that data to be there regardless of what states the phone goes through. If at all possible, this data should be automatically backed up to a server or desktop computer to facilitate quickly restoring it if the device's long-term storage fails. There are two fundamental questions that you need to answer with regard to your mobile device application's long-term storage model:

1. *Should the data be stored in a file or in a database?* If you only have a small amount of data to store, a text file is probably your best bet. If your stored file needs maximum portability between devices, XML is a great choice. On the other hand, if your application is working with a large amount of data that needs to be randomly accessed, if the data needs to be secured, or if you want to be able to use rich querying, transaction, or synchronization abilities, a database is the best choice. The main downsides of using a database are the additional size and processing overhead required along with any additional setup steps that may be required to deploy your application.

2. *If a database is used, should it be on or off the device?* Just as with desktop applications, it is possible to directly access databases running on servers or to host databases locally. The advantage of an on-device database is availability; it will be there whether or not you have a connection to a server. If a large amount of data needs to be accessed, a local database may be much more efficient than pushing query results down a comparatively slow wireless connection. The downside of a local database is the additional application deployment complexity and on-device footprint required to host the database. It is also important to know that different mobile devices have different levels of support for hosting local databases. For example, as of this writing, the SQL CE database was supported on Pocket PCs but not

Smartphones. If your application is unable to have a database on the local device, you will most likely need to devise a custom mechanism for caching the most important, frequently accessed, or expensive-to-obtain data on the local device.

Flash or RAM File Storage for Your Data?

Mobile devices usually employ one of two strategies for long-term information storage. Data is either stored into flash memory or it is stored in a RAM file system.

Flash memory is memory that does not require constant power to keep its contents stable. Flash memory can either come in the form of a removable card (for example, Secure Digital, Compact Flash) or be permanently built in to the device. Today flash memory is available in large-capacity formats; 512MB cards are not uncommon now, and the numbers are going up. Flash memory is also less power consumptive than RAM because it does not need to be electrically refreshed continually. However, flash memory is slower to access than volatile RAM; this is particularly true for writing data. Also any storage bits in flash memory can usually only be updated a limited number of times before they wear out; this number is typically above several hundred thousand writes, which is large but not endless. Although great advances have been made in flash memory to increase its flexibility, it is still not as flexible as RAM. Flash memory is presently suitable to use as a disk replacement but not as a replacement for volatile program RAM.

It is also worth noting that SIM cards in GSM mobile phones contain flash memory to hold a limited amount of data as well. This data space was traditionally used for storing the mobile phone's address book, but on newer phones most of this data is stored in the phone's storage for quicker and more flexible access. SIM card storage is still useful for storing specific "secrets" such as cryptographic certificates and keys, but is used less and less for general storage needs due to the availability of other general-purpose flash memory.

Think of flash memory as conceptually similar to a hard drive but with no moving parts. The USB storage keys you can stick into your PC are also flash memory. As with hard drives, flash memory usually has a file system built on top of it to allow it to be easily accessed in a structured way.

The other common method for persisting information long-term on devices is by using a RAM-based file system. In contrast to flash file systems, RAM file systems use a portion of a device's available memory to hold a file system there. RAM-based storage results in fast file access for both reading and writing but consumes significantly more power than flash. RAM file systems require some power even when the devices are turned off; should the device's battery be removed or run out of energy the file system's contents will be lost. This makes RAM file systems more susceptible to loss than flash systems. On many devices, including Windows CE / Pocket PC–based devices, files are typically stored in RAM file systems using compression algorithms. This provides greater capacity but incurs a processing penalty because data streams must be compressed during reads and writes. RAM file systems are fast, typically significantly faster than flash storage, but not as fast as in-memory application data.

Devices can support both flash and RAM file systems simultaneously the same way a desktop can support multiple hard drives. Even closely related devices can differ significantly in their long-term storage models. For example, the Pocket PC and Smartphones differ in the model they use for long-term data storage. By default, Pocket PCs offer a RAM file system; this is a reason why Pocket PC devices have bigger batteries than Smartphones. Smartphones primarily use flash for file system storage. Both Pocket PC and Smartphone devices support having flash memory cards inserted to them dynamically; this allows the devices to access songs, pictures, or any other data that may be on the cards.

The capacity and efficiency of file storage on different classes of devices is yet another reason why "write once, run anywhere" strategies for mobile device applications tend to produce unsatisfactory results. How well your mobile application can move data into and out of memory is dependent on the storage medium being used and the capacity present on the device. It is important to know what storage formats target devices support and to consider how your application will utilize these facilities. Knowing this will enable you to optimize your on-device data access and storage strategy based on your application's performance and reliability needs. An explicit understanding of long-term storage mechanisms will also aid you in efficiently porting a mobile application from one device class to another.

.NET Compact Framework Specific: ADO.NET

ADO.NET is powerful and multilayered programming model for working with relational data of all kinds. ADO.NET is available on desktops and servers as part of the .NET Framework and on devices as part of the .NET Compact Framework. The .NET Compact Framework's support for ADO.NET is a subset of the desktop and server programming model.

A key innovation in the ADO.NET data model for servers, desktops, and devices is that the ADO.NET DataSet itself is completely separated from the source of the data. Once data is in an ADO.NET DataSet, it can be serialized as XML and stored to a local file or it can be sent over a network to a server, desktop, or mobile device. No persistent connection is held between the ADO.NET DataSet and the databases where the data was acquired from; this is great for server scalability because persistent connections are detrimental to server scalability.

You Do Not Need to Use the DataSet Object in Your Application to Work with Databases

DataSets are wonderful abstractions, but are not always the right choice for every data access need. For read-only applications, it may make sense to work directly with the data coming out of the ADO.NET DataReader object and store it in the most efficient format for the task you are trying to accomplish. More on this later in the chapter.

The Very Basics of ADO.NET DataSets

ADO.NET offers many powerful concepts that can at first seem complicated and daunting to developers coming from other data access models. In reality, ADO.NET is quite easy to use, but it requires the developer to think in its model and this means letting go of the concept of the data cursor as the central mechanism for working with data.

To gain a better understanding, it is worth contrasting ADO.NET with its predecessor technology, ADO. As its name implies, an ADO.NET DataSet is closer to the mathematical idea of a "set of data" than it is to the traditional ADO idea of a record set that represents rows of records in a table and provides a cursor to iterate over them. ADO.NET DataSets are "cursorless," meaning that there is no concept of having a current record and a cursor that switches the context between records. In an ADO.NET DataSet all the records simply exist in a set and can be accessed nonsequentially without the need to cursor between current records. DataSets are also not table specific; an ADO.NET DataSet can contain any number of tables of data as well as information about the relations between tables. Old-style ADO RecordSet objects allow the iteration of one table of information, whereas ADO.NET DataSet objects allow the exploration of one or more tables of data.

The ADO.NET DataView and DataTable objects exist to bridge this "set-based" approach with the row-based model of working with data.

A DataSet can contain any number of DataTable objects. A data table is basically an array of objects similar to a table in a database. DataViews are objects that present filters and sorts on top of DataTable objects, allowing the contents of a DataSet to be distilled down to the data that is immediately interesting to your application. DataView objects can also provide a sorted view on the data so that it is ordered in the most convenient manner for your application's use and display. Any number of DataView objects can be associated with a DataTable, each with its own sorting and filtering criteria to supply a custom view onto the data.

The desktop and server .NET Framework supports both "untyped" and "typed" DataSets. The .NET Compact Framework specifically only supports "untyped DataSets." This sounds limiting, but in reality is not because typed DataSets are just classes that are built on top of untyped DataSets that bind strongly typed field names onto the underlying untyped DataSet elements. Because a typed DataSet is built on top of an untyped DataSet class, it actually represents a convenient-to-use but slightly slower abstraction. Applications that use untyped DataSets properly by looking up and caching the DataColumn objects of the fields they use (as opposed to looking up the fields by name every time they are used) will get as good or better performance than developers using typed DataSets.

A Very Brief Example of Using DataSets, DataTables, and XML

An example is useful in showing some of the basics of working with ADO.NET DataSets. The .NET Framework documentation offers a comprehensive description of ADO.NET and DataSets. This example only shows the very basics of creating and using a DataSet to set the context for discussing the use of ADO.NET on mobile devices.

The code in Listing 14.1 enables you to build the application shown in Figure 14.1. Do the following to build the application:

1. Start Visual Studio .NET (2003 or later) and create a C# Smart Device Application.
2. Choose Pocket PC as the target platform. (A project will be created for you and Pocket PC Form designer will appear.)
3. Add a Button control to the form designer. (It will be named button1.)
4. Add a TextBox to the form designer. (It will be named textBox1.)
5. Change the MultiLine property of the TextBox to be true and resize the TextBox to take up most of the form.
6. Change the ScrollBar property of the TextBox to be vertical.

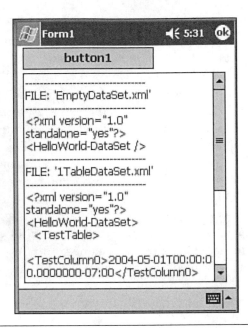

Figure 14.1 A simple example showing the creation of an ADO.NET DataSet.

7. Double-click the Button in the designer and fill in the code for
   `button1_Click()` in the listing.
8. Enter all of the remaining code in Listing 14.1.
9. Go back to the Form designer.
10. Set the MinimizeBox property of the form to false. At runtime this
    will give the form an OK box at the top-right corner that makes it
    easy to close the form and exit the application; this is very useful for
    repeated testing.
11. Run the application and click the Button; you should be able to re-
    produce the output shown in Figure 14.1.

Listing 14.1 Basic Creation and Use of an ADO.NET DataSet

```
//The DataSet we are going to load
System.Data.DataSet m_myDataSet;
//Constants we will use
const string FILE_EMPTY_DATASET = "EmptyDataSet.xml";
const string FILE_1TABLE_DATASET = "1TableDataSet.xml";
const string dividerLine = "---------------------------\r\n";
const string nextLine = "\r\n";
```

```
//---------------------------------------------------------
//Load the contents of a file and append it to the text
//in textBox1
//---------------------------------------------------------
private void addFileContentsToTextBox(string fileName)
{
  //Open the file and read in its contents
  System.IO.StreamReader myStreamReader;
  myStreamReader = System.IO.File.OpenText(fileName);
  string fileText = myStreamReader.ReadToEnd();
  //Close the file
  myStreamReader.Close();

  //Append the contents to the text in the text box
  textBox1.Text = textBox1.Text +
    dividerLine+ "FILE: '" + filcName + "'" + nextLine +
    dividerLine + fileText + nextLine;
}


//---------------------------------------------------------
//1. Creates a dataset,
//     persists dataset out as XML,
//     displays results in text box
//
//2. Adds a data table to the dataset,
//     adds two typed columns to the data table,
//     adds to rows to the data table
//     persists dataset out as XML,
//     displays results in text box
//---------------------------------------------------------
private void button1_Click(object sender, System.EventArgs e)
{
  //Clear the contents of the text box
  textBox1.Text = "";

  //=======================================
  //1. Create a new dataset
  //=======================================
  m_myDataSet = new System.Data.DataSet("HelloWorld-DataSet");

  //Write out the ADO.NET DataSet contents as XML and show
  //the file in the textbox
  m_myDataSet.WriteXml(FILE_EMPTY_DATASET);
  addFileContentsToTextBox(FILE_EMPTY_DATASET);
```

```
//===========================================
//2. Add a data table to the ADO.NET dataset
//   and add 2 rows of data to the data table
//===========================================
System.Data.DataTable myTestTable;
myTestTable = m_myDataSet.Tables.Add("TestTable");


//-----------------------------------
//Add 2 columns to the Table
//-----------------------------------
//Add a date column to the DataTable in the DataSet
myTestTable.Columns.Add("TestColumn0",
                        typeof(System.DateTime));
//Add a string colum to the DataTable in the DataSet
myTestTable.Columns.Add("TestColumn1", typeof(string));


//-----------------------------------
//Add data rows to the Table
//-----------------------------------
//Add a row of data to the data table
object[] rowOfData;
rowOfData = new object[2];
//Column 0 is a date type
rowOfData[0] = System.DateTime.Today;
//Column 1 is a string type
rowOfData[1] = "a string of data today";
myTestTable.Rows.Add(rowOfData);

//Add a 2nd row of data to the data table
object[] rowOfData2;
rowOfData2 = new object[2];
//Column 0 is a date type
rowOfData2[0] = System.DateTime.Today.AddDays(1);

//Column 1 is a string type
rowOfData2[1] = "tomorrow's string";
myTestTable.Rows.Add(rowOfData2);

//Write out the ADO.NET DataSet contents as XML and show
//the file in the textbox
m_myDataSet.WriteXml(FILE_1TABLE_DATASET);
addFileContentsToTextBox(FILE_1TABLE_DATASET);
} //End function
```

Tracking Changes in Data

ADO.NET DataSet objects automatically keep track of changes made to the data in them, including the creation, deletion, and change of rows of data in data tables. These changes can then be accepted or rejected and the accepted changes committed to a database when appropriate. If the source of the data is distributed among several databases, the data can even be updated using distributed transactions.

It is important to understand that ADO.NET DataSet objects do not know anything about the databases where the data permanently resides; for this, DataAdapter classes are used. The purpose of an ADO.NET Data-Adapter class is to move data between an ADO.NET DataSet's objects and long-term storage. All ADO.NET DataAdapter classes are custom code; the developer writes whatever logic is required to connect to, get data from, and update data to the data source being worked with. ADO.NET DataSets are essentially small in-memory databases and DataAdapter classes are written to synchronize DataSet data with database data; whether that database is on a device or server is known only to the data adapter's code.

DataAdapter objects can either exist on the client or on the server. If the data adapter is located on a server, a copy of the ADO.NET DataSet's data must be passed from client to server in order to be given to the data adapter there. The transfer of this DataSet from client to server is usually done by serializing the DataSet as XML, sending it to the server, and having the server reconstruct the DataSet from the XML. ADO.NET has built-in support to enable this. This model works well with Web services. Often there is a desire to remove the need for client devices to know about the underlying databases being accessed; this makes for a simpler architecture by centralizing access to the database on the server. In these cases, an ADO.NET DataSet's data is typically passed from a client device to a Web service running on the server. The Web service reloads the XML data into an ADO.NET DataSet and then passes it on to an ADO.NET data adapter, which then makes any necessary updates to the server. It is worth noting that ADO.NET DataSets have built-in efficiency mechanisms such as allowing you to pass only the DataSet data that has changed up to the server (known as a "diffgram"); this eliminates the need to move the whole DataSet's data around when only a few rows have changed.

Two Models for Use with ADO.NET

Because ADO.NET offers a layered approach to working with data, it enables you to choose the right level of programming abstraction appropriate for your mobile device application's needs and performance demands.

ADO.NET High-Level DataSet Centric Approach

At the highest level of data access abstraction, the .NET Compact Framework offers ADO.NET DataSets along with DataTable and DataView objects. Figure 14.2 shows the different logical tiers for this kind of an application. As discussed above, central to this model is the ADO.NET DataSet.

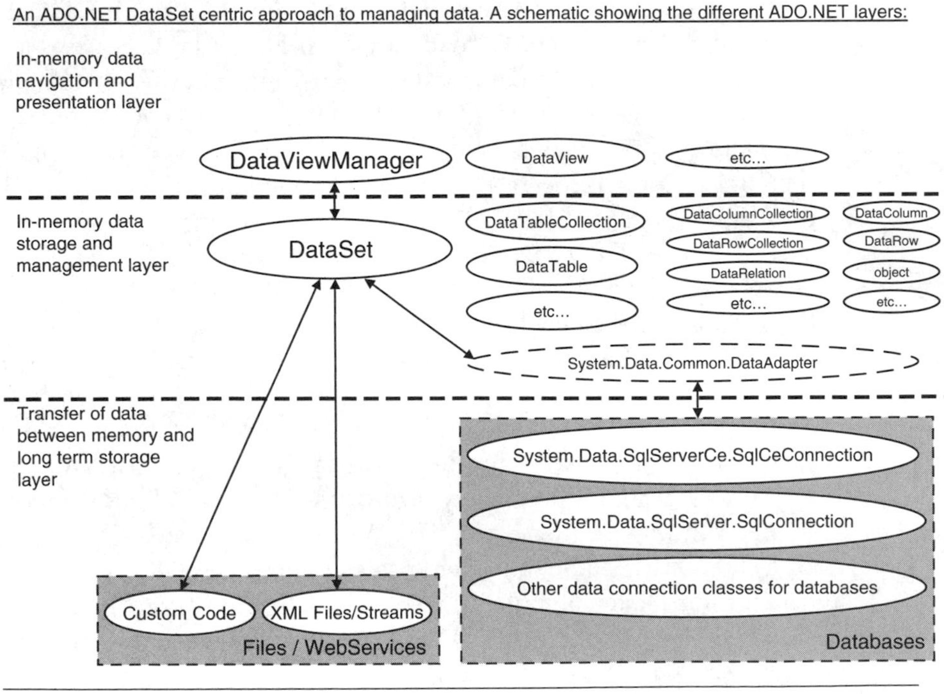

An ADO.NET DataSet centric approach to managing data. A schematic showing the different ADO.NET layers:

Figure 14.2 An ADO.NET DataSet centric approach to working with data.

ADO.NET Lower-Level Approach Using Data Connectors

The ADO.NET DataSet offers a powerful model for working with data but this comes at a cost of in-memory overhead for having additional objects created to abstract and manage your application's data and its interrelations. Sometimes this overhead may not be necessary or appropriate; in these cases, a lower-level alternative is worth considering. An alternative to the DataSet centric approach that still utilizes the lower-level abstractions of ADO.NET is shown in Figure 14.3. This model builds a custom data management model on top of the data connection objects that ADO.NET data providers supply. For example, SQL Server supplies a System.Data.SqlClient.SqlConnection class to access its database, and SQL CE supplies a System.Data.SqlServerCe.SqlCeConnection to do the same. These classes are typically used in conjunction with DataAdapter classes to transfer data to and from DataSet objects, but they can also be used on their own to move data into and out of your own data formats. This model can be significantly more memory efficient when the mobile application's data access needs are narrower in scope than the rich general-purpose features offered by the ADO.NET DataSet model. Figure 14.3 schematically shows what this relationship looks like.

An alternative to the ADO.NET DataSet centric approach.

This model uses custom logic for in-memory data management, presentation and navigation. ADO .NET database connection objects are still used. A schematic showing the different layers:

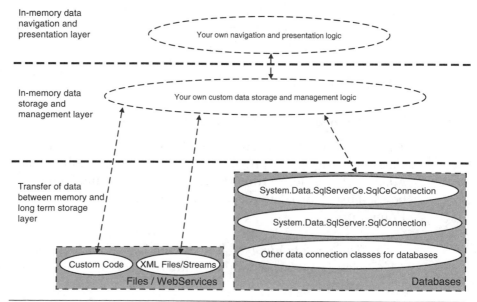

Figure 14.3 An alternative to using ADO.NET DataSets.

In choosing to use a lower-level approach, your application takes explicit responsibility for managing data loaded into memory, tracking any necessary changes, and committing these changes back to long-term storage as appropriate. The lower overhead of working at a lower abstraction level comes at the cost of more development responsibility to design and maintain an efficient data model.

The ADO.NET DataSet programming model is a great way of working with relational data, but it is not appropriate in every context. It is important to understand when and when not to use ADO.NET for your data access needs.

When to Use ADO.NET DataSets

It is appropriate to use ADO.NET DataSets if you have significant in-memory data-manipulation needs or the data needs to be traversed in a complex relational way. Because ADO.NET effectively maintains a small in-memory relational database for you that tracks changes made to the data, it can be a great way to automatically manage a set of highly dynamic data as well as to navigate relationships between pieces of data. ADO.NET DataSet objects are a good choice when (1) the size of the data you need to work with is not too great relative to the mobile device's memory capacity, *and* (2) the data is of a dynamic nature that requires the tracking and propagation of changes.

ADO.NET DataSet objects allow the transfer of data to and from long-term storage. This transfer is accomplished via one of three ways: (1) using DataAdapter classes that connect to databases via data connection objects, (2) serialization to or from XML files and streams, or (3) custom serialization code that reads data from or places data into the DataSet objects. The following list briefly describes each of these data-transfer methods.

Using DataAdapter Classes to Interact with Databases

The ADO.NET type System.Data.Common.DataAdapter is an *abstract* class, meaning that it provides a template other database-specific Data-Adapter classes derive from but is not a complete implementation that can be used itself. Two data adapters are shipped alongside the .NET Compact Framework:

1. *The SqlDataAdapter*—The System.Data.SqlClient.SqlDataAdapter class is used when working with SQL Server databases running on servers.

2. *The SqlCeDataAdapter*—The System.Data.SqlServerCe.SqlCe-DataAdapter is used when working with SQL CE databases running on the mobile device.

Third-party data adapters can be used to connect to other data sources. You can also author your own DataAdapter class if you have a custom data source you want to connect to.

Regardless of the data adapter chosen, DataAdapter objects work through "Command" objects that are attached to them. Unlike the Data-Adapter class, there is no root Command class from which other database-specific Command classes derive; the concept of a "Command" class is just a concept that various data adapters use. SqlDataAdapter objects have Sql-Command objects associated with them; SQL CE SqlCeDataAdapter objects have SqlCECommand objects, and so on. The Command objects in turn have Connection objects associated with them that map the commands to specific database instances; for example, a SqlCommand would use a Sql-Connection object to execute commands on a specific SQL Server connection. These Command objects execute the queries or other database commands that need to be performed to get data from or place data into the databases your application is using. The Command objects understand how to perform specific actions on the database they work with and execute SQL commands to select, update, insert, or delete data in them. For example, the SQLDataAdapter class has four properties for these four commands: the properties are named SelectCommand, UpdateCommand, DeleteCommand, and InsertCommand. Each of these properties is of type SqlCommand. Similarly, the SqlCeDataAdapter also has four properties with the same names, but the type of the properties is SQLCeCommand.

To recap: Data adapters broker communication between ADO.NET DataSets and databases. The data adapters typically use Command objects to do this. Command objects are specific to each type of database. Command objects in turn typically are associated with Connection objects that own the connection with a specific server. A Command object is typically the owner of SQL statements such as `Select * from Customers`, and the Connection objects own the logical connection with the database that gets these commands sent to them.

When you are building .NET desktop and server applications, Visual Studio .NET offers design-time tools to aid you in the configuration of data adapters and their associated Command classes; this simplifies accessing databases considerably. In contrast, creating and using a data adapter with the .NET Compact Framework will require you to manually write code for the DataAdapter and Command objects to configure them to work with your data sources. In the future, automated tools may also support the .NET Compact Framework and the DataAdapter and DataCommand classes for popular databases, but for now you are on your own. Because the desktop and server database tools work by autogenerating source code for applications, it can often be useful to look at the code generated and adapt this code for running on devices; some significant differences will exist but it is a good starting point.

Using XML Files and Streams to Store and Transfer Data

Storing an ADO.NET DataSet object's contents in an XML file can be thought of as "a poor man's database." Your application's data is stored in a text file in a format that can later be reloaded into memory as an ADO.NET DataSet. This is similar to getting a DataSet returned via a Web service request. In contrast to storing data in a database, using an XML text file for storage does not give your application the benefits of rich transactions and data integrity offered by modern databases. Despite this model's limitations for storing large amounts of data or providing transactional updates, it can be useful in storing small amounts of data (for example, 20KB XML files) or moving data up to a server via an XML stream. Think of XML-persisted DataSets as a simple way to package up a small to moderate amount of application state for later reuse.

When writing the contents of a DataSet to an XML file or stream it is important to look at the options offered by the System.Data.XmlWriteMode enumeration. For performance reasons, it is recommended to write out the XML schema (that is, use System.Data.XmlWriteMode.WriteSchema) when persisting DataSets to XML. Writing out the schema of the data along with the data itself can make reloading the XML into a DataSet significantly faster; if the schema is not explicitly persisted with the DataSet it will need to be dynamically inferred when the data is reloaded, and this requires additional work. Listing 14.2 shows a very simple example of DataSet to XML persistence. The sample allows the specification of the WriteSchema parameter.

To run the sample, add the code in Listing 14.2 to the code in Listing 14.1, and add a Button control that calls the `writeDataSetToFile` function.

Listing 14.2 Using XMLWriteMode When Persisting ADO.NET DataSets

```
//------------------------------------------------------------
//This function exists because the .NET Compact Framework does
//not support the overload:
// "public void WriteXml(string, XmlWriteMode);"
```

```
//
//as a "public" member (it is private)
//-----------------------------------------------------------
void writeDataSetToFile(System.Data.DataSet ds,
                        string filename,
                        System.Data.XmlWriteMode xmlWriteMode)
{

  //Create an XML TextWriter to write out our XML
  System.Xml.XmlWriter xmlWriter;
  xmlWriter = new System.Xml.XmlTextWriter(filename,
                    System.Text.Encoding.Default);

  //NOTE: This overload is not public!
  //ds.WriteXml(filename, xmlWriteMode);
  //Instead use...

  ds.WriteXml(xmlWriter, xmlWriteMode);
  xmlWriter.Close(); //It is important to close the file!
}
```

Using Custom Logic to Get Data into and out of ADO.NET DataSets

As described previously, ADO.NET DataSet objects have built-in support for persisting to XML. However, this XML format is not arbitrary; it is a specific XML schema intended for ADO.NET DataSets. If your application needs to write out to or read in from a different XML schema or any other format, you can do so by writing custom logic. The DataSet model is flexible enough to support any kind of persistence you dream up. Because the ADO.NET DataSet maintains a simple in-memory database independent of storage format, you can persist an ADO.NET DataSet into any format (for example, custom XML, binary, simple text) that is appropriate for your needs. The only caveat to doing this is to make sure you have a good reason for taking on this extra design work.

When writing custom deserialization code to populate a DataSet your application's code will need to programmatically build the tables, columns, and relational definitions and then populate the tables with the data you are importing. Similarly, when custom persisting a DataSet, your application logic will have to iterate through all the tables and persist out the data using whatever mechanism you require. A hybrid model can also be used to read from and write to different data sources; for example, a DataSet might be automatically populated by a SQLDataAdapter that connects to a SQL database and later this data may be serialized to a custom format local to the device. The ADO.NET DataSet does not care how data got placed into it or where the data came from.

Working with Untyped DataSets

The desktop and server .NET Framework offer the concept of a "typed DataSet." A typed DataSet is a strongly typed set of wrapper classes implemented via object inheritance on top of DataSet, DataTable, and other ADO.NET data objects. These inherited classes allow access to the underlying tables and rows in the DataSet using strongly typed class members with names matching the names of the tables and columns being worked with. For example, instead of using the late bound column name look up `myDataRow["CustomerFirstName"]` or requiring the use of a column index (for example, `myDataRow[2]`), the developer can use the early bound myDataRow.CustomerFirstName property. This design-time binding is what makes the DataSet "typed." The source code for typed DataSet's classes is automatically generated by the Visual Studio .NET design-time environment.

NOTE: It is important to note that strongly typed DataSets are not more efficient than untyped DataSets. This is a common and understandable misconception; it seems like early binding should be more efficient. However, typed DataSet early binding simply defers down to the DataSet's untyped core objects. Typed DataSet classes are not faster; they are simply easier to use. Having strongly typed wrapper objects allows design-time features such as auto statement completion to aid in developing code that uses the DataSet. Using strongly typed wrapper classes also allows some kinds of syntactical errors to be found at design time instead of at runtime. Beyond this, there is no performance advantage.

The .NET Compact Framework does not support compiling the desktop autogenerated typed DataSet code. This means that the most common way to work with a ADO.NET DataSet using the .NET Compact Framework is to work directly with the untyped DataSet class and its subordinate DataTable, DataColumn, and DataRow classes. Other than adding some complexity to your code and requiring you to be diligent to make sure you do not have typos in column or field names (a common error) code there are no disadvantages to using untyped DataSets. The fastest performance is achieved by working directly with the untyped DataSet classes themselves and not going through any wrapper layers.

Bringing Typed ADO.NET DataSets to Mobile Devices

Visual Studio .NET has design-time support for turning a data schema definition into typed DataSet source code. Unfortunately the .NET Compact Framework does not support all the types, properties, and methods present in this source code.

If you take the typed DataSet source code generated for a desktop project and copy/paste it into a .NET Compact Framework project, you will get a few compilation errors when you compile the project. The compilation errors fall into three categories:

1. Some of these errors are due to class and function meta data attributes that are not supported by the .NET Compact Framework; this meta data can be commented out. For example, the meta data attribute `[System.Component-Model.ToolboxItem(`**`true`**`)]` is not supported and can be commented out.

2. Some of these errors are due to missing exception types; more generic exceptions can be thrown instead. For example, because the .NET Compact Framework does not define the exception `new StrongTypingException()` the generic exception `new Exception()` can be used instead.

3. Some of these errors are due to autogenerated code that relies on functionality that the .NET Compact Framework does not support; functions using this functionality can be commented out.

It is not particularly difficult to get desktop project typed DataSet code to compile with the .NET Compact Framework; doing so may be a good way to borrow some useful typed DataSet concepts and use them in your mobile device application.

Rather then taking desktop code and trimming down, a more robust way to go about supporting typed DataSet access would be to create your own typed DataSet, DataTable, and DataRow classes from scratch by deriving strongly typed classes from these core ADO.NET types and then only importing selected pieces of desktop project autogenerated code as needed.

Building from the bottom up and adding code only as needed is a much more robust way to go versus taking desktop code and trying to trim it down until things work. You will end up with a much better-understood, engineered and maintainable piece of code if built from the ground up. Desktop code should be thought of as something to learn from but not to copy directly.

Getting the Best Performance from ADO.NET DataSet Objects

When working with DataSets, it is important to keep efficiency in mind. It is almost equally as easy to write efficient ADO.NET code as it is to write poorly performing code. A common inefficiency mistake developers make is to look up tables and columns using their string names rather than using more efficient indexing mechanisms. This is particularly important for accessing fields inside rows of data because this is an operation that is often done in loops iterating over significant numbers of rows. When accessing a field of data inside a data row, there are three ways to reference the item. In order of increasing performance, they are as follows:

1. *String-based field lookup*—For example: `myRow["myColumnName"]`; this is the slowest way because the string name of the column must be compared with available columns to find the correct field.
2. *Integer index-based field lookup*—For example: `myRow[2]`; this is a moderate improvement over string-based lookup because an integer is used. To use this mechanism, your code must look up and cache the integer index of the column in advance.
3. *Column object-based field lookup*—For example: `myRow-[myColumnObject]`; where `myColumnObject` represents an object of type System.Data.DataColumn. This is a significant improvement in performance over the previous two mechanisms. To use this mechanism, your code must cache the column object that represents the field you want to use.

Listing 14.3 contains code to test the relative performance of the three different approaches described above. The code simulates the common data processing task of record lookup and modification.

The scenario:

Mobile devices are being used to allow agents working for a transportation company to make changes to customer travel information while in the field. A situation such as a big snowstorm occasionally occurs that requires the ability to change the travel plans of a set of customers waiting in a travel terminal or currently in mid-transport on a train or airplane. These customers have connections that need to be updated and travel plans that need to be revised. The simplest way to accomplish this is to arm the employees with mobile devices that contain the travel information for the customers. Having a mobile device application allows multiple agents to go out and solve the customers' problems without forcing customers to queue up in a line and often allows them to have new travel arrangements completed even before their current train or airplane completes its trip. The mobile devices contain a downloaded list of customers and their travel details. To make finding customers' records fast and less error-prone, the mobile devices are equipped with readers that can scan in a passenger's credit card number and do lookups based on this key. After customers' records are found, their travel date can be updated with new information.

Our test code will simplify this scenario and use only customer name, travel date, and credit card number in its data table. In reality, of course, there is much more data that would need to be accessed, but this simplified example contains all the basic components; there is on-device data, there is the need to look it up, and the need to make changes to it. Because real-world scenarios would do even more data lookups, the performance results for real-world scenarios should be able to be extrapolated from this simple test.

Table 14.1 shows the results of running the test on a physical Pocket PC device. Unsurprisingly, the text-based column lookup (column A) performs the worst, completing the test in 32.82 seconds. Integer-based lookup (column B) offers a respectable 8 percent improvement by completing the test in 30.28 seconds. Data column-based lookup (column C) offers a 28 percent improvement over string-based lookup in the test case below. These gains are significant and point to the benefits of caching DataColumn objects when doing loop operations that look up data in data tables.

Table 14.1 Physical Pocket PC Performance Processing 500 Interations × 201 Data Rows

Trial #	(A) Text Index (Seconds)	(B) Integer Index (Seconds)	(C) DataColumn Object Index (Seconds)
1	32.538	30.09	23.554
2	33.063	30.387	23.491
3	32.87	30.372	23.582
Average	32.82	30.28	23.54
Relative performance	100%	92%	72%

The code in Listing 14.3 belongs inside a form in a Pocket PC project. Do the following to build and run the application:

1. Start Visual Studio .NET (2003 or later) and create a C# Smart Device Application.
2. Choose Pocket PC as the target platform. (A project will be created for you and a Pocket PC Form designer will appear.)

3. Add a Button control to the Form. Rename it **buttonRunTest**.
4. Double-click the Button in the Form designer. In the event handler function generated and hooked up for you, enter the `buttonRunTest_Click()` code shown in Listing 14.3.
5. Enter the rest of the code into the same class.
6. Set the MinimizeBox property of the form to false. At runtime, this will give the form an OK box at the top right that makes it easy to close the form and exit the application; this is very useful for repeated testing.
7. Run the application by pressing F5. Click the button to run the three performance tests in series. A message box should be shown following each test containing the test results.

Listing 14.3 Comparing the Performance of Different DataSet Access Methods

```
System.Data.DataSet m_myDataSet; //Dataset for test

//Column and table indexes to cache
private bool m_indexesLookedUp = false;
private const int INVALID_INDEX = -1;
private int  m_IndexOfTestColumn_CreditCard = INVALID_INDEX;
private int  m_IndexOfTestColumn_TravelDate = INVALID_INDEX;
private int  m_IndexOfTestTable = INVALID_INDEX;

//Data columns and table to cache
System.Data.DataColumn m_TestColumn_CreditCard;
System.Data.DataColumn m_TestColumn_TravelDate;
private System.Data.DataTable m_TableCustomerInfo;

//3 different kinds of tests we can run
public enum testType
{ textColumnLookup,  cachedIndexLookup,  cachedColumnObject }

//These determine the size of the test
const int DUMMY_ROWS_OF_DATA = 100;
const int NUMBER_TEST_ITERATIONS = 500;

//Datatable information
const string TABLE_NAME_PASSENGERINFO = "CustomerTravelInfo";
const string COLUMN_NAME_DATE_OF_TRAVEL = "DateOfTravel";
const string COLUMN_NAME_PASSENGER_NAME = "PassengerName";
const string COLUMN_NAME_PASSENGER_CREDIT_CARD = "PassengerCreditCard";
```

```csharp
const string TEST_CREDIT_CARD = "IvoCard-987-654-321-000";

//------------------------------------------------------------
//Creates the dataset
//------------------------------------------------------------
private void createDataSet()
{
  //1. Create a new DataSet
m_myDataSet = new System.Data.DataSet("TravelService Dataset");

  //2. Add a DataTable to the ADO.NET DataSet
  System.Data.DataTable myTestTable;
 myTestTable = m_myDataSet.Tables.Add(TABLE_NAME_PASSENGERINFO);

  //Add 2 columns to the table
  //Add a date column to the DataTable in the DataSet
  myTestTable.Columns.Add(COLUMN_NAME_DATE_OF_TRAVEL,
    typeof(System.DateTime));
  //Add a string colum to the DataTable in the DataSet
  myTestTable.Columns.Add(COLUMN_NAME_PASSENGER_NAME,
    typeof(string));

  //Add a string colum to the DataTable in the DataSet
    myTestTable.Columns.Add(COLUMN_NAME_PASSENGER_CREDIT_CARD,
    typeof(string));

  //Data to place into the data row
  object[] objArray;
  objArray = new object[3];

  //-----------------------------------
  //Add data rows to the table
  //-----------------------------------
  System.Text.StringBuilder buildTestString;
  buildTestString = new System.Text.StringBuilder();
  for(int addItemsCount = 0; addItemsCount < DUMMY_ROWS_OF_DATA;
addItemsCount++)
  {
    //Pick a travel day for the passenger
    objArray[0] = System.DateTime.Today.AddDays(addItemsCount);

    //Pick a name for the passenger
    buildTestString.Length = 0;
    buildTestString.Append("TestPersonName");
```

```
  buildTestString.Append(addItemsCount);
  objArray[1] = buildTestString.ToString();

  //Assign the passenger a text credit card number
  buildTestString.Length = 0;
  buildTestString.Append("IvoCard-000-000-0000-");
  buildTestString.Append(addItemsCount);
  objArray[2] = buildTestString.ToString();

  //Add the items in the array to the dataset row
  myTestTable.Rows.Add(objArray);
}

//Add the item we want to search for in our test...
objArray[0] = System.DateTime.Today;
objArray[1] = "Ms. TestPerson";
objArray[2] = TEST_CREDIT_CARD;

//Add the items in the array to the dataset row
myTestTable.Rows.Add(objArray);
} //End function


//-------------------------------------------------------
//Look up and cache all the dataset indexes we will need
//-------------------------------------------------------
private void cacheDataSetInfo()
{
  //Exit if we've already loaded the indexes
  if (m_indexesLookedUp == true) {return;}

  //Cache the index of the table
  m_IndexOfTestTable =
    m_myDataSet.Tables.IndexOf(TABLE_NAME_PASSENGERINFO);

  //-------------------------------------------------------
  //Iterate through all the columns in our table definition
  //and cache the indexes of the ones we want
  //-------------------------------------------------------
  m_TableCustomerInfo = m_myDataSet.Tables[m_IndexOfTestTable];

  int dataColumnCount = m_TableCustomerInfo.Columns.Count;
  System.Data.DataColumn myColumn;
  for(int colIdx = 0; colIdx < dataColumnCount;)
```

```
    {
      myColumn = m_TableCustomerInfo.Columns[colIdx];

      //Only try a lookup if we haven't already
      if (m_IndexOfTestColumn_CreditCard == INVALID_INDEX)
      {
        //See if the name matches
        if (myColumn.ColumnName ==
            COLUMN_NAME_PASSENGER_CREDIT_CARD)
        {
          //Cache the index
          m_IndexOfTestColumn_CreditCard = colIdx;

          //Cache the column
          m_TestColumn_CreditCard = myColumn;
          goto next_loop_iteration; //Skip other compares...
        } //Endif string compare
      } //Endif

      if (m_IndexOfTestColumn_TravelDate == INVALID_INDEX)
      {
        //See if the name matches
        if (myColumn.ColumnName ==
            COLUMN_NAME_DATE_OF_TRAVEL)
        {
          //Cache the index
          m_IndexOfTestColumn_TravelDate = colIdx;
          //Cache the column
          m_TestColumn_TravelDate = myColumn;
          goto next_loop_iteration; //Skip other compares...
        } //Endif string compare
      } //Endif

next_loop_iteration:
    colIdx++;
  }
  m_indexesLookedUp = true;
}


//-----------------------------------------------
//Run the test...
//-----------------------------------------------
void changeDayOfTravel_test(testType kindOfTest)
{
```

```csharp
//Show wait cursor
System.Windows.Forms.Cursor.Current =
  System.Windows.Forms.Cursors.WaitCursor;

//Start at a known date....
System.DateTime newDate;
newDate = System.DateTime.Today;
changeDayOfTravel_textColumnLookup(TEST_CREDIT_CARD, newDate);

//TEST CODE ONLY!!!
//Calling garbage collector in code will SLOW DOWN your app!
System.GC.Collect();
const int testNumber = 0;

//Set up properly depending on which test we are running
switch(kindOfTest)
{
  case testType.textColumnLookup:
    PerformanceSampling.StartSample(testNumber,
          "Text based Column lookup.");
    break;

  case testType.cachedIndexLookup:
    PerformanceSampling.StartSample(testNumber,
                "Cached Column Index lookup.");
    break;

  case testType.cachedColumnObject:
    PerformanceSampling.StartSample(testNumber,
                "Cached Column objects");
    break;

  default:
    throw new Exception("Unknown state!");
}

//Run the test!
for(int testCount = 0;
    testCount < NUMBER_TEST_ITERATIONS; testCount++)
{
  //Move the date forward one day
  newDate = newDate.AddDays(1);
  int numberRecordsChanged = 0;
```

```csharp
//Which kind of test are we running?
switch(kindOfTest)
{
  case testType.textColumnLookup:
    //BAD PERFORMANCE: Look up all names using STRINGS
    numberRecordsChanged =
        changeDayOfTravel_textColumnLookup(
                TEST_CREDIT_CARD, newDate);
    break;

  case testType.cachedIndexLookup:
    //BETTER PERFORMANCE: Use cached indexes
    numberRecordsChanged =
      changeDayOfTravel_cachedColumnIndex(
                TEST_CREDIT_CARD, newDate);
    break;

  case testType.cachedColumnObject:
    //BEST PERFORMANCE: Use cached colum objects
    numberRecordsChanged =
      changeDayOfTravel_CachedColumns(
                TEST_CREDIT_CARD, newDate);
    break;
}

//Make sure the test is running as expected...
if(numberRecordsChanged != 1)
{
  System.Windows.Forms.MessageBox.Show(
    "No matching records found. Test aborted!");
  return;
}
}
//Get the time it took to run the test
PerformanceSampling.StopSample(testNumber);

//Normal cursor
System.Windows.Forms.Cursor.Current =
  System.Windows.Forms.Cursors.Default;

//Show the test results
string runInfo = NUMBER_TEST_ITERATIONS.ToString() + "x" +
  DUMMY_ROWS_OF_DATA.ToString() + ": ";
System.Windows.Forms.MessageBox.Show(runInfo +
```

```
                PerformanceSampling.GetSampleDurationText(testNumber));
}


//POOR PERFORMANCE SEARCH FUNCTION
private int changeDayOfTravel_textColumnLookup(
        string creditCardNumber, System.DateTime newTravelDate)
{
  int numberRecordsChanged = 0;
  //Look up the table name
  System.Data.DataTable dataTable_Customers;
  //BAD PERFORMANCE: Look up table by string comparison!
  dataTable_Customers =
    m_myDataSet.Tables[TABLE_NAME_PASSENGERINFO];

  foreach(System.Data.DataRow currentCustomerRow in
                        dataTable_Customers.Rows)
  {
    string currentCreditCard;
    //BAD PERFORMANCE: Look up table by string comparison!
    currentCreditCard = (string)
      currentCustomerRow[COLUMN_NAME_PASSENGER_CREDIT_CARD];
    //See if this is the credit card we are looking for
    if(creditCardNumber == currentCreditCard)
    {
      //Change the date of travel
      //BAD PERFORMANCE: Look up column by string comparison!
      System.DateTime currentTravelDate = (System.DateTime)
          currentCustomerRow[COLUMN_NAME_DATE_OF_TRAVEL];

      if(currentTravelDate != newTravelDate)
      {
        //BAD PERFORMANCE: Look up column by string comparison!
        currentCustomerRow[COLUMN_NAME_DATE_OF_TRAVEL] =
            newTravelDate;
        numberRecordsChanged++;
      }
    } //endif: string compare
  } //end foreach

    return numberRecordsChanged; //# updated records
  }


//SLIGHTLY BETTER PERFORMANCE FUNCTION
private int changeDayOfTravel_cachedColumnIndex(
```

```csharp
      string creditCardNumber, System.DateTime newTravelDate)
{
  int numberRecordsChanged = 0;
  //Look up the table name
  System.Data.DataTable dataTable_Customers;
  //BETTER PERFORMANCE: use a cached index
  dataTable_Customers =
    m_myDataSet.Tables[m_IndexOfTestTable];

  foreach(System.Data.DataRow currentCustomerRow in
        dataTable_Customers.Rows)
  {
    string currentCreditCard;
    //BETTER PERFORMANCE: User a cached column index!
    currentCreditCard = (string)
      currentCustomerRow[m_IndexOfTestColumn_CreditCard];
  //See if there is a card number matches...
    if(creditCardNumber == currentCreditCard)
    {
      //Change the date of travel
      //BETTER PERFORMANCE: User a cached column index!
      System.DateTime currentTravelDate = (System.DateTime)
          currentCustomerRow[m_IndexOfTestColumn_TravelDate];

      if(currentTravelDate != newTravelDate)
      {
        //BETTER PERFORMANCE: User a cached column index!
        currentCustomerRow[m_IndexOfTestColumn_TravelDate] =
                      newTravelDate;
        numberRecordsChanged++;
      }
    }
  }
  return numberRecordsChanged;   //# updated records
}

//BEST PERFORMANCE FUNCTION
private int changeDayOfTravel_CachedColumns(
      string creditCardNumber, System.DateTime newTravelDate)
{
  int numberRecordsChanged = 0;
  //Look up the table name
  System.Data.DataTable dataTable_Customers =
                      m_TableCustomerInfo;
```

```csharp
     foreach(System.Data.DataRow currentCustomerRow in
             dataTable_Customers.Rows)
     {
       string currentCreditCard;
       //BEST PERFORMANCE: User a cached column index!
       currentCreditCard = (string)
           currentCustomerRow[m_TestColumn_CreditCard];
       //See if there is a card number matches...
       if(creditCardNumber == currentCreditCard)
       {
         //Change the date of travel
         //BEST PERFORMANCE: User a cached column index!
         System.DateTime currentTravelDate = (System.DateTime)
             currentCustomerRow[m_TestColumn_TravelDate];
         if(currentTravelDate != newTravelDate)
         {
           //BEST PERFORMANCE: User a cached column index!
           currentCustomerRow[m_TestColumn_TravelDate] =
                 newTravelDate;
           numberRecordsChanged++;
         }
       }
     }
     return numberRecordsChanged;   //# updated records
}

//Button click event
private void buttonRunTest_Click(object sender,
                                    System.EventArgs e)
{
   createDataSet();   cacheDataSetInfo();

   //BAD PERFORMANCE: Use string to based lookups
   changeDayOfTravel_test(testType.textColumnLookup);

   //BETTER PERFORMANCE: Use integer based lookups
   changeDayOfTravel_test(testType.cachedIndexLookup);

   //BEST PERFORMANCE: Use column object based lookups
   changeDayOfTravel_test(testType.cachedColumnObject);
}
```

When Not to Use ADO.NET DataSet Objects

If your mobile device application's data is mostly read-only, if you have a large amount of data you need to keep in memory, or if your data's relationships are relatively simple, it is worth considering a customized data management model. ADO.NET DataSet objects are efficiently implemented, but they are a general-purpose data management model. Significant size and performance benefits can be realized by creating a specific data model that most efficiently meets your needs. The key to size efficiency is reducing the number of objects that need to be allocated to hold your data; fewer objects generally result in lower memory pressure and better application performance.

Table 14.2 and Listing 14.4 show the results of using an optimized custom data format for storing rows of data. The test code in Listing 14.4 accomplishes the same functional task as the code above in Listing 14.3 but does so using simple typed arrays of data instead of an ADO.NET DataSet. This benefits the application's performance in two specific ways:

1. *Execution performance*—As can be seen in Table 14.2, the custom data format runs in 38 percent of the time that the ADO.NET text index solution does. Comparing it to the optimized "column object" lookup shows that the custom data format solution runs in almost half the time as the most optimized ADO.NET result we could achieve with the code above (12.32 / 23.54 = 52.3 percent).

2. *Lower memory pressure*—Because the custom data format solution has only the minimum of objects required to hold the data and does not have any of the additional overhead of ADO.NET DataSets, our application will have lower memory pressure. All else being equal, this means fewer garbage collections and more working room for other code in our application. This result is not reflected in the table but is an overall application-wide performance advantage.

Of course, a custom data format solution has some disadvantages compared to ADO.NET as well. Most notably, if the data is going to need to be updated to a server, our code will need to manually keep track of changes made to the data. This means introducing at least one more column of Boolean data to indicate which rows have been updated. This may be easy for simple tabular data, but will be more complicated for data that has rich relationships between multiple tables of data. In addition, ADO.NET offers rich DataView objects to do sorting and filtering of data that are not available in custom data implementations. With richness comes overhead, and your application will need to make a prudent trade-off between the richness of ADO.NET and the potentially higher efficiency of a custom implementations. For device applications, the choice of high efficiency is often worth the additional design burdens that custom data models require.

Table 14.2 Physical Pocket PC Performance Contrasting Custom Format with ADO.NET Datasets

Trial	(A) Text Index (Seconds)	(B) Integer Index (Seconds)	(C) DataColumn Index (Seconds)	(D) Custom Data Format (s)
	(ADO.NET)	(ADO.NET)	(ADO.NET)	(Custom)
1	32.538	30.09	23.554	12.268
2	33.063	30.387	23.491	12.335
3	32.87	30.372	23.582	12.358
Average	32.82	30.28	23.54	12.32
Relative performance	100%	92%	72%	38%

The code in Listing 14.4 belongs inside a form in a Pocket PC project. Do the following to build and run the application:

1. Start Visual Studio .NET (2003 or later) and create a C# Smart Device Application.
2. Choose Pocket PC as the target platform. (A project will be created for you and a Pocket PC Form designer will appear.)
3. Add a Button control to the form and rename it **buttonRunTest**.
4. For the control above, double-click the button in the form designer. In the event handler function generated and hooked up for you, enter the `buttonRunTest_Click()` code shown in Listing 14.4.
5. Enter the rest of the code into the same class.
6. Set the MinimizeBox property of the form to false. At runtime this will give the form an OK box at the top right that makes it easy to close the form and exit the application; this is very useful for repeated testing.
7. Run the application by hitting F5. Click the Button to run the performance test. A MessageBox should show the results of the test.

Listing 14.4 Testing the Performance of Using a Custom Data Format Instead of a DataSet

```csharp
//These determine the size of the test
const int DUMMY_ROWS_OF_DATA = 100;
const int NUMBER_TEST_ITERATIONS = 500;

const string TABLE_NAME_PASSENGERINFO = "CustomerTravelInfo";
const string TEST_CREDIT_CARD = "IvoCard-987-654-321-000";

string [] m_data_creditCards;
string [] m_data_names;
System.DateTime [] m_data_travelDates;

//-----------------------------------------------------------
//Creates the arrays of data (instead of using a dataset)
//-----------------------------------------------------------
private void createDataSet()
{
  //========================================
  //1. Create the space for our data
  //========================================
  m_data_creditCards = new string[DUMMY_ROWS_OF_DATA + 1];
  m_data_names = new string[DUMMY_ROWS_OF_DATA + 1];
  m_data_travelDates =
      new System.DateTime[DUMMY_ROWS_OF_DATA + 1];

  //-----------------------------------
  //Add the rows of data
  //-----------------------------------
  System.Text.StringBuilder buildTestString;
  buildTestString = new System.Text.StringBuilder();
  for(int addItemsCount = 0; addItemsCount < DUMMY_ROWS_OF_DATA;
      addItemsCount++)
  {
    //Pick a travel day for the passenger
    m_data_travelDates[addItemsCount] =
      System.DateTime.Today.AddDays(addItemsCount);

    //-----------------------------------
    //Pick a name for the passenger
    //-----------------------------------
    //Clear the text of the string
    buildTestString.Length = 0;
```

```
    buildTestString.Append("TestPersonName");
    buildTestString.Append(addItemsCount);
    m_data_names[addItemsCount] = buildTestString.ToString();


    //-----------------------------------
    //Assign the passenger a text credit card number
    //-----------------------------------
    //A string for the third dataset column value
    buildTestString.Length = 0;
    buildTestString.Append("IvoCard-000-000-0000-");
    buildTestString.Append(addItemsCount);
    m_data_creditCards[addItemsCount] =
                        buildTestString.ToString();
  }


  //Add the item we want to search for in our test...
  //Pick a day for the first dataset column value
  m_data_travelDates[DUMMY_ROWS_OF_DATA] =
                            System.DateTime.Today;
  //A string for the second dataset column  value
  m_data_names[DUMMY_ROWS_OF_DATA] = "Ms. TestPerson";
  //A string credit-card ID
  m_data_creditCards[DUMMY_ROWS_OF_DATA] = TEST_CREDIT_CARD;
} //End function


//--------------------------------------------------
//Run the test...
//--------------------------------------------------
void changeDayOfTravel_test()
{
  //Show wait cursor
  System.Windows.Forms.Cursor.Current =
    System.Windows.Forms.Cursors.WaitCursor;

  //Start at a known date....
  System.DateTime newDate;
  newDate = System.DateTime.Today;
  changeDayOfTravel_CustomArrays(TEST_CREDIT_CARD, newDate);

  //TEST CODE ONLY!!!
  //Do NOT call the garbage collector in production
  //code. It will SLOW DOWN your application performance
  System.GC.Collect();
  const int testNumber = 0;
```

```csharp
        //Start the timer running for the test
        PerformanceSampling.StartSample(testNumber,
                     "Custom Array implementation");

        //Run the test!
        for(int testCount = 0;
          testCount < NUMBER_TEST_ITERATIONS; testCount++)
        {

            //Move the date forward one day
            newDate = newDate.AddDays(1);
            int numberRecordsChanged = 0;

            //Look up all names using STRINGS
            numberRecordsChanged =
                  changeDayOfTravel_CustomArrays(
                  TEST_CREDIT_CARD, newDate);

            //Make sure the test is running as expected...
            if(numberRecordsChanged != 1)
            {
              System.Windows.Forms.MessageBox.Show(
                "No matching records found. Test aborted!");
              return;
            }
        }
        //Get the time it took to run the test
        PerformanceSampling.StopSample(testNumber);

        //Normal cursor
        System.Windows.Forms.Cursor.Current =
          System.Windows.Forms.Cursors.Default;

        //Show the test results
        string runInfo = NUMBER_TEST_ITERATIONS.ToString() + "x" +
          DUMMY_ROWS_OF_DATA.ToString() + ": ";
        System.Windows.Forms.MessageBox.Show(runInfo +
          PerformanceSampling.GetSampleDurationText(testNumber));
    }

    private int changeDayOfTravel_CustomArrays(
      string creditCardNumber, System.DateTime newTravelDate)
    {
      int numberRecordsChanged = 0;
```

```csharp
//Look at each item in the array
for(int index = 0; index <= DUMMY_ROWS_OF_DATA; index++)
{
  string currentCreditCard;
  currentCreditCard = m_data_creditCards[index];

  //If there is a match, update the record
  if(creditCardNumber == currentCreditCard)
  {
    //Change the date of travel
    System.DateTime currentTravelDate =
      m_data_travelDates[index];

    //Only count the update if the date does not match
    if(currentTravelDate != newTravelDate)
    {
      m_data_travelDates[index] =
        newTravelDate;
      numberRecordsChanged++;
    }
  }
}
//Return the number of records we updated
return numberRecordsChanged;
}

private void buttonRunTest_Click(object sender,
                                 System.EventArgs e)
{
  createDataSet();
  changeDayOfTravel_test();
}
```

An Example of Using Custom Data Management and On-Device Databases

To illustrate custom in-memory representation and management of data read in from a database, it is useful to return an example from a previous chapter. For this example, we will consider again the foreign-language vocabulary game we designed the user interface for in Chapter 13, "Step 2: Design the Right User Interface." Previously we examined user interface design issues for this mobile application and now we will investigate the storage and in-memory representation of the vocabulary words themselves. Because the dictionary of words that we would like to use for this mobile application is potentially large, it is desirable to store the data in a database for fast access, efficiency, and flexibility reasons. The data is primarily read-only in nature; the user may add additional words occasionally, but dynamic updates to the existing data are not a primary requirement. In addition, the structure of the data is simple and can easily be represented in a single database table. All of these reasons—the potentially large number of records, the low frequency of updates, and the simplicity of the data's structure—make the ADO.NET DataSet approach overkill for our needs. We can build an optimized solution that uses the lower-level SQL CE data reader (System.Data. SqlServerCe.SqlCeDataReader) to execute a query on our device's local SQL CE database. The query will return our application a forward-only cursor to data meeting our query criteria. This data can then be custom loaded into memory and stored in a format specifically designed to work with vocabulary-word data efficiently. For simplicity and speed, these objects will be placed into arrays. This can save us a significant amount of time and object allocation over a generic DataSet approach because we are only allocating objects we know we will use in our application.

It is worth noting that for simplicity the example does two things that would be unlikely in a real mobile device application:

1. *It fills the contents of the database using the same application that loads the data from the database.* If we knew at design time all the data that was needed by the application at runtime, there is little need for an external database; the application could just populate its in-memory data structures directly from code and forego the overhead of any database. In a real version of this application, we would create and populate the database by one of the three following mechanisms: (a) downloading a fully populated database file to the device, the database having been prebuilt by us earlier; (b) synchronizing the SQL CE database with a server-based SQL server; and (c) running and then discarding a single-purpose application that created and populated the database.

2. *It loads all of the data into memory at once.* As noted above, the vocabulary dictionary for our application is potentially large. If we have 20,000 vocabulary words in our database, we probably do not want to read them all into memory at once. The user receives no particular benefit from us doing this because they only get to work with a small set of words at any given time. What we should do is choose a reasonable limit for the number of vocabulary words our application will load into memory at any given time; the application can then periodically refresh the in-memory cache with new words. For example, if

we want to keep an in-memory dictionary of no more than 500 words out of a total database dictionary of 20,000, only 1 of 40 words needs be loaded into memory at any given time. It would be easy to update the code that reads in vocabulary words to give each word it encountered a 1/40 random probability of being loaded. Other strategies for keeping the in-memory word count down are also possible such as grouping the words into related sets that are loaded together (for example, easy words, more difficult words, very difficult words). In any case, we want our mobile device application to have a memory management system that makes sure only a limited number of words are loaded into memory at any given time so that regardless of the size of the database our application performs in a predictable and acceptable way.

The code in Listing 14.5 belongs inside a form in a Pocket PC project. The code in Listings 14.6, 14.7, and 14.8 are separate classes listed in their entirety. Do the following to build and run the application:

1. Start Visual Studio .NET (2003 or later) and create a C# Smart Device Application.
2. Choose Pocket PC as the target platform. (A project will be created for you and a Pocket PC Form designer will appear.)
3. Add a project reference to SqlServerCe. This can be done by right-clicking the References node in the Solution Explorer TreeView and

After creation of database…   After loading from database…

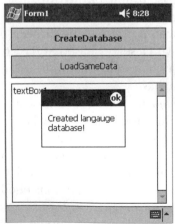

Figure 14.4 Example of non–DataSet-using data management.

then selecting the System.Data.SqlServerCe item. This reference allows our application to use classes in the System.Data.SqlServerCe assembly, giving us access to the SQL CE programming model.

4. Add the following controls to the form:
   a. A button, rename it **buttonCreateDatabase**.
   b. A button, rename it **buttonLoadGameData**.
   c. A text box, leave it named **textBox1**.
5. Set TextBox's Multiline property to True.
6. Set the TextBox's ScrollBars property to Vertical.
7. For each of the Button controls above, double-click the button in the Form designer. In the event handler function generated and hooked up for you, enter the button<*ButtonName*>_Click code shown in Listing 14.5.
8. Set the MinimizeBox property of the form to false. At runtime this will give the form an OK box at the top right that makes it easy to close the form and exit the application; this is very useful for repeated testing.
9. To the project, add a class called DatabaseAccess, erase all the default code that was placed into the class editor, and enter the code in Listing 14.6.
10. To the project, add a class called GameData, erase all the default code that was placed into the class editor, and enter the code in Listing 14.7.
11. To the project, add a class called VocabularyWord, erase all the default code that was placed into the class editor, and enter the code in Listing 14.8.
12. Run the application by pressing F5. The application's user interface should look similar to that shown in Figure 14.4. Click the buttonCreateDatabase to create and populate the SQL CE database. Click the buttonLoadGameData to load the contents of the database into memory for use; this should display the vocabulary words in the text box.

Listing 14.5 Custom Data Management Sample—Code That Goes Inside Form1.cs

```
//Creates the database
private void buttonCreateDatabase_Click(object sender,
                                        System.EventArgs e)
{
  DatabaseAccess.CreateAndFillDatabase();
}
```

```
//Loads the data from the database and displays it
private void buttonLoadGameData_Click(object sender,
                                        System.EventArgs e)
{
  //Clear the text box
  textBox1.Text = "";

  //Load the data for the words
  GameData.InitializeGameVocabulary();

  //Go through each of the words and add it to our text list
  System.Text.StringBuilder thisStringBuilder;
  thisStringBuilder = new System.Text.StringBuilder();
  foreach(VocabularyWord thisWord in GameData.AllWords)
  {
    thisStringBuilder.Append(thisWord.EnglishWord);
    thisStringBuilder.Append(" = ");
    thisStringBuilder.Append(
            thisWord.GermanWordWithArticleIfExists);
    thisStringBuilder.Append("\r\n"); //New line
  }
  //Show the list of word in the text box
  textBox1.Text = thisStringBuilder.ToString();
}
```

Listing 14.6 Custom Data Management Sample—Code for DatabaseAccess.cs

```
//----------------------------------------------------------
//Database access code
//
//This class manages our applications database access
//----------------------------------------------------------

using System;

internal class DatabaseAccess
{
const string DATABASE_NAME = "LearnGerman.sdf";
const string CONNECT_STRING =
      "Data Source = "+DATABASE_NAME+"; Password = ''";

const string TRANSLATIONTABLE_NAME = "TranslationDictionary";
const string TRANSLATIONTABLE_ENGLISH_COLUMN =  "EnglishWord";
```

```csharp
const string TRANSLATIONTABLE_GERMAN_COLUMN =  "GermanWord";
const string TRANSLATIONTABLE_GERMANGENDER_COLUMN =
       "GermanGender";
const string TRANSLATIONTABLE_WORDFUNCTION_COLUMN =
       "WordFunction";

internal const int DS_WORDS_COLUMNINDEX_ENGLISHWORD = 0;
internal const int DS_WORDS_COLUMNINDEX_GERMANWORD = 1;
internal const int DS_WORDS_COLUMNINDEX_GERMANGENDER = 2;
internal const int DS_WORDS_COLUMNINDEX_WORDFUNCTION = 3;

static public System.Data.IDataReader GetListOfWords()
{
  System.Data.SqlServerCe.SqlCeConnection conn = null;

  conn = new System.Data.SqlServerCe.SqlCeConnection(
            CONNECT_STRING);
  conn.Open();

  System.Data.SqlServerCe.SqlCeCommand cmd =
            conn.CreateCommand();

  cmd.CommandText = "select " +
    TRANSLATIONTABLE_ENGLISH_COLUMN                 + ", "
    + TRANSLATIONTABLE_GERMAN_COLUMN                + ", "
    + TRANSLATIONTABLE_GERMANGENDER_COLUMN          + ", "
    + TRANSLATIONTABLE_WORDFUNCTION_COLUMN          + " "
    + "from " + TRANSLATIONTABLE_NAME;

  //Execute the database command
  System.Data.SqlServerCe.SqlCeDataReader myReader =
    cmd.ExecuteReader(System.Data.CommandBehavior.SingleResult);

  return myReader;
}


//-------------------------------------------------
//Creates and a database if needed
//-------------------------------------------------
static public void CreateDatabaseIfNonExistant()
{
  if (System.IO.File.Exists(DATABASE_NAME) == false)
  {
    CreateAndFillDatabase();
```

```
    }
}


//----------------------------------------------------
//Creates and fills a database
//----------------------------------------------------
static public void  CreateAndFillDatabase()
{
  //Delete the database if it's there
  if (System.IO.File.Exists(DATABASE_NAME))
  { System.IO.File.Delete(DATABASE_NAME);   }

  //Create a new database
  System.Data.SqlServerCe.SqlCeEngine sqlCeEngine;
  sqlCeEngine = new System.Data.SqlServerCe.SqlCeEngine(
              CONNECT_STRING);
  sqlCeEngine.CreateDatabase();


  //----------------------------------------------------
  //Try to connect to the database
  //and populate it with data
  //----------------------------------------------------
  System.Data.SqlServerCe.SqlCeConnection conn = null;
  try
  {
    conn = new System.Data.SqlServerCe.SqlCeConnection(
          CONNECT_STRING);
    conn.Open();

    System.Data.SqlServerCe.SqlCeCommand cmd =
          conn.CreateCommand();

    //Create a translation table
    //Fields:
    //   1. EnglishWord
    //   2. GermanWord
    //   3. Gender of word
    //   4. Type of word
    cmd.CommandText = "CREATE TABLE " + TRANSLATIONTABLE_NAME +
      " (" +
      TRANSLATIONTABLE_ENGLISH_COLUMN       + " ntext" + ", " +
      TRANSLATIONTABLE_GERMAN_COLUMN        + " ntext" + ", " +
      TRANSLATIONTABLE_GERMANGENDER_COLUMN + " int"   + ", " +
      TRANSLATIONTABLE_WORDFUNCTION_COLUMN + " int"   +
```

```
      ")";
    cmd.ExecuteNonQuery();

    //Fill the database with words
    FillDictionary(cmd);
  }
  catch (System.Exception eTableCreate)
  {
    System.Windows.Forms.MessageBox.Show(
    "Error occured adding table :" + eTableCreate.ToString());
  }
  finally
  {
    //Always close the database when we are done
    conn.Close();
  }

  //Tell the user
  System.Windows.Forms.MessageBox.Show(
      "Created language database!");
}

static private void FillDictionary(
      System.Data.SqlServerCe.SqlCeCommand cmd)
{
  //Verbs
  InsertEnglishGermanWordPair(cmd, "to pay", "zahlen",
            VocabularyWord.WordGender.notApplicable,
            VocabularyWord.WordFunction.Verb);
  InsertEnglishGermanWordPair(cmd, "to catch", "fangen",
            VocabularyWord.WordGender.notApplicable,
            VocabularyWord.WordFunction.Verb);
  //Add more words...

  //Pronouns
  InsertEnglishGermanWordPair(cmd, "What", "was",
            VocabularyWord.WordGender.notApplicable,
            VocabularyWord.WordFunction.Pronoun);
  //Add more words...

  //Adverb
  InsertEnglishGermanWordPair(cmd, "where", "wo",
            VocabularyWord.WordGender.notApplicable,
            VocabularyWord.WordFunction.Adverb);
```

```
InsertEnglishGermanWordPair(cmd, "never", "nie",
         VocabularyWord.WordGender.notApplicable,
         VocabularyWord.WordFunction.Adverb);
//Add more words...

//Preposition
InsertEnglishGermanWordPair(cmd, "at the", "am",
         VocabularyWord.WordGender.notApplicable,
         VocabularyWord.WordFunction.Preposition);

//Adjective
InsertEnglishGermanWordPair(cmd, "invited", "eingeladen",
         VocabularyWord.WordGender.notApplicable,
         VocabularyWord.WordFunction.Verb);

InsertEnglishGermanWordPair(cmd, "yellow", "gelbe",
         VocabularyWord.WordGender.notApplicable,
         VocabularyWord.WordFunction.Adjective);
InsertEnglishGermanWordPair(cmd, "one", "eins",
         VocabularyWord.WordGender.notApplicable,
         VocabularyWord.WordFunction.Adjective);
InsertEnglishGermanWordPair(cmd, "two", "zwei",
         VocabularyWord.WordGender.notApplicable,
         VocabularyWord.WordFunction.Adjective);

//Masculine nouns
InsertEnglishGermanWordPair(cmd, "Man", "Mann",
         VocabularyWord.WordGender.Masculine,
         VocabularyWord.WordFunction.Noun);
InsertEnglishGermanWordPair(cmd, "Marketplace", "Marktplatz",
         VocabularyWord.WordGender.Masculine,
         VocabularyWord.WordFunction.Noun);
InsertEnglishGermanWordPair(cmd, "Spoon", "Löffel ",
         VocabularyWord.WordGender.Masculine,
         VocabularyWord.WordFunction.Noun);

//Feminine nouns
InsertEnglishGermanWordPair(cmd, "Woman", "Frau",
         VocabularyWord.WordGender.Feminine,
         VocabularyWord.WordFunction.Noun);
InsertEnglishGermanWordPair(cmd, "Clock", "Uhr",
         VocabularyWord.WordGender.Feminine,
         VocabularyWord.WordFunction.Noun);
InsertEnglishGermanWordPair(cmd, "Cat", "Katze",
```

```
                         VocabularyWord.WordGender.Feminine,
                         VocabularyWord.WordFunction.Noun);

        //Neuter nouns
        InsertEnglishGermanWordPair(cmd, "Car", "Auto",
                         VocabularyWord.WordGender.Neuter,
                         VocabularyWord.WordFunction.Noun);
        InsertEnglishGermanWordPair(cmd, "Book", "Buch",
                         VocabularyWord.WordGender.Neuter,
                         VocabularyWord.WordFunction.Noun);
    }


    //-------------------------------------------------
    //Inserts a word into the database
    //-------------------------------------------------
    static private void InsertEnglishGermanWordPair(
                     System.Data.SqlServerCe.SqlCeCommand cmd,
                     string englishWord, string germanWord,
                     VocabularyWord.WordGender germanWordGender,
                     VocabularyWord.WordFunction wordFunction)
    {
      cmd.CommandText = "INSERT INTO " + TRANSLATIONTABLE_NAME +
       "("+ TRANSLATIONTABLE_ENGLISH_COLUMN + ", " +
       TRANSLATIONTABLE_GERMAN_COLUMN + ", " +
       TRANSLATIONTABLE_GERMANGENDER_COLUMN + ", " +
       TRANSLATIONTABLE_WORDFUNCTION_COLUMN +
         ")  VALUES ('"
         + englishWord + "', '"
         + germanWord +  "', '"
         + System.Convert.ToString(((int) germanWordGender))+ "', '"
         + System.Convert.ToString(((int) wordFunction))
         + "')";

      cmd.ExecuteNonQuery();
    }
} //End of class
```

Listing 14.7 Custom Data Management Sample—Code for GameData.cs

```
//---------------------------------------------------------
//In-Memory Data Management Code
//
//This code manages the in-memory representation of the code
//---------------------------------------------------------
```

```csharp
using System;

internal class GameData
{
//Array-Lists to store the data we have loaded in
private static System.Collections.ArrayList
                m_vocabularyWords_All;
private static System.Collections.ArrayList
                m_vocabularyWords_Nouns;
private static System.Collections.ArrayList
                m_vocabularyWords_Verbs;
private static System.Collections.ArrayList
                m_vocabularyWords_Adjectives;
private static System.Collections.ArrayList
                m_vocabularyWords_Adverbs;
private static System.Collections.ArrayList
                m_vocabularyWords_Prepositions;

public static bool isGameDataInitialized
{
  //The game data is initialized if we have loaded the words
  get {return (m_vocabularyWords_All != null);}
}

//Returns the collection of all words we have
public static System.Collections.ArrayList AllWords
{
  get
  {
    //If the data has not been initialized, load it
    if (m_vocabularyWords_All == null)
        {InitializeGameVocabulary();}
    return m_vocabularyWords_All;
  }
}

//Returns the collection of all nouns we have
public static System.Collections.ArrayList Nouns
{
  get
  {
    //If the data has not been initialized, load it
    if (m_vocabularyWords_Nouns == null)
        {InitializeGameVocabulary();}
```

```
      return m_vocabularyWords_Nouns;
  }
}


//===========================================================
//Loads the data in from our database
//===========================================================
static public void InitializeGameVocabulary()
{
  //Create a new array list to hold our words
  m_vocabularyWords_All = new System.Collections.ArrayList();
  m_vocabularyWords_Nouns = new System.Collections.ArrayList();
  m_vocabularyWords_Verbs = new System.Collections.ArrayList();
  m_vocabularyWords_Adjectives =
                          new System.Collections.ArrayList();
  m_vocabularyWords_Adverbs =
                          new System.Collections.ArrayList();
  m_vocabularyWords_Prepositions =
                          new System.Collections.ArrayList();

  System.Data.IDataReader dataReader;
  dataReader = DatabaseAccess.GetListOfWords();

  VocabularyWord newWord;
  //Go through all of the records
  while(dataReader.Read())
  {
    //Place the data for the word we just read in into a class
    newWord = new VocabularyWord(
      dataReader.GetString(
        DatabaseAccess.DS_WORDS_COLUMNINDEX_ENGLISHWORD),

      dataReader.GetString(
        DatabaseAccess.DS_WORDS_COLUMNINDEX_GERMANWORD),

      (VocabularyWord.WordGender) dataReader.GetInt32(
        DatabaseAccess.DS_WORDS_COLUMNINDEX_GERMANGENDER),

      (VocabularyWord.WordFunction) dataReader.GetInt32(
        DatabaseAccess.DS_WORDS_COLUMNINDEX_WORDFUNCTION)
      );

    //Add the new word to the array list
    m_vocabularyWords_All.Add(newWord);
```

```
        //Words can belong to more than one group, so check
        //using a logical AND to see if the word meets a
        //given category
        if((newWord.getWordFunction &
            VocabularyWord.WordFunction.Noun) != 0)
        {m_vocabularyWords_Nouns.Add(newWord);}

        if((newWord.getWordFunction &
            VocabularyWord.WordFunction.Verb) != 0)
        {m_vocabularyWords_Verbs.Add(newWord);}

        if((newWord.getWordFunction &
            VocabularyWord.WordFunction.Adjective) != 0)
        {m_vocabularyWords_Adjectives.Add(newWord);}

        if((newWord.getWordFunction &
            VocabularyWord.WordFunction.Adverb) != 0)
        {m_vocabularyWords_Adverbs.Add(newWord);}

        if((newWord.getWordFunction &
            VocabularyWord.WordFunction.Preposition) != 0)
        {m_vocabularyWords_Prepositions.Add(newWord);}

    }
    //Close the data reader
    dataReader.Close();
}
} //End class
```

Listing 14.8 Custom Data Management Sample—Code for VocabularyWord.cs

```
using System;
//-----------------------------------------------
//Holds the data for a vocabulary word
//-----------------------------------------------
internal class VocabularyWord
{

[System.FlagsAttribute] //Indicates values can be logically ORed
public enum WordFunction
{
  Noun = 1,
  Verb = 2,
```

```
      Pronoun = 4,
      Adverb = 8,
      Adjective = 16,
      Preposition = 32,
      Phrase = 64
    }

  public enum WordGender
  {
    notApplicable = 0,
    Masculine = 1,
    Feminine = 2,
    Neuter = 3,
  }

  private string m_englishWord;
  private string m_germanWord;
  private VocabularyWord.WordGender m_germanGender;
  private VocabularyWord.WordFunction m_wordFunction;

  public string EnglishWord {get {return m_englishWord;}}
  public string GermanWord {get {return m_germanWord;}}
  public WordFunction getWordFunction
          {get {return m_wordFunction;}}
  public WordGender GermanGender {get {return m_germanGender;}}

  //--------------------------------------------------------
  //Returns the German word, prefixed with an article
  //(for example, 'der', 'die', 'das' if it exists)
  //--------------------------------------------------------
  public string GermanWordWithArticleIfExists
  {
    get
    {
      if (m_germanGender == WordGender.notApplicable)
      {
        return this.GermanWord;
      }

      return this.GenderArticle + " " + this.GermanWord;

    }
  } //End Property
```

```
public string GenderArticle
{
  get
  {
    switch (m_germanGender)
    {
      case WordGender.Masculine:
        return "der";
      case WordGender.Feminine:
        return "die";
      case WordGender.Neuter:
        return "das";
    }
    return "";
  }
}

public VocabularyWord(string enlgishWord, string germanWord,
        WordGender germanGender, WordFunction wordFunction)
{
  m_englishWord = enlgishWord;
  m_germanWord = germanWord;
  m_germanGender = germanGender;
  m_wordFunction = wordFunction;
}
}   //End class
```

Options for Storing Long-Term Data

There exist many different options for storing mobile application data. Data can be stored in binary files, text files, or in databases. (A database can be considered a special purpose binary file.) The storage of the data can occur off the device or on the device. Long-term data can be synchronized between devices and servers. Below are described the benefits and drawbacks of the most common choices along with suggestions on how to go about making long-term storage decisions in your mobile application's design.

Storage of Data in XML Files on Device

- *Benefits*—Text files can be a great way to store moderate amounts of long-term data. XML files offer a nice balance between custom data formats and structured formats and are an improvement over generic text files. XML files can easily be passed between desktops, servers, and devices and can be interpreted by different applications with little difficulty. For simplicity and flexibility, it is hard to beat XML files.

- *Drawbacks*—Text files are verbose, and XML files are particularly verbose. If your mobile applications works with a lot of data they need to store efficiently, an XML file will not be appropriate for their needs. Also, because XML files are formatted text, they are easily readable and offer no data protection; for this reason, their use for sensitive information storage should be avoided unless you have a reliable mechanism for encrypting the files. Note: See the chapter on XML performance for further guidelines on using XML efficiently for data storage.

Storage of Data in SQL CE Databases on Device

- *Benefits*—The on-device database engine is a powerful concept. Having an on-device database allows your application to store, manage, and query large amounts of information locally. SQL CE databases can be password encrypted and thus can offer data protection for sensitive information. Partnerships can be set up between SQL CE databases and server-based SQL databases allowing for rich automated synchronization between them. For applications that deal with a lot of data that needs to be managed locally, it is probably the best choice.
- *Drawbacks*—The largest drawback of using an on-device database is the need to ensure the database engine is installed on your target devices. The SQL CE database itself takes up a significant chunk of storage space on the device (1 to 3MB) and usually needs to be installed onto devices because it is not often part of a device's ROM image. Because of the space requirements, not all classes of devices support hosting the SQL CE database engine. For example, although the Pocket PC supports hosting SQL CE, the Smartphone presently does not. In addition to size, there is the need to consider synchronization requirements. Moving data stored on one local device database to another computer will require business logic to be written; you may need to package the data as an ADO.NET DataSet or use a custom format to move data between devices.

Storage of Data in Off-Device (Server) SQL Databases

- *Benefits*—Storing and accessing data on a server-based database can be a useful way to access an almost limitless amount of data.
- *Drawbacks*—Connectivity is required to get data from the server or update data on the server. If your mobile device application uses an external database as its primary data source, plan on writing custom logic to temporarily store the data locally if the server connection is lost; it is an extremely bad user experience to lose the data when an attempt to perform a server update fails. Intermittent network failure is an inherent challenge for mobile devices and your mobile application will have to deal with this reality.

A second potential drawback to accessing data on a server is the need to deal with private network access rules and firewalls. Most server databases containing valuable information are located inside protected environments behind firewalls. These firewalls may not allow your mobile application to connect to the database server when the device is outside the private network. If access to data on a protected server is required, you will need to consider how to enable that access.

Accessing Off-Device Data via Web Services

- *Benefits*—Web services are increasingly being used to wrap access to private data sources. Access to information in databases can be exposed via Web services without exposing the underlying databases themselves. Web services usually work through HTTP or HTTPS network protocols; these protocols are generally firewall friendly. If a network already supports an outward-facing Web server, it is a relatively straightforward process to build a Web service hosted on that Web server.

  Newer database engines increasingly support returning data as XML without the need for an intermediary Web server. These databases effectively offer their own Web services. XML returned directly by a database will not necessarily be in the ADO.NET XML DataSet format, but any returned XML can be parsed and processed on your device if this is the best way to work with the data.

  In both cases, data can be exchanged with mobile devices using ADO.NET DataSets streamed as XML or via other XML formats. The choice of communicating directly with a database or insulating the database by using a Web server intermediary should be based on security, performance, and ease of development and deployment criteria.

- *Drawbacks*—As with using an off-device database for storage, network access to a Web service cannot be guaranteed at all times. To be useful and robust, your mobile device application must always have a fallback strategy to work with cached data locally if the network is not available.

 A second drawback is efficiency of communication. Because Web services use XML as their communication mechanism, they are more verbose than specialized formats such as those used to synchronize databases. If you have a large amount of data you need to download or upload, you might want to consider a direct access mechanism to the database that uses the most efficient protocol available.

SQL CE

Smaller amounts of simply structured data may be manageable in an XML file, but past a certain point of size and complexity a formal database adds a great deal of value and will simplify your mobile application development. Although there are no absolute rules for when to use a database versus an XML file, as the data size starts getting larger a true database adds increasing value. As a rule of thumb, if your mobile device application is going to be working with more than a hundred rows of data or the information needs to be stored in multiple tables, it probably makes sense to use an on-device database such as SQL CE.

 Good documentation exists online that describes SQL CE. Those interested in learning detailed specifics about SQL CE should search the MSDN online (or Visual Studio product) documentation for "SQL Server CE." Instead of attempting to repeat the detailed documentation already available there, this section briefly overviews SQL CE and then describes the important decisions that must be made when developing mobile application code that works with on-device databases such as SQL CE. For a simple example showing how to use SQL CE, see Listings 14.5, 14.6, 14.7, and 14.8 earlier in this chapter.

What Is SQL CE?

Formally named SQL Server CE, SQL CE is a database engine for mobile and embedded devices. It offers relatively rich functionality for storing, querying, and synchronizing structured data with servers. Multiple SQL CE databases can be created on a single device. Each database is represented in a single binary file on the device; these files can be manually copied from one device to another or synchronized automatically with a server database. A SQL CE database's contents can be password encrypted to offer a reasonable level of data security in case a device is lost, stolen, or has its data contents copied surreptitiously.

SQL CE offers a subset of the database functionality present on its larger desktop and server SQL Server sibling. SQL CE supports storing relational data in tables and supports a significant portion of the desktop SQL data types and query syntax for adding, retrieving, and modifying data. Notably, SQL CE does not presently support stored procedures or named parameters in queries.

Other Mobile Device Databases and Database Licensing Models

It is worth noting that other software venders also make on-device databases that can be run on mobile devices. These are conceptually similar to SQL CE, but each will have its own strengths and weaknesses with regard to synchronization abilities, database features, and pricing model.

An important characteristic of SQL CE is that it is freely usable and distributable with your application without the need for a special runtime license or royalty. For synchronization with SQL servers, an appropriate SQL client license is required—the same way a client license is required to connect a desktop application directly to SQL Server.

Historically, Microsoft has also had a second database on mobile devices called CEDB (Windows CE Database). This is a limited-functionality database and its usage in newer applications is discouraged; the CEDB database may not be present in future devices. Because this is already a legacy technology, no direct .NET Compact Framework mechanism for accessing this database was built. If your application needs to access the CEDB, you will need to call native code or use a .NET wrapper class created by a third party. There exist two good alternatives to using CEDB: For relatively small amounts of data, XML files can be used; for larger amounts of data, SQL CE is the best choice.

SQL CE Standalone and Synchronized Modes

SQL CE can be used in one of three modes:

1. *Standalone*—In this usage model, the SQL CE database serves as a standalone database on the device. Think of this as similar to using a local SQL Server or the Access runtime on a desktop application to manage a local database. One of the main challenges in standalone

SQL CE usage is devising a strategy to populate the database. Your application can either dynamically populate the database with external data pulled down to the device at runtime or you can use a pre-filled database file that is copied onto the device. These models can also be combined; data can be dynamically added to a preexisting database file that was downloaded to the device. Which database population strategy is best depends on the nature of your application. If you are using a prefilled database, the easiest way to provision devices with this data is to build a master copy of the database on a Pocket PC as part of your development process and then copy this database file off of the device and onto your development machine. This prepopulated database can then be copied to all target devices as part of your application's deployment.

2. *Synchronized with SQL server through a Web server (IIS)*– This mechanism is known as RDA, or remote data access. This is a simple method of synchronization where the SQL server that contains the master copy of the data has no special relationship to SQL CE databases synchronizing with it. SQL CE databases access the server data just like any other client application of the database except that the access occurs through a Web server interface. Because the server database does not need to keep track of what data any of the synchronized SQL CE clients are holding, the RDA strategy has low server overhead and scales well. An unlimited number of devices can have local SQL CE databases that are synchronized with a master SQL server in this manner. Data synchronization occurs through a special SQL CE synchronization engine that runs on top of Windows Internet Information Server (a Web server). Because the synchronization is Web server–based, it can be done over a public network if desired. The SQL server has no knowledge that client databases are synchronizing with its data, so the responsibility for ensuring data that changes get updated on client and server is left to the mobile device application. For more information on RDA, read the help topic titled "Using Remote Data Access" in Microsoft's "SQL Server CE Books Online"; this documentation ships as part of Visual Studio .NET (2003 or later). To sum up: RDA = low overhead and high scalability, but at the cost of needing to handle data updates manually. RDA is a great choice when the data being synchronized with is being used in a mostly read-only way.

3. *Synchronized directly with SQL Server: This mechanism is known as merge replication*—Merge replication creates a partnership between

a device-local SQL CE database and the SQL server it is synchronizing with. This is a powerful model because the SQL server has intimate knowledge of what data each partnered SQL CE client is holding; updates to data both on device and server can be handled in a much more automated and systematic way versus synchronization via RDA. Because SQL Server needs to maintain information regarding each partnering SQL CE client, this model does not scale as well as the RDA model; supporting a huge number of clients will be taxing on the server. Regardless, when the most robust synchronization behavior is needed, it is an excellent choice. For more information on merge replication read the topic titled "Using Replication" in Microsoft's "SQL Server CE Books Online."

SQL CE Multiple Application Usage

Presently, SQL CE supports only one concurrent connection to any given database. This rule is true for both inside a single application as well as across application boundaries. Each database is stored in a separate file; these files cannot be opened concurrently using SQL CE. This means that although multiple databases can be open simultaneously on the same device, any single database can only have one concurrent connection to it at any time. If an application attempts to open a SQL CE database file already opened by another application or already opened by itself, an exception will be thrown by the database engine and the second connection attempt will fail.

If your application is using a database that does not need to be shared with other applications, you only need to ensure that your code does not attempt to establish more than one simultaneous connection to the database; the database connection should be managed as an application global resource. If your application is working with a SQL CE database that may be shared with other mobile device applications, you need to do two additional things in your mobile application's design:

1. You should ensure that your mobile application does not hold an open database connection any longer than absolutely necessary. A connection should be established only right before database access is required and freed as soon as possible following the database access. Your application should be designed not to require a constant database connection.

2. You should code defensively and assume that the database will already be opened every time you try to access it. Your application should have a model for informing the user that the database is cur-

rently in use by another local application so that he can take steps to close the other application or force it to release its database connection. Your mobile device application should also have a model for deferring the database access until a database connection can be established; the application should not stall if the database cannot be connected to.

SQL CE Is Not Available on All Device Types

It is important to know that SQL CE is presently not available for Smartphone devices. This is primarily due to size, memory, and storage constraints. Pocket PC devices have a battery-powered RAM file system they can use for fast file system access; Smartphones use flash RAM for their longer-term storage needs and have smaller amounts of working RAM; both of these factors make running a database engine on the Smartphone less desirable.

If you are building two versions of an application, one for a Pocket PC and another intended for a Smartphone device, you should consider this to be another design decision you will need to think about. The Smartphone application will not only have different user interface demands than the Pocket PC application, it will also have different data-storage capabilities. The amount of data a Smartphone application will keep in long-term storage is usually smaller than the amount of data a similar Pocket PC application will store. It may be acceptable to use SQL CE on the Pocket PC application and to use an XML-persisted data file on a Smartphone.

Visual Studio .NET 2005 and SQL CE, Older and Wiser

The next version of SQL CE and the .NET Compact Framework will offer two important data access improvements for working with SQL CE.

1. The SqlCeResultSet class will enable developers to cursor over and update data directly in a SQL CE database. This makes it easier to build applications that work intimately with databases rather than favoring the use of higher-level abstractions such as the ADO.NET DataSet.

2. Multiuser access will be supported by SQL CE. This means that multiple on-device applications will be able to simultaneously open and work with the same databases. This eliminates some of the problems outlined above with concurrent on-device database access.

Are these new feature additions for you and your application? The answer is "maybe." Many mobile application developers choose to target mobile devices that already have the needed target runtimes in device ROM because this simplifies application deployment. (For some devices, this is the only option, but this is the subject of a future chapter.) For these kinds of applications, it will take some time for the critical mass of devices to be available that have the updated components in ROM. However, if you have the option of installing an updated runtime and database engine, these features may be a compelling reason to do so.

Summary

As with performance, memory management, and user interface design, building a successful data access model for your mobile applications requires both discipline and experimentation. The good news is that much of your desktop data access knowledge can be applied when designing mobile application data access code. The bad news is that little of your preexisting desktop code will be of use and that specifics of devices must be kept in mind to build great mobile applications.

The most important data access consideration is determining how your data access strategy will deal with the offline needs of your users. The reality is that a mobile application will be frequently disconnected from database servers, sometimes "by design" and sometimes due to network failures. Dealing with intermittent connectivity will be a specific focus of the next chapter, but is a key thing to keep in mind when designing your data access strategy. If the user wants instant access to the data, it will need to be cached locally on the device.

Depending on how your mobile device application will be used, it may need to connect to data sources via a variety of different connectivity models. Some connectivity such as Wi-Fi is fast and inexpensive, and some slow and expensive. The need to support connections over public networks or via virtual private networks may also add requirements to your design. When designing your mobile application's data access model, it is important to map out what these connectivity scenarios will look like and how they will effect your data access and synchronization needs. It is important to think about what kind of data will be stored locally on the device, how this data will be stored and accessed, and how the data will be synchronized with servers.

Data access programming frameworks often offer layered approaches to working with data. As with working with XML frameworks, there are lower-level forward-only models that are stateless, and there are full-service models built on top of these that are highly stateful. ADO.NET offers such a selection of choices. As a developer, you can either work at a high level of abstraction using ADO.NET DataSets to manage your data in memory or you can work at a low level of abstraction directly using the data-reader and data-connection classes that communicate directly with databases. As with gas stations, full service is nice but costs more; in the case of data access, you will be paying for higher-level data access services with in-memory state and this ultimately means lower application performance. If you choose to work at a low level of abstraction, you can store the loaded data in the most efficient format for your mobile application's needs but take on the burden of managing that data efficiently.

For small amounts of data, data that requires lots of dynamic updates or data with complex relationships, the full-service ADO.NET DataSet model has a lot to offer. When using DataSets, be sure to use the most efficient ways of accessing the data. For working with DataRows inside DataTable objects, this means using cached DataColumn object indexes to access fields.

For the best possible performance when working with larger amounts of data, your application should consider a custom data model that is highly optimized to the task at hand. This can directly increase performance as well as reduce the overall memory load on your application. When choosing to use a custom lower-level approach, it is important to keep the model as simple and memory efficient as possible. Always instrument your code and test the performance of your design versus the existing higher-level data access models!

For storing longer-term data locally on devices, there are two recommended models, either storing the data in an XML file or storing it using a device-local database such as SQL CE. Both of these options are available whether you are using the higher-level ADO.NET DataSet model or using lower-level customized mechanisms for working with data. As long as the amount of data being worked with is relatively small (for example, on the order of 50KB of XML), an XML file is an excellent and flexible choice. For larger amounts of data, a real database engine becomes increasingly useful. Again, instrumenting your code and producing metrics you can compare is the only way to ensure you are making good design decisions.

As with user interface design, "write once, run anywhere" proves an elusive goal for mobile application data access design. For the best possible performance, you will want to tune your mobile application's data access and data storage models for the specific devices the application will run on. If you are building multiple versions of your application for different device classes, you may choose different data storage models for each device class depending on the capabilities of the device and the needs of your application.

Data access technologies are both relevant and extremely useful on today's rich mobile devices. The interesting design challenges are in choosing the right model for your application's needs and in keeping this model flexible enough to be tuned as real-world experiences dictate.

CHAPTER 15

Step 4: Get Your Communications Model Right

"The medium is the message..."

—Marshall McLuhan (1911–1980), Communications theorist.
(Encarta 2004, Quotations)

"E. T. phone home."

—E. T. (E.T. - The Extra-Terrestrial, 1982),
the extraterrestrial who just wanted to call home

"If anything can go wrong, it probably will and at the worst possible time."

—Murphy's Law

Introduction to Mobile Application Communications

Each of the three seemingly unrelated quotes above have something insightful to say about mobile application communications strategy.

Marshall McLuhan's prophetic statement "The medium is the message" implied that the nature of society is fundamentally altered by the evolving technology of communication. He postulated that a significant part of the character of a society was the way it communicates. To put it another way, communication technologies are not just something that a society uses; rather, the communications technologies used greatly affect that society. A similar analogy holds true for software; an application does not just use communications, rather the nature of the application is greatly affected by how it communicates. This is particularly true for software that runs on mobile devices. A fundamental characteristic of your mobile device application is how it communicates with the world around it. The means of communication should not be considered a "thing your application does" but rather a core behavioral attribute of the application itself.

Many communications technologies are available for mobile application developers to choose from; this list grows every year. Some communications capabilities are built in to hardware such as mobile phones and some are enabled via extensibility mechanisms such as plug-in cards. Each of these successive technologies is not just a faster and cheaper version of the technologies preceding it but rather a complex system with its own strengths and weaknesses that is struggling for its evolutionary survival in the communications jungle. It is important to understand the ramifications of the communications choices you make in your mobile application's design. For instance, an application that uses Wi-Fi for its communication will in some important ways behave differently than one that uses Bluetooth to communicate with a GPRS mobile phone to access the network; these in turn work differently from wired network connections and body area network protocols such as ZigBee (if interested, see: `http://www.zigbee.org/`).

Just as there is no universally best means of transportation, there is no best means of communication for your mobile application. Even without consideration of cost, a mule may be much more useful than an all-terrain vehicle if you are climbing a rocky slope and a train may be vastly superior to an airplane if you are traveling in between proximate metropolitan centers. So it is with communications mechanisms; more expensive, faster, or newer technologies do not necessarily offer the best solutions to your mobile application's needs. It is important to understand the nature of the communications options open to you and to make wise decisions that meet your needs.

Turning to the second quote, it is worth being suspicious as to what insights a 1980s family-friendly movie about a visiting alien can teach us about mobile application communication. The message here is simple: Even for people of advanced technology, it can sometimes be difficult to resolve communications problems and "phone home." E. T. had to cobble together Speak&Spells and home hardware equipment to get in touch with the folks back home; mercifully our experience will (we hope!) be a little more robust. In any case effective communications require good design and flexibility to deal with challenges that will unexpectedly arise. To access the network resources that your mobile application needs, you may have to deal with obstacles such as unreliable connections, uncooperative firewalls, and mobile networks that seem to enjoy making "improvements" to the packets, HTTP headers, or streams being used to push data around. Mobile communications networks are and will remain more heterogeneous environments than fixed-line networks, and as with other aspects of mobile application design a "one size fits all" approach to communications is not likely to prove successful. Getting things to work correctly will require experimentation, insight, good design, even better testing, and possibly a bit of Speak&Spell scavenging of your own to make sure that you can send and receive messages to and from "home."

As for the third quote, Murphy's law is self-explanatory. If there is a chance that communications will fail at an inappropriate and inconvenient time, practice has shown that it will. This does not mean that your mobile application's end users are doomed to have an unreliable experience. It does, however, mean that ensuring that they have a great mobile device experience is up to your application's logic. Robust communications despite intermittent connections are quite possible. It is important to plan ahead for communications challenges and code defensively.

Coding for Mobile Networking

Most interesting applications interact with resources outside of the application itself. They interact with the operating system, the device's local resources, and networked resources. Each level of increasing interaction brings with it increasing application power but also diminished control. Increased interaction with off-device resources brings with it the increased probability of intermittent communications failures. The most important thing to remember when you are writing code that communicates over a network is that you are no longer in full control of the outcome.

The paragraphs below give a framework for thinking about increasing levels of interdependence between your application and the resources surrounding it.

- *Closed system computing*—When writing an algorithm to process data that the application has full ownership of, you are in full control of your application's destiny. Everything that happens in this system is happening because of code that you can inspect and can get a full and detailed understanding of. If your algorithm allocates and releases memory, it is giving up a slight bit of control to the runtime to manage that memory, but still you can have a very high degree of confidence that you are in control of the system. These situations approximate a closed system over which you have full determinacy of the outcome.

- *Cooperative computing with the operating system*—When writing code that interacts with the runtime and operating system, you are giving up some more control to the runtime and operating system in exchange for rich services provided by them. Presenting a user interface on a modern computing device is usually an example of this; the user interface is a cooperative effort between your application's code and the operating system. The underlying operating system and runtime operate the user interface for you and send your application events and messages when interesting things occur. In this mode of software development, you are no longer in control of a closed system; you are now in a cooperative system where your application and the runtime cooperate to provide a rich experience for the user. Although you cannot be sure exactly what is going on in the underlying system, you can still make very good assumptions about the behavior of the application as a whole. For example, while your application is giving up low-level details of how its user interface operates, it is a fair assumption that it is still in full charge of everything that goes into the user interface and is not sharing that resource with any other applications.

- *Cooperative computing with other applications running on the device*—Your mobile device can assume that it has full control of its user interface because the operating system and runtime environment have set up logical boundaries between the individual resources of different applications; what's mine is mine and what's yours is yours. When your mobile application starts working with resources global to the device such as local files and databases, it must be mindful that it is not the only potential client for these resources. The operating system serves as the honest broker of these resources, but it cannot guarantee your application exclusive and full access to any given resource at all times. Additionally, there is the possibility of running out of resources; for instance, if other applications use up all of the available file system space, your application must respond robustly to this unfortunate circumstance. When working with shared resources, it is important to code defensively and to understand that every attempt to access a shared resource can fail. Thought must also be given to what happens when a resource is accessed simultaneously by different applications; some types of resources lock access to a single party at a time, some allow concurrent access but do not make guarantees on the coherency of the data during updates, and some resources guarantee atomic reads and writes of data. Understanding the concurrency behavior of any device-global resource your application uses is important for ensuring its robust behavior.

- *Cooperative computing with the network at large*—When your application relies on services provided over a network, it is taking on two additional sources of potential unreliability. Access to networked resources may fail because the computer at the other end of the network may be uncooperative. Things may also go wrong because any of the steps in the networking chain that connects the two computers may fail to behave as expected.

  Adding further complexity is the fact that networked resources may fail in the middle of communications; this is something that happens very rarely in device-local communications. For example, although it is possible that reading from a local file system file may fail, the chances of this happening are vanishingly small; a hard drive may occasionally crash, but this is rare, and when it does your application has bigger problems to worry about than the file it was reading. The chance of failure is so small that many operating systems regularly perform read and write operations to local storage unbeknownst to the applications running on top of the OS. When reading a file over a network, the chances of failure midstream are dramatically higher, higher still if the network is wireless, and even greater yet if the mobile device is roaming between network cells while reading the files. Failure may not occur all the time, but it occurs enough of the time that it must be accounted for and dealt with robustly.

Described next are guidelines for building robust networked mobile applications.

Do Not Build a Communication-Dependent Application

Just as a group of people acting in concert can achieve more than a single person acting alone, a mobile application interacting with the networked world around it can offer a far richer experience than a mobile application that is self-contained. For a group of people in an organization to be effective in meeting goals, the organization must robustly deal with failures in communication and failures in individual people; no single interaction can be critical path or the organization will fail without it. The same is true for mobile devices. A mobile device can greatly benefit from interacting with the world around it, but it should not be reliant on interaction at any given time. This point is both obvious and surprisingly often ignored.

Your mobile application should look at each network access as an opportunity and not a necessity. For most mobile devices, networked communication is something that is available "approximately on demand," meaning that a user of a mobile application can usually go to a physical location where they have network access but that the device itself cannot rely on constantly being in a network-connected state. This is very different from a desktop computer that is wired to a network and also significantly different from a laptop computer that may be used while stationary in a network "hot spot." Although few people walk around train stations with their laptops open and typing, many people walk around these same stations tapping into their mobile phones. The difference is a matter of degree, but the distinction is significant.

Thinking about network access as intermittent results in two useful design guidelines:

1. *Download and cache useful data ahead of time when a network connection is available*. It is important to consider what kind of information will be most useful when your application is offline and to make sure it is downloaded and available on the device when needed. While it is useful to manage on-device resources by deferring allocation until needed, off-device information should be downloaded and hoarded to prepare for the application being offline. For example, a connection to an on-device database can be deferred until it is actually needed. In contrast, relevant data in an off-device database should be downloaded ahead of time when a network connection is available. Ideally the downloading of information should be done as a background task that does not block the application's user interface. Having predownloaded information can also significantly speed up an application's performance, especially when the data is commonly accessed by the application or user and would otherwise need to be downloaded on demand.

2. *Queue data for upload and allow it to be uploaded when an appropriate network connection becomes available*. Users want a responsive experience when working with device-local applications. If the user updates data on a mobile phone application and the application requires an immediate server connection to process that data, the experience will be high latency and unreliable. A far better model is to reliably queue updates on the client and offer either automated or manual batch uploads of the data to servers as available. The data upload code should also be robust enough to defer work until later if a reliable connection cannot presently be established.

Two Examples of Commutations Strategies

Synchronizing Calendar, Contact, and E-Mail Information on a Mobile Phone

A good example of the two principles described above is the synchronization model used by Microsoft's Smartphone and Pocket PC Phone. Both of these devices contain an e-mail application that allows for periodic synchronization of e-mail, calendar data, and contacts with an Exchange messaging server.

Different users have different preferences and needs for the synchronization of this information. To minimize data traffic, the mobile application enables the user to configure which kinds of data to synchronize locally on the device. For example, I may choose only to synchronize my calendar appointments and contact information, leaving e-mail for my laptop. Appropriate size constraints can also be specified such as choosing to synchronize all forward calendar appointments but only those going back 2 weeks and limiting each downloaded e-mail to the first 3KB of data.

The devices' e-mail, contacts, and calendaring application also allows the specification of how often synchronization should take place and whether the synchronization should be manual or automatic. The most appropriate settings for each user are based on the kind of data being synchronized and the user's need for that data to be kept up-to-date. For most users, calendar appointments change less often than their e-mail inbox, and contact lists change even less frequently. My personal preference is to manually synchronize data while walking outside before and after work or as needed during the day; others I know tend to synchronize their data more frequently using automated updates. The synchronization model is highly dependent on the usage patterns of the user and the application.

To accomplish the synchronization of this information, devices use a dedicated synchronization service called ActiveSync. The ActiveSync engine periodically makes a mobile network connection to the Internet to connect to the user's Exchange server and then synchronizes the data. This synchronization consists of two operations:

1. Uploading all of the batched updates. Any changes made locally to the calendar, e-mails, or contacts are synchronized.

2. Downloading data that meets the local filter criteria. New appointments, contacts, and e-mail headers are downloaded as appropriate.

This model strikes a good balance between keeping the data up-to-date and conserving bandwidth. If the appointments information for a date were only downloaded on demand as the user selected each day on his or her mobile device's calendar, it would be impossible to get calendar information when a mobile network connection was not available or when an e-mail server was down. Even with live connections, the user would have to suffer annoying latencies in accessing or uploading data. On the other hand, if all possible information were downloaded from the server the synchronization would be slow and bandwidth costs would be prohibitive. Clearly a user-driven balance is needed.

Maintaining a smart cache on the device, keeping it current enough to meet the user's needs, and enabling the user to configure what and when data is synchronized provides the user a robust experience.

Sending and Receiving SMS Messages on Mobile Phones

SMS messages are short text messages sent between mobile phones. SMS is a surprisingly compelling technology for allowing a few lines of text to be sent between mobile phone users. By charging a nominal per-message fee, mobile phone networks derive a huge amount of revenue for a very small amount of bandwidth; per-bit SMS messages are much more lucrative than voice communications! SMS is thus a "killer application," and it is hard to argue that mobile phone makers and mobile network operators have not done something right with this technology.

SMS message transfer has one great strength and one annoying weakness:

1. *The SMS advantage: decoupled transmission and reception*—If an SMS message is sent from one mobile phone to another, the receiving mobile phone does not need to be online at the time of transmission. If you are flying across the Atlantic when someone sends your phone an SMS message, the mobile network infrastructure will happily queue up the message on its servers and deliver it to you when you land and turn your mobile phone back on. This is equally true if the receiving phone is temporarily inaccessible to the network because it is on a subway underground, in an elevator, or skiing on a part of a hill that is out of site from the cell tower. For this reason, it is a great mechanism for sending short messages such as "Meet me at Longhorn's Grill at 5 pm. ivo." The sender and receiver can communicate in short sentences without both needing to be online at the same time.

2. *The SMS disadvantage: dumb client applications that cannot cache messages when offline*—Presently most mobile phones do not have an automated mechanism for queuing outbound SMS messages. When an SMS message is typed in by the user and "sent" transmission is attempted, usually several times, it fails if the network cannot be accessed. This is an example of a synchronous application model where communication is immediately attempted and will either succeed for fail before control is returned to the user. A far better client application model would be to attempt to send the message synchronously and if it fails to go through immediately, to queue up the transmission for when network access is restored. The sending user could be notified by the phone when his SMS message finally went through to the server.

As with the previous example, there are important lessons to be learned here. It is worth asking why the current generation of mobile phones have this client-side SMS limitation. The answer is that building an asynchronous communication model is more complicated; it requires client-side logic to keep the SMS message sending system running in the background, it requires logic to handle resends, it requires the concept of an outbound queue, and to do well it requires a user interface model that unobtrusively notifies the user when queued up SMS messages are finally sent. Previous generations of mobile phones had less-sophisticated application models and building this kind of a system was not deemed worth the additional programming complexity. Today's phones, however, have both richer user interfaces and application models that more easily support background processing. It is reasonable to assume that future mobile phone operating systems and applications will support caching outbound SMS messages the same way that many now support caching outbound e-mails, contact information, and calendar appointments to be synchronized with servers.

Never Block Your User Interface Thread for Any Extended Period of Time

Communication is inherently a synchronous operation; your mobile device application will have a block of data that it will want to move up to a server or down from a server, and moving this data will take some amount of time. Because the amount of time required for transmission to an external server, desktop, or other device is inherently out of your application's direct control, it is important not to perform these kinds of operations on the user interface thread of your application.

A mistake that application developers commonly make is to first build all of their communications systems to run synchronously on the user interface thread with the goal of moving this communication to a background thread later in the application development cycle. As a general rule of thumb, this will not produce acceptable results. There are several reasons developers fall into this trap:

- *It is easier to design and debug synchronous communications.* This is undoubtedly true. It is much easier to design and debug application logic that runs synchronously. For this reason it is recommended that you *do* design and debug your communications logic by running it synchronously with your application's user interface logic. The communications routines you write should be synchronous functions. However, as soon as these communications functions are written and their base functionality is tested, they should be made to run asynchronously to the user interface's application logic.

- *It is faster to write synchronous code.* This is also true. When milestone deadlines loom, it is very easy to convince yourself that the only way to make the deadline is to cut corners and make the communications logic run synchronous to the user interface.
- *As long as asynchronous operation is kept in mind and designed into the application it will be easy to move operations to be asynchronous later.* This is false. Keeping the need to run asynchronously in mind when designing synchronous communications routines is undoubtedly helpful in making these systems asynchronous in the future, but it is simply not enough. The truth is that despite all efforts to the contrary synchronous dependencies will be built in to code that uses synchronous routines. Human beings are simply not good at tracking all of the implicit assumptions that creep into application logic and fixing these kinds of problems is very difficult in later stages of an application's development.

The best methodology to use when designing communications code that needs to keep the user interface responsive is to follow the four guidelines below:

1. *Design your communications routines as discrete well-encapsulated functions.* The best way to prepare your communications routines for running asynchronously is to make sure they are well encapsulated. A communications routine that sends data up to a server should be passed a static copy of that data. It should be the sole owner of this copy; the function should not need to access any global or shared state to get that data. Similarly, a communications routine that reads data from a server should not modify any global application state until it has read in all the data. This principle is important because having two threads work on global application state at the same time is a recipe for complexity, data corruption, and unreliability. The user interface thread should have sole access to the data that it is working with, the communications routines should have another copy, and the two systems should only interact at very cleanly defined and well-tested points.

2. *Test your communications routines by calling them synchronously.* As noted above, it is much easier to test and debug communications code when it is running synchronously on the application's user interface thread. For this reason, there is little benefit in testing code running on a background thread before the bugs are worked out when running the code synchronously with the user interface.

I recommend placing a big button on your form called "test Save Code" and use it to test and debug your communications routines. The reason I recommend using the "big button" approach is because it looks ugly and you will remember to remove it; if the code is hooked up to the user interface in a well-integrated way, there is a strong chance it will be kept that way.

3. *Stress test your communications routines by calling them asynchronously in difficult circumstances using a test application.* Background threaded code is always more complex than code called synchronously. Moreover, tracking down the kinds of subtle data corruption and state management bugs that can occur when code on different threads interacts in unexpected ways is tricky business made more so by all of the rich application feature code that surrounds the code being debugged. The best way to ensure a robust system is to stress test the code in a simplified environment designed to place the code into difficult states and also have it instrumented to detect abnormal circumstances. It is worth considering building a stress application that attempts to run multiple streams of code asynchronously and carefully inspects the internal state to look for any unexpected results. Doing this kind of testing may point out restrictions you should place on the code being executed to prevent it from getting into potentially risky states; for instance, the code for executing a background task could actively prevent multiple instances of that task running concurrently on different threads if this were identified to be problematic and unnecessary. Communications code that is tested, hardened, and debugged in this way can be integrated into your application with a much higher degree of confidence than code that is optimistically assumed to be correct.

4. *Once tested, immediately move the communications routines to run on a background worker thread in your application.* After your basic communications code has been debugged synchronously and tested asynchronously, it is ready to be moved into asynchronous operation in your application. Your application should have a clean and consistent model for running code on a background work thread and the same model should be used for all of your asynchronous communications needs. When you integrate communications code into your application's user interface, it should always be integrated using this asynchronous execution model. *Do not* integrate synchronous communications calls into your user interface with the plan to change them later to run asynchronously when time allows; the longer the code sits there, the more dependencies it will gain.

As a rule of thumb, it is far easier to take an asynchronous system and run it synchronously than it is to go the other way. To run an asynchronous system synchronously, your application simply calls the asynchronous code and then goes into a loop that waits for the asynchronous code to finish before moving on. To try to make synchronous communication asynchronous, you will have to identify all of the application state that the communications routines touch and make an isolated copy of that data, you will need to create a background threading model to call code from, you will need to redesign the way the communications code interacts with any user interface elements because often user interface controls cannot be robustly accessed from other threads (this is a common mistake and definitely not robust when using the .NET Compact Framework! <Control>.Invoke() must be used for cross-thread communication to user interface elements), you will need to come up with a way to notify the user interface of communications problems, you will need to deal with error conditions, and you will need to design a model for communicating commands and status between the user interface and communications code. All of this is very difficult to build in after the fact and attempts at taking synchronous operations in mobile applications and making them asynchronous will at the very least require significant redesign and typically will introduce instability and bugs into your application. Design off-device communicating code to be asynchronous from the start and you will be much happier with the results.

NOTE: See Chapter 9, "Performance and Multithreading," for a discussion of running code on a background thread.

Work at the Highest Level of Abstraction That Is Adaptable to Your Needs

As with desktop and server code, it is a good idea to work at the highest level of abstraction feasible.

For instance, when working with Internet protocols, if you can work at the level of Web services using SOAP requests/responses, it is recommendable to do so; the built-in abstractions will save you a lot of time by making your Web requests simply appear to be method calls. If for performance or customization needs you need to go down a level, HTTP or HTTPS requests and responses offer a fairly high degree of abstraction and also tend to be firewall friendly. Should you find out that for some reason HTTP requests/responses cannot be adapted to serve your needs, you have the option of moving to sockets-level communication and using streams built on top of sockets.

Working at the sockets level of abstraction requires taking on a significant burden of complexity because you will have to design your own communications protocols to interact with servers rather than using the simple and well-tested HTTP request/response mechanisms. If your application needs to communicate with a server that requires socket-level communication, it is recommended that you look at building a server-side proxy component that communicates with the socket interface and in turn exposes a HTTP or a Web services interface to your application. Because server-to-server communication is generally more reliable than device-to-server communication, doing this may significantly reduce the complexity of your device-side code and increase the reliability of your mobile application.

Only in extreme cases does it make sense to work at a level of communications below the socket level and work with the TCP/IP protocol stack. If your application requires this kind of communication, you will very likely be writing a significant amount of native C language code to work with protocols. The added complexity and required testing this demands is almost never justified by the end application payoff. The higher-level protocols are well tested and your mobile application is taking on an enormous burden to achieve this level of reliability in using its own custom communications protocols. The same also goes for using non-TCP/IP communications; TCP/IP may not be the most ideal communications mechanism for many tasks, but it is very difficult to achieve the level of testing and proven reliability that has gone into these stacks. Unless you are planning on inventing a new commercial protocol and putting the huge amount of design and testing into the effort that this requires, it is a fool's errand to reinvent the wheel to try to get a perfect protocol for your needs. An 80 percent suitable wheel that exists today and has been tested for years is much better than trying to build a new wheel from scratch. Before you go off inventing a new communications protocol or switch to using a lower layer in the communications stack, you should explicitly prove that the existing higher-level communications protocol cannot be used creatively to meet your mobile application's needs.

Always Expect Failure

The key principle in writing communications code is dealing robustly with failure. Traditional communications technologies are often described as a multilayered stack of increasing abstractions starting at the physical layer, ranging through link layers, protocol layers, and up to the application layer. Most of these layers work in a similar way on mobile devices. Each layer typically has some built-in robustness facilities for error detection and dealing with small interruptions in communication. In most cases, you will not need to worry about the specifics of the lower layers of communication; this is pretty much the same as when writing desktop or server code. The only difference is that mobile networks are more subject to intermittent failures than fixed-line networks or stationary wireless networks.

When writing robust communications code, it is extremely important to keep a careful eye on how resources are cleaned up when something goes wrong. Communication can be a complex endeavor involving the establishment of multiple connections and allocation of different system resources in a chained set of steps. When something goes wrong during communications, it is important to clean up thoroughly, discard any system resources your application is holding, and if you are using the .NET Compact Framework make sure to proactively call `Dispose()` on any resources that support this method. Calling `Dispose()` is important because it immediately releases the underlying system resources rather than waiting for the garbage collector to eventually close handles and release locked resources. The C# `using` keyword (for example, `using(myObject) {...your code...}`) can also be a great help here because it not only ensures that `Dispose()` is called under successful circumstances but but also when an exception is thrown inside the `using` code block. It is important to note that some classes like the .NET System.Net.Sockets.Socket class do not have a public `Dispose()` method but rather have a `Close()` method that must be called to release the resources held by the object. Be sure to carefully read the available documentation for whatever communications object you are using to ensure that you fully understand its resource reclamation rules and procedures.

If you inadvertently leave resources open when dealing with error conditions, you are inviting a situation where future communication attempts will fail. Without proper cleanup, an intermittent loss of a network connection will very possibly result in a situation where future attempts to establish a connection fail because a needed local resource was left in an exclusive-access open state earlier and cannot be reopened. Future attempts to reestablish communications will fail even though the physical network connection has been restored. This situation is no different when writing desktop or server code except for the fact that intermittent network failures are more common when the communicating device is both mobile and wireless. Error conditions matter more because they occur more.

There may also be additional cleanup functions exposed by the communications classes and it may be necessary to call these to ensure a graceful exit. If a communications channel needs to be closed manually, be sure to call its `Close()` or `Dispose()` method as appropriate and to wrap that call in error trapping code to deal with the possibility of failure. Under some conditions, an error may occur in your application not due to a communication disruption but due to another source such as when parsing server responses that do not meet your code's expectations. Depending on the application and networked service, it may be important to close down communication in an orderly way. For example, if your application is doing socket-based communication to a custom service that has the concept of logon and logoff, it may be important to try to close communications in an orderly fashion if the application gets into an unexpected state. Rather than just calling `Close()`, your application may want to send whatever logout command is appropriate to the server and then call `Shutdown()` on the socket to finish communications before calling `Close()`. It is important to understand the connection and disconnection patterns of the services your mobile application is using.

Throwing and Catching Exceptions Can Lead to Dangling Connections and Performance Concerns!

Exceptions are just that: They are exceptional circumstances that must be handled by the runtime environment and application code. Throwing an exception starts a complex runtime process as stacks are crawled upward looking for exception handlers, local variables are discarded, and other potentially costly runtime housekeeping chores take place. From a performance perspective, this is typically more expensive than detecting the error-causing condition in advance and preempting the need for an exception to be thrown. As with other performance questions, the final proof is always in the empirical measurements. In addition, because the normal flow of your application's logic is disrupted by a thrown exception, it is possible that important communications cleanup code may be skipped. This can leave communications resources dangling and cause problems down the road for your application.

Using and handling exceptions in your application is a good idea, but it is also important to understand when not to use exceptions. No exceptions should be thrown or have to be to be handled during the *normal execution* of your application. It is not appropriate to use exception generating and catching code to test normal premises in your application because this is a wasteful and convoluted operation. When it is possible to verify things about your communications through normal algorithmic code rather than though attempting an operation and catching an exception if it fails, it is preferable to do so. If your exception handlers are being triggered during normal application execution, it is a good idea to revisit the code and see whether preemptive steps can be taken to prevent the exception from being thrown in the first place.

See Chapter 7, "Step 1: Start with Performance, Stay with Performance," for a sample that compares runtime exception handling with normal algorithmic code.

Listing 15.1 shows a trivial file I/O example to illustrate some of the different points of failure between local and remote file access. Although you can place the code inside a mobile device application's form and run the example, it is probably not worth the effort; the code is there primarily for inspection purposes. As can be seen in the comments in the code, not only is the opening of a file more failure prone when accessing a server, but the actual reading from and writing to a file is also subject to failure due to loss of network access. This failure potential is increased by each layer of communication that separates your device from the data it is accessing. If a wireless network is used, the signal may be lost as the device moves. If a virtual private network is used to access the data through a firewall, this server may fail at any point. If the connection is going through a mobile telephone network, the mobile network may drop the connection. Although each of these layers may be fairly reliable themselves, the compounding of them means that the causes of failure can multiply. For this reason, it is worth being careful when porting local file system code to access remote servers. Code that works robustly locally may be making assumptions that will cause intermittent failures when accessing remote data sources. Two precautionary measures are recommended:

1. *Wrap all remote server access in a try/catch exception block.* Any operation that takes place over a remote connection can fail. Any blocks of code that access off-device resources should be wrapped in exception catching code that deals with this eventuality.
2. *Perform your remote communications compactly and close the connection quickly.* The longer you have a remote socket, file, database connection or any other networked resource open, the greater the opportunity is for something to go wrong. For this reason, it is important to cleanly encapsulate your network communication code to open a connection, do the necessary work, and close the connection before moving on to other work. It is a bad idea to leave a dangling connection open to a networked resource.

Listing 15.1 Trivial File I/O Code That Notes Local vs. Server Differences

```
private void button1_Click(object sender, System.EventArgs e)
{
//Write a file locally
WriteFile("\\testfile.txt");

//Replace server name with your own server and uncomment.
```

```csharp
//Write a file on a network share:
//"\\MyFileServer\MyFileShare"
//WriteFile("\\\\MyFileServer\\MyFileShare\testfile.txt");

System.Windows.Forms.MessageBox.Show("Success");
}

private void button2_Click(object sender, System.EventArgs e)
{
//Read the file locally
int numberLinesInFile;
numberLinesInFile = CountNumberLinesInFile("\\testfile.txt");
//Display the number of lines read in
System.Windows.Forms.MessageBox.Show(
  "Successfully read file " + numberLinesInFile.ToString() +
  " Lines.");

//Replace server name with your own server and uncomment.
/*      //Write the file from a network share:
    //"\\MyFileServer\MyFileShare"
    numberLinesInFile = CountNumberLinesInFile(
      "\\\\MyFileServer\\MyFileShare\testfile.txt");

    //Display the number of lines read in
    System.Windows.Forms.MessageBox.Show(
      "Successfully read file " +
      numberLinesInFile.ToString() +
      " Lines.");
*/
}

private void WriteFile(string filename)
{
//-------------------------------------------------------
//CREATING A FILE:
//
//For local files:
// This could fail if:
// 1. The file already exists and we can not overwrite it
// 2. There is no more room on the file system
//
//For server-based files:
// This could fail for the above reasons as well as because
// of network connectivity issues to the server, server
```

```csharp
//  security issues, etc.
//-------------------------------------------------------

System.IO.StreamWriter myStreamWriter =
  System.IO.File.CreateText(filename);


//------------------------------------------------------------
//WRITING TO A FILE:
//
//For local files:
//  If we successfully opened the file we should be able
//  to write to it as long as we do not run out of disk
//  space.
//
//For server-based files:
//  This could fail for the above reasons as well as because
//  our network connection to the server was lost
//------------------------------------------------------------
myStreamWriter.WriteLine("Hello!");
myStreamWriter.WriteLine("MyTextFile!");
myStreamWriter.WriteLine("GoodBye!");


//----------------------------------------------------
//CLOSE THE FILE:
//As above there is a much higher possibility that
//this could fail when accessing a file on a network
//share
//----------------------------------------------------
myStreamWriter.Close();
}

private int CountNumberLinesInFile(string filename)
{
int numberLinesInput = 0;


//----------------------------------------------------------
//OPEN A FILE:
//
//For local files:
//  It is possible for local device file access to trigger
//  an exception here if the file is inaccessible
//
//For server-based files:
//  In addition to all the reasons possible for failure
```

```
//    when opening a local file there are failures possible
//    because of network access problems, server security
//    problems, etc.
//---------------------------------------------------------
System.IO.StreamReader myStreamReader =
  System.IO.File.OpenText(filename);

  string inputLine;
  //Read in the file line by line
  do
  {
    //----------------------------------------------------------
    //INPUT A LINE:
    //
    //For local files:
    //    If the file was successfully opened, this call should
    //    never fail.
    //
    //For server-based files:
    //    Wireless network access issues that occur during our
    //    file access make it very possible for this code to
    //    fail and throw an exception
    //----------------------------------------------------------
    inputLine = myStreamReader.ReadLine();

    //If we have not returned 'null' it means that we have
    //not hit the end of the file. Up the line count.
    if(inputLine != null)
    {
      numberLinesInput++;
    }
    //Continue execution as long as we have a file to read
  } while(inputLine != null);

  //---------------------------------------------------
  //CLOSE THE FILE:
  //As above there is a higher possibility that
  //this could fail when accessing a file on a network
  //share
  //---------------------------------------------------
  myStreamReader.Close();

//Return the number of lines in the file
return numberLinesInput;
}
```

Simulate Communications Failures to Test Your Application's Robustness

It is highly advisable to test all communications error conditions by explicitly triggering intermittent communications failures and seeing how your mobile application responds to these cases. It is equally important to test how the next attempt at network access behaves after your application has attempted to clean up from a previous communications error.

Simulate Communications Failures via Client-Side Code

Listing 15.2 shows a mechanism to enable you to test your mobile application's robustness in recovering from communications failures. The code snippet contains conditionally compiled code that can be enabled by placing #define DEBUG_SIMULATE_FAILURES at the top of your source file. The function writeDataToSocket() below is called in the normal course of communications. To test the application's response to failure in this communication, the application can set the variable g_failureCode = SimulatedFailures.failInNextWriteSocketCode at any point during the application's execution. When the communications code is subsequently called, it will throw an exception the first time but not subsequent times. This allows testing to simulate the situation where a network connection suddenly drops off and causes a communications failure but is then restored. This kind of use of conditionally compiled testing code is a quick-and-dirty but very effective way to instrument your code to simulate real-world failure conditions.

Writing communications code that is carefully designed and code reviewed by peers is a good idea, but is not sufficient; the code must be tested under explicit failure conditions. There is no substitute for real-world testing, but at the same time causing real-world communications failures for every possible case is difficult. The only real alternative is to try to simulate and explore each possible failure path. Given that communications failures will occur and will cause unusual code paths to be exercised the only way to gain confidence in the robustness of your code is to cause the error conditions to occur in a controlled environment and verify that your application recovers well from them.

Listing 15.2 Simulating Communications Failure to Test Your Application

```csharp
//-----------------------------------------------------------
//A global variable we want to use to indicate that we
//should throw an exception during communications
//-----------------------------------------------------------
#if DEBUG_SIMULATE_FAILURES
//Variable that holds next pending failure
static SimulatedFailures g_failureCode =
          SimulatedFailures.noFailurePending;

//List of failures that we want to simulate
public enum SimulatedFailures
{
  noFailurePending,   //No test failures pending

  //Simulated failures:
  failInNextWriteSocketCode,
  failInNextWebServiceCall,
  failInNextFileIODuringFileOpen,
  failInNextFileIODuringFileRead
  //etc.
}
#endif //DEBUG_SIMULATE_FAILURES


//-----------------------------------------------------------
//The function we are using to communicate data...
//-----------------------------------------------------------
private void writeDataToSocket(
  System.Net.Sockets.Socket mySocket,
  byte[] dataToSend)
{
  //-----------------------------------------------------------
  //Only compile this code in if we are testing network failures
  //-----------------------------------------------------------
#if DEBUG_SIMULATE_FAILURES
//If this is the failure we want to test, throw an Exception
if (g_failureCode ==
SimulatedFailures.failInNextWriteSocketCode)
{
  //Reset the failure so it does not occur next time
  //this function is called
  g_failureCode  = SimulatedFailures.noFailurePending;
```

```
    throw new Exception("Test communications failure: " +
            g_failureCode.ToString());
}
#endif

  //Send the data as normal...
  mySocket.Send(dataToSend);
} //end function
```

Simulate Communications Failures via Server-Side Code

Just as it is possible to insert testing code on a device to simulate error conditions, it is also advisable to stress test your application's communications experience by simulating failures and delays on server-side code. By instrumenting your server code, it is possible to force servers to abruptly terminate a request or to indefinitely hang in the middle of sending a response. In these cases, your mobile application must be able to continue providing its end user a highly responsive and robust experience despite the errors. Testing by simulating errors thrown on the client as well as causing failures and delays on server-side code is a good way to ensure this is the case. For example, in the case of calling a Web service, an easy way to do this is to pass an extra parameter up with the Web service request that indicates an error condition it wants to test. By default, the testing parameter can indicate normal operation and other values for that parameter could indicate that the Web service should throw an error or cause a long delay before sending a response. The client calling the specially instrumented Web service can then intermittently make a request that will generate one of these conditions and make it possible to test its response.

Keep Data-Synchronization Progress Transparent to the User

It is important for user peace of mind to know the status of their data. Just as e-mail programs offer the user a notion of an "outbox" that contains untransmitted mail and printer queues allow the user to inspect "pending jobs," your application should offer a transparent view into the synchronization status of the user's data.

There is a balance to be reached in exposing synchronization data to users. The balance is between offering users a clear view into what is going on with their data and interrupting the users with status information they do not care about. By default, when synchronization occurs smoothly the user does not want to be interrupted by modal dialogs that pop up stating, "Data uploaded successfully!" Similarly the user would probably prefer not to be interrupted every 30 seconds by large text flashing in front of them stating "I am attempting to connect to the server again."

For this reason, it is often useful to have a small graphical indicator on your mobile device application's screen that lets users know at a glance what the status of their data's transmission is. What kind of graphic to use and where to place it will depend on the user interface guidelines of the particular device you are working with. Some devices such as Pocket PCs offer ample room for a line of text on the screen that gives a summary of the communications status. On other devices, such as Smartphones, screen real estate is limited and only a few words of text or a small icon's worth of information may be possible. At a minimum, the user should be provided with the following summary information:

- *Knowledge of pending communication tasks*—If there are communications tasks that are stored in the local queue, the user should be made aware of this. It should be possible for the user to drill down into this data and examine which tasks are pending and to manually force a communications attempt when they think it will succeed.
- *Knowledge of the completion of communication tasks*—The end user wants to know when pending tasks are successfully completed. It is a good idea to have a visual mechanism for informing the user that all is well.
- *Knowledge of problems preventing communication*—If communications tasks have been attempted on the user's behalf and have failed, the user should be made aware of this. It is possible the user may want to take action based on this information. They may choose to attempt to remedy the communications problem themselves, for example by coming above ground from a subway station and then attempting to synchronize or aborting the pending work because it is no longer relevant. In either case, it is useful for end users to know that the work that was being done on their behalf was not successful.

It is, of course, important to give the right level of information to the user; information such as "Patient312.xml transfer pending available socket port 8080 communication to ServerXYZ" is probably meaningless to most users, whereas the information "Upload pending: 'Bob Smith' patient evaluation" is much more useful.

The end goal of providing relevant communications status information to the users is to make them an active participant in the communications process. Users feel much more empowered when they have a clear conceptual understanding of what is going on. There may be things the end user can do to help the communications process along, or users may just need to content themselves with an understanding of the successes and failures that are occurring. In either case, the anxiety level of users is lower when they have a transparent view into the communications processes that occur on their behalf.

Assume That Data Transmission Rates and Latencies Will Vary

Some networks operate dramatically faster than others. In addition, networks can become congested as increasing numbers of devices attempt to communicate simultaneously. Latency rates for establishing connections as well as for sending requests and receiving responses will vary. A device operating at the periphery of a network's transmission range may need to attempt multiple sends or receives of packets of information in order to get the data through. For all these reasons, it is important for your application to deal robustly with the reality of variable bandwidth and latency times. Testing in a controlled environment is good and will enable you to make the greatest progress in writing your application, but it is important to plan for the reality that in real-world usage communications rates will vary. It is important to ensure that the application user's experience remains a good one despite all this variability.

Implement Needed Communications Security Early in Your Design

Because mobile devices often communicate over public networks and over wireless channels, it is important to think about what data security is required, how it will be built in to your application, and what effects it will have on the application's deployment and performance. There exist many ways of encrypting communications today; one of the most popular and easy to use is HTTPS and SSL. SSL stands for Secure Sockets Layer, and HTTPS is Web communication built on top of SSL.

Fundamentally, your application will need to decide (1) whether it requires secure communication, (2) which networks it will communicate over, and (3) how any needed security will be implemented.

In most ways, secure communications works a lot like unsecured communication but with some additional setup steps and operational overhead. When secure communications are required over a public network, your application may need to attach digital certificates to Web requests and verify the veracity of data that is sent back down to it. When communications are encrypted and decrypted, additional computation takes place on both ends of the line and this will have some performance effects; how big these effects are must be tested. Although the core communication code works very similarly to unsecured communication, additional steps are required. These steps take time to design and incur some runtime performance penalty. If your application requires secure communication, it is best to design this in early and test it. As with asynchronous communications, security code is not something you want to try to retrofit into an already completed design. When encrypted communications are required, having the code needed for secure communication built in and performance tested with your application will save you a great deal of redesign down the road.

Communications and Networking Options

A mobile application can utilize many different communications mechanisms to move information onto or off the device. It is important to realize that there is no uniquely best communications mechanism. Each mechanism has its own strengths, weaknesses, and appropriate usage scenarios. Some communications mechanisms are peer to peer, some are body-area network oriented, and others are Internet or LAN oriented. When looking at a given communications need, it is helpful to draw up a list of the potential solution technologies and map out how a solution using those technologies would work. In almost all cases, there will be more than one potentially applicable solution, and deciding which mechanisms are best suited for your mobile application needs is a matter of both creativity and hard-nosed analysis. Below are described some of the most common communications mechanisms.

Wi-Fi: Local Area Networking

Also known as 802.11 (in all of its flavors, 802.11a, b, g, etc.), Wi-Fi is essentially short-distance Ethernet-based communication done wirelessly; it is a communications mechanism for local area networks (LANs). Wi-Fi has many things to recommend it: It is popular, conceptually easy to use, it supports relatively high-bandwidth communications (for example, often 10Mbps or better), it is easy to set up, and Wi-Fi communications tend to be inexpensive. A Wi-Fi base station connects to the network and usually provides wireless access in a diameter of a few hundred feet if not obstructed (see Figure 15.1). Communicating over Wi-Fi is generally programmatically identical to communicating over an Ethernet cable. As a general-purpose "I need network connectivity" solution, it is a great choice. There are, however, several things to consider when using Wi-Fi for communications:

- *Do you do Wi-Fi?*—Not all mobile devices support Wi-Fi. Most laptops today have Wi-Fi built in, but most mobile phones do not. Some mobile devices will allow a Wi-Fi card to be added, commonly via a Compact Flash or Secure Digital card. In the future, more devices will support Wi-Fi, but this will not be a ubiquitous choice.

- *Your Wi-Fi or somebody else's?*—If you have a fixed amount of area that needs network access, it is feasible to set up your own Wi-Fi connections. If your mobile application needs to work in the world at large but does not need continuous network connections, using a third-party Wi-Fi network is reasonable as well. In most places today, it is relatively easy to find a reputable "Wi-Fi hot spot" in a hotel or in a city at large if the mobile application's user is willing to look for one. However, despite user enthusiasm and a great deal of hype, it is unlikely that good Wi-Fi access options will blanket the earth any time soon. Even if there were more blanket Wi-Fi coverage, different Wi-Fi services would have different payment models and access rights, ranging from free to expensive. Free networks come with few guarantees. Some Wi-Fi networks will allow access to the Internet at large and some only to the local LAN. All Wi-Fi access is not equal. When traveling along large stretches of highway or making your way through a city of any reasonable size, you will find a lot of empty space dotted with a frequent but not ubiquitous patchwork of Wi-Fi base stations.

- *Security*—Sending packets over a Wi-Fi connection is like shouting from the roof of a building; everyone who wants can hear you. This is not as bad as it sounds because Wi-Fi networks can offer various degrees of built-in encryption support, ranging from shared secret keys between the Wi-Fi base station and the devices to certificate/public key–based security (which is highly secure). Even when communicating over a public unencrypted Wi-Fi channel, it is easy to use SSL (Secure Sockets Layer) or HTTPS (Secure HTTP) communications to encrypt your application layer communication. If you are transmitting important data, be prepared to encrypt it.

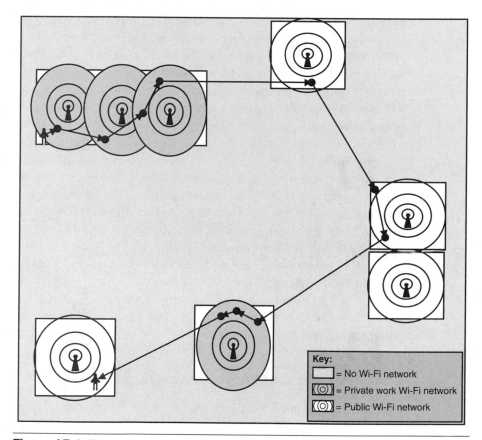

Figure 15.1 The nomadic wanderings of a Wi-Fi user. Wi-Fi enables pockets of high bandwidth communications. Wi-Fi-dependent applications require the user to travel to a Wi-Fi hot spot to get connectivity. While the mobile application is synchronizing, the user is typically not moving in between Wi-Fi access points (that is, not roaming).

- *Power consumption*—Wi-Fi is not a particularly power-efficient communications mechanism. As devices and their batteries become smaller and smaller, the power budget to support Wi-Fi communications becomes smaller. This means that there is a practical limit to how small a device can be and still support usable Wi-Fi communications. Doubtless hardware and software innovation will occur in this area, but today problems remain.

A Few Words on WiMax

WiMax, also known as 802.16 and 802.20, is an emerging standard intended to blend the best of Wi-Fi with the best of mobile telephone networks and provide high-bandwidth Wi-Fi-like packet-based networking over large areas and potentially allow roaming between access points. Whereas 802.11 (Wi-Fi) is intended for wireless LANs (local area networks), these new standards are intended to enable wireless MANs (metropolitan area networks) covering much larger radiuses than Wi-Fi. Like any new standard, WiMax will almost certainly take some time to emerge but it does offer significant promise for faster communications at lower costs. Traditional fixed-line network operators, mobile network operators, and communications hardware manufacturers all have significant competitive interests in this area and how this communications landscape will develop is anyone's guess at this point. The author of this book makes no predictions other than to offer his opinion that it will be an interesting and wild ride for the next few years. As with all the wireless communications mechanisms discussed here, working with WiMax will require your application to deal with intermittent network access and heterogeneous networks consisting of Wi-Fi, WiMax, 2.5G, 3G, and other networking technologies.

See `http://grouper.ieee.org/groups/802/16/` and `http://grouper.ieee.org/groups/802/20/` for more information on these emerging standards.

Bluetooth: Personal Area Networking

Bluetooth, a communications mechanism for personal area networks (PANs), is intended to network together the kinds of devices users may have around themselves in their immediate environment. PDAs, laptops, mobile phones, printers and perhaps even vending machines and kiosks are all potential Bluetooth networking targets. Bluetooth's intent is to allow various different devices that come into proximity to one another to form ad hoc relationships. As Figure 15.2 shows, there are two kinds of computing devices that Bluetooth connects, personal devices carried by an individual and external devices that the owner of a Bluetooth-enabled device may come into contact with.

A common misnomer about Bluetooth is that it is just "one thing" or a single communications protocol; actually it is not. Although built on top of a core networking stack, the most important thing about Bluetooth is the "profiles" that are built on top of it. Bluetooth itself is a low-level communications mechanism, but almost all the interesting work happens at the level of Bluetooth profiles. The practical implication of this is that unless two different devices happen to support the same Bluetooth profiles, they will have little to say to one another. For instance, a Bluetooth printer that supports the Bluetooth "Basic Printing Profile" may be dimly aware of the fact that

Personal Area Networks (PANs) network devices are carried by the user and allow conversations with computing appliances the user comes into temporary contact with.

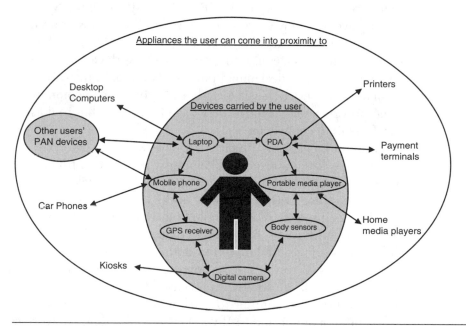

Figure 15.2 Personal area network schematic.

there is a remote control in the same room that supports the "A/V Remote Control Profile," but the two devices have nothing meaningful to say to one another unless they share a common set of profiles. A list of supported profiles is available on the Bluetooth organization's Web site, `www.bluetooth.org`.

In practice, the need for two devices to have matching profiles is not as limiting as it sounds because of two reasons: (1) Common devices that would benefit from talking to one another tend to support sets of overlapping profiles; and (2) Although there are many profiles, in practice a few dominate the areas interesting to mobile devices. Common profiles exist for synchronizing PDA-type information and for using your mobile phone as a network connections hub.

Importantly a profile also exists for using a Bluetooth device as a RS-232 serial port; this is appropriately called the Serial Port Profile. This allows a Bluetooth device to appear as a COM port and supports old-style serial communications. Many legacy information sources have traditionally used

RS-232 serial port communication, and these communications protocols have gained wide acceptance over the years. Traditionally, these devices have hooked into computers using a RS-232 cable. A prime example of this that is relevant to mobility is GPS (Global Positioning System) receivers. These have for many years used a NMEA (National Marine Electronics Association) serial protocol to transfer global positioning information from a location sensor to a computing device. These devices are now going wireless; and instead of designing brand new protocols, many of the next generation of these devices have elected just to continue to communicate with the same proven serial protocols they have in the past but to do so over a wireless Bluetooth connection.

Programming using Bluetooth follows a similar pattern to working with the profiles listed above. A developer working with Bluetooth can either work with low-level Bluetooth APIs, possibly via sockets if the device supports a mapping between sockets and Bluetooth, or they can work using profile-specific APIs. For example, if a Bluetooth device is being accessed via the Serial Port Profile, the developer can dispense with any need to think about Bluetooth altogether and simply work with COM port APIs. The choice is up to you, but as noted earlier in this chapter more abstract higher-level APIs are almost always easier to work with. Even the serial port APIs can be much simpler to work with than delving into the details of Bluetooth communications. If you have the possibility of working with simpler, more abstracted APIs it is recommendable to do so.

If you are programming with the .NET Compact Framework version 1.1, you will need to call into native code to access Bluetooth functionality unless a third party has already built specific managed-code wrappers for you to use. The .NET Compact Framework version 1.1 has no built-in support either for working with Bluetooth or with the COM serial port. There is, however, good sample code on www.gotdotnet.com that can show you how to call into native code to accomplish low-level communications tasks such as serial port access.

Note: Because Bluetooth was designed specifically with mobile devices in mind, it tends to have fairly good power-consumption characteristics, but there are even more specialized communications mechanisms available if needed. In addition to personal area network technologies such as Bluetooth, there also exist lower-power-consumption body area network (BAN) technologies such as Zig-Bee (IEEE 802.15). These BAN networking protocols are suitable for embedded sensors and other kinds of devices that require very low power consumption.

Mobile Phone Networks/Cellular

The principal advantage of mobile phone network communication is broad area availability. The wide-area coverage of mobile phone networks is so pervasive that it is easy to forget how novel this facility really is; it truly offers the possibility of "data almost anywhere." This advantage is tempered by three disadvantages: generally lower bandwidth, generally higher data-transfer costs, and fragmented network standards. Even with these disadvantages, mobile phone networks are important potential conduits for your mobile application's data. It is important to understand something about them to make proper usage of the services they offer.

Modern mobile phone networks offer both voice and data channels for communications. Mobile phone network data channels offer applications the ability to send and receive data at moderate to good data rates. The actual data rate will vary considerably for different network technologies as well as due to local contention by other mobile devices to use the data facilities. Just as an unlimited number of phone conversations cannot be supported by a single mobile communications base station (a.k.a. "cell tower"), there is a fixed amount of data bandwidth that must be shared by different users. This is also true for other technologies such as Wi-Fi, but an important difference is that because a mobile phone network base station serves a much larger radius than a Wi-Fi base station, the bandwidth can more easily be diluted by a large number of users.

Mobile network technology is fragmented by region as well as by technical generation. A full discussion of this subject would fill its own book and probably be out of date before it was published. For reference, here are a few of the most relevant terms:

- *Mobile Network technology: GSM and CDMA phone networks*— Traditionally, Europe and the Middle East have used GSM mobile technology standards, and North America and Korea have used CDMA. (Older North American networks used TDMA, and Japan used yet another standard.) This line is staring to blur as increasingly some North American mobile phone operators have started to offer GSM services; these services are typically first available in high-population areas. GSM radio frequencies used in North America and Europe differ, and to use a mobile phone in both environments an appropriate "dual-band" or "tri-band" phone is required; thankfully these phones are quite common today, and rich mobile devices commonly offer this capability. There are also efforts to produce single phones that can communicate using different standards (for example, CDMA and GSM on the same phone); these may or may not prove to be viable in the marketplace. At the same time, newer standards such as CDMA2000 (the 3G successor to CDMA) and W-CDMA (the 3G successor to GSM) are also replacing older standards. Mobile standards are converging, but it will be many years before the concept of an affordable phone that works anywhere in the world is a reality.

■ *Technological generation: 2.5G, 3G, Beyond 3G.* These G numbers refer to the generation of the mobile network technology. Generally speaking, the higher the number, the faster the network. For most mobile device data purposes, 2.5G is the first generation that has practical value. 2.5G for GSM mobile networks is generally referred to as GPRS (General Packet Radio Service). 3G networks offer significantly higher data rates, but are relatively new, and there are business challenges in deploying these networks widely. 3G handsets can typically roam and operate in 2.5G environments with 2.5G data rates. UMTS (Universal Mobile Telecommunications System) is another name for 3G data services. Anything beyond this (4G and so on) is generally referred to as "Beyond 3G"; as of the writing of this book, these are still on the drawing board. Note: Mobile data communication is also possible on "2G" networks; 2G networks typically use the voice channel for data communications so that accessing the data network is akin to making a phone call. A 2G mobile phone network is a first-generation digital network; 1G = analog communication.

If all of this sounds confusing, it's because it is. The global world of mobile phone communications is a mess today! Moreover, it is likely to remain a global patchwork of different systems and generations of technologies for some time to come. The reason for this is primarily financial; it costs a huge amount of money to license radio spectrum from governments as well as to deploy and operate mobile networks. This means that rolling out new networks is a costly endeavor and is generally done in a patchwork "wire the most lucrative markets first" basis. Network upgrades are expensive, often requiring new base stations and customer handsets. Movement to a new generation of technology requires deploying parallel overlapping networks that allow network operators to continue supporting existing paying customers while developing new services. Further complicating this ecosystem is the fact that many mobile telephone network operators view Wi-Fi as both a threat and potential opportunity; different carriers are taking different approaches to giving their existing mobile telephone customers access to Wi-Fi hot spots with common billing mechanisms. The following are some guidelines for navigating the mobile network choices available for use by mobile applications:

1. *Abstract the network technology.* Thankfully, as a mobile application developer, you can be abstracted from most of the lower-level details of mobile communications technologies. A socket connection to a Web server is the same on 2.5G or 3G networks, and the socket does not care whether the underlying radio technology is CDMA, GSM, or something else. The important learning here is to work at the highest level of technological abstraction that is possible. HTTP requests and responses are a good high level of abstraction, sockets are one level lower but also neutral to the networks used. The farther you can get away from the device's radio interface, the more portable your mobile application will be. There is no reason why a properly designed mobile application should not run unaltered on a GSM or CDMA network.

2. *Deal gracefully with lower data rates.* Although 3G networks can offer considerably higher throughput, for the foreseeable future it is reasonable to assume that your target mobile devices will probably operate in a mixed 2.5G and better environment. For a 2.5G network, it is reasonable to assume a base communications speed of around 20Kb/second; 20 kilobits/s = 2.5KB a second. It is possible your application will get higher data rates when running on better networks, but equally possible your data rates will be lower on crowded networks; this is somewhere around the speed of an analog phone modem. A second consideration is latency; a 2.5G mobile data channel will almost certainly have higher communications latency than a wired Internet connection; this is important if you are expecting instant (below 1 second) response times. If your mobile device application is going to use mobile telephone network communications, it is important to be able to respond robustly to lower network data rates and higher latency. A reasonable rule of thumb to consider in your designs is "when downloading data larger than 20KB, it is appropriate to keep track of the amount of time the download is taking and to consider aborting the operation if the download will take an unreasonably long time." The actual size threshold and maximum wait time are of course determined by the nature of the application, the communications networks being used, and the end user's expectations. The mobile application's end user should not be left waiting an indefinite amount of time for data to arrive even if the data is

being downloaded on a background thread; measure the download rate in progress and set the user's expectations appropriately.

3. *Understand the monetary cost of communications.* Although some older (mostly 2G) data connections mechanisms charged by the time duration of a connection, most mobile telephone network data services charge based on the total number of bits transferred. Rates may vary significantly between home networks and roaming networks. All of this will have a direct effect on the cost to the user of using your mobile device application to communicate. There are no definitive rules about what cost of communication is appropriate or inappropriate; this will depend on the nature of your application. When choosing a mobile communications technology, it is worth measuring your upload and download sizes and comparing estimated prices using different models of communication.

Mobile Phone Network, Wi-Fi, or Both?

Increasingly, rich mobile phone devices are coming with Wi-Fi support either built in or available via a plug-in card; Compact Flash and Secure Digital Wi-Fi cards are two of the most popular formats. Alternatively, laptops and specialized mobile computing devices that have Wi-Fi support built in often have the ability of adding mobile telephone network access via plug-in cards.

Given that added features mean added price and power consumption, does it make sense to have a mobile device that communicates over mobile telephone and Wi-Fi networks? The answer is, "It depends on the application," which is another way of saying, "It depends on *your* design."

For many applications, it should be a design goal to work well when deployed to devices using either Wi-Fi or mobile telephone networks. Generally speaking, the more popular and useful an application, the more likely that users will want to run it on different kinds of network hardware. Users will want to take advantage of high bandwidth where it's available, but still need to use the applications acceptably on slower networks. As long as your application is using high-level networking technologies such as sockets or HTTP, this should not be a technical problem because both of these levels of communication abstract the underlying network protocols.

When working with different mobile telephone or Wi-Fi networks, it is important for your mobile application to be aware of the *measured* (not theoretical) throughput that the communications channel is providing. It is one thing to "work fine as long as the user has an infinite amount of time to wait" and quite another thing to "always provide the user an acceptable experience." If your mobile application is going to be run on devices that support both Wi-Fi and mobile telephone network communications, you may want to allow the application to run in two different modes, a low-bandwidth and high-bandwidth mode. The low-bandwidth mode should transfer only essential data and cache the rest of the data until a high-bandwidth connection can be established.

Consider the example of a traffic-accident investigator. Suppose that our investigator spends his or her days traveling to accident scenes generating accident reports and taking digital photographs as evidence. It is important that an accident be reported as quickly as possible; all parties to the accident have insurance claims that need to be filed, medical processes may need to be initiated, cars may need to be towed to various locations, and so on. For all of these reasons, a quickly submitted accident report is essential. Of longer-term importance is the evidence relating to the accident; for this, detailed photographs are invaluable. An application integrated into the mobile telephone the investigator carries with him could be of great use in making this process more efficient. Upon arriving on the scene of an accident, the investigator initiates a new accident report on a mobile device. The mobile device application enables the investigator to input the essential information about the accident, such as the license plate numbers of the cars involved, the driver's licenses of the drivers, passenger contact information, and an initial assessment of the accident. As soon as this information is ready, it can immediately be uploaded to a server using a mobile telephone connection. Because the information is mostly text and the size is relatively small, the upload process is quick and easily accomplished over a mobile telephone network. With this information entered into the system, the process of helping the parties involved recover can immediately begin; everyone benefits. Our accident investigator can now get down to the detailed work: taking detailed photographs, recording voice notes, and gathering additional information. Some of this information can be uploaded immediately if it is of use, but the bulk of the information can be cached on the device, saving the investigator from a time-consuming and expensive upload. Later, when our investigator returns to his or her office or goes to a location that offers Wi-Fi access, the investigator's mobile application can upload the digital photographs, recorded voice notes, and other large-size data.

It is important not to overdesign a network access model by trying to outguess the mobile application's user. It may be possible to gather a great deal of information about available networks and automatically perform smart high-bandwidth and low-bandwidth communications on behalf of the mobile application's user; alternatively, it may not. Trying to automate network access decisions is a good thing, but not at the expense of offering the user the final choice. In the end, it is the end users who will need to use your mobile application in the field and they will be the best people to make the appropriate communications decisions. Your application should supply them with the right kind of information and empower them to make the communications decisions that make sense for them. Allowing the user to set communications preferences, enabling the user to attempt communications on demand, and allowing them to defer operations that are not meeting their expectations are good ways to do this. A proper balance must be struck between giving users too little control and giving them an overly complex array of options. Some guidelines include the following:

- *Allow the user to set basic communications preferences.* When possible, your mobile application should have a scalable set of information transfer options that allow the application's users to tune the application based on network bandwidth and their own needs. Allowing users to scale the number of database records for download (for example, small, medium, full) or allowing the users the option to download only text information and defer the download of related image data are two examples of user-settable preferences.
- *Give the user the ability to attempt communications "on demand."* Often the mobile application's end user will be in the best position to make connectivity decisions. For example, if Wi-Fi or mobile telephone network connectivity is required, a mobile device user can walk to a physical location that offers this connectivity. After the user has entered a space where she knows that the needed connectivity is available, she should immediately be able to command the mobile application to attempt synchronization. Putting the end user in the driver's seat is very empowering.
- *Allow users to defer operations that do not meet their expectations.* Try as you might, it is nearly impossible to predict and respond robustly to all communications challenges. A network may be congested and offer lower throughput, proxy servers may be having problems, or any number of other communications problems could occur that prevent your mobile application from meeting its user's expectations. You should write robust code to deal with these situations. Just as importantly, you should enable end users to take charge of the situation and command the application to stop trying to communicate and to defer operations until later. Your mobile application must provide the necessary information to enable users to make intelligent communications decisions, and then it must respond to the users' wants. Listing the number of attempts or the "% complete" of a communication operation and enabling users to cancel or defer the

operation if it is not progressing at the rate they need are examples of empowering users to make these kinds of intelligent decisions.

Figure 15.3 shows a schematic example of mobile communications occurring using both mobile telephone network and Wi-Fi communications. As can be seen in the diagram, mobile telephone networks offer wide areas of coverage with relatively few "dead spots" where communication is not possible. In contrast, Wi-Fi networks have much lower area coverage but offer high-bandwidth data-transfer opportunities. Mobile device users can use the mobile telephone network to perform frequent small-sized data transfers as needed in the field, but can queue up larger transfers until they get to a high-bandwidth Wi-Fi hot spot.

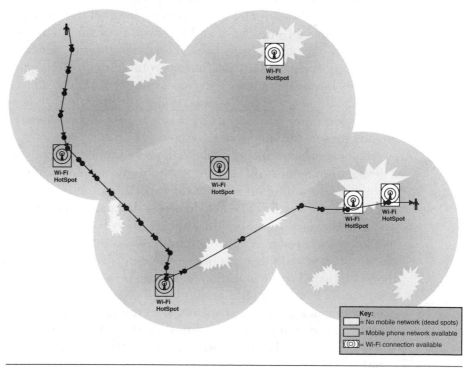

Figure 15.3 The nomadic wanderings of a mobile phone and Wi-Fi user. Mobile phone network data connections offer broad coverage but usually at lower data rates than Wi-Fi connections. When the user is roaming in a wide area, the mobile network offers near-continual connectivity to server data. The user may choose to specifically go to a Wi-Fi network hot spot when large data transfers are required. In addition, Wi-Fi may be available in some "dead spots" (for example, underground) where broad mobile phone networks are not available.

Cradle / PC Cable

Cradle-based communication is data transfer that occurs directly to or through an intermediary computer when the device is hooked up to that computer using a physical cable. Instead of having a direct network connection, the mobile device communicates to a desktop or laptop computer. The device either synchronizes data with the computer or uses it as its means to gain access to the network. Note: For network access through a host computer, the synchronization software must support this feature; for instance, starting with the Pocket PC 2002, versions of Microsoft's ActiveSync software support the ability for a device to tunnel through a desktop to get to the Internet. Different device technologies will have different software to enable this kind of "pass-through" support.

The benefit of cradle-based communication is its relative simplicity. Existing owners of rich mobile devices often have all the software and cables needed to make things work and the owners of these computers usually have their computers already hooked up to the Internet. Cradle-based communication is particularly useful for prototyping, testing, and debugging purposes because it allows easy access to networked resources in a controlled environment. Cradle-based communication is also inexpensive because it does not rely on any network access infrastructure that is not already present for laptops or desktops.

The major shortcoming of cradle-based communication is that it tethers a device to computers that support the required synchronization software. A mobile device solution that relies on a specific set of host computers to allow data transfer will not be able to access data "any time, anywhere." However, if the mobile solution you are developing does not require instantaneous access to networks, but instead only requires periodic synchronization of data that can be done through a PC's network connection, the PC-tethered communication model can be a good choice. As with Wi-Fi access, it is possible to use cradle-based communication to complement other communications mechanisms; for example, relatively small amounts of data can be sent and received in the field using mobile telephone networks while larger data items are left cached on the device for later synchronization via a PC connection.

Network Cable

Using Ethernet cable-based communications for mobile devices is very similar to Wi-Fi-based communication. Although mostly the same, the two models differ in the following ways:

- *Network cables are more location dependent than Wi-Fi.* A Wi-Fi base station has a communications diameter of a few hundred feet, which is significantly longer than most cables; in this sense, Wi-Fi is more mobile than network cable. As a practical matter, if flexible network access is required throughout a relatively bounded space such as the interior of a building, Wi-Fi is often less expensive than wiring the whole area with cables. However, anywhere you can reach a network cable is network accessible; in areas where a Wi-Fi signal cannot easily reach, a physical cable may be the only option for connectivity.
- *Network cables offer some security advantages over Wi-Fi.* Although Wi-Fi networks can be configured to communicate using encrypted channels, they are still broadcasting over the air. A wired scenario offers protection against others eavesdropping on the radio signals; this protection is not bulletproof, but it is one level of increased security. Note: If you are connecting to or through a public network, this increased security is minimal; you will need to rely on encrypted communications to meet your security needs. (This is a good idea in any case.)
- *Extra hardware will probably be required.* Although most of today's laptops have both wired and wireless networking capabilities built in, this is not true for most mobile devices. Due to added size, power consumption, and manufacturing cost, this is likely to remain the case. An external network card (usually Compact Flash or Secure Digital) will often be required to support network cable-based communication.

As with cradle-based communication, a physical network cable connection can prove very useful when prototyping and debugging mobile device solutions. However, it is important to realize that connectivity speeds and reliability characteristics will be much lower for many wireless communication mechanisms; although wired network connections are a useful tool, they are not sufficient to develop and test an application that will be run on wireless networks.

IrDA

At low levels of abstraction, IrDA (Infrared Data Association) is simply serial-based communication over an infrared channel; with higher-level programming models, it is significantly more than this. A sophisticated multichannel programming model has been built on top of IrDA, and it can be an excellent and flexible communications choice (see www.irda.org for full details).

IrDA is a useful technology for device peer-to-peer communications because it is inexpensive and nearly ubiquitous. Because IrDA technology does not cost much to manufacture, is small, and does not consume a lot of power, it is integrated into many mobile devices, including Pocket PCs and Smartphones. To communicate, two devices are physically lined up to one another and then a conversation is initiated.

For mobile application development, IrDA is of interest for two reasons: First, like Bluetooth, IrDA can be used to enable a device to communicate with external networks through another device; for example, my PDA can use my mobile phone to make a data connection; this tunnel-through communications capability is somewhat limited by the need to physically keep the devices lined up for the duration of the communication, a limitation Bluetooth does not have. Second, and perhaps more interestingly, IrDA can be used to share information between two different devices; the classic example of this is "beaming" or "squirting" an address book entry from one mobile device to another. Because the bandwidth of IrDA is reasonable, a fair amount of information can be transferred by "squirting" it from one device to another.

Point-to-Point Networking with IrDA

Before "peer-to-peer" networking, there came "point-to-point" networking, and for this IrDA is king. IrDA-based communication offers an easy and relatively high-bandwidth mechanism for exchanging data between adjacent devices. Although lacking some of the "luster of the new" that personal area networking technology such as Bluetooth has, it has the virtue of being tried, tested, and easy to work with. If your users do not mind pointing two devices at one another, IrDA may well be the right peer-to-peer technology for your mobile application's needs.

IrDA is a mature technology that often goes unnoticed and is underutilized by application developers. I believe this is due to a lack of awareness of how easy to use and flexible IrDA actually is. In the .NET Compact Framework, IrDA programming is exposed via a sockets interface very similar to the sockets interface used for TCP/IP (Internet) communication. The principal difference between using sockets for Internet communication and sockets for IrDA communication is the concept of a "named port."

When using TCP/IP and sockets, each machine has its own IP address (for example, 200.198.126.81) and a list of potential numbered ports it can use for communications. Servers open up the ports they want to listen for request on. A client device can then request a conversation with a server by specifying both the machine's IP address and the port it wants to connect to. With IrDA point-to-point communication, one device's IrDA port is lined up with another device's, so no addressing scheme is needed to locate a server. If an application wants to expose an IrDA socket interface to transmit its owner's contact information, it might open an IrDA socket it names OwnerContactInfo. Similarly, a photo album application that wants to allow other devices to download photos from it may open an IrDA socket called PhotoDownloadService. Client applications on other devices that want to connect to these services ask for them by name.

A conversation between a Web browser and server goes something like this:

1. Server: Opens port 80 for listening for incoming requests.
2. Browser: "Hello server number '200.198.126.81,' can I have a connection to Port 80?"
3. Server: "Yes you can, here is a port connection for you to use for communications."
4. Browser: Takes the connection it has been given and starts a conversation on it that results in the downloading of several files.

A similar conversation using sockets over IrDA would go as follows:

1. Receiving device: Creates a named port ReceiveAppXYZData.
2. Sending device: "Hello, I would like to make a connection to a device listening on port ReceiveAppXYZData."
3. Receiving device: "Yes, I am listening on that port. Let's make a connection."
4. Sending device: Takes the connection it has been given and starts a conversation on it that results in the sending of data.

When two devices are in physical proximity, socket-based IrDA communication is a simple and effective way to exchange information.

IrDA Sockets and the .NET Compact Framework

As noted previously, the .NET Compact Framework offers a socket interface for working with IrDA. If you are familiar with using sockets for Internet (TCP/IP) communications, there are only a few small differences you need to understand to make use of sockets over IrDA. The sample code shows how to use IrDA Sockets to communicate between two devices.

> ### *Presently .NET Sockets Support for IrDA Is Only Available in the .NET Compact Framework; It Is Not Available on the Desktop .NET Framework*
>
> IrDA support is built in to version 1.1 of the .NET Compact Framework, but is not available in version 1.1 of the desktop .NET Framework. This is a case where the .NET Compact Framework led the way in introducing a technology interesting to mobile devices. Future versions of the desktop .NET Framework may support IrDA sockets programming, but until then if you want to communicate between desktop computers and the .NET Compact Framework you will need to call into native code on the desktop to access IrDA functionality. On the positive side, the desktop native code should not be too complicated because the Windows native code sockets APIs support using IrDA; the C/C++ code should look relatively similar to the C# or VB.NET code you use on the device. For more information, look in the Windows Platform SDK under the topics "IrDA Programming with Windows sockets" and "IrDA and Windows sockets reference."

The code in Listings 15.3, 15.4, and 15.5 show how to transmit the contents of a file from one device onto another using IrDA. Do the following to build and run the application:

1. Start Visual Studio .NET (2003 or later) and create a C# Smart Device Application.
2. Choose Pocket PC as the target platform. (A project will be created for you and Pocket PC Form designer will appear.)
3. Add a project reference to System.Net.IrDA. The System.Net.IrDA.DLL component is not referenced by projects by default, so a reference must explicitly be added so that this namespace is available to your application. Note: System.Net.IrDA.DLL is a core part of the .NET Compact Framework and is installed on any device that has the .NET Compact Framework present. It just happens not to be referenced by default in Visual Studio .NET device projects.
4. Add the following controls to the form:
   a. A button; rename it **buttonTestFileSend**.
   b. A button; rename it **buttonTestFileReceive**.
5. For each of the Button controls above, double-click the button in the Form designer. In the event handler function generated, enter the `button<ButtonName>_Click` in Listing 15.3. Note: Be sure also to include any code in Listing 15.3 that is outside the two function definitions.

6. Set the MinimizeBox property of the form to false. At runtime this will give the form an OK box at the top right that makes it easy to close the form and exit the application; this is very useful for repeated testing.

7. Add a new class to your project, name it **IrDAFileSend**, and enter the code in Listing 15.4 into the class.

8. Add a new class to your project, name it **IrDAFileReceive**, and enter the code in Listing 15.5 into the class.

9. Deploy and run the application to two different Pocket PCs (or smart phones).

10. On the first Pocket PC, press the buttonTestFileReceive button. You should see the application's window caption display text indicating that it is waiting for an incoming file.

11. On the second Pocket PC, press the buttonTestFileSend button. You should see the application's window caption display text indicating that it is waiting for a device to send the file to.

12. Point the two devices' IrDA ports at one another. The file should get transferred from one device to the other and message boxes should pop up on both devices indicating the transmission was successful.

Result: A file from the second Pocket PC should be transmitted to the first Pocket PC. You can verify this by starting the Pocket PC File Explorer, going to the My Device root directory, and clicking the file myTestReceiveFile; this will open the file up in PocketWord and show the contents of the file.

After you have successfully tested the application synchronously, try to call the IrDA send and receive functions asynchronously. You will need to write code on both devices for your user interface thread to periodically poll the state of the IrDAFileSend or IrDAFileReceive classes to see whether it has completed.

> **Presently .NET Compact Framework IrDA Sockets Code Will Run on Physical Devices That Have IrDA Hardware Such as Pocket PCs and Smart Phones, but the Code Will Not Run Properly in the Emulator**
>
> If you try to create or connect to an IrDA socket with code running in a Pocket PC, Smartphone, or Windows CE emulator, your application will probably encounter a runtime exception. This means that unlike most other .NET Compact Framework features your IrDA code will need to be designed and tested using a real physical device. Although this is not a blocking difficulty, it does mean that the design and testing process will be a bit more complex because to test IrDA code you will need two physical devices running the .NET Compact Framework, one to act as the IrDA server and one to act as the client. Because of this added complexity, it is recommended to write and test your IrDA communications code separately from the rest of your application using the simplest possible application model to work out the kinks in the communication. After you have all the kinks worked out of your IrDA code, you can then bring it into your larger application.

Listing 15.3 Test Code to go Inside a Form Class to Test IrDA Transmit and Receive

```
//The name we want to give to our IrDA socket
const string myIrDASocketName = "IrDaTestFileTransmit";

private void buttonTestFileSend_Click(object sender,
                                      System.EventArgs e)
{
  //Create a simple text file we want to send
  const string fileName = "\\myTestSendFile.txt";
  System.IO.StreamWriter textFileStream;
  textFileStream = System.IO.File.CreateText(fileName);
  textFileStream.WriteLine("Today...");
  textFileStream.WriteLine("is a nice day");
  textFileStream.WriteLine("to go swim");
  textFileStream.WriteLine("in the lake");
  textFileStream.Close();

  IrDAFileSend irdaFileSend;
  irdaFileSend = new IrDAFileSend(fileName, myIrDASocketName);
  //We have 2 options: 1 - Sync, 2 - Async

  //1. Call the function synchronously
  //and block the thread until the
```

```
//file is sent

//1a. Let the user know we're waiting to send
this.Text = "Trying to send...";
//1b. Wait until we find a client and then send the file
irdaFileSend.LoopAndAttemptIRSend();
//1c. Let the user the file has been transmitted
System.Windows.Forms.MessageBox.Show("File sent!");
this.Text = "IrDA: Sent!";

//2. Call the function async and set
//up a background thread to do the sending

//irdaFileSend.LoopAndAttemptIRSendAsync();
//NOTE: If we call the function async, we want to
//occasionally check if it is finished by
//calling 'irdaFileSend.Status'
}

private void buttonTestFileReceive_Click(object sender,
                                         System.EventArgs e)
{
  //If our destination file exists, delete it
  const string fileName = "\\myTestReceiveFile.txt";
  if (System.IO.File.Exists(fileName))
  {
    System.IO.File.Delete(fileName);
  }

  IrDAFileReceive irdaFileReceive;
  irdaFileReceive = new IrDAFileReceive(fileName,
                                        myIrDASocketName);
  //We have 2 options: 1 - Sync, 2 - Async

  //1. Call the function synchronously
  //and block the thread until the
  //file is received

  //1a. Let the user know we're waiting to receive
  this.Text = "Waiting to receive...";
  //1b. Wait until someone contacts us and sends the file
  irdaFileReceive.WaitForIRFileDownload();
  //1c. Let the user know we've got the sent file
  this.Text = "IrDA: received!";
  System.Windows.Forms.MessageBox.Show("File received!");
```

```
//2. Call the function async and set
//up a background thread to do the receive

//irdaFileReceive.WaitForIRFileDownloadAsync();
//NOTE: If we call the function async, we want to
//occasionally check if it is finished by
//calling 'irdaFileReceive.Status'
}
```

Listing 15.4 IrDAFileSend class

```
//=============================================================
//This class is an IrDA client. It looks for an IrDA
//server with a matching IrDA service name and when found
//it streams the data of a file to it.
//=============================================================
class IrDAFileSend
{
private string m_descriptionOfLastSendAttempt;
private string m_IrDAServiceName;
private string m_fileToSend;
private bool m_wasSenderStopped;

public enum SendStatus
{
  AttemptingToSend,
  Finished_Successfully,
  Finished_Aborted,
  Finished_Error
}

private SendStatus m_SendStatus;
public SendStatus Status
{
  get
  {
    //Lock prevents concurrent read/write to m_SendStatus
    lock(this) {return m_SendStatus;}
  }
}
private void setStatus(SendStatus newStatus)
{
```

```
      //Lock prevents concurrent read/write to m_SendStatus
      lock(this) {m_SendStatus = newStatus;}
}


public string ErrorText
{
   get {return m_descriptionOfLastSendAttempt;}
}


//-----------------------------------------------------------
//CONSTRUCTOR
//-----------------------------------------------------------
public IrDAFileSend(string fileToSend, string irdaServiceName)
{
   //The name of the IrDA socket we want to look for
   m_IrDAServiceName = irdaServiceName;
   //The file we want to send
   m_fileToSend = fileToSend;
}


//-----------------------------------------------------------
//Starts a new thread to try to send the file
//-----------------------------------------------------------
public void LoopAndAttemptIRSendAsync()
{
   //We are in send mode
   setStatus(SendStatus.AttemptingToSend);
   //User has not aborted us yet
   m_wasSenderStopped = false;

   //This is the function we want the new thread to start running
   System.Threading.ThreadStart threadEntryPoint;
   threadEntryPoint =
      new System.Threading.ThreadStart(LoopAndAttemptIRSend);

   //-------------------------------------------
   //Create a new thread and start it running
   //-------------------------------------------
   System.Threading.Thread newThread =
      new System.Threading.Thread(threadEntryPoint);

   newThread.Start(); //Go!
}
```

```csharp
//-------------------------------------------------------------
//Goes in loops and tries to send the file via IR
//-------------------------------------------------------------
public void LoopAndAttemptIRSend()
{
  System.Net.Sockets.IrDAClient irDASender;
  System.IO.Stream streamOutToIrDA ;
  System.IO.Stream streamInFromFile;

  //User has not aborted us yet
  m_wasSenderStopped = false;
  setStatus(SendStatus.AttemptingToSend);

  //-------------------------------------------------------------
  //Continually loop and try to send the message until
  //-------------------------------------------------------------
  while(true)
  {
    //These should all be null going in and out of the
    //'sendStream(...)' call unless an exception is thrown!
    irDASender = null;
    streamOutToIrDA = null;
    streamInFromFile = null;

    //Attempt to send the stream
    bool bSuccess;
    try
    {
      bSuccess = sendStream(
        out m_descriptionOfLastSendAttempt,
        ref streamOutToIrDA,
        ref irDASender,
        ref streamInFromFile
        );
    }
    catch(System.Exception eUnexpected) //Unexpected error!!!
    {
      setStatus(SendStatus.Finished_Error); //Note the failure
      m_descriptionOfLastSendAttempt =
        "Unexpected error in IR send loop. " +
        eUnexpected.Message;
```

```
//--------------------------------------------------
//Clean up any resources we may have allocated
//--------------------------------------------------
if(streamOutToIrDA != null)
{
  try {streamOutToIrDA.Close();}
  catch{};//Swallow any error
  streamOutToIrDA = null;
}

if(streamInFromFile != null)
{
  try {streamInFromFile.Close();}
  catch{};//Swallow any error
  streamInFromFile = null;
}

if (irDASender != null)
{
  try {irDASender.Close();}
  catch{}; //Swallow any error
  irDASender = null;
}
return; //Exit
}

//See if we succeeded
if (bSuccess == true)
{
  m_descriptionOfLastSendAttempt = "Success!";
  setStatus(SendStatus.Finished_Successfully);
  return;
}

//See if there was a user driven abort
if (m_wasSenderStopped == true)
{
  m_descriptionOfLastSendAttempt = "User Aborted.";
  setStatus(SendStatus.Finished_Aborted);
  return;
}

//Otherwise...We have not found an IrDA server with a
//matching service name yet. We will loop and keep
```

```
      //looking for one.
  }


  //We will never hit this point in execution
}


//------------------------------------------------------------
//Attempt to send an I/O stream (for example, a file) over IR
//[ret]:
//   true: We sent the file successfully
//   false: The file was not sent successfully
//------------------------------------------------------------
private bool sendStream(out string errorDescription,
  ref System.IO.Stream streamOutToIrDA,
  ref System.Net.Sockets.IrDAClient irDASender,
  ref System.IO.Stream streamInFromFile
)
{
  errorDescription = "";
  //----------------------------------------------------------
  //Create a new IRDA client
  //----------------------------------------------------------
  try
  {
    //--------------------------------------------------------
    //This will return pretty quickly. It will peek out there
    //and will return if no one is listening.
    //--------------------------------------------------------
    irDASender =
      new System.Net.Sockets.IrDAClient(m_IrDAServiceName);
  }


  catch (System.Exception eCreateClient)
  {
    //A number of things could have happened here
    //#1: No devices may be listening
    //#2: A device may be listening, but may not care
    //   (may refuse our conversation)
    errorDescription = eCreateClient.Message;
    return false;
  }


  //At this point a number of things could happen:
  //#1: We have gotten a connection from an IR receiving device
```

```
//#2: The IR request has been canceled (someone called STOP).
if (m_wasSenderStopped == true)
{
  irDASender.Close();
  irDASender = null;
  return false;
}


//=========================================
//SEND THE DATA!
//=========================================
//Open the file we want to send
streamInFromFile = System.IO.File.OpenRead(m_fileToSend);
//Open the IrDA socket we want to sent out to
streamOutToIrDA = irDASender.GetStream();

const int BUFFER_SIZE = 1024;
byte[] inBuffer = new byte[BUFFER_SIZE];
int bytesRead;
int iTestAll = 0;
int iTestWrite = 0;
do
{
  //Read the bytes in from the file
  bytesRead = streamInFromFile.Read(inBuffer, 0, BUFFER_SIZE);
  iTestAll = iTestAll + 1;

  //Write the bytes out to our output stream
  if (bytesRead > 0)
  {
    streamOutToIrDA.Write(inBuffer, 0, bytesRead);
    iTestWrite = iTestWrite + 1;
  }

}while(bytesRead > 0);

//Clean up output stream
streamOutToIrDA.Flush(); //Finish writing any output
streamOutToIrDA.Close(); //Close the stream
streamOutToIrDA = null;

//Clean up local file
streamInFromFile.Close();
streamOutToIrDA  = null;
```

```
    //Clean up IrDA port
    irDASender.Close();
    irDASender = null;

    //Success!!!
    return true;
}
} //end class
```

Listing 15.5 IrDAFileReceive Class

```
//---------------------------------------------------------
//Allows the reception of a file over IrDA (infrared port)
//
//This class is NOT re-entrant and should not be called by more
//than one caller at a time. If multiple simultaneous IR
//sessions are desired, they should be done by creating
//different instances of this class.
//---------------------------------------------------------
public class IrDAFileReceive
{
private bool m_wasListenerStopped;
private string m_IrDAServiceName;
private string m_fileNameForDownload;
private string m_errorDuringTransfer;
private System.Net.Sockets.IrDAListener m_irListener;
private ReceiveStatus m_ReceiveStatus;

public string ErrorText
{get {return m_errorDuringTransfer;}}
//-------------------------------------------------------------
//This notes the status of the receive
//-------------------------------------------------------------
public enum ReceiveStatus
{
  NotDone_SettingUp,
  NotDone_WaitingForSender,
  NotDone_Receiving,
  Done_Success,
  Done_Aborted,
  Done_ErrorOccured
}
```

```
//-------------------------------------------------------
// Returns the state of transfer
//-------------------------------------------------------
public ReceiveStatus Status
{
  get
  {
    //Thread safety to avoid read and write at same time
    lock(this)
    {
      return m_ReceiveStatus;
    } //end lock
  } //end get
} //end property

private void setStatus(ReceiveStatus newStatus)
{
  //Thread safety to avoid read and write at same time
  lock(this)
  {
    m_ReceiveStatus = newStatus;
  } //end lock
}


//-------------------------------------------------------------
// [in] filename: Filename we want to the IR file into
//-------------------------------------------------------------
public IrDAFileReceive(string filename, string irdaServiceName)
{
  //The name of the IrDA socket we want to open
  m_IrDAServiceName = irdaServiceName;

  //The filename we want to save the received data to
  m_fileNameForDownload = filename;
}


//-------------------------------------------------------------
//Allows you to receive a file asynchronously over IR
//
// [in] filename: Filename to write to
//-------------------------------------------------------------
public void WaitForIRFileDownloadAsync()
{
  //Note that we are now in setup mode
```

```
      setStatus(ReceiveStatus.NotDone_SettingUp);
      //----------------------------------------------------------
      //Create a new thread
      //----------------------------------------------------------
      System.Threading.ThreadStart threadEntryPoint;
      threadEntryPoint =
        new System.Threading.ThreadStart(WaitForIRFileDownload);

      System.Threading.Thread newThread =
        new System.Threading.Thread(threadEntryPoint);

      //Start the thread running
      newThread.Start();
    }


    //----------------------------------------------------------
    //Opens up an IR port and waits to download a file
    //----------------------------------------------------------
    public void WaitForIRFileDownload()
    {
      System.IO.Stream outputStream = null;
      System.Net.Sockets.IrDAClient irdaClient = null;
      System.IO.Stream irStreamIn = null;

      try
      {
        //========================================================
        //Setup and download the file!
        //========================================================
        internal_WaitForIRFileDownload(ref outputStream, ref irdaClient,
                    ref irStreamIn);
      }
      catch //Swallow any errors that occurred
      {
        setStatus(ReceiveStatus.Done_ErrorOccured);
      }


      //==========================================
      //Cleanup all resources
      //==========================================
      //Close our input stream
      if(irStreamIn != null)
      {
        try {irStreamIn.Close();}
```

```
      catch {} //Swallow any errors that occured
    }
    //Close the IrDA client
    if(irdaClient != null)
    {
      try {irdaClient.Close();}
      catch {} //Swallow any errors that occured
    }
    //Close the file we have been writing to
    if(outputStream != null)
    {
      try {outputStream.Close();}
      catch {} //Swallow any errors that occured
    }
    //Close the listener if it's running
    if (m_irListener != null)
    {
      //Set first so code running on another thread will
      //abort if it is set
      m_wasListenerStopped = true;
      try {m_irListener.Stop();} catch{} //Swallow any errors
      m_irListener = null;
    }
  }


  private void internal_WaitForIRFileDownload(
      ref System.IO.Stream outputStream,
      ref System.Net.Sockets.IrDAClient irdaClient,
      ref System.IO.Stream irStreamIn
  )
  {
    //----------------------------------------------------------
    //Open an input file to stream into
    //----------------------------------------------------------
    outputStream = System.IO.File.Open(
      m_fileNameForDownload,
      System.IO.FileMode.Create);

    //=========================================
    //STATUS UPDATE
    //=========================================
    setStatus(ReceiveStatus.NotDone_WaitingForSender);
```

```
//------------------------------------------------------------
//Open a listener
//------------------------------------------------------------
try
{
  m_wasListenerStopped = false;
  m_irListener =
    new System.Net.Sockets.IrDAListener(m_IrDAServiceName);
  m_irListener.Start();
}
catch(System.Exception eListener)
{
  m_errorDuringTransfer = "Error creating listener - " +
    eListener.Message;
  goto exit_sub_with_error;
}

//See if we got aborted
if (m_wasListenerStopped == true)
{ goto exit_sub_with_abort; }

//------------------------------------------------------
//Accept a connection
//------------------------------------------------------
try
{
  //--------------------------------------------------------
  //Execution will stop here until we get pinged by a device
  //or the listener was halted on another thread
  //--------------------------------------------------------
  irdaClient = m_irListener.AcceptIrDAClient();
}
catch(System.Exception eClientAccept)
{
  //If the listening is stopped by another thread calling cancel,
  // an exception will be thrown and we will be here.
  if (m_wasListenerStopped == true)
  {goto exit_sub_with_abort; }

  //If it was not a matter of the listening service being
  //stopped, some other exception has occurred. Deal with it.
  m_errorDuringTransfer = "Error accepting connection - " +
    eClientAccept.Message;

  goto exit_sub_with_error;
```

```
}

//At this point we will be in 1 of 2 states, ether:
//#1: We have gotten a connection from an IR sending device
//#2: The IR request has been canceled (by someone calling STOP)
//     (in which the code below will throw an exception)
//See if we got aborted
if (m_wasListenerStopped == true)
{goto exit_sub_with_abort;}

//==========================================
//STATUS UPDATE
//==========================================
setStatus(ReceiveStatus.NotDone_Receiving);

//------------------------------------------------------------
//Open a receiving stream
//------------------------------------------------------------
try
{
  irStreamIn = irdaClient.GetStream();
}
catch(System.Exception exGetInputStream)
{
  m_errorDuringTransfer = "Error getting input stream - " +
    exGetInputStream.Message;
  goto exit_sub_with_error;
}
//Get ready to receive the data!
const int BUFFER_SIZE = 1024;
byte[] inBuffer = new byte[BUFFER_SIZE];
int bytesRead = 0;
do
{
  //Read the bytes in from the IR port
  bytesRead = irStreamIn.Read(inBuffer, 0, BUFFER_SIZE);

  //Write the bytes out to our output stream
  if (bytesRead > 0)
  {outputStream.Write(inBuffer, 0, bytesRead);}
}while (bytesRead > 0);

outputStream.Flush(); //Finish writing any output
```

```
//==========================================
//STATUS UPDATE: SUCCESS
//==========================================
setStatus(ReceiveStatus.Done_Success);
return; //No errors


//==========================================
//FAILURE...
//==========================================
exit_sub_with_abort:
  //STATUS UPDATE: Aborted (but no error)
  setStatus(ReceiveStatus.Done_Aborted);
  return;

exit_sub_with_error:

  //STATUS UPDATE: ERROR!!!!
  setStatus(ReceiveStatus.Done_ErrorOccured);
}
} //end class
```

Memory Cards

Before the advent of inexpensive and widely deployed networking technology, there was the concept of the "sneaker net." This literally meant walking the data from one computer to another with the data stored on a physical transferable medium such as a magnetic disk; people were the network transport and the physical media the packets. With all of the remarkable networking technology available today, it is easy to forget how useful physically movable storage is. Often the fastest practical way to move large amounts of data from one computer or mobile device to another is just to place it onto a storage card and physically transfer it between the devices.

Today removable memory cards come with staggeringly large capacities; 256MB of storage is common, 512MB is not uncommon, and 1GB storage cards are already available at reasonable prices. Storage capacity keeps growing exponentially. These cards come in a variety of form factors, including USB memory keys, Compact Flash cards that can plug easily into laptop PCMICA slots using an inexpensive pass-through sleeve, and Secure Digital cards. Most of these storage elements simply appear as a removable hard drive when inserted into a mobile device or computer.

There is a great deal of merit in a "sneaker net" approach when large amounts of data need to be transferred. On-device databases such as SQL CE can be stored on memory cards and prepopulated with large amounts of data along with any other data required such as directories full of images. Storage cards can be loaded with data on one machine and have data unloaded from them as needed by mobile devices; thus the data's server and the data's client do not need to be online at the same time. As a communications mechanism, think of storage cards as a batch processing solution; they provide the ability to move a large amount of data in bulk but do not offer a live connection to new data on the network. A useful model is to use storage cards to move lots of data initially without requiring prolonged network access and then subsequently use online communications to perform incremental updates to that data. Storage cards are a relatively simple and "low-tech" communications mechanism but they should not be overlooked because of this.

Pushing Information to a Device

The fact that much of mobile device communications centers on mobile devices initiating conversations with servers is not by accident. After a connection with a server is established, it is easy to push data up to a server or pull data down from a server. Most communication with servers uses abstractions such as sockets or HTTP, which are built on top of Internet TCP/IP protocols. In TCP/IP communications, each device on the network has its own IP address. An IP address is like a phone number, with the caveat that some IP addresses are permanent, some are long lived, and some are far more transient. An understanding of the transient nature of some IP addresses is important to understand which communications models are practical for mobile device applications and which are not.

Internet servers have IP addresses that rarely change. In addition, there exist mechanisms for looking up the IP address based on friendly URL names. The most popular Internet name lookup service is called DNS, which stands for Domain Naming System; it translates friendly names such as `www.microsoft.com` or `www.yahoo.com` to IP addresses. These DNS servers maintain replicated databases that map names to IP addresses. This works well because the server IP addresses rarely change.

Things work in a fairly similar way inside intranets. A server, desktop, or laptop name is registered and associated with an IP address. Sometimes these IP addresses are fixed, but usually internal IP addresses are loaned to computers by servers known as DHCP servers. DHCP stands for Dynamic Host Configuration Protocol, and as you might imagine the DHCP server's task is to loan out IP addresses to client computers who ask for them. Again the assumption is that these IP addresses do not change very often. A server that changed IP addresses very often would be a burden on the network because its address would require constant updating and lookup by client computers. Devices that appear and disappear on the network often because they are constantly roaming between different parts of the network or being turned on and off often will end up changing IP addresses frequently.

If a mobile device is going to be confined to a specific network topology (for example, inside a single corporate network), the addressing challenge for mobile devices is relatively straightforward. In these cases, one of two solutions is possible: (1) simply assigning the mobile device a fixed IP address, which is the simplest but least-flexible solution, or (2) building a custom mapping server that gets called by devices to register their IP address whenever they change; other devices can query this server for the address of a given device.

For devices that roam through different networks, the problem is far more complex. A static IP address is not permissible because it relies on the consent of the operating network, which may have already handed out or reserved any given IP address that the device may want to use. The presence of proxy servers, NATs (Network Address Translators), and firewalls present additional problems. Proxy servers, NATs, and firewalls allow specific kinds of outgoing requests and route responses back to the computing devices that made the requests; they do not generally allow unsolicited incoming requests to devices inside the networks. A device inside a network making server requests does not need to be aware of these complexities, but any party attempting to access a device from outside the network does.

The net result of all this is that for roaming mobile devices it is very difficult to send requests down to the devices; there is no good generic model for accomplishing this. This results in an asymmetry; it is far easier to make requests from a device than it is to send requests to a device.

But Won't IPv6 Solve All These Problems?

The answer is "maybe in the long run," but as the famous economist John Maynard Keynes stated, "Long run is a misleading guide to current affairs. In the long run we are all dead." It will take many years for IPv6 to fully filter out into the world, and in any case network security components such as firewalls are here to stay. The implication of this is that servers will remain easier to address than mobile devices. Mobile devices that travel constantly through different network topologies will require special mechanisms to address them.

In some cases, it is useful to be able to push information down to a mobile device. As noted previously, for custom static network topologies this is not a large problem; the mobile device can have a fixed or specially registered IP address and simply open up a socket and wait for requests to come in. For general-purpose mobile devices that roam through different networks, this is a challenge. The challenge can be addressed in several ways:

- *Mobile phones can use SMS message reception*—Most mobile phones today support the widely popular SMS (Short Message Service) mechanism for pushing short streams of data down to devices. SMS offers a convenient universal addressing scheme: the device's phone number. Usually these SMS messages are text messages for the user to read, but this need not be the only use. Because SMS messages are limited to about 160 characters of information, a good model for using SMS to push information to a device is "push to pull"; a specific SMS message's arrival triggers a local application to access a server and download a larger amount of information.
- *E-mail messages*—Many rich mobile devices support receiving e-mail notifications either to a phone-specific e-mail address or to the user's regular e-mail address. Sending specific messages to a device that are intended to be interpreted by a local application is a powerful way to push data down to a device.
- *Polling*—Polling is simply occasionally making a call from the device to a server to see whether new information intended for the device is pending.

Of the three mechanisms described above, polling is the least sophisticated and by far the easiest to implement. Only in cases where a polling-based solution proves to be inadequate should other mechanisms be looked at.

Presently when developing with the .NET Compact Framework v1.1 there is no built-in library support for intercepting or viewing incoming e-mail or SMS messages; to do this, native code will have to be written and fairly sophisticated operations will need to be performed. Accessing incoming e-mail and SMS messages is not infeasible, but it is a significant amount of work. This work needs to be justified by proving that a less-elegant but simpler solution is not sufficient to meet your mobile application's needs. Writing low-level messaging code is interesting work, but is hardly ever a high-productivity task; weigh the alternatives and choose wisely.

Accessing Incoming SMS Messages on a Microsoft Smartphone

There are two ways for working with SMS messages on a Microsoft Smartphone: (1) working at a low level by building your own filter to inspect incoming messages, or (2) working at a high level using the "CE Messaging API" to look at messages after they have arrived. Both presently require C/C++ native code to access the necessary operating system functionality.

1. Building Your Own Low-Level SMS Filter for Incoming Messages

The Smartphone OS offers advanced developers two ways to register their own filters for handling SMS messages. This can be done by building and registering an on-device SMS provider or by building and registering a component that implements the IMailRuleClient interface.

In principle both of these approaches are similar to developing an ISAPI filter for Internet Information Server; multiple filters are can run simultaneously, and the first filter whose criteria matches incoming requests is given the request to handle. (For example, in ISAPI ,*.ASP Web page requests are routed to one handler, and *.ASPX Web page requests are routed to another based on the file extension.) Building ISAPI filters for Internet Information Server is a sophisticated feature demanding careful design and testing. Just as almost all Web developers do not require their own custom ISAPI filters, almost all mobile device developers do not require their own SMS provider or IMailRuleClient component. Nevertheless the flexibility is there if needed.

■ SMS Providers

SMS providers get to examine the headers of incoming SMS messages and decide what application to deliver them to. This is true for both binary and text SMS messages. However, as a practical matter, many "locked" Smartphones will not allow you to implement your own SMS provider because it may violate the security policy of the phone's issuer.

More information about building an SMS provider can be found in the Smartphone SDK by searching for the term "SMS Provider" or looking in the "Short Message Service" section of the "Smartphone Adaptation Kit for Mobile Operators" documentation.

■ IMailRuleClient

For Smartphone 2003 and later devices, it is possible to implement and register a component implementing the IMailRuleClient interface. This is a higher-level approach versus building an SMS provider and is preferable because it is intended for application developers as opposed to mobile network operators issuing the phones. IMailRuleClient allows a component to inspect incoming SMS messages and respond to them. This may be a more feasible approach than writing your own SMS provider but will still require the component to be signed with an authorized cryptographic key if the mobile phone's issuer demands this.

More information on IMailRuleClient can be found by searching for IMailRule-Client or "CEMAPI" on MSDN online.

2. Using CEMAPI for Higher-Level SMS Message Access

CEMAPI offers a higher-level mechanism to access *text* SMS messages that have been routed into the Smartphone's e-mail inbox. CEMAPI offers a set of interfaces for navigating the device's message store and for creating and viewing messages. Your mobile application can periodically poll the device's inbox to check for new SMS messages that may be intended for it. Search for "CEMAPI" in the Smartphone SDK for more information about working with a Pocket PC or Smartphone's inbox.

Web Services

The industry momentum behind Web services makes it a technology that is impossible to ignore. Just as the HTML-enabled proprietary sources of information are wrapped and exposed to end users using a standardized presentation model, so do Web services wrap and expose proprietary information sources to other applications. Web services allow applications to communicate using a commonly agreed upon high-level standardized XML-based language.

The primary intent of HTML was to allow text-based documents to be linked together in a web. This turned out to be such a good idea that application programming models were built on top of the document presentation model, resulting in dynamically generated documents; HTML grew well beyond its original intent. The original intent of Web services was to allow different servers to communicate with one another using a standard XML-based communications protocol. Just as with HTML, Web services technologies have grown past their original design goals and are now commonly used to link client applications to servers as well. Web services are the XML-based glue for linking together client and server applications.

Calling a Web service from a desktop application is a fairly trivial matter. Today desktop computers are online most of the time, and fast networks are available to provide high-bandwidth and low-latency communications. Web services can also be leveraged from mobile devices, but to do so effectively developers must take into account the differences in connectivity, bandwidth, and latency and tune a mobile application's usage of Web services accordingly.

A Very Brief Description of Web Services

A vast amount of literature already exists that describes Web services technologies. This information is available both online and in book form. For a detailed introduction to Web services, I recommend starting with MSDN's online documentation. However, to set the stage for further discussions on calling Web services from mobile devices, a very brief description of Web services is offered here.

Web services use specifically formatted XML messages to send and receive requests for computing services. A Web services "call" is a request from one computing device to another to perform some processing and usually return a result. Web services have the following characteristics:

- *Use of the SOAP protocol*—SOAP stands for Simple Object Access Protocol and is a dialect of XML. Most commonly SOAP is used to call methods on a server and get results back. SOAP packages up a requested method's name and along with the method's parameters in XML and ships the XML up to the server for processing. The server receives the XML SOAP request, parses it to extract the method's name and parameters, and then calls the method. When the server method's processing is complete, a SOAP result is returned to the client as XML. The client parses the returned XML, extracts the results, and gives them to the calling program.

- *Use of WSDL documents*—WSDL stands for Web Service Description Language. A WSDL document is a dialect of XML that describes a Web service. A WSDL document details what methods a Web service has, what parameters each method takes, and what the return values look like for each method. WSDL documents are typically machine generated and returned upon request from a Web services server. Software development tools download WSDL documents from Web service servers and generate client-side code to make it easy to call the described Web services on those servers. Each Web service has its own associated WSDL document.

- *Probable use of HTTP or HTTPS communications protocols for making requests and receiving responses*—Although Web services can in theory run using a variety of different communications transports, including SMTP e-mail transports, in practice most Web service requests are sent via HTTP or HTTPS. This means that most Web services run on the same kinds of Web servers that serve HTML-based applications. This is particularly useful because HTTP and HTTPS requests are typically allowed through firewalls; making

Web services access as simple as Web page access. If a given Web server can be accessed by your mobile application, Web services running on that server can also be accessed.

In addition to these basic Web services characteristics, additional layers of technology are being designed to go on top of SOAP and WSDL to address more sophisticated needs. For example, specifications such as WS-Reliability and WS-Security address reliable delivery and integrated security needs. More specifications are being created, debated, evolved, and standardized all the time. Web services technologies will expand and evolve greatly over the next 10 years. Programming tools and frameworks that take advantage of these new standards will tend to lag the emerging standards by a few years.

Calling Web Services from a Mobile Device

The ability for mobile devices to interact with the same kinds of Web services as desktop and server applications is a great boon for mobile application developers. Any device that can access Web pages has the built-in connectivity necessary to call Web services.

It is one thing to be able to call Web services and quite another to be able to do so easily. By analogy, it is relatively easy to download HTML, but much more work to transform that HTML into a meaningful visual experience for end users. For this reason, layered programming libraries exist to make working with Web services easier. In increasing order of abstraction, the layers are as follows:

- *The ability to make HTTP/HTTPS requests*—In theory, if your mobile application can make a request of a Web server you can call a Web service.
- *The ability to generate and parse XML*—Because the language of conversation in Web services is XML, the ability to parse and generate XML greatly simplifies working with Web services.
- *The ability to generate and parse SOAP messages*—SOAP messages are a specific grammar built on top of XML. A programming library that allows your application to work at the conceptual level of SOAP requests and responses is much easier to work with than building these requests manually and interpreting the XML responses.
- *The ability to autogenerate proxy code for Web services client applications*—Some software development tools are capable of downloading the WSDL documents that describe Web services and

automatically generating the Web service client code needed to build the SOAP requests and parse returned SOAP responses. Auto-generated Web services client code greatly simplifies calling Web services. Instead of needing to write code to manually construct SOAP requests, send them to servers, and parse the results returned, developers can treat Web services requests as simple method calls. For example, a Web service that adds two numbers together can simply be called as follows:

```
MyWebService myWS = new MyWebService();
int result = myWS.AddTwoNumbers(2, 8);
```

A Web services client-side proxy class called MyWebService contains all of the needed logic to create the SOAP request, send it to the server, and parse the SOAP response.

The .NET Compact Framework supports all of the levels of abstraction described above in the same way that the desktop and server .NET Framework does. At the time of this writing, other mobile device technologies (for example, J2ME, native code) did not yet support some of the higher levels of abstraction, but Web services are such an important technology that it is likely that almost all future versions of mobile programming frameworks will make Web services easy to call. However, mobile runtime deployment takes time (often new hardware needs to be rolled out with new runtimes and libraries on the devices) and if you are working with a mobile device programming technology that does not yet have built-in support for Web services, you should be prepared to do some extra lower-level coding to generate the requests and parse the responses.

Creating a Web Service Using .NET

To create a Web service to test with, you will need to be running Internet Information Server (IIS) either on your local desktop or a server accessible to the mobile device you are testing. The IIS installation will need to have the proper server-side extensions for working your development tool as well; the Visual Studio .NET setup installer can help you configure these on IIS.

To create a Web service, follow these steps:

1. Start Visual Studio .NET and create a new C# ASP.NET Web service project. The development tool will ask you for a location to create the Web service. For example, specifying `http://localhost/ WebService1` will create a Web service on your desktop machine,

and `http://MyWebServer/WebService1` will create a Web service called WebService1 on a server named MyWebServer.

    Result: A class called Service1 will be created, and a file called
Service1.asmx will be deployed to the Web server you specified.

2. Create a public Web method in the Service1 class. The snippet code
in Listing 15.6 shows a simple method exposed as a Web service.
Type the code into the Service1 class you created in Step 1.

3. Press F5 to deploy and run the Web service project. A Web page will
automatically be created for the Web service that shows what methods the Web service exposes and enables you to try calling the methods through a Web browser. To test the Web service, use a Web
browser to navigate to the address of the Web service and class you
specified in Steps 1 and 2 (for example, `http://MyWebServer/`
`WebService1/Service1.asmx`).

Listing 15.6 Simple Web Service

```
//This code snippet goes inside the Service1 class
//in the file "Service1.asmx".
//
//"[WebMethod]" is a meta-data attribute that tells the Web
// service engine that this method should be web accessible

[WebMethod]
public int AddTwoNumbers(int x, int y)
{
return x + y;
}
```

Calling a Web Service from a Device Using the .NET Compact Framework

NOTE: Code running on a physical or emulated device is running on a different
logical machine from your development machine; even if the emulator is running
on the same physical machine as your Web server, it will not share the same machine name.

    Because of this, you *cannot* use the URL `//localhost/WebService1` to
locate the Web service from the device; you must use the hosting machine's actual name (for example, `//myDevMachine1/WebService1`), just as if you
were calling the Web service from another PC.

Calling a Web service from a device works almost exactly like calling a Web service from a desktop or server application. To call a Web service from a mobile device, follow these steps:

1. Start Visual Studio .NET and create a new C# Smart Device Application.

2. In the Project menu, select Add Web Reference. This will bring up a dialog that lets you browse and find the Web service you want to reference. Enter the URL of the Web service you created above (for example, `http://MyWebServer/WebService1/Service1.asmx`).

3. In the Add Web Reference dialog, enter the text **MyTestWebService** in the Web Reference Name text box, and then click the Add Reference button. This will download the WSDL document that describes the Web service and then create a local proxy class in your project that enables you to easily call the Web service.

4. Place a button on your application's form and double-click the button. This will bring you to the button's event handler code.

5. Enter the following lines of code:

```
//Create an instance of the local proxy object
MyTestWebService.Service1 myWebService;
myWebService = new MyTestWebService.Service1();

//Tell the local proxy to call the web service
int sum = myWebService.AddTwoNumbers(2,3);

//Show the result of the Web service call!
System.Windows.Forms.MessageBox.Show(sum.ToString());
```

6. Run your application and call the Web service.

In the preceding example, we chose to test calling the Web service synchronously. Synchronous calls are easy to test and debug, but in real-world scenarios we would almost certainly choose to call the Web service asynchronously. The autogenerated proxy class has facilities built in to it to enable this. To call the Web service asynchronously call `myWebService.BeginAddTwoNumbers(...parameters...)`. Each Web service method in the local proxy class has a Begin* method to invoke the Web service asynchronously and an End* method to get the results back.

Mobile Device Challenges When Using Web Services

Although consuming Web services from a mobile device is in many ways similar to utilizing Web services from a server or desktop computer, there are some important differences. The sections below describe challenges that are either specific to or magnified on mobile devices.

Support for "Browser Cookies" Will Vary

A "cookie" is a piece of device-local data that is owned and managed by a specific Web site. Cookie data "owned" by a Web site gets sent up to the server along with the rest of a HTTP request. For instance, `www.Mywebaddress.com` and `www.Yourwebaddress.com` both could maintain separate cookies on a client machine accessing their Web sites. If a computing device and application support client-side cookies, every time the Web address or subaddress (for example, `www.Mywebad-dress.com/somepath/somepath1`) is sent an HTTP request, the cookie data for the site is sent up to the server with the request. Cookies are often used to maintain per-client preferences on a Web site. A client-side cookie that is passed up with every request can be desirable from a server's perspective because it eliminates the need for the server (or group of servers acting together in a Web farm) to maintain server-side "session state" and can increase a Web application's scalability by allowing it to be stateless between requests. A Web site that lists the weather in your city and your four favorite stock listings is probably using client-side cookies to either maintain this data explicitly in the cookie or to hold a unique ID in the cookie that allows the server to look up the data in a server database. Cookies can be used to store short-term session data such as items in a Web "shopping cart" or longer-term data that persists over different sessions such as a user's long-term stock or weather-information preferences. However, client-side cookies have several important limitations:

- *They are client and machine specific.* If a Web application is using client-side cookies, those cookies will need to be re-created if the user accesses the Web application from a different machine. This means that preferences stored as client cookies do not travel with the user to different machines.
- *They are not always secure.* A Web application should not store valuable information in a cookie because that involves passing the valuable information back and forth with every call as well as keeping a

copy of the information on the client machine where another malicious application may be able to access it through a client-side vulnerability. Sensitive information should be kept securely on a server and only passed around as needed.

- *They take up extra transmission space.* Because cookies are passed around with every Web request, they are using bandwidth. When passed over mobile phone networks, this extra baggage wastes time and costs money. The larger the cookie, the more bandwidth that is wasted.

- *Cookies have a limited capacity.* There is a limit to the amount of data a client-side cookie can hold.

In addition to the general limitations listed here, client-side cookies have another disadvantage when used with Web services: complexity. A Web service conversation can be viewed as a series of well-defined requests passed between a client and a server. Often these requests can be represented as method calls with parameters being passed in and results being passed back. Using cookies while calling Web services represents a second hidden channel of communication between the client and server, and this can cause confusion. Listing 15.7 shows a Web service being called without using cookies, and Listing 15.8 shows how the same example might look if cookies were used to replace some of the parameters being passed.

Listing 15.7 Web Service Calls with Only Explicit Parameters Being Passed

```
//0. Establish a session
int sessionID = someWebService.LogOn(userCredentials);
//
//...Lots of other code gets run...
//
//1. Call a Web service and create a new order
int orderID = someWebService.CreateNewOrder(sessionID, userInfo,
productInfo);
//
//...Lots of other code gets run...
//
//2. Confirm the order with the server
someWebService.ConfirmPayment(sessionID, orderID, paymentInfo);
//
//...Lots of other code gets run...
//
//3. Confirm the shipping address
```

```
someWebService.ConfirmShipping(sessionID, orderID, shippingAddress);
//
//...Lots of other code gets run...
//
//4. Finalize order
someWebService.FinalizeOrder(sessionID, orderID);
```

This code is relatively simple to follow. In Step 1, a new order is created and an orderID is returned to use in subsequent calls. This orderID is passed into each subsequent call, and it is clear that each of the Web service calls can identify the order being processed using the orderID that is passed in.

Instead of using an explicit orderID, the Web service implementer could have stuffed this information into a client-side cookie. In this case, the client-side code would look like Listing 15.8.

Listing 15.8 Web Service Calls with Implicit Parameters Passed via Cookies

```
//0. Establish a session
//Although you can't see it, this will pass back a client cookie!
int sessionID = someWebService.LogOn(userCredentials);

//1. Call a Web service and create a new order
//Although you can't see it, this will pass up a client cookie!
//Although you can't see it, this will pass back a client cookie!
someWebService.CreateNewOrder(userInfo, productInfo);
//
//...Lots of other code gets run...
//
//2. Confirm the order with the server
//Although you can't see it, a client-side cookie is passed
//up to the server containing the "orderID". Sneaky!
someWebService.ConfirmPayment(paymentInfo);
//
//...Lots of other code gets run...
//
//3. Confirm the shipping address
//Although you can't see it, a client-side cookie is passed
//up to the server containing the "orderID". Sneaky!
someWebService.ConfirmShipping(shippingAddress);
//
//...Lots of other code gets run...
//
```

```
//4. Finalize order
//Although you can't see it, a client-side cookie is passed
//up to the server containing the "orderID". Sneaky!
someWebService.FinalizeOrder();
```

The code above looks fairly simple, but as noted in the comments there is a second channel of communication that is hidden from the programmer. Hidden parameters are being passed back and forth between the client and the server via cookies. This is a good reason not to use client-side cookies when designing Web services. It is far better to explicitly pass all the parameters needed for a Web service request than to rely on an opaque second channel to hold this information.

Many mobile device platforms either do not support client-side cookies or their support differs substantially from what desktop computers and programming frameworks offer. Specifically, the .NET Compact Framework running on Smartphones, Pocket PCs, or Windows CE devices does not automatically support passing cookies back and forth via Web service requests. If you want to take any cookies sent down by a server and send them back up to the server in a subsequent request, you will have to write code to read the cookies from one HTTPWebResponse's headers and write them out into the subsequent HTTPWebRequest's headers. In the case of calling Web services, this will require that you examine and modify the client-side Web service proxy code that is autogenerated for you by Visual Studio .NET. This is by no means impossible, but it is extra work that you will need to be aware of. This is an important difference between desktop and device programming framework support.

Despite the fact that the use of client-side cookies is discouraged when building Web services, some services may use them to store session data such as logon information. If a Web service works when calling it from a desktop computer but mysteriously fails when calling it from a mobile device, cookie usage may be to blame. If possible, check with the Web service's author to see whether the service is using cookies; this is always easier than trying to reverse engineer what is going on. If it is not possible to get this information from the Web service's author, you can try to test this empirically by changing the cookie policy on the desktop computer; this is specified in Internet Explorer in the Tools->Options dialog under the Privacy tab. In addition, if you want to delve into low-level Web services client code, you can examine the client-side cookies collection returned in the HTTPResponse of a Web request. If client-side cookie dependencies are at fault, you have three possible courses of action: (1) Get the Web service to support a cookie-less access model, which in any case is good engineering; (2) build a server-based wrapper Web service that serves as an intermediary between mobile devices and the offending Web service (this wrapper will need to explicitly maintain cookie data for its clients); or (3) write your own device-side code to explicitly handle collecting the cookies returned by any Web server responses and packing them back into subsequent Web requests.

Often the First Call to a Web Service Has Additional Latency

The first call your mobile application makes to a Web service can incur significant performance overhead. Several things need to take place when a Web service call is first made:

1. *Code may have to be loaded.* If XML, Web service, network, and other client-side classes have not been loaded into memory yet, they will need to be loaded and compiled before they can be used to call Web services. All of this takes time, possibly a few seconds.
2. *The address of the Web service may need to be looked up.* For example, if you are calling a Web service on `www.myWebService.com`, this address will need to be mapped into an IP address (for example, 200.134.81.26) to locate the server. This lookup occurs by asking a DNS server to translate the Web address into an IP address. Name lookup requests from DNS servers take time; the request has to be packed up, sent to the DNS server, and your mobile application will have to wait for the reply before actually contacting the server with the Web service you want to call. Most mobile devices should cache this address locally so that subsequent requests to the server do not require DNS lookup. Name resolution can take a significant amount of time and can easily be the largest source of latency when calling a Web service for the first time. As a general rule, looking up a local network name (for example, `//myLocalServer`) should be quicker than looking up a World Wide Web name (for example, `www.myWebServer.com`).

When measuring the response times of Web services, it is useful to separate the measurement into two parts: (1) Measure the response time for the first call; (2) measure the average response time for subsequent Web service calls.

Because Web service requests rely on resources out of your application's immediate control, it is always a good idea to make these calls asynchronously to your application's user interface thread. Despite this there will be cases where the mobile application's user makes a request for information or attempts to perform a transaction and needs to wait for its completion before moving on. In these cases, it is worth doing everything possible to speed up the server communication. If your application knows that it is going to need to call a Web service on behalf of a user, it may be worth making a background "dummy call" to that same Web service prior to the user needing to make a real request. The "dummy call" will preload any necessary classes into memory and cache any IP addresses needed for subsequent calls.

Passing Large Amounts of Data via a Web Service Request Is Inefficient

Although it is possible to pass an array of 2,000 integers up to a Web service or to download an array of the same from a Web service, it is never a good idea to do so. Web services are optimized for flexibility and HTTP protocol friendliness. For this reason, Web services use a large amount of text relative to the information being passed. For example, the number 32 can be represented in 1 byte of data as 00100000. Passing an integer, 32, as XML looks roughly like `<int>32</int>`, which is about 14 bytes of data; the same holds true for other kinds of data. The properties that make Web services and XML flexible also make them inefficient for moving larger amounts of data around.

If your Web service needs to transfer a significant amount of data, the best way to do this is to have the Web service return a pointer to a binary data file rather than streaming the data as XML. A good example is a Web service that returns photographic images. Although it is possible for a Web service to return an image as an array of bytes or integers coded in XML, it is far more efficient to return a string that contains a URL pointing to a binary file that can be downloaded by the mobile application (for example, `//somewebserver/someshare/somedir/somefile.jpg`). This is exactly what Web browsers do; they download human-readable text and layout information as HTML and the HTML contains links to the binary image files that go into the layout. It is important to think carefully about the kind of data being moved around and to optimize for it if it is large.

Chatty Mobile Network Conversations Are Very Expensive

Each request sent to a server requires a conversation to be started, negotiated, and completed; this incurs communications overhead. Five separate Web service calls, each with one parameter, will be much more wasteful than one request that contains five parameters. In addition, because of the intermittent nature of mobile communications, making five smaller requests instead of one larger request creates a higher probability of failure during the conversation between device and server. This means complex cleanup logic will need to be written to recover when things do go wrong mid-conversation. A single Web services call has both a lower chance of communications failure as well as simpler cleanup logic if things do go wrong.

NOTE: When using Web services, it is still better to transfer binary data via a second request rather than trying to stream a large amount of data as XML. Because binary data becomes very verbose when expressed in XML, it will require a long amount of time to transfer. Long transfer times increase the odds of failure during the transfer. A better model is to make a single Web service call to pass all the data that can be passed reasonably efficiently as XML and subsequent calls to transfer binary files such as images. Listing 15.11 contains code to download a file from a Web server and store it locally. If multiple files' worth of binary data need to be transferred, it may also be useful to experiment with combing all the binary data into a single compressed file; this single combined file can be sent as binary data and decompressed at the other end.

Listing 15.9 shows a chatty Web service conversation with multiple requests and responses. Listing 15.10 shows the same conversation being batched up and processed in one request/response cycle. Whenever possible, it is a good idea to consolidate multiple requests into a smaller number of larger requests.

Listing 15.9 A Chatty Conversation with Multiple Web Service Calls

```
//--------------------------------
//Create and process an order
//--------------------------------
//0. Establish a session
int sessionID = someWebService.LogOn(userCredentials);
//1. Call a Web service and create a new order
int orderID = someWebService.CreateNewOrder(sessionID, userInfo,
productInfo);
//2. Call the Web service and pass in payment info
someWebService.ConfirmPayment(sessionID, orderID, paymentInfo);
//3. Call the Web service and pass in shipping information
someWebService.ConfirmShipping(sessionID, orderID, shippingAddress);
```

```
//4. Call the Web service and finalize the order
someWebService.FinalizeOrder(sessionID, orderID);
```

Listing 15.10 A Batched Conversation with a Single Web Service Call

```
//------------------------------------------------
//Create and process an order in a batch request
//that combines:
// 0. Session initiation
// 1. Creating a new order
// 2. Confirming payment
// 3. Confirming shipping
// 4. Finalizing the order
//------------------------------------------------
//Do everything at once
someWebService.BatchCreateOrder(userCredentials, userInfo,
                            paymentInfo, shippingAddress);
```

Listing 15.11 is sample code that downloads a binary file from a server and stores it locally on the device. This code may be useful if you need to download files such as images from a server.

Listing 15.11 Code to Download a File from a Web Server

```
//-----------------------------------------------------------
//Performs a synchronous download of a file on a Web server
//of a file and stores it to a local file system
// [in] httpWhereFrom: URL to file
//      (for example, "http://someserver/somefile.jpg")
// [in] filenameWhereTo: File location to write the file to
//      (for example, "\\localfile.jpg")
//-----------------------------------------------------------
public void downloadFileToLocalStore(string httpWhereFrom,
  string filenameWhereTo)
{
  System.IO.FileStream myFileStream = null;
  System.IO.Stream myHTTPResponseStream = null;
  System.Net.WebRequest myWebRequest = null;
  System.Net.WebResponse myWebResponse = null;
```

```
//If the location we want to write to exists, delete it
if(System.IO.File.Exists(filenameWhereTo) == true)
{
  System.IO.File.Delete(filenameWhereTo);
}

try
{
  //Create a Web request
  myWebRequest =
    System.Net.HttpWebRequest.Create(httpWhereFrom);
  //Get the response
  myWebResponse - myWebRequest.GetResponse();
  //Get the stream for the response
  myHTTPResponseStream = myWebResponse.GetResponseStream();

  //Create a local file to stream the response to
  myFileStream = System.IO.File.OpenWrite(filenameWhereTo);

  //This buffer size can be tuned
  const int buffer_length = 4000;
  byte [] byteBuffer = new byte[buffer_length];
  int bytesIn;

  //Read in the file and stream it to a local file
  do
  {
    //Read data in
    bytesIn = myHTTPResponseStream.Read(byteBuffer,
      0, buffer_length);

    //Write data out
    if(bytesIn != 0)
    {
      myFileStream.Write(byteBuffer, 0, bytesIn);
    }
  }while(bytesIn != 0);
}

catch(Exception myException) //Download failed!
{
  //Something bad happened. Let's clean up
  attemptCleanup_ThrowNoExceptions(myFileStream,
              myHTTPResponseStream, myWebResponse);
```

```
    //Now that we've cleaned up, rethrow the exception
    //So that the application knows something went wrong!
    throw myException;
  }


  //Download has succeeded!

  //Lets close everything down.
  try
  {
    //Normal clean up.
    myFileStream.Close();            myFileStream = null;
    myHTTPResponseStream.Close();  myHTTPResponseStream = null;
    myWebResponse.Close();           myWebResponse = null;
  }
  catch(Exception myException) //Failure during a close!
  {
    //Something bad happened. Let's clean up
    attemptCleanup_ThrowNoExceptions(myFileStream,
                    myHTTPResponseStream, myWebResponse);

    //Now that we've cleaned up, rethrow the exception
    //So that the application knows something went wrong!
    throw myException;
  }


  //Success!
}


//-------------------------------------------
//Tries to close and clean up everything
//Traps any exceptions that might be thrown.
//-------------------------------------------
void attemptCleanup_ThrowNoExceptions(
System.IO.FileStream myFileStream,
System.IO.Stream myHTTPResponseStream,
System.Net.WebResponse myWebResponse)
{
  if(myFileStream != null)
  {
    try
    { myFileStream.Close(); }
    catch
    {} //Do nothing.
```

```
    }

    if(myHTTPResponseStream != null)
    {
      try
      { myHTTPResponseStream.Close(); }
      catch
      {} //Do nothing.
    }

    if(myWebResponse != null)
    {
      try
      { myWebResponse.Close(); }
      catch
      {} //Do nothing.
    }
} //end function
```

Working with Heterogeneous Network Topologies Can Be Challenging

Desktop and server computers sit in relatively stable network topologies; things may behave well or poorly, but they usually behave fairly consistently. Part of this stability is due to the greater maturity of desktop networking, and part of it is due to the simple fact that the pieces do not move very often. A laptop roaming through different Wi-Fi environments may experience some variance, but because Wi-Fi is intended to mimic wired connectivity the variances are usually moderate; some allowances may have to be made for bandwidth differences, proxy settings, and security configuration. Using a mobile telephone network for data communication can add further complexities because bandwidth and reliability can vary significantly. A mobile device that roams in between different mobile telephone operators' networks will add still more variance and intricacies. By using widely tested and supported Web protocols for communication, Web services can be useful in abstracting many of the details of communication networks, but there are still a few things that must be kept in mind if your mobile application is going to function well across a wide range of networks:

- *Generally data rates will be slower, connection latencies will be higher and both will be more variable.* Inevitably the data rates you experience on wireless networks will be lower than wired systems.

What may not be obvious at first glance is that establishing a network communication channel may take more time as well. All of this will have a direct effect on how well Web services requests perform on different mobile networks. Some mobile phone networks' data facilities will be significantly faster and lower latency than others. It is important to keep this in mind as you develop and test your Web services.

- *Proxy servers may need to be set up manually.* Solutions that run on corporate networks often access the Internet via a proxy server that sits between the intranet and the World Wide Web. While desktop and laptop computers often have these proxy connections set up automatically mobile devices may not. If you are experiencing problems calling a Web service from a mobile application, it is often a good idea to try to see whether the Web browser on that device can access the same Web server. If you cannot access the server with a Web browser, you probably need to manually configure the proxy settings on the device.

- *GPRS connections and other mobile network connections may need to be configured manually.* Similar to corporate proxy servers, many mobile networks have the concept of an access point through which Internet communication occurs. On 2.5G GSM networks, this is known as a GPRS connection and may need to be configured manually for each mobile network the device roams onto. The device may need to have usernames, passwords, and DNS addresses configured. As with proxy servers, a good test for a working connection is to see whether the Web browser on the device is capable of accessing the Internet. If the Web browser is working, the Internet connection for your mobile application is probably good.

- *Different mobile phone networks may behave in unexpected ways.* Internet access via mobile telephone networks is still somewhat of a work in progress. In the old days (two to three years ago), phones came with hard-wired functionality for voice and limited data services; this was easy for mobile phone network operators to test because they knew what kind of requests were going to be made through their networks. Today we are in the middle of an explosion of flexible multipurpose phone hardware. Although mobile telephone network infrastructure is steadily moving toward good support of smart phones that are generic application platforms, this transformation is not yet complete. Because of this, there may still be some hard-coded server infrastructure that is expecting specific client applications and protocols. For example, a few years ago we encountered a mobile network that was always sending back HTTP responses that were compressed and thus indecipherable to client applications that were expecting plain-text data. This caused Web service responses to appear as scrambled information bearing no resemblance to the XML data expected back. The reason for this was that the Internet browser on the client phones knew to expect compressed data and how to decompress it, but this facility was not available to other applications. Temporary workarounds were required to enable generic client applications to pass in a modified HTTP request header that explicitly insisted on uncompressed responses. It is reasonable to assume that most of these kinds of issues are ironed out now, but doubtless a few "gotchas" still remain to be discovered. For this reason, it is recommended that you take a layered approach to diagnosing problems that occur. If problems occur while accessing a Web service, I recommend the following sequence of debugging steps: (1) Try calling the Web service from a desktop application; if this does not work then things are broken in a non–device-specific way. (2) Try to browse the Web from the client device; if this works it means you have Internet connectivity. (3) Try to download files from the same Web server in question using a .NET Compact Framework System.Net.HttpWebRequest as shown in Listing 15.11; if this works and the file downloaded is intelligible, the data is getting to your application properly. (4) Try calling the Web service from a desktop application with client-side cookies turned off. (5) Step through the autogenerated Web service client-side code in your application line by line to see exactly where things are going wrong. These kinds of problems can be frustrating to debug when they occur; a disciplined and step-by-step approach will yield the best results.

There is no substitute for testing on the networks your solution will be deployed on. If your mobile solution is intended to roam between different networks, you will benefit greatly from testing on different mobile networks to get a feel for what variances your application will have to deal with.

Summary

Communication is essential for doing almost any kind of meaningful work. Mobile devices, because they travel through the physical world with their users, are in a unique position to give their users on-demand information and services. With this flexibility comes its own set of challenges. As a mobile application developer, you need to ensure that your application resiliently and flexibly handles wide ranges of communications bandwidth, variable latencies, intermittent connection failures, and different modes of communication. It is important to design your mobile application's communications mechanisms robustly and with the user's needs in mind. This can be substantially more complex than building an effective communications model for servers, desktops, or laptop computers, which tend to deal with a much smaller set of communications variables.

Your mobile application should be designed in such a way that it can take advantage of networks when and as they become available, but it should not be dependent on network access. Access to a communications network should instead be treated opportunistically; use it to good effect when it's there, but do not rely on it. It is important to put the end users in control of network access; they may be able to make intelligent connectivity decisions that are simply not possible to automate into your application logic. Only the end users are able to walk outside to get network connectivity or can tell the device that they are about to go underground where network coverage will not exist. Whenever possible, the end user of the mobile device should be given the ability to initiate or halt network operations. End users may also want to set synchronization preferences based on their own needs and knowledge of available network conditions.

When accessing a networked resource, your application's thread is ceding control for a potentially indeterminate amount of time. For this reason, it is highly recommended that all network access that does not have a definite and short timeout threshold specified should take place on a background thread. Keeping the user interface responsive is the only way to keep end users in control of their experience with your application.

Coding defensively and simulating intermittent network failure should both be standard development practices. Because mobile devices move in and out of networks, the chance of intermittent network failure is much higher than on desktop or laptop computers. It is important that your application respond robustly to all communications failures. In cases of communications disruption, it is also important that your application properly release resources that it may have allocated during the communication attempt. It is very easy to inadvertently keep a socket connection or file open that will cause subsequent network access to fail. Instrumenting your code to throw intermittent test exceptions during communications tasks is a good way to test the robustness of your cleanup code and your application's ability to resiliently resume communications later.

There are many potential mechanisms for providing mobile applications with communications capabilities. These range from personal area networking technologies such as Bluetooth to the very wide area networks provided by mobile phone infrastructure. Wi-Fi is playing an increasingly important role as a provider of high-bandwidth communications in small-radius hot spots. In addition to these technologies, there are other less-glamorous but still very useful mechanisms to consider. Device-in-cradle network connections through a PC and Ethernet cable connectivity offer good network access capabilities. Memory cards that can be inserted into devices offer the ability to move large amounts of information by using a physical medium. Finally there is IrDA, which offers point-to-point communication between devices as well as communication to and through laptop computers. These communications mediums cover a wide range of possibilities, and none is superior for all tasks. It is important to think creatively about what your mobile application's communications needs are and how these can be achieved with simplicity, reliability, and convenience for the end user. Often a combination of the technologies listed above can be used to give the mobile application's users the flexibility to meet their communications needs.

Web services offer a useful way to interact with Internet- and intranet-based applications. By using standard XML, usually passed via HTTP or HTTPS protocols, Web services can allow your mobile application to take advantage of existing Web infrastructure to meet its communications needs. It is, however, important to realize that Web services offer useful abstractions but at the expense of incurring considerable overhead. XML is a verbose format, and it can take longer to push data around a network if the XML messages being passed are of considerable size. In addition, domain naming servers may need to be called to look up IP addresses, adding further overhead to your mobile application's communications. These challenges are by no means unique to mobile devices; but due to the fact that mobile network communication is usually slower and tends to be less robust than wired networking, these challenges need to be considered carefully. Other than in testing scenarios, Web service calls should always be made asynchronously to keep the application's user interface responsive. The number of separate Web service calls required to accomplish a task should be kept to a minimum because communications latencies on mobile networks can make chatty conversations expensive. Binary data such as image information should not be passed as XML; instead, Web services should return URLs to the data so that it can be downloaded as a binary file by the mobile device. Web services are very useful and will be increasingly used to connect different systems, but they must be used prudently to achieve good performance on mobile devices.

Mobile application communications provide a rich variety of options for software developers to choose from. Along with all these choices comes the responsibility of choosing the most appropriate options to meet your application users' needs and cost requirements. Extra thought must be given to designing failure-tolerant and user-tailored communications mechanisms that provide the right balance of automation and end-user control. Because of all of the communications possibilities available, significant innovation is possible in building better mobile applications. As with other areas of mobile device software design, the field is wide open and experimentation is the best way to come up new and innovative approaches to meet your mobile application's communications needs.

CHAPTER 16

Step 5: Packaging and Deploying Your Mobile Application

It ain't over 'til it's over.

—Yogi Berra, 1925 (Encarta 2004, Quotations)

Introduction

In software development, accomplishment means getting the finished software to the intended audience. For mobile device software, this means getting the applications you create onto users' devices. The final measure of the quality of a product is the utility and joy it brings its users. To achieve its goals, a mobile application must actually get to the target devices, and this means it must be packaged and deployed to each user's mobile device.

This book has as its focus the goal of imparting the engineering wisdom and spurring the creative thinking required to enable developers to build great mobile applications. Although packaging and deployment is beyond the scope of "writing mobile code," it is important, and this chapter provides an overview of the decisions you need to make to successfully deploy your mobile application.

Because the details of application packaging and deployment are specific to each device type and programming technology used, this chapter gives only a general overview of the issues involved. Different detailed packaging steps are required for different technologies; J2ME/J2SE, the .NET Compact Framework, and various types of native code technologies all have specific steps that must be taken to package up and deploy applications. Different device types such as PDAs, smart phones, and custom-engineered devices all have software installation processes that vary in their details. Mobile network operators issue phones to their customers and often offer software for dynamic download onto those devices; they have their own policies for software installation and provisioning. Each device technology and mobile network operator has their own associated documentation, often available for download from the Web. This short chapter focuses on the broad outlines and gives you a mental framework in which to think about packaging and deployment issues. Additional links to .NET Compact Framework-specific packaging and deployment articles are listed in Appendix A, "Additional Resources for the .NET Compact Framework"; fairly good online articles and samples exist to walk you through some of the details. In addition, professional installation tools are available that can significantly reduce the number of manual steps involved in mobile device application packaging and provisioning; these are certainly worth having a look at. In any case, it is important to understand what the issues and possibilities are for mobile application deployment.

To successfully deploy your mobile application, you need to answer the following questions:

1. If you are targeting devices that are not "open devices," are there any requirements from the issuer of the devices that need to be met?
2. Are there additional components that also need to be deployed for your application to function on all of the devices you are targeting?
3. How will the end user install your application?

These issues are addressed in the following sections.

Does Your Mobile Application Need to Be Signed?

Mobile devices can be placed into three categories:

1. *Fixed-purpose devices*—These are devices that ship with all the software on them that they are going to allow their users to access. There is no facility for adding additional software after device deployment. The original mobile phones of not too many years ago were such systems. Today the main reason for having a fixed-purpose device is to guarantee reliability and security. A closed system can be tested exhaustively. The only way to get your software onto a fixed-purpose system is to have it included in the device's ROM image either when the device is first manufactured or when its ROM is flash upgraded.

Most interesting mobile device platforms today are not fixed-purpose systems.

2. *Open devices*—These are devices that have no restrictions on what software can be installed on them. The user is free to place any software they want on the device and does not need permission from anyone to do so. Most PDA/Pocket PC types of devices are open systems, and some smart phone devices are open systems.

3. *Restricted-extensibility devices*—These are devices that allow only approved applications to be installed on them. Any application that wants to run on a restricted-access device needs the consent of the third party that controls access to the device. In the case of mobile phones, this is typically the mobile network operator that issued the device. Applications deployed to restricted-access devices must be cryptographically signed before deployment.

A cryptographic signature is a small piece of information that is attached to an application. The signature is based on two things: (1) a unique binary hash code that is generated by running an algorithm over the bytes of the application, and (2) a cryptographic key held by an individual or organization signing the application; usually this key comes in two parts consisting of a secret private part and a derivative public part that is difficult to reverse engineer. A signed application's signature is verified on the device against a set of approved keys. The signature is used to assert the identity of the party that signed the application. If the application's binary image is modified in any way, the signature becomes invalid. Similarly, if a different key is used to sign the application, a different signature will be produced. A device that offers restricted installation of applications maintains a list of approved signatory keys. Any application that is attempted to be installed or run on the device is checked by code on the device to make sure it has been signed by an approved party; if it has not, the application is not allowed to run. Alternatively, missing or unapproved signatures may prompt the device to ask the user if she wants to continue with the potentially unsafe operation; the choice to allow this is up to the device manufacturer and distributor.

NOTE: It is possible for a manufacturer to ship multiple versions of a device, some that are "open" and some that are "restricted access."

The Microsoft Smartphone is an example of such a device. Some manufacturers and their mobile network operating partners ship these as "open devices," allowing any applications to be installed on the devices. Others ship them with "restricted extensibility," allowing only approved applications to be installed.

A device purchased directly from a device manufacturer is usually an open device. If you are doing application development and testing, you will want an open device that allows your application to be deployed onto the device from the development tool without requiring it to be signed. Check for this capability when buying devices for development purposes.

If your mobile application is intended to be run on mobile devices that restrict what applications can be used on the device, the application will need to be signed. Usually this involves submitting your application's binary to a third party that is in possession of the signing keys that the device checks applications for. It is important to understand that the signature model is independent of how an application is brought onto a device. An application might be downloaded from the Web, installed via a flash memory card or downloaded from a PC; the on-device signature checker usually does not care. To run the application, it must pass the same signature check.

Contact the mobile network operators issuing the phones you want to target to get specific information explaining how to get applications approved and cryptographically signed. Many mobile phone operators issuing smart phones have some kind of a developer partnering program you can join. Technology vendors also often have certification and partnering programs to aid developers in bringing applications to mobile network operators. For instance, Microsoft has its Mobile2Market program for this purpose (see Appendix A).

Why Do Some Device Issuers Require Applications to Be Signed?

Mobile network operators are the main distributors of mobile devices that require application signatures to install and run new software. This is primarily done for one of three reasons:

1. *To control the business model for applications running on devices they have issued*—Mobile network operators often subsidize the costs of the phones they issue users. Because of this, they need a model to recoup their handset subsidies. Some mobile network operators want to ensure that they receive a share of mobile application revenue for applications running on their devices. Some mobile network operators want to ensure that only applications that they deem useful to their business are deployed on their devices. Some mobile network operators may want to ensure the quality and content of applications deployed to their devices.

2. *To control support costs for devices they have issued*—A mobile network operator that offers a large number of phones to their users is going to worry about support costs. Any time users have a handset problem and call their mobile network operator, the provider incurs support costs. This is particularly problematic if a mobile application on a device aberrantly or maliciously causes unauthorized network usage or prevents use of the mobile phone for normal operations. A mobile network operator may want to ensure that only an approved set of high-quality and supported applications can be run on devices they offer to large numbers of users.

3. *To safeguard their networks*—Mobile network operators worry about aberrant or malicious applications running on their devices causing disruptions to their valuable communications networks. Their nightmare scenario is a virus spreading to mass numbers of mobile phones and initiating a denial-of-service attack onto the mobile network that prevents the network from being commercially used.

There is a natural tension between the mobile network operators' desire to control the capabilities of phones they issue and the quicker innovation potential of open platforms. A centrally controlled model may offer stability, but an open platform offers the dynamic possibility of unplanned invention. This is similar to the predicable stability of planned economies versus the creative chaos of capitalistic systems. Different mobile operators are experimenting with different models, each trying to find the right mix of control versus freedom. Add to this debate the desire by different parties to give mobile phones settable per-application security settings (for example, for accessing the network, displaying user interface, accessing the device's file system) and it is safe to say that this debate will be ongoing for some years to come. In the end it is likely that something close to the open model will prevail, but with safeguards put into place to ensure that critical functionality cannot be accessed without the mobile operator's consent on mobile devices that they issue. It is also conceivable that other phone-issuing parties will get into the act as well. A corporation that outfits their employees with rich smart phones may want to place policy on the phones it issues that restricts the set of applications that can be run to those it deems trustable. In the end, the party issuing the mobile device to the user will have the strongest say. People buying directly from manufacturers are likely to get an open device, and people receiving phones issued by a third party will likely get a set of extensibility capabilities that are to some degree skewed in the interests of that party.

Installation of Runtimes and Other Required Components

If you have a specific device configuration in mind for your mobile application, you can optimize your installation for that device. On the other hand, if your mobile application is intended to run on the largest possible set of devices, you need to consider what the least common denominator device has on it and make allowances for dealing with components that some devices may be missing. This problem can be broken down into two different parts: (1) Target devices missing the runtime required by your application, and (2) target devices missing components that your application uses.

Dynamic Deployment of Runtimes to Mobile Devices

The ability to dynamically install the core runtime libraries required by your mobile application is important if you are targeting multiple generations of devices. For example, whereas the .NET Compact Framework v1.1 is supported on Pocket PC 2000, 2002, 2003, and later devices, no Pocket PC 2000 devices have it pre-installed in ROM, and most 2002 devices do not have it pre-installed either. It is only with the 2003 generation of Pocket PC devices that the .NET Compact Framework became a standard part of the platform. If your application is built to run on top of the .NET Compact Framework v1.1 and you want to run on the largest range of hardware, some devices will need to have this runtime dynamically installed in order for your application to run. This leaves you three options:

1. *Only run on devices that have the needed runtime installed.* This is, of course, the simplest but least flexible option.
2. *Package the needed runtime with the application installation.* This is the most full-service option but is also the most cumbersome because it requires potentially unneeded runtime components to be carried around with the application's setup program and requires potentially complex installation logic because different types of hardware may require different builds of the runtime. If most of your target devices already have the needed runtime version installed, it is a lot of effort for little gain.
3. *Require users of devices without the needed runtime to manually install it.* Ideally your installation logic should be able to detect the presence or absence of needed runtime components. If only a minority of your target devices will require dynamic installation of components, it is probably sufficient to inform those device's users of the prerequisite and direct them to further installation instructions.

NOTE: Only some device classes support dynamic installation of runtimes and components.

As described previously, some devices are open and allow installation of software, and some devices allow only restricted software installations that may not include the ability to dynamically install a runtime. Additionally, only some device classes are capable of dynamic installation of runtimes for technical reasons. For example, the Microsoft Smartphone and Pocket PC treat file system memory differently, making it reasonable to support installing the .NET Compact Framework in a Pocket PC's RAM file system if needed but making this option infeasible for Microsoft Smartphones, which require the runtime to be ROM installed (although applications can be stored in the Smartphone's file system). For this reason, it is important to understand your target device's specification and extensibility capabilities.

Versioning of runtimes becomes an important consideration as well. Regardless of runtime technology used (for example, .NET Compact Framework, J2ME, J2SE, native code), updated runtime releases will occasionally occur and versioning will require consideration.

Many runtimes are backward compatible; for example, version 1.3 of a runtime may be capable of running code written targeting versions 1.1 and 1.2. If backward version compatibility is not supported, you have two options:

1. Probably the simplest solution is to produce a version of your application for each version of the runtime you want to support; this requires extra development and testing on your part but makes for the best end user experience.
2. The second option is to attempt to install the needed runtime version as described above.

Dynamic Installation of Needed Application Components

Components are any additional on-device technologies that your application is leveraging that are not part of the core runtime or operating system. For example, a popular component for mobile enterprise applications is a device-local database engine. Third-party graphing controls that your mobile application can use are another example. Along with the components themselves may come additional files. For example, an application that uses a mobile database engine may also have a prepopulated database file containing the data for the application to use at runtime.

Unlike runtimes, it is usually not reasonable to assume that the bulk of your target devices will come with the components your application requires pre-installed. As with runtimes, if your application needs these components you are left with two choices: (1) Your application installation can bring the needed components with it and install them as needed, or (2) your application installation can ship without the components but let users know whether they need to install them separately. The choice you make should be governed by the likelihood of end users having the components already installed and the additional size the components add to your setup.

Packaging and Installation Options

There are several potential options for the delivery and installation of your application. Which mechanism is best is based on the complexity of your application, its component dependencies, and the way end users will use your mobile application.

Copy and Run / Download and Run

If your application has no dependencies that need to come with it, the simple "copy and run" installation is the easiest approach to take. As the name implies, installation simply consists of copying the application locally, and thereafter the application can be run.

Missing in this approach is device-local registration of the application. If the application needs to be registered with the mobile device so that it can appear as navigation option for users of the mobile device, additional setup code will be required.

Device-Driven Install

A device-driven install is very similar to installing a desktop application on a PC. A special-purpose application is run to install the application locally onto the mobile device. The setup application itself may need to be signed if the device requires applications to be signed. The user typically downloads and runs the setup, possibly by finding it via an Internet browser. Third-party setup tools can help you with this.

A device local installer typically has the flexibility to install needed components, copy needed files, and perform needed pre- and post-installation steps.

Desktop-Driven Install

A desktop-driven install is usually a device-installation program that is initiated from a desktop computer. This model is most common when a partnership exists between a desktop PC and a mobile device that it synchronizes with. The desktop application can run a setup application that communicates with a mobile device and installs the necessary software.

Desktop-based installations have two principal benefits: (1) Computer users are used to running setup applications on their computers, and (2) desktop computers that synchronize with mobile devices can use this synchronization process to push updated applications and data to devices.

As above, third-party setup tools can help build desktop-driven installs.

Install via Memory Card

A memory-card-based install is a device installation that is initiated by the insertion of a storage card into a device. This kind of installation is very similar to a desktop computer's CD-ROM autorun installation where a setup process is initiated by the insertion of a CD-ROM or DVD into the computer. This kind of installation works by having a specially named file present at a predefined location in the storage medium that the device's operating system looks for when the storage card is inserted.

Memory-card-based installation can be an excellent choice if a memory card is going to be used to store application data anyway. For example, a mobile application that uses a 200MB database of information on a storage card that is plugged into a device is a natural choice for memory-card-based application installation. A 4MB install for the application, its runtime, and other needed components can easily piggyback on top of the 200MB of data being brought to the device via the storage card anyway.

Once again, a third-party setup tool can be an aid in building this kind of an install.

Developer Tool–Based Installation

If your mobile device application only needs to be deployed to a small number of devices (for instance, 20 devices), a viable option may be just to let the development tool handle it for you. Development tools often have excellent facilities for downloading applications and needed components and can spare you the need to build and debug your own installation scripts.

The downside of this approach is that it really does not scale. It will not work for deploying applications to restricted-access devices nor will it scale to anything but a small number of devices. If there is a good chance your mobile application will need to be deployed to a larger number of devices in the future, you need to think about an installation mechanism that does not require developer tool participation. If you are building a custom-use application intended only to be used on a small number of devices, however, this solution may meet your needs.

ROM-Based Installation

An option sometimes available when building a mobile application for custom hardware or when working closely with the issuer of mobile devices is placing the mobile application into the device's ROM image. Customized mobile devices are often provisioned with a set of built-in applications.

In addition, many modern devices have the ability to re-flash the ROM image in a device, allowing the issuer to periodically update the device's capabilities. Usually re-flashing requires the cryptographic key to "unlock" the device's ROM image.

Although it is not technically challenging, getting your application onto a mobile device's ROM image requires a close relationship with the device's issuer (which can be challenge unto itself).

Summary

The best advice for mobile application developers who want to build applications for deployment to a large number of mobile devices is to test the deployment early in the development cycle and make it a requirement for exiting each development milestone thereafter. Developing setup and installation technologies is always more work than anticipated; it is also less exciting than building the application itself, and therefore often gets put on the back burner in favor of more interesting tasks. This is true for desktop and server applications and even truer for mobile devices. The heterogeneous nature of mobile devices, the potential need to involve the third parties that issue the devices, and the need to test on different types of devices make this an important area to address. Package early, package often, and test the installation on the target hardware onto which you plan to deploy.

CHAPTER 17

Afterword

Any sufficiently advanced technology is indistinguishable from magic.
—Arthur C. Clark, author of *2001: A Space Odyssey* and one of the fathers
of satellite communications (Encarta 2004, Quotations)

If you have read this far, thank you for your attention! I hope you have enjoyed the book and that it has been both inspiring and educational. If you are skimming through this chapter and mulling a purchase decision, I hope you buy the book and read it!

I am often asked where I think things are headed with mobile devices. Without getting too specific (which is doomed to failure), I'd like to offer the following thoughts:

- *The "personal computer" is not going away or being replaced by mobile devices.* I often hear statements such as, "Last year 500 million mobile phones were sold and 100 million PCs. The PC is going away and going to be replaced by mobile phones that connect to the Internet." These kinds of statements assume that mobile devices serve the same purposes as personal computers; this is incorrect. For raw interactivity with the user, flexibility of purpose, richness of display, and in-depth experience, it is almost impossible to imagine replacing the personal computer. Try to imagine writing a book on a mobile phone or designing complicated spreadsheets on a PDA; it is just not possible, nor is it compelling. Personal computers, with their large screens, rich input and output capabilities, and truly awesome computing power and storage capacity, serve a very important purpose in giving their users an encompassing information experience. However, personal computers are evolving and bifurcating. The desktop computer does indeed appear to be fading away and is probably destined to be replaced by laptops on one end and personal/home servers on the other end. The desktop PC may be on its way out, but the personal computer continues to become more important than ever.

Mobile devices will play an increasing role in interacting with these computers, pushing data in, pulling data out, and probably in identifying ourselves to them, but the personal computer is here to stay.

■ *Mobile devices will become our constant companions.* In the old days people carried pocket watches with them. These devices were one of the first examples of personal technology that traveled with its owner and gave the owner valuable on-demand information. The form factor was correct, and the utility was indisputable; people needed to know what time it was. It fit in peoples' pockets and offered unobtrusive and valuable information. As increased technology enabled miniaturization and mass manufacturing brought down prices, watches moved from pockets to peoples' wrists. There was no need for the devices to be pocket-sized, so they got smaller. Digital technology came to watches, further reducing prices and increasing functionality, but the devices remained primarily read-only. Early and present-day digital watches offer some services their owners can interact with, but they are mostly read-only because of their form factor. Remember how hard it was to push buttons on digital watch calculators? Separately, mobile phones have emerged. Mobile phones offered the promise of portable two-way interaction, first starting off quite large but then quickly moving into the sweet spot form factor of "fits nicely in my pocket." Perhaps fittingly, mobile phones all have clocks on them as well, bringing us back to the pocket watch but with vastly greater capabilities. Technology has improved, prices have continued to fall, and adoption rates have risen to staggering numbers. These devices have moved from being fixed-purpose timepieces and telephones to being mobile computing platforms, but they have not moved to peoples' wrists because the current form factor is more useful for two-way interaction. Like the pocket watches of yesteryear, mobile phones are always with us and offer us information on demand, but now the interaction is definitely two-way. Mobile devices, and specifically mobile phones, are becoming the constant companions we keep in our pockets and pull out when we need information or services. Their size is well suited for comfortable portability, battery lives now span multiple days, the screen is suitable for displaying a useful quantity of rich information, and their already impressive communications capabilities are sufficient to bring a wide array of services to us. Most of what is needed today is just better software, both on the devices and the servers they talk to. As extensible computing platforms, mobile devices offer great promise to bring their users the information and services they need anywhere and at any time, online and offline. Just as many of us now find it hard to imagine how we got by before mobile phones and the Internet, today's and tomorrow's rich mobile devices will offer us services so valuable and compelling that they will quickly weave themselves into the fabric of our daily activities. Just as people in former times occasionally took out their pocket watches and quickly glanced at them to glean valuable information, so too will people everywhere soon habitually and almost unconsciously take out and glance at their mobile phones, perhaps tapping a few things into them and then placing them back into their pockets having been informed and served. More exotic form factors such as eyepiece displays and car-piece computers may yet make their mark, but for my money I'm betting on the pocket watch.

- *Mobile devices will become ever more aware of their surrounding environment.* Knowledge of time and date is something computer application programmers take for granted today. Knowledge of location, environment, and the device owner's context will be capabilities mobile devices will gain in the coming years. This knowledge will increase piecemeal and incrementally because there are many aspects to this knowledge that must be mastered and the task is complex. This knowledge is not a single factor but many small factors that when exposed to application developers in a meaningful way will bring the capabilities of mobile devices well past where they are today.

- *Mobile devices will contain lots of specific-purpose small and midsized applications.* Desktop computers lend themselves to large and engrossing applications that surround their users with data and invite them to explore and work with that data. Mobile applications work best when they give users a highly focused experience that provides them with exactly the needed information or the immediate services they want with a minimum of application navigation. Rather than a single large application, rich mobile devices are better suited for many small to mid-sized applications, each offering a highly focused user experience for accomplishing a specific set of tasks. The challenge with this model is keeping the user interface consistent in all the applications so that the user is given a single unified experience when using the device. The user, tomorrow even more than today, will become unaware of the concept of separate applications on the device; there will only be rich capabilities that the user switches comfortably between. Success means that the user does not notice the imperfections and weld lines that glue the pieces together, but instead sees only the smooth polished whole.

- *We are at the beginning.* It is only recently that mobile devices have become small, cheap, powerful, and connected enough to serve as capable software applications platforms. Because of this, most of today's state of the art in mobile device programming technologies has focused on bringing device-appropriate versions of desktop and server technologies down to mobile platforms. This is a necessary first step, but it is only the beginning. Having now brought the appropriate desktop and server technologies down to devices, the really interesting work is ready to begin. This work will consist of developing new capabilities and programming models that originate on mobile devices. These innovations will initiate on mobile devices and cross over to laptops, desktops, and servers as appropriate. Concepts such as knowledge of the environment surrounding the device, knowledge of communications capabilities, and knowledge of the individual using the device are natural areas for innovation to begin on devices and later find its way out to larger and less-mobile computing platforms. It is going to be an exciting ride.

Mobile devices offer the unprecedented capability to bring information and services directly to users in ways that can truly be described as "anytime, anywhere." It is hard to overestimate the potential for these kinds of improvements in increasing people's productivity, increasing their enjoyment, helping maintain their health, improving services for the elderly and disabled, and most importantly helping people communicate better with the world around them. Software enables developers to paint in the realm of ideas, and good engineering practices allow these ideas to be transformed into useful inventions. I hope this book has gone some small step in helping you understand and take advantage of the promise that mobile software development offers.

—Ivo Salmre

Additional Resources for the .NET Compact Framework

Online Resources

The Web is a big place, and there are plenty of high-quality mobile development resources on it that are worth taking a look at. There is unfortunately also a lot of random information to sift through. I have listed a few good places to start below. Unfortunately, the Web being a dynamic place means that URLs tend to change over time. Whenever possible, I have listed the specific title and author of the articles; if the URLs do not work, you should still have enough information to find the relevant resource.

Code Sharing

- www.GotDotNet.com is a community code-sharing site set up by Microsoft. It is a favorite code-sharing site of mine because it enables one to see what other people have been downloading most. In this way, it serves as a good way to rank the most popular and useful pieces of sample code. On GotDotNet, search in the "User Samples" section and search for samples listed under ".NET Compact Framework," and then click the Downloads header. A list of posted .NET Compact Framework samples sorted by popularity will display.
- www.OpenNETCF.org is a code-sharing site set up by independent professionals and enthusiasts to share code, news, articles, and discussions about the .NET Compact Framework. It has a source-code license that is supportive of commercial use of code on the site and is well worth taking a good look at. OpenNetCf.org also has some fairly significant shared-source development projects going on.

Newsgroups

Quite a few active "question-and-answer" forums are available for .NET Compact Framework developers. These can be accessed using a newsgroup viewer or via the Web site `http://msdn.microsoft.com/newsgroups/`.

A few of the more relevant newsgroups include the following:

- `microsoft.public.dotnet.framework.compactframework`
- `microsoft.public.pocketpc.developer`
- `microsoft.public.pocketpc.developer.networking`
- `microsoft.public.smartphone.developer`

As with any public newsgroup and discussion, there are good answers and bad answers. Newsgroups are a good place to look for hints and ideas about how to solve blocking problems, but the information is available on a "no refunds, no guarantees" basis.

General Mobility Development

For the latest and greatest news on the .NET Compact Framework and other Microsoft mobile development technologies, check out these Web sites:

- `http://msdn.microsoft.com/mobility/`
- `http://msdn.microsoft.com/mobility/prodtechinfo/devtools/netcf/faq/default.aspx`

To develop Microsoft Smartphone applications using Visual Studio .NET 2003, you will need to download and install the SDK for Windows Mobile 2003-based Smartphones from the following site:

- `http://msdn.microsoft.com/mobility/windowsmobile/downloads/`

For a terrific frequently asked questions live Wiki document, access the following site:

- `http://wiki.opennetcf.org/ow.asp?CompactFrameworkFAQ`

Specifics on Interacting with Native Code

Calling native code from VB.NET or C# is not particularly difficult, but you do need to be aware of some specific rules and facts. The best way to learn these is by example.

- The basics of working with native code from the .NET Compact Framework
  "An Introduction to P/Invoke and Marshaling on the Microsoft .NET Compact Framework"
  by Jon Box, Dan Fox, Quilogy
  `http://msdn.microsoft.com/library/default.asp?url=`
  `/library/en-us/dnnetcomp/html/netcfintrointerp.asp`
- The ins and outs of calling native code from the .NET Compact Framework
  "Advanced P/Invoke on the Microsoft .NET Compact Framework"
  by Jon Box, Dan Fox, Quilogy
  `http://msdn.microsoft.com/library/default.asp?url=`
  `/library/en-us/dnnetcomp/html/netcfadvinterop.asp`
- Passing asynchronous messages from native code into managed code with the .NET Compact Framework
  "Asynchronous Callbacks from Native Win32 Code"
  by Maarten Struys, PTS Software
  `http://msdn.microsoft.com/library/default.asp?url=`
  `/library/en-us/dnnetcomp/html/AsynchCallbacks.asp`

Working with Mobile Network Operators

Microsoft offers guidelines and a partner program for building, certifying, and deploying applications to phones issued by mobile network operators.

- A short link that will redirect you to the more detailed content below
  Mobile2Market short URL
  `http://www.mobile2market.com`
- Mobile2Market certification and marketing program
  `http://msdn.microsoft.com/mobility/windowsmobile/`
  `partners/mobile2market/default.aspx`
- A list of mobile network operators, operator-specific guidelines, and contact points
  `http://msdn.microsoft.com/mobility/windowsmobile/`
  `partners/mobile2market/smartphoneapps/default.aspx`

Deployment and Installation

Setup technologies are ever evolving and specific to the kind of application you are developing and the hardware you are targeting. As with native code interaction, examples are the best way to learn what you need to.

A good place to get deployment and installation instructions for .NET Compact Framework applications is in the MSDN product documentation that ships with Visual Studio .NET. You can find a useful device-deployment example by following the help path *Visual Studio .NET > Developing with Visual Studio .NET > Designing Distributed Applications > Developing for Devices > Samples and Walkthroughs > Smart Device Walkthroughs > Generating Custom CAB Files for Device Projects*.

- A walkthrough of building a setup application for a Pocket PC
  "Developing and Deploying Pocket PC Setup Applications"
  By Ralph Arvesen, Vertigo Software, Inc.
  `http://msdn.microsoft.com/library/default.asp?url=`
  `/library/en-us/dnnetcomp/html/netcfdeployment.asp`
- Details on dynamically installing the .NET Compact Framework on devices in case you ever need to do this
  "Creating an MSI Package That Detects and Updates the .NET Compact Framework"
  by Stan Adermann, Microsoft Corporation
  `http://msdn.microsoft.com/library/default.asp?url=`
  `/library/en-us/dnnetcomp/html/netcfdepl.asp`
- Professional installation development tools. Today some makers of desktop and server installation tools have expanded their offerings to embrace mobile device development. InstallShield's offerings for mobile devices are certainly worth looking at.
  `http://www.installshield.com`
  Note: I list InstallShield because it is a well-known and popular installation tool. If you are using other installation tools, it is certainly worth looking at their Web sites to see what mobile device support they offer.

Optimizing Performance

The following article has some excellent tips and best practices for tuning performance as well as details about how to get profiling information from the .NET Compact Framework that will enable you to analyze your algorithm's performance. It is great reading to keep you in the right "performance mindset" when building your mobile application.

- ■ "Developing Well-Performing .NET Compact Framework Applications"
  by Dan Fox, Jon Box, Quilogy
  `http://msdn.microsoft.com/library/default.asp?url=`
  `/library/en-us/dnnetcomp/html/netcfperf.asp`

Visual Basic .NET Samples

Why VB.NET and C#?

The debate between VB.NET developers and C# developers is never ending and that's a good thing! Both camps have things to learn from one another. For my part, having worked with both languages for years and specifically having worked as part of the Visual Basic design team years back, I offer the following observations. Both languages can be used to accomplish just about any programming task; it is just a question of emphasis. I find Visual Basic .NET with its traditional Visual Basic emphasis on coding productivity extremely well suited for end-application development. C#, on the other hand, has an advantage in rigor that makes it somewhat better suited for framework design. Both seem about equally well suited for designing reusable components that fall somewhere in between standalone applications and comprehensive programming libraries. In addition, both languages offer nondefault options that make the languages approach one another; for example, the Visual Basic .NET language offers the Option Strict On directive, which I strongly suggest placing at the top of any module you write as a way to catch many kinds of common syntactic and logic errors. Both languages also learn from one another with each successive version borrowing useful concepts pioneered by one another; for this reason there is a good creative tension between the two languages. A feature I particularly like in Visual Basic .NET is its treatment of events; the `AddHandler` and `Handles` keywords (used in the code below) are more elegant and declarative than their current C# variants. Because it is most convenient to see example code in the language one is most familiar with, I am placing VB.NET versions of almost all the book's listings here in the appendix. Not listed are examples too trivial to bother translating because they are short and very easily understandable to both Visual Basic and C# developers. Wherever possible, common Visual Basic coding practices have been followed, meaning that the code below is not a direct translation of the C# code but rather a somewhat more "VB-ish" version; however, the samples are functionally equivalent, and it should be easy for those interested to compare the Visual Basic and C# languages and make their own decision on preference. Happy coding!

Chapter 5 (State Machines) Samples

Listing 5.1 Sample Code for State Machine for Multiple-Choice Game

```
Option Explicit On
Class MyStateMachineClass

Private Enum GameState
    StartScreen
    AskQuestion
    CongratulateUser
    ScoldUser
End Enum


Private m_CurrentGameState As GameState


'------------------------------------------------
'The state machine that drives our user interface
'and manages other application state based on the
'mode the user is currently in
'------------------------------------------------
Private Sub StateChangeForGame(ByVal newGameUIState _
                               As GameState)


    'See which state the application is being brought into
    Select Case (newGameUIState)

      Case GameState.StartScreen
        'If we are coming from a state that does not allow
        'transition to this state, throw an exception
        If ((m_CurrentGameState <> GameState.CongratulateUser) _
        AndAlso (m_CurrentGameState <> GameState.ScoldUser)) Then

            Throw New System.Exception("Illegal State Change!")
        End If

        'UNDONE: Place code here to
```

```vbnet
        ' 1. Hide, Show, Move UI controls into place
        ' 2. Set up what ever variables/game-state needed
        '    for this mode
        '
        ' SetUpGameStateForStartScreen()

    Case GameState.AskQuestion
        'If we are coming from a state that does not allow
        'transition to this state, throw an exception
        If ((m_CurrentGameState <> GameState.StartScreen) _
AndAlso (m_CurrentGameState <> GameState.CongratulateUser) _
AndAlso (m_CurrentGameState <> GameState.ScoldUser)) Then

            Throw New System.Exception("Illegal State Change!")
        End If

        'UNDONE: Place code here to
        ' 1. Hide, Show, Move UI controls into place
        ' 2. Set up what ever variables/game-state needed
        '    for this mode
        '
        ' SetUpGameStateForAskQuestion()

    Case GameState.CongratulateUser
        'If we are coming from a state that does not allow
        'transition to this state, throw an exception
        If (m_CurrentGameState <> GameState.AskQuestion) Then
          Throw New System.Exception("Illegal State Change!")
        End If

        'UNDONE: Place code here to
        ' 1. Hide, Show, Move UI controls into place
        ' 2. Set up what ever variables/game-state needed
        '    for this mode
        '
        ' SetUpGameStateForCongratulateUser()

    Case GameState.ScoldUser
        'If we are coming from a state that does not allow
        'transition to this state, throw an exception
        If (m_CurrentGameState <> GameState.AskQuestion) Then

            Throw New System.Exception("Illegal State Change!")
        End If
```

```
                    'UNDONE: Place code here to
                    ' 1. Hide, Show, Move UI controls into place
                    ' 2. Set up what ever variables/game-state needed
                    '    for this mode
                    '
                    ' SetUpGameStateForScoldUser()

                Case Else
                    Throw New System.Exception("Unknown state!")
                End Select

            'Store the new requested state as our current state
            m_CurrentGameState = newGameUIState
        End Sub
        End Class
```

Listing 5.2 Application State Being Changed Implicitly (Bad Design!)

```
'Code that gets run when the form is loaded
Private Sub Form1_Load(ByVal sender As System.Object, ByVal _
                    e As System.EventArgs) Handles MyBase.Load

    TextBox1.Visible = True
    ListBox1.Visible = False
End Sub

'Data
Private m_someImportantInfo As String

'The user has clicked the button and wants to move on to the
'next step in this application. Hide the text box and show
'list box in its place.
Private Sub Button1_Click(ByVal sender As System.Object, ByVal _
                    e As System.EventArgs) Handles Button1.Click

    m_someImportantInfo = TextBox1.Text
    TextBox1.Visible = False
    ListBox1.Visible = True
End Sub
```

Listing 5.3 Application State Being Changed Explicitly (Good Design)

```
Private m_someImportantInfo As String
'Define the states the application can be in
Enum MyStates
  step1
  step2
End Enum


'-----------------------------------------------------
'The central function that is called
'whenever the application state needs
'to be changed
'-----------------------------------------------------
Sub ChangeApplicationState(ByVal newState As MyStates)
  Select Case newState
  Case MyStates.step1
    TextBox1.Visible = True
    ListBox1.Visible = False

  Case MyStates.step2
    m_someImportantInfo = TextBox1.Text
    TextBox1.Visible = False
    ListBox1.Visible = True
  End Select
End Sub


'-----------------------------------------------------
'The user has clicked the button and wants to move on to the
'next step in this application. Hide the text box and show
'list box in its place.
'-----------------------------------------------------
Private Sub button1_Click(ByVal sender As Object, ByVal _
                          e As System.EventArgs)
  'Call a central function to change the state
  ChangeApplicationState(MyStates.step2)
End Sub


'-----------------------------------------------------
'Code that gets run when the form is loaded
'-----------------------------------------------------
Private Sub Form1_Load(ByVal sender As Object, _
               ByVal e As System.EventArgs)
  'Call a central function to change the state
```

```
      ChangeApplicationState(MyStates.step1)
End Sub
```

Listing 5.4 Code for the Background Thread Prime Number Calculator

```
Option Strict On
Imports System
Public Class FindNextPrimeNumber

'States we can be in.
Public Enum ProcessingState
  notYetStarted
  waitingToStartAsync
  lookingForPrime
  foundPrime
  requestAbort
  aborted
End Enum


Private m_startTickCount As Integer
Private m_endTickCount As Integer
Private m_startPoint As Long
Private m_NextHighestPrime As Long
Private m_processingState As ProcessingState


'---------------------------------------------------
'A very simple state machine.
'---------------------------------------------------
Public Sub setProcessingState(ByVal nextState _
                              As ProcessingState)
    '-------------------------------------------------
    'Some very simple protective code to make sure
    'we can't enter another state if we have either
    'successfully finished, or successfully aborted
    '-------------------------------------------------
    Dim currentState As ProcessingState
    currentState = getProcessingState()
    If ((currentState = ProcessingState.aborted) _
      OrElse (currentState = ProcessingState.foundPrime)) Then
      Return
    End If
```

```vb
    'Thread concurrency protection
    SyncLock (Me)
      'Allow the state change
      m_processingState = nextState
    End SyncLock
End Sub


Public Function getProcessingState() As ProcessingState
    Dim currentState As ProcessingState
    'Thread concurrency protection
    SyncLock (Me)
      currentState = m_processingState
    End SyncLock

    Return currentState
End Function


Public Function getTickCountDelta() As Integer
    If (getProcessingState() = _
          ProcessingState.lookingForPrime) Then
      Throw New Exception( _
        "Still looking for prime! No final time calculated")
    End If

    Return m_endTickCount - m_startTickCount
End Function


'---------------------------------------------------
'Returns the prime
'---------------------------------------------------
Public Function getPrime() As Long
    If (getProcessingState() <> ProcessingState.foundPrime) Then
      Throw New Exception("Prime number not calculated yet!")
    End If

    Return m_NextHighestPrime
End Function

'Class constructor
Public Sub New(ByVal startPoint As Long)
    setProcessingState(ProcessingState.notYetStarted)
    m_startPoint = startPoint
End Sub
```

```vb
'-----------------------------------------------------------
'Creates a new worker thread that will call
' "findNextHighestPrime()"
'-----------------------------------------------------------
Public Sub findNextHighestPrime_Async()
  Dim threadStart As System.Threading.ThreadStart
  threadStart = _
    New System.Threading.ThreadStart( _
          AddressOf findNextHighestPrime)

  Dim newThread As System.Threading.Thread
  newThread = New System.Threading.Thread(threadStart)

  'Set our processing state to say that we are looking
  setProcessingState(ProcessingState.waitingToStartAsync)
  newThread.Start()
End Sub


'-----------------------------------------------------------
'This is the main worker function. This synchronously starts
'looking for the next prime number and does not exit until
'either:
' (a) The next prime is found
' (b) An external thread to this thread tells us to abort
'-----------------------------------------------------------
Public Sub findNextHighestPrime()
  'If we've been told to abort, don't even start looking
  If (getProcessingState() = ProcessingState.requestAbort) Then
    GoTo finished_looking
  End If

  'Set our processing state to say that we are looking
  setProcessingState(ProcessingState.lookingForPrime)

  m_startTickCount = System.Environment.TickCount
  Dim currentItem As Long
  'See if it's odd
  If ((m_startPoint And 1) = 1) Then
    'It's odd, start at the next odd number
    currentItem = m_startPoint + 2
  Else
    'It's even, start at the next odd number
    currentItem = m_startPoint + 1
  End If
```

```vb
    'Look for the prime item.
    While (getProcessingState() = ProcessingState.lookingForPrime)
      'If we found the prime item, return it
      If (isItemPrime(currentItem) = True) Then
        m_NextHighestPrime = currentItem
        'Update our state
        setProcessingState(ProcessingState.foundPrime)
      End If

      currentItem = currentItem + 2
    End While

finished_looking:
      'Exit. At this point we have either been
      'told to abort the search by another thread, or
      'we have found and recorded the next highest prime number

      'Record the time
      m_endTickCount = System.Environment.TickCount

    'If an abort was requested, note that we have aborted
    'the process.
    If (getProcessingState() = ProcessingState.requestAbort) Then
      setProcessingState(ProcessingState.aborted)
    End If
End Sub

'Helper function that looks to see if a specific item
'is a prime number.
Private Function isItemPrime(ByVal potentialPrime _
                                    As Long) As Boolean

  'If it's even, it's not prime
  If ((potentialPrime And 1) = 0) Then
    Return False
  End If

  'We want to look up until just past the square root
  'of the item
  Dim end_point_of_search As Long
  end_point_of_search = _
      CLng(System.Math.Sqrt(potentialPrime) + 1)
```

```vb
    Dim current_test_item As Long = 3
    While (current_test_item <= end_point_of_search)

        '-------------------------------
        'Check to make sure we have not been asked to abort!
        '-------------------------------
        If (getProcessingState() <> _
          ProcessingState.lookingForPrime) Then
            Return False
        End If

        'If the item is divisible without remainder,
        'it is not prime
        If (potentialPrime Mod current_test_item = 0) Then
            Return False
        End If

        'advance by two
        current_test_item = current_test_item + 2
    End While

    'The item is prime
    Return True
End Function
End Class
```

Listing 5.5 Test Code to Call the Background Thread Prime Number Calculator Above

```vb
'------------------------------------------------------------
'Code to process the Click event of Button1 on the form
'
'Call the prime number function on this thread!
'(This will block the thread)
'------------------------------------------------------------
    Private Sub Button1_Click(ByVal sender As System.Object, _
            ByVal e As System.EventArgs) Handles Button1.Click
    Dim testItem As Long
    testItem = System.Convert.ToInt64("123456789012345")

    Dim nextPrimeFinder As FindNextPrimeNumber
    nextPrimeFinder = New FindNextPrimeNumber(testItem)
```

```vbnet
nextPrimeFinder.findNextHighestPrime()
Dim nextHighestPrime As Long
nextHighestPrime = nextPrimeFinder.getPrime()

MsgBox(CStr(nextHighestPrime))

    'How long did the caclulation take?
Dim calculation_time As Integer
calculation_time = nextPrimeFinder.getTickCountDelta()
MsgBox(CStr(calculation_time) + " ms")
End Sub


'------------- --------------------------------------------
'Code to process the Click event of Button2 on the form
'
'Call the prime number function on another thread!
'(This will not
'block this thread)
'We will use a state machine to track the progress
'----------------------------------------------------------
Private Sub Button2_Click(ByVal sender As System.Object, _
        ByVal e As System.EventArgs) Handles Button2.Click
  Dim testItem As Long
  testItem = System.Convert.ToInt64("123456789012345")

  Dim nextPrimeFinder As FindNextPrimeNumber
  nextPrimeFinder = New FindNextPrimeNumber(testItem)

    '-----------------------------------
    'Do the processing on another thread
    '-----------------------------------
  nextPrimeFinder.findNextHighestPrime_Async()

  'Go in a loop and wait until we either find the result
  'or it is aborted
  While ((nextPrimeFinder.getProcessingState() <> _
     FindNextPrimeNumber.ProcessingState.foundPrime) _
    And _
    (nextPrimeFinder.getProcessingState() <> _
    FindNextPrimeNumber.ProcessingState.aborted))

    'TEST CODE ONLY:
    'Show a message box, allow the user to dismiss it
    'This will help pass the time!
```

```
        MsgBox("Still Looking...Click OK")

        'We could abort the search by calling:
        'nextPrimeFinder.setProcessingState(
        '   FindNextPrimeNumber.ProcessingState.requestAbort)
    End While

    'If we aborted the search, exit gracefully
    If (nextPrimeFinder.getProcessingState() = _
    FindNextPrimeNumber.ProcessingState.aborted) Then
        MsgBox("Search was aborted!")
        Return
    End If

    Dim nextHighestPrime As Long
    nextHighestPrime = nextPrimeFinder.getPrime()
    MsgBox(CStr(nextHighestPrime))

    'How long did the calculation take?
    Dim calculation_time As Integer
    calculation_time = nextPrimeFinder.getTickCountDelta()
    MsgBox(CStr(calculation_time) + " ms")
End Sub
```

Chapter 7 (Performance Introduction) Samples

Listing 7.1 Performance Sampling Code to Instrument Your Code With

```
Option Strict On
Imports System

Friend Class PerformanceSampling
'Arbitrary number, but 8 seems like enough samplers for
'most uses.
Const NUMBER_SAMPLERS As Integer = 8

Private Shared m_perfSamplesNames(NUMBER_SAMPLERS) As String
Private Shared m_perfSamplesStartTicks(NUMBER_SAMPLERS) As _
                                                        Integer
Private Shared m_perfSamplesDuration(NUMBER_SAMPLERS) As Integer
```

```vbnet
'----------------------------------------------------
'Take a start tick count for a sample
'----------------------------------------------------
Friend Shared Sub StartSample(ByVal sampleIndex As Integer, _
                             ByVal sampleName As String)

  m_perfSamplesNames(sampleIndex) = sampleName

  m_perfSamplesStartTicks(sampleIndex) = _
    System.Environment.TickCount()
End Sub


'----------------------------------------------------
'Take a start tick count for a sample
'----------------------------------------------------
Friend Shared Sub StopSample(ByVal sampleIndex As Integer)
  Dim stopTickCount As Integer = System.Environment.TickCount

  'The counter resets itself every 24.9 days
  '(which is about 2 billion ms)
  'we'll account for this unlikely possibility
  If (stopTickCount >= m_perfSamplesStartTicks(sampleIndex)) _
  Then
    'In almost all cases we will run this code.
    m_perfSamplesDuration(sampleIndex) = _
        stopTickCount - m_perfSamplesStartTicks(sampleIndex)
  Else
    'We have wrapped back around to zero and should account
    'for this
    m_perfSamplesDuration(sampleIndex) = stopTickCount + _
(Integer.MaxValue - m_perfSamplesStartTicks(sampleIndex)) + 1
  End If
End Sub


'----------------------------------------------------
'Return the length of a sample we have taken
'(length in milliseconds)
'----------------------------------------------------
Friend Shared Function GetSampleDuration(ByVal sampleIndex _
                                As Integer) As Integer
  Return m_perfSamplesDuration(sampleIndex)
End Function
```

```
'Returns the number of seconds that have elapsed
'during the sample period
Friend Shared Function GetSampleDurationText(ByVal _
                        sampleIndex As Integer) As String
  Return m_perfSamplesNames(sampleIndex) + ": " + _
    System.Convert.ToString( _
      (m_perfSamplesDuration(sampleIndex) / CDbl(1000.0)) _
      ) + " seconds."
End Function
End Class
```

Listing 7.2 Test Code Showing Use of Timing Instrumentation Code Above

```
Private Sub Button1_Click(ByVal sender As System.Object, _
   ByVal e As System.EventArgs) Handles Button1.Click

  Const TEST_SAMPE_INDEX As Integer = 2 'Choose any valid index
  'Start sampling
  PerformanceSampling.StartSample(TEST_SAMPE_INDEX, _
     "TestSample")

  'Show the message box
  MsgBox("Hit OK to finish Sample")

  'Stop sampling
  PerformanceSampling.StopSample(TEST_SAMPE_INDEX)

  'Show the results
  MsgBox(PerformanceSampling.GetSampleDurationText( _
  TEST_SAMPE_INDEX))
End Sub
```

Listing 7.3 Three Different Levels of User Responsiveness

```
'Place captions on the buttons
  Private Sub Form1_Load(ByVal sender As System.Object, _
      ByVal e As System.EventArgs) Handles MyBase.Load
    Button1.Text = "Bad experience"
    Button2.Text = "Better experience"
    Button3.Text = "Even Better"
  End Sub
```

```
'----------------------------------------
'Example of a bad experience:
'    - No visual indication is given when work is started
'    - No visual indication is given when work is ended
'    - User interface is unresponsive during work
'    - End user is left to guess when the task completes
'----------------------------------------
Private Sub Button1_Click(ByVal sender As System.Object, _
    ByVal e As System.EventArgs) Handles Button1.Click
    'Simulate work by pausing for 4 seconds
    System.Threading.Thread.Sleep(4000)
End Sub


'----------------------------------------
'Example of a better experience:
'    + A visual indication is given when work is started
'      (Wait cursor appears)
'    + A visual indication is given when work is ended
'      (Wait cursor disappears)
'    - User interface is unresponsive during work
'    + End user knows when task is completed and UI is reponsive
'      again
'----------------------------------------
Private Sub Button2_Click(ByVal sender As System.Object, _
    ByVal e As System.EventArgs) Handles Button2.Click

    System.Windows.Forms.Cursor.Current = _
        System.Windows.Forms.Cursors.WaitCursor

    'Simulate work by pausing for 4 seconds
    System.Threading.Thread.Sleep(4000)

    System.Windows.Forms.Cursor.Current = _
        System.Windows.Forms.Cursors.Default
End Sub


'----------------------------------------
'Example of an even better experience:
'    + A visual indication is given when work is started
'      (Wait cursor appears)
'    + Additional text is displayed telling the user what is
'      going on
'    + A visual indication is given when work is ended
'      (Wait cursor disappears)
```

```vb
'   - User interface is unresponsive during work
'   + End user knows when task is completed and UI is
'     responsive again
'   + Text tells user what happened
'----------------------------------------
Private Sub Button3_Click(ByVal sender As System.Object, _
        ByVal e As System.EventArgs) Handles Button3.Click
  'Give user text that explains what is going on
  Label1.Text = "Wait! Doing work!"
  'Force the UI to update the text
  '(otherwise it will wait until it processes the repaint
  'message, this may be after we exit this function)
  Label1.Update()

  'Show wait cursor
  System.Windows.Forms.Cursor.Current = _
    System.Windows.Forms.Cursors.WaitCursor

  'Simulate work by pausing for 2.8 seconds
  System.Threading.Thread.Sleep(2800)

  'Optional Incremental status update
  Label1.Text = "Wait! Almost done!"
  Label1.Update()

  'Simulate work by pausing for 1.2 seconds
  System.Threading.Thread.Sleep(1200)

  'Give text indication that we are done
  '(Update whenever UI normally updates)
  Label1.Text = "Success!"
  'Get rid of the wait cursor
  System.Windows.Forms.Cursor.Current = _
  System.Windows.Forms.Cursors.Default
End Sub
```

Listing 7.4 Performance Comparison Between Exception-Throwing Algorithm and Non-Exception-Throwing Algorithm

```vb
'==========================================================
'Note: This sample uses the "PerformanceSampling" class
'         defined earlier in this chapter. Make sure this
'         class is included in your project.
'==========================================================
```

```
'TEST FUNCTION:
'
'Attempt to add 'n1' and 'n2' together and return the result
' in 'n3'
'
' return:
'    TRUE: If the result is positive
'    FALSE: If the result is negative
'============================================================
Function returnFalseIfLessThanZero_Add2Numbers( _
          ByVal n1 As Integer, ByVal n2 As Integer, _
          ByRef n3 As Integer) As Boolean

  n3 = n1 + n2

  'Is the item less than 0?
  If (n3 < 0) Then
    Return False
  End If

  Return True
End Function


'============================================================
'TEST FUNCTION:
'
'Attempt to add 'n1' and 'n2' together and return the result
' in 'n3'
'
'This function THROWS AN EXCEPTION if 'n3' is less than 0.
'Otherwise TRUE is returned
'============================================================
Function exceptionIfLessThanZero_Add2Numbers( _
          ByVal n1 As Integer, ByVal n2 As Integer, _
          ByRef n3 As Integer) As Boolean

  n3 = n1 + n2

  'Is the item less than 0?
  If (n3 < 0) Then
    Throw New Exception("Less than 0!")
  End If
  Return True
End Function
```

```vb
'===========================================================
'Calls a simple function a large number of times and
'measures the total execution time.
'
'The function called DOES NOT raise an exception
'===========================================================
Private Sub buttonRunNoExceptionCode_Click(ByVal sender As _
            System.Object, ByVal e As System.EventArgs) Handles _
            buttonRunNoExceptionCode.Click
  Const TEST_NUMBER As Integer = 0
  Dim numberItterations As Integer
  numberItterations = _
    CInt(textBoxNumberAttempts.Text)

  'Show the number of iterations we are going to perform
  ListBox1.Items.Add("=>" + numberItterations.ToString() + _
                        " Iterations")

  Dim count_SumLessThanZero As Integer
  Dim dataOut As Integer

  '-----------------------------------------------------------
  'Start the performance timer
  '-----------------------------------------------------------
  PerformanceSampling.StartSample(TEST_NUMBER, "No Exception")
  '-----------------------------------------------------------
  'Run the loop that calls the function
  '-----------------------------------------------------------
  count_SumLessThanZero = 0
  Dim sumGreaterThanZero As Boolean
  Dim i As Integer
  While (i < numberItterations)

    '=======================
    'Call the test function!
    '=======================
    sumGreaterThanZero = _
      returnFalseIfLessThanZero_Add2Numbers(-2, -3, dataOut)

    If (sumGreaterThanZero = False) Then
      count_SumLessThanZero = count_SumLessThanZero + 1
    End If
```

```vb
        i = i + 1
    End While


    '------------------------------------------------------------
    'Stop the performance timer
    '------------------------------------------------------------
    PerformanceSampling.StopSample(TEST_NUMBER)


    '------------------------------------------------------------
    'Output the results to the user
    '------------------------------------------------------------
    If (count_SumLessThanZero = numberItterations) Then
      MsgBox("Test Passed")
      ListBox1.Items.Add( _
      PerformanceSampling.GetSampleDurationText(TEST_NUMBER))
    Else

      MsgBox("Something is wrong with the test")
    End If
End Sub


'============================================================
'Calls a simple function a large number of times and
'measures the total execution time.
'
'The function called DOES raise an exception
'============================================================
Private Sub buttonRunExceptionCode_Click(ByVal sender As _
            System.Object, ByVal e As System.EventArgs) Handles _
          buttonRunExceptionCode.Click
  Const TEST_NUMBER As Integer = 1

  'Get the number of iterations
  Dim numberItterations As Integer
  numberItterations = _
    CInt(textBoxNumberAttempts.Text)

  'Show the number of iterations we are going to perform
  ListBox1.Items.Add("=>" + numberItterations.ToString() + _
                          " Iterations")

  Dim count_SumLessThanZero As Integer
  Dim dataOut As Integer
```

```vbnet
'------------------------------------------------------------
'Start the performance timer
'------------------------------------------------------------
PerformanceSampling.StartSample(TEST_NUMBER, _
                                "Catch Exception")


'------------------------------------------------------------
'Run the loop that calls the function
'------------------------------------------------------------
count_SumLessThanZero = 0
Dim sumGreaterThanZero As Boolean
Dim i As Integer
While (i < numberItterations)
  Try
  '======================
  'Call the test function!
  '======================
  sumGreaterThanZero = _
    exceptionIfLessThanZero_Add2Numbers(-2, -3, dataOut)

  Catch
    count_SumLessThanZero = count_SumLessThanZero + 1
  End Try

  i = i + 1
End While 'end of loop

'------------------------------------------------------------
'Stop the performance timer
'------------------------------------------------------------
PerformanceSampling.StopSample(TEST_NUMBER)


'------------------------------------------------------------
'Output the results to the user
'------------------------------------------------------------
If (count_SumLessThanZero = numberItterations) Then

  MsgBox("Test Passed")
  ListBox1.Items.Add( _
    PerformanceSampling.GetSampleDurationText(TEST_NUMBER))
Else
  MsgBox("Something is wrong with the test")
End If
End Sub
```

Chapter 8 (Performance and Memory) Samples

Listing 8.1 Ways of Deferred Loading, Caching, and Releasing Graphics Resources

```
Option Strict On
Public Class GraphicsGlobals

Private Shared s_Player_Bitmap1 As System.Drawing.Bitmap
Private Shared s_Player_Bitmap2 As System.Drawing.Bitmap
Private Shared s_Player_Bitmap3 As System.Drawing.Bitmap
Private Shared s_Player_Bitmap4 As System.Drawing.Bitmap
Private Shared s_colPlayerBitmaps As _
                System.Collections.ArrayList

    '-----------------------------------------------
    'Releases all the resoruces
    '-----------------------------------------------
    Public Shared Sub g_PlayerBitmapsCollection_CleanUp()

        'If we don't have any bitmaps loaded, there is nothing
        'to clean up
        If (s_colPlayerBitmaps Is Nothing) Then Return

        'Tell each of these objects to free up
        'whatever nonmanaged resources they are
        'holding.
        s_Player_Bitmap1.Dispose()
        s_Player_Bitmap2.Dispose()
        s_Player_Bitmap3.Dispose()
        s_Player_Bitmap4.Dispose()

        'Clear each of these variables, so they do not keep
        'the objects in memory
        s_Player_Bitmap1 = Nothing
        s_Player_Bitmap2 = Nothing
        s_Player_Bitmap3 = Nothing
        s_Player_Bitmap4 = Nothing

        'Get rid of the array list
        s_colPlayerBitmaps = Nothing
    End Sub
```

```vb
'----------------------------------------------------
'Function: Returns Collection of Bitmaps
'----------------------------------------------------
Public Shared Function g_PlayerBitmapsCollection() _
                    As System.Collections.ArrayList
    '--------------------------------------------------
    'If we have already loaded these, just return them
    '--------------------------------------------------
    If Not (s_colPlayerBitmaps Is Nothing) Then
        Return s_colPlayerBitmaps
    End If

    'Load the bitmaps as resources from our executuable binary
    Dim thisAssembly As System.Reflection.Assembly = _
      System.Reflection.Assembly.GetExecutingAssembly()

    Dim thisAssemblyName As System.Reflection.AssemblyName = _
      thisAssembly.GetName()

    Dim assemblyName As String = thisAssemblyName.Name

    'Load the bitmaps
    s_Player_Bitmap1 = New System.Drawing.Bitmap( _
      thisAssembly.GetManifestResourceStream(assemblyName _
      + ".Hank_RightRun1.bmp"))

    s_Player_Bitmap2 = New System.Drawing.Bitmap( _
      thisAssembly.GetManifestResourceStream(assemblyName + _
      ".Hank_RightRun2.bmp"))

    s_Player_Bitmap3 = New System.Drawing.Bitmap( _
      thisAssembly.GetManifestResourceStream(assemblyName + _
      ".Hank_LeftRun1.bmp"))

    s_Player_Bitmap4 = New System.Drawing.Bitmap( _
      thisAssembly.GetManifestResourceStream(assemblyName + _
      ".Hank_LeftRun2.bmp"))


    'Add them to the collection
    s_colPlayerBitmaps = New System.Collections.ArrayList
    s_colPlayerBitmaps.Add(s_Player_Bitmap1)
    s_colPlayerBitmaps.Add(s_Player_Bitmap2)
```

```vb
    s_colPlayerBitmaps.Add(s_Player_Bitmap3)
    s_colPlayerBitmaps.Add(s_Player_Bitmap4)

    'Return the collection
    Return s_colPlayerBitmaps
End Function



Private Shared s_blackPen As System.Drawing.Pen
Private Shared s_whitePen As System.Drawing.Pen
Private Shared s_ImageAttribute As _
          System.Drawing.Imaging.ImageAttributes

Private Shared s_boldFont As System.Drawing.Font

'-------------------------------- --------
'Called to release any drawing resources we
'may have cached
'---------------------------------------
Private Shared Sub g_CleanUpDrawingResources()

    'Clean up the black pen, if we've got one
    If Not (s_blackPen Is Nothing) Then
      s_blackPen.Dispose()
      s_blackPen = Nothing
    End If

    'Clean up the white pen, if we've got one
    If Not (s_whitePen Is Nothing) Then
      s_whitePen.Dispose()
      s_whitePen = Nothing
    End If

    'Clean up the ImageAttribute, if we've got one
    'Note: This type does not have a Dispose() method
    'because all of its data is managed data
    If Not (s_ImageAttribute Is Nothing) Then
      s_ImageAttribute = Nothing
    End If

    'Clean up the bold font, if we've got one
    If Not (s_boldFont Is Nothing) Then
      s_boldFont.Dispose()
      s_boldFont = Nothing
```

```vb
      End If
End Sub


'-------------------------------------
'This function enables us to access the
'cached black pen
'-------------------------------------
Private Shared Function g_GetBlackPen() As System.Drawing.Pen

  'If the pen does not exist yet, create it
  If (s_blackPen Is Nothing) Then
    s_blackPen = New System.Drawing.Pen( _
      System.Drawing.Color.Black)
  End If


  'Return the black pen
  Return s_blackPen
End Function


'-------------------------------------
'This function enables us to access the
'cached white pen
'-------------------------------------
Private Shared Function g_GetWhitePen() As System.Drawing.Pen

  'If the pen does not exist yet, create it
  If (s_whitePen Is Nothing) Then
    s_whitePen = New System.Drawing.Pen( _
      System.Drawing.Color.White)
  End If


  'Return the white pen
  Return s_whitePen
End Function


'-------------------------------------
'This function enables us to access the
'cached bold font
'-------------------------------------
Private Shared Function g_GetBoldFont() As System.Drawing.Font
  'If the pen does not exist yet, create it
  If (s_boldFont Is Nothing) Then
    s_boldFont = New System.Drawing.Font( _
      System.Drawing.FontFamily.GenericSerif, _
```

```vbnet
            10, System.Drawing.FontStyle.Bold)
    End If

    'Return the bold font
    Return s_boldFont
End Function


'---------------------------------------------
'This function enables us to access the
'cached imageAttributes we use for bitmaps
'with transparency
'---------------------------------------------
Private Shared Function g_GetTransparencyImageAttribute() As _
           System.Drawing.Imaging.ImageAttributes

    'If it does not exist, create it
    If (s_ImageAttribute Is Nothing) Then

        'Create an image attribute
        s_ImageAttribute = _
          New System.Drawing.Imaging.ImageAttributes

        s_ImageAttribute.SetColorKey(System.Drawing.Color.White, _
          System.Drawing.Color.White)
    End If

    'Return it
    Return s_ImageAttribute
End Function
End Class
```

Listing 8.2 Common Code Used in All Test Cases Below

```vbnet
'Number of times we want to repeat the test
Const LOOP_SIZE As Integer = 8000
'----------------------------------------------------
'This function resets the contents of our test
'array, so we can run the test algorithm
'over and over
'----------------------------------------------------
Private Sub ResetTestArray(ByRef testArray() As String)
  If (testArray Is Nothing) Then
    ReDim testArray(5)
```

```
End If

    testArray(0) = "big_blue_duck"
    testArray(1) = "small_yellow_horse"
    testArray(2) = "wide_blue_cow"
    testArray(3) = "tall_green_zepplin"
    testArray(4) = "short_blue_train"
    testArray(5) = "short_purple_dinosaur"
End Sub
```

Listing 8.3 A Test Case Showing Wasteful Allocations (a Typical First Implementation of a Function)

```
Private Sub Button2_Click(ByVal sender As System.Object, _
        ByVal e As System.EventArgs) Handles Button2.Click
    'Run the garbage collector so we know we're starting
    'from a clean slate for our test.
    'ONLY CALL DURING TESTING! Calling the GC manually will
    'slow(down)
    'overall application throughput!
    System.GC.Collect()
    Dim testArray() As String = Nothing


    '-------------------------------------------
    'Go through the items in the array and
    'look for ones where the middle word is
    '"blue". Replace the "blue" with "orange"
    '-------------------------------------------


    'Start the stopwatch for our test!
    PerformanceSampling.StartSample(0, "WastefulWorkerClass")
    Dim workerClass1 As WastefulWorkerClass

    Dim outerLoop As Integer
    For outerLoop = 1 To LOOP_SIZE

        'Set up the data in the array we want to do our test on
        ResetTestArray(testArray)

        Dim topIndex = testArray.Length - 1
        Dim idx As Integer
        For idx = 0 To topIndex
```

```
'------------------------------------
'Create an instance of a helper class
'that dissects our string into 3 pieces
'
'This is wasteful!
'------------------------------------
workerClass1 = New WastefulWorkerClass(testArray(idx))

'If the middle word is "blue", make it "orange"
If (workerClass1.MiddleSegment = "blue") Then
  'Replace the middle item
  workerClass1.MiddleSegment = "orange"
  'Replace the word
  testArray(idx) = workerClass1.getWholeString()
End If

Next 'inner loop
Next 'outer loop
'Get the time we completed our test
PerformanceSampling.StopSample(0)
MsgBox(PerformanceSampling.GetSampleDurationText(0))
End Sub
```

Listing 8.4 The Worker Class for our First Test Case

```
Option Strict On
Imports System

Public Class WastefulWorkerClass
Private m_beginning_segment As String
Public Property BeginSegment() As String
  Get
    Return m_beginning_segment
  End Get
  Set(ByVal Value As String)
    m_beginning_segment = Value
  End Set
End Property

Private m_middle_segment As String
Public Property MiddleSegment() As String
  Get
    Return m_middle_segment
```

```vbnet
      End Get
    Set(ByVal Value As String)
      m_middle_segment = Value
    End Set
  End Property


  Private m_end_segment As String
  Public Property EndSegment() As String
    Get
      Return m_end_segment
    End Get
    Set(ByVal Value As String)
      m_end_segment = Value
    End Set
  End Property


  Public Sub New(ByVal in_word As String)
    Dim index_segment1 As Integer

    'Look for a "_" in the string
    index_segment1 = in_word.IndexOf("_", 0)

    'If there is no "_", the first segment is the whole thing
    If (index_segment1 = -1) Then
      m_beginning_segment = in_word
      m_middle_segment = ""
      m_end_segment = ""
      Return
    Else 'If there is a "_", split it

      'If the "_" is the first char, the 1st segment is ""
      If (index_segment1 = 0) Then
        m_beginning_segment = ""
      Else
        'The first segment
        m_beginning_segment = in_word.Substring(0, index_segment1)
      End If

      'Find the second "_"
      Dim index_segment2 As Integer
      index_segment2 = in_word.IndexOf("_", index_segment1 + 1)

      'Second "_" does not exist
      If (index_segment2 = -1) Then
```

```
            m_middle_segment = ""
            m_end_segment = in_word.Substring(index_segment1 + 1)
        Return
    End If


        'Set the end segment
        m_middle_segment = in_word.Substring(index_segment1 + 1, _
                            index_segment2 - index_segment1 - 1)

        m_end_segment = in_word.Substring(index_segment2 + 1)
    End If
End Sub


'Returns the whole 3 segments joined by "-"s
Public Function getWholeString() As String

    Return m_beginning_segment + "_" + m_middle_segment + "_" + _
            m_end_segment
End Function
End Class
```

Listing 8.5 A Test Case Showing Slightly Reduced Object Allocations (a Typical Refinement of a First Function Implementation)

```
Private Sub Button3_Click(ByVal sender As System.Object, _
        ByVal e As System.EventArgs) Handles Button3.Click

'Run the garbage collector so we start from a "clean"
'state for our test
'ONLY CALL DURING TESTING! Calling the GC manually will slow
'down overall application throughput!
System.GC.Collect()

Dim testArray() As String = Nothing

'-------------------------------------------
'Go through the items in the array and
'look for ones where the middle word is
'"blue". Replace the "blue" with "orange"
'-------------------------------------------

'Start the stopwatch!
PerformanceSampling.StartSample(1, "LessWasteful")
```

```
'------------------------------------------------
'LESS WASTEFUL: Allocate the object before we get in the
'loop
'------------------------------------------------
Dim workerClass1 As LessWastefulWorkerClass
workerClass1 = New LessWastefulWorkerClass

Dim outerLoop As Integer
For outerLoop = 1 To LOOP_SIZE
  'Set up the data in the array we want to do our test on
  ResetTestArray(testArray)
  Dim topIndex As Integer = testArray.Length - 1
  Dim idx As Integer
  For idx = 0 To topIndex
    '------------------------------------------------
    'Instead of reallocating the object, let's just reuse
    'it
    '------------------------------------------------
    'workerClass1 = new WastefulWorkerClass(
    '                   testArray(topIndex))
    workerClass1.ReuseClass(testArray(idx))

    'If the middle word is "blue", make it "orange"
    If (workerClass1.MiddleSegment = "blue") Then
      'Replace the middle item
      workerClass1.MiddleSegment = "orange"
      'Replace the word
      testArray(idx) = workerClass1.getWholeString()
    End If
  Next 'inner loop
Next 'outer loop

'Stop the stopwatch!
PerformanceSampling.StopSample(1)
MsgBox(PerformanceSampling.GetSampleDurationText(1))
End Sub
```

Listing 8.6 The Worker Class for Our Second Test Case

```
Option Strict On
Imports System

Public Class LessWastefulWorkerClass
```

```vb
    If (index_segment1 = -1) Then
      m_beginning_segment = in_word
      Return

    Else 'If there is a "_", split it

      If (index_segment1 = 0) Then
      Else

        m_beginning_segment = in_word.Substring(0, _
                                 index_segment1)
      End If

      Dim index_segment2 As Integer
      index_segment2 = in_word.IndexOf("_", index_segment1 + 1)

      If (index_segment2 = -1) Then
        m_end_segment = in_word.Substring(index_segment1 + 1)
        Return
      End If

      'Set the end segment
      m_middle_segment = in_word.Substring(index_segment1 + 1, _
                           index_segment2 - index_segment1 - 1)
      m_end_segment = in_word.Substring(index_segment2 + 1)

    End If
End Sub

Public Function getWholeString() As String

  Return m_beginning_segment + "_" + m_middle_segment + "_" + _
                   m_end_segment
End Function
End Class
```

Listing 8.7 A Test Case Showing Significantly Reduced Object Allocations (Typical of Doing Significant Algorithm Optimizations on the First Implementation)

```vb
Private Sub Button5_Click(ByVal sender As System.Object, _
          ByVal e As System.EventArgs) Handles Button5.Click
  'Run the garbage collector, so we start from a
  'clean slate for our test
```

```vb
Private m_beginning_segment As String
Public Property BeginSegment() As String
  Get
     Return m_beginning_segment
  End Get
  Set(ByVal Value As String)
    m_beginning_segment = Value
  End Set
End Property


Private m_middle_segment As String
Public Property MiddleSegment() As String
  Get
     Return m_middle_segment
  End Get
  Set(ByVal Value As String)
    m_middle_segment = Value
  End Set
End Property


Private m_end_segment As String
Public Property EndSegment() As String
  Get
     Return m_end_segment
  End Get
  Set(ByVal Value As String)
    m_end_segment = Value
  End Set
End Property


Public Sub ReuseClass(ByVal in_word As String)
  '----------------------------------------
  'To reuse the class, clear all the internal state
  '----------------------------------------
  m_beginning_segment = ""
  m_middle_segment = ""
  m_end_segment = ""

  Dim index_segment1 As Integer

  'Look for a "_" in the string
  index_segment1 = in_word.IndexOf("_", 0)

  'If there is no "_", the first segment is the whole thing
```

```vbnet
'ONLY CALL DURING TESTING! Calling the GC manually will slow
'down overall application throughput!
System.GC.Collect()

Dim testArray() As String = Nothing


'---------------------------------------------
'Go through the items in the array and
'look for ones where the middle word is
'"blue". Replace the "blue" with "orange"
'---------------------------------------------


'Start the stopwatch for the test
PerformanceSampling.StartSample(2, "DeferredObjects")

'---------------------------------------------------
'Less wasteful: Allocate the object before we get in the
'loop
'---------------------------------------------------
Dim workerClass1 As LessAllocationsWorkerClass
workerClass1 = New LessAllocationsWorkerClass

Dim outerLoop As Integer
For outerLoop = 1 To LOOP_SIZE
    'Set up the data in the array we want to do our test on
    ResetTestArray(testArray)
    Dim topIndex As Integer = testArray.Length - 1
    Dim idx As Integer
    For idx = 0 To topIndex
        '----------------------------------------------------
        'Less wasteful:
        'Instead of reallocating the object, let's just reuse it
        'Also: The implementation does NOT create additional
        'strings
        '----------------------------------------------------
        'workerClass1 = new WastefulWorkerClass(
        '                   testArray[topIndex])
        workerClass1.ReuseClass(testArray(idx))

        'If the middle word is "blue", make it "orange"
        '----------------------------------------------------
        'Less wasteful:
        'This compare does not need to create any additional
        'strings
        '----------------------------------------------------
```

```
        If (workerClass1.CompareMiddleSegment("blue") = 0) Then
            'Replace the middle item
            workerClass1.MiddleSegment = "orange"
            'Replace the word
            testArray(idx) = workerClass1.getWholeString()
        End If
    Next 'inner loop
  Next 'outer loop
  'Stop the stopwatch!
  PerformanceSampling.StopSample(2)
  MsgBox(PerformanceSampling.GetSampleDurationText(2))
End Sub
```

Listing 8.8 The Worker Class for Our Third Test Case

```
Option Strict On
Imports System

Public Class LessAllocationsWorkerClass

Public WriteOnly Property MiddleSegment() As String
  Set(ByVal Value As String)
    m_middleSegmentNew = Value
  End Set
  End Property


Private m_middleSegmentNew As String
Private m_index_1st_undscore As Integer
Private m_index_2nd_undscore As Integer
Private m_stringIn As String


Public Sub ReuseClass(ByVal in_word As String)
    '----------------------------------------
    'To reuse the class, clear all the internal state
    '----------------------------------------
    m_index_1st_undscore = -1
    m_index_2nd_undscore = -1
    m_middleSegmentNew = Nothing
    m_stringIn = in_word   'This does not make a string copy

    'Look for a "_" in the string
    m_index_1st_undscore = in_word.IndexOf("_", 0)
```

```vb
    'If there is no "_", the first segment is the whole thing
    If (m_index_1st_undscore = -1) Then
      Return
    End If


    'Look for the second "_"
    m_index_2nd_undscore = in_word.IndexOf("_", _
                            m_index_1st_undscore + 1)
End Sub

Public Function CompareMiddleSegment(ByVal compareTo As _
  String) As Integer
  'If there is no second underscore, there is no middle
  If (m_index_2nd_undscore < 0) Then
    'If we are comparing to an empty string, then this is a
    'match
    If ((compareTo = Nothing) OrElse (compareTo = "")) Then
      Return 0
    End If

    Return -1
  End If

  'Compare the middle segment to the first and second segments
  Return System.String.Compare(m_stringIn, _
    m_index_1st_undscore + 1, _
    compareTo, _
    0, _
    m_index_2nd_undscore - m_index_1st_undscore - 1)
End Function


Public Function getWholeString() As String
  'If we've been given no new middle segment, return the
  'original
  If (m_middleSegmentNew = Nothing) Then
    Return m_stringIn
  End If

  'Build the return string
  Return m_stringIn.Substring(0, m_index_1st_undscore + 1) + _
    m_middleSegmentNew + m_stringIn.Substring( _
        m_index_2nd_undscore, _
        m_stringIn.Length - m_index_2nd_undscore)

End Function
End Class
```

Listing 8.9 Comparing String Usage to StringBuilder in Algorithms

```
Const COUNT_UNTIL As Integer = 300
Const LOOP_ITERATIONS As Integer = 40
'-------------------------------------------------------
'NOT VERY EFFICIENT!
'
'Use regular strings to simulate building a typical set of
'strings
'-------------------------------------------------------
  Private Sub Button1_Click(ByVal sender As System.Object, _
        ByVal e As System.EventArgs) Handles Button1.Click

    'Do a garbage collection before we start running, to start
    'us from a clean state.
    'ONLY CALL DURING TESTING! Calling the GC manually will slow
    'down overall application throughput!
    System.GC.Collect()
    Dim numberToStore As Integer

    PerformanceSampling.StartSample(0, "StringAllocaitons")
    Dim total_result As String
    Dim outer_loop As Integer
    For outer_loop = 1 To LOOP_ITERATIONS
      'Clear out the old result
      total_result = ""

      'Count up to 'x_counter' and append the test of each count
      'to our working string
      Dim x_counter As Integer
      For x_counter = 1 To COUNT_UNTIL
        total_result = total_result + numberToStore.ToString() _
                    + ", "

        'Advance the counter
        numberToStore = numberToStore + 1
      Next
    Next
    PerformanceSampling.StopSample(0)

    'Display the length of the string
    MsgBox("String Length: " + total_result.Length.ToString())
    'Display string
    MsgBox("String : " + total_result)
```

```
      'Display the time it tool to run
      MsgBox(PerformanceSampling.GetSampleDurationText(0))
End Sub


'------------------------------------------------------
'MUCH MORE EFFICIENT!
'
'Use the string builder to simulate building a fairly typical
'set of strings
'------------------------------------------------------
Private Sub Button2_Click(ByVal sender As System.Object, _
          ByVal e As System.EventArgs) Handles Button2.Click
   'Do a garbage collection before we start running, to start
   'us from a clean state.
   'ONLY CALL DURING TESTING! Calling the GC manually will slow
   'down overall application throughput!
   System.GC.Collect()
   Dim sb As System.Text.StringBuilder = _
         New System.Text.StringBuilder

   Dim total_result As String
   Dim numberToStore As Integer

   PerformanceSampling.StartSample(1, "StringBuilder")
   Dim outer_loop As Integer
   For outer_loop = 1 To LOOP_ITERATIONS

      'Clear the string builder
      sb.Length = 0
      'Clear out our old result string
      total_result = ""

      'Count up to 'x_counter' and append the test of each count
      'to our working string
      Dim x_counter As Integer
      For x_counter = 1 To COUNT_UNTIL
        sb.Append(numberToStore)
        sb.Append(", ")

        'Advance the counter
        numberToStore = numberToStore + 1
      Next
      'Pretend we're doing something with the string...
      total_result = sb.ToString()
```

```
      Next

    PerformanceSampling.StopSample(1)

    'Display the length of the string
    MsgBox("String Length: " + total_result.Length.ToString())
    'Display string
    MsgBox("String : " + total_result)
    'Display the time it tool to run
    MsgBox(PerformanceSampling.GetSampleDurationText(1))
End Sub
```

Chapter 9 (Performance and Multithreading) Samples

Listing 9.1 Code to Manage Single-Task Execution on a Background Thread

```
Option Strict On
Imports System
Public Class ThreadExecuteTask

'States we can be in.
Public Enum ProcessingState
    '----------------
    'Initial state
    '----------------
    'Not doing anything interesting yet
    notYetStarted

    '----------------
    'Working states
    '----------------
    'We are waiting for the background thread to start
    waitingToStartAsync
    'Code is running in the background thread
    running
    'Requesting that the calculation be aborted
    requestAbort
    '----------------
    'Final states
    '----------------
```

```
    'Final State: We have successfully completed background
    'execution
    done
    'Final State: We have aborted the background execution
    'before finishing
    aborted
End Enum


Private m_processingState As ProcessingState

Public Delegate Sub ExecuteMeOnAnotherThread(ByVal _
    checkForAborts As ThreadExecuteTask)

Private m_CallFunction As ExecuteMeOnAnotherThread
Private m_useForStateMachineLock As Object


Public Sub New(ByVal functionToCall As ExecuteMeOnAnotherThread)
    'Create an object we can use for a lock for the
    'state machine transition function
    m_useForStateMachineLock = New Object

    'Mark our execution as ready to start
    m_processingState = ProcessingState.notYetStarted

    'Store the function we are supposed to call on the new
    'thread
    m_CallFunction = functionToCall

    '-----------------------------------------------------
    'Create a new thread and have it start executing on:
    ' this.ThreadStartPoint()
    '-----------------------------------------------------
    Dim threadStart As System.Threading.ThreadStart
    threadStart = _
        New System.Threading.ThreadStart(AddressOf ThreadStartPoint)

    Dim newThread As System.Threading.Thread
    newThread = New System.Threading.Thread(threadStart)

    'Mark our execution as ready to start (for determinism,
    'it is important to do this before we start the thread!)
    setProcessingState(ProcessingState.waitingToStartAsync)
```

```vb
        'Tell the OS to start our new thread async.
        newThread.Start()
        'Return control to the caller on this thread
    End Sub


    '--------------------------------------------------------
    'This function is the entry point that is called on the
    'new thread
    '--------------------------------------------------------
    Private Sub ThreadStartPoint()
        'Set the processing state to indicate we are running on
        'a new thread!
        setProcessingState(ProcessingState.running)

        'Run the user's code, and pass in a pointer to our class
        'so that code can occasionally call to see if an abort has
        'been requested
        m_CallFunction(Me)

        'If we didn't abort, change the execution state to indicate
        'success
        If (m_processingState <> ProcessingState.aborted) Then
                'Mark our execution as done
            setProcessingState(ProcessingState.done)
        End If

        'Exit the thread...
    End Sub


    '--------------------------------------------------
    'The state machine.
    '--------------------------------------------------
    Public Sub setProcessingState(ByVal nextState As _
                                    ProcessingState)
        'We should only allow one thread of execution to try
        'to modify the state at any given time.
        SyncLock (m_useForStateMachineLock)
                'If we are entering the state we are already in,
            'do nothing.
            If (m_processingState = nextState) Then
                    Return
            End If
```

```vbnet
'-------------------------------------------------
'Some very simple protective code to make sure
'we can't enter another state if we have either
'successfully finished, or successfully aborted
'-------------------------------------------------
If ((m_processingState = ProcessingState.aborted) _
  OrElse (m_processingState = ProcessingState.done)) Then
      Return
End If


'Make sure the state transition if valid
Select Case (nextState)
      Case ProcessingState.notYetStarted
    Throw New Exception _
      ("Cannot enter 'notYetStarted' state")


Case ProcessingState.waitingToStartAsync
  If (m_processingState <> ProcessingState.notYetStarted) _
  Then
    Throw New Exception("Invalid state transition")
  End If


Case ProcessingState.running
  If (m_processingState <> _
      ProcessingState.waitingToStartAsync) Then
    Throw New Exception("Invalid state transition")
  End If


Case ProcessingState.done
  'We can complete work only if we have been running.
  'It is also possible that the user requested an
  'abort, but we finished the work before aborting
  If ((m_processingState <> ProcessingState.running) _
    AndAlso _
  (m_processingState <> ProcessingState.requestAbort)) Then
      Throw New Exception("Invalid state transition")
  End If


  Case ProcessingState.aborted
    If (m_processingState <> _
      ProcessingState.requestAbort) Then
      Throw New Exception("Invalid state transition")
    End If
End Select
```

```
      'Allow the state change
      m_processingState = nextState
    End SyncLock
  End Sub

  Public ReadOnly Property State() As ProcessingState
    Get
      Dim currentState As ProcessingState
        'Prevents simultanious read/write of the state variable
        SyncLock (m_useForStateMachineLock)
          currentState = m_processingState
        End SyncLock
        Return currentState
    End Get
  End Property
End Class
```

Listing 9.2 Test Example for Work to Be Done on a Background Thread

```
Option Strict On
Imports System
'-----------------------------------------------------------
'Test code we will use to try background thread execution
'-----------------------------------------------------------
Public Class Test1
  Public m_loopX As Integer


    '-----------------------------------------------------------
    'The function that gets called on a background thread
    '
    ' [in] threadExecute: The class managing our thread's
    '                      execution. We can check this to see if
    '                      we should abort our calculation.
    '-----------------------------------------------------------
  Public Sub ThreadEntryPoint(ByVal threadExecute As _
                                    ThreadExecuteTask)
    'This message box will be shown in the context of the thread
    'it is running in
    MsgBox("In TEST")


    '-----------------------------
    '60 times
    '-----------------------------
```

```
      For m_loopX = 1 To 60
         'If an abort has been requested, we should quit
         If (threadExecute.State = _
            ThreadExecuteTask.ProcessingState.requestAbort) Then

            threadExecute.setProcessingState( _
               ThreadExecuteTask.ProcessingState.aborted)
            Return
         End If

         'Simulate work: Wait 1/3 second
         System.Threading.Thread.Sleep(333)
      Next
   End Sub
End Class
```

Listing 9.3 Code to Test and Run the Sample Code Above

```
'The class that will manage our new thread's execution
Private m_threadExecute As ThreadExecuteTask
'The class with the method we want to run async
Private m_testMe As Test1

'-------------------------------------------------------
'This code needs to be run before the other code because
'it starts the background execution!
'
'Create a new thread and get the execution going
'-------------------------------------------------------
Private Sub buttonStartAsyncExecution_Click(ByVal sender _
   As System.Object, ByVal e As System.EventArgs) _
   Handles buttonStartAsyncExecution.Click

'Create an instance of the class we
'want to call a method on, in another thread
m_testMe = New Test1

'Package the class' method entry point up in a delegate
Dim delegateCallCode As _
   ThreadExecuteTask.ExecuteMeOnAnotherThread

delegateCallCode = _
   New ThreadExecuteTask.ExecuteMeOnAnotherThread(AddressOf _
                       m_testMe.ThreadEntryPoint)
```

```
'Tell the thread to get going!
m_threadExecute = New ThreadExecuteTask(delegateCallCode)
End Sub

'Cause an illegal state transition (will raise an exception)
Private Sub buttonCauseException_Click(ByVal sender As _
    System.Object, ByVal e As System.EventArgs) _
    Handles buttonCauseException.Click

m_threadExecute.setProcessingState( _
      ThreadExecuteTask.ProcessingState.notYetStarted)
End Sub

'Request the async code to abort its work
Private Sub buttonAbort_Click(ByVal sender As System.Object, _
      ByVal e As System.EventArgs) Handles buttonAbort.Click
    m_threadExecute.setProcessingState( _
      ThreadExecuteTask.ProcessingState.requestAbort)
End Sub


'Check the status of our execution
Private Sub buttonCheckStatus_Click(ByVal sender As System.Object _
ByVal e As System.EventArgs) Handles ButtonCheckStatus.Click
'Ask the thread management class what state it's in
MsgBox(m_threadExecute.State.ToString())

'Ask the class with the method running on the thread how it's
progressing
MsgBox(m_testMe.m_loopX.ToString())
End Sub
```

Listing 9.4 Code That Goes into the Smartphone Form1.cs Class

```
'----------------------------------------------------
'All this code belongs inside a Form1.cs class
'----------------------------------------------------

'The object that will do our background calculation
Private m_findNextPrimeNumber As FindNextPrimeNumber
'----------------------------------------------------------
'Update the status text...
'----------------------------------------------------------
```

```vb
Sub setCalculationStatusText(ByVal text As String)
  Label1.Text = text
End Sub

Private Sub menuItemExit_Click(ByVal sender As _
       System.Object, ByVal e As System.EventArgs) _
       Handles menuItemExit.Click

  Me.Close()
End Sub

'-----------------------------------------------------------
'Menu item for starting the background calculation
'-----------------------------------------------------------
  Private Sub menuItemStart_Click(ByVal sender As _
       System.Object, ByVal e As System.EventArgs) _
       Handles menuItemStart.Click

  'What number do we want to start looking at
  Dim startNumber As Long = _
    System.Convert.ToInt64(TextBox1.Text)

  'Set up the background calculation
  m_findNextPrimeNumber = New FindNextPrimeNumber(startNumber)

  'Start the background processing running...
  m_findNextPrimeNumber.findNextHighestPrime_Async()

  'Set up the timer that will track the calculation
  Timer1.Interval = 400 '400 ms
  Timer1.Enabled = True
  End Sub

'-----------------------------------------------------------
'Menu item for "Aborting" a calculation under progress
'-----------------------------------------------------------
  Private Sub menuItemAbort_Click(ByVal sender As _
      System.Object, ByVal e As System.EventArgs) _
      Handles menuItemAbort.Click

  'If we are not doing a calculation, do nothing.
  If (m_findNextPrimeNumber Is Nothing) Then Return

  'Set the thread up to abort
```

```vb
m_findNextPrimeNumber.setProcessingState( _
   FindNextPrimeNumber.ProcessingState.requestAbort)

'Let the user instantly know we are getting
'ready to abort...
setCalculationStatusText("Waiting to abort..")
End Sub


'-------------------------------------------------------
'This timer gets called on the UI thread and enables
'us to keep track of progress on our background
'calculation
'-------------------------------------------------------
Private Sub Timer1_Tick(ByVal sender As System.Object, _
      ByVal e As System.EventArgs) Handles Timer1.Tick

   'If we get called and we have no prime number
   'we are looking for, turn off the timer
   If (m_findNextPrimeNumber Is Nothing) Then
      Timer1.Enabled = False
      Return
   End If


   '------------------------------------------------
   'If we've been aborted, throw out the prime seeker
   'and turn off the timer
   '------------------------------------------------
   If (m_findNextPrimeNumber.getProcessingState = _
     FindNextPrimeNumber.ProcessingState.aborted) Then
       Timer1.Enabled = False
     m_findNextPrimeNumber = Nothing
     setCalculationStatusText("Prime search aborted")
     Return
   End If


   '------------------------------------------------
   'Did we find the right answer?
   '------------------------------------------------
   If (m_findNextPrimeNumber.getProcessingState = _
     FindNextPrimeNumber.ProcessingState.foundPrime) Then
       Timer1.Enabled = False

     'Show the result
     setCalculationStatusText("Found! Next Prime = " + _
```

```
        m_findNextPrimeNumber.getPrime().ToString())

    m_findNextPrimeNumber = Nothing
    Return
End If


    '--------------------------------------------
    'The calculation is progressing. Give the
    'user an idea of the progress being made...
    '--------------------------------------------
    'Get the two output values
    Dim numberCalculationsToFar As Long
    Dim currentItem As Long
    m_findNextPrimeNumber.getExecutionProgressInfo( _
        numberCalculationsToFar, currentItem)

    setCalculationStatusText("In progress. Looking at: " & _
        CStr(currentItem) & " . " + _
        CStr(numberCalculationsToFar) + _
        " calculations done for you so far!")
End Sub
```

Listing 9.5 Code for the FindNextPrimeNumber.cs Class

```
Option Strict On
Imports System
Public Class FindNextPrimeNumber
'States we can be in.
Public Enum ProcessingState
  notYetStarted
  waitingToStartAsync
  lookingForPrime
  foundPrime
  requestAbort
  aborted
End Enum


Private m_startPoint As Long
Private m_NextHighestPrime As Long

'How many items have been searched?
Private m_comparisonsSoFar As Long
'What is the current item we are doing a prime search for?
```

```vb
Private m_CurrentNumberBeingExamined As Long
'Called to get an update on how the calculation is progressing
Public Sub getExecutionProgressInfo( _
                ByRef numberCalculationsSoFar As Long, _
                ByRef currentItemBeingLookedAt As Long)

    'NOTE: We import this thread lock to make sure that
    'we are not reading these values while they are in the
    'middle of being written out. Because 'm_comparisonsSoFar'
    'and 'm_CurrentNumberBeingExamined' may be
    'accessed from multiple threads, any read or write
    'operation to them needs to be synchronized with "lock" to
    'ensure that reads and writes are atomic.
    SyncLock (Me)
        numberCalculationsSoFar = m_comparisonsSoFar
        currentItemBeingLookedAt = m_CurrentNumberBeingExamined
    End SyncLock

End Sub

Private m_processingState As ProcessingState
'--------------------------------------------------
'A very simple state machine.
'--------------------------------------------------
Public Sub setProcessingState(ByVal nextState As _
                                ProcessingState)
    '--------------------------------------------------
    'Some very simple protective code to make sure
    'we can't enter another state if we have either
    'successfully finished, or successfully aborted
    '--------------------------------------------------

    If ((m_processingState = ProcessingState.aborted) _
      OrElse (m_processingState = ProcessingState.foundPrime)) _
    Then
        Return
    End If

    'Allow the state change
    m_processingState = nextState
End Sub

Public ReadOnly Property getProcessingState() As ProcessingState
    Get
```

```vbnet
        Return m_processingState
    End Get
End Property


'----------------------------------------------------
'Returns the prime
'----------------------------------------------------

Public Function getPrime() As Long
    If (m_processingState <> ProcessingState.foundPrime) Then
        Throw New Exception("Prime number not calculated yet!")
    End If
    Return m_NextHighestPrime

End Function

'Class constructor
Public Sub New(ByVal startPoint As Long)
    setProcessingState(ProcessingState.notYetStarted)
    m_startPoint = startPoint
End Sub


'------------------------------------------------------------
'Creates a new worker thread that will call
' "findNextHighestPrime()"
'------------------------------------------------------------

Public Sub findNextHighestPrime_Async()
    Dim threadStart As System.Threading.ThreadStart
    threadStart = _
        New System.Threading.ThreadStart(AddressOf _
                findNextHighestPrime)

    Dim newThread As System.Threading.Thread
    newThread = New System.Threading.Thread(threadStart)

    'Set our processing state to say that we are looking
    setProcessingState(ProcessingState.waitingToStartAsync)
    newThread.Start()
End Sub


'------------------------------------------------------------
'This is the main worker-function. This synchronously starts
'looking for the next prime number and does not exit until
'either:
' (a) The next prime is found
' (b) An external thread to this thread tells us to abort
'------------------------------------------------------------
```

```vb
Public Sub findNextHighestPrime()
  'If we've been told to abort, don't even start looking
  If (m_processingState = ProcessingState.requestAbort) Then
      GoTo finished_looking
  End If

  'Set our processing state to say that we are looking
  setProcessingState(ProcessingState.lookingForPrime)

  Dim currentItem As Long
  'See if it's odd
  If ((m_startPoint And 1) = 1) Then
      'It's odd, start at the next odd number
    currentItem = m_startPoint + 2
  Else
      'It's even, start at the next odd number
    currentItem = m_startPoint + 1
  End If

  'Look for the prime item.
  While (m_processingState = ProcessingState.lookingForPrime)
      'If we found the prime item, return it
    If (isItemPrime(currentItem) = True) Then
          m_NextHighestPrime = currentItem
        'Update our state
        setProcessingState(ProcessingState.foundPrime)
    End If

    currentItem = currentItem + 2
  End While

finished_looking:
      'Exit. At this point we have either been
      'Told to abort the search by another thread, or
      'we have found and recorded the next highest prime number

      'If an abort was requested, note that we have aborted
      'the process.
    If (m_processingState = ProcessingState.requestAbort) Then
          setProcessingState(ProcessingState.aborted)
    End If
End Sub

'Helper function that looks to see if a specific item
```

```vbnet
'is a prime number.
Private Function isItemPrime(ByVal potentialPrime _
                                As Long) As Boolean
  'If it's even, it's not prime
  If ((potentialPrime And 1) = 0) Then
      Return False
  End If


  'We want to look up until just past the square root
  'of the item
  Dim end_point_of_search As Long
  end_point_of_search = _
      CLng(System.Math.Sqrt(potentialPrime)) + 1


  Dim current_test_item As Long = 3
  While (current_test_item <= end_point_of_search)
      '---------------------------------
    'Check to make sure we have not been asked to abort!
      '-------------------------------
    If (m_processingState <> ProcessingState.lookingForPrime) _
    Then
          Return False
    End If


    'If the item is divisible without remainder,
    'it is not prime
    If (potentialPrime Mod current_test_item = 0) Then
          Return False
    End If


    'advance by two
    current_test_item = current_test_item + 2
      '-------------------------------------------------------
    'Up the count of items we have examined
      '-------------------------------------------------------
    'NOTE: We import this thread lock to make sure that
    'we are not reading these values while they are in the
    'middle of being written out. Because 'm_ccmparisonsSoFar'
    'and 'm_CurrentNumberBeingExamined' may be
    'accessed from multiple threads, any read or write
    'operation to them needs to be synchronized with "lock" to
    'ensure that reads and writes are atomic.
    SyncLock (Me)
          m_CurrentNumberBeingExamined = potentialPrime
```

```
            m_comparisonsSoFar = m_comparisonsSoFar + 1
        End SyncLock
    End While


    'The item is prime
    Return True
End Function
End Class
```

Chapter 10 (Performance and XML) Samples

Listing 10.1 Using the XML DOM to Save and Load Data from a File

```
Option Strict On
Option Compare Binary
Imports System


'-------------------------------------------------
'Shows saving and loading data imports the
'XML Document Object Model
'-------------------------------------------------
Public Class SaveAndLoadXML_UseDOM
    'XML Tags we will use in our document
    Const XML_ROOT_TAG As String = "AllMyData"
    Const XML_USERINFO_TAG As String = 'UserInfo'
    Const XML_USERID_TAG As String = "UserID"
    Const XML_NAMEINFO_TAG As String = "Name"
    Const XML_FIRSTNAME_TAG As String = "FirstName"
    Const XML_LASTNAME_TAG As String = 'LastName'


    '----------------------------------------------------------
    'Loads the state of the user
    '
    ' [in] fileName: The name of the file we are saving to
    ' [out] userId:     UserID we have loaded
    ' [out] firstName: User's FirstName we have loaded
    ' [out] lastName:User's LastName we have loaded
    '----------------------------------------------------------
    Public Shared Sub XML_LoadUserInfo(ByVal fileName As String, _
```

```vbnet
ByRef userId As Integer, ByRef firstName As String, _
ByRef lastName As String)

'Start out with null values
userId = 0
firstName = ""
lastName = ""
'Assume we have not loaded the user data
Dim gotUserInfoData As Boolean = False

Dim xmlDocument As System.Xml.XmlDocument = _
    New System.Xml.XmlDocument

xmlDocument.Load(fileName)

'Grab the root node
Dim rootElement As System.Xml.XmlElement
rootElement = _
  CType(xmlDocument.ChildNodes(0), System.Xml.XmlElement)

'Make sure the root node matches our expected text
'Otherwise, this could just be some random other XML file
If (rootElement.Name <> XML_ROOT_TAG) Then
      Throw New Exception("Root node not of expected type!")
End If

'----------------------------------------
'A simple machine that iterates through all the nodes
'----------------------------------------
Dim childOf_RootNode As System.Xml.XmlElement
For Each childOf_RootNode In _
        rootElement.ChildNodes

  'If it's a UserInfo node, we want to look inside it
  If (childOf_RootNode.Name = XML_USERINFO_TAG) Then
        gotUserInfoData = True   'We found the user data

    '----------------------------------------
    'Load each of the subitems
    '----------------------------------------
    Dim child_UserDataNode As System.Xml.XmlElement
    For Each child_UserDataNode In _
          childOf_RootNode.ChildNodes
            'UserID
```

```vb
              If (child_UserDataNode.Name = XML_USERID_TAG) Then
                  userId = CInt(child_UserDataNode.InnerText)
                'UserName
              ElseIf (child_UserDataNode.Name = XML_NAMEINFO_TAG) Then
                Dim child_Name As System.Xml.XmlElement
                For Each child_Name In child_UserDataNode.ChildNodes
                  'FirstName
                  If (child_Name.Name = XML_FIRSTNAME_TAG) Then
                    firstName = child_Name.InnerText
                  'LastName
                  ElseIf (child_Name.Name = XML_LASTNAME_TAG) Then
                    lastName = child_Name.InnerText
                  End If

                Next 'End of UserName parsing loop
              End If '"End if" for "is UserName?"

          Next 'End of UserInfo parsing loop
        End If '"End if" for "is UserInfo"?

      Next  'End of root node parsing loop

      If (gotUserInfoData = False) Then
          Throw New Exception("User data not found in XML!")
      End If
End Sub


    '-----------------------------------------------------------
    'Saves the state of the user
    '
    ' [in] fileName: The name of the file we are saving to
    ' [in] userId:    UserID we want to save
    ' [in] firstName: User's FirstName we want to save
    ' [in] lastName: User's LastName we want to save
    '-----------------------------------------------------------
Public Shared Sub XML_SaveUserInfo(ByVal fileName As String, _
    ByVal userId As Integer, ByVal firstName As String, _
    ByVal lastName As String)

    Dim xmlDocument As System.Xml.XmlDocument = _
                      New System.Xml.XmlDocument


      '-----------------------------------------------------------
      'Add the top-level document element
      '-----------------------------------------------------------
```

```vb
Dim rootNodeForDocument As System.Xml.XmlElement
rootNodeForDocument = xmlDocument.CreateElement( _
                        XML_ROOT_TAG)
xmlDocument.AppendChild(rootNodeForDocument)


'-----------------------------------------------------------
'Add the data for the user info
'-----------------------------------------------------------
Dim topNodeForUserData As System.Xml.XmlElement
topNodeForUserData = xmlDocument.CreateElement( _
                        XML_USERINFO_TAG)
rootNodeForDocument.AppendChild(topNodeForUserData)


'-----------------------------------------------------------
'Add the UserID value to our document
'-----------------------------------------------------------
'Create a subnode for the namespace info
Dim subNodeForUserID As System.Xml.XmlElement
subNodeForUserID = _
    xmlDocument.CreateElement(XML_USERID_TAG)
subNodeForUserID.InnerText = _
    System.Convert.ToString(userId)
'Attach the UserID subnode to the top-level node
topNodeForUserData.AppendChild(subNodeForUserID)


'-----------------------------------------------------------
'Add all the NameInfo values to our document
'-----------------------------------------------------------
'Create a subnode for the namespace info
Dim subNodeForNameInfo As System.Xml.XmlElement
subNodeForNameInfo = xmlDocument.CreateElement( _
                        XML_NAMEINFO_TAG)
'FirstName
Dim subNodeFirstName As System.Xml.XmlElement
subNodeFirstName = xmlDocument.CreateElement( _
                        XML_FIRSTNAME_TAG)
subNodeFirstName.InnerText = firstName

'LastName
Dim subNodeLastName As System.Xml.XmlElement
subNodeLastName = xmlDocument.CreateElement( _
                        XML_LASTNAME_TAG)
subNodeLastName.InnerText = lastName
```

```
'Attach the first And last name subnodes to the NameInfo
'parent note
subNodeForNameInfo.AppendChild(subNodeFirstName)
subNodeForNameInfo.AppendChild(subNodeLastName)

'Attach the NameInfo subnode (with its children too) to
'the top-level node
topNodeForUserData.AppendChild(subNodeForNameInfo)


'-----------------------------------------------------------
'Save the document
'-----------------------------------------------------------
Try
      xmlDocument.Save(fileName)
Catch ex As System.Exception
      MsgBox( _
    "Error occurred saving XML document - " + ex.Message)
End Try
End Sub      'End of function
End Class 'End of class
```

Listing 10.2 Calling the XML Save and Load Code

```
Private Sub Button1_Click(ByVal sender As System.Object, _
      ByVal e As System.EventArgs) Handles Button1.Click

  Const FILENAME As String = "TestFileName.XML"

  'Save imports the XML DOM
  SaveAndLoadXML_UseDOM.XML_SaveUserInfo(FILENAME, 14, "Ivo", _
                                      "Salmre")

  'Save imports the forward only XMLWriter
  'SaveAndLoadXML_UseReaderWriter.XML_SaveUserInfo(FILENAME, _
  '                                   18, "Ivo", "Salmre")

  Dim userID As Integer
  Dim firstName As String
  Dim lastName As String

  'Load imports the XML DOM
  SaveAndLoadXML_UseDOM.XML_LoadUserInfo(FILENAME, userID, _
                              firstName, lastName)
```

```
'Load imports the forward only XML Reader
'SaveAndLoadXML_UseReaderWriter.XML_LoadUserInfo(FILENAME, _
'            userID, firstName, lastName)

  MsgBox("Done! " + _
     userID.ToString() + ", " + lastName + ", " + firstName)
End Sub
```

Listing 10.3 Using the Forward-Only XML Reader/Writers to Save and Load XML Data from a File

```
Option Strict On
Option Compare Binary
Imports System
Public Class SaveAndLoadXML_UseReaderWriter

'XML Tags we will use in our document
Const XML_ROOT_TAG As String = "AllMyData"
Const XML_USERINFO_TAG As String = "UserInfo"
Const XML_USERID_TAG As String = "UserID"
Const XML_NAMEINFO_TAG As String = "Name"
Const XML_FIRSTNAME_TAG As String = "FirstName"
Const XML_LASTNAME_TAG As String = "LastName"

'The set of states we are tracking as we read in data
Private Enum ReadLocation
  inAllMyData
  inUserInfo
  inUserID
  inName
  inFirstName
  inLastName
End Enum


'-----------------------------------------------------------
'Saves the state of the user
'
' (in) fileName:  The name of the file we are saving to
' (in) userId:    UserID we have loaded
' (in) firstName: User's FirstName we have loaded
' (in) lastName:  User's LastName we have loaded
'-----------------------------------------------------------
Public Shared Sub XML_SaveUserInfo(ByVal fileName As String, _
```

```vbnet
ByVal userId As Integer, ByVal firstName As String, _
ByVal lastName As String)

Dim xmlTextWriter As System.Xml.XmlTextWriter
xmlTextWriter = New System.Xml.XmlTextWriter(fileName, _
                    System.Text.Encoding.Default)


'Write out the contents of the document!
'<Root>
xmlTextWriter.WriteStartElement(XML_ROOT_TAG)

'<Root>
xmlTextWriter.WriteStartElement(XML_USERINFO_TAG)
'<Root><UserID>

'<Root><UserInfo>
xmlTextWriter.WriteStartElement(XML_NAMEINFO_TAG)
'<Root><UserInfo><Name>
xmlTextWriter.WriteStartElement(XML_FIRSTNAME_TAG)
'<Root><UserInfo><Name><FirstName>
xmlTextWriter.WriteString(firstName) 'Value being written
xmlTextWriter.WriteEndElement() 'Close first name
'<Root><UserInfo><Name>
xmlTextWriter.WriteStartElement(XML_LASTNAME_TAG)
'<Root><UserInfo><Name><LastName>
xmlTextWriter.WriteString(lastName) 'Value being written
xmlTextWriter.WriteEndElement() 'Close last name
'<Root><UserInfo><Name>
xmlTextWriter.WriteEndElement() 'Close Name
'<Root><UserInfo>

'<Root><UserInfo>
xmlTextWriter.WriteStartElement(XML_USERID_TAG)
'<Root><UserInfo><UserID>

'Value being written
xmlTextWriter.WriteString(userId.ToString())
xmlTextWriter.WriteEndElement() 'Close UserID
'<Root><UserInfo>

xmlTextWriter.WriteEndElement() 'Close UserInfo
'<Root>

xmlTextWriter.WriteEndElement() 'Close Document
```

```
   xmlTextWriter.Close()
End Sub


'-----------------------------------------------------------
'Loads the state of the user
'
' (in) fileName:    The name of the file we are saving to
' (out) userId:     UserID we have loaded
' (out) firstName: User's FirstName we have loaded
' (out) lastName:  User's LastName we have loaded
'-----------------------------------------------------------
Public Shared Sub XML_LoadUserInfo(ByVal fileName As String, _
  ByRef userId As Integer, ByRef firstName As String, _
  ByRef lastName As String)

  Dim currentReadLocation As ReadLocation

  'Start out with null values
  userId = 0
  firstName = ""
  lastName = ""


  Dim xmlReader As System.Xml.XmlTextReader = _
      New System.Xml.XmlTextReader(fileName)

  xmlReader.WhitespaceHandling = _
     System.Xml.WhitespaceHandling.None

  Dim readSuccess As Boolean

  readSuccess = xmlReader.Read()
  If (readSuccess = False) Then
      Throw New System.Exception("No XML data to read!")
  End If

  'Make sure we recognize the root tag.
  If (xmlReader.Name <> XML_ROOT_TAG) Then
      Throw New System.Exception( _
          "Root tag different from expected!")
  End If

  'Note where we are in the document
  currentReadLocation = ReadLocation.inAllMyData
```

```
'------------------------------------------------
'Loop through our document and read what we need
'------------------------------------------------
While (readSuccess)

  Select Case (xmlReader.NodeType)
          'Called when we enter a new element
    Case System.Xml.XmlNodeType.Element

      Dim nodeName As String = xmlReader.Name
      LoadHelper_NewElementEncountered(nodeName, _
            currentReadLocation)


      '--------------------------------------------------
      'Here's where we can actually extract some text and
      'get the data we are trying to load
      '--------------------------------------------------
    Case System.Xml.XmlNodeType.Text

      Select Case currentReadLocation
        Case ReadLocation.inFirstName
          firstName = xmlReader.Value

        Case ReadLocation.inLastName
          lastName = xmlReader.Value

        Case ReadLocation.inUserID
          userId = CInt(xmlReader.Value)
      End Select

      'End of Case "System.Xml.XmlNodeType.Text"


      '--------------------------------------------------
      'Gets called when we have encountered the end of
      'an element
      '
      'We may want to switch our state based on what node
      'we are exiting to indicate that we are going back
      'to that node's parent
      '--------------------------------------------------
    Case System.Xml.XmlNodeType.EndElement
      Dim continueParsing As Boolean
      continueParsing = LoadHelper_EndElementEncountered( _
                  currentReadLocation)
```

```
            If (continueParsing = False) Then
                GoTo finished_reading_wanted_data
            End If

        Case Else
            'There is no harm in having other XML node types, but
            'in our sample XML parsing we should note this occurrence
            MsgBox( _
                "Unexpected XML type encountered" + xmlReader.Name)

    End Select 'End of case statement based current type of XML
        'element the parser is on.

    'Go to the next node
    readSuccess = xmlReader.Read()
End While

'If we made it to this point without exiting the UserInfo
'XML tag, something went wrong with the XML data we were
'reading.
Throw New Exception("Cculd not find UserInfo in XML!")

finished_reading_wanted_data:
    'Close the file, we're done with it!
    xmlReader.Close()
End Sub


'-----------------------------------------------------------
'Helper logic that decides what state we should enter
'when we encounter an exit tag.
'-----------------------------------------------------------
Private Shared Function LoadHelper_EndElementEncountered( _
            ByRef currentReadLocation As ReadLocation) _
            As Boolean

    Select Case (currentReadLocation)
        'If we are leaving the Name node, we are going back
        'up to the UserInfo
    Case ReadLocation.inName
        currentReadLocation = ReadLocation.inUserInfo

        'If we are leaving the FirstName node, we are going
        'back up to the Name node
    Case ReadLocation.inFirstName
        currentReadLocation = ReadLocation.inName
```

```vbnet
              'If we are leaving the LastName node, we are going back
              'up to the Name node
           Case ReadLocation.inLastName
             currentReadLocation = ReadLocation.inName

              'If we are leaving the UserID node, we are going back
              'up to the UserInfo node
           Case ReadLocation.inUserID
             currentReadLocation = ReadLocation.inUserInfo

              'If we are leaving the UserInfo node, we have just
              'finished reading in the UserID, FirstName,
              'and LastName.
              '
              'We can exit the loop, because we have all the information
              'we want!
           Case ReadLocation.inUserInfo
                   Return False   'We should stop parsing
        End Select

     Return True 'Continue parsing
  End Function


  Private Shared Sub LoadHelper_NewElementEncountered( _
          ByVal nodeName As String, _
          ByRef currentReadLocation As ReadLocation)


      '-----------------------------------------------------------
      'We have entered a new element!
      '
      'What state we can enter is dependent on what state we are
      'presently in
      '-----------------------------------------------------------
      Select Case (currentReadLocation)
         'If we're in the AllMyData node, here are the nodes
         'we can enter
         Case (ReadLocation.inAllMyData)

           If (nodeName = XML_USERINFO_TAG) Then
             currentReadLocation = ReadLocation.inUserInfo
           End If

         'If we're in the UserInfo node, here are the nodes
         'we can enter
```

```vb
        Case (ReadLocation.inUserInfo)
            If (nodeName = XML_USERID_TAG) Then
                currentReadLocation = ReadLocation.inUserID

        ElseIf (nodeName = XML_NAMEINFO_TAG) Then
                currentReadLocation = ReadLocation.inName
        End If

        'If we're in the Name node, here are the nodes
        'we can enter
        Case (ReadLocation.inName)
          If (nodeName = XML_FIRSTNAME_TAG) Then
            currentReadLocation = ReadLocation.inFirstName

          ElseIf (nodeName = XML_LASTNAME_TAG) Then
            currentReadLocation = ReadLocation.inLastName
          End If
    End Select
End Sub
End Class
```

Chapter 11 (Performance and Graphics) Samples

Listing 11.1 Populating and Clearing a TreeView Control Using Alternative Strategies

```vb
'-------------------------------------------------------------
'Note #1: This sample uses the PerformanceSampling class
'         defined earlier in this book. Make sure this class
'         is included in your project.
'Note #2: This code need to be inserted into a Form class that
'         has a TreeView control and buttons hooked up to the
'         xxx_Click functions below.
'-------------------------------------------------------------
'Number of items to place into the tree view
Const NUMBER_ITEMS As Integer = 800


'-------------------------------------------------
'Code for: "Fill: Baseline" Button
'
'"Unoptimized" Approach to filling a TreeView
'-------------------------------------------------
```

```vb
Private Sub UnOptimizedFill_Click(ByVal sender As _
   System.Object, ByVal e As System.EventArgs) _
   Handles UnOptimizedFill.Click

   'To make sure we're testing the same thing, make sure
   'the array is clear
    If (TreeView1.Nodes.Count > 0) Then
        TreeView1.BeginUpdate()
      TreeView1.Nodes.Clear()
      TreeView1.EndUpdate()
      TreeView1.Update()
    End If
   'For more consistent measurement, collect the garbage
   'before running. Do not do this in production code!
   System.GC.Collect()

   'Start the test timer
   PerformanceSampling.StartSample(0, "TreeViewPopulate")

   'Fill the TreeView
   Dim i As Integer
   For i = 1 To NUMBER_ITEMS
     TreeView1.Nodes.Add("TreeItem" + CStr(i))
   Next

   'Stop the test timer and show the results
   PerformanceSampling.StopSample(0)
   MsgBox(PerformanceSampling.GetSampleDurationText(0))
End Sub

'---------------------------------------------
'Code for: "Clear: Baseline" Button
'
'"Unoptimized" Approach to filling a TreeView
'---------------------------------------------
Private Sub UnOptimizedClear_Click(ByVal sender As _
      System.Object, ByVal e As System.EventArgs) _
      Handles UnOptimizedClear.Click

   'For more consistent measurement, collect the garbage
   ' before running
   System.GC.Collect()

   'Start the test timer
```

```vb
    PerformanceSampling.StartSample(1, "TreeViewClear")
    TreeView1.Nodes.Clear()

    PerformanceSampling.StopSample(1)
    MsgBox(PerformanceSampling.GetSampleDurationText(1))
End Sub


'---------------------------------------------
'Code for: "Fill: BeginUpdate" Button
'
'"Using BeginUpdate()" Approach
'---------------------------------------------
Private Sub UseBeginEndUpdateForFill_Click(ByVal sender As _
   System.Object, ByVal e As System.EventArgs) _
   Handles UseBeginEndUpdateForFill.Click

    'To make sure we're testing the same thing, make sure
    'the array is clear
    If (TreeView1.Nodes.Count > 0) Then
        TreeView1.BeginUpdate()
      TreeView1.Nodes.Clear()
      TreeView1.EndUpdate()
      TreeView1.Update()
     End If

    'For more consistent measurement, collect the garbage
    ' before running. DO NOT DO THIS IN PRODUCTION CODE!
    System.GC.Collect()

    'Start the test timer
    PerformanceSampling.StartSample(2, _
                "Populate - Use BeginUpdate")

    'Fill the TreeView
    TreeView1.BeginUpdate()
    Dim i As Integer
    For i = 1 To NUMBER_ITEMS
        TreeView1.Nodes.Add("TreeItem" + i.ToString())
    Next
    TreeView1.EndUpdate()

    'Stop the test timer and show the results
    PerformanceSampling.StopSample(2)
    MsgBox(PerformanceSampling.GetSampleDurationText(2))
End Sub
```

```
'---------------------------------------------
'Code for: "Clear: BeginUpdate" Button
'
'"Using BeginUpdate()" Approach
'---------------------------------------------
Private Sub UseBeginEndUpdateForClear_Click(ByVal sender As _
    System.Object, ByVal e As System.EventArgs) _
    Handles UseBeginEndUpdateForClear.Click

    'For more consistent measurement, collect the garbage
    ' before running. DO NOT DO THIS IN PRODUCTION CODE!
    System.GC.Collect()

    'Start the test timer
    PerformanceSampling.StartSample(3, "Clear - Use BeginUpdate")

    TreeView1.BeginUpdate()
    TreeView1.Nodes.Clear()
    TreeView1.EndUpdate()

    'Stop the test timer and show the results
    PerformanceSampling.StopSample(3)
    MsgBox(PerformanceSampling.GetSampleDurationText(3))
End Sub


'---------------------------------------------
'Code for: "Fill: Use Array" Button
'
'"Using Array" Approach
'---------------------------------------------
Private Sub FillArrayBeforeAttachingToTree_Click(ByVal _
    sender As System.Object, ByVal e As System.EventArgs) _
    Handles FillArrayBeforeAttachingToTree.Click

    'To make sure we're testing the same thing, make sure
    ' the array is clear
    If (TreeView1.Nodes.Count > 0) Then
        TreeView1.BeginUpdate()
        TreeView1.Nodes.Clear()
        TreeView1.EndUpdate()
        TreeView1.Update()
    End If

    'For more consistent measurement, collect the garbage before
```

```
'running.  DO NOT DO THIS IN PRODUCTION CODE!
System.GC.Collect()

'Start the test timer
PerformanceSampling.StartSample(4, "Populate - Use Array")


'Allocate space for our array of tree nodes
Dim newTreeNodes() As System.Windows.Forms.TreeNode
ReDim newTreeNodes(NUMBER_ITEMS - 1)

'Fill up the array
Dim i As Integer
For i = 0 To NUMBER_ITEMS - 1
        newTreeNodes(i) = _
    New System.Windows.Forms.TreeNode("TreeItem" + _
        i.ToString())
Next

'Connect the array to the TreeView
TreeView1.BeginUpdate()
TreeView1.Nodes.AddRange(newTreeNodes)
TreeView1.EndUpdate()

'Stop the test timer and show the results
PerformanceSampling.StopSample(4)
MsgBox(PerformanceSampling.GetSampleDurationText(4))
End Sub
```

Listing 11.2 Dynamic Population of a TreeView Control

```
'Dummy text to put in the placeholder child nodes
Const dummy_node As String = "_dummynode"
'Tag we will use to indicate a node
Const node_needToBePopulated As String = "_populateMe"
'Text we will use for our top-level nodes
Const nodeText_Neighborhoods As String = "Neighborhoods"
Const nodeText_Prices As String = "Prices"
Const nodeText_HouseType As String = "HouseTypes"
```

```
'----------------------------------------------------------------
'Click event handler for our button
'
'Sets up our TreeView to show incremental filling of the
'tree
'----------------------------------------------------------------

Private Sub Button1_Click(ByVal sender As System.Object, _
    ByVal e As System.EventArgs) Handles Button1.Click

  Dim tnNewNode As TreeNode

  'Turn off UI updates before we fill in the tree
  TreeView1.BeginUpdate()
  'Throw out any old data
  TreeView1.Nodes.Clear()

  '---------------------------
  ''Neighborhoods' node
  '---------------------------
  'Add the top-level 'Neighborhoods' node.
  tnNewNode = TreeView1.Nodes.Add("Neighborhoods")

  'Set a tag on the node that indicates that we will
  'dynamically fill in the node
  tnNewNode.Tag = node_needToBePopulated
  'This dummy child node only exists so that the node has
  'at least one child node and therefore the tree node is
  'expandable.
  tnNewNode.Nodes.Add(dummy_node)

  '---------------------------
  ''Price' node
  '---------------------------
  tnNewNode = TreeView1.Nodes.Add("Price")

  'Set a tag on the node that indicates that we will
  'dynamically fill in the node
  tnNewNode.Tag = node_needToBePopulated

  'This dummy child node only exists so that the node has
  'at least one child node and therefore the tree node is
  'expandable.
  tnNewNode.Nodes.Add(dummy_node)
```

```
'-----------------------------
''HouseType' node
'-----------------------------
tnNewNode = TreeView1.Nodes.Add("HouseType")

'Set a tag on the node that indicates that we will
'dynamically fill in the node
tnNewNode.Tag = node_needToBePopulated

'This dummy child node only exists so that the node has
'at least one child node and therefore the tree node is
'expandable.
tnNewNode.Nodes.Add(dummy_node)

'Resume the UI updates
TreeView1.EndUpdate()
End Sub


''-------------------------------------------------------
''BeforeExpand event handler for our TreeView
''NOTE: Unlike with C#, This event handler
''        DOES NOT require you to tinker with the code in
''        "InitializeComponent()" (don't do this!)
''        You can just choose the event the regular way
''        via the VB editors event drop-down list
''
''Called when a user asks to expand a node that has at least
''one child node. This is called before the node's children
''are shown and gives us a chance to dynamically populate the
''TreeView control.
''-------------------------------------------------------
Private Sub TreeView1_BeforeExpand(ByVal sender As Object, _
    ByVal e As System.Windows.Forms.TreeViewCancelEventArgs) _
    Handles TreeView1.BeforeExpand

'Get the node that is about to be expanded
Dim tnExpanding As System.Windows.Forms.TreeNode
tnExpanding = e.Node

'If the node is not marked 'need to be populated' the
'node is fine 'as is.'
If Not (tnExpanding.Tag Is node_needToBePopulated) Then
    Return 'Allow things to contine without hinderance
End If
```

```
'-----------------------------------------------------
'Dynamic tree population required.
'We know the node needs to be populated, figure out which
'node it is
'-----------------------------------------------------
If (tnExpanding.Text = nodeText_Neighborhoods) Then
    PopulateTreeViewNeighborhoods(tnExpanding)
  Return 'done adding items!
Else
  'Check other possibilities for tree nodes we need to add.
  MsgBox("UN-DONE: Add code to dynamically populate this node")

  'Remove the tag from the node so we don't run this
  'code again
  tnExpanding.Tag = ""
End If
End Sub


'-----------------------------------------------------
'This function is called to dynamically add child nodes
'To the "Neighborhood" node
'-----------------------------------------------------
Sub PopulateTreeViewNeighborhoods(ByVal tnAddTo As TreeNode)
  Dim tvControl As TreeView
  tvControl = tnAddTo.TreeView

  tvControl.BeginUpdate()
  'Clear the dummy sub-node we have in there
  tnAddTo.Nodes.Clear()

  'Declare four nodes we want to make children
  'of the node that was passed in.
  Dim newNeighborhoodNodes() As TreeNode
  ReDim newNeighborhoodNodes(3)
  newNeighborhoodNodes(0) = New TreeNode("Capitol Hill")
  newNeighborhoodNodes(1) = New TreeNode("Chelsea")
  newNeighborhoodNodes(2) = New TreeNode("Downtown")
  newNeighborhoodNodes(3) = New TreeNode("South Bay")
  'Add the child nodes to the tree view
  tnAddTo.Nodes.AddRange(newNeighborhoodNodes)

  tvControl.EndUpdate()
End Sub
```

Listing 11.3 Programmatic TextBox Update Causes Event Code to Be Run

```
Private m_eventTriggerCount As Integer

Private Sub Button1_Click(ByVal sender As System.Object, _
      ByVal e As System.EventArgs) Handles Button1.Click
  'This triggers a TextChanged event
  'same as if the user typed in text
  TextBox1.Text = "Hello World"
End Sub


Private Sub TextBox1_TextChanged(ByVal sender As _
    System.Object, ByVal e As System.EventArgs) _
    Handles TextBox1.TextChanged

  m_eventTriggerCount = m_eventTriggerCount + 1
  'Update a label to show the number of events
  Label1.Text = "Events: #" + CStr(m_eventTriggerCount)
  'List each of the events
  ListBox1.Items.Add(m_eventTriggerCount.ToString() + _
  TextBox1.Text)
End Sub
```

Listing 11.4 Using a State Model for Updates and Instrumentation to Better Understand and Control Event Processing

```
'----------------------------------------------------------------
'To enable event instrumentation:
'    #Const EVENTINSTRUMENTATION = 1
'
'To disable event instrumentation:
'    #Const EVENTINSTRUMENTATION = 0
'----------------------------------------------------------------
#Const EVENTINSTRUMENTATION = 1


'----------------------------------------------------------------
'A flag that tells control event handlers if they should
'exit without doing any work
'----------------------------------------------------------------
Private m_userInterfaceUpdateOccuring As Boolean

'Counters for event occurrences
```

```vb
Private m_radioButton1ChangeEventCount As Integer
Private m_textBox1ChangeEventCount As Integer


'-----------------------------------------------------------
'Code we only want to include if we are running in an
'instrumented mode. This code has relatively high execution
'overhead and we only want to compile it in and run it if
'we are doing diagnostics.
'-----------------------------------------------------------
#If EVENTINSTRUMENTATION <> 0 Then
Private m_instrumentedEventLog As System.Collections.ArrayList
'-----------------------------------------------------------
'Logs the occurrence of an event into an array we can inspect
'
'Note: No attempt is made to keep the size of the
'       logging array bounded, so the longer the application
'       runs the larger this array will become
'-----------------------------------------------------------
Private Sub instrumented_logEventOccurrence(ByVal eventData _
                                            As String)
    'Create the event log if it has not already been created
    If (m_instrumentedEventLog Is Nothing) Then
        m_instrumentedEventLog = _
            New System.Collections.ArrayList
    End If

    'Log the event
    m_instrumentedEventLog.Add(eventData)
End Sub


'-----------------------------------------------------------
'Show the list of events that have occurred
'Note: This implementation is pretty crude.
'       You may want instead to show the events
'       list in a separate dialog that pops up for the
'       purpose.
'-----------------------------------------------------------
Private Sub instrumentation_ShowEventLog()
  Dim listItems As _
      System.Windows.Forms.ListBox.ObjectCollection

  listItems = listBoxEventLog.Items

  'Clear the items in the list
```

```
listItems.Clear()
'If there are no events, exit
If (m_instrumentedEventLog Is Nothing) Then
    listItems.Add("0 Events")
  Return
End If


'At the top of the list show the total of events we
'have counted
listItems.Add(m_instrumentedEventLog.Count.ToString() + _
            " Events")
'List the items in reverse order, so the most recent are
'displayed first
Dim logItem As String
Dim listIdx As Integer
For listIdx = _
  m_instrumentedEventLog.Count - 1 To 0 Step -1

    logItem = CStr(m_instrumentedEventLog(listIdx))
    listItems.Add(logItem)
  Next
End Sub
#End If


'-----------------------------------------------------------
'RadioButton1 Changed event
'-----------------------------------------------------------
Private Sub RadioButton1_CheckedChanged(ByVal sender As _
      System.Object, ByVal e As System.EventArgs) _
      Handles RadioButton1.CheckedChanged

  'If our application is updating the data in the
  'user interface we do not want to treat this as
  'a user triggered event. If this is the case
  'exit and do nothing.
  If (m_userInterfaceUpdateOccuring = True) Then
    Return
  End If

  'Count the number of times this event has been called
  m_radioButton1ChangeEventCount = _
    m_radioButton1ChangeEventCount + 1

#If (EVENTINSTRUMENTATION <> 0) Then
```

```
        'Log the occurrence of the event
        instrumented_logEventOccurrence("radioButton1.Change:" + _
          m_radioButton1ChangeEventCount.ToString() + ":" + _
          RadioButton1.Checked.ToString()) 'value
    #End If
    End Sub


    '--------------------------------------------------------------
    'Button1 click event
    'Simulates a case where code updates the user interface
    'potentially causes event code to be run
    '--------------------------------------------------------------
    Private Sub Button1_Click(ByVal sender As System.Object, _
        ByVal e As System.EventArgs) Handles Button1.Click

        'Indicate that we do not want the event handlers
        'to process events right now because we are updating
        'the user interface.
        '
        'm_userInterfaceUpdateOccuring   = true

        RadioButton1.Checked = True
        TextBox1.Text = "Hello World"

        'We are done updating the user interface
        m_userInterfaceUpdateOccuring = False
    End Sub


    '--------------------------------------------------------------
    'TextBox changed event handler
    '--------------------------------------------------------------
    Private Sub TextBox1_TextChanged(ByVal sender As System.Object _
        , ByVal e As System.EventArgs) Handles TextBox1.TextChanged

        'If our application is updating the data in the
        'user interface we do not want to treat this as
        'a user triggered event. If this is the case
        'exit and do nothing.
        If (m_userInterfaceUpdateOccuring = True) Then
            Return
        End If

        'Count the number of times we execute this event
        m_textBox1ChangeEventCount = m_textBox1ChangeEventCount + 1
```

```vbnet
#If EVENTINSTRUMENTATION <> 0 Then
  'Log the occurrence of the event
  instrumented_logEventOccurrence("textBox1.Change:" + _
    m_textBox1ChangeEventCount.ToString() + ":" + _
    TextBox1.Text.ToString()) 'Value
#End If
End Sub



Private Sub buttonShowEventLog_Click(ByVal sender As _
      System.Object, ByVal e As System.EventArgs) _
      Handles buttonShowEventLog.Click

#If EVENTINSTRUMENTATION <> 0 Then
  instrumentation_ShowEventLog()
#End If
End Sub
```

Listing 11.5 Calling a Controls Update() Method to Show Progress Text

```vbnet
'----------------------------------------------------
'This code belongs in a Form containing a single
'Button (button1) and a Label (label1)
'----------------------------------------------------
Private Sub Button1_Click(ByVal sender As System.Object, _
    ByVal e As System.EventArgs) Handles Button1.Click
  'Show a wait cursor
  System.Windows.Forms.Cursor.Current = _
          System.Windows.Forms.Cursors.WaitCursor

  Dim testString As String
  Dim loop3 As Integer
  For loop3 = 1 To 100 Step 10
      Label1.Text = loop3.ToString() + "% Done..."
      '!!!!!!!!!!!!!!!!!!!!!!!!!!!!!!!!!!!!!!!!!!!!!!!!!!!
      'Uncomment the line below to show progress updates!
      '!!!!!!!!!!!!!!!!!!!!!!!!!!!!!!!!!!!!!!!!!!!!!!!!!!!
      'Label1.Update()

      testString = ""
      Dim loop2 As Integer
      For loop2 = 1 To 1000
```

```
          testString = testString + "test"
      Next
   Next
   Label1.Text = "Done!"

   'Remove the wait cursor
   System.Windows.Forms.Cursor.Current = _
           System.Windows.Forms.Cursors.Default
End Sub
```

Listing 11.6 Drawing into an Off-Screen Bitmap and Sending It to a Picture Box

```
'-----------------------------------------------------------
'Draw into a bitmap. Send the bitmap to a PictureBox
'-----------------------------------------------------------
Private Sub Button1_Click(ByVal sender As System.Object, _
     ByVal e As System.EventArgs) Handles Button1.Click

   'Create a new bitmap
   Dim myBitmap As System.Drawing.Bitmap
   myBitmap = New System.Drawing.Bitmap(PictureBox1.Width, _
                                   PictureBox1.Height)
   '----------------------------------------------------
   'Create a graphics object so we can draw in the bitmap
   '----------------------------------------------------
   Dim myGfx As System.Drawing.Graphics
   myGfx = System.Drawing.Graphics.FromImage(myBitmap)

   'Paint our bitmap all yellow
   myGfx.Clear(System.Drawing.Color.Yellow)

   'Create a pen
   Dim myPen As System.Drawing.Pen
   myPen = New System.Drawing.Pen(System.Drawing.Color.Blue)


   '----------------------------------------------------
   'Draw an ellipse
   '----------------------------------------------------
   myGfx.DrawEllipse(myPen, 0, 0, myBitmap.Width - 1, _
                  myBitmap.Height - 1)

   'Create a solid brush
   Dim myBrush As System.Drawing.Brush
```

```
'-------------------------------------------------------
'Draw the text with the brush
'-------------------------------------------------------
myBrush = New System.Drawing.SolidBrush( _
                        System.Drawing.Color.Black)
'Note: We are useing the Font object from the Form
myGfx.DrawString("Hello!", Me.Font, myBrush, 2, 10)


'-------------------------------------------------------
'Important! Clean up after ourselves
'-------------------------------------------------------
myGfx.Dispose()
myPen.Dispose()
myBrush.Dispose()


'-------------------------------------------------------
'Tell the picture box that it should display the
'bitmap we just created and drew on.
'-------------------------------------------------------
PictureBox1.Image = myBitmap
End Sub
```

Listing 11.7 Creating a Graphics Object for a Form

```
'------------------------------------------------------------
'Creates a Graphics object for a Form and draws onto it
'------------------------------------------------------------
Private Sub Button1_Click(ByVal sender As System.Object, _
    ByVal e As System.EventArgs) Handles Button1.Click

  'Create a Graphics object for the Form
  Dim myGfx As System.Drawing.Graphics
  myGfx = Me.CreateGraphics()

  'Create a Brush
  Dim myBrush As System.Drawing.Brush
  myBrush = New System.Drawing.SolidBrush( _
                          System.Drawing.Color.DarkGreen)

  'Fill the rectangle
  myGfx.FillRectangle(myBrush, 4, 2, 60, 20)
```

```
'-------------------------------------
'Important: Clean up!
'-------------------------------------
myBrush.Dispose()
myGfx.Dispose()
End Sub
```

Listing 11.8 Hooking into the Paint Function for a Form

```
'Brushes we want to cache, so we don't need to create/dispose them
'all the time
Private m_brushBlue As System.Drawing.Brush
Private m_brushYellow As System.Drawing.Brush
'Just for fun, lets count the number of times we are called
Private m_paintCount As Integer


'-----------------------------------------------------------
'We are overriding our base classes 'Paint' event. This means
'every time the Form gets called to paint itself, this
'function will get called.
'-----------------------------------------------------------
Protected Overrides Sub OnPaint(ByVal e As PaintEventArgs)
    'Important: Call the base class and allow it to do its
    'paint work
    MyBase.OnPaint(e)

    'Up the count of the number of times we have been called
    m_paintCount = m_paintCount + 1


    '-----------------------------------------------------------
    'Important:
    'Instead of creating a graphics object, we are being lent one
    'for the duration of this call. This means that it is not
    'our job to .Dispose() of the object
    '-----------------------------------------------------------
    Dim myGfx As System.Drawing.Graphics
    myGfx = e.Graphics


    '-----------------------------------------------------------
    'Because this painting needs to occur quickly, let's cache the
    'brushes so we don't need to create/dispose them every time
    'we are called
    '-----------------------------------------------------------
```

```
If (m_brushBlue Is Nothing) Then
    m_brushBlue = New System.Drawing.SolidBrush( _
                        System.Drawing.Color.Blue)
End If
If (m_brushYellow Is Nothing) Then
    m_brushYellow = New System.Drawing.SolidBrush( _
                    System.Drawing.Color.Yellow)
End If


'------------------------------------------------------------
'Do the drawing
'------------------------------------------------------------
myGfx.FillRectangle(m_brushBlue, 2, 2, 100, 100)
myGfx.DrawString("PaintCount: " + CStr(m_paintCount), _
                        Me.Font, m_brushYellow, 3, 3)


    'Exit: Nothing we want to call .Dispose() on.
End Sub
```

Listing 11.9 A Simple Custom Control That Changes Colors and Fires a Custom Event

```
'A very simple custom control
Public Class myButton
Inherits System.Windows.Forms.Control
'-----------------------------------------------------
'Objects we need for drawing
'-----------------------------------------------------
Private m_RectangleBrush As System.Drawing.Brush
Private m_TextBrush As System.Drawing.Brush
Private m_RectangleColor As System.Drawing.Color


'-----------------------------------------------------
'The event we want to expose. This is a public delegate.
'-----------------------------------------------------
Public Event EventButtonTurningBlue(ByVal sender As Object, _
                        ByVal e As System.EventArgs)

'The constructor
Public Sub New()
  MyBase.New()
```

```vbnet
      'Note: We should write a "Dispose()" function and
      'destructor that clean up these objects

      'Create the brushes we will need
      m_RectangleColor = System.Drawing.Color.Black

      m_RectangleBrush = New System.Drawing.SolidBrush( _
                         m_RectangleColor)

      m_TextBrush = New System.Drawing.SolidBrush( _
                         System.Drawing.Color.White)
  End Sub


  '--------------------------------------------------------
  'Internal response to being clicked is to cycle
  'through three different button colors
  '--------------------------------------------------------
  Protected Overrides Sub OnClick(ByVal e As System.EventArgs)
      '------------------------------------------------
      'Important: Call the base implementation. This
      'will allow any event handlers hooked up to this
      'control to be called
      '------------------------------------------------
      MyBase.OnClick(e)

      '--------------------------------------------------------
      'Select our new brush color based on the last brush color
      '--------------------------------------------------------
      If (m_RectangleColor.Equals(System.Drawing.Color.Black)) Then
          m_RectangleColor = System.Drawing.Color.Blue

          '!!!!!!!!!!!!!!!!!!!!!!!!!!!!!!!!!!!!!!!!!!!!!!!!!!
          'Trigger an event!
          '!!!!!!!!!!!!!!!!!!!!!!!!!!!!!!!!!!!!!!!!!!!!!!!!!!
          'Call the event, pass no event arguments
          RaiseEvent EventButtonTurningBlue(Me, Nothing)
      ElseIf (m_RectangleColor.Equals(System.Drawing.Color.Blue)) _
      Then
          m_RectangleColor = System.Drawing.Color.Red
      Else
          m_RectangleColor = System.Drawing.Color.Black
      End If
```

```
'-------------------------------------------------------
'Release the old brush
'-------------------------------------------------------

m_RectangleBrush.Dispose()


'-------------------------------------------------------------
'Create the new brush we want to draw the background with
'-------------------------------------------------------------

m_RectangleBrush = _
   New System.Drawing.SolidBrush(m_RectangleColor)


'-------------------------------------------------------------
'Tell the operating system that our control needs to be
'redrawn as soon as reasonable
'-------------------------------------------------------------

  Me.Invalidate()
End Sub


'-------------------------------------------------------------
'Just for fun let's count how many times we get painted
'-------------------------------------------------------------
Private m_paintCount As Integer
Protected Overrides Sub OnPaint( _
        ByVal e As System.Windows.Forms.PaintEventArgs)
    '-------------------------------------------------------------
    'Important: Call the base class and allow it to do its
    'paint work
    '-------------------------------------------------------------

    MyBase.OnPaint(e)


    'Up the count of the number of times we have been called
    m_paintCount = m_paintCcunt + 1


    '-------------------------------------------------------------
    'Important:
    'Instead of creating a graphics object, we are being lent one
    'for the duration of this call. This means that it is not
    'our job to .Dispose() of the object
    '-------------------------------------------------------------

    Dim myGfx As System.Drawing.Graphics
    myGfx = e.Graphics

    'Draw the rectangle
    myGfx.FillRectangle(m_RectangleBrush, 0, 0, _
                        Me.Width, Me.Height)
```

```
'Draw the text
myGfx.DrawString("Button! Paint: " + m_paintCount.ToString(), _
                    Me.Parent.Font, m_TextBrush, 0, 0)
End Sub
End Class
```

Listing 11.10 Code to Place inside a Form to Create an Instance of the Custom Control

```
'Our new button
Private m_newControl As myButton


'---------------------------------------------------
'This code will get hooked up as our event handler
'---------------------------------------------------
Private Sub CallWhenButtonTurningBlue(ByVal sender As Object, _
                            ByVal e As System.EventArgs)

  MsgBox("Button is about to turn blue!")
End Sub


'---------------------------------------------------
'This function is to be hooked up to the click event
'of Button1
'---------------------------------------------------
Private Sub Button1_Click(ByVal sender As System.Object, _
      ByVal e As System.EventArgs) Handles Button1.Click
    '---------------------------------------------------
    'To keep things simple, allow only one instance of
    'the control.
    '---------------------------------------------------
    If Not (m_newControl Is Nothing) Then Return

    'Create an instance of our button
    m_newControl = New myButton
    'Tell it where it should be located inside its parent
    m_newControl.Bounds = New Rectangle(10, 10, 150, 40)


    '-------------------------------------
    'Connect up an event handler
    '-------------------------------------
    AddHandler m_newControl.EventButtonTurningBlue, _
          AddressOf CallWhenButtonTurningBlue
```

```
    'Add it to the list of controls in this Form.
    'This will make it visible
    Me.Controls.Add(m_newControl)
End Sub
```

Listing 11.11 Three Useful Ways to Cache Graphical Resources

```
Imports System
Imports System.Drawing

Friend Class GraphicsGlobals
'==========================================================
'Approach 1: Create the resource on demand
'            and keep cached afterward.
'
'External code gets access view the public properties, but
'the variable itself is internal to the class
'==========================================================
Private Shared s_bluePen As Pen
Public Shared ReadOnly Property globalBluePen() As Pen
  Get
      'If we have not created a
    If (s_bluePen Is Nothing) Then
      s_bluePen = New System.Drawing.Pen( _
                    System.Drawing.Color.Blue)
    End If
    Return s_bluePen
  End Get
End Property


'==========================================================
'Approach 2:
'Globally load and cache a bunch of commonly
'used Pens, ImageAttributes, Fonts, and brushes
'
'External code gets access to the public members,
'no accessors functions needed.
'==========================================================
Public Shared g_blackPen As Pen
Public Shared g_whitePen As Pen
Public Shared g_ImageAttribute As Imaging.ImageAttributes
Private Shared s_alreadyInitialized As Boolean
Public Shared g_boldFont As Font
```

```vb
Public Shared g_smallTextFont As Font
Public Shared g_greenBrush As Brush
Public Shared g_yellowBrush As Brush
Public Shared g_redBrush As Brush
Public Shared g_blackBrush As Brush


'===========================================================
'Needs to be called before anyone accesses the globals above
'===========================================================
Public Shared Sub InitializeGlobals()
  If (s_alreadyInitialized = True) Then Return
  g_blackPen = New System.Drawing.Pen(Color.Black)
  g_whitePen = New System.Drawing.Pen(Color.White)
  g_ImageAttribute = New _
          System.Drawing.Imaging.ImageAttributes
  g_ImageAttribute.SetColorKey(Color.White, Color.White)
  g_boldFont = New Font(FontFamily.GenericSerif, _
                    10, FontStyle.Bold)
  g_smallTextFont = New Font(FontFamily.GenericSansSerif, _
                    8, FontStyle.Regular)

  g_blackBrush = New SolidBrush(System.Drawing.Color.Black)
  g_greenBrush = New SolidBrush( _
                        System.Drawing.Color.LightGreen)
  g_yellowBrush = New SolidBrush(System.Drawing.Color.Yellow)
  g_redBrush = New SolidBrush(System.Drawing.Color.Red)

  s_alreadyInitialized = True
End Sub


'==========================================================
'Approach 3: Return an array of related resources.
'           Cache the resources locally so that multiple
'           requests do not load duplicate (wasteful)
'           versions
'
'==========================================================
Private Shared m_CaveMan_Bitmap1 As Bitmap
Private Shared m_CaveMan_Bitmap2 As Bitmap
Private Shared m_CaveMan_Bitmap3 As Bitmap
Private Shared m_CaveMan_Bitmap4 As Bitmap
Private Shared m_colCaveManBitmaps As _
                System.Collections.ArrayList
```

```vbnet
'-----------------------------------------------------------
'Create and load an array of images for a sprite
'-----------------------------------------------------------
Public Shared Function g_CaveManPictureCollection() As _
                          System.Collections.ArrayList

    'Only load the bitmaps if we do not have them loaded yet
    If (m_CaveMan_Bitmap1 Is Nothing) Then
        '-----------------------------------------------------
        'Load the bitmaps. These bitmaps are stored as embedded
        'resources in our binary application
        '
        'Loading the images from external files would be similar
        'but slightly simpler (we could just specify the file
        'name in the bitmaps constructor).
        '-----------------------------------------------------
        'Get a reference to our binary assembly
        dim thisAssembly  as System.Reflection.Assembly = _
              System.Reflection.Assembly.GetExecutingAssembly()

        'Get the name of the assembly
        Dim thisAssemblyName As System.Reflection.AssemblyName = _
                                  thisAssembly.GetName()
        Dim assemblyName As String = thisAssemblyName.Name

        'Load the bitmaps as binary streams from our assembly
        m_CaveMan_Bitmap1 = New System.Drawing.Bitmap( _
            thisAssembly.GetManifestResourceStream( _
            assemblyName + ".Hank_RightRun1.bmp"))

        m_CaveMan_Bitmap2 = New System.Drawing.Bitmap( _
            thisAssembly.GetManifestResourceStream( _
            assemblyName + ".Hank_RightRun2.bmp"))

        m_CaveMan_Bitmap3 = New System.Drawing.Bitmap( _
            thisAssembly.GetManifestResourceStream( _
            assemblyName + ".Hank_LeftRun1.bmp"))

        m_CaveMan_Bitmap4 = New System.Drawing.Bitmap( _
            thisAssembly.GetManifestResourceStream( _
            assemblyName + ".Hank_LeftRun2.bmp"))

        'Add them to the collection
        m_colCaveManBitmaps = New System.Collections.ArrayList
```

```
            m_colCaveManBitmaps.Add(m_CaveMan_Bitmap1)
            m_colCaveManBitmaps.Add(m_CaveMan_Bitmap2)
            m_colCaveManBitmaps.Add(m_CaveMan_Bitmap3)
            m_colCaveManBitmaps.Add(m_CaveMan_Bitmap4)
        End If

        'Return the collection
        Return m_colCaveManBitmaps
    End Function
End Class
```

Chapter 13 (User Interface Design) Samples

Listing 13.1 Use of State Machine to Experiment with Two Different UI Layouts

```
#Const PLAYFIELD_ON_BOTTOM = 0   'Show PLAYFIELD below UI
'#Const PLAYFIELD_ON_BOTTOM = 1 'Show PLAYFIELD above UI
'-------------------------------------------------------------
'EVENT HANDLER: Called when form is loaded
'-------------------------------------------------------------
Private Sub Form1_Load(ByVal sender As System.Object, _
    ByVal e As System.EventArgs) Handles MyBase.Load

  'Set the shared properties of our visual interface
  SetStartControlPositionAndState()
  'Set the dynamic properties based on the state we're entering
  StateChangeForGameUI(GameUIState.startScreen)
End Sub


'-------------------------------------------------------------
'The state machine that drives showing hand hiding buttons
'-------------------------------------------------------------
Private Enum GameUIState
  startScreen = 1
  waitForNextQuestion = 2
  waitForUserToStateKnowledge = 4
  waitForUserToAnswerMultipleChoice = 8
End Enum
'Current state of game
Private m_GameUIState As GameUIState
```

```vb
'==============================================================
'State machine used for driving the user interface
'==============================================================
Private Sub StateChangeForGameUI(ByVal newGameUIState As _
                                        GameUIState)

  m_GameUIState = newGameUIState
 Select Case (newGameUIState)
      Case GameUIState.startScreen
          buttonAskQuestion.Visible = True
          buttonAskQuestion.Text = "Start"

          'Hide the text box
          textBoxAskQuestion.Visible = False

          SetAnswerButtonVisibility(False)
          SetDifficultyButtonVisibility(False)

     Case GameUIState.waitForNextQuestion
       setQuestionText("List answer details here... " + vbCrLf + _
          "Lots of space to write..." + vbCrLf + _
          "Waiting for user to select next question...")
       textBoxAskQuestion.Visible = True

          buttonAskQuestion.Text = "Next"
          buttonAskQuestion.Visible = True
          'Make sure the button is displayed on top
          buttonAskQuestion.BringToFront()
          SetAnswerButtonVisibility(False)
          SetDifficultyButtonVisibility(False)

#If PLAYFIELD_ON_BOTTOM <> 0 Then 'PLAYFIELD is below UI
    textBoxAskQuestion.Height = pictureBoxGameBoard.Top - 2
#Else 'PLAYFIELD is above user controls

        textBoxAskQuestion.Top = pictureBoxGameBoard.Top + _
          pictureBoxGameBoard.Height + 2
        textBoxAskQuestion.Height = Me.Height - _
          textBoxAskQuestion.Top
#End If

     Case GameUIState.waitForUserToStateKnowledge

        SetTextForVocabularyQuestion()
```

```vbnet
            textBoxAskQuestion.Visible = True
            buttonAskQuestion.Visible = False
            SetAnswerButtonVisibility(False)
            SetDifficultyButtonVisibility(True)


#If PLAYFIELD_ON_BOTTOM <> 0 Then 'PLAYFIELD is below UI
            textBoxAskQuestion.Height = _
                    buttonShowAnswers_AdvancedVersion.Top - 2
#Else 'PLAYFIELD is above user controls

            textBoxAskQuestion.Top = _
              buttonShowAnswers_AdvancedVersion.Top + _
              buttonShowAnswers_AdvancedVersion.Height + 2

            textBoxAskQuestion.Height = Me.Height - _
              textBoxAskQuestion.Top
#End If

        Case GameUIState.waitForUserToAnswerMultipleChoice
            buttonAskQuestion.Visible = False
            SetDifficultyButtonVisibility(False)
            'Enable the buttons so they can be clicked by the user
            SetAnswerButtonEnabled(True)
            SetAnswerButtonVisibility(True)


#If PLAYFIELD_ON_BOTTOM <> 0 Then 'PLAYFIELD is below UI
            textBoxAskQuestion.Height = buttonAnswer0.Top - 2
#Else 'PLAYFIELD is above user controls
            'Position the text box to make good use of the screen
            textBoxAskQuestion.Top = buttonAnswer5.Top + _
              buttonAnswer5.Height + 2
            textBoxAskQuestion.Height = Me.Height - _
              textBoxAskQuestion.Top
#End If
        End Select
End Sub
'============================================================
'Sets up the shared layout of our user interface.
'These are all the items whose positions will remain fixed
'The user interface state machine will make changes to other
'properties
'============================================================
```

```
Private Sub SetStartControlPositionAndState()
  pictureBoxGameBoard.Width = 240
  pictureBoxGameBoard.Height = 176

  'Set the size of the multiple-choice answer buttons
  Const answerButtons_dx As Integer = 117
  Const answerButtons_dy As Integer = 18

  buttonAnswer0.Width = answerButtons_dx
  buttonAnswer0.Height = answerButtons_dy
  buttonAnswer1.Size = buttonAnswer0.Size
  buttonAnswer2.Size = buttonAnswer0.Size
  buttonAnswer3.Size = buttonAnswer0.Size
  buttonAnswer4.Size = buttonAnswer0.Size
  buttonAnswer5.Size = buttonAnswer0.Size

  buttonShowAnswers_AdvancedVersion.Width = answerButtons_dx
  buttonShowAnswers_AdvancedVersion.Height = 24
  buttonShowAnswers_SimpleVersion.Size = _
    buttonShowAnswers_AdvancedVersion.Size

  'Pixels between adjacent buttons
  Const dx_betweenButtons As Integer = 3
  Const dy_betweenButtons As Integer = 2

  Const answerbuttons_beginX As Integer = 3

  'Make a background image for our bitmap, so we can see it
  'in our testing
  Dim gameBoard As System.Drawing.Bitmap
  gameBoard = New System.Drawing.Bitmap( _
      pictureBoxGameBoard.Width, pictureBoxGameBoard.Height)

  Dim gameboard_gfx As System.Drawing.Graphics
  gameboard_gfx = System.Drawing.Graphics.FromImage(gameBoard)
  gameboard_gfx.Clear(System.Drawing.Color.Yellow)
  Dim myPen As System.Drawing.Pen = New System.Drawing.Pen( _
      System.Drawing.Color.Blue)
  gameboard_gfx.DrawRectangle(myPen, 2, 2, _
            gameBoard.Width - 4, gameBoard.Height - 6)
  myPen.Dispose()
  gameboard_gfx.Dispose()
  pictureBoxGameBoard.Image = gameBoard
```

```vb
'Position the text box that contains the questions we ask
'as well as detailed answers to users
textBoxAskQuestion.Left = 0
textBoxAskQuestion.Width = 240

buttonAskQuestion.Width = 64
buttonAskQuestion.Height = 20

#If PLAYFIELD_ON_BOTTOM <> 0 Then 'PLAYFIELD is below UI
    Const answerbuttons_beginY As Integer = 42
    Const showanswers_beginY As Integer = 77
    '---------------------------------------------
    'Set up the "Easy" or "Hard" option buttons for the game
    '---------------------------------------------
    buttonShowAnswers_AdvancedVersion.Top = showanswers_beginY
    buttonShowAnswers_SimpleVersion.Top = showanswers_beginY


    '---------------------------------------------
    'Set up the multiple-choice answers
    '---------------------------------------------
    'Set the control that the others will line up based on
    buttonAnswer0.Top = answerbuttons_beginY

    'Place Picture Box below the controls
    pictureBoxGameBoard.Top = _
        (answerButtons_dy + dy_betweenButtons) * 3 + _
        answerbuttons_beginY

    buttonAskQuestion.Top = 0
    buttonAskQuestion.Left = 174

    textBoxAskQuestion.Top = 0
#Else 'PLAYFIELD is above user controls
    Const answerbuttons_beginY As Integer = 174


    '-----------------------------------------------------
    'Set up the "Easy" or "Hard" option buttons for the game
    '-----------------------------------------------------
    buttonShowAnswers_AdvancedVersion.Top = answerbuttons_beginY
    buttonShowAnswers_SimpleVersion.Top = answerbuttons_beginY


    '---------------------------------------------
    'Set up the multiple-choice answers
    '---------------------------------------------
```

```
       'Set the control that the others will line up based on
       buttonAnswer0.Top = answerbuttons_beginY

       pictureBoxGameBoard.Top = 0

       buttonAskQuestion.Top = answerbuttons_beginY
       buttonAskQuestion.Left = 174
   #End If

       buttonShowAnswers_AdvancedVersion.Left = answerbuttons_beginX
       buttonShowAnswers_SimpleVersion.Left = _
           buttonShowAnswers_AdvancedVersion.Left + _
           answerButtons_dx + dx_betweenButtons

       pictureBoxGameBoard.Left = 0
       pictureBoxGameBoard.Width = 240
       pictureBoxGameBoard.Height = 172


       buttonAnswer0.Left = answerbuttons_beginX

       buttonAnswer1.Left = buttonAnswer0.Left + answerButtons_dx + _
                       dx_betweenButtons
       buttonAnswer1.Top = buttonAnswer0.Top

       'next row
       buttonAnswer2.Left = buttonAnswer0.Left
       buttonAnswer2.Top = buttonAnswer0.Top + answerButtons_dy + _
                       dy_betweenButtons

       buttonAnswer3.Left = buttonAnswer2.Left + answerButtons_dx + _
                       dx_betweenButtons
       buttonAnswer3.Top = buttonAnswer2.Top

       'next row
       buttonAnswer4.Left = buttonAnswer2.Left
       buttonAnswer4.Top = buttonAnswer2.Top + answerButtons_dy + _
                       dy_betweenButtons

       buttonAnswer5.Left = buttonAnswer4.Left + answerButtons_dx + _
                       dx_betweenButtons
       buttonAnswer5.Top = buttonAnswer4.Top
   End Sub
```

```vb
'--------------------------------------------------------------
'A helper function that enables us to set the visibility
'state of the buttons that show vocabulary answers
'--------------------------------------------------------------
Private Sub SetAnswerButtonVisibility(ByVal visibleState _
                                      As Boolean)
  buttonAnswer0.Visible = visibleState
  buttonAnswer1.Visible = visibleState
  buttonAnswer2.Visible = visibleState
  buttonAnswer3.Visible = visibleState
  buttonAnswer4.Visible = visibleState
  buttonAnswer5.Visible = visibleState
End Sub


'--------------------------------------------------------------
'A helper function called to set the visibility state of some
'controls
'--------------------------------------------------------------
Private Sub SetDifficultyButtonVisibility(ByVal visibleState _
                                          As Boolean)
  buttonShowAnswers_AdvancedVersion.Visible = visibleState
  buttonShowAnswers_SimpleVersion.Visible = visibleState
End Sub


'--------------------------------------------------------------
'A helper function that enables us to set the visibility
'of the buttons that show vocabulary answers
'--------------------------------------------------------------
Private Sub SetAnswerButtonEnabled(ByVal enabledState _
                                   As Boolean)
  buttonAnswer0.Enabled = enabledState
  buttonAnswer1.Enabled = enabledState
  buttonAnswer2.Enabled = enabledState
  buttonAnswer3.Enabled = enabledState
  buttonAnswer4.Enabled = enabledState
  buttonAnswer5.Enabled = enabledState
End Sub


'--------------------------------------------------------------
'Sets the text in the text box and buttons necessary
'to ask a question.
'
'In a real implementation, this function would look up
'the vocabulary questions dynamically
'--------------------------------------------------------------
```

```vb
Private Sub SetTextForVocabularyQuestion()
    setQuestionText("What is the English word for 'der Mensch'?")

    buttonAnswer0.Text = "Four"
    buttonAnswer1.Text = "Person"
    buttonAnswer2.Text = "Three"
    buttonAnswer3.Text = "To Jump"
    buttonAnswer4.Text = "Newspaper"
    buttonAnswer5.Text = "Brother"
End Sub
'Called to evaluate a user selected a multiple-choice answer
Private Sub evaluateMultipleChoiceAnswer(ByVal buttonClicked _
    As Button, ByVal selection As Integer)
    'Note: In the non-prototype implementation, the correct
    'answer would be a dynamic value, not always "button #1"

    'If the user did not select the correct answer, disable
    'the button pressed
    If (selection <> 1) Then
        'The answer selected was not the correct one
        buttonClicked.Enabled = False
    Else
        'User got the right answer, move on with the game
        StateChangeForGameUI(GameUIState.waitForNextQuestion)
    End If
End Sub


'Abstracts setting the question text
Sub setQuestionText(ByVal textIn As String)
    textBoxAskQuestion.Text = textIn
End Sub


'------------------------------------------------------------
'EVENT HANDLER: User wants to see next question
'------------------------------------------------------------
Private Sub buttonAskQuestion_Click(ByVal sender As Object, _
    ByVal e As System.EventArgs) Handles buttonAskQuestion.Click

    SetTextForVocabularyQuestion()
    StateChangeForGameUI(GameUIState.waitForUserToStateKnowledge)
End Sub
```

```vb
'--------------------------------------------------------------
'EVENT HANDLER:
'User wants to answer the question displayed and what's
'the hardest list of options possible to challenge him/her
'--------------------------------------------------------------
Private Sub buttonShowAnswers_AdvancedVersion_Click( _
      ByVal sender As Object, ByVal e As System.EventArgs) _
      Handles buttonShowAnswers_AdvancedVersion.Click
  'Set the state of the game to show the multiple-choice
  'options
  StateChangeForGameUI( _
          GameUIState.waitForUserToAnswerMultipleChoice)
End Sub


'--------------------------------------------------------------
'EVENT HANDLER:
'User wants to answer the question displayed and what's
'the simplest list of options possible to challenge him/her
'--------------------------------------------------------------
Private Sub buttonShowAnswers_SimpleVersion_Click( _
        ByVal sender As Object, ByVal e As System.EventArgs) _
        Handles buttonShowAnswers_SimpleVersion.Click
  'Set the state of the game to show the multiple-choice
  'options
  StateChangeForGameUI( _
          GameUIState.waitForUserToAnswerMultipleChoice)
End Sub


'EVENT HANDLER: A multiple-choice answer button was clicked
Private Sub buttonAnswer0_Click(ByVal sender As Object, ByVal _
     e As System.EventArgs) Handles buttonAnswer0.Click
  evaluateMultipleChoiceAnswer(buttonAnswer0, 0)
End Sub


'EVENT HANDLER: A multiple-choice answer button was clicked
Private Sub buttonAnswer1_Click(ByVal sender As Object, ByVal _
     e As System.EventArgs) Handles buttonAnswer1.Click
  evaluateMultipleChoiceAnswer(buttonAnswer1, 1)
End Sub


'EVENT HANDLER: A multiple-choice answer button was clicked
Private Sub buttonAnswer2_Click(ByVal sender As Object, ByVal _
     e As System.EventArgs) Handles buttonAnswer2.Click
  evaluateMultipleChoiceAnswer(buttonAnswer2, 2)
End Sub
```

```
'EVENT HANDLER: A multiple-choice answer button was clicked
Private Sub buttonAnswer3_Click(ByVal sender As Object, ByVal _
    e As System.EventArgs) Handles buttonAnswer3.Click
  evaluateMultipleChoiceAnswer(buttonAnswer3, 3)
End Sub


'EVENT HANDLER: A multiple-choice answer button was clicked
Private Sub buttonAnswer4_Click(ByVal sender As Object, ByVal _
    e As System.EventArgs) Handles buttonAnswer4.Click
  evaluateMultipleChoiceAnswer(buttonAnswer4, 4)
End Sub


'EVENT HANDLER: A multiple-choice answer button was clicked
Private Sub buttonAnswer5_Click(ByVal sender As Object, ByVal _
    e As System.EventArgs) Handles buttonAnswer5.Click
  evaluateMultipleChoiceAnswer(buttonAnswer5, 5)
End Sub
```

Listing 13.2 Dynamic Creation of Controls on a Form at Runtime

```
'------------------------------------------------------------
'Counter for the number of button controls we create
'------------------------------------------------------------
Private m_nextNewButtonIndex As Integer


'------------------------------------------------------------
'EVENT HANDLER: Click event handler for the button we have
'              on our form.
'
'This function creates a new button, attaches it to our
'form and hooks up a "Click" event handler for it
'------------------------------------------------------------
Private Sub buttonCreateNewButtons_Click(ByVal sender As _
  System.Object, ByVal e As System.EventArgs) _
  Handles buttonCreateNewButtons.Click

    'Eventually we will start creating new buttons off the
    'bottom of the screen, so lets stop at 8
    If (m_nextNewButtonIndex > 8) Then
        Return
    End If
```

```vb
'----------------------------------------------------------
'Create the button (not yet attached to our form)
'set its location, size, and text
'----------------------------------------------------------
Const newButtonHeight As Integer = 15
Dim newButton As System.Windows.Forms.Button
newButton = New System.Windows.Forms.Button
newButton.Width = 100
newButton.Height = newButtonHeight
newButton.Left = 2
newButton.Top = (newButtonHeight + 2) * m_nextNewButtonIndex
newButton.Text = "New Button " + _
                 m_nextNewButtonIndex.ToString()

'----------------------------------------------------------
'Attach an event handler to the "Click" event of this
'control.
'----------------------------------------------------------
AddHandler newButton.Click, _
                          AddressOf Me.ClickHandlerForButtons

'----------------------------------------------------------
'Attach this button to the form. This will actually
'create the button on the form!
'----------------------------------------------------------
newButton.Parent = Me

    'Increment our counter for the next button we create
    m_nextNewButtonIndex = m_nextNewButtonIndex + 1
End Sub

'----------------------------------------------------------
'Event handler we will dynamically hook up to our new
'buttons
'----------------------------------------------------------
Private Sub ClickHandlerForButtons(ByVal sender As Object, _
                              ByVal e As System.EventArgs)

    Dim buttonCausingEvent As Button = _
              CType(sender, System.Windows.Forms.Button)

    'Bring up a message box announcing that we have received
    'the event
    MsgBox("Click event from:" + vbCrLf + buttonCausingEvent.Text)
End Sub
```

```vb
                        'advance the insert point
                        If (currentCharIndex <= selectionStart) Then
                           selectionStart = selectionStart + 1
                        End If
                     End If


                     'This character is fine now, advance to the next char
                     currentCharIndex = currentCharIndex + 1
                  Else
                     '------------------------------------------------------
                     'The character  needs to be a digit
                     '------------------------------------------------------
                     If (System.Char.IsDigit(currentChar) = False) Then
                        'Remove a character
                        m_sb.Remove(currentCharIndex, 1)
                        'If we removed a character before the insert point
                        'retreat the insert point
                        If (currentCharIndex < selectionStart) Then
                           selectionStart = selectionStart - 1
                        End If

                        'Don't advance the char count, we need to look at
                        'the character that took the place of the one we
                        'have removed
                     Else
                           'The character is a digit, all is well.
                           currentCharIndex = currentCharIndex + 1
                     End If
                  End If
               End While

               'If we are over the length, truncate it
               If (m_sb.Length > SSNumberLength) Then
                  m_sb.Length = SSNumberLength
               End If

               'Return our new string
               Return m_sb.ToString()
            End Function


            Private m_in_OnChangeFunction As Boolean
            Protected Overrides Sub OnTextChanged(ByVal e As EventArgs)
```

```vb
'-----------------------------------------------------
'If we change the .Text property, we will get called
're-entrantly. In this case we want to do nothing, and
'just exit the function without passing on the event
'to anyone else.
'-----------------------------------------------------
If (m_in_OnChangeFunction = True) Then
      Return
End If

'Note that we are now in the OnChanged function
'so we can detect re-entrancy (see code above)
m_in_OnChangeFunction = True

'Get the current .Text property
Dim oldText As String = Me.Text
'Get the current SelectionStart Index
Dim selectionStart As Integer = Me.SelectionStart
'Format the string so it meets our needs
Dim newText As String = formatText_NNN_NN_NNNN(oldText, _
                            selectionStart)

'If the text differs from the original, update the
'.Text property
If (oldText <> newText) Then
   'This will cause us to get called reentrantly
   Me.Text = newText
   'Update the location of the insert point
   Me.SelectionStart = selectionStart
End If

'Because we have just forced the text entry into the
'right format, if the length matches the length of
'the Social Security number we know that it is in
'the format ###-##-####.
If (Me.Text.Length = SSNumberLength) Then
    'Yes, we have a full Social Security number
   m_inputIsFullValidEntry = True
Else
    'No, we do note have a full Social Security number yet
   m_inputIsFullValidEntry = False
End If

'Call our base class and let anyone who wants
```

```
'to know that the text has changed get called
MyBase.OnTextChanged(e)

'Note that we are exiting our code now and want to turn
'off the re-entrancy check.
m_in_OnChangeFunction = False
End Sub


Protected Overrides Sub OnKeyPress( _
            ByVal e As System.Windows.Forms.KeyPressEventArgs)
   'Because we know we don't want any letters in our input, _
   'just ingore them if we detect them.
   Dim keyPressed As Char = e.KeyChar
   If (System.Char.IsLetter(keyPressed)) Then
       'Tell the system we have handled the event
     e.Handled = True
     Return
   End If
   'Process the keypress as normal
   MyBase.OnKeyPress(e)
End Sub
End Class
```

Listing 13.4 Code in Form to Create the Custom TextBox Control

```
'----------------------------------------------------------
'The variable to hold our new text box control
'----------------------------------------------------------
Private m_filteredTextBox As SocialSecurityTextBox
'----------------------------------------------------------
'EVENT HANDLER: Create an instance of our custom control
'               and place it onto the Form
'----------------------------------------------------------
Private Sub Button1_Click(ByVal sender As System.Object, _
      ByVal e As System.EventArgs) Handles Button1.Click

   'Create, position, and host the control
   m_filteredTextBox = New SocialSecurityTextBox
   m_filteredTextBox.Bounds = _
         New System.Drawing.Rectangle(2, 2, 160, 20)

   'Hook up the event handler
```

```vb
    AddHandler m_filteredTextBox.TextChanged, _
      AddressOf Me.textBox_TextChanged

    'Set the parent
    m_filteredTextBox.Parent = Me

    'Select the control
    m_filteredTextBox.Focus()

    'Disable this button so a second SocialSecurityTextBox does
    'not get created on top of this one
    Button1.Enabled = False
End Sub


'------------------------------------------------------------------
'EVENT HANDLER: This gets dynamically hooked up when the control
'                 is created
'------------------------------------------------------------------
Private Sub textBox_TextChanged(ByVal sender As Object, _
                                ByVal e As System.EventArgs)

    If (m_filteredTextBox.IsFullValidInput = True) Then
        label1.Text = "FULL SOCIAL SECURITY NUMBER!!!"
    Else
        Label1.Text = "Not full input yet..."
    End If
End Sub
```

Listing 13.5 Code in Form to Demonstrate Use of Transparencies

```vb
'--------------------------------------------------------
'Dimensions for our bitmaps and the onscreen PictureBox
'--------------------------------------------------------
Const bitmap_dx As Integer = 200
Const bitmap_dy As Integer = 100
'--------------------------------------------------------
'Creates and draws the background image
'--------------------------------------------------------
Private m_backgroundBitmap As System.Drawing.Bitmap
Sub CreateBackground()
    If (m_backgroundBitmap Is Nothing) Then
        m_backgroundBitmap = New Bitmap(bitmap_dx, bitmap_dy)
    End If
```

```
'Make the bitmap white
Dim gfx As System.Drawing.Graphics
gfx = System.Drawing.Graphics.FromImage(m_backgroundBitmap)
gfx.Clear(System.Drawing.Color.White)

'Draw a bunch of text in black
Dim myBrush As System.Drawing.Brush
myBrush = New System.Drawing.SolidBrush( _
                        System.Drawing.Color.Black)

Dim y As Integer
For y = 0 To bitmap_dy Step 15
    gfx.DrawString("I am the BACKGROUND IMAGE...hello", _
            Me.Font, myBrush, 0, y)
Next

'Clean up
myBrush.Dispose()
gfx.Dispose()
End Sub


'-----------------------------------------------------
'Creates and draws the foreground image
'-----------------------------------------------------
Private m_foregroundBitmap As System.Drawing.Bitmap
Sub CreateForeground()
  If (m_foregroundBitmap Is Nothing) Then
      m_foregroundBitmap = New Bitmap(bitmap_dx, bitmap_dy)
  End If
  'Make the whole bitmap blue
Dim gfx As System.Drawing.Graphics
gfx = System.Drawing.Graphics.FromImage(m_foregroundBitmap)
gfx.Clear(System.Drawing.Color.Blue)

'Draw some shapes in yellow
Dim yellowBrush As System.Drawing.Brush
yellowBrush = New System.Drawing.SolidBrush( _
                        System.Drawing.Color.Yellow)
gfx.FillEllipse(yellowBrush, 130, 4, 40, 70)
gfx.FillRectangle(yellowBrush, 5, 20, 110, 30)
gfx.FillEllipse(yellowBrush, 60, 75, 130, 20)

'Clean up
yellowBrush.Dispose()
```

```vb
    gfx.Dispose()
End Sub


'------------------------------------------------------
'Sets the size and left hand location of the PictureBox
'------------------------------------------------------
Private Sub SetPictureBoxDimensions()
  PictureBox1.Width = bitmap_dx
  PictureBox1.Height = bitmap_dy
  PictureBox1.Left = 20
End Sub


'-----------------------------------------------------------
'EVENT HANDLER: Display the background image in the PictureBox
'-----------------------------------------------------------
Private Sub buttonDrawBackground_Click(ByVal sender As Object, _
 ByVal e As System.EventArgs) Handles buttonDrawBackground.Click

    SetPictureBoxDimensions()
    CreateBackground()
    PictureBox1.Image = m_backgroundBitmap
End Sub


'-----------------------------------------------------------
'EVENT HANDLER: Display the foreground image in the PictureBox
'-----------------------------------------------------------
Private Sub buttonDrawForeground_Click(ByVal sender As Object, _
ByVal e As System.EventArgs) Handles buttonDrawForeground.Click

  SetPictureBoxDimensions()
  CreateForeground()
  PictureBox1.Image = m_foregroundBitmap
End Sub


'-----------------------------------------------------------
'EVENT HANDLER: Overlay the FOREGROUND image ON TOP OF the
'               BACKGROUND image. Use a TRANSPARENCY MASK
'               so that the color YELLOW in the FOREGROUND
'               image becomes transparent and shows the
'               contents of the BACKGROUND IMAGE
'-----------------------------------------------------------
Private Sub buttonDrawBackgroundPlusForeground_Click(ByVal _
    sender As Object, ByVal e As System.EventArgs) _
    Handles buttonDrawBackgroundPlusForeground.Click
```

```vb
        SetPictureBoxDimensions()
        CreateForeground()
        CreateBackground()
        'Get the grahics of the background image because that
        'is what we are going to draw on top of.
        Dim gfx As System.Drawing.Graphics
        gfx = System.Drawing.Graphics.FromImage(m_backgroundBitmap)


        '--------------------------------------------------------
        'Create an ImageAttributes class. This class enables us
        'to set the TRANSPARANCY COLOR for our draw operation
        '--------------------------------------------------------
    Dim trasparencyInfo As System.Drawing.Imaging.ImageAttributes
        trasparencyInfo = New System.Drawing.Imaging.ImageAttributes
        '--------------------------------------------------------
        'Set the transparency color
        '--------------------------------------------------------
        trasparencyInfo.SetColorKey(System.Drawing.Color.Yellow, _
                                System.Drawing.Color.Yellow)


        'Set our drawing rectangle
        Dim rect As System.Drawing.Rectangle = _
                    New System.Drawing.Rectangle(0, 0, _
                        m_backgroundBitmap.Width, _
                        m_backgroundBitmap.Height)


        '--------------------------------------------------------
        'Draw the FOREGROUND on top of the BACKGROUND bitmap and
        'use the transparency color in the ImageAttributes to
        'give us a transparent window onto the background
        '--------------------------------------------------------
        gfx.DrawImage(m_foregroundBitmap, _
                    rect, _
                    0, 0, _
                    m_foregroundBitmap.Width, _
                    m_foregroundBitmap.Height, _
                    System.Drawing.GraphicsUnit.Pixel, _
                    trasparencyInfo)
        'Cleanup
        gfx.Dispose()


        'Show the results in the bitmap
        PictureBox1.Image = m_backgroundBitmap
    End Sub
```

Listing 13.6 Code in Form to Demonstrate Loading of Embedded Resources

```vb
'----------------------------------------------------------
'Load the image and display it in a PictureBox
'----------------------------------------------------------
Private Sub Button1_Click(ByVal sender As System.Object, _
    ByVal e As System.EventArgs) Handles Button1.Click

    LoadImageFromResource()
    PictureBox1.Image = m_myBitmapImage
End Sub


Private m_myBitmapImage As System.Drawing.Bitmap
'------------------------------------------------
'Loads an image that is stored as a binary
'resource inside our assembly
'------------------------------------------------
Public Sub LoadImageFromResource()
  'If we have already loaded the bitmap
  'no point in doing it again.
  If Not (m_myBitmapImage Is Nothing) Then
    Return
  End If


  '-----------------------------------------------------
  'Get a reference to our application's binary assembly
  '-----------------------------------------------------
  Dim thisAssembly As System.Reflection.Assembly = _
    System.Reflection.Assembly.GetExecutingAssembly()


  '-------------------------------------------
  'Get the name of the assembly
  '-------------------------------------------
  Dim thisAssemblyName As System.Reflection.AssemblyName = _
                          thisAssembly.GetName()
  Dim assemblyName As String = thisAssemblyName.Name


  '---------------------------------------------------------
  'Stream the image in from our assembly and create an
  'in-memory bitmap
  '
  'Note: The ResourceStream name is CASE SENSITIVE
  '      be sure the image name matches EXACTLY with
  '      filename of the image file you add to the project
```

```
'-------------------------------------------------------
m_myBitmapImage = New System.Drawing.Bitmap( _
    thisAssembly.GetManifestResourceStream( _
                            assemblyName + ".MyImage.PNG"))
End Sub
```

Chapter 14 (Data) Samples

Listing 14.1 Basic Creation and Use of an ADO.NET Data Set

```
'The data set we are going to load
Private m_myDataSet As System.Data.DataSet
'Constants we will use
Const FILE_EMPTY_DATASET As String = "EmptyDataSet.xml"
Const FILE_1TABLE_DATASET As String = "1TableDataSet.xml"
Const dividerLine As String = _
    "---------------------------" + vbCrLf


'-------------------------------------------------------
'Load the contents of a file and append it to the text
'in textBox1
'-------------------------------------------------------
Private Sub addFileContentsToTextBox(ByVal fileName As String)
    'Open the file and read in its contents
    Dim myStreamReader As System.IO.StreamReader
    myStreamReader = System.IO.File.OpenText(fileName)
    Dim fileText As String = myStreamReader.ReadToEnd()
    'Close the file
    myStreamReader.Close()

    'Append the contents to the text in the text box
    TextBox1.Text = TextBox1.Text + _
        dividerLine + "FILE: '" + fileName + "'" + vbCrLf + _
        dividerLine + fileText + vbCrLf
End Sub


'-------------------------------------------------------
'1. Creates a data set
'      persists DataSet out as XML,
'      displays results in textbox
'
```

```vb
'2. Adds a data table to the data set
'    adds two typed columns to the data table
'    adds to rows to the data table
'    persists data set out as XML,
'    displays results in text box
'-----------------------------------------------------------
Private Sub Button1_Click(ByVal sender As System.Object, _
            ByVal e As System.EventArgs) Handles Button1.Click

    'Clear the contents of the text box
    TextBox1.Text = ""
    '==========================================
    '1. Create a new data set
    '==========================================
    m_myDataSet = New System.Data.DataSet("HelloWorld-DataSet")

    'Write out the ADO.NET DataSet contents as XML and show
    'the file in the textbox
    m_myDataSet.WriteXml(FILE_EMPTY_DATASET)
    addFileContentsToTextBox(FILE_EMPTY_DATASET)

    '==========================================
    '2. Add a data table to the ADO.NET data set
    '    and add two rows of data to the data table
    '==========================================
    Dim myTestTable As System.Data.DataTable
    myTestTable = m_myDataSet.Tables.Add("TestTable")

    '------------------------------------
    'Add two columns to the table
    '------------------------------------
    'Add a date column to the data table in the data set
    myTestTable.Columns.Add("TestColumn0", _
                        GetType(System.DateTime))
    'Add a string colum to the data table in the data set
    myTestTable.Columns.Add("TestColumn1", GetType(String))

    '------------------------------------
    'Add data rows to the table
    '------------------------------------
    'Add a row of data to the data table
    Dim rowOfData() As Object
    ReDim rowOfData(1)
    'Column 0 is a date type
```

```
rowOfData(0) = System.DateTime.Today
'Column 1 is a string type
rowOfData(1) = "a string of data today"
myTestTable.Rows.Add(rowOfData)

'Add a second row of data to the data table
Dim rowOfData2() As Object
ReDim rowOfData2(1)
'Column 0 is a date type
rowOfData2(0) = System.DateTime.Today.AddDays(1)

'Column 1 is a string type
rowOfData2(1) = "tomorrow's string"
myTestTable.Rows.Add(rowOfData2)

'Write out the ADO.NET data set contents as XML and show
'the file in the text box
m_myDataSet.WriteXml(FILE_1TABLE_DATASET)
addFileContentsToTextBox(FILE_1TABLE_DATASET)
End Sub
```

Listing 14.2 Using XMLWriteMode When Persisting ADO.NET Data Sets

```
'------------------------------------------------------------
'This function exists because the .NET Compact Framework does
'not support the overload:
' "public Sub WriteXml(string, XmlWriteMode)"
'
'as a "public" member (it is private)
'------------------------------------------------------------
Sub writeDataSetToFile(ByVal ds As System.Data.DataSet, _
             ByVal filename As String, _
             ByVal xmlWriteMode As System.Data.XmlWriteMode)

  'Create an XML TextWriter to write out our XML
  Dim xmlWriter As System.Xml.XmlWriter
  xmlWriter = New System.Xml.XmlTextWriter(filename, _
                         System.Text.Encoding.Default)

  'NOTE: This overload is not public!
  'ds.WriteXml(filename, xmlWriteMode)
  'Instead use...
```

```
   ds.WriteXml(xmlWriter, xmlWriteMode)
   xmlWriter.Close() 'It is important to close the file!
End Sub
```

Listing 14.3 Comparing the Performance of Different Data Set Access Methods

```
Private m_myDataSet As System.Data.DataSet 'Data set for test
'Column and table indexes to cache
Private m_indexesLookedUp As Boolean = False
Private Const INVALID_INDEX As Integer = -1
Private m_IndexOfTestColumn_CreditCard _
        As Integer = INVALID_INDEX
Private m_IndexOfTestColumn_TravelDate _
        As Integer = INVALID_INDEX
Private m_IndexOfTestTable As Integer = INVALID_INDEX

'Data columns and table to cache
Private m_TestColumn_CreditCard As System.Data.DataColumn
Private m_TestColumn_TravelDate As System.Data.DataColumn
Private m_TableCustomerInfo As System.Data.DataTable

Public Enum testType 'Three different kinds of tests we can run
  textColumnLookup
  cachedIndexLookup
  cachedColumnObject
End Enum

'These determine the size of the test
Const DUMMY_ROWS_OF_DATA As Integer = 100
Const NUMBER_TEST_ITERATIONS As Integer = 500

'Datatable information
Const TABLE_NAME_PASSENGERINFO As String = "CustomerTravelInfo"
Const COLUMN_NAME_DATE_OF_TRAVEL As String = "DateOfTravel"
Const COLUMN_NAME_PASSENGER_NAME As String = "PassengerName"
Const COLUMN_NAME_PASSENGER_CREDIT_CARD As String = _
                                    "PassengerCreditCard"
Const TEST_CREDIT_CARD As String = "IvoCard-987-654-321-000"


'-----------------------------------------------------------
'Creates the data set
'-----------------------------------------------------------
```

```vb
Private Sub createDataSet()
  '1. Create a new data set
 m_myDataSet = New System.Data.DataSet("TravelService Dataset")

  '2. Add a data table to the ADO.NET data set
  Dim myTestTable As System.Data.DataTable
 myTestTable = m_myDataSet.Tables.Add(TABLE_NAME_PASSENGERINFO)

  'Add two columns to the table
  'Add a date column to the data table in the data set
  myTestTable.Columns.Add(COLUMN_NAME_DATE_OF_TRAVEL, _
    GetType(System.DateTime))
  'Add a string colum to the data table in the data set
  myTestTable.Columns.Add(COLUMN_NAME_PASSENGER_NAME, _
    GetType(String))

  'Add a string colum to the data table in the data set
  myTestTable.Columns.Add(COLUMN_NAME_PASSENGER_CREDIT_CARD, _
                                          GetType(String))
  'Data to place into the data row
  Dim objArray() As Object
  ReDim objArray(2)

  '-------------------------------------
  'Add data rows to the table
  '-------------------------------------
  Dim buildTestString As System.Text.StringBuilder
  buildTestString = New System.Text.StringBuilder
  Dim addItemsCount As Integer
  For addItemsCount = 1 To DUMMY_ROWS_OF_DATA
      'Pick a travel day for the passenger
    objArray(0) = System.DateTime.Today.AddDays(addItemsCount)

    'Pick a name for the passenger
    buildTestString.Length = 0
    buildTestString.Append("TestPersonName")
    buildTestString.Append(addItemsCount)
    objArray(1) = buildTestString.ToString()

    'Assign the passenger a text credit card number
    buildTestString.Length = 0
    buildTestString.Append("IvoCard-000-000-0000-")
    buildTestString.Append(addItemsCount)
    objArray(2) = buildTestString.ToString()
```

```vb
        'Add the items in the array to the data set row
        myTestTable.Rows.Add(objArray)
    Next

    'Add the item we want to search for in our test.
    objArray(0) = System.DateTime.Today
    objArray(1) = "Ms. TestPerson"
    objArray(2) = TEST_CREDIT_CARD

    'Add the items in the array to the data set row
    myTestTable.Rows.Add(objArray)
End Sub


'---------------------------------------------------------
'Look up and cache all the data set indexes we will need
'---------------------------------------------------------
Private Sub cacheDataSetInfo()
    'Exit if we've already loaded the indexes
    If (m_indexesLookedUp = True) Then Return

    'Cache the index of the table
    m_IndexOfTestTable = _
        m_myDataSet.Tables.IndexOf(TABLE_NAME_PASSENGERINFO)

    '----------------------------------------------------------
    'Iterate through all the columns in our table definition
    'and cache the indexes of the ones we want
    '----------------------------------------------------------
    m_TableCustomerInfo = m_myDataSet.Tables(m_IndexOfTestTable)

    Dim dataColumnCount As Integer
    dataColumnCount = m_TableCustomerInfo.Columns.Count
    Dim myColumn As System.Data.DataColumn
    Dim colIdx As Integer
    While (colIdx < dataColumnCount)
        myColumn = m_TableCustomerInfo.Columns(colIdx)

        'Only try a lookup if we haven't already
        If (m_IndexOfTestColumn_CreditCard = INVALID_INDEX) Then

            'See if the name matches
            If (myColumn.ColumnName = _
COLUMN_NAME_PASSENGER_CREDIT_CARD) Then
```

```
        'Cache the index
        m_IndexOfTestColumn_CreditCard = colIdx

        'Cache the column
        m_TestColumn_CreditCard = myColumn
        GoTo next_loop_iteration 'Skip other compares...
      End If 'Endif string compare
    End If

    If (m_IndexOfTestColumn_TravelDate = INVALID_INDEX) Then
        'See if the name matches
      If (myColumn.ColumnName = _
          COLUMN_NAME_DATE_OF_TRAVEL) Then

        'Cache the index
        m_IndexOfTestColumn_TravelDate = colIdx
        'Cache the column
        m_TestColumn_TravelDate = myColumn
        GoTo next_loop_iteration 'Skip other compares.
      End If 'Endif string compare
    End If

next_loop_iteration:
    colIdx = colIdx + 1
  End While
  m_indexesLookedUp = True
End Sub


'------------------------------------------------
'Run the test.
'------------------------------------------------
Sub changeDayOfTravel_test(ByVal kindOfTest As testType)
  'Show wait cursor
  System.Windows.Forms.Cursor.Current = _
    System.Windows.Forms.Cursors.WaitCursor

  'Start at a known date.
  Dim newDate As System.DateTime
  newDate = System.DateTime.Today
  changeDayOfTravel_textColumnLookup(TEST_CREDIT_CARD, newDate)

  'TEST CODE ONLY!!!
  'Calling garbage collector in code will SLOW DOWN your app!
  System.GC.Collect()
  Const testNumber As Integer = 0
```

```vb
'Set up properly depending on which test we are running
Select Case (kindOfTest)
    Case testType.textColumnLookup
    PerformanceSampling.StartSample(testNumber, _
        "Text based Column lookup.")

  Case testType.cachedIndexLookup
    PerformanceSampling.StartSample(testNumber, _
            "Cached Column Index lookup.")

  Case testType.cachedColumnObject
    PerformanceSampling.StartSample(testNumber, _
            "Cached Column objects")

  Case Else
    Throw New Exception("Unknown state!")
End Select

'Run the test!
Dim testCount As Integer
For testCount = 1 To NUMBER_TEST_ITERATIONS
    'Move the date forward one day
  newDate = newDate.AddDays(1)
  Dim numberRecordsChanged As Integer = 0

  'Which kind of test are we running?
  Select Case (kindOfTest)
    Case testType.textColumnLookup
      'BAD PERFORMANCE: Look up all names imports STRINGS
      numberRecordsChanged = _
          changeDayOfTravel_textColumnLookup( _
                TEST_CREDIT_CARD, newDate)

    Case testType.cachedIndexLookup
      'BETTER PERFORMANCE: Use cached indexes
      numberRecordsChanged = _
        changeDayOfTravel_cachedColumnIndex( _
                TEST_CREDIT_CARD, newDate)

    Case testType.cachedColumnObject
      'BEST PERFORMANCE: Use cached column objects
      numberRecordsChanged = _
        changeDayOfTravel_CachedColumns( _
                TEST_CREDIT_CARD, newDate)
    End Select
```

```
        'Make sure the test is running as expected.
        If (numberRecordsChanged <> 1) Then
            MsgBox("No matching records found. Test aborted!")
          Return
        End If
    Next
    'Get the time it took to run the test
    PerformanceSampling.StopSample(testNumber)

    'Normal cursor
    System.Windows.Forms.Cursor.Current = _
      System.Windows.Forms.Cursors.Default

    'Show the test results
    Dim runInfo As String = NUMBER_TEST_ITERATIONS.ToString() + _
      "x" + DUMMY_ROWS_OF_DATA.ToString() + ": "

    MsgBox(runInfo + _
      PerformanceSampling.GetSampleDurationText(testNumber))
End Sub


'POOR PERFORMANCE SEARCH FUNCTION
Private Function changeDayOfTravel_textColumnLookup( _
        ByVal creditCardNumber As String, _
        ByVal newTravelDate As System.DateTime) As Integer
    Dim numberRecordsChanged As Integer
    'Look up the table name
    Dim dataTable_Customers As System.Data.DataTable
    'BAD PERFORMANCE: Look up table by string comparison!
    dataTable_Customers = _
      m_myDataSet.Tables(TABLE_NAME_PASSENGERINFO)

    Dim currentCustomerRow As System.Data.DataRow
    For Each currentCustomerRow In dataTable_Customers.Rows
      Dim currentCreditCard As String

      'BAD PERFORMANCE: Look up table by string comparison!
      currentCreditCard = CType( _
      currentCustomerRow(COLUMN_NAME_PASSENGER_CREDIT_CARD), _
      String)

      'See if this is the credit card we are looking for
      If (creditCardNumber = currentCreditCard) Then
        'Change the date of travel
```

```vb
'BAD PERFORMANCE: Look up column by string comparison!
Dim currentTravelDate As System.DateTime = CType( _
    currentCustomerRow(COLUMN_NAME_DATE_OF_TRAVEL), _
    System.DateTime)

If (currentTravelDate <> newTravelDate) Then
    'BAD PERFORMANCE: Look up column by string comparison!
    currentCustomerRow(COLUMN_NAME_DATE_OF_TRAVEL) = _
        newTravelDate
    numberRecordsChanged = numberRecordsChanged + 1
End If
    End If 'endif: string compare
Next 'end for each


    Return numberRecordsChanged 'Number updated records
End Function

'SLIGHTLY BETTER PERFORMANCE FUNCTION
Private Function changeDayOfTravel_cachedColumnIndex( _
    ByVal creditCardNumber As String, ByVal newTravelDate _
    As DateTime) As Integer

    Dim numberRecordsChanged As Integer
    'Look up the table name
    Dim dataTable_Customers As System.Data.DataTable
    'BETTER PERFORMANCE: use a cached index
    dataTable_Customers = _
        m_myDataSet.Tables(m_IndexOfTestTable)

    Dim currentCustomerRow As System.Data.DataRow
    For Each currentCustomerRow In dataTable_Customers.Rows
        Dim currentCreditCard As String
        'BETTER PERFORMANCE: User a cached column index!
        currentCreditCard = CType(currentCustomerRow( _
            m_IndexOfTestColumn_CreditCard), String)
        'See if there is a card number matches.
        If (creditCardNumber = currentCreditCard) Then
            'Change the date of travel
            'BETTER PERFORMANCE: User a cached column index!
            Dim currentTravelDate As System.DateTime = CType( _
            currentCustomerRow(m_IndexOfTestColumn_TravelDate), _
            System.DateTime)
```

```vb
    If (currentTravelDate <> newTravelDate) Then
        'BETTER PERFORMANCE: User a cached column index!
        currentCustomerRow(m_IndexOfTestColumn_TravelDate) = _
                        newTravelDate
        numberRecordsChanged = numberRecordsChanged + 1
    End If
  End If
Next
Return numberRecordsChanged  'Number updated records
End Function


'BEST PERFORMANCE FUNCTION
Private Function changeDayOfTravel_CachedColumns( _
    ByVal creditCardNumber As String, _
    ByVal newTravelDate As System.DateTime) As Integer
  Dim numberRecordsChanged As Integer

  'Look up the table name
  Dim dataTable_Customers As System.Data.DataTable = _
                    m_TableCustomerInfo

  Dim currentCustomerRow As System.Data.DataRow
  For Each currentCustomerRow In dataTable_Customers.Rows
    Dim currentCreditCard As String
    'BEST PERFORMANCE: User a cached column index!
    currentCreditCard = CType( _
        currentCustomerRow(m_TestColumn_CreditCard), _
        String)

    'See if there is a card number that matches.
    If (creditCardNumber = currentCreditCard) Then
        'Change the date of travel
      'BEST PERFORMANCE: User a cached column index!
      Dim currentTravelDate As System.DateTime = CType( _
        currentCustomerRow(m_TestColumn_TravelDate), _
        System.DateTime)

      If (currentTravelDate <> newTravelDate) Then
        'BEST PERFORMANCE: User a cached column index!
        currentCustomerRow(m_TestColumn_TravelDate) = _
            newTravelDate
        numberRecordsChanged = numberRecordsChanged + 1
      End If
    End If
```

```vb
    Next
    Return numberRecordsChanged   'Number updated records
End Function

'Button click event
Private Sub buttonRunTest_Click(ByVal sender As Object, _
    ByVal e As System.EventArgs) Handles buttonRunTest.Click

    createDataSet()
    cacheDataSetInfo()

    'BAD PERFORMANCE: Use string-based lookups
    changeDayOfTravel_test(testType.textColumnLookup)

    'BETTER PERFORMANCE: Use integer-based lookups
    changeDayOfTravel_test(testType.cachedIndexLookup)

    'BEST PERFORMANCE: Use column object-based lookups
    changeDayOfTravel_test(testType.cachedColumnObject)
End Sub
```

Listing 14.4 Testing the Performance of Using a Custom Data Format Instead of a Data Set

```vb
'These determine the size of the test
Const DUMMY_ROWS_OF_DATA As Integer = 100
Const NUMBER_TEST_ITERATIONS As Integer = 500

Const TABLE_NAME_PASSENGERINFO As String = "CustomerTravelInfo"
Const TEST_CREDIT_CARD As String = "IvoCard-987-654-321-000"

Private m_data_creditCards() As String
Private m_data_names() As String
Private m_data_travelDates() As System.DateTime


'-------------------------------------------------------------
'Creates the arrays of data (instead of imports a data set)
'-------------------------------------------------------------

Private Sub createDataSet()
    '=======================================
    '1. Create the space for our data
    '=======================================
```

```
    ReDim m_data_creditCards(DUMMY_ROWS_OF_DATA)
    ReDim m_data_names(DUMMY_ROWS_OF_DATA)
    ReDim m_data_travelDates(DUMMY_ROWS_OF_DATA)

    '-----------------------------------
    'Add the rows of data
    '-----------------------------------
    Dim buildTestString As System.Text.StringBuilder
    buildTestString = New System.Text.StringBuilder
    Dim addItemsCount As Integer
    For addItemsCount = 0 To DUMMY_ROWS_OF_DATA
        'Pick a travel day for the passenger
        m_data_travelDates(addItemsCount) = _
            System.DateTime.Today.AddDays(addItemsCount)

        '-----------------------------------
        'Pick a name for the passenger
        '-----------------------------------
        'Clear the text of the string
        buildTestString.Length = 0
        buildTestString.Append("TestPersonName")
        buildTestString.Append(addItemsCount)
        m_data_names(addItemsCount) = buildTestString.ToString()

        '-----------------------------------
        'Assign the passenger a text credit card number
        '-----------------------------------
        'A string for the third data set column value
        buildTestString.Length = 0
        buildTestString.Append("IvoCard-000-000-0000-")
        buildTestString.Append(addItemsCount)
        m_data_creditCards(addItemsCount) = _
                            buildTestString.ToString()
    Next

    'Add the item we want to search for in our test.
    'Pick a day for the first data set column value
    m_data_travelDates(DUMMY_ROWS_OF_DATA) = _
                            System.DateTime.Today
    'A string for the second data set column value
    m_data_names(DUMMY_ROWS_OF_DATA) = "Ms. TestPerson"
    'A string credit card ID
    m_data_creditCards(DUMMY_ROWS_OF_DATA) = TEST_CREDIT_CARD
End Sub
```

```vb
'-------------------------------------------------
'Run the test.
'-------------------------------------------------
Sub changeDayOfTravel_test()
  'Show wait cursor
  System.Windows.Forms.Cursor.Current = _
    System.Windows.Forms.Cursors.WaitCursor

  'Start at a known date.
  Dim newDate As System.DateTime
  newDate = System.DateTime.Today
  changeDayOfTravel_CustomArrays(TEST_CREDIT_CARD, newDate)

  'TEST CODE ONLY!!!
  'Do NOT call the garbage collector in production
  'code. It will SLOW DOWN your application performance
  System.GC.Collect()
  Const testNumber As Integer = 0

  'Start the timer running for the test
  PerformanceSampling.StartSample(testNumber, _
              "Custom Array implementation")

  'Run the test!
  Dim testCount As Integer
  For testCount = 1 To NUMBER_TEST_ITERATIONS

    'Move the date forward one day
    newDate = newDate.AddDays(1)
    Dim numberRecordsChanged As Integer

    'Look up all names' import STRINGS
    numberRecordsChanged = _
        changeDayOfTravel_CustomArrays( _
        TEST_CREDIT_CARD, newDate)

    'Make sure the test is running as expected.
    If (numberRecordsChanged <> 1) Then
        MsgBox("No matching records found. Test aborted!")
      Return
    End If
  Next
  'Get the time it took to run the test
  PerformanceSampling.StopSample(testNumber)
```

```vbnet
    'Normal cursor
    System.Windows.Forms.Cursor.Current = _
      System.Windows.Forms.Cursors.Default

    'Show the test results
    Dim runInfo As String = NUMBER_TEST_ITERATIONS.ToString() + _
      "x" + DUMMY_ROWS_OF_DATA.ToString() + ": "
    MsgBox(runInfo + _
      PerformanceSampling.GetSampleDurationText(testNumber))
  End Sub


  Private Function changeDayOfTravel_CustomArrays( _
    ByVal creditCardNumber As String, ByVal newTravelDate _
    As System.DateTime) As Integer

    Dim numberRecordsChanged As Integer

    'Look at each item in the array
    Dim index As Integer
    For index = 0 To DUMMY_ROWS_OF_DATA
      Dim currentCreditCard As String
      currentCreditCard = m_data_creditCards(index)

      'If there is a match, update the record
      If (creditCardNumber = currentCreditCard) Then
        'Change the date of travel
        Dim currentTravelDate As System.DateTime = _
          m_data_travelDates(index)

        'Only count the update if the date does not match
        If (currentTravelDate <> newTravelDate) Then
              m_data_travelDates(index) = _
            newTravelDate
          numberRecordsChanged = numberRecordsChanged + 1
        End If
      End If
    Next
    'Return the number of records we updated
    Return numberRecordsChanged
  End Function


  Private Sub buttonRunTest_Click(ByVal sender As Object, _
        ByVal e As System.EventArgs) Handles buttonRunTest.Click
    createDataSet()
    changeDayOfTravel_test()
  End Sub
```

Listing 14.5 Custom Data Management Sample—Code That Goes Inside Form1.cs

```
'Creates the database
Private Sub buttonCreateDatabase_Click(ByVal sender As Object, _
ByVal e As System.EventArgs) Handles buttonCreateDatabase.Click

    DatabaseAccess.CreateAndFillDatabase()
End Sub

'Loads the data from the database and displays it
Private Sub buttonLoadGameData_Click(ByVal sender As Object, _
   ByVal e As System.EventArgs) Handles buttonLoadGameData.Click

    'Clear the text box
    TextBox1.Text = ""
    'Load the data for the words
    GameData.InitializeGameVocabulary()

    'Go through each of the words and add it our text list
    Dim thisStringBuilder As System.Text.StringBuilder
    thisStringBuilder = New System.Text.StringBuilder
    Dim thisWord As VocabularyWord
    For Each thisWord In GameData.AllWords
        thisStringBuilder.Append(thisWord.EnglishWord)
      thisStringBuilder.Append(" = ")
      thisStringBuilder.Append( _
            thisWord.GermanWordWithArticleIfExists)
      thisStringBuilder.Append(vbCrLf) 'New line
    Next
    'Show the list of word in the text box
    TextBox1.Text = thisStringBuilder.ToString()
End Sub
```

Listing 14.6 Custom Data Management Sample—Code for DatabaseAccess.cs

```
Option Strict On
'------------------------------------------------------------
'Database access code: This class manages our database access
'------------------------------------------------------------
Imports System

Friend Class DatabaseAccess
Const DATABASE_NAME As String = "LearnGerman.sdf"
```

```vb
Const CONNECT_STRING As String = _
      "Data Source = " + DATABASE_NAME + "; Password = ''"

Const TRANSLATIONTABLE_NAME As String = "TranslationDictionary"
Const TRANSLATIONTABLE_ENGLISH_COLUMN As String = "EnglishWord"
Const TRANSLATIONTABLE_GERMAN_COLUMN As String = "GermanWord"
Const TRANSLATIONTABLE_GERMANGENDER_COLUMN As String = _
      "GermanGender"
Const TRANSLATIONTABLE_WORDFUNCTION_COLUMN As String = _
      "WordFunction"

Friend Const DS_WORDS_COLUMNINDEX_ENGLISHWORD As Integer = 0
Friend Const DS_WORDS_COLUMNINDEX_GERMANWORD As Integer = 1
Friend Const DS_WORDS_COLUMNINDEX_GERMANGENDER As Integer = 2
Friend Const DS_WORDS_COLUMNINDEX_WORDFUNCTION As Integer = 3

Public Shared Function GetListOfWords() As _
               System.Data.IDataReader

  Dim conn As System.Data.SqlServerCe.SqlCeConnection = Nothing

  conn = New System.Data.SqlServerCe.SqlCeConnection( _
            CONNECT_STRING)
  conn.Open()

  Dim cmd As System.Data.SqlServerCe.SqlCeCommand = _
            conn.CreateCommand()

  cmd.CommandText = "select " + _
    TRANSLATIONTABLE_ENGLISH_COLUMN + ", " _
    + TRANSLATIONTABLE_GERMAN_COLUMN + ", " _
    + TRANSLATIONTABLE_GERMANGENDER_COLUMN + ", " _
    + TRANSLATIONTABLE_WORDFUNCTION_COLUMN + " " _
    + "from " + TRANSLATIONTABLE_NAME

  'Execute the database command
  Dim myReader As System.Data.SqlServerCe.SqlCeDataReader = _
      cmd.ExecuteReader(System.Data.CommandBehavior.SingleResult)

  Return myReader
End Function


'--------------------------------------------------
'Creates a database if needed
'--------------------------------------------------
```

```vb
Public Shared Sub CreateDatabaseIfNonExistant()
  If (System.IO.File.Exists(DATABASE_NAME) = False) Then
    CreateAndFillDatabase()
  End If
End Sub


'--------------------------------------------------
'Creates and fills a database
'--------------------------------------------------
Public Shared Sub CreateAndFillDatabase()
  'Delete the database if it's there
  If (System.IO.File.Exists(DATABASE_NAME)) Then
   System.IO.File.Delete(DATABASE_NAME)
  End If

  'Create a new database
  Dim sqlCeEngine As System.Data.SqlServerCe.SqlCeEngine
  sqlCeEngine = New System.Data.SqlServerCe.SqlCeEngine( _
            CONNECT_STRING)
  sqlCeEngine.CreateDatabase()


  '--------------------------------------------------
  'Try to connect to the database
  'and populate it with data
  '--------------------------------------------------
  Dim conn As System.Data.SqlServerCe.SqlCeConnection = Nothing
  Try
    conn = New System.Data.SqlServerCe.SqlCeConnection( _
        CONNECT_STRING)
    conn.Open()

    Dim cmd As System.Data.SqlServerCe.SqlCeCommand = _
        conn.CreateCommand()

    'Create a translation table
    'Fields:
    '   1. EnglishWord
    '   2. GermanWord
    '   3. Gender of word
    '   4. Type of word
    cmd.CommandText = "CREATE TABLE " + TRANSLATIONTABLE_NAME _
      + " (" + _
      TRANSLATIONTABLE_ENGLISH_COLUMN + " ntext" + ", " + _
      TRANSLATIONTABLE_GERMAN_COLUMN + " ntext" + ", " + _
```

```vb
            TRANSLATIONTABLE_GERMANGENDER_COLUMN + " int" + ", " + _
            TRANSLATIONTABLE_WORDFUNCTION_COLUMN + " int" + ")"
        cmd.ExecuteNonQuery()


        'Fill the database with words
        FillDictionary(cmd)
    Catch eTableCreate As System.Exception
MsgBox("Error occured adding table :" + eTableCreate.ToString())
    Finally
        'Always close the database when we are done
        conn.Close()
    End Try


    'Tell the user
    MsgBox("Created language database!")
End Sub


Private Shared Sub FillDictionary( _
        ByVal cmd As System.Data.SqlServerCe.SqlCeCommand)
    'Verbs
    InsertEnglishGermanWordPair(cmd, "to pay", "zahlen", _
            VocabularyWord.WordGender.notApplicable, _
            VocabularyWord.WordFunction.Verb)
    InsertEnglishGermanWordPair(cmd, "to catch", "fangen", _
            VocabularyWord.WordGender.notApplicable, _
            VocabularyWord.WordFunction.Verb)
    'Add more words.


    'Pronouns
    InsertEnglishGermanWordPair(cmd, 'What', "was", _
            VocabularyWord.WordGender.notApplicable, _
            VocabularyWord.WordFunction.Pronoun)
    'Add more words.


    'Adverb
    InsertEnglishGermanWordPair(cmd, 'where', "wo", _
            VocabularyWord.WordGender.notApplicable, _
            VocabularyWord.WordFunction.Adverb)
    InsertEnglishGermanWordPair(cmd, "never", "nie", _
            VocabularyWord.WordGender.notApplicable, _
            VocabularyWord.WordFunction.Adverb)
    'Add more words.


    'Preposition
```

```
InsertEnglishGermanWordPair(cmd, "at the", "am", _
        VocabularyWord.WordGender.notApplicable, _
        VocabularyWord.WordFunction.Preposition)

'Adjective
InsertEnglishGermanWordPair(cmd, "invited", "eingeladen", _
        VocabularyWord.WordGender.notApplicable, _
        VocabularyWord.WordFunction.Verb)

InsertEnglishGermanWordPair(cmd, "yellow", "gelbe", _
        VocabularyWord.WordGender.notApplicable, _
        VocabularyWord.WordFunction.Adjective)
InsertEnglishGermanWordPair(cmd, "one", "eins", _
        VocabularyWord.WordGender.notApplicable, _
        VocabularyWord.WordFunction.Adjective)
InsertEnglishGermanWordPair(cmd, "two", "zwei", _
        VocabularyWord.WordGender.notApplicable, _
        VocabularyWord.WordFunction.Adjective)

'Masculine nouns
InsertEnglishGermanWordPair(cmd, "Man", "Mann", _
        VocabularyWord.WordGender.Masculine, _
        VocabularyWord.WordFunction.Noun)
InsertEnglishGermanWordPair(cmd, "Marketplace", "Marktplatz", _
        VocabularyWord.WordGender.Masculine, _
        VocabularyWord.WordFunction.Noun)
InsertEnglishGermanWordPair(cmd, "Spoon", "Löffel ", _
        VocabularyWord.WordGender.Masculine, _
        VocabularyWord.WordFunction.Noun)

'Feminine nouns
InsertEnglishGermanWordPair(cmd, "Woman", "Frau", _
        VocabularyWord.WordGender.Feminine, _
        VocabularyWord.WordFunction.Noun)
InsertEnglishGermanWordPair(cmd, "Clock", "Uhr", _
        VocabularyWord.WordGender.Feminine, _
        VocabularyWord.WordFunction.Noun)
InsertEnglishGermanWordPair(cmd, "Cat", "Katze", _
        VocabularyWord.WordGender.Feminine, _
        VocabularyWord.WordFunction.Noun)

'Neuter nouns
InsertEnglishGermanWordPair(cmd, "Car", "Auto", _
        VocabularyWord.WordGender.Neuter, _
        VocabularyWord.WordFunction.Noun)
```

```vb
        InsertEnglishGermanWordPair(cmd, "Book", "Buch", _
                VocabularyWord.WordGender.Neuter, _
                VocabularyWord.WordFunction.Noun)
    End Sub


    '------------------------------------------------
    'Inserts a word into the database
    '------------------------------------------------
    Private Shared Sub InsertEnglishGermanWordPair( _
      ByVal cmd As System.Data.SqlServerCe.SqlCeCommand, _
      ByVal englishWord As String, ByVal germanWord As String, _
      ByVal germanWordGender As VocabularyWord.WordGender, _
      ByVal wordFunction As VocabularyWord.WordFunction)

        cmd.CommandText = "INSERT INTO " + TRANSLATIONTABLE_NAME + _
          "(" + TRANSLATIONTABLE_ENGLISH_COLUMN + ", " + _
        TRANSLATIONTABLE_GERMAN_COLUMN + ", " + _
        TRANSLATIONTABLE_GERMANGENDER_CCLUMN + ", " + _
        TRANSLATIONTABLE_WORDFUNCTION_CCLUMN + _
          ")  VALUES ('" _
          + englishWord + "', '" _
          + germanWord + "', '" _
          + System.Convert.ToString(+ _
              CType(germanWordGender, Integer)) + "', '" _
          + System.Convert.ToString(CType(wordFunction, Integer)) _
          + "')"

        cmd.ExecuteNonQuery()
    End Sub
End Class
```

Listing 14.7 Custom Data Management Sample—Code for GameData.cs

```vb
Option Strict On
'------------------------------------------------------------
'In-memory data management code
'
'This code manages the in-memory representation of the code
'------------------------------------------------------------
Imports System

Friend Class GameData
'Array-Lists to store the data we have loaded in
```

```vb
Private Shared m_vocabularyWords_All As _
    System.Collections.ArrayList
Private Shared m_vocabularyWords_Nouns As _
    System.Collections.ArrayList
Private Shared m_vocabularyWords_Verbs As _
    System.Collections.ArrayList
Private Shared m_vocabularyWords_Adjectives As _
    System.Collections.ArrayList
Private Shared m_vocabularyWords_Adverbs As _
    System.Collections.ArrayList
Private Shared m_vocabularyWords_Prepositions As _
    System.Collections.ArrayList


Public Shared ReadOnly Property _
        isGameDataInitialized() As Boolean
  Get
  'The game data is initialized if we have loaded the words
    Return Not (m_vocabularyWords_All Is Nothing)
  End Get
End Property


'Returns the collection of all words we have
Public Shared ReadOnly Property _
        AllWords() As System.Collections.ArrayList
  Get
      'If the data has not been initialized, load it
    If (m_vocabularyWords_All Is Nothing) Then
        InitializeGameVocabulary()
    End If
    Return m_vocabularyWords_All
  End Get
End property

'Returns the collection of all nouns we have
Public Shared ReadOnly Property _
        Nouns() As System.Collections.ArrayList
  Get
      'If the data has not been initialized, load it
    If (m_vocabularyWords_Nouns Is Nothing) Then
        InitializeGameVocabulary()
    End If
    Return m_vocabularyWords_Nouns
  End Get
End Property
```

```vbnet
'============================================================
'Loads the data in from our database
'============================================================
Public Shared Sub InitializeGameVocabulary()
    'Create a new array list to hold our words
    m_vocabularyWords_All = New System.Collections.ArrayList
    m_vocabularyWords_Nouns = New System.Collections.ArrayList
    m_vocabularyWords_Verbs = New System.Collections.ArrayList
    m_vocabularyWords_Adjectives = _
                            New System.Collections.ArrayList
    m_vocabularyWords_Adverbs = _
                            New System.Collections.ArrayList
    m_vocabularyWords_Prepositions = _
                            New System.Collections.ArrayList


    Dim dataReader As System.Data.IDataReader
    dataReader = DatabaseAccess.GetListOfWords()


    Dim newWord As VocabularyWord
    'Go through all of the records
    While (dataReader.Read())
        Dim thisword_gender As VocabularyWord.WordGender
        Dim thisword_function As VocabularyWord.WordFunction
        thisword_gender = CType(dataReader.GetInt32( _
            DatabaseAccess.DS_WORDS_COLUMNINDEX_GERMANGENDER), _
            VocabularyWord.WordGender)


        thisword_function = CType(dataReader.GetInt32( _
            DatabaseAccess.DS_WORDS_COLUMNINDEX_WORDFUNCTION), _
            VocabularyWord.WordFunction)


        'Place the data for the word we just read into a class
        newWord = New VocabularyWord( _
            dataReader.GetString( _
            DatabaseAccess.DS_WORDS_COLUMNINDEX_ENGLISHWORD), _
            dataReader.GetString( _
            DatabaseAccess.DS_WORDS_COLUMNINDEX_GERMANWORD), _
            thisword_gender, thisword_function)


        'Add the new word to the array list
        m_vocabularyWords_All.Add(newWord)


        'Words can belong to more than one group, so check
        'imports a logical AND to see if the word meets a
```

```vb
'given category
If ((newWord.getWordFunction And _
    VocabularyWord.WordFunction.Noun) <> 0) Then
  m_vocabularyWords_Nouns.Add(newWord)
End If

If ((newWord.getWordFunction And _
    VocabularyWord.WordFunction.Verb) <> 0) Then
  m_vocabularyWords_Verbs.Add(newWord)
End If

If ((newWord.getWordFunction And _
    VocabularyWord.WordFunction.Adjective) <> 0) Then
  m_vocabularyWords_Adjectives.Add(newWord)
End If

If ((newWord.getWordFunction And _
    VocabularyWord.WordFunction.Adverb) <> 0) Then
  m_vocabularyWords_Adverbs.Add(newWord)
End If

If ((newWord.getWordFunction And _
    VocabularyWord.WordFunction.Preposition) <> 0) Then
  m_vocabularyWords_Prepositions.Add(newWord)
End If

End While
'Close the data reader
dataReader.Close()
End Sub
End Class
```

Listing 14.8 Custom Data Management Sample—Code for VocabularyWord.cs

```vb
Option Strict On
Imports System
'------------------------------------------------
'Holds the data for a vocabulary word
'------------------------------------------------
Friend Class VocabularyWord

<System.FlagsAttribute()> _
```

```vbnet
Public Enum WordFunction
  Noun = 1
  Verb = 2
  Pronoun = 4
  Adverb = 8
  Adjective = 16
  Preposition = 32
  Phrase = 64
End Enum

Public Enum WordGender
  notApplicable = 0
  Masculine = 1
  Feminine = 2
  Neuter = 3
End Enum

Private m_englishWord As String
Private m_germanWord As String
Private m_germanGender As VocabularyWord.WordGender
Private m_wordFunction As VocabularyWord.WordFunction

Public ReadOnly Property EnglishWord() As String
  Get
    Return m_englishWord
  End Get
End Property
Public ReadOnly Property GermanWord() As String
Get
  Return m_germanWord
End Get
End Property
Public ReadOnly Property getWordFunction() As WordFunction
Get
  Return m_wordFunction
End Get
End Property
Public ReadOnly Property getWordGender() As WordGender
Get
  Return m_germanGender
End Get
End Property
```

```vb
'----------------------------------------------------------
'Returns the German word, prefixed with an article
'(e.g. 'der', 'die', 'das' if it exists)
'----------------------------------------------------------
Public ReadOnly Property GermanWordWithArticleIfExists() _
                                                    As String
Get
  If (m_germanGender = WordGender.notApplicable) Then
    Return Me.GermanWord
  End If

  Return Me.GenderArticle + " " + Me.GermanWord
End Get
End Property

Public ReadOnly Property GenderArticle() As String
Get
  Select Case (m_germanGender)
  Case WordGender.Masculine
    Return "der"
  Case WordGender.Feminine
    Return "die"
  Case WordGender.Neuter
    Return "das"
  End Select
  Return ""
End Get
End Property

Public Sub New(ByVal enlgishWord As String, ByVal germanWord _
  As String, ByVal germanGender As WordGender, _
  ByVal wordFunction As WordFunction)

  m_englishWord = enlgishWord
  m_germanWord = germanWord
  m_germanGender = germanGender
  m_wordFunction = wordFunction
End Sub
End Class
```

Chapter 15 (Communications) Samples

Listing 15.1 Trivial File I/O Code That Notes Local vs. Server Differences

This is just a series of function calls. It should be easy for VB programmers to follow the C# code.

Listing 15.2 Simulating Communications Failure to Test Your Application

```
'Conditional compile flags for our insturmented code
#Const DEBUG_SIMULATE_FAILURES = 1 'Simulate failures
'#Const DEBUG_SIMULATE_FAILURES = 0 'Don't simulate failures


'------------------------------------------------------------
'A global variable we want to use to indicate that we
'should throw an exception during communications
'------------------------------------------------------------
#If DEBUG_SIMULATE_FAILURES <> 0 Then
'Variable that holds next pending failure
Shared g_failureCode As SimulatedFailures = _
         SimulatedFailures.noFailurePending

'List of failures that we want to simulate
public enum SimulatedFailures
  noFailurePending  'No test failures pending

  'Simulated failures:
  failInNextWriteSocketCode
  failInNextWebServiceCall
  failInNextFileIODuringFileOpen
  failInNextFileIODuringFileRead
  'etc.
End Enum
#End If 'DEBUG_SIMULATE_FAILURES


'------------------------------------------------------------
'The function we import to communicate data.
'------------------------------------------------------------
Private Sub writeDataToSocket( _
  ByVal mySocket As System.Net.Sockets.Socket, _
  ByVal dataToSend() As Byte)
```

```vbnet
'-------------------------------------------------------------
'Only compile this code in if we are testing network failures
'-------------------------------------------------------------
#If DEBUG_SIMULATE_FAILURES <> 0 Then
'If this is the failure we want to test, throw an Exception
If (g_failureCode = _
SimulatedFailures.failInNextWriteSocketCode) Then
    'Reset the failure so it does not occur next time
    'this function is called
    g_failureCode = SimulatedFailures.noFailurePending

    Throw New Exception("Test communications failure: " + _
            g_failureCode.ToString())
End If
#End If

    'Send the data as normal.
    mySocket.Send(dataToSend)
End Sub
```

Listing 15.3 Test Code to Go Inside a Form Class to Test IrDA Transmit and Receive

```vbnet
'The name we want to give to our IrDA socket
Const myIrDASocketName As String = "IrDaTestFileTransmit"

Private Sub buttonTestFileSend_Click(ByVal sender As Object, _
    ByVal e As System.EventArgs) Handles buttonTestFileSend.Click

    'Create a simple text file we want to send
    Const fileName As String = "\myTestSendFile.txt"
    Dim textFileStream As System.IO.StreamWriter
    textFileStream = System.IO.File.CreateText(fileName)
    textFileStream.WriteLine("Today...")
    textFileStream.WriteLine("is a nice day")
    textFileStream.WriteLine("to go swim")
    textFileStream.WriteLine("in the lake")
    textFileStream.Close()

    Dim irdaFileSender As IrDAFileSend
    irdaFileSender = New IrDAFileSend(fileName, myIrDASocketName)
    'We have 2 options: 1 - Sync, 2 - Async
```

```vb
'1. Call the function synchronously
'and block the thread until the
'file is sent

'1a. Let the user know we're waiting to send
Me.Text = "Trying to send..."
'   '1b. Wait until we find a client and then send the file
irdaFileSender.LoopAndAttemptIRSend()

'1c. Let the user know the file has been transmitted
MsgBox("File sent!")
Me.Text = "IrDA: Sent!"

'2. Call the function async and set
'up a background thread to do the sending

'irdaFileSend.LoopAndAttemptIRSendAsync()
'NOTE: If we call the function async, we want to
'occasionally check if it is finished by
'calling 'irdaFileSend.Status'
End Sub


Private Sub buttonTestFileReceive_Click(ByVal sender As Object _
, ByVal e As EventArgs) Handles buttonTestFileReceive.Click

'If our destination file exists, delete it
Const fileName As String = "\myTestReceiveFile.txt"
If (System.IO.File.Exists(fileName)) Then
    System.IO.File.Delete(fileName)
End If


Dim irdaFileReceiver As IrDAFileReceive
irdaFileReceiver = New IrDAFileReceive(fileName, _
                                    myIrDASocketName)
'We have 2 options: 1 - Sync, 2 - Async

'1. Call the function synchronously
'and block the thread until the
'file is received

'1a. Let the user know we're waiting to receive
Me.Text = "Waiting to receive..."
'1b. Wait until someone contacts us and sends the file
irdaFileReceiver.WaitForIRFileDownload()
```

```
    '1c. Let the user know we've got the sent file
    Me.Text = "IrDA: received!"
    MsgBox("File received!")

    '2. Call the function async and set
    'up a background thread to do the receive

    'irdaFileReceive.WaitForIRFileDownloadAsync()
    'NOTE: If we call the function async, we want to
    'occasionally check if it is finished by
    'calling 'irdaFileReceive.Status'
End Sub
```

Listing 15.4 IrDAFileSend Class

```
Option Strict On
'============================================================
'This class is an IrDA client. It looks for an IrDA
'server with a matching IrDA service name and when found
'it streams the data of a file to it.
'============================================================
Class IrDAFileSend
Private m_descriptionOfLastSendAttempt As String
Private m_IrDAServiceName As String
Private m_fileToSend As String
Private m_wasSenderStopped As Boolean

Public Enum SendStatus
    AttemptingToSend
    Finished_Successfully
    Finished_Aborted
    Finished_Error
End Enum

Private m_SendStatus As SendStatus
Public ReadOnly Property Status() As SendStatus
    Get
        'Lock prevents concurrent read/write to m_SendStatus
        SyncLock (Me)
            Return m_SendStatus
        End SyncLock
    End Get
End Property
```

```vbnet
Private Sub setStatus(ByVal newStatus As SendStatus)
    'Lock prevents concurrent read/write to m_SendStatus
    SyncLock (Me)
      m_SendStatus = newStatus
    End SyncLock
End Sub


Public ReadOnly Property ErrorText() As String
Get
  Return m_descriptionOfLastSendAttempt
End Get
End Property


'------------------------------------------------------------
'CONSTRUCTOR
'------------------------------------------------------------
Public Sub New(ByVal fileToSend As String, _
               ByVal irdaServiceName As String)
  'The name of the IrDA socket we want to look for
  m_IrDAServiceName = irdaServiceName
  'The file we want to send
  m_fileToSend = fileToSend
End Sub


'------------------------------------------------------------
'Starts a new thread to try to send the file
'------------------------------------------------------------
Public Sub LoopAndAttemptIRSendAsync()
  'We are in send mode
  setStatus(SendStatus.AttemptingToSend)
  'User has not aborted us yet
  m_wasSenderStopped = False

  'This is the function we want the new thread to start running
  Dim threadEntryPoint As System.Threading.ThreadStart
  threadEntryPoint = _
    New System.Threading.ThreadStart(AddressOf _
                                      LoopAndAttemptIRSend)

  '-------------------------------------------
  'Create a new thread and start it running
  '-------------------------------------------
  Dim newThread As System.Threading.Thread = _
    New System.Threading.Thread(threadEntryPoint)
```

```vb
    newThread.Start() 'Go!
End Sub


'-------------------------------------------------------------
'Goes in loops and tries to send the file via IR
'-------------------------------------------------------------
Public Sub LoopAndAttemptIRSend()
    Dim irDASender As System.Net.Sockets.IrDAClient
    Dim streamOutToIrDA As System.IO.Stream
    Dim streamInFromFile As System.IO.Stream

    'User has not aborted us yet
    m_wasSenderStopped = False
    setStatus(SendStatus.AttemptingToSend)


    '-------------------------------------------------------------
    'Continually loop and try to send the message until
    '-------------------------------------------------------------
    While (True)
        'These should all be null going in and out of the
        ''sendStream(...)' call unless an exception is thrown!
        irDASender = Nothing
        streamOutToIrDA = Nothing
        streamInFromFile = Nothing

        'Attempt to send the stream
        Dim bSuccess As Boolean
        Try
            bSuccess = sendStream(m_descriptionOfLastSendAttempt, _
                streamOutToIrDA, irDASender, streamInFromFile)

        Catch eUnexpected As System.Exception 'Unexpected error!!!
            setStatus(SendStatus.Finished_Error) 'Note the failure

            m_descriptionOfLastSendAttempt = _
        "Unexpected error in IR send loop. " + eUnexpected.Message


            '-------------------------------------------------
            'Clean up any resources we may have allocated
            '-------------------------------------------------
            If Not (streamOutToIrDA Is Nothing) Then
              Try
                  streamOutToIrDA.Close()
              Catch
```

```vb
        'Swallow any error
      End Try
      streamOutToIrDA = Nothing
    End If


    If Not (streamInFromFile Is Nothing) Then
      Try
        streamInFromFile.Close()
      Catch
        'Swallow any error
      End Try
      streamInFromFile = Nothing
    End If


    If Not (irDASender Is Nothing) Then
      Try
        irDASender.Close()
      Catch
        'Swallow any error
      End Try
      irDASender = Nothing
    End If
    Return 'Exit
  End Try


  'See if we succeeded
  If (bSuccess = True) Then
    m_descriptionOfLastSendAttempt = "Success!"
    setStatus(SendStatus.Finished_Successfully)
    Return
  End If


  'See if there was a user-driven abort
  If (m_wasSenderStopped = True) Then
    m_descriptionOfLastSendAttempt = "User Aborted."
    setStatus(SendStatus.Finished_Aborted)
    Return
  End If


  'Otherwise ... We have not found an IrDA server with a
  'matching service name yet. We will loop and keep
  'looking for one.
End While
```

```vbnet
    'We will never hit this point in execution
End Sub


'-----------------------------------------------------------
'Attempt to send an i/o stream (e.g. a file) over IR
'(ret):
'   true: We sent the file successfully
'   false: The file was not sent successfully
'-----------------------------------------------------------
Private Function sendStream(ByRef errorDescription As String, _
  ByRef streamOutToIrDA As System.IO.Stream, _
  ByRef irDASender As System.Net.Sockets.IrDAClient, _
  ByRef streamInFromFile As System.IO.Stream) As Boolean

  errorDescription = ""
  '-----------------------------------------------------------
  'Create a new IRDA client
  '-----------------------------------------------------------
  Try
      '-----------------------------------------------------------
      'This will return pretty quickly. It will peek out there
      'and will return if no one is listening.
      '-----------------------------------------------------------
      irDASender = _
        New System.Net.Sockets.IrDAClient(m_IrDAServiceName)

  Catch eCreateClient As System.Exception
      'A number of things could have happened here
      '1: No devices may be listening
      '2: A device may be listening, but may not care
      '   (may refuse our conversation)
      errorDescription = eCreateClient.Message
    Return False
  End Try

  'At this point a number of things could happen:
  '1: We have gotten a connection from an IR receiving device
  '2: The IR request has been canceled (someone called STOP).
  If (m_wasSenderStopped = True) Then
    irDASender.Close()
    irDASender = Nothing
    Return False
  End If
```

```vb
'==========================================
'SEND THE DATA!
'==========================================
'Open the file we want to send
streamInFromFile = System.IO.File.OpenRead(m_fileToSend)
'Open the IrDA socket we want to sent out to
streamOutToIrDA = irDASender.GetStream()

Const BUFFER_SIZE As Integer = 1024
Dim inBuffer() As Byte
ReDim inBuffer(BUFFER_SIZE)
Dim bytesRead As Integer
Dim iTestAll As Integer
Dim iTestWrite As Integer
'Loop...
Do
    'Read the bytes in from the file
  bytesRead = streamInFromFile.Read(inBuffer, 0, BUFFER_SIZE)
  iTestAll = iTestAll + 1

  'Write the bytes out to our output stream
  If (bytesRead > 0) Then
        streamOutToIrDA.Write(inBuffer, 0, bytesRead)
    iTestWrite = iTestWrite + 1
  End If

Loop While (bytesRead > 0)

'Clean up output stream
streamOutToIrDA.Flush() 'Finish writing any output
streamOutToIrDA.Close() 'Close the stream
streamOutToIrDA = Nothing

'Clean up local file
streamInFromFile.Close()
streamOutToIrDA = Nothing

'Clean up IrDA port
irDASender.Close()
irDASender = Nothing

'Success!!!
Return True
End Function
End class
```

Listing 15.5 IrDAFileReceive Class

```
'------------------------------------------------------------
'Allows the reception of a file over IrDA (InfraRed port)
'
'This class is NOT re-entrant and should not be called by more
'than one caller at a time. If multiple simultaneous IR
'sessions are desired, they should be done by creating
'different instances of this class.
'------------------------------------------------------------
Public Class IrDAFileReceive

Private m_wasListenerStopped As Boolean
Private m_IrDAServiceName As String
Private m_fileNameForDownload As String
Private m_errorDuringTransfer As String
Private m_irListener As System.Net.Sockets.IrDAListener
Private m_ReceiveStatus As ReceiveStatus

Public ReadOnly Property ErrorText() As String
Get
   Return m_errorDuringTransfer
End Get
End Property


'------------------------------------------------------------
'This notes the status of the receive
'------------------------------------------------------------
Public Enum ReceiveStatus
  NotDone_SettingUp
  NotDone_WaitingForSender
  NotDone_Receiving
  Done_Success
  Done_Aborted
  Done_ErrorOccured
End Enum


'------------------------------------------------------------
' Returns the state of transfer
'------------------------------------------------------------
Public ReadOnly Property Status() As ReceiveStatus
Get
  SyncLock (Me)
      Return m_ReceiveStatus
```

```vb
      End SyncLock
    End Get
    End Property


    Private Sub setStatus(ByVal newStatus As ReceiveStatus)
      'Thread safty to aSub read and write at same time
      SyncLock (Me)
          m_ReceiveStatus = newStatus
      End SyncLock 'end lock
    End Sub


    '------------------------------------------------------------
    ' (in) filename: Filename we want to the IR file into
    '------------------------------------------------------------
    Public Sub New(ByVal filename As String, _
                   ByVal irdaServiceName As String)
      'The name of the IrDA socket we want to open
      m_IrDAServiceName = irdaServiceName

      'The filename we want to save the received data to
      m_fileNameForDownload = filename
    End Sub


    '------------------------------------------------------------
    'Allows you to receive a file asynchronously over IR
    '
    ' (in) filename: Filename to write to
    '------------------------------------------------------------
    Public Sub WaitForIRFileDownloadAsync()
      'Note that we are now in setup mode
      setStatus(ReceiveStatus.NotDone_SettingUp)
      '------------------------------------------------------------
      'Create a new thread
      '------------------------------------------------------------
      Dim threadEntryPoint As System.Threading.ThreadStart
      threadEntryPoint = _
        New System.Threading.ThreadStart(AddressOf _
                                    WaitForIRFileDownload)

      Dim newThread As System.Threading.Thread = _
        New System.Threading.Thread(threadEntryPoint)

      'Start the thread running
      newThread.Start()
    End Sub
```

```vb
'-----------------------------------------------------------
'Opens up an IR port and waits to download a file
'-----------------------------------------------------------
Public Sub WaitForIRFileDownload()
  Dim outputStream As System.IO.Stream
  Dim irdaClient As System.Net.Sockets.IrDAClient
  Dim irStreamIn As System.IO.Stream

  Try
    '========================================================
    'Set up and download the file!
    '========================================================
    internal_WaitForIRFileDownload(outputStream, irdaClient, _
              irStreamIn)
  Catch 'Swallow any errors that occurred
      setStatus(ReceiveStatus.Done_ErrorOccured)
  End Try


  '============================================
  'Clean up all resources
  '============================================
  'Close our input stream
  If Not (irStreamIn Is Nothing) Then
    Try
      irStreamIn.Close()
    Catch 'Swallow any errors that occured
    End Try
  End If
  'Close the IrDA client
  If Not (irdaClient Is Nothing) Then
    Try
      irdaClient.Close()
    Catch 'Swallow any errors that occured
    End Try
  End If
  'Close the file we have been writing to
  If Not (outputStream Is Nothing) Then
    Try
      outputStream.Close()
    Catch 'Swallow any errors that occured
    End Try
  End If
  'Close the listener if its running
  If Not (m_irListener Is Nothing) Then
```

```vbnet
      'Set first so code running on another thread will
      'abort if it is set
      m_wasListenerStopped = True
      Try
        m_irListener.Stop()
      Catch 'Swallow any errors
      End Try
      m_irListener = Nothing
   End If
End Sub


Private Sub internal_WaitForIRFileDownload( _
    ByRef outputStream As System.IO.Stream, _
    ByRef irdaClient As System.Net.Sockets.IrDAClient, _
    ByRef irStreamIn As System.IO.Stream)
  '----------------------------------------------------------
  'Open an input file to stream into
  '----------------------------------------------------------
  outputStream = System.IO.File.Open( _
    m_fileNameForDownload, _
    System.IO.FileMode.Create)


  '==========================================
  'STATUS UPDATE
  '==========================================
  setStatus(ReceiveStatus.NotDone_WaitingForSender)


  '----------------------------------------------------------
  'Open a listener
  '----------------------------------------------------------
  Try
      m_wasListenerStopped = False
    m_irListener = _
      New System.Net.Sockets.IrDAListener(m_IrDAServiceName)
    m_irListener.Start()
  Catch eListener As System.Exception
      m_errorDuringTransfer = "Error creating listener - " + _
      eListener.Message
    GoTo exit_sub_with_error
  End Try

  'See if we got aborted
  If (m_wasListenerStopped = True) Then
    GoTo exit_sub_with_abort
  End If
```

```
'---------------------------------------------------------
'Accept a connection
'---------------------------------------------------------
Try
    '---------------------------------------------------------
    'Execution will stop here until we get pinged by a device
    'or the listener was halted on another thread
    '---------------------------------------------------------
    irdaClient = m_irListener.AcceptIrDAClient()
Catch eClientAccept As System.Exception
    'If the listenting is stopped by another thread calling cancel
    ' an exception will be thrown and we will be here.
    If (m_wasListenerStopped = True) Then
        GoTo exit_sub_with_abort
    End If

    'If it was not a matter of the listening service being
    'stopped, some other exception has occurred. Deal with it.
    m_errorDuringTransfer = "Error accepting connection - " + _
        eClientAccept.Message

    GoTo exit_sub_with_error
End Try

'At this point we will be in 1 of 2 states, either:
'1: We have gotten a connection from an IR sending device
'2: The IR request has been canceled (by someone calling STOP)
'    (in which the code below will throw an exception)
'See if we got aborted
If (m_wasListenerStopped = True) Then
    GoTo exit_sub_with_abort
End If

'========================================
'STATUS UPDATE
'========================================
setStatus(ReceiveStatus.NotDone_Receiving)

'---------------------------------------------------------
'Open a receiving stream
'---------------------------------------------------------
Try
    irStreamIn = irdaClient.GetStream()
Catch exGetInputStream As System.Exception
```

```vbnet
                m_errorDuringTransfer = "Error getting input stream - " + _
                    exGetInputStream.Message
                GoTo exit_sub_with_error
            End Try

            'Get ready to receive the data!
            Const BUFFER_SIZE As Integer = 1024
            Dim inBuffer() As Byte
            ReDim inBuffer(BUFFER_SIZE)

            Dim bytesRead As Integer
            Do
                'Read the bytes in from the IR port
                bytesRead = irStreamin.Read(inBuffer, 0, BUFFER_SIZE)

                'Write the bytes out to our output stream
                If (bytesRead > 0) Then
                    outputStream.Write(inBuffer, 0, bytesRead)
                End If
            Loop While (bytesRead > 0)

            outputStream.Flush() 'Finish writing any output

            '=========================================
            'STATUS UPDATE: SUCCESS
            '=========================================
            setStatus(ReceiveStatus.Done_Success)
            Return 'No errors

            '=========================================
            'FAILURE.
            '=========================================
exit_sub_with_abort:
            'STATUS UPDATE: Aborted (but no error)
            setStatus(ReceiveStatus.Done_Aborted)
            Return

exit_sub_with_error:
            'STATUS UPDATE: ERROR!!!
            setStatus(ReceiveStatus.Done_ErrorOccured)
        End Sub
End Class
```

Listing 15.6 Simple Web Wervice

```
'This code snippet goes inside the Service1 class
'in the file "Service1.asmx.vb".
'
'"<WebMethod>" is meta data that tells the Web service
'engine that this method should be exposed as a Web service

<WebMethod()> _
Public Function AddTwoNumbers(ByVal x As Integer, _
    ByVal y As Integer) As Integer
  Return x + y
End Function
```

Listing 15.7 Web Service Calls with Only Explicit Parameters Being Passed

This is just a series of function calls. It should be easy for VB programmers to follow the C# code.

Listing 15.8 Web Service Calls with Implicit Parameters Passed via Cookies

This is just a series of function calls. It should be easy for VB programmers to follow the C# code.

Listing 15.9 A Chatty Conversation with a Multiple Web Service Calls

This is just a series of function calls. It should be easy for VB programmers to follow the C# code.

Listing 15.10 A Batched Conversation with a Single Web Service Call

This is just a series of function calls. It should be easy for VB programmers to follow the C# code.

```vb
'-------------------------------------------------------------
'Accept a connection
'-------------------------------------------------------------
Try
    '-------------------------------------------------------------
    'Execution will stop here until we get pinged by a device
    'or the listener was halted on another thread
    '-------------------------------------------------------------
    irdaClient = m_irListener.AcceptIrDAClient()
Catch eClientAccept As System.Exception
    'If the listenting is stopped by another thread calling cancel
    ' an exception will be thrown and we will be here.
    If (m_wasListenerStopped = True) Then
        GoTo exit_sub_with_abort
    End If

    'If it was not a matter of the listening service being
    'stopped, some other exception has occurred. Deal with it.
    m_errorDuringTransfer = "Error accepting connection - " + _
        eClientAccept.Message

    GoTo exit_sub_with_error
End Try

'At this point we will be in 1 of 2 states, either:
'1: We have gotten a connection from an IR sending device
'2: The IR request has been canceled (by someone calling STOP)
'     (in which the code below will throw an exception)
'See if we got aborted
If (m_wasListenerStopped = True) Then
    GoTo exit_sub_with_abort
End If

'=========================================
'STATUS UPDATE
'=========================================
setStatus(ReceiveStatus.NotDone_Receiving)

'-------------------------------------------------------------
'Open a receiving stream
'-------------------------------------------------------------
Try
    irStreamIn = irdaClient.GetStream()
Catch exGetInputStream As System.Exception
```

Listing 15.11 Code to Download a File from a Web Server

```
'-------------------------------------------------------------
'Performs a synchronous download of a file on a Web server
'of a file and stores it to a local file system
' (in) httpWhereFrom: URL to file
'      (e.g. "http:'someserver/somefile.jpg")
' (in) filenameWhereTo: File location to write the file to
'      (e.g. "\localfile.jpg")
'-------------------------------------------------------------
Public Sub downloadFileToLocalStore(ByVal httpWhereFrom As _
  String, ByVal filenameWhereTo As String)
  Dim myFileStream As System.IO.FileStream = Nothing
  Dim myHTTPResponseStream As System.IO.Stream = Nothing
  Dim myWebRequest As System.Net.WebRequest = Nothing
  Dim myWebResponse As System.Net.WebResponse = Nothing

  'If the location we want to write to exists, delete it
  If (System.IO.File.Exists(filenameWhereTo) = True) Then
      System.IO.File.Delete(filenameWhereTo)
  End If

  Try
      'Create a Web request
    myWebRequest = _
      System.Net.HttpWebRequest.Create(httpWhereFrom)
    'Get the response
    myWebResponse = myWebRequest.GetResponse()
    'Get the stream for the response
    myHTTPResponseStream = myWebResponse.GetResponseStream()

    'Create a local file to stream the response to
    myFileStream = System.IO.File.OpenWrite(filenameWhereTo)

    'This buffer size can be tuned
    Const buffer_length As Integer = 4000
    Dim byteBuffer() As Byte
    ReDim byteBuffer(buffer_length)
    Dim bytesIn As Integer

    'Read in the file and stream it to a local file
    Do
      'Read data in
      bytesIn = myHTTPResponseStream.Read(byteBuffer, _
        0, buffer_length)
```

```
          'Write data out
        If (bytesIn <> 0) Then
           myFileStream.Write(byteBuffer, 0, bytesIn)
        End If
     Loop While (bytesIn <> 0)


  Catch myException As Exception  'Download failed!
       'Something bad happened. Let's clean up
     attemptCleanup_ThrowNoExceptions(myFileStream, _
         myHTTPResponseStream, myWebResponse)


     'Now that we've cleaned up, rethrow the exception
     'so that the application knows something went wrong!
       Throw myException
  End Try


  'Download has succeeded!

  'Let's close everyting down.
  Try
       'Normal clean up.
       myFileStream.Close()
       myFileStream = Nothing

       myHTTPResponseStream.Close()
       myHTTPResponseStream = Nothing

       myWebResponse.Close()
       myWebResponse = Nothing
  Catch myException As Exception  'Failure during a close!
        'Something bad happened. Let's clean up
     attemptCleanup_ThrowNoExceptions(myFileStream, _
          myHTTPResponseStream, myWebResponse)


     'Now that we've cleaned up, rethrow the exception
     'so that the the application knows something went wrong!
       Throw myException
  End Try
     'Success!
End Sub


'-------------------------------------------
'Tries to close and clean up everything
'Traps any exceptions that might be thrown.
'-------------------------------------------
```

```
Sub attemptCleanup_ThrowNoExceptions( _
  ByVal myFileStream As System.IC.FileStream, _
  ByVal myHTTPResponseStream As System.IO.Stream, _
  ByVal myWebResponse As System.Net.WebResponse)

  If Not (myFileStream Is Nothing) Then
    Try
      myFileStream.Close()
    Catch 'Do nothing.
    End Try
  End If

  If Not (myHTTPResponseStream Is Nothing) Then
    Try
      myHTTPResponseStream.Close()
    Catch 'Do nothing.
    End Try
  End If

  If Not (myWebResponse Is Nothing) Then
    Try
      myWebResponse.Close()
    Catch 'Do nothing.
    End Try
  End If
End Sub
```

Index